# Enterprise Information Systems

**A Pattern-Based Approach**    *Third Edition*

## Cheryl L. Dunn
*Florida State University*

## J. Owen Cherrington
*Brigham Young University*

## Anita S. Hollander
*University of Tennessee*

Boston   Burr Ridge, IL   Dubuque, IA   Madison, WI   New York
San Francisco   St. Louis   Bangkok   Bogotá   Caracas   Kuala Lumpur
Lisbon   London   Madrid   Mexico City   Milan   Montreal   New Delhi
Santiago   Seoul   Singapore   Sydney   Taipei   Toronto

ENTERPRISE INFORMATION SYSTEMS: A PATTERN-BASED APPROACH

Published by McGraw-Hill/Irwin, a business unit of The McGraw-Hill Companies, Inc., 1221 Avenue of the Americas, New York, NY, 10020. Copyright © 2005, 2000, 1996 by The McGraw-Hill Companies, Inc. All rights reserved. No part of this publication may be reproduced or distributed in any form or by any means, or stored in a database or retrieval system, without the prior written consent of The McGraw-Hill Companies, Inc., including, but not limited to, in any network or other electronic storage or transmission, or broadcast for distance learning.

Some ancillaries, including electronic and print components, may not be available to customers outside the United States.

This book is printed on acid-free paper.

Domestic          1 2 3 4 5 6 7 8 9 0 DOC/DOC 0 9 8 7 6 5 4
International      1 2 3 4 5 6 7 8 9 0 DOC/DOC 0 9 8 7 6 5 4

ISBN      0-07-240429-9

Vice president and editor-in-chief: *Robin J. Zwettler*
Publisher: *Stewart Mattson*
Executive editor: *Tim Vertovec*
Senior developmental editor: *Kimberly D. Hooker*
Marketing manager: *Richard Kolasa*
Senior producer, Media technology: *Ed Przyzycki*
Lead project manager: *Pat Frederickson*
Freelance project manager: *Rich Wright, Omega Publishing Services*
Production supervisor: *Debra R. Sylvester*
Designer: *Kami Carter*
Supplement producer: *Lynn M. Bluhm*
Senior digital content specialist: *Brian Nacik*
Cover image: *© Corbis*
Typeface: *10/12 Times New Roman*
Compositor: *ElectraGraphics, Inc.*
Printer: *R. R. Donnelley*

Library of Congress Control Number: 2003116879

INTERNATIONAL EDITION ISBN 0-07-111120-4
Copyright © 2005. Exclusive rights by The McGraw-Hill Companies, Inc. for manufacture and export. This book cannot be re-exported from the country to which it is sold by McGraw-Hill.
The International Edition is not available in North America.

First and foremost, we dedicate this book to God, without whom this book would not exist.

We dedicate this book to our families, who sacrificed time with us and who encouraged us to persevere as we completed this book.

We also dedicate this book to Bill McCarthy, the true innovator whose ideas form the foundation of this book.

# Letter to the Instructor

Dear Colleague,

We are excited to introduce *Enterprise Information Systems: A Pattern-Based Approach,* third edition, a major revision of *Accounting, Information Technology, and Business Solutions,* second edition. This edition has a brand new title given that over 75 percent of the content is new, including topics not typically found in other AIS texts.

## WHY THESE MAJOR CHANGES?

- This edition follows an innovative approach to teaching information systems—REA, which looks at the relationship between an organization's critical resources, events, and agents. REA, developed by Bill McCarthy of Michigan State University, is a framework for creating an enterprisewide database that can be used to retrieve information for multiple business purposes. Using traditional diagrams and an alternative grammar format, students will be able to separate the substance from the form of the REA framework. This edition goes beyond the business process level of coverage of the REA enterprise ontology previously addressed. We've drilled down the high-level value system view to the more detailed value chain level and illustrated how the transaction cycles fit together to form the value chain, which enables your students to see the "big picture."

- This edition is built on the idea that a separation between accounting information systems and management information systems should not exist. We believe patterns help people see the "big picture" of enterprises more clearly and therefore help design better systems. We believe you cannot identify anything that we need to account for that we do not also need to manage; nor can we identify anything we need to manage that we do not also need to account for. In this edition, we will show how a well-designed REA-based accounting information system *is* the enterprise information system.

- This edition covers such topics as enterprise systems integration, representation and patterns, value system and value chain modeling, information retrieval via SQL and QBE queries, view integration and implementation compromises, and inter- versus intra-enterprise systems. We've also moved the coverage on internal controls later in the text based on the belief that the REA framework can enhance and structure our thinking about internal controls, but internal controls don't facilitate our thinking about the REA framework.

This textbook offers your students a unique alternative to the more traditional forms of accounting information systems (or other types of information systems). We do not present the traditional approach as a basis for comparison; rather we simply present what we believe is the most current and innovative method to designing enterprise information systems.

# About the Authors

## Cheryl L. Dunn   *Florida State University*

Cheryl L. Dunn (PhD, Michigan State University) is Associate Professor of Accounting at Florida State University. Cheryl also has served as visiting associate professor in the Master of Science in Accountancy program at the University of Notre Dame. She formerly served on the faculty of Grand Valley State University.

Cheryl has written many articles for scholarly journals such as *Decision Sciences, Journal of Information Systems, International Journal of Accounting Information Systems,* and *Advances in Accounting Information Systems* as well as a chapter in the American Accounting Association research monograph *Researching Accounting as an Information Systems Discipline.* Her primary teaching and research interests are in conceptual modeling, enterprise information systems design, and database financial reporting. She has been awarded research grants by the International Center for Automated Information Research and Florida State University. She serves as book review editor for *Journal of Information Systems* and on the editorial board of the *International Journal of Accounting Information Systems.* She has also held various positions for the Information Systems section of the American Accounting Association.

## J. Owen Cherrington   *Brigham Young University*

J. Owen Cherrington (PhD, University of Minnesota) is the Mary & Ellis Distinguished Professor of Accounting and Information Systems at Brigham Young University and the founding director of the Rollins Center for eBusiness. Owen previously served on the faculties of Utah State University and Pennsylvania State University. He also served as the Director of the Information Systems faculty and programs in the Marriott School of BYU.

Owen has an extensive list of publications including four major college textbooks in introductory accounting, cost and managerial accounting, information systems, and CPA review. He has published over 40 articles and monographs in professional books and journals. He has also written training materials or conducted training programs for IBM, AICPA, Utah Association of CPAs, and Ernst & Young. Owen holds teaching as a high priority. He has taught business ethics, analysis and design of information systems, management consulting, and e-business. He has won numerous awards and recognitions, including the Marriott School Outstanding Faculty and Teaching Awards, the NAC Outstanding Faculty Award, the Exxon Outstanding Teaching Award, the Wm. C. Brown Teaching Excellence Award, and the Utah Association of CPAs Outstanding Educator Award.

## Anita Sawyer Hollander   *University of Tennessee*

Anita Sawyer Hollander (PhD, University of Tennessee–Knoxville) is a visiting lecturer at the University of Tennessee. She teaches and is involved in curriculum development in the eMBA program. Formerly, Anita was Chapman Professor at the University of Tulsa where she served as director of the School of Accounting and chair of the MIS department. She also was associate professor at the Florida State University. Anita was selected as a 1999–2000 Carnegie Foundation Pew Scholar, one of only three business professors selected nationwide to receive this honor.

Anita's research interests include financial information system architectures and the effect of information system design and use on the role of the information providers within organizations. Anita has published in numerous journals. She has been active in the American Accounting Association (AAA) and the American Institute of Certified Public Accountants (AICPA). Anita served as chairperson of the Information Systems Section of the AAA, on the AICPA Technology Curriculum and Competency Model Task Force, and on an AICPA Pre-Professional Competencies Task Force charged with identifying the critical core competencies of successful accounting program graduates. Anita's teaching interest is information systems. She has been named for several teaching awards: University of Tulsa Innovation in Teaching award, two Florida State University Beta Alpha Psi Professor of the Year awards, a Florida State University Teaching award, and a State of Florida Legislature Teaching Incentive Program Award. She was also honored with the TU Mortar Board Professor of the Year.

# Putting the Big Picture Together

## REA Integrated Throughout

This text follows the REA model, an innovative approach to teaching information systems, developed by Bill McCarthy of Michigan State University. The REA model is the framework for analyzing the relationship between an organization's critical **R**esources, **E**vents, and **A**gents. The new text title reflects the fact this approach considers the enterprisewide implications of information systems rather than simply the accounting implications.
Students will benefit from this theoretical foundation for enterprise systems because it provides a glimpse of what is possible in enterprise systems yet also permits comparison to existing systems. While existing software can be used to demonstrate the constructs in this approach, REA is software-independent and therefore stands the test of time.

### THE REA ENTERPRISE ONTOLOGY

McCarthy proposed a generalized model for accounting systems after analyzing many accounting transactions and identifying the common features of the transactions.[3] McCarthy and Geerts have further developed the constructs of the original model to form an enterprise domain ontology. This ontology is called the REA Enterprise Ontology because three of the principle constructs are **R**esources, **E**vents, and **A**gents. **Resources** are things of economic value (with or without physical substance) that are provided or consumed by an enterprise's activities and operations. Examples of resources found in many enterprises are cash, raw

**EXHIBIT 4–6  Simplified Extended REA Business Process Level Pattern**

Diagram Format

## Pattern-Based Approach

People use patterns every day in learning. We apply patterns we have seen before to help us understand new situations. This textbook **encourages students to apply the object patterns** (things and relationships between them) and **script patterns** (logical sequences of events) that make up the REA enterprise ontology to help them understand enterprises and transaction cycles/business processes.

### PATTERNS

People use **patterns** of various kinds every day in understanding the environment around them. Patterns allow us to make predictions about future events and to make sense of the present based on our past experiences. Patterns are used in learning from the time that we are very young children throughout the rest of our lives. Preschoolers and early elementary school students are given a row of symbols such as

♥♦♥♦♥__

and are asked to fill in the blank with the appropriate symbol. Go ahead; figure out what goes in the blank. It probably didn't take you very long to identify the correct answer as ♦!

As students progress, patterns may be more complicated, for example,

♣♦♥♣♦♥♣♦♦___

Of course the correct answer is ♣.

Try this one, which is a little more complex:

⊕⊠⊖⊞⊗⊞⊖⊠⊕⊞___

The answer is ⊗ and requires recognition that the + × — pattern is embedded inside the

# Real-World and Practical Examples

Real-world examples incorporated into each chapter through Case in Point boxes help reinforce concepts. The running cases throughout the text help students better connect the theory with practical problems and solutions. The Robert Scott Woodwinds examples in Chapters 2 through 4 tie together the value system modeling, value chain modeling, business process modeling, and database implementation. Practical examples using hypothetical but realistic distributors are provided in Chapters 8, 9, 10, 12, and 13. In Chapter 11 a hypothetical cookie manufacture helps to make the conversion cycle more concrete.

.

## Case in Point

Sunbeam and Cott are two companies that run multiple warehouse management systems (WMS). In such environments data must be manually keyed from one system to the other, inviting the possibilities for errors and data inconsistency. Sunbeam runs two WMS in 12 warehouses and its IT staff has to write additional interfaces between the two WMS and its back-end systems. Cott's CIO, Douglas Neary, configured its billing, shipping, and invoicing systems to periodically synchronize with one another and uses business intelligence applications to recognize anomalies in the data. In about half of Cott's warehouses Neary has written interfaces between the legacy ERP system and WMS, thereby eliminating the need to manually rekey inventory transactions into the ERP system.

Source: M. Levinson, "How to Get Your House in Order," *CIO Magazine*, September 15, 2002, www.cio.com.

### ELECTRONIC COMMERCE SOLUTIONS AND INTER-ENTERPRISE SYSTEM DESIGN

## Integration of Microsoft Access

Students walk through applications of several course concepts using Microsoft Access. Even students who have never used Access should find it easy to use as they follow the examples explained in narrative form and illustrated in the screen captures. The actual implementation of the conceptual models as illustrated by the screen captures helps students to make abstract concepts more concrete

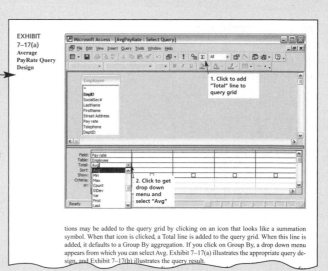

**EXHIBIT 7–17(a)** Average PayRate Query Design

tions may be added to the query grid by clicking on an icon that looks like a summation symbol. When that icon is clicked, a Total line is added to the query grid. When this line is added, it defaults to a Group By aggregation. If you click on Group By, a drop down menu appears from which you can select Avg. Exhibit 7–17(a) illustrates the appropriate query design, and Exhibit 7–17(b) illustrates the query result.

# Relevancy

Students will be better prepared for the business process understanding portion on the new CPA exam. Chapter 3 goes **beyond the business process level only coverage** of REA enterprise ontology included in most textbooks. Business process understanding is a topic experts agree students need to better understand. Enterprise resource planning systems training has been criticized for focusing too much on software and not enough on understanding the business processes the software represents.

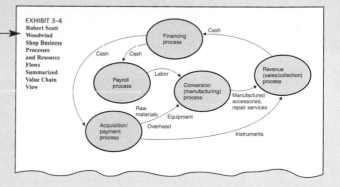

EXHIBIT 3–4
Robert Scott Woodwind Shop Business Processes and Resource Flows Summarized Value Chain View

# End-of-Chapter Material

The end-of-chapter questions offer a range from very simple multiple choice and review questions to more thought-provoking discussion questions and applied learning problems that require a higher level of understanding to complete. This range of questions allows students to **adequately assess and expand their knowledge** of chapter concepts.

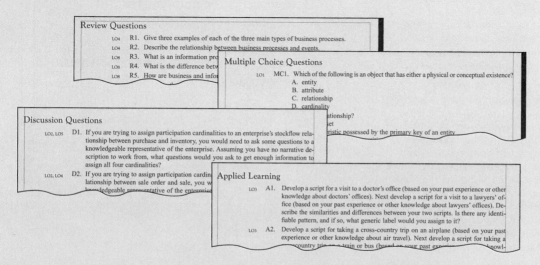

**Review Questions**

LO4  R1.  Give three examples of each of the three main types of business processes.
LO4  R2.  Describe the relationship between business processes and events.
LO8  R3.  What is an information pro
LO8  R4.  What is the difference betw
LO8  R5.  How are business and infor

**Multiple Choice Questions**

LO1  MC1.  Which of the following is an object that has either a physical or conceptual existence?
    A.  entity
    B.  attribute
    C.  relationship
    D.  cardinality

lationship?
set
ristic possessed by the primary key of an entity

**Discussion Questions**

LO2, LO5  D1.  If you are trying to assign participation cardinalities to an enterprise's stockflow relationship between purchase and inventory, you would need to ask some questions to a knowledgeable representative of the enterprise. Assuming you have no narrative description to work from, what questions would you ask to get enough information to assign all four cardinalities?

LO2, LO4  D2.  If you are trying to assign participation cardin lationship between sale order and sale, you w knowledgeable representative of the enterprise

**Applied Learning**

LO3  A1.  Develop a script for a visit to a doctor's office (based on your past experience or other knowledge about doctors' offices). Next develop a script for a visit to a lawyers' office (based on your past experience or other knowledge about lawyers' offices). Describe the similarities and differences between your two scripts. Is there any identifiable pattern, and if so, what generic label would you assign to it?

LO3  A2.  Develop a script for taking a cross-country trip on an airplane (based on your past experience or other knowledge about air travel). Next develop a script for taking a country trip on a train or bus (based on your past expe

# Cutting Edge Coverage

*Enterprise Information Systems,* Third Edition, covers topics not typically found in other AIS textbooks, including chapters on enterprise system integration, representation and patterns, value system and value chain modeling, information retrieval via SQL and QBE queries, view integration and implementation compromises, inter- versus intra-enterprise systems, and more extensive coverage than is found in other textbooks on the conversion, payroll, and financing cycles.

A comprehensive company example is offered throughout Chapters 2, 3, and 4 to provide step-by-step application of the chapter concepts and thereby make the theoretical concepts more concrete.

This edition provides a shift in focus for the transaction cycle chapters from repetitive application of the same internal controls in each cycle to the use of information and example queries for each transaction cycle. Internal controls are still covered, but they are covered later in the text based on the belief that the REA framework can enhance and structure our thinking about internal controls, but internal controls don't facilitate our thinking about the REA framework.

**Chapter Highlights include:**

This discussion as to why enterprise systems should be integrated, why they are often not fully integrated, what types of integration are often used, and recommendations for the focal points of efforts to reengineer enterprise systems is not typically found in AIS textbooks.

This coverage of representation and patterns is also a first in the AIS textbook arena. A strong link is formed for students between the real objects and activities in enterprises and the representations of those objects and activities in enterprise information systems.

This chapter goes beyond the business process level only coverage of the REA enterprise ontology included in most textbooks. This chapter incorporates recent REA research advances that modeling of enterprises value systems and value chains. By illustrating the high-level value system view, then drilling down to demonstrate how business processes fit together to form a value chain, this chapter enables students to see the big picture of enterprises more clearly.

**1**  An Introduction to Integrated Enterprise Information Systems

**2**  Representation and Patterns: An Introduction to the REA Enterprise Ontology

**3**  The REA Enterprise Ontology: Value System and Value Chain Modeling

x

# to Help Students Succeed

Recognizing that presentation of the REA enterprise ontology only in diagram format sometimes makes it difficult for students to differentiate the REA pattern from the diagramming toolset, this chapter portrays the REA pattern for the business process level using both the traditional diagram format and an alternative grammar format. This enables students to separate the substance from the form of the REA framework.

This chapter clearly delineates the differences between conceptual models, logical models, and physical implementation to enable students to understand the different types of decisions made for what to include in each. This is accomplished with a step-by-step approach used to convert conceptual models to the relational logical model and via the use of screen shot examples to illustrate the physical implementation of those logical relational tables.

Many concrete examples of queries using Structured Query Language and Query By Example (with screen shots) facilitate students' understanding of information retrieval issues for relational databases.

Coverage of each cycle chapter includes the complete REA pattern, with instigation, commitment, economic increment, economic decrement, and economic reversal events along with all appropriate relationships. These chapters provide extensive querying examples to facilitate students' understanding of both the design and use of REA-based information systems.

4   The REA Enterprise Ontology: Business Process Modeling

5   Task Level Modeling

6   Relational Database Design: Converting Conceptual REA Models to Relational Databases

7   Information Retrieval from Relational Databases

8   The Sales/Collection Business Process

9   The Acquisition/Payment Business Process

11  The Conversion Business Process

12  The Human Resource Business Process

13  The Financing Business Process

This chapter on view integration and implementation compromise is a first among AIS textbooks. Its placement after the first two cycle chapters enables students to immediately begin to see how the models for each separate cycle may be combined to form an integrated enterprise database.

This chapter uses the REA framework as a means for structuring students' thinking about internal controls. Such an approach may result in more complete specification and analysis of system and business process controls than would an unstructured approach.

This chapter demonstrates the relevancy of the REA enterprise ontology by placing it in the context of ongoing developments in Enterprise Resource Planning (ERP) systems and Electronic commerce technologies.

**10** View Integration and Implementation Compromises

**14** Enterprise System Risks and Controls

**15** ERP Systems and E-Commerce: Intra- and Inter-Enterprise Modeling

# Supplements and Technology

**INSTRUCTOR SUPPLEMENT CD-ROM (007 2405198) includes:**

**Solutions Manual:** prepared by Cheryl Dunn, includes the solutions to all end-of-chapter review questions, discussion questions, and applied learning problems. Two alternative 15-week syllabi are provided to assist instructors in preparing for class.

**Test bank:** prepared by Cheryl Dunn, offers an assortment of true-false, multiple choice, and long problems that instructors can choose in creating exams.

**PowerPoint presentations:** prepared by Cheryl Dunn with the assistance of Lisa M. Casey, a complete set of slides that cover the key concepts presented in each chapter.

## Online Learning Center

www.mhhe.com/dunn3e

For instructors, the book's website contains the Instructor's Resource and Solutions Manual, PowerPoint slides, example Access database files, additional projects and cases, text and supplement updates, and links to other useful resources.

The student section of the site features PowerPoint slides, Internet exercises, additional projects and cases, learning objectives, and key terms with definitions.

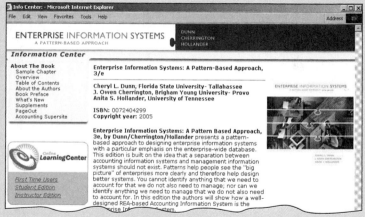

Keeping your course current can be a job in itself, and now McGraw-Hill does that job for you. PowerWeb extends the learning experience beyond the core textbook by offering all of the latest news and developments pertinent to accounting and information systems, without the clutter and dead links of a typical online search.

PowerWeb offers timely articles and links culled by a real-world expert in accounting and information systems. PowerWeb users can also take advantage of self-grading quizzes, interactive glossaries, and exercises, and study tips.

Both instructors and students will appreciate the Online Learning Center's links to many of McGraw-Hill's most popular sites, including PageOut.

# Acknowledgments

Our greatest acknowledgement for this textbook is to Bill McCarthy of Michigan State University. Bill is the founder of the REA enterprise ontology that forms the focal point of this textbook. We have done our best to faithfully present his ideas so as to make them more accessible to instructors and students across the globe. We appreciate Bill's many insights and his permission to use or adapt many of the examples he himself uses in teaching REA to his students. Our heartfelt thanks to you, Bill!

We also acknowledge insights gained over the past several years to participants of the regularly occurring SMAP (semantic modeling of accounting phenomena) workshop organized by Julie Smith David at Arizona State University and Bill McCarthy. A better group of people with whom to exchange both research and teaching ideas about the REA enterprise ontology simply does not exist.

We thank Julie Smith David at Arizona State University for the wonderful idea of using cookie-baking as an example to which students can easily relate in understanding the conversion cycle.

We thank Greg Gerard at Florida State University for patiently class-testing pre-publication editions of this text and Microsoft PowerPoint presentations with his undergraduate AIS students. We thank the students in Gerard's and Cheryl Dunn's systems classes at Florida State University and the University of Notre Dame who used pre-publication editions of this textbook and helped us identify errors and ambiguous paragraphs. We also acknowledge Cheryl's graduate assistant, Daniel Selby, for his help in developing end-of-chapter questions and some Cases in Point.

We also thank the many people who participated in focus groups, completed questionnaires, and reviewed the manuscript. Our sincerest thanks to them all:

**Janie Chang**
*San Jose State University*

**Gordon Chapman**
*Eastern Washington University*

**Deb Cosgrove**
*University of Nebraska–Lincoln*

**Henry Davis**
*Eastern Illinois University*

**James Davis**
*Clemson University*

**Guido Geerts**
*University of Delaware*

**Gregory Gerard**
*Florida State University*

**Kathy Hurtt**
*University of Wisconsin*

**Frederick Jones**
*University of Massachusetts*

**Steven Muzatko**
*University of Wisconsin–Green Bay*

**Linda Parsons**
*George Mason University*

**Gary Peters**
*University of Arkansas*

**Austin Reitenga**
*University of Texas at San Antonio*

**Barbara Waddington Ross**
*Eastern Michigan University*

**Nazik Roufaiel**
*Ithaca College*

**Georgia Saemann**
*University of Wisconsin–Milwaukee*

**Gary Schneider**
*University of San Diego*

**Herbert Snyder**
*North Dakota State University*

**Darrell Walden**
*University of Richmond*

**Ting J. Wang**
*University of Wisconsin–Milwaukee*

**Roman Wong**
*Southern Illinois University*

We also appreciate the efforts of the McGraw-Hill/Irwin team. In particular we would like to thank Stewart Mattson, publisher; Tim Vertovec, executive editor; Kimberly Hooker, senior developmental editor; Rich Kolasa, senior marketing manager; Kami Carter, designer; Lynn Bluhm, supplements producer; Pat Frederickson, lead project manager; Debra Sylvester, production supervisor; and freelance project manager, Rich Wright—Omega Publishing.

*Cheryl L. Dunn*

*J. Owen Cherrington*

*Anita Sawyer Hollander*

# Brief Contents

1   An Introduction to Integrated
    Enterprise Information Systems   1

2   Representation and Patterns: An
    Introduction to the REA Enterprise
    Ontology   19

3   The REA Enterprise Ontology:
    Value System and Value Chain
    Modeling   35

4   The REA Enterprise Ontology:
    Business Process Modeling   51

5   Task Level Modeling   91

6   Relational Database Design:
    Converting Conceptual REA Models
    to Relational Databases   121

7   Information Retrieval from Relational
    Databases   161

8   The Sales/Collection Business
    Process   199

9   The Acquisition/Payment Business
    Process   259

10  View Integration and Implementation
    Compromises   311

11  The Conversion Business
    Process   345

12  The Human Resource Business
    Process   385

13  The Financing Business Process   409

14  Enterprise System Risks
    and Controls   431

15  ERP Systems and E-Commerce: Intra-
    and Inter-Enterprise Modeling   475

# Table of Contents

## Chapter 1
**An Introduction to Integrated Enterprise Information Systems    1**

Introduction    1
Enterprise System Software and Degrees of Integration    2
Stovepiped Operations and Stovepiped Systems    5
*Breaking Down Stovepipes by Reengineering Business Processes    6*

## Chapter 2
**Representation and Patterns: An Introduction to the REA Enterprise Ontology    19**

Representation and Modeling    19
Patterns    21
*Object Patterns    22*
*Script Patterns    23*
The REA Enterprise Ontology    24
*An Example Enterprise    25*
*RSWS Value System    26*
*RSWS Value Chain    27*
*Task Level    30*
Concluding Comments    30

## Chapter 3
**The REA Enterprise Ontology: Value System and Value Chain Modeling    35**

Value Systems and Value Chains    35
Value System Level REA Modeling    40
Value Chain Level REA Modeling    42
*Step 1: Write the Entrepreneurial Script    44*
*Step 2: Connect the Scenes with Resource Flows    45*
*Step 3: Specify the Economic Exchange Events within Each Scene    45*
Concluding Comments    47

## Chapter 4
**The REA Enterprise Ontology: Business Process Modeling    51**

Introduction    51
Conceptual Modeling Constructs    52
Conceptual Modeling Notations    55
Pattern Discovery    59
REA Core Pattern    62
*REA Business Process Modeling Step 1: Identify Economic Exchange Events    63*
*REA Business Process Modeling Step 2: Attach Resources to Economic Events    64*
*REA Business Process Modeling Step 3: Attach External Agents to Economic Events    64*
*REA Business Process Modeling Step 4: Attach Internal Agents to Economic Events    64*
*REA Business Process Modeling Step 5: Attribute Assignment    64*
*REA Business Process Modeling Step 6: Participation Cardinality Assignment    67*
*REA Business Process Modeling Step 7: Validate Model    70*
*REA Business Process Level Extensions    82*

## Chapter 5
**Task Level Modeling    91**

Introduction    91
System Flowcharting    94
*The Basic Elements of System Flowcharts    94*
*Flowcharting Element 1: Symbols    95*
*Flowcharting Element 2: Flow Lines    100*
*Flowcharting Element 3: Area of Responsibility    101*
Preparation Conventions    101
*Left to Right, Top to Bottom    101*
*All Documents Must Have an Origin and Termination    101*
*Keep Flowcharts Uncluttered    101*

*Make Sure the Progress of a Document
Is Clear   102*
*Make Sure Your Flowchart Is Complete: Represent
Each Input, Processing, Output, and Storage
Step   102*
System Flowchart Summary   102
File Types, Media, and Processing Methods   102
   *File Types   103*
   *Media   103*
   *Processing Methods   105*
Data Flow Diagrams   106
Data Flow Diagram Symbols   106
   *Process   106*
   *Data Sources and Sinks   106*
   *Data Stores   107*
   *Data Flow Lines   107*
Constraints   107
   *General Rules   107*
   *Process   109*
   *Data Store   109*
   *Source/Sink   109*
   *Data Flow   109*
Levels of Data Flow Diagrams   110
   *Context Diagram   110*
   *Subsequent Level DFDs   110*
Comparing Flowcharts and Data Flow
Diagrams   112
Concluding Comments   114

## Chapter 6
### Relational Database Design: Converting Conceptual REA Models to Relational Databases   121

Introduction   121
Converting Conceptual Models into Relational
Logical Models   122
Relationship Attribute Placement   135
Physical Implementation of Relational Model
in Microsoft Access   137
   *Creating and Working with Databases   138*
   *Deleting Existing Relationships   148*
   *Entering Data into Microsoft Access Tables   148*
Concluding Comments   150

## Chapter 7
### Information Retrieval from Relational Databases   161

Introduction   161
Querying Relational Databases   162
Relational Algebra   163
   *PROJECT Example   164*
   *SELECT Example   164*
   *JOIN Examples   165*
Structured Query Language   169
   *PROJECT Example   170*
   *SELECT Example   170*
   *Combining SELECT and PROJECT in SQL   170*
   *JOIN Examples   171*
   *Using Mathematical, Special Comparison,
   and Logical Operators in SQL Queries   172*
   *Using Calculations and Aggregation Functions
   in SQL Queries   172*
Query by Example in Microsoft Access   174
   *Familiarization with Database   175*
   *Starting a Query and Adding the Appropriate Tables
   and/or Queries   178*
Parameter Queries   189
Concluding Comments   191

## Chapter 8
### The Sales/Collection Business Process   199

Introduction   199
Sales/Collection Business Process in an Enterprise
Value System   200
Sales/Collection Business Process in Enterprise
Value Chains   200
Sales/Collection Business Process Level REA
Models   202
   *Instigation Events (Marketing Events, Customer
   Inquiries)   202*
   *Mutual Commitment Events (Customer Orders,
   Rentals, Service Agreements)   206*
   *Economic Decrement Event (Sale, Shipment, Rental,
   or Service Engagement)   207*
   *Economic Increment Event (Cash Receipt)   213*
   *Economic Decrement Reversal Event (Sales Returns
   and Sales Allowances)   217*

Information Needs and Measures in the
Sales/Collection Process   220
   *Resource Queries in the Sales/Collection
   Process   221*
   *Event Queries in the Sales/Collection Process   228*
   *Agent Queries in the Sales/Collection Process   229*
Relationship Queries in the Sales/Collection
Process   231
   *Duality Relationship Queries in the Sales/Collection
   Process   231*
   *Stockflow Relationship Queries in the
   Sales/Collection Process   237*
   *Fulfillment Relationship Queries in the
   Sales/Collection Process   241*
   *Proposition Relationship Queries in the
   Sales/Collection Process   244*
   *Reservation Relationship Queries in the
   Sales/Collection Process   244*
   *Participation Relationship Queries in the
   Sales/Collection Process   246*
   *Queries Requiring Multiple Relationships in the
   Sales/Collection Process   246*
Concluding Comments   251

## Chapter 9
### The Acquisition/Payment Business Process   259

Introduction   259
Acquisition/Payment Business Process in an
Enterprise Value System   260
Acquisition/Payment Business Process Level
REA Models   262
   *Instigation Events—Need Identification and Request
   for Goods/Services   262*
   *Mutual Commitment Events (Purchase Orders,
   Rental Agreements, Service Agreements)   265*
   *Economic Increment Event (Purchase [Receipt
   of Goods], Rental, or Service Acquisition)   269*
   *Economic Decrement Event (Cash
   Disbursement)   273*
   *Economic Increment Reversal Event (Purchase
   Returns and Allowances)   275*

Information Needs and Measures in the
Acquisition/Payment Process   279
   *Resource Queries in the Acquisition/Payment
   Process   279*
   *Event Queries in the Acquisition/Payment
   Process   285*
   *Agent Queries in the Acquisition/Payment
   Process   287*
Relationship Queries in the Acquisition/Payment
Process   288
   *Duality Relationship Queries in the
   Acquisition/Payment Process   288*
   *Stockflow Relationship Queries in the
   Acquisition/Payment Process   294*
   *Fulfillment Relationship Queries in the
   Acquisition/Payment Process   295*
   *Proposition Relationship Queries in the
   Acquisition/Payment Process   298*
   *Reservation Relationship Queries in the
   Acquisition/Payment Process   299*
   *Participation Relationship Queries in the
   Acquisition/Payment Process   299*
   *Queries Requiring Multiple Relationships in the
   Acquisition/Payment Process   300*
Concluding Comments   304

## Chapter 10
### View Integration and Implementation Compromises   311

Introduction   311
View Integration   312
Implementation Compromise   318
   *Conceptual Level Modeling Compromises   318*
   *Logical Level Modeling Compromises   320*
   *Physical Implementation Compromises   321*
Information Needs That Require Data
from Multiple Business Processes   324
Concluding Comments   338

## Chapter 11
### The Conversion Business Process   345

Conversion Business Process in an Enterprise
Value System   345

Conversion Business Process Level REA
Models   346

*Economic Increment Event: Production Run   349*
*Economic Decrement Event: Material Issuance   351*
*Economic Decrement Event: Labor Operation   353*
*Economic Decrement Event: Machine
Operation   358*
*Commitment to Economic Increment Event:
Production Order   359*
*Commitment to Economic Decrement Event:
Materials Requisition   361*
*Custody Relationship   365*
*Association (Responsibility) Relationship   365*
*Reciprocal Relationship   366*
*Linkage Relationships   367*

Information Needs and Measures in the
Conversion Process   371

*Resource Queries in the Conversion Process   371*
*Event Queries in the Conversion Process   371*
*Agent Queries in the Conversion Process   373*
*Duality Relationship Queries in the Conversion
Process   373*
*Stockflow Relationship Queries in the Conversion
Process   374*
*Fulfillment Queries in the Conversion Process   375*
*Reservation Queries in the Conversion Process   376*
*Participation Queries in the Conversion
Process   376*
*Linkage Queries in the Conversion Process   377*

Concluding Comments   378

## Chapter 12
## The Human Resource Business
## Process   385

Human Resource Business Process in an
Enterprise Value System   385
Human Resource Business Process Level REA
Models   387

*Resources   389*
*Instigation Events—Need Identification and Request
for Labor   389*
*Mutual Commitment Event (Labor Schedule)   392*
*Economic Increment Event (Labor Acquisition)   393*
*Economic Decrement Event (Cash
Disbursement)   395*

Information Needs and Measures in the Human
Resource Process   397

*Resource Queries in the Human Resource
Process   398*
*Event Queries in the Human Resource Process   399*
*Agent Queries in the Human Resource Process   400*
*Duality Relationship Queries in the Human Resource
Process   400*
*Stockflow Relationship Queries in the Human
Resource Process   401*
*Fulfillment Queries in the Human Resource
Process   402*
*Reservation Queries in the Human Resource
Process   402*
*Participation Queries in the Human Resource
Process   403*

Concluding Comments   404

## Chapter 13
## The Financing Business Process   409

Financing Business Process in an Enterprise Value
System   409
Financing Business Process Level REA
Models   411

*Resources   413*
*Instigation Events—Need Identification and Request
for Cash   413*
*Mutual Commitment Event (Financing
Agreement)   414*
*Economic Increment Event (Cash Receipt)   419*
*Economic Decrement Event (Cash
Disbursement)   420*

Information Needs and Measures in the Financing
Process   422

*Resource Queries in the Financing Process   423*
*Event Queries in the Financing Process   423*
*Agent Queries in the Financing Process   424*
*Duality and Fulfillment Relationship Queries in the
Financing Process   424*
*Stockflow Relationship Queries in the Financing
Process   425*
*Reservation Queries in the Financing Process   426*
*Participation Queries in the Financing Process   426*

Concluding Comments   427

## Chapter 14
## Enterprise System Risks and Controls   431

The Relationships between Risks, Opportunities, and Controls   431
- *Risks   431*
- *Opportunities and Objectives   432*
- *Controls   432*

Components of Internal Control Systems   434
- *Control Environment   434*
- *Risk Assessment   435*
- *Control Activities   435*
- *Information and Communication   436*
- *Monitoring   436*

Risk Identification   437
- *Economy and Industry Risks   437*
- *Enterprise Risks   439*
- *Business Process Risks   440*
- *Information Process Risks   441*
- *Controls for Economy and Industry Risks   441*
- *Controls for Enterprise Risks   441*
- *Controls for Business Process Risks   442*
- *Event and Relationship Risks and Controls   447*
- *Economic Increment Event Risks and Controls   450*
- *Controls for Information Process Risks   452*
- *Software Processing Controls   455*
- *Application Controls   457*

Concluding Comments   468

## Chapter 15
## ERP Systems and E-Commerce: Intra- and Inter-Enterprise Modeling   475

Intra-Enterprise Systems: ERP and the REA Enterprise Ontology   476
- *Goals and Methods of ERP Software and the REA Enterprise Ontology   476*
- *Intra-Enterprise Integration   479*

Electronic Commerce Solutions and Inter-Enterprise System Design   481

Inter-Enterprise Systems: E-Commerce and the REA Enterprise Ontology   483

## Glossary of Terms and Concepts   489
## Index   505

# Chapter **One**

# An Introduction to Integrated Enterprise Information Systems

## LEARNING OBJECTIVES

The objectives of this chapter are to provide a definition for integrated enterprise information systems, discuss the need for integrated information systems in enterprises, and assess the extent to which current enterprise information systems are integrated. After studying this chapter, you should be able to

1. Define integrated enterprise information system
2. Identify impediments to integrating the components of enterprise information systems
3. Explain the need to eliminate stovepipes in operations and information systems
4. Identify artificial constructs versus natural phenomena in enterprise activities as opportunities for effective reengineering

## INTRODUCTION

Before we can engage in a detailed discussion of integrated enterprise information systems, we must define some terms so that we are all using the same vocabulary. Let's start with the phrase, "integrated enterprise information system." That phrase contains several terms to be defined. Let's start by defining the term *enterprise*. For this book we are defining **enterprise** as an organization established to achieve a particular undertaking involving industrious, systematic activity. Most enterprises are for-profit business organizations; however, not-for-profit organizations are also enterprises. Whether the undertaking of an enterprise is profit driven or charitably motivated, the enterprise needs an information system to support its activities. An **information system** is defined as the network of all communication channels used within an organization. Notice that the concept *information system* is not synonymous with the concept *computer technology*. Certainly computer technology is an important component of most modern information systems; however, the information system is much more inclusive. Any paths by which enterprise employees and

1

business partners impart and receive information (e.g., telephone conversations, written documents, or fax transmittals) are included in the enterprise information system.

**Integration** is defined in most dictionaries as the combination of parts into a whole. This definition may bring to your mind the disassembled pieces of a jigsaw puzzle, and their assembly into one completed picture, as in Exhibit 1–1. To achieve the integration of these pieces into the finished whole, each piece must be connected to another piece that fits and which in turn fits with another piece. The integration of pieces in most jigsaw puzzles is a relatively simple task that has a single correct solution. A picture on the box in which the puzzle pieces are stored illustrates how the assembled end product should look. The puzzle solver uses that illustration to help determine how to integrate the pieces. For this book, the puzzle pieces we are interested in combining into a whole are the building blocks of an enterprise information system, and there is not a sole predefined solution. Thus, the pieces we need to integrate are less similar to jigsaw puzzle pieces and are more similar to various children's building blocks, such as Legos, K'nex, Tinkertoys, and so on. To build something from such building blocks, a person may start with a predefined solution (e.g., a picture of an end product to build) and follow a set of directions to arrive at that solution. However, a person may instead visualize something to build, and then start integrating the pieces, gradually shaping the desired end product. The builder's visualization may change as the product takes shape and additional possibilities are identified. As with jigsaw puzzles, these specialized building pieces must fit together in a certain way. Unlike jigsaw puzzles, these pieces may be correctly assembled in many different ways.

Putting all these terms together, we define *an integrated enterprise information system as a set of communication channels in a business organization, combined together in such a way as to form one network by which information is gathered and disseminated.*

## ENTERPRISE SYSTEM SOFTWARE AND DEGREES OF INTEGRATION

Today many enterprises have what they consider to be integrated information systems. What you might picture in your mind as an integrated information system, however, might

**EXHIBIT 1–1**
**Integration of Jigsaw Puzzle Pieces**

**EXHIBIT 1–2**
**Lego and
K'nex Lincoln
Log Trains**

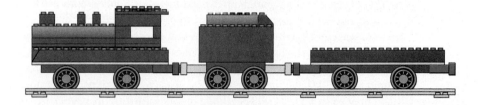

not be consistent with the systems they actually have in place. Remember that integration can be achieved to various degrees.

Consider the following example as a rough analogy of the degrees to which information systems may be integrated: Two children decide to build train cars. One builds a train car using Legos; the other builds a train car using K'nex Lincoln Logs. (See Exhibit 1–2.)

They decide they want to hook the train cars together and run them on the same track. Because Legos and K'nex have different types of connectors, the children must determine how to connect the train cars. One approach they could take is to tie the train cars together with string. Such a connection would work, but is not ideal because it is likely to be loose and to result in the back car swaying to and fro while the cars are in motion. Another approach is for one of the children to start over and build a new train car out of the same type of blocks as the other child's train car. That would result in the best fit for connecting the train cars together. Of course, that approach would involve an incredible amount of cooperation on the part of one of the children, each of which is likely to want the other child to rebuild. Unless one of the children either recognizes that the other child's building blocks were better for building trains, or one of the children bribes the other child in some way to rebuild, or unless one of the children would rather build trains than use them, it is conceivable that a mediator (such as a parent) will need to step in and declare which train should be rebuilt or that the two children will decide not to connect their trains at all.

Other possible integration solutions for the train car example would require some intervention from either the Legos and K'nex manufacturers or from a third-party manufacturer. One such solution is to have these manufacturers collaborate to build a special combination building block that has a Lego compatible connector on one end and a K'nex compatible connector on the other end. Another similar solution is for the Lego manufacturer to build a special building block that has a Lego compatible connector on one end and a generic type of connector on the other end, and for the K'nex manufacturer to build another special building block that has a K'nex compatible connector on one end and a generic type of connector on the other end. Then, the Lego end can be connected to the Lego train car and the K'nex end

In 1979 IBM was using more than 300 noncomplex applications to support financial reporting requirements alone. In isolation, each system appeared very straightforward. However, these 300+ financial applications were fed data by thousands of other systems that provided the details of economic transactions. Attempting to maintain and control such an information system became nearly impossible and far more costly than necessary. IBM initiated several reengineering projects aimed at consolidating these many systems, but still ended up with multiple systems.

can be connected to the K'nex train car and their two generic ends can be attached together. Of course the manufacturers would need to develop standards for the specifications of the generic connectors. As long as the integration needed is exclusively between cars (i.e., the only connections needed are at the edges) these solutions are likely to work as well as the rebuilding option. Also important to note is that for any of these integration solutions to work, the train cars must have the same size wheelbase to operate on a common track.

You may be wondering what building blocks for toy trains have to do with enterprise system integration. Admittedly it is a rough analogy, but think of information systems software applications built by various divisions, departments, or even individual users in an enterprise as the train cars in our toy example. The hardware platform and operating system serve as the track on which the train cars run. Just as train cars built to run on different tracks cannot be connected to run together on the same track, software applications built to run on different operating systems cannot be connected to run together on the same operating system. In the train car example, we would need to take one car to the end of its track, unload whatever the train car was transporting, reload it onto the train car on the next track and take it the rest of the way to its destination. In an enterprise system we need to print the data from one system and rekey it into the other, or preferably we may download it into a generic format from the one system and upload it into the other system. Depending on the extent of interaction between the integrated pieces of our system, such an integration solution may be adequate. However, such a solution is not ideal, just as the string tying the train cars together was not ideal. Such a system is filled with redundancy (duplication of data), which leads to data inconsistencies. For example, an enterprise's marketing department software and its credit department software may each capture data about customers. When a customer calls to change his address and telephone number, if those data are stored separately in each software application, they must be changed in both places or the result will be data inconsistency.

Current developments in enterprise systems have sought to solve the problem of disparate software applications in organizations. Many large companies and even some midsized companies have implemented enterprise resource planning **(ERP) system software** such as Oracle Applications, PeopleSoft, or SAP in an effort to get all of their corporate data into a common database. Others have developed internal enterprise system software applications instead of purchasing packaged enterprise software solutions.

Although a goal of enterprise software is to provide one integrated enterprisewide system with a common database, in reality most implementations of these software packages do not achieve seamless integration. Some of the ERP software packages themselves are combinations of separate applications for manufacturing, materials resource planning (MRP), general ledger, human resources, procurement, and order entry. Programming code forms connections between the modules of these applications in much the same way the combination Lego/K'nex pieces could be manufactured for the purpose of connecting the train cars in our toy example. Within a specific enterprise software package implemented uniformly throughout an enterprise, the connections are likely to be solid; so if a sale order is entered into the order entry module, information flows through to the warehouse, manufacturing, and accounting modules. However, many enterprises do not implement the same enterprise software package uniformly throughout their organizations. Instead they take a best-of-breed approach in which they choose one software package that best fits their **business process** for manufacturing, a different software package that best fits their human resource business process, and yet another software package that best fits their procurement process.

## STOVEPIPED OPERATIONS AND STOVEPIPED SYSTEMS

A recognized problem in integrating enterprise information systems is that stovepiped operations lead to stovepiped systems, and stovepiped systems perpetuate stovepiped operations. Let's examine what this means. First of all, what are stovepiped operations? In Exhibit 1–3 we illustrate the notion of **stovepipes.** Looking at the stovepipes you can see that only at the very top does anything flow back and forth between them. The walls of each functional area go straight up, so no pathways of communication connect the stovepipes. The only openings through which communication can flow are at the top. Second, consider the form of most enterprises. Most are made up of departments that have different functions; sometimes these departments are called functional areas. Typical departments in enterprises may include accounting/finance, customer service, human resources, information systems, logistics, manufacturing, marketing, and procurement. Employees in each of these areas are typically focused on what they, as individuals, need to do for their jobs. In today's economic environment, employees are trained to specialize in something. Assembly line workers specialize in a few specific tasks, which they repeat over and over each day. Credit managers specialize in making a few specific decisions, which they make over and over each day. Accountants specialize in journalizing a limited number of types of transactions, and they make those entries over and over. These departments consisting of people similarly trained in specialized activities serve as stovepipes. Other authors have described these functional areas as silos or islands. The common theme of these descriptors is that each functional area is relatively isolated from the other functional areas and decisions may be made without a realization of how they may affect the other functional areas. The isolation of functional areas need not be physical; two departments that are located on the same floor of the same building may not fully understand each other's operations and objectives, nor how they fit together within the broad scope of the enterprise.

**EXHIBIT 1–3**
**Stovepiped System**

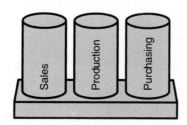

Even the members of top management in organizations tend to be specialists—the CFO (chief financial officer) focuses on financial decisions, while the COO (chief operations officer) focuses on daily operations, and the CIO (chief information officer) focuses on information systems issues. Yet these top-level executives provide the primary pathways of communication by which the functional areas of many enterprises pass information back and forth. Is it any wonder, then, that in most enterprises, separate information systems were created to support the separate, specialized functions? Thus enterprises have accounting information systems, marketing information systems, personnel information systems, and so on. And just as each of the children who built train cars in our toy example is unlikely to want to rebuild a toy just for the sake of matching the other child's, the builders of these stovepiped systems are not likely to want to rebuild their systems to match other systems in the enterprise. The specialized areas must be given a mandate from top management or they must be given a strong incentive for wanting to rebuild their systems—or preferably, both!

Now that you understand how stovepiped operations generate stovepiped systems, consider how stovepiped systems perpetuate stovepiped operations. When decision making is based on information obtained from within one functional area, those decisions are likely to be made from a narrow perspective. When systems are not integrated, decision makers are unlikely to obtain information from multiple areas, because of the enormous effort required to obtain information from multiple systems. If decisions are not based on integrated information, then enterprises may not realize the advantages that such information may provide.

## Breaking Down Stovepipes by Reengineering Business Processes

Many top-level corporate executives have recognized the problem of stovepiped departments or functional areas. Some have tried to break down the stovepipes by encouraging interdepartmental interactions. Some enterprises assign building space so people from different departments are next to each other, with the thought that those employees will develop friendships with each other and perhaps engage in cross-departmental topic discussions. For some enterprises such physical integration of employees from different departments may not be possible or practical. For example, it wouldn't make sense to physically locate a member of an assembly line in an office with a credit manager.

Michael Hammer recommends that enterprises get rid of traditional departments and focus instead on workflow processes. Known as a champion of **reengineering,** Hammer recognizes that most enterprise workflow processes are cross-functional and that passing information from one department to another in a nonintegrated enterprise system environment takes unnecessary time. He also recognizes that to take full advantage of their information system capabilities, enterprises need to do more than just automate their existing processes. In a 1990 article he wrote

> It is time to stop paving the cowpaths. Instead of embedding outdated processes in silicon
> and software, we should obliterate them and start over. . . . use the power of modern
> information technology to radically redesign our business processes in order to achieve
> dramatic improvements in their performance. (p. 104)[1]

[1]M. Hammer, "Business Process Reengineering: Don't Automate, Obliterate," *Harvard Business Review,* July–August 1990, pp. 104–12.

Hammer encouraged enterprises to carefully examine every step in their business processes and question the necessity of each and every step. Many reengineering efforts that have been publicized have focused on streamlining workflow and reducing head count. Other reengineering efforts have focused on consolidating disparate information systems to eliminate duplication of effort in collecting, maintaining, and reporting information. An example of a reengineering effort made to streamline workflow and reduce head count was undertaken by Ford Motor Company and is described in Hammer's article. Economic times were tough and the entire automotive industry was in cost-cutting mode. Management believed Ford would realize a significant cost savings by reengineering its accounts payable (A/P) department. Initially managers hoped to cut Ford's accounts payable head count (redirecting the displaced workers to more challenging, meaningful, and revenue-generating positions) by 20 percent. Upon comparing itself to Mazda, a much smaller automotive manufacturer, managers realized that even accounting for the size difference, Ford should be able to cut its A/P staff by 80 percent. The reengineers started by taking a close look at the existing A/P processing function, which began when the purchasing department wrote a purchase order (PO) and sent a copy to the A/P department (and one to the vendor, of course). The vendor sent the goods to the material control department and an invoice to the A/P department (not necessarily at the same time). Upon receipt of the goods, material control staff prepared a receiving report and sent a copy to A/P. An A/P clerk compared the three documents received (PO, vendor invoice, and receiving report) and matched them on 14 data items. If the 14 fields all matched, the clerk issued payment to the vendor. Most of the time and effort in accounts payable was devoted to reconciling the mismatches.

Ford could have chosen to pave the cowpaths by simply automating the existing process. Instead of the purchasing department, the vendor, and the material control department sending paper documents to A/P, they could have each entered the data into an information system that would automatically compare the 14 fields on the three documents and issue an electronic payment to the vendors for whom there were no mismatches. The mismatches would still need to be flagged for human intervention. This would have sped up the process by eliminating the lead time associated with transferring paper documents to A/P, by eliminating the manual matching process, and by eliminating the issuance of manual checks for those transactions with no mismatches. The faster lead time would undoubtedly have enabled some reduction of head count and also would have enabled Ford to take advantage of more early payment discounts. However, Ford did even better. The reengineers questioned the purpose of the three-way match, and whether mismatches could be prevented from the start rather than being detected after they had already entered the system. The three-way match is an age-old internal control that serves the purpose of ensuring that companies don't pay for something they didn't order and/or that they didn't receive. Notice two risks the three-way match mitigates: (1) they might receive (and pay for) goods they didn't order, and (2) they might pay for goods they didn't receive. Ford's more effective procedure had the purchasing department entering POs into an integrated information system. Upon receipt of goods, material control clerks immediately entered the receipt information into the system and had the computer check to see if the item numbers and the quantities agreed (within predetermined acceptable ranges). If they agreed, the shipment was accepted; if they disagreed, the shipment was rejected. Vendors quickly learned not to deliver a shipment that didn't match the order! This control mitigates the first risk of receiving goods that were not ordered. Ford mitigated the second risk of paying for goods not received by issuing payment based on goods receipts rather than basing payments on invoices. In fact, Ford asked its vendors to not send invoices and even threw away the invoices that were received! Upon the acceptance of a shipment of goods, the computer automatically flagged the record for payment and the check was issued within the early payment discount period.

We started this discussion saying that Ford reengineered its accounts payable function. But is that really true? Actually, Ford reengineered its Acquisition/Payment business process. The Acquisition/Payment process (that we describe further in Chapter 9) is sometimes called the expenditures cycle or the procure-to-pay process. The reengineering project involved three of the major events found in this business process: the ordering of goods, the receipt of goods, and the payment for goods, and cut across three different departments (purchasing, material control, and Accounts Payable). That meant many people had to change their job functions. This radical change approach paid off for Ford, which achieved a 75 percent reduction in head count, and improved accuracy of inventory information with fewer discrepancies between the physical inventory records and the financial inventory records. Vendors enjoyed on-time payments, although they had to get used to not sending invoices. One vendor complained that their own system didn't allow them not to print an invoice; Ford countered that the vendor could print the invoice as its system required, but then just throw it away rather than wasting postage to mail it to Ford.

Ford's reengineers are not the only ones to question an age-old accounting practice such as the three-way match internal control. McCarthy questions the need for debits and credits to accomplish accounting.[2] He proposed an alternative accounting model that he labeled as the REA (Resources-Events-Agents) accounting model. In a series of papers in the years since, Geerts and McCarthy have proposed expansion of the REA accounting model into an enterprise domain ontology that can be used as a foundation for building enterprise systems to provide information not just for accounting purposes but also for most decision-making needs.[3] The premise is that the **base objects** (the foundational building blocks) in an enterprise information system should not be reflective of a certain view (decision-making need) within the enterprise, but that they should reflect the real underlying activities in which the enterprise engages. Systems containing foundational building blocks that represent a particular view of data (e.g., debits, credits, journals, and ledgers) are view-driven. Systems whose foundational building blocks are representations of the actual underlying activities are event-driven. You may not have heard the term *ontology* before. Ontology is the study of what things exist. Domain ontologies attempt to define things that are relevant to specific application domains. The purpose of the REA enterprise ontology is to define constructs common to all enterprises and demonstrate how those constructs may be represented in an integrated enterprise information system. Effective REA modeling requires and enables thorough understanding of an enterprise's environment, business processes, risks, and information needs.

[2]W. E. McCarthy, "The REA Accounting Model: A Generalized Framework for Accounting Systems in a Shared Data Environment," *The Accounting Review,* July 1982, pp. 554–77.

[3]G. L. Geerts and W. E. McCarthy, "Modeling Business Enterprises as Value-Added Process Hierarchies with Resource-Event-Agent Object Templates," in *Business Object Design and Implementation,* edited by J. Sutherland, D. Patel, C. Casanave, G. Hollowell, and J. Miller (London: Springer-Verlag, 1997), pp. 94–113. Also see "An Accounting Object Infrastructure for Knowledge-Based Enterprise Models," *IEEE Intelligent Systems and Their Application* 14, no. 4 (1999), pp. 89–94; "The Ontological Foundation of REA Enterprise Information Systems," presented to the American Accounting Association annual meeting, Philadelphia, Pennsylvania, 2000; and "An Ontological Analysis of the Economic Primitives of the Extended-REA Enterprise Information Architecture," *International Journal of Accounting Information Systems* 3, no. 1 (March 2002), pp. 1–16.

# Case in Point

The term *enterprise system* for many people brings to mind ERP software. Such software has the same objective as the **REA ontology**—to store enterprise information one time, in a disaggregated format from which it can be retrieved by many different users for use in making many different types of decisions. O'Leary compared the REA ontology with SAP, the market leader in enterprise resource planning software.[4] He concluded that many similarities exist between the underlying SAP models and the REA pattern, but that the SAP models contain many **artificial constructs** as base objects, which is something REA discourages.[5] In other words, while parts of ERP software use representations of underlying business activities as the foundational building blocks, they use many artificial view-driven base objects as well. His analysis confirms that REA provides a good theoretical foundation for studying enterprise system design.

Like REA models, ERP software packages are representations of business processes. If the software is not an adequate representation of an enterprise's existing business processes, either the business process must be changed or the software must be changed. Either type of change is problematic. When an enterprise customizes ERP software to fit its business processes, considerable care must be taken to avoid creating bugs in the software. The software changes take extra time, and every time the vendor upgrades the software the customizations need to be redone. On the other hand, when an enterprise changes its business processes, people must change. People don't like to change. If change management in such cases is not handled well, the software implementation is doomed to fail. Most failed ERP software implementations have been blamed on people issues as opposed to technological software issues. Some practitioners have pinpointed one of the biggest problems as lack of education about the underlying business processes for system users.

In the chapters that follow, we introduce you to a set of building blocks that are the best blocks for interoperability because they focus on the common elements of the reality of most enterprises. They focus on real things, not artificial constructs. The best news is that even if you do not agree that these are the best building blocks for designing integrated enterprise information systems, the discussions in this book will lead you to thoroughly analyze the major business processes that are common to most enterprises. By developing a strong understanding of business processes, you will gain the business-and-people processes education so many ERP software users lack (see Case in Point nearby). The REA

[4]D. E. O'Leary, "On the Relationship Between REA and SAP," presented to the American Accounting Association Annual Meeting, San Diego, CA, 1999.

[5]C. L. Dunn and W. E. McCarthy, "The REA Accounting Model: Intellectual Heritage and Prospects for Progress," *Journal of Information Systems* 11, no. 1 (1997), pp. 31–51.

ontology approach attempts to eliminate stovepipes and is based on a set of building blocks that could be used by all enterprises, and by all functional areas within an enterprise. Wherever two areas of an enterprise (or two different enterprises) use these same building blocks as the foundation of their database design, their systems may be effectively integrated.

## Key Terms and Concepts

| | | |
|---|---|---|
| Artificial constructs, *9* | ERP system software, *4* | Reengineering, *6* |
| Base object, *8* | Information system, *1* | Stovepipe, *5* |
| Business process, *5* | Integration, *2* | |
| Enterprise, *1* | REA ontology, *9* | |

## Review Questions

LO3  R1.  What does it mean to have a stovepiped enterprise?

LO3  R2.  What does it mean to have stovepiped systems?

LO2  R3.  What are some impediments enterprises may encounter in their efforts to integrate their information systems?

LO4  R4.  What does the phrase *paving the cowpaths* mean with respect to reengineering?

LO1, LO2  R5.  What are three common types of integration attempts currently used by enterprises?

## Multiple Choice Questions

LO2  MC1.  Most failed software implementations have been blamed on:
   a.  Technological software issues
   b.  People issues
   c.  a. and b.
   d.  None of the above

LO4  MC2.  What are domain ontologies?
   a.  Foundational building blocks
   b.  Base objects
   c.  Attempts to define things that are relevant
   d.  None of the above

LO2  MC3.  What do most ERP users lack?
   a.  Business-and-people processes education
   b.  Understanding of stovepipe organizations
   c.  People skills
   d.  Keystoke and transaction training

LO4  MC4.  The REA ontology approach is intended to:
   a.  Understand software specific issues
   b.  Define artificial constructs
   c.  Encourage the use of structured data blocks
   d.  Eliminate stovepipes

LO4    **MC5.** What is the REA ontology based on?

        a. A set of building blocks that can be used by all enterprises and functional areas

        b. Debits and credits

        c. A set of building blocks that can be used by a few enterprises and functional areas

        d. Enterprise domain

## Discussion Questions

LO1    **D1.** What are the different degrees to which an information system may be integrated, and what are the pros and cons to each approach?

LO3    **D2.** Explain the statement, "Stovepiped operations lead to stovepiped systems; stovepiped systems perpetuate stovepiped operations."

LO4    **D3.** Read Michael Hammer's article on reengineering. Is reengineering the same as automating or computerizing the traditional methods of conducting business? Explain.

LO2    **D4.** Suppose you wanted to implement REA enterprise ontology concepts when you enter the workplace. What obstacles and challenges are you likely to face?

LO4    **D5.** Would you describe the REA enterprise ontology as used for accounting systems as automating traditional methods of accounting or as reengineering accounting methods? Why?

## Applied Learning

LO1, LO2, LO3, LO4    **A1.** Reengineering the Business School.

This chapter included discussions of functional silos or stovepipes in business and the need to reengineer business processes and information systems to better share information across functions. Consider your college or university's business school.

**Required:**

a. Describe the structure of your business school (e.g., what departments or other subdivisions exist within the business school; who is in charge of those areas; where are faculty offices located for each department or subdivision; to what extent do faculty members from different departments or other subdivisions coauthor research and/or team teach; how many business courses are team-taught; does anything about the structure of your business school seem remarkable).

b. Based on your description in part (a), to what extent do you think functional silos are present in your college or university's business school?

c. How does the presence (or absence) of stovepipes in the form of the business school affect your curriculum?

d. What are your recommendations about how your business school could be reengineered? Explain.

LO1, LO2, LO3    **A2.** Management Misinformation Systems

Five assumptions people typically make about information systems follow. The author, Russell L. Ackoff, contends these are erroneous assumptions and identifies reasons why he feels they are in error.[6] The objective of this assignment is to help you to begin

[6]Russell L. Ackoff, "Management Misinformation Systems," *Management Science* 14, no. 4 (December 1967), pp. B-147–B-156.

to identify factors that distinguish good information systems from bad information systems.

### Assumption 1—Give Them More

Most MIS's are designed on the assumption that the critical deficiency under which most managers operate is the *lack of relevant information*. I do not deny that most managers lack a good deal of information that they should have, but I do deny that this is the most important informational deficiency from which they suffer. It seems to me that they suffer more from an *overabundance of irrelevant information*.

This is not a play on words. The consequences of changing the emphasis of an MIS from supplying relevant information to eliminating irrelevant information is considerable. If one is preoccupied with supplying relevant information, attention is almost exclusively given to the generation, storage, and retrieval of information: hence emphasis is placed on constructing data banks, coding, indexing, updating files, access languages, and so on. The ideal which has emerged from this orientation is an infinite pool of data into which a manager can reach to pull out any information he wants. If, on the other hand, one sees the manager's information problem primarily, but not exclusively, as one that arises out of an overabundance of irrelevant information, most of which was not asked for, then the two most important functions of an information system become *filtration* (or evaluation) and *condensation*. The literature on MIS's seldom refers to these functions let alone considers how to carry them out.

My experience indicates that most managers receive much more data (if not information) than they can possibly absorb even if they spend all of their time trying to do so. Hence they already suffer from an information overload. They must spend a great deal of time separating the relevant documents. For example, I have found that I receive an average of forty-three hours of unsolicited reading material each week. The solicited material is usually half again this amount.

I have seen a daily stock status report that consists of approximately six hundred pages of computer printout. The report is circulated daily across managers' desks. I've also seen requests for major capital expenditures that come in book size, several of which are distributed to managers each week. It is not uncommon for many managers to receive an average of one journal a day or more. One could go on and on.

Unless the information overload to which managers are subjected is reduced, any additional information made available by an MIS cannot be expected to be used effectively.

Even relevant documents have too much redundancy. Most documents can be considerably condensed without loss of content. My point here is best made, perhaps, by describing briefly an experiment that a few of my colleagues and I conducted on the Operations Research (OR) literature several years ago. By using a panel of well-known experts we identified four OR articles that all members of the panel considered to be "above average," and four articles that were considered to be "below average." The authors of the eight articles were asked to prepare "objective" examinations (duration thirty minutes) plus answers for graduate students who were to be assigned the articles for reading. (The authors were not informed about the experiment.) Then several experienced writers were asked to reduce each article to $\frac{2}{3}$ and $\frac{1}{3}$ of its original length only by eliminating words. They also prepared a brief abstract of each article. Those who did the condensing did not see the examinations to be given to the students.

A group of graduate students who had not previously read the articles was then selected. Each one was given four articles randomly selected, each of which was in one of its four versions: 100%, 67%, 33%, or abstract. Each version of each article was read by two students. All were given the same examinations. The average scores on the examinations were compared.

For the above-average articles there was no significant difference between average test scores for the 100%, 67%, and 33% versions, but there was a significant *decrease* in average test scores for those who had read only the abstract. For the below-average articles there was no difference in average test scores among those who had read the 100%, 67%, and 33% versions, but there was a significant *increase* in average test scores of those who had read only the abstract.

The sample used was obviously too small for general conclusions but the results strongly indicate the extent to which even good writing can be condensed without loss of information. I refrain from drawing the obvious conclusions about bad writing.

It seems clear that condensation as well as filtration, performed mechanically or otherwise, should be an essential part of an MIS, and that such a system should be capable of handling much, if not all, of the unsolicited as well as solicited information that a manager receives.

## Assumption 2—The Manager Needs the Information That He Wants

Most MIS designers "determine" what information is needed by asking managers what information they would like to have. This is based on the assumption that managers know what information they need and want it.

For a manager to know what information he needs he must be aware of each type of decision he should make (as well as does make) and he must have an adequate model of each. These conditions are seldom satisfied. Most managers have some conception of at least some of the types of decisions they must make. Their conceptions, however, are likely to be deficient in a very critical way, a way that follows from an important principle of scientific economy: the less we understand a phenomenon, the more variables we require to explain it. Hence, the manager who does not understand the phenomenon he controls plays it "safe" and, with respect to information, wants "everything." The MIS designer, who has even less understanding of the relevant phenomenon than the manager, tries to provide even more than everything. He thereby increases what is already an overload of irrelevant information.

For example, market researchers in a major oil company once asked their marketing managers what variables they thought were relevant in estimating the sales volume of future service stations. Almost seventy variables were identified. The market researchers then added about half again this many variables and performed a large multiple linear regression analysis of sales of existing stations against these variables and found about thirty-five to be statistically significant. A forecasting equation was based on this analysis. An OR team subsequently constructed a model based on only one of these variables, traffic flow, which predicted sales better than the thirty-five variable regression equation. The team went on to *explain* sales at service stations in terms of the customers' perception of the amount of time lost by stopping for service. The relevance of all but a few of the variables used by the market researchers could be explained by their effect on such perception.

The moral is simple: one cannot specify what information is required for decision making until an explanatory model of the decision process and the system involved has been constructed and tested. Information systems are subsystems of control systems. They cannot be designed adequately without taking control into account. Furthermore, whatever else regression analyses can yield, they cannot yield understanding and explanation of phenomena. They describe and, at best, predict.

### Assumption 3—Give a Manager the Information He Needs and His Decision Making Will Improve

It is frequently assumed that if a manager is provided with the information he needs, he will then have no problem in using it effectively. The history of OR* stands to the contrary. For example, give most managers an initial tableau of a typical "real" mathematical programming, sequencing, or network problem and see how close they come to an optimal solution. If their experience and judgment have any value they may not do badly, but they will seldom do very well. In most management problems there are too many possibilities to expect experience, judgment, or intuition to provide good guesses, even with perfect information.

Furthermore, when several probabilities are involved in a problem the unguided mind of even a manager has difficulty in aggregating them in a valid way. We all know many simple problems in probability in which untutored intuition usually does very badly (e.g., What are the correct odds that 2 of 25 people selected at random will have their birthdays on the same day of the year?). For example, very few of the results obtained by queuing theory, when arrivals and service are probabilistic, are obvious to managers; nor are the results of risk analysis where the manager's own subjective estimates of probabilities are used.

The moral: it is necessary to determine how well managers can use needed information. When, because of the complexity of the decision process, they can't use it well, they should be provided with either decision rules or performance feedback so that they can identify and learn from their mistakes.

**Hint:** In deciding whether you agree or disagree with the author you may want to consider the definitions of data and information once more. When the author refers to some of the above items as information, is it really information or is it data?

### Assumption 4—More Communication Means Better Performance

One characteristic of most MIS's which I have seen is that they provide managers with better current information about what other managers and their departments and divisions are doing. Underlying this provision is the belief that better interdepartmental communication enables managers to coordinate their decisions more effectively and hence improves the organization's overall performance. Not only is this not necessarily so, but it seldom is so. One would hardly expect two competing companies to become more cooperative because the information each acquires about the other is improved. This analogy is not as farfetched as one might first suppose. For example, consider the following very much simplified version of a situation I once ran into. The simplification of the case does not affect any of its essential characteristics.

A department store has two "line" operations: buying and selling. Each function is performed by a separate department. The Purchasing Department primarily controls one variable—how much of each item is bought. The Merchandising Department controls the price at which it is sold. Typically, the measure of performance applied to the Purchasing De-

---

***Note:** OR stands for Operation Research. It is an academic subject area dealing with the application of mathematical models and techniques to business decisions.

partment was the turnover rate of inventory. The measure applied to the Merchandising Department was gross sales; this department sought to maximize the number of items sold times their price.

Now by examining a single item let us consider what happens in this system. The merchandising manager, using his knowledge of competition and consumption, set a price which he judged would maximize gross sales. In doing so he utilized price-demand curves for each type of item. For each price the curves show the expected sales and values on an upper and lower confidence band as well. (See Figure 1). When instructing the Purchasing Department how many items to make available, the merchandising manager quite naturally used the value on the upper confidence curve. This minimized the chances of his running short which, if it occurred, would hurt his performance. It also maximized the chances of being overstocked, but this was not his concern, only the purchasing manager's. Say, therefore, that the merchandising manager initially selected price $P_1$ and requested that amount $Q_1$ be made available by the Purchasing Department.

In this company the purchasing manager also had access to the price-demand curves. He knew the merchandising manager always ordered optimistically. Therefore, using the same curve he read over from $Q_1$ to the upper limit and down to the expected value from which he obtained $Q_2$, the quantity he actually intended to make available. He did not intend to pay for the merchandising manager's optimism. If merchandising ran out of stock, it was not his worry. Now the merchandising manager was informed about what the purchasing manager had done so he adjusted his price to $P_2$. The purchasing manager in turn was told that the merchandising manager had made this readjustment so he planned to make only $Q_3$ available. If this process (made possible only by perfect communication between departments) had been allowed to continue, nothing would have been bought and nothing would have been sold. This outcome was avoided by prohibiting communication between the two departments and forcing each to guess what the other was doing.

I have obviously caricatured the situation in order to make the point clear: When organizational units have inappropriate measures of performance which put them in conflict with each other, as is often the case, communication between them may hurt organizational performance, not help it. Organizational structure and performance measurement must be

**FIGURE 1**
**Price-Demand Curve**

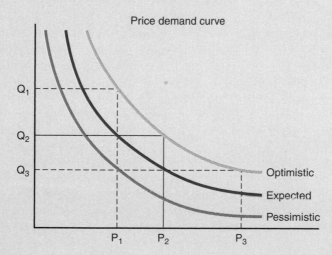

taken into account before opening the flood gates and permitting the free flow of information between parts of the organization.

### Assumption 5—A Manager Does Not Have to Understand How an Information System Works, Only How to Use It

Most MIS designers seek to make their systems as innocuous and unobtrusive as possible to managers lest they become frightened. The designers try to provide managers with very easy access to the system and assure them that they need to know nothing more about it. The designers usually succeed in keeping managers ignorant in this regard. This leaves managers unable to evaluate the MIS as a whole. It often makes them afraid to even try to do so lest they display their ignorance publicly. In failing to evaluate their MIS, managers delegate much of the control of the organization to the system's designers and operators who may have many virtues, but managerial competence is seldom among them.

Let me cite a case in point. A chairman of the board of a medium-size company asked for help on the following problem. One of his larger (decentralized) divisions had installed a computerized production—inventory control and manufacturing—manager information systems about a year earlier. It had acquired about $2,000,000 worth of equipment to do so. The board chairman had just received a request from the Division for permission to replace the original equipment with newly announced equipment which would cost several times the original amount. An extensive "justification" for so doing was provided with the request. The chairman wanted to know whether the request was really justified. He admitted to complete incompetence in this connection.

A meeting was arranged at the Division at which I was subjected to an extended and detailed briefing. The system was large but relatively simple. At the heart of it was a reorder point for each item and a maximum allowable stock level. Reorder quantities took lead time as well as the allowable maximum into account. The computer kept track of stock, ordered items when required and generated numerous reports on both the state of the system it controlled and its own "actions."

When the briefing was over I was asked if I had any questions. I did. First I asked if, when the system had been installed, there had been many parts whose stock level exceeded the maximum amount possible under the new system. I was told there were many. I asked for a list of about thirty and for some graph paper. Both were provided. With the help of the system designer and volumes of old daily reports I began to plot the stock level of the first listed item over time. When this item reached the maximum "allowable" stock level it had been reordered. The system designer was surprised and said that by sheer "luck" I had found one of the few errors made by the system. Continued plotting showed that because of repeated premature reordering the item had never gone much below the maximum stock level. Clearly the program was confusing the maximum allowable stock level and the reorder point. This turned out to be the case in more than half of the items on the list.

Next I asked if they had many paired parts, ones that were only used with each other; for example, matched nuts and bolts. They had many. A list was produced and we began checking the previous day's withdrawals. For more than half of the pairs the differences in the numbers recorded as withdrawn were very large. No explanation was provided.

Before the day was out it was possible to show by some quick and dirty calculations that the new computerized system was costing the company almost $150,000 per month more than the hand system which it had replaced, most of this in excess inventories.

The recommendation was that the system be redesigned as quickly as possible and that the new equipment not be authorized for the time being.

The questions asked of the system had been obvious and simple ones. Managers should have been able to ask them but—and this is the point—they felt themselves incompetent to do so. They would not have allowed a hand-operated system to get so far out of their control.

No MIS should ever be installed unless the managers for whom it is intended are trained to evaluate and hence control it rather than be controlled by it.

### Required:

This assignment should be performed in groups of four to six people. After each group discusses the assumptions and contentions, it should come to a group consensus that agrees or disagrees with the author. Write a one-page report summarizing your group's conclusions and justifications. In addition, develop a one-sentence statement that describes what a good information system should have or should do in response to each assumption and contention.

## Answers to Multiple Choice Questions

MC1. B; MC2. C; MC3. A; MC4. D; MC5. A.

# Chapter **Two**

# Representation and Patterns: An Introduction to the REA Enterprise Ontology

## LEARNING OBJECTIVES

The objective of this chapter is to help you understand how to analyze and create representations of enterprises that serve as the core foundation for their information systems. After studying this chapter, you should be able to

1. Explain the importance of representation and modeling in enterprise system design and use
2. Identify various types of patterns and recognize patterns in the world around you
3. Describe the purpose and the components of the four levels of the REA ontology
4. Describe the usefulness of the REA pattern as a framework for database design

## REPRESENTATION AND MODELING

You may be wondering why **representation** and modeling are important for understanding enterprise information systems. The general answer to this question is that we can't understand enterprise information systems without **models** that serve as representations of the systems and their underlying **reality.**[1] The systems are too large and complex for most people to comprehend in their entirety. The creation and use of models to help build and understand complex things in life is common. Engineers who build automobiles create models before they create the real cars. Automotive repairpersons use models to help them understand the cars on which they work. Architects create models of the buildings they design; once the

---

[1]Much of the material on representation and patterns is based on materials prepared by Professor William E. McCarthy at Michigan State University. The script material is also based on books written by Roger Schank, including *Tell Me A Story,* Northwestern University Press 1990; *The Connoisseur's Guide to the Mind,* Summit Books 1991; and *Dynamic Memory Revisited,* Cambridge University Press 1999.

building is built, other users may need to refer to the model to understand some aspect of the building (such as where the support beams are located).

To design and understand enterprise information systems, we must be able to develop and understand representations of the enterprise's reality. Representations are surrogates for the real constructs; in other words, they are **symbols** of those constructs. To design an information system that closely resembles the underlying reality of the enterprise about which the information is stored, we must build a set of symbols that represent that reality. Some models are better than others. Consider an example of model cars. Picture a molded plastic toy car designed for use by a baby or toddler. For safety reasons, such a toy may be created with no removable parts that could choke a baby—the wheels wouldn't turn, and the doors wouldn't open. Contrast that with a model car that an adult constructs from a kit. Such a model may have doors and a trunk that open, headlights that light up, perhaps a battery-operated convertible top or even a power source that propels it across the floor. Which is the better representation, and why? Most would consider the adult model car the better representation because it is more like a real automobile than is the baby's toy car.

In modeling enterprise systems, our symbol representations must not only map as directly as possible to the underlying reality but they must also be convertible into a computerized format. In the case of designing enterprise databases, that means we must be able to create paper-based representations of the enterprise reality and then convert the paper models into a format compatible with a database software package.

Representations may be created at different levels of abstraction. More specifically, a representation may symbolize individual **objects** or categories of objects. In database design, individual objects are sometimes referred to as tokens, and categories of objects are known as **types.** For example, see Exhibit 2–1.

Exhibit 2–1 demonstrates that the reality of shapes can be represented in different formats and at various levels of abstraction. Each shape is represented at the token level by a word that once upon a time was created as a representation for that shape. The string of characters s-q-u-a-r-e is a representation of the square shape. A **token** is an individual instance of something. For example *Fred's little red Corvette* is a token. Please understand

**EXHIBIT 2–1**
**Representation at Token and Type Levels of Abstraction**

Adapted from: G. L. Geerts and W. E. McCarthy, "An Ontological Analysis of the Economic Primitives of the Extended-REA Enterprise Information Architecture," *International Journal of Accounting Information Systems* 3, no. 1 (March 2002), pp. 1–16.

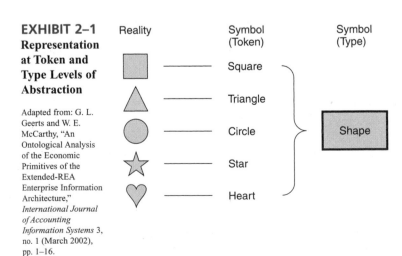

that it is not the fact that the shapes are represented by words that makes the middle column of Exhibit 2–1 a token-level representation; it is the fact that each individual instance in the reality is represented as a separate token. For the Corvette example, the tokens in the middle column could include *Fred's little red Corvette, Samantha's hot pink Corvette, Sally's little green Corvette,* or *Andrew's royal blue Corvette.*

The shapes (reality) in the first column of Exhibit 2–1 also may be represented at the type level. A type is a category of instances that have something in common with each other. The box with the word *shape* inside it in the third column of Exhibit 2–1 is a type-level representation of the individual shape instances. Each separate shape fits into the *shape* category. *Corvette* is a type, of which *Fred's little red Corvette* and *Samantha's hot pink Corvette* are tokens.[2] This reality-to-category mapping is a very important concept in building enterprise system models, because often we need to represent categories of things as well as the individual things themselves. Imagine an enterprise that has 4,000 different inventory items, 895 employees, 25 different cash accounts, 12 branch locations, and engages in thousands of transactions each day. A system must be built to store data about all those individual things, but the conceptual model of the system must represent those things at the type level to make the complexity manageable.

# PATTERNS

People use **patterns** of various kinds every day in understanding the environment around them. Patterns allow us to make predictions about future events and to make sense of the present based on our past experiences. Patterns are used in learning from the time that we are very young children throughout the rest of our lives. Preschoolers and early elementary school students are given a row of symbols such as

♥♦♥♦♥__

and are asked to fill in the blank with the appropriate symbol. Go ahead; figure out what goes in the blank. It probably didn't take you very long to identify the correct answer as ♦!

As students progress, patterns may be more complicated, for example,

♣♦♥♠♣♦♥♠___

Of course the correct answer is ♣.

Try this one, which is a little more complex:

⊕⊠⊖⊞⊗⊟⊕⊠⊖⊞___

The answer is ⊗ and requires recognition that the + × — pattern is embedded inside the ○□○□ pattern.

---

[2]Types also exist at different levels of detail; we have subtypes and supertypes (Corvette is a subtype of car, which is a subtype of vehicle). We will save this level of complexity for later chapters.

# Object Patterns

Some patterns serve the purpose of associating like objects with each other. For example, an early learning pattern was (and perhaps still is) popular on the children's television show "Sesame Street." A group of four objects was shown on the screen and a song said something like, "One of these things just doesn't belong here; one of these things just isn't the same." The children were asked to identify which thing was different. Simple patterns of this type might include three things that are identical (e.g., three pictures of the same cow) and one unique thing (e.g., a picture of an airplane). A slightly harder pattern of this type could include three things that could be combined into a category, contrasted with another thing that doesn't fit the category. For example, a group could include a cow, a dog, a monkey, and an airplane; of course it is the airplane that is not like the others. Even more advanced patterns of this type might include three things that are related to each other by some kind of domain (e.g., a cow, a barn, and a tractor are related to each other as part of the farm domain) and one thing that is unrelated to that domain (e.g., a monkey). Note that it is particularly complicated if the object that is unrelated to the domain common to the other three is part of a different domain with at least one of the other objects. In this example, cow and monkey are part of the animal domain, but barn and tractor don't fit that domain.

In conceptual modeling, object patterns consist of expected groupings of things and the relationships between them. Let's use the farm example. What things and activities would you expect to find on a farm? A partial list would include

- Animals
- Crops
- Barn
- Silo
- Farmer
- Tractor
- Harvesting equipment
- Field
- Harvesting of crops
- Feeding of animals
- Caring for animals

What relationships between these objects would you expect to find on the farm? A partial list would include

- Animals take shelter in the barn
- Crops (unharvested) grow in the field
- Crops (harvested) are stored in the silo
- Farmer participates in harvesting of crops
- Crops participate in harvesting of crops
- Farmer responsible for caring for animals
- Animals benefit from caring for animals
- Farmer drives the tractor
- Harvesting equipment is used in harvesting of crops

You can probably think of additional objects, activities, and relationships between them that you could expect to find on a farm—these lists are intended just to get you thinking. How do you know what things are likely to be part of the farm's reality? You probably know from past experience. That experience could have been personal (e.g., from visiting or growing up on a farm) or secondhand (e.g., from seeing a farm on television or hearing stories about a farm on which your grandfather was raised).

You may not have realized you had a farm object pattern stored in your memory! In fact, you have many object patterns stored in your long-term memory. Whether the information is actually stored as a pattern or whether you simply have an indexing scheme that triggers recall of those objects from various parts of your memory is a matter of debate among academic researchers, but that distinction is unimportant for purposes of this book. Our goal is to lead you along a lifelong path of using pattern matching to solve problems. When you are faced with what looks like a new problem, this approach requires you to find some similarity to old problems for which you have already developed a solution. You may then apply the old solution to the new problem, adapting the solution for anything that is different in the new situation. For enterprise system modeling, you will need to think about what objects you expect to find in an enterprise, match the reality to your expectations, and adapt as necessary. Such an approach enables you to avoid having to reinvent the wheel every time you design or evaluate a new enterprise system.

## Script Patterns

Whereas object patterns focus on objects and the relationships between them, **script patterns** are sequences of events that typically occur in combination with each other. Imagine you are in a friend's house and he came in from his car and said he had just come from the grocery store. If you are a polite person, you will likely ask if he would like you to help him carry in the groceries. How do you know he has groceries to carry? Based on past experience, you have stored in your memory a script pattern for a sequence of events that frequently occur when someone goes to the grocery store. That script leads you to infer he drove to the grocery store (not necessarily from home), took groceries off the store shelves, transported the groceries to the checkout lane, placed the groceries on the checkout counter so the prices could be summed and the groceries could be bagged, paid for the groceries, and drove home. The script that is evoked in your mind is not necessarily accurate for the particular situation. Perhaps the friend was looking for only one thing, and was unable to find it, so he came home empty-handed, or perhaps he went to the grocery store because it contained a postal station and he needed to mail a letter. In spite of exceptions, the script patterns you have developed based on your past experiences help you more often than not in understanding your present and future experiences.

**Context** is important in determining which script is invoked, and part of what determines someone's knowledge is that person's ability to invoke the most appropriate script for a situation. For example, imagine that someone starts to tell you a story that begins with the following sentences. "Once upon a time a boy named Jimmy met a girl named Melissa. They fell in love." You likely have at least two scripts to invoke based on those sentences, and you need to know more about the context to guess the ending. If you are told that the story is a traditional romance, you are likely to guess the ending reads something like this: "They lived happily ever after." If you are told the story is a romantic tragedy, you are likely to guess the ending reads more like this: "One of them died and the other was very sad."

To thoroughly understand the enterprise domain and to completely represent the phenomena of the enterprise in its information system we must identify object patterns that communicate things in the enterprise that are usually associated with each other, and we must also identify script patterns that communicate typical sequences of events. A combination of such patterns for a particular domain is known as a domain ontology.

# THE REA ENTERPRISE ONTOLOGY

McCarthy proposed a generalized model for accounting systems after analyzing many accounting transactions and identifying the common features of the transactions.[3] McCarthy and Geerts have further developed the constructs of the original model to form an enterprise domain ontology. This ontology is called the REA Enterprise Ontology because three of the principle constructs are **R**esources, **E**vents, and **A**gents. **Resources** are things of economic value (with or without physical substance) that are provided or consumed by an enterprise's activities and operations. Examples of resources found in many enterprises are cash, raw materials, finished goods inventory, equipment, employee labor, and land. (Note: this is not a comprehensive list!) **Events** are activities within an enterprise that need to be planned, controlled, executed, and evaluated. A carefully designed REA model includes only those events that are necessary and in a sense natural, as opposed to those that could be eliminated without changing the substance of the enterprise and thus are in a sense artificial. We return to this distinction later. For this chapter we focus only on economic events, which are those events that increase or decrease one or more resources in the enterprise. Later in the book we introduce other types of events. **Agents** are individuals, departments, divisions, or organizations that participate in the control and execution of events.

The **REA ontology** views enterprises at four levels of detail.[4] The first level of detail is called the value system level. A **value system level REA model** focuses on the resources that are exchanged between the enterprise and its various external business partners such as suppliers, customers, creditors/investors, and employees. A supply chain is made up of the value system level models of interconnected business partners. The second level of detail is called the value chain level. A **value chain level REA model** focuses on the resource flows between interconnected business processes and on the economic events that accomplish the resource flows. The term *business process* is a term widely used in practice to mean anything from a single activity of producing a report to an entire transaction cycle. For this textbook, business process describes an entire transaction cycle. The commonly interconnected

---

[3]The REA Ontology material included in this chapter is based on the McCarthy 1982 paper (see footnote 1) and on the following papers: G. Geerts and W. E. McCarthy, "Modeling Business Enterprises as Value-Added Process Hierarchies with Resource-Event-Agent Object Templates" in J. Sutherland and D. Patel, eds., *Business Object Design and Implementation* (London: Springer-Verlag, 1997), pp. 94–113. See also "Using Object Templates from the REA Accounting Model to Engineer Business Processes and Tasks," *The Review of Business Information Systems* 5, no. 4 (Fall 2001), pp. 89–108; "An Accounting Object Infrastructure for Knowledge-Based Enterprise Models," *IEEE Intelligent Systems and Their Application* 14, no. 4 (1999), pp. 89–94; "The Ontological Foundation of REA Enterprise Information Systems," presented to the American Accounting Association annual meeting, Philadelphia, Pennsylvania, 2000; and "An Ontological Analysis of the Economic Primitives of the Extended-REA Enterprise Information Architecture," *International Journal of Accounting Information Systems* 3, no. 1 (March 2002), pp. 1–16.

[4]Geerts and McCarthy describe the REA ontology as a three-level architecture consisting of the value chain, business process, and task levels; however, many professors also find it helpful to discuss the value system level.

business processes included in a value chain level REA model are the **financing process,** the **acquisition/payment process,** the **human resources process,** the **conversion process** (manufacturing), and the **sales/collection process.** Each of these processes is discussed in more detail later in this chapter and in later chapters. The third level of detail is the business process level. A **business process level REA model** focuses on one or more transaction cycles in an enterprise's value chain, expanding the representation to include various types of resources, events, agents, and relationships among them. The fourth level of detail is the task level. A **task level REA model** focuses on the individual steps involved in accomplishing events in an enterprise. Tasks are activities that may be changed or eliminated and therefore should not serve as foundational elements in an enterprise information system.

The value system level is an object pattern that depicts a macro level view of the firm, with the objects being the enterprise itself, its external business partners, and the resources that are exchanged between them. The value chain level is based on a script pattern. McCarthy proposes that there is a **business-entrepreneur script** (with several possible variations) that serves as a starting point for modeling enterprises. The script says (from the enterprise's point of view)

- The enterprise gets some money
- The enterprise engages in value-added exchanges, such as
  - Purchase equipment and raw materials
  - Purchase labor
  - Manufacture finished goods
  - Sell finished goods
- The enterprise pays back the money and lives off the profit

Variations on this script include value-added exchanges that involve performing services rather than manufacturing and selling finished goods, and any of a number of other revenue-generating and resource-expending activities that are not covered in this version of the script. The value chain level models should be created with this overall script in mind, but adjusted and embellished as appropriate for the particular enterprise being modeled.

Scripts consist of scenes and involve actors, roles, and props. You have probably experienced a dramatic production (e.g., a play, musical, or opera) either as an actor or as an audience member. Members of the audience are typically given a program that outlines the scenes that will take place in the drama. Each scene involves actors and actresses playing roles according to a written script. Sometimes props (physical items used to help communicate the message of the scene) are used. The value chain level is somewhat analogous to the program given to the audience—it provides an outline of the scenes (internal business processes) that will take place for the enterprise. Each scene in the value chain then needs to be portrayed as a business process level REA object pattern model. The REA object pattern identifies the roles and props involved in the scene's events, and also relates the events within a scene to each other.

## An Example Enterprise

Robert Scott Woodwind Shop (RSWS) is a fictitious enterprise (based on a real enterprise) we use to illustrate many of the concepts throughout this book. To help separate fact from fiction, Robert Scott is a real person and truly is an accomplished woodwind instrument repairman, player, and teacher. His primary line of business has been woodwind instrument repair, and many concert musicians claim he is the best in the world because he has near perfect pitch and can detect subtle tone and pitch changes that other repairmen can't hear. He provides repair services and he manufactures clarinet mouthpieces, clarinet barrels, oboe reeds, and bassoon reeds. In years past he sold a few instruments and taught some lessons to a few lucky students. He never took on more work than he could perform by himself, with a little help now and then from whichever one of his children showed an interest in learning how to perform some of the simpler repair or manufacturing activities. To keep his workload manageable, he never advertised; word of mouth proved sufficient to generate enough business to support his family while doing something he loved with a minimal amount of administrative work. He is currently in semiretirement and has only limited need for an information system to maintain complete control of his tiny sole proprietorship. To make this an appropriate enterprise for which to discuss the need for an integrated enterprise information system, we have scaled up this example to include a high volume of transactions and multiple locations, thus necessitating the use of multiple employees, division of labor, and other complicating factors that evolve small sole proprietorships into large corporations that need integrated enterprise information systems.

RSWS as a whole has two types of financing: debt and equity. The debt financing reflects occasional loans RSWS obtains from banks to help with short-term cash flow needs. As RSWS expanded in volume, and needed additional cash infusions to purchase new equipment, rent new store buildings, and pay employees, Robert Scott made the decision to change from a sole proprietorship to a corporation. He completed all the necessary legal paperwork and sold shares of stock representing ownership interest to a dozen of his concert musician friends.

RSWS generates revenues in four ways. First, RSWS purchases woodwind instruments from its suppliers at wholesale prices and sells them to its customers at retail prices. Second, RSWS purchases woodwind instruments from its suppliers at wholesale prices and rents them to customers who are not yet sure they want to buy an instrument. Most often these rentals are made to the parents of schoolchildren who are just beginning to play an instrument and the parents want some evidence that their child's interest in the instrument is more than just a passing fancy. Third, RSWS manufactures various instrument parts and accessories and sells them to customers. For example, RSWS manufactures clarinet barrels, clarinet mouthpieces, oboe reeds, and bassoon reeds. This involves purchasing the equipment and raw materials and performing the labor and machining operations needed to transform the raw materials into the finished goods. Fourth, RSWS performs repair services for customers. This involves evaluating the customer's woodwind instrument to diagnose the problem, purchasing any repair parts that are needed (or taking them from stock), and performing the labor and machining operations needed to repair the instrument.

## RSWS Value System

From this summary of RSWS's operations, we can identify RSWS's external business partners and the resources that are exchanged among them. Exhibit 2–2 illustrates RSWS's value system level REA model. The external business partners for RSWS include investors, creditors, suppliers, customers, and employees. At first glance, you may wonder why employees are considered to be external business partners. After all, they perform services on

**EXHIBIT 2–2**
**RSWS Value**
**System Level**
**REA Model**

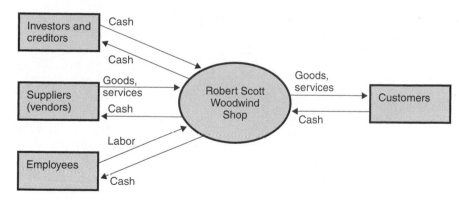

behalf of RSWS. Although they perform services on behalf of RSWS, they are being paid by RSWS to perform those services and as such are external business partners. We return to the distinction of employees' functioning as internal agents and external business partners later. The resource RSWS receives from its investors and creditors is cash, and the resource RSWS gives to its investors and creditors is also cash. Investors and creditors are willing to give cash to RSWS because they expect to receive an amount of cash that is worth more to them than the cash they initially gave up (with the excess being interest, dividends, and/or capital appreciation). The resources RSWS receives from its suppliers are goods and services. This generic label covers specific resources such as raw materials inventory, machinery and equipment, advertising services, accounting services, and many other goods and services. The resource RSWS gives to its suppliers in exchange for these goods and services is cash. Suppliers are willing to give goods and services to RSWS because they expect to receive an amount of cash that is worth more to them than the goods and services they gave up. The resource RSWS receives from its employees is labor. In exchange, RSWS gives cash to its employees. The employees are willing to give labor to RSWS because they expect to receive an amount of cash that is worth more to them than the labor (time and effort) they gave up. The resource RSWS receives from its customers is cash. The resources RSWS gives to its customers are goods and services. This generic label includes instruments, clarinet barrels and mouthpieces, oboe and bassoon reeds, repair services, and the temporary use of instruments (rentals), as well as other potential goods and services. RSWS is willing to give these goods and services to its customers because it expects to receive cash that is worth more to RSWS than the goods and services given up.

Note that the value system level REA model is based on expectations rather than actuality (as are all levels of the REA model). Some customers may not fulfill their end of the exchange bargain and RSWS will have given up goods and services without receiving the expected cash. Likewise it is possible that RSWS will not succeed in its endeavors and its investors will not receive cash in excess of their initial investment. Regardless of what actually occurs, the model must allow for the expected exchanges.

## RSWS Value Chain

Once the external business partners and the resource exchanges between them are identified, we can proceed to develop a model of RSWS's internal business processes and the

**EXHIBIT 2–3**
**RSWS Value Chain Level REA Model (Summarized Version)**

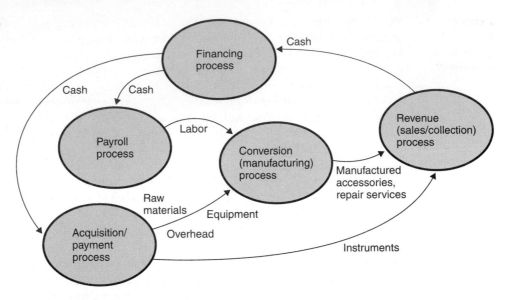

resource flows that link them together. Such a model is called a value chain level model, and an example is illustrated as Exhibit 2–3. This model is based on the business-entrepreneur script discussed earlier in this chapter. Comparing the standard script to the value system model we identify that RSWS has a financing business process (cash is exchanged with investors and creditors), a human resources process (cash is exchanged for labor with employees), an acquisition/payment process (cash is exchanged for goods and services with suppliers) a conversion process (accessories are manufactured and instruments are repaired), and a sales/collection process (goods and services are exchanged for cash with customers).

Each resource flow on this model represents an output from one process and an input to a related process. Starting at the top and working counterclockwise, cash from the financing process is used in the payroll process and in the acquisition/payment process. Within the payroll process, the labor that is acquired in exchange for the cash becomes an output that then serves as an input to the conversion process. Within the acquisition/payment process, the acquired raw materials, equipment, and overhead services (such as utilities) become outputs of that process and inputs to the conversion process. The acquired instruments become outputs of the acquisition/payment process and inputs to the revenue process. The raw materials, equipment, labor, and overhead services that are input to the conversion process are converted into manufactured accessories and repair services that are output to the revenue process. The instruments that are input to the revenue process are exchanged for cash, which becomes the output of the revenue process and serves as an input to the financing process. Resources continue to flow throughout the chain until the enterprise is dissolved.

The value chain level model shown in Exhibit 2–3 is somewhat summarized, using only one bubble to represent each business process. To concentrate on the exchange events and the resource flows resulting from the exchange events, some of the bubbles may be more appropriately decomposed into smaller, less complex parts. For example, the bubble Acquisition/Payment Process could be broken down into two parts: acquire goods and acquire services. Cash would be the inflow resource for each of those separate bubbles, raw materials and equipment would be the outflow resources from acquire goods that become inputs to the conversion process bubble, and overhead would be the outflow resource from acquire services that becomes an input to the conversion process bubble. The decision as to whether to decompose these depends on whether the acquisitions of goods and services are combined into a single set with the same data attributes captured for them. We discuss value chain level models in more depth and illustrate them in more detail in Chapter 3.

As we discuss in Chapter 3, developing a value chain level model provides a great deal of insight about the enterprise and is useful for understanding the enterprise's mission, strategy, and overall operations. Facilitating high-level strategic analysis is certainly a goal of the REA enterprise ontology. The primary goal, though, is to provide a structure for the creation of an enterprisewide database in which to store disaggregated transaction data. Once an enterprise's business processes have been identified, along with the specification of the resource flows and the events that caused the resource flows, a pattern has been established from which an enterprisewide database may be designed. To develop the business process level model, each bubble in the value chain level model is further specified as to the resources, events, agents, and the various types of relationships between them. The components of the business process level REA model will be discussed in more detail in Chapter 4; however, an illustration of the basic business process model for the acquisition of materials is included as Exhibit 2–4. In this exhibit, the purchase of materials is an economic event, which increases the materials resource. The disbursement of cash is another economic event, which decreases the cash resource. The model also shows the participation of agents in those events. The purchasing agent processes the purchase on behalf of RSWS and the supplier is the external agent from whom the materials are purchased. The supplier is the external agent to whom payment is sent, and the accounts payable clerk processes the payment on behalf of RSWS.

Exhibit 2–4 is oversimplified to provide a manageable example; additional complexities that provide more realism are introduced and discussed in later chapters. In Chapter 4 we describe how models like the one in Exhibit 2–4 are derived and further explain what the

**EXHIBIT 2–4**
**Business Process Level Core Model: Acquisition/Payment Process**

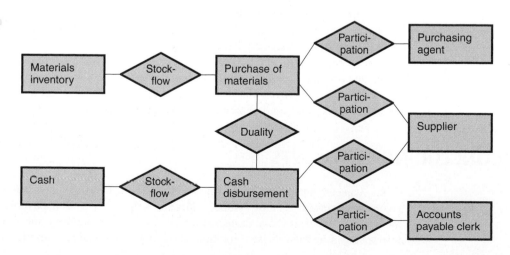

symbols and the names of the constructs shown mean. For now, you need to understand that each rectangle represents a resource, an event, or an agent. The resources shown are *materials inventory* and *cash*. The events shown are *purchase of materials* and *cash disbursement*. The *purchasing agent, supplier,* and *accounts payable clerk* are agents. You also need to understand that each of these rectangular constructs corresponds to a table in the enterprisewide database and that the relationships between them (represented by the diamond symbols) determine how the database tables are linked to each other. The set of relational database tables in Exhibit 2–5 corresponds to the model in Exhibit 2–4. Additional information beyond that available in Exhibit 2–4 was needed to derive these tables; that information is explained in Chapter 4 and the process for deriving the table structures and entering data into the tables is discussed in Chapter 6. For now the purpose of Exhibit 2–5 is to show you a small piece of a deliverable obtained from the REA ontology: an operational enterprisewide transaction database.

One goal of this book is to teach you the basics of designing such a deliverable as the partial relational database illustrated in Exhibit 2–5. There are complexities involved in scaling up such a design and optimizing its performance that are beyond the scope of this book. Courses or modules on interface design, networking and client-server computing also are recommended. Thus when you master the material covered in this book you have only a partial toolset to use in designing a working enterprise database for a real-world enterprise. The toolset you acquire by mastering the material in this book also can help you to use and evaluate relational database tables (such as those shown in Exhibit 2–5) in real-life organizations. Such issues are discussed in later chapters.

## Task Level

The final level of detail in the REA ontology is the task level. Recall that any activities that are not an essential part of an enterprise's operations—in other words those activities that can be reengineered away—should not serve as foundational building blocks for an integrated enterprise information system and thus should not become base objects in the enterprisewide database. However, enterprises need to be able to document all activities and to include information about them in their enterprise system. A variety of workflow activities are possible and no pattern has yet been identified to represent the task level. Further, a variety of representation techniques for documenting workflow activities are used in practice, including narrative descriptions, system flowcharts, data flow diagrams, process models, and fishbone diagrams. For this reason we do not provide a standard representation for tasks for the RSWS example. Although a specific pattern has not yet been discovered for tasks, we describe two of those representation techniques later in the textbook. The ability to document tasks and to interpret task documentation is important for designing, using, and evaluating enterprise information systems.

## CONCLUDING COMMENTS

In this chapter we discussed techniques for representing elements of an enterprise's reality in a conceptual model (set of symbols on paper) that serves as a basis for designing an enterprisewide database. We discussed the REA enterprise ontology and illustrated how the enterprise can be viewed from multiple perspectives to ensure the database is designed to

**EXHIBIT 2–5  RSWS Business Process Level Database Tables: Acquisition/Payment Process**

Cash

| Account Number | Account type | Account Location |
|---|---|---|
| 1223 | Checking | Fourth-Second Bank |
| 3445 | Petty cash | File drawer, room 222 |
| 4556 | Payroll imprest | True American Bank |

Cash Disbursement

| Disbursement ID | Date | Amount | Cash Account | Supplier ID | APClerk ID |
|---|---|---|---|---|---|
| CD1 | November 5 | $1,230.00 | 1223 | S2 | E8 |
| CD2 | November 5 | $9,778.65 | 4556 | | |
| CD3 | November 6 | $2,476.00 | 1223 | S3 | E9 |

Materials Inventory

| Item ID | Description | Standard Unit Cost |
|---|---|---|
| M210 | Cork set, standard oboe | $5.00 |
| M220 | Spring set, standard oboe | $9.00 |
| M321 | Cane, ½" width × 12" length | $1.00 |

Purchase

| Purchase ID | Date | Amount | Supplier ID | PurchAgent ID | Disbursement ID |
|---|---|---|---|---|---|
| P1 | November 1 | $1,230.00 | S2 | E2 | CD1 |
| P2 | November 1 | $2,476.00 | S3 | E2 | CD3 |
| P3 | November 3 | $ 500.00 | S1 | E3 | |

Materials Inventory—Purchase

| Item ID | Purchase ID | Quantity Purchased | Actual Unit Cost |
|---|---|---|---|
| M210 | P1 | 66 | $5.00 |
| M220 | P1 | 100 | $9.00 |
| M220 | P2 | 200 | $9.00 |
| M321 | P2 | 676 | $1.00 |
| M210 | P3 | 100 | $5.00 |

Accounts Payable Clerk

| APClerk ID | Last Name | First Name | Date of Birth | Telephone |
|---|---|---|---|---|
| E7 | Hitchcock | Henry | October 31 | 555-1000 |
| E8 | Ingalls | Ingrid | January 3 | 555-1012 |
| E9 | Jacobs | Jennifer | February 2 | 555-1027 |

Purchasing Agent

| PurchAgent ID | Last Name | First Name | Date of Birth | Purchase Limit |
|---|---|---|---|---|
| E2 | Benson | Betty | September 22 | $25,000.00 |
| E3 | Corbett | Carlos | April 26 | $20,000.00 |
| E4 | Daniels | Doris | June 21 | $19,000.00 |

Supplier

| Supplier ID | Name | Address | City | State |
|---|---|---|---|---|
| S1 | We Know Woodwinds | 123 Ensemble Ave. | Highbrow | MA |
| S2 | Adverteaser | 118 Stephens | Greenfield | MI |
| S3 | Emersmith | 6830 Newfound | Kansas City | MO |

capture information consistent with the enterprise's value-adding activities and overall strategy. The coverage of these topics in this chapter provides only a high level overview. In the remaining chapters of this book we provide more details regarding each level of the ontology.

## Key Terms and Concepts

| | | |
|---|---|---|
| Acquisition/payment process, *25* | Human resources process, *25* | Script pattern, *23* |
| Agents, *24* | Model, *19* | Symbols, *20* |
| Business-entrepreneur script, *25* | Object, *20* | Task level REA model, *25* |
| Business process level REA model, *25* | Pattern, *21* | Token, *20* |
| Context, *23* | REA ontology— 4 Levels, *24* | Type, *20* |
| Conversion process, *25* | Reality, *19* | Value chain level REA model, *24* |
| Events, *24* | Representation, *19* | Value system level REA model, *24* |
| Financing process, *25* | Resources, *24* | |
| | Sales/collection process, *25* | |

## Review Questions

LO1   **R1.**   What is a model? Why do we create models of systems?

LO3   **R2.**   What is a business process?

LO1, LO3   **R3.**   Is it better to make one model of an entire enterprise, or several smaller models of individual processes? Why?

LO1   **R4.**   What is the difference between token and type level representation?

LO2   **R5.**   What is the difference between an object pattern and a script pattern?

LO3   **R6.**   What are the four levels of the REA ontology and what type of pattern (object or script) exists at each level?

## Multiple Choice Questions

LO3   **MC1.**   Relationships in the business process level REA model are based on:
   A.  Events
   B.  Expectations
   C.  Actuality
   D.  Software

LO3   **MC2.**   In order from the top down, the hierarchy levels in the REA enterprise ontology are
   A.  Task, business process, value chain, value system
   B.  Business process, task, value system, value chain
   C.  Value chain, value system, business process, task
   D.  Value system, value chain, business process, task

LO3   **MC3.**   Which REA ontology level focuses on an object pattern of events within one or more transaction cycles?
   A.  Task
   B.  Business process

C. Value system

D. Value chain

LO3  MC4. Which REA ontology level focuses on the resource flows between interconnected business processes?

A. Task

B. Business process

C. Value system

D. Value chain

LO3, LO4  MC5. For which level of the REA ontology has a specific pattern not yet been discovered?

A. Task

B. Business process

C. Value system

D. Value chain

## Discussion Questions

LO4  D1. Dramatic productions follow scripts that contain scenes, actors, props, and roles. Describe how each of these components maps into the levels of the REA enterprise ontology. Do you believe it is useful to think about enterprises from the script perspective? Why or why not?

LO2  D2. The chapter gave an example of a romantic script that some would say is the theme for most chick flicks (i.e., movies that tend to appeal to a largely female audience). Write a similar script for the types of action/adventure movies that tend to appeal to a mostly male audience. What (if anything) do romantic and action movie scripts have in common?

LO3  D3. The chapter gave an example of a business process level core model including resources, events, and agents for the acquisition/payment process for Robert Scott Woodwinds. What do you think some of the resources, events, and agents would be for the business process level core model for the revenue cycle for Robert Scott Woodwinds? Include at least two resources, two events, and three types of agents.

LO4  D4. Do you think activities that could be reengineered away should serve as foundational building blocks in an enterprise information system? Why or why not?

LO4  D5. The REA ontology was originally created as an accounting model intended to replace the traditional double-entry model Assets = Liabilities + Owners' Equity. Using your knowledge of the traditional double-entry accounting model, what are the essential parts of accounting that cannot be reengineered away? In other words, what makes up the essence of accounting? What parts of the traditional double-entry model are artifacts that could be replaced with other methods or approaches?

## Applied Learning

LO2  A1. Picture in your mind a pizza (or other food) delivery retailer of your choice. Using the knowledge you have based on your previous experiences with ordering pizza (or other food), combined with your general business understanding, try to guess what the value system level model for this enterprise includes. You may either draw a value system level model similar to Exhibit 2–2, or you may prepare a matrix as follows:

| External Business Partner | Resources Flowing from External Business Partner | Resources Flowing to External Business Partner |
|---|---|---|
|  |  |  |
|  |  |  |

LO2   A2. Midsize University in Make-Believe Land has a library. You have never been to Midsize University or even to Make-Believe Land before. You have been asked to create an object model for Midsize University's library. This model illustrates the sets of things in the library and the relationships between those sets of things. You will earn a bonus if you can complete the model in a very short time frame. Your flight to Make-Believe Land has been delayed for four hours, which is going to make it very difficult to finish on time. Whatever you can complete now will help you to meet your bonus deadline, so you start sketching a model while you are waiting for your plane. Either prepare a model in diagram format, with boxes to represent the things and lines connecting those things that are related, or prepare a list of things you expect to need in your model and a list of the relationships you expect to find between them.

## Answers to Multiple Choice Questions

MC1. B; MC2. D; MC3. B; MC4. D; MC5. A.

# Chapter **Three**

# The REA Enterprise Ontology: Value System and Value Chain Modeling

## LEARNING OBJECTIVES

The objectives of this chapter are to describe the components of a typical enterprise's value system and value chain and to discuss the procedures for developing models of enterprise value systems and value chains. After studying this chapter, you should be able to:

1. Identify an enterprise's external business partners
2. Identify the resources that are exchanged between an enterprise and its business partners
3. Develop a value system level REA model for an enterprise
4. Identify the business processes (transaction cycles) in an enterprise
5. Identify the resource flows between an enterprise's internal business processes
6. Identify the economic events that cause the resource flows between an enterprise's internal business processes
7. Develop a value chain level REA model for an enterprise
8. Explain how enterprises create value and describe Porter's Value Chain Model
9. Explain how evaluating enterprise activities at the value system and value chain levels facilitates understanding the business process level

## VALUE SYSTEMS AND VALUE CHAINS

We introduced the concepts of value systems and value chains in Chapter 2; we examine them more closely in this chapter. You may be surprised to learn that many of the critical steps of building an information system have little to do with programming a computer. The process begins with identifying the need for a business solution and acquiring a better understanding of the environment you plan to support and/or improve. You must examine that environment (the enterprise) from different perspectives and at different levels

35

of detail. We believe the first level of detail you should consider is the least detailed—the big picture view that we call the value system level. You may have heard the saying "they couldn't see the forest for the trees" used to describe those so mired in detail that they forget the big picture of what they are trying to accomplish. We believe that looking at the forest level of an enterprise first and trying to develop a plan for analyzing the enterprise a section at a time will help you keep your perspective and avoid getting mired in the detail. Obviously there is plenty of detail in which to get mired, so try to keep picturing the end goal and the plan for getting there to keep you on the path.

Examining the **value system** level of a firm includes thinking about the enterprise's mission and strategy. Understanding this level is crucial because later you must ensure that activities within the enterprise's business processes are consistent with its overall mission and **strategy.** The REA ontology is about much more than developing information systems; it is about understanding enterprises.

Everything an enterprise does should create value for its **customers** according to Michael Porter in *Competitive Advantage.*[1] Creating value has a cost. For example, an enterprise that assembles automobiles creates something of value but also must pay for various inputs (e.g., materials, supplies, and time of employees). Porter computes an organization's **margin** as the difference between value and cost. This calculation includes all value and all cost, much of which is difficult to measure financially, but which the REA value chain model can capture if measurements are available.

The concept of creating value applies to both for-profit and not-for-profit organizations. For-profit organizations try to maximize their margins. Not-for-profit organizations, such as charitable or governmental entities, seek to maximize the goods and services they provide with the **resources** (funds) they receive. Over the long run, charitable and governmental organizations seek to optimize their services while matching outflows to inflows. Whether for-profit or not-for-profit, viable organizations provide goods and services that customers value in a cost-effective way. The main difference between for-profit and not-for-profit enterprises is that at the value system level, the input resources and output resources are paired with different external business partners. That is, some of the partners who give resources to the not-for-profit enterprises do not receive resources directly from the not-for-profit enterprises and some of the partners who receive resources from the not-for-profit enterprises do not give resources to the not-for-profit enterprises. The overall notion of input resources being transformed into output resources is still valid because one would expect that if the not-for-profit organization failed to provide the expected goods and services, its contributing external business partners would discontinue their contributions.

Every organization seeks to create value by providing goods and services customers want. For example:

- A grocery store creates value by providing food in a clean and convenient location for customers to purchase.

- An airline company creates value by safely transporting passengers and cargo in a timely manner.

- An automobile manufacturer creates value by producing safe, reliable vehicles to transport people and cargo.

[1]M. Porter, *Competitive Advantage: Creating and Sustaining Superior Performance* (New York: Free Press, 1985), p. 12.

# Case **in Point**

In the late 1970s and early 1980s when gas prices were rapidly rising and our oil supplies were in doubt, most new car buyers favored smaller, more gas-efficient automobiles. America's automobile manufacturers had several lean years as they modified their automobile design to smaller, fuel-efficient vehicles. Over the next decade as the percentage of small cars increased, most parking lots adjusted the size of the parking stalls from 8 or 9 feet wide to 7 feet wide. But since 1987 the size of America's cars has been getting bigger. In sprawling Western and Southwestern cities, the popularity of sport-utility vehicles and pickup trucks can make parking a hassle. Parking lots with larger parking stalls are now able to charge a premium price. Parking problems will likely increase as the popularity of the Hummer increases. The Hummer is the civilian adaptation of a military vehicle that is 8 feet wide, including the mirrors.*

*Neal Templin, "Big Cars and Little Spaces Cause Mayhem," *The Wall Street Journal,* March 11, 1998, pp. B1, 8.

- A municipality creates value by providing essential community services (e.g., police protection, fire protection, emergency services, and utilities) to its citizens.

Enterprises that provide goods and services of value to their customers will survive and grow while those that do not will shrink and die. Due to competition for scarce resources, each enterprise must provide value in a cost-effective manner. Although some organizations manage to defer their demise through deceit, disguise, or political influence, ultimately every organization has to answer to the final arbiter of value—the customer.

Because enterprises need increased adaptability, effectiveness, and efficiency to remain competitive, most organizations find it essential to differentiate between the various business activities in which they engage. Obviously, organizations must look internally at each of their functions and develop capabilities in each area. They also must effectively integrate and coordinate all business functions. However, in today's business world, an organization's performance is increasingly affected by the world around it. You might work for the most internally cost-effective organization you can imagine, but it might be an unsuccessful organization. Why? Perhaps the organization has competitors who better meet the needs of customers, do a good job of outsourcing some business functions, or do a better job of creating effective strategic alliances with trading partners.[2]

To really understand and analyze an organization, you must understand more than internal operations and functions. You must look outside the organization at the industry, the **suppliers,** the customers, and all the other parties that affect organization performance. In other words, you must examine the enterprise at its value system level, and also consider how the enterprise's value system interacts with the value systems of the other enterprises in its **supply chain.** An enterprise supply chain encompasses all of the enterprises involved in providing a product or service to an end customer. For example, Robert Scott Woodwind Shop purchases instruments from its suppliers as part of its value system level activities. Those suppliers had value systems of their own to make those instruments available for

[2]Outsourcing occurs when one organization finds another organization to perform some work. This is usually done when the outsourcing organization can't complete the work (e.g., they do not have the capacity or the expertise) or when they identify another organization that can complete the work in a more cost-effective manner.

**EXHIBIT 3–1** **Porter's Generic Value Chain**

Source: Michael Porter, *Competitive Advantage: Creating and Sustaining Superior Performance* (New York: Free Press, 1985).

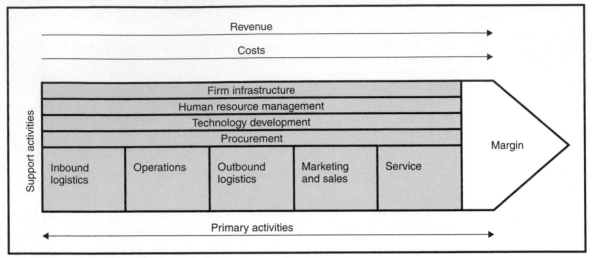

sale to RSWS. Likely RSWS buys the instruments from the manufacturers; their value system levels would involve purchasing raw materials, labor, and manufacturing equipment from their suppliers. Those suppliers had value systems to make those items available for sale.

Eventually managers must look at the entire supply chain to streamline interenterprise activities and gain efficiencies in operations. However, the best first step is to focus on the enterprise in the context of its immediate business partners, then to focus on the enterprise value chain and the **internal business processes** that comprise that chain. Once you understand the enterprise in the context of its immediate business partners and its internal processes, examine the more distant links on its supply chain.

To complete a thorough cradle-to-grave analysis, many people use the value chain analysis approach originally proposed by Michael Porter.[3] Porter illustrated that each firm is a "collection of activities that are performed to design, produce, market, deliver, and support its product." You can see Porter's Generic Value Chain in Exhibit 3–1.

Although this diagram looks different from the value chain diagrams we use in this textbook, both types of value chain diagrams encompass the same set of activities. Porter's value chain is defined as a set of business activities that add value or usefulness to an organization's products or services; the REA ontology defines the **value chain** as a set of business processes through which resources flow, with the assumption that value is added to the resources within each business process. The value chain is intended to show total value and consists of value activities and margin. Value activities are the physical and technological activities performed by an organization. Porter presented two types of value ac-

[3]M. Porter, *Competitive Advantage: Creating and Sustaining Superior Performance* (New York: Free Press, 1985); and *Competitive Strategy Techniques for Analyzing Industries and Competitors* (New York: Free Press, 1980).

tivities in his generic value chain: primary and support. **Primary value activities** consist of the events that create customer value and provide organization distinctiveness in the marketplace. They are the critical activities in running a business. **Support value activities** facilitate accomplishing the primary activities. Margin is the difference between total value and the cost of performing the value activities.

Porter's *primary* value activities include the following categories:

- **Inbound logistics**—activities associated with receiving, storing, and disseminating inputs to the products or services
- **Operations**—activities associated with transforming inputs into the final products or services
- **Outbound logistics**—activities associated with collecting, storing, and physically distributing the products or services
- **Marketing and sales**—activities associated with providing a means by which customers can buy products and the means for inducing them to buy
- **Service**—activities associated with providing service to enhance or maintain the value of the products or services

Porter's *support* value activities include:

- **Procurement**—the function of purchasing inputs to a firm's value chain
- **Technology development**—the know-how, procedures, or technology embedded in processes that are intended to improve the product, services, and/or process
- **Human resource management**—activities involved in recruiting, hiring, training, developing, and compensating all types of personnel
- **Firm infrastructure**—activities that support the entire value chain (e.g., general management, planning, finance, accounting, legal, government affairs, and quality management)

In REA value chain analysis we also differentiate value activities in three event categories—operating events, information events, and decision/management events. We define and discuss these categories in Chapter 4.

Value system and value chain analyses are valuable because they compel you to understand the internal operations of a firm as well as the forces and parties outside the firm that affect its ability to create value. The direct actions of an organization are only part of its overall value chain process. It is also important to look at external linkages, such as the activities of customers and suppliers, to understand the ability of an organization to create value. For example, some organizations may be more successful at creating value because they elicit quality responses from their customers and use the feedback to quickly change or upgrade their products. Other organizations may achieve success because they have worked effectively with their suppliers to reduce costs and improve the ability to respond to customer desires. A thorough analysis of the value system and value chain helps you to understand all the activities that are strategically relevant to an organization, not just the portion of activities in which an organization directly participates or controls. In Exhibit 3–2 we illustrate how the value system and value chain activities are linked. In this diagram note that Suppliers encompasses suppliers of every type of resource, including employees, investors, and creditors, as well as those who supply products and services.

**EXHIBIT 3–2**
**Relating Value
System
and Value
Chain Levels**

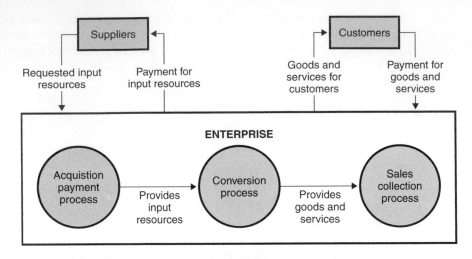

# VALUE SYSTEM LEVEL REA MODELING

To develop a value system level REA model you must answer the question, "Who are the enterprise's **external business partners**?" To answer this question, focus on **resource flows** and ask the question this way, "To whom does the enterprise give resources and from whom does the enterprise receive resources?" Recall from Chapter 2 that resources are defined as things that have economic value to the enterprise. Recall also from Chapter 2 that we are taking a pattern-based approach to developing enterprise information systems. Thus we want to consider what is true for most enterprises and then make adjustments as necessary for our particular enterprise. Most enterprise resources fit into one of the following categories:

- Cash
- Inventory (raw materials, finished goods, merchandise, parts, and supplies)
- Labor
- Property, plant, and equipment
- Insurance
- Services (such as advertising or government services)
- Utilities (water and energy)

To determine an enterprise's external business partners, a helpful step is to examine which of these resources the enterprise provides or uses and then determine to whom they provide the resources and from whom they acquire the resources. To make matters even simpler, in the current economic environment cash is the universal resource for which most other resources are exchanged. Very seldom do companies engage in barter transactions (**exchanges** of a noncash resource for a different noncash resource). Therefore by concentrating on identifying the various partners to whom the enterprise pays cash and from whom the enterprise receives cash, you very likely have identified all the appropriate external business partners. Typically the external business partners fit into the following categories:

- Vendors or suppliers (of various types of inventory, equipment, utilities, insurance, and services)
- Employees
- Investors and creditors
- Customers

Sometimes examining the cash outflows of an enterprise does not reveal a resource received in exchange. For example, when an enterprise pays cash to government agencies (such as the Internal Revenue Service) what resource does the enterprise receive in exchange? Some resources the government provides are easy to identify, such as a license to do business, or police and fire protection services. However, the amounts paid in taxes and fees to the government often exceed an identifiable resource received in exchange and we must simply label the resource as government services. Payments to charitable organizations pose a similar dilemma. If an enterprise donates money to a university, what resource does it receive in exchange? The enterprise must believe it receives a resource, because enterprises are assumed to make economically rational decisions. The enterprise may expect goodwill, an increased reputation in the community (in effect, advertising), or an advantage in recruiting the university's students. Based on the assumption that the enterprise does in fact receive resources in exchange for these payments, hopefully you have figured out that government agencies and charitable organizations would be included in the external business partner category of vendors or suppliers.

Once the resources an enterprise uses are identified and the external business partners with whom these resources are exchanged are determined, the information is portrayed in a diagram. The enterprise being modeled is represented as a circle or oval in the center of the diagram. Each external business partner is represented as a square or rectangle; these are placed around the outside of the circle that represents the enterprise. Arrows are drawn between the circle and the squares as appropriate to indicate the actual resource exchanges between the enterprise and its business partners. Let's examine the RSWS example introduced in Chapter 2 to determine how the value system level REA model was constructed. The value system diagram from that example is reproduced in Exhibit 3–3.

The first step in constructing this model is to examine the various resources RSWS uses in its operations. Cash is certainly used by RSWS. Let's consider how the cash is used, to

**EXHIBIT 3–3**
**Robert Scott Woodwind Shop REA Value System Level Model**

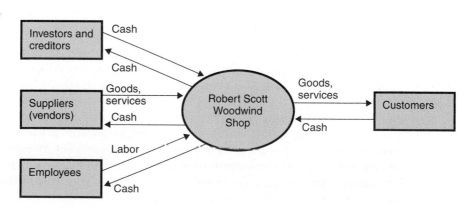

whom it is paid, and from whom it is received. We identify that cash is received from investors (for equity financing), from creditors (for debt financing), and from customers. Thus we draw a rectangle to represent the set of investors and creditors and another rectangle to represent the set of customers. Cash is received from investors and creditors because they expect to receive cash in exchange, therefore we simply draw an arrow from investors and creditors to RSWS and label it cash to represent those cash inflows. We draw another arrow from RSWS to investors and creditors to represent cash outflows to investors and creditors (e.g., for interest payments, dividends, principal repayments, and treasury stock purchases). Next we draw an arrow from customers to RSWS and label it cash to represent the cash inflows from customers. We realize that the reason customers give RSWS cash is because they expect RSWS to provide goods (e.g., instruments, accessories), repair services, or the use of goods (i.e., rental of instruments). Therefore we draw an arrow from RSWS to customers to indicate that RSWS provides those resources to its customers.

We then inspect the narrative to determine what types of cash payments are made and to whom. We identify cash payments made to employees and realize that those payments are made in exchange for labor provided by our employees. Therefore we draw a rectangle to represent the set of employees. We draw an arrow from RSWS to employees to represent the cash outflows to employees and we draw an arrow from employees to RSWS to represent the labor inflow from employees. You might notice that there is no arrow to represent benefits such as health insurance paid to employees. Is it because RSWS doesn't offer any such benefits or is it because they have forgotten to represent them? The answer is neither. Payments made for health insurance for employees is a cash outflow to suppliers made by RSWS on behalf of the employees. The actual insurance is an outflow from the health insurance supplier to the employees and is outside the scope of RSWS's value system model, which only examines the direct resource flows between RSWS and its external business partners. This leads us to the other external business partner for RSWS—the suppliers (some enterprises may call these vendors). Suppliers is the set of all nonemployee individuals or organizations from which an enterprise acquires goods and services. We draw a rectangle to represent the set of suppliers, an arrow from RSWS to suppliers to indicate the cash outflow, and an arrow from suppliers to RSWS to indicate the inflow of goods and services.

## VALUE CHAIN LEVEL REA MODELING

Once the value system level analysis is complete, much of the initial value chain analysis has also been completed. This level of analysis focuses on the resource flows between its internal business processes. A *business process* is a series of activities that accomplishes a business objective: adding value to input resources. Once you have identified the resources flowing into and out of the enterprise, examine what the company does with its input resources and how it generates its output resources. As business processes use up resources, they should be producing resources worth more to the enterprise than those used up. As noted earlier, enterprises create value by developing and providing the goods and services customers desire. Goods and services are provided through a series of business processes. Regardless of the type of goods or services provided, each organization has at least three business processes (see Exhibit 3–2):

1. *Acquisition/payment process:* The objective of the acquisition/payment process is to acquire, maintain, and pay for the resources needed by the organization. Many resources are required including human resources, property, plant, equipment, financial resources, raw materials, and supplies. Resources are acquired from external entities like suppliers or vendors. These are the inputs required by the organization to provide goods and services to its customers. Because the acquisition of financial resources and the acquisition of human resources have complexities not found in the acquisition of other goods and services, many enterprises separate these activities into additional business processes, called the *financing process* and the *human resources process,* that we cover separately in later chapters.

2. *Conversion process:* The objective of the conversion process is to convert the acquired resources into goods and services for customers. The raw inputs are transformed into finished goods and services by this process.

3. *Sales/collection process:* The objective of the sales/collection process is to sell and deliver goods and services to customers and collect payment. The finished goods and services from the conversion process are sold to customers (external entities) in exchange for their payment, usually in the form of cash.

Creating a value chain model that illustrates the linkages between these processes requires understanding of two very important concepts in the REA ontology: *duality* and *stockflow.* These concepts characterize the core economic phenomena of an exchange. As noted earlier, enterprises are assumed to make rational economic decisions. Rational economic theory precludes decision makers from giving up something with no expectation of anything in exchange. For every event in which an enterprise gives something up we expect a related event in which the enterprise receives something. The causal relationship between a give event and a take event is a **duality relationship.** Stockflow is defined as the **inflow** or **outflow** of a resource. Stockflow relationships exist between give events and resources (these stockflows are outflows) and between take events and resources (these stockflows are inflows). The value chain level of the REA ontology is constructed based on these two concepts. Geerts and McCarthy say, "Duality relationships are the glue that binds a firm's separate economic events together into rational economic processes, while stockflow relationships weave these processes together into an enterprise value chain."[4]

The first step in creating a value chain model is to write the enterprise script to identify the business processes that need to be included in the value chain. We use the value system level model along with whatever other information we have such as a narrative description about the enterprise's activities. The second step in creating a value chain model is to draw the resource flows to link the business processes together. The third step is to determine the economic exchange events and the duality relationships that make up the core of each business process in the value chain. An example will clarify these steps.

Let's revisit our RSWS example. In Exhibit 2–3 (reprinted here as Exhibit 3–4) we portrayed a summarized value chain level that would be the result of the first two steps. After going through steps 1 and 2 to reconstruct this model, we discuss step 3 and illustrate the resulting detailed value chain model.

---

[4]G. Geerts and W. E. McCarthy, "Modeling Business Enterprises as Value-Added Process Hierarchies with Resource-Event-Agent Object Templates," in J. Sutherland and D. Patel, eds., *Business Object Design and Implementation* (London: Springer-Verlag, 1997), pp. 94–113.

**EXHIBIT 3–4**
**Robert Scott Woodwind Shop Business Processes and Resource Flows Summarized Value Chain View**

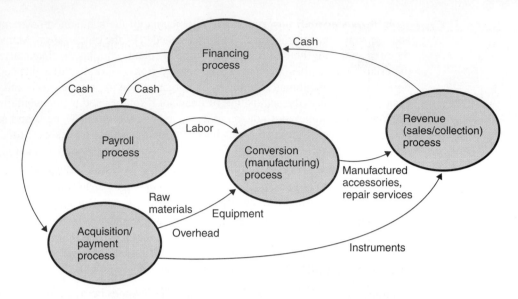

## Step 1: Write the Entrepreneurial Script

To complete this step, we examine the typical scenes of the entrepreneurial business script to see which of the typical scenes RSWS has. Based on our value system level analysis, the typical script pattern, and the narrative description of RSWS we write RSWS's script as follows:

- RSWS gets cash from investors and creditors
- RSWS engages in value-adding activities
  - uses cash to buy instruments, raw materials, and overhead from vendors
  - uses cash to acquire labor from employees
  - uses materials, equipment, and overhead to manufacture accessories and to provide repair services
  - sells instruments, accessories, and repair services to customers for cash
- RSWS pays cash to investors and creditors

The first and last scenes together comprise the financing process; in scene 2, the subscenes are (in order) the acquisition/payment process; the human resources (payroll) process; the conversion process; and the sales/collection process. Keep in mind that all of these scenes and subscenes come directly from our value system level analysis except for the "uses materials, equipment, and overhead to manufacture accessories and to provide repair services." Because the subscene doesn't involve resource exchanges with external business partners, it is not modeled at the value system level. Thus you must be careful when developing your value chain model to include not only the scenes that you derive from the value system level but also any business processes that add value via internal resource transformations.

## Step 2: Connect the Scenes with Resource Flows

Once all the scenes are identified they need to be combined to form a value chain (at which point no distinction is made between scenes and subscenes). The resource flows provide the link from one scene to the next. Once the cash is acquired in the financing process, it is used as input for the acquisition/payment and human resource processes, where it is transferred out to external business partners in exchange for instruments, raw materials, overhead, and labor. Because the value chain model only illustrates the internal processes, we don't show the cash outflows from the acquisition and payroll processes to the external partners, nor do we show the related resource inflows from those external partners. From this perspective we view the acquisition process as one that uses up cash and produces materials, equipment, overhead, and instruments; and we view the payroll process as one that uses up cash and produces labor. We view the conversion process as one that transforms the labor, materials, equipment, and overhead into the accessories and repair service resources. The sales/collection process is then viewed as one that uses up instruments, accessories, and repair services and obtains cash. The assumption is that in each of these scenes the resources produced are worth more than the resources used up; thus value is added to the enterprise in each link of the chain.

## Step 3: Specify the Economic Exchange Events within Each Scene

The third step in creating the value chain diagram adds more detail to the diagram that clarifies how each scene's representation in the value chain diagram provides the starting point for a business process level model representation. This step entails depicting the economic exchange events inside each scene's bubble on the value chain diagram. Each scene must contain at least one economic increment (take) event and at least one economic decrement (give) event. You can use the resource flows to determine what events are needed. This analysis also helps you to determine whether a scene in your value chain should be decomposed into multiple scenes. The general rule to follow for this step is that each process must have an economic decrement event to match up with each resource inflow and an economic increment event to match up with each resource outflow. The idea is that if a resource is flowing into a process, the process must include an event that uses it up (either by transferring it to an external partner or by transforming it into a different resource). Similarly, if a resource is flowing out of a process, the process must include an event that produced the resource (either by transferring it in from an external business partner or by creating it as a transformation of some other resources).

In our RSWS example, let's add detail first to the financing process. Because cash is a resource inflow to that process, the process must include an event that uses it up (i.e., a cash disbursement event). Cash is also a resource outflow from financing, so the process must include an event that acquired it (i.e., a cash receipt event). The cash receipt and cash disbursement events are linked via a duality relationship. So we draw two event boxes inside the financing process bubble and connect them via a diamond (relationship symbol) labeled with the word *duality*. We label the events *cash receipt* and *cash disbursement*. Note that even though the cash flows from the financing process to multiple other processes, the data attributes of all cash receipts are likely the same so we consider cash receipts for all purposes as part of the same event set. The fact that cash got used for different purposes doesn't matter.

Next we examine the payroll process. Because cash is a resource inflow, the process must include an event that uses it up (i.e., a cash disbursement event). Notice that the enterprise will likely have only one cash disbursement event set that encompasses all cash disbursements made for all purposes, but we must depict the event set in each business process that uses cash. The payroll process generates labor as its resource outflow, so there must be an event within the payroll process that obtains that labor (labor acquisition, an event that transfers the labor in). So we draw two event boxes inside the payroll process bubble and connect them via a diamond (relationship symbol) labeled with the word *duality*. We label the events *cash disbursement* and *labor acquisition*.

The acquisition/payment process is similar to the payroll process. Cash is a resource inflow to acquisition/payment, so the process must have an event that uses it up (i.e., a cash disbursement event). The acquisition/payment process has instruments, materials, services, and equipment as outflows, so the process must include an event that obtains those things from external sources (i.e., an acquisition event set). Here we must determine whether the same data attributes are recorded for acquisitions of each of these types of items. For any that are different, the events should be modeled separately and the recommendation would be to make separate acquisition cycle bubbles. Let's say we determine that RSWS records all acquisitions using a common set of forms and captures the same data attributes for them. Thus we need only one acquisition event set and only one acquisition process (scene). We draw two event boxes inside the acquisition/payment process bubble and connect them via a diamond labeled with the word *duality*. We label the events *cash disbursement* and *acquisition*.

Next we examine the conversion process. The conversion process is typically the most complicated scene. Our value chain diagram shows input resource flows as materials, equipment, labor, and overhead. That indicates our conversion process must have events that use up each of those items. We determine that raw materials are used up as they are issued into a manufacturing or repair job so we draw a box labeled *material issue*. We note that employee labor is used up through the employees' involvement in labor operations, so we draw a box labeled *labor operation*. Equipment and overhead are used up in machine operations, so we draw a box labeled *machine operation*. Next we need to determine what event produces the finished accessories and/or repaired instruments. We determine that for RSWS every repair service and each production run for a batch of parts or accessories is considered to be a *work in process job*. Thus we add a box labeled *WIP Job*. We realize that the material issues, labor operations, and machine operations are **economic decrement events** (they use up resources) that are matched with the WIP job, which is an economic increment event (it produces resources). Therefore we draw a diamond symbol to connect all four boxes and label it as *duality*.

Now all our scenes are detailed except for the Sales/Collection process. We see that the input resources are the instruments (from the acquisition process), and the manufactured accessories and repair services (from the conversion process). The instruments get changed into cash either by selling them or renting them to customers. The repair services and manufactured accessories are also changed into cash by selling them to customers. As with the acquisition process, we need to make a choice as to whether there is a common sale event set for which the same set of data attributes can be maintained, or whether the activities are dissimilar enough to warrant being maintained as separate event sets. For this example, we assume RSWS uses the same set of forms and captures the same data attri-

**EXHIBIT 3–5**   **Robert Scott Woodwinds Shop Detailed Value Chain**

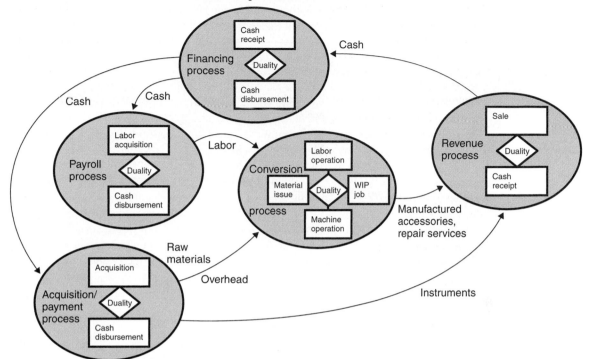

butes for each of these revenue-generating activities, so we combine them into one economic decrement event called *sale.* The output resource flow is cash, indicating that the process must include an event that produces or obtains the cash, in other words an economic increment event called cash receipt. We draw two boxes with a duality relationship connecting them; we label one box *sale* and the other box *cash receipt.* Now our value chain is complete (see Exhibit 3–5) and may be used to facilitate creation of the business process level models for RSWS. We discuss that process in detail in Chapter 4.

# CONCLUDING COMMENTS

In this chapter we have provided a patterned approach for developing models of enterprises at two levels of detail—the value system level and the value chain level. This approach facilitates your understanding of how business enterprises work. As you go about your daily activities, pay attention to the business enterprises with which you interact and look for these script patterns. When you go out to eat at a restaurant, or order pizza, see if you can picture the value system and value chain for that restaurant or pizza place. When you go shopping at different kinds of stores: grocery, convenience, department, or electronics, see if you can identify the value system and value chain patterns for those stores. Consider what they have in common and any differences they may have. Think about the possibilities of using the things they have in common as base objects in an information system and keeping the things that are unique as nonfoundational elements in the information system. Think about how such an approach could lead to enterprise systems that may be integrated with solid connections rather than tied together with string.

## Key Terms and Concepts

| | | |
|---|---|---|
| Customer, *36* | Internal business | Resource flow, *40* |
| Duality relationship, *43* | process, *38* | Service, *39* |
| Economic event, *46* | Margin, *36* | Strategy, *36* |
| Exchange, *40* | Marketing and sales, *39* | Supplier, *37* |
| External business | Operations, *39* | Supply chain, *37* |
| partner, *40* | Outbound logistics, *39* | Support value |
| Firm infrastructure, *39* | Outflow, *43* | activities, *39* |
| Human resource | Primary value | Technology |
| management, *39* | activities, *39* | development, *39* |
| Inbound logistics, *39* | Procurement, *39* | Value chain, *38* |
| Inflow, *43* | Resource, *36* | Value system, *36* |

## Review Questions

LO4  R1. What is a business process? Describe each of the major business processes found in most enterprises.

LO8  R2. What does it mean to create value? How do enterprises create value?

LO8  R3. What is an enterprise's margin as defined by Michael Porter?

LO2  R4. Differentiate between the objectives of a profit and a not-for-profit enterprise.

LO8  R5. Give an example of a primary value activity for a retail store.

LO8  R6. Give an example of a support value activity for a retail store.

LO1–LO3  R7. To begin creating a value system model, what does the chapter recommend as the first thing you should try to identify?

LO6  R8. What do duality relationships consist of?

LO5, LO6  R9. What is the difference between a stock inflow and a stock outflow? What types of events are associated with stock inflows and with stock outflows?

LO6, LO7  R10. When you are creating a value chain level REA model, if you have two resource inflows and one resource outflow for a transaction cycle, what do you know about the events in that cycle?

## Multiple Choice Questions

LO8  MC1. Which events in Porter's value chain create customer value and provide organization distinctiveness in the marketplace?
   A. Primary activities
   B. Support activities
   C. Operational activities
   D. Value activities

LO6, LO7     MC2.   Which of the following is usually represented as a value activity in the REA value chain?
- A. The generation of an aged accounts receivable report
- B. The sending of a bill to a customer
- C. The sale of goods to a customer
- D. The decision as to whether to discontinue a product line

LO3     MC3.   Which level of the REA enterprise ontology represents the big-picture view?
- A. Value system
- B. Value chain
- C. Business process
- D. Task

LO8     MC4.   Which of the following is considered a primary value activity, as opposed to a support activity, in Porter's value chain?
- A. Procurement
- B. Accounting
- C. General management
- D. Inbound and outbound logistics

LO7     MC5.   To which other internal business process are manufactured goods typically made available by the conversion process?
- A. Financing
- B. Revenue
- C. Payroll
- D. Acquisition/payment

## Discussion Questions

LO8     D1.   If only enterprises that truly create value survive, how do tobacco companies stay in business? How do illegal drug markets survive?

LO1, LO2     D2.   Do some events occur outside enterprise boundaries? Should information system designers focus on events that lie beyond an enterprise's boundaries?

LO4     D3.   All business organizations have at least three broad business processes: acquisition/payment, conversion, and sales/collection. Into which of these processes do each of the following activities belong? Explain your response.
- a. Delivering a new product to a customer
- b. Hiring new employees
- c. Paying for a new capital tool
- d. Assembling subcomponents for a finished product.

LO9     D4.   Why is it useful to try to understand an enterprise's activities at the value system and value chain levels rather than simply beginning with the business process level?

LO5–LO7     D5.   Is it easier for you to first think about the resource flows associated with a transaction cycle and then use that knowledge to identify the economic events in the cycle, or is it easier to first think about the economic events in a cycle and then use that knowledge to identify the related resource flows?

## Applied Learning

LO1–LO7   A1.   Owen's Farm owns approximately 50 acres of peach trees. Migrant farmworkers perform almost all of the work. In the late winter and early spring they prune the trees. During the midspring they thin the fruit on the trees, and in late summer and early autumn they pick the fruit.

The farm manager does most of the other work, such as spraying the trees, irrigating, and selling the fruit. Spray concentrate, fruit boxes, and other supplies are purchased on account from the local food co-op stores. Fruit is sold on account to major grocery chains such as Kroger and Albertson's.

### Required:

a. Draw a value system level diagram for Owen's Farm.

b. Assuming the various activities that need to be performed in the conversion process are considered labor operations, draw a value chain level diagram for Owen's Farm.

LO1–LO7   A2.   Visit a local movie theater. Observe what you can about the economic activities of the theater (e.g., ticket sales, concession sales, movie showing). Consider what must also happen that you are unable to observe (e.g., theater's purchase of concessions and ingredients for concessions from suppliers; acquisition of movies to show).

### Required:

a. Create a value system level model for the movie theater (as best you can tell).

b. Create a value chain level diagram for the movie theater (as best you can tell).

## Answers to Multiple Choice Questions

MC1. A; MC2. C; MC3. A; MC4. D; MC5. B.

# Chapter **Four**

# The REA Enterprise Ontology: Business Process Modeling

## LEARNING OBJECTIVES

The objective of this chapter is to present a template pattern for modeling enterprise business processes (transaction cycles) that serves as the structure for an enterprisewide database. After studying this chapter, you should be able to:

1. Explain each of the constructs in entity-relationship conceptual modeling and the notation used to represent each construct in diagrammatic and grammar formats
2. Assign cardinalities to represent the participation of REA entities in prescribed relationships
3. Explain the concept of pattern discovery and apply pattern-based thinking
4. Identify the economic exchanges that form the core of business processes, the commitment events that lead to economic exchange events, and the instigation events that lead to mutual commitment events
5. Identify resources involved in instigation, commitment, and economic events
6. Identify internal and external agents involved in instigation, commitment, and economic events
7. Create a conceptual model for a business process following the REA pattern
8. Explain the differences among business processes, operating events, and information process events

## INTRODUCTION

In this chapter we focus on modeling one **business process** at a time; in a later chapter we discuss the procedures needed to integrate the individual business process models to create a complete database. In this chapter we present the REA pattern for modeling the business process level. The REA pattern is independent of any particular modeling notation. It can be communicated using (1) narrative descriptions, (2) diagrams of various types with different notations, (3) structured grammar, (4) predicate logic notation, (5) tags such as are used in XML and XBRL, (6) programming language notation, and probably using other means that we haven't identified. It is very difficult for some people to separate the pattern that is REA from the notation used to communicate the pattern. Therefore we present the REA pattern using diagram and structured grammar notations in this chapter. Both of these notations are derived from an underlying set of constructs called entity-relationship modeling. The REA pattern is actually separable from entity-relationship modeling (the same pattern can be applied in object-oriented models and other forms of modeling). Most of the REA literature has used entity-relationship models to portray the pattern constructs. These types of models seem to be the easiest to understand, so we focus on that modeling technique.

# CONCEPTUAL MODELING CONSTRUCTS

Entity-relationship modeling has been the most commonly used tool for presenting REA business process level patterns. Before we discuss the details of the REA business process level pattern, we need to introduce the constructs of the entity-relationship modeling tool. You've actually already seen some of these constructs represented in the examples we have shown. The four constructs we discuss are entities, relationships, attributes, and participation cardinalities.

An **entity** is a real-world object that has a separate physical or conceptual existence. Entities that possess identical characteristics (but may have different values for those characteristics) form an entity set. In entity-relationship (ER) models, the word *entity* nearly always means entity set. An entity set may be a thing or an event. For example, an enterprise's customers form an entity set called *Customer*. The customers share a set of characteristics (e.g., CustomerID, name, address, telephone number, credit limit, and account balance due). Each customer in the set may have different values for these characteristics, but they are expected to possess these characteristics. Because the word *entity* is used synonymously with entity set, the word *instance* is used to refer to a specific member of the entity set. The specific customer whose ID is C1234, named Brenda Brenton, who lives at 236 Bonair St., Lansing, MI 48917, whose telephone number is (517) 555-2236, whose credit limit is $4,000, whose account balance due is $100 is an instance of the Customer entity.

A **relationship** is an association between entities. Notice that because entities are set level constructs, in the ER model relationships also are actually sets of relationships. Consider an entity Student and an entity Course. The relationship between them may be called Enrollment. Exhibit 4–1 illustrates a relationship set between the student entity set and the course entity set.

Notice that to describe instances of the relationship set, we need to use characteristics of both of the related entity sets. Instances of the enrollment set in Exhibit 4–1 are

- Margaret enrolled in Accounting 201
- Margaret enrolled in Economics 242
- Joe enrolled in Accounting 201
- Joe enrolled in MIS 179
- Frank enrolled in MIS 179

**EXHIBIT 4–1**
**Students,**
**Courses,**
**and the**
**Enrollment**
**Relationship**

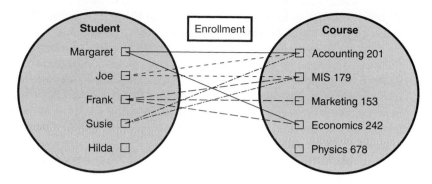

- Frank enrolled in Marketing 153
- Frank enrolled in Economics 242
- Susie enrolled in Accounting 201
- Susie enrolled in MIS 179

Relationships also may possess characteristics of their own. For example, the enrollment relationship may possess a grade earned characteristic that reflects the result of a student's enrollment in a course. People sometimes are confused about distinguishing an entity from a relationship that can possess characteristics of its own. Notice that to fully describe the characteristic of a relationship, you must use both entities in the description (the characteristic is a grade earned by a *student* in a *course*). To fully describe the characteristic of an entity, you need only use that entity in the description (e.g., Social Security number of a student). The relationship therefore does not have separate existence, whereas the entity does.

An **attribute** is a characteristic possessed by an entity or a relationship. Several kinds of attributes are distinguished in entity-relationship modeling. A **primary key attribute** is used to uniquely and universally describe each instance of an entity or relationship. For a primary key to be unique, each instance must have a different data value for that attribute. For a primary key to be universal, each instance must possess a data value for that attribute. Consider the Student entity and some possible attributes we could use to uniquely and universally identify each instance in the set of students. Could we use Last Name? No; it is likely that more than one student will share the same last name so it would not be unique. Could we use Driver's License Number? No; it is likely that some students will not possess a driver's license so it would not be universal. If the school in question is in the United States, it may be reasonable to use social security number, substituting an equivalent government-assigned identification number for non-US citizens. In cases where there is not a naturally occurring attribute that uniquely and universally describes each instance (or if there is one but for some reason the enterprise doesn't want to use it), a primary key may be arbitrarily assigned. For example, the university may decide that using a social security number as the primary key value for a student table will make that number available to too many users of the database. (You will understand why primary keys are more available than other attribute values after you have completed Chapter 6.) Because privacy issues associated with social security numbers make its widespread availability undesirable, the university may choose to assign student ID numbers with which to universally and uniquely identify each student. In some cases it may be possible to uniquely and universally identify an instance of an entity or relationship using a combination of two (or more) attributes. For example, to identify instances of the Enrollment relationship between Student and Course, we can't use student ID (not unique, since the same student may enroll in multiple courses) or course ID (not unique, since the same course may have multiple students enrolled). However, a combination of the student ID attribute with the course ID attribute would suffice as a primary key. Such a key is called a **concatenated primary key**.

A **simple attribute** is an attribute that cannot be further decomposed; whereas a **composite attribute** may be decomposed into other attributes. An example of a commonly used composite attribute is address, which may be decomposed into street address, city, state or province, country, and postal code. In general, it is best to store only simple attributes to facilitate querying and maintenance of the data once they are entered. For example, to query all customers who live in a particular city, it will be most efficient if city is stored as a separate attribute rather than as part of address.

A **derivable attribute** is an attribute that can be derived (computed) from the values of other attributes in the database. For example, a student's overall grade point average is an attribute that is computed based on all of the instances of grade earned in the enrollment relationship for that student. There are two types of derivable attributes: those for which the derived value will not change if new data are entered into the database (i.e., a **static derivable attribute**), and those for which the derived value will change if new data are entered into the database (i.e., a **volatile derivable attribute**). Student's overall grade point average is an example of a volatile derivable attribute. Each time a student completes another course, the value for overall gpa must be recalculated. "Total sale amount" as an attribute of the Sale entity is an example of a static derivable attribute. This attribute may be calculated as the sum of the quantity multiplied by the selling price of each item sold. For example, we may compute the total sale amount for Sale 1 as $100. As we enter data for Sales 2 through 50 into the database, that new data do not change the value we computed as the total amount for Sale 1. In general, derivable attributes should not be stored in a relational database, because they take up valuable storage space. Ignoring the cost of storage space, from a theoretical perspective we recommend storing static derivable attributes if they are likely to be needed as base elements in queries, because those queries are much less complex and more efficient. For example, the total sale amount is likely to be needed as a base element in other queries such as "accounts receivable as of the balance sheet date" or "total sales for region Y during the marketing campaign." We do not recommend storing volatile derivable attributes unless the database software is capable of storing them as triggers (in essence storing the formula by which the data value is computed instead of storing an actual data value). However, keep in mind that the conceptual level model is independent of a particular logical model or specific physical implementation. Therefore the conceptual level model should include derivable attributes attached to the entity or relationship they describe. In fact, the decision to exclude derivable attributes from relational tables should not be made until the physical implementation level, at which point the specific software has been chosen and its capability of storing triggers is known.

**Participation cardinalities** are assigned to represent business rules for how many times an instance of an entity set is allowed to participate in a relationship. **Minimum par-**

**ticipation cardinalities** represent the minimum number of times each instance of an entity set must participate in a relationship. The possible values for a minimum participation cardinality are zero and one. This indicates whether an entity's participation in a relationship is considered optional or mandatory. If minimum participation is zero, any particular instance of the entity set is not required to participate in the relationship at all. If the minimum participation is one, each instance of the entity set must participate in the relationship at least once. **Maximum participation cardinalities** represent the maximum number of times each instance of an entity set may participate in a relationship. The possible values for a maximum participation cardinality are one and many. The term *many* for cardinalities is somewhat misleading because it actually means more than one. So if the maximum participation of an entity happens to be two, it would be depicted as many.

*Abstraction relationships* often are used in conceptual modeling to represent categories of entities or hierarchies of entities. One abstraction relationship is called **typification;** it allows us to store characteristics about categories, or types, of entities. For example, a university may want to track certain characteristics of the categories of students, such as the tuition rate per credit hour or the maximum number of credits which students in the category are allowed to take per semester. Another commonly used abstraction relationship is called **generalization;** it allows us to store entity subtypes and supertypes with an "is-a" relationship between them. Subtype entities contain more specific instances of supertype entities. For example, the entities oboe, bassoon, and English horn all participate in an "is-a" relationship with the double-reed instrument entity. Generalization relationships may even be chained to form a hierarchy; for example, oboe is a double-reed instrument, a double-reed instrument is a woodwind instrument, a woodwind instrument is a musical instrument. Another example is an accountant is an employee, a truck driver is an employee, and a cashier is an employee. Generalization relationships are used in conceptual modeling when some of the characteristics that we want to include in the model are common to all subtype entities but some are unique to particular subtypes. The subtype entities inherit the characteristics of the supertype as well as possessing their own attributes. For example, we might include a set of common attributes for all employees in an enterprise, such as employee id, last name, first name, address, telephone number, and date of birth. However, there may be unique attributes that we need to store for some employees. Perhaps we need to store the CPA license number and state of issuance for the employees who are accountants, but we realize that attribute will be blank (null) for our other employees. Similarly we may need to store the driver's license numbers for our truck driver employees, but we have no need to store that attribute for our other employees. And perhaps we want to store a bond rating for our cashiers but not for our other employees. Some insurance companies issue bond ratings for employees as part of a policy paid for by the enterprise to mitigate losses from employee fraud. Many enterprises require employees who handle cash to be rated by these companies. The process of being rated is sometimes referred to as *being bonded.*

# CONCEPTUAL MODELING NOTATIONS

Entity-relationship models usually are portrayed in diagram format; however, there is no requirement that diagrams be used, and several different notations exist. Chen introduced the entity-relationship model and his is one of the notations we have chosen to illustrate in this textbook edition.[1] If you have studied entity-relationship models in another course, you may have used different notation. It may seem disconcerting that there is not just one notation that everyone uses for entity-relationship modeling. The differences in notation are particularly pronounced for cardinalities. You must not let these differences frustrate you any more than you can let the fact that there are more than a thousand languages spoken across the globe. You must simply be aware of the different notations and make sure you understand which language an enterprise has used when you are trying to interpret its system documentation. At least with different spoken languages, the words look different on paper so you can immediately recognize whether you are reading English, Spanish, or Japanese! Just as most English-speaking Americans can't distinguish between Japanese and Chinese characters, you may not be able to tell exactly what language the nonfamiliar notation is, but you will at least recognize that it is not the same as a language you know. With entity-relationship notation (especially for cardinalities) you must be very careful because at first glance it may look similar but upon closer examination you may find it is backward from your approach. You must become multilingual with regard to entity-relationship modeling notations!

To get you started on the path to being multilingual for entity-relationship modeling notations, we use two notations in many parts of this textbook. One, as noted earlier, is the Chen notation, which is a diagrammatic format. We also use a structured grammar representation called Backus-Naur form (BNF) grammar as a linguistic alternative for people who prefer text to graphics.[2] In this textbook we refer to the Chen notation as ER diagrams and the BNF notation as ER grammar.

Exhibit 4–2 displays the ER diagram and ER grammar notations for entities and attributes, relationships, and participation cardinalities using purchase and cash disbursement as examples (and the **duality relationship** between them).

As you can see, entities are represented in ER diagrams as rectangles labeled with the entity names. The attributes of each entity are attached to the entity via lines with small circles on the ends of them. To indicate which attribute is the primary key, its circle is darkened. For a concatenated primary key, the circles of all attributes comprising the primary key should be darkened. In ER grammars, an entity is represented as the word *Entity* and the entity's name, separated by a colon. The attributes are included as a list following the word *Attributes* and a colon. The primary key attribute is listed preceded by the word *Identifier* and a colon. For a concatenated primary key, all attributes comprising the primary key are listed as the Identifier.

Most relationships are represented in ER diagrams as diamonds labeled with the relationship names connected to the related entities. Participation cardinalities are listed along the connection lines (we discuss cardinalities next). The exception is generalization, which is represented by an arrow drawn from the subtype entity to the supertype entity. No cardinalities are assigned to generalization relationships. In ER grammars, a relationship is represented as the word *Relationship* and the relationship's name, separated by a colon. Then follows a statement *Connected Entities:* followed by the names of the entities that participate in the relationship. Participation cardinalities indicating each entity's participation in the relationship immediately precede each entity's name in the Connected Entities statement.

---

[1]P. P. Chen, "The Entity Relationship Model—Toward a Unified View of Data," *ACM Transactions on Database Systems,* March 1976, pp. 9–36.

[2]C. Batini, S. Ceri, and S. B. Navathe, *Conceptual Database Design: An Entity-Relationship Approach* (San Francisco: Benjamin Cummings, 1992).

**EXHIBIT 4–2**

ER Diagram Notation

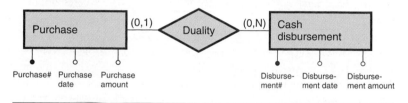

ER Grammar Notation

Entity: Purchase
Attributes: Purchase#
       Purchase date
       Purchase amount
Identifier: Purchase#

Entity: Cash disbursement
Attributes: Disbursement#
       Disbursement date
       Disbursement amount
Identifier: Disbursement#

Relationship: Duality
Connected entities: (0,N) Cash disbursement
                         (0,1) Purchase

Let's discuss cardinality notation further. To keep the notation to one character per cardinality, in the Chen notation *many* is denoted as N. In this notation, the minimum and maximum participation of an entity in a relationship are listed in the format (min,max) next to the entity itself. For example, (0,N) next to Student in the Enrollment relationship would indicate that the minimum participation of Student in Enrollment is 0 and the maximum participation is N (many). This says that at least one instance of the set of students (e.g., Hilda) may exist in the university's database without ever having enrolled in a course, and that at least one instance of the set of students (e.g., Frank) may participate in the enrollment relationship multiple times (i.e., may be enrolled in multiple courses).

Examine Exhibit 4–1 again. What do you think the participation cardinalities (min, max) are for Course in the Enrollment relationship? To answer this question, look at each instance in the Course set. Does at least one instance of Course exist without a related instance of Student? Yes, no student has ever enrolled for Physics 678 in this university's database. Therefore the minimum participation is 0 for Course. Is at least one instance of Course related to multiple instances of Student? Yes, Accounting 201, MIS 179, and Economics 242 are each related to multiple instances of Student. Therefore the maximum participation is N for Course. The Student to Course relationship is thus a (0,N)–(0,N) relationship.

Nearly every diagrammatic notation in practice represents entities with rectangles (or rounded rectangles). Notations vary as to whether they represent relationships using diamonds, some other symbol, or just connection lines. It is usually reasonably easy to tell at a glance what the entities and relationships are in any notation. Cardinalities are sometimes more difficult to interpret across notations. To clarify cardinalities and to illustrate the difference between the Chen notation and two other notations, examine Exhibit 4–3.

**EXHIBIT 4–3**
Comparing
Participation
Cardinality
Notations

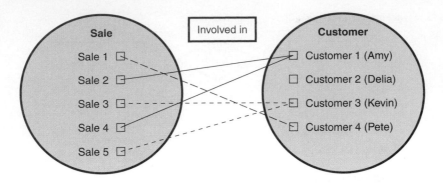

We ask (and answer) four questions to determine what this picture of reality shows:

1: Can at least one instance of sale exist without a related instance of customer?

  • No, each instance of sale involves a customer.

2: Can at least one instance of sale involve more than one customer?

  • No, each instance of sale involves only one customer.

3: Can at least one instance of customer exist without a related instance of sale?

  • Yes, customer 2 (Delia) is unconnected to any sale.

4: Can at least one instance of customer be involved in more than one sale?

  • Yes, customer 1 (Amy) is involved in sale 2 and sale 4.

(Note: Customer 3 (Kevin) is also involved in multiple sales, but once we find one customer that is involved in multiple sales we can answer the question as "Yes" and there is no need to look further.)

These same four questions are asked and answered no matter what participation cardinality notation is used; the difference is simply in where the answers to the questions are placed and what notation is used to communicate the answers. Following Chen's example, we believe the most logical place to put the answers is next to the first entity in the question, with the minimum participation followed by the maximum participation. Alternative cardinality notations such as the widely used Crow's Foot and the notation that was used in the first and second editions of this textbook (HDC notation) place the answers to the minimum and maximum cardinality questions next to the second entity in the questions. Crow's Foot notation places the minimums closest to the center of the relationship and the maximums closest to the entities. HDC notation lists the minimum first, followed by the maximum. Interestingly, Crow's Foot and HDC notations do not represent relationships with diamonds (only with a connection line between the related entities) nor do they assign names to the relationships. We believe it is important to be able to represent relationships with symbols in which names can be included.

Table 4–1 displays the notation that would be used for the relationship and its cardinalities based on the answers to the four questions that determine a picture of reality.

**TABLE 4–1   Conceptual Modeling Notation Comparison**

| | Chen (used in current edition of textbook) | Crow's Foot | HDC |
|---|---|---|---|
| Notation for each cardinality | Min zero = (0, Min one = (1, Max one = ,1) Max many = ,N) | Min zero = ⊖ Min one = ⊢ Max one = ⊢ Max many = ⟨ | Min zero = (0, Min one = (1, Max one = ,1) Max many = ,*) |
| Answer placement | Sale (Q1, Q2) Customer (Q3, Q4) | Min symbol closest to relationship center on opposite entity's side; max symbol closest to opposite entity. Sale (Q4, Q3) ------ (Q1, Q2) Customer | Sale (Q3, Q4) Customer (Q1, Q2) |
| Solution to Exhibit 4–1 (attributes are left off to increase readability) | Diagram format Grammar format Relationship: participation Connected entities: (1,1) Sale (0,N) Customer | | |

# PATTERN DISCOVERY

Now that you have some understanding of the notation that is used to represent the constructs that comprise the business process level of the REA ontology, we can discuss this level in more detail. To begin, let's revisit some of the history and the development goals of REA ontology. McCarthy proposed REA in 1982 as a generalized model for accounting systems after analyzing hundreds of accounting transactions. Note that REA is not a pattern McCarthy created as a prescription for the entities and relationships that enterprises *should* have in their underlying business processes. Rather, REA is the pattern McCarthy discovered in an enterprise's business processes. The prescriptive nature of his 1982 research was that if we realize the pattern exists in the enterprise's underlying business processes, then we should build systems that not only match that pattern but also match the underlying reality as closely as possible. At that point, McCarthy's discovery was limited to what we refer to as the REA core pattern that we introduced as the business process level pattern in Chapter 2. After focusing on this core pattern, we discuss extensions to the pattern that

McCarthy and other colleagues (most notably Geerts) have discovered since then. The ontological soundness of some of these extensions is being investigated. Additional extensions to the pattern will likely be discovered in years to come. For now, we believe they are worthy of discussion in their current state of development.

You may be wondering why the pattern underlying all enterprises isn't obvious to everyone and why such patterns haven't been searched for and already discovered. Even when a pattern is quite straightforward, sometimes it takes a certain perspective to be able to see it. Separating a complex reality into parts that are relevant and irrelevant for a particular context can be quite difficult. One can't be focused on the form of the activities in which the enterprise is involved to see patterns—you must focus on the substance of what occurs. It is very easy to focus on the form with surface level similarities and differences and miss the substance and deep level commonalities between enterprise processes.

In Chapter 2 we introduced the notion of script patterns that have been researched extensively by Schank in his quest to figure out how to make computers that can think and learn like human beings. His most famous script example is restaurants. Unless you had previously read Schank's ideas in another book or heard about them in a class you took, you probably never realized that you have a restaurant script (and possible variations of the restaurant script) in your memory that you retrieve and adapt as necessary to allow you to understand your environment whenever you go to a restaurant. Close your eyes for a few moments and picture yourself going out to dinner at a fancy restaurant (but don't forget to open your eyes and continue reading when you are through imagining that scenario).

What did you see happening? Probably you pictured some combination of the following:

- Was greeted by host or hostess upon entry into building
- Waited in lobby area until seating was available
- Was seated by host or hostess at a table in dining area
- Was provided with a menu that included descriptions and prices of available products
- Ordered beverage from waiter or waitress
- Received beverage from waiter or waitress
- Ordered food from waiter or waitress
- Stayed at table conversing with companion and sipping beverages while food was prepared by cooks in the kitchen
- Received food from waiter or waitress
- Gave waiter or waitress payment for food and beverages (and possibly tip)
- Waiter or waitress took payment to cashier
- Waiter or waitress returned any change due to you
- Left tip for waiter or waitress (if not done earlier with food payment)
- Left restaurant

This list is not necessarily comprehensive and may include more or less detail in each step than was included in your list, but likely there was significant overlap.

Now close your eyes again and picture yourself going out to lunch at a fast-food restaurant (once again, be sure to open them and continue reading when you finish imagining the scenario).

The following list is likely a fairly good representation of what you imagined.

- Entered restaurant and approached the cashier's counter
- Examined menu board posted on wall while waiting in line at the counter
- Ordered food and beverage from cashier
- Paid cashier for food and beverage
- Waited at cashier's counter while food was prepared by cooks in the kitchen
- Seated yourself in the dining area
- Ate food
- Threw trash away
- Left restaurant

How are the two restaurant scripts different? How are they similar? One of the many obvious differences between them is the order in which the activities occur. In sit-down restaurants, we typically pay for our meal after we eat; in fast-food restaurants we pay for our meal before we eat. In sit-down restaurants, we sit down before we examine a menu, order food, or receive food. In fast-food restaurants, we examine the menu, order food, and receive food before we sit down. It is easy to focus on differences, particularly in the physical flow of what occurs. Other variations of the script are possible. For example, if the restaurant you pictured in your mind was a Japanese steakhouse you may have imagined the food being prepared at your table with the cook entertaining you in the process of preparing your food. The first time you go to such a restaurant, you immediatcly notice that there is something different about this restaurant and you create a Japanese steakhouse variation in your repertoire of restaurant scripts.

To find a pattern that applies to all restaurants, we focus on those elements of these descriptions that are necessary for this to be considered a restaurant. The essential constructs seem to be "customer ordered food," "customer received food," "customer ate food," and "customer paid for food." If you went to a restaurant where normal operations did not involve you ordering food, receiving food, eating food, and paying for food (not necessarily in that order), you would not know what to think! We can add to this core restaurant pattern, although we will not try to complete the example to its full potential; we just want to give you the idea of the thought processes involved. We need to sift away all the details that make the scripts different from each other—not that the different details are not important, but we can't include them in a pattern unless we can discover a conceptual commonality among them. Let's look at an example of discovering a conceptual commonality. Although details—such as who prepared the food, who received payment for the food and beverages, who received the order from the customer, and where the food was prepared differed—the fact that a restaurant employee was involved in taking orders, preparing the food, and receiving payment, and the fact that a location for food preparation was identified can become part of the pattern. Similarly in modeling enterprises to determine what data need to be stored in enterprisewide databases, we want to store the identifiable pattern of necessary elements as base objects and ensure the other details may be stored by enterprises to which they apply, and left out by enterprises to which they do not apply.

For some management and decision-making activities, physical workflow differences are important and physical workflow and information flow certainly need to be documented.

Those things do not matter for the storage structure of the data. They can matter for how and when data are input and retrieved, but they do not matter for the actual storage structure, which is what REA is all about. The core elements we identified in our restaurant script do not describe workflow, and indeed to form a pattern for the restaurants we do not require the activities to happen in a prescribed order. Similarly in REA models, we are less concerned about the order in which events occur and are more interested in tracking data attributes and relationships to other relevant phenomena.

# REA CORE PATTERN

When McCarthy examined the hundreds of accounting transactions to try to identify a pattern in the underlying reality that could be represented in conceptual modeling symbols and translated into computer readable form, he took a similar approach. The first core pattern he noticed was the relationship of one **economic event** to another economic event as part of an exchange. Though different events were involved in various transactions, they had something in common; there was always a decrement economic event (one in which something is given up) that could be paired with an increment economic event (one in which something is received). He also noticed that the exchange was not always immediate and that there was no rule as to whether the increment or the decrement event happened first. Sometimes there was a significant time lag between the events, for which double-entry bookkeeping entries created an account to allow the entries to balance—to keep both sides of the Assets = Liabilities + Equity equation equal with each other. McCarthy labeled these timing differences **claims.** You may recognize some of these timing differences as accounts receivable, deferred revenue, prepaid expenses, accounts payable, and wages payable. He also noticed that although the thing received or given up was different for various transactions, that thing always had economic value and could be thought of as a **resource.** Finally, he noticed each event making up the exchange involved not only a what (the resource) but also a who. In fact each event typically involved at least one person operating as an agent of the enterprise and another person or company who was an external business partner. He thus proposed the **REA core pattern** shown in Exhibit 4–4. Although McCarthy proposed the pattern in diagram form, we also display the corresponding grammar notation.

McCarthy also recognized that each core pattern was actually the core of a different transaction cycle, so he recommended applying this pattern to each transaction cycle in an enterprise to model the core constructs of its daily operations. In 1982 McCarthy had not formally developed the value chain level; he simply recognized that enterprises' economic activities followed an identifiable pattern in which causally related give and take events are associated with resources and agents. In the years since, he published the value chain script pattern and has informally described how that compares to the value system level.

Although McCarthy started identifying the pattern at the business process level and then worked his way up to levels of less detail, it is useful to start from the big picture and work down. We can use the value system and value chain level models described in Chapters 2 and 3 to help develop business process level models. Let's revisit the RSWS example from those chapters. Recall that RSWS is Robert Scott Woodwind Shop and that it is an enterprise generating revenue by selling instruments, renting instruments, providing re-

**EXHIBIT 4–4**
**Core REA**
**Pattern**

Adapted from W. E.
McCarthy, "The REA
Accounting Model: A
Generalized
Framework for
Accounting Systems
in a Shared Data
Environment," *The
Accounting Review,*
July 1982, pp. 554–77.

Diagram format

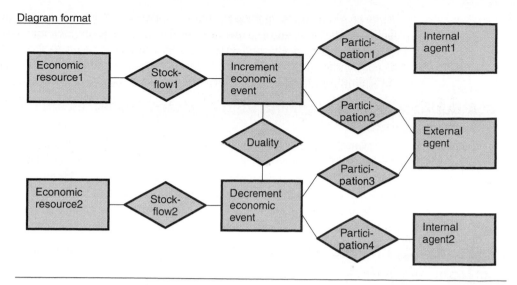

Grammar format
Entity: Increment economic event
Entity: Decrement economic event
Entity: Economic resource1
Entity: Economic resource2
Entity: External agent
Entity: Internal agent1
Entity: Internal agent2

Relationship: Duality
Connected entities:  Increment economic event
                                   Decrement economic event
Relationship: Stockflow1
Connected entities: Increment economic event
                                   Economic resource1

Relationship: Stockflow2
Connected entities: Decrement economic event
                                   Economic resource2
Relationship: Participation1
Connected entities: Increment economic event
                                   Internal agent1
Relationship: Participation2
Connected entities: Increment economic event
                                   External agent
Relationship: Participation3
Connected entities: Decrement economic event
                                   External agent
Relationship: Participation4
Connected entities: Decrement economic event
                                   Internal agent2

pair services, and selling manufactured accessories such as clarinet barrels and mouth-pieces. Recall that to engage in these revenue-generating activities RSWS must purchase instruments, raw materials, fixed assets, and various services from suppliers. RSWS must also purchase labor from employees, and use that labor in addition to the materials, fixed assets, and services to manufacture accessories and repair instruments. The value system and value chain models from that example are displayed in Exhibit 4–5. We focus on the acquisition/payment process as an example. The steps we follow in creating a business process level model from these higher-level models are as follows:

## REA Business Process Modeling Step 1: Identify Economic Exchange Events

The first step is to identify the economic exchange events that form the core of the business process. To do this, consider the **resource inflows** and **resource outflows** for the business process for which you are constructing a model and determine what economic exchange events provide and use up these resources. Represent the economic exchange events with a duality relationship between them. Note that if you already prepared a value chain level model, you have already completed this step, and the economic exchange events and duality relationship are inside the bubble for that business process on the value chain. So you can simply copy that to your business process level model.

## REA Business Process Modeling Step 2: Attach Resources to Economic Events

The second step is to attach the resources identified in step 1 to the appropriate events via **stockflow relationships.** If there are multiple inflow resources, determine whether the same attributes need to be stored for each inflow resource. Combine resources for which the same attributes are stored; keep separate resources for which different attributes are stored. Similarly if there are multiple outflow resources, combine resources for which the same attributes are stored and keep separate those for which different attributes are stored.

## REA Business Process Modeling Step 3: Attach External Agents to Economic Events

The third step is to attach the appropriate **external agents** to the events via participation relationships. To determine the appropriate external agents, examine the value system level and determine which external agent represents the one that gives and receives the same resource flows as are represented in your business process level model. That is the external agent for your model. If you did not prepare a value system level model, examine any narrative description you may have for the process or ask someone knowledgeable from the enterprise which external business partners participate in those economic events.

## REA Business Process Modeling Step 4: Attach Internal Agents to Economic Events

The fourth step is to attach the appropriate **internal agents** to the events via participation relationships. Internal agents are not reflected anywhere in the value system and value chain levels, so to determine the appropriate internal agents you must examine any narrative description you may have for the process or ask someone knowledgeable from the enterprise which type of employees are responsible for each of the economic events in the process. Keep in mind that sometimes multiple internal agents participate in an event. For example, one type of employee may perform an event and another type of employee may authorize the event. Assuming the enterprise wants to track information about both roles, it needs to establish separate relationships for each role.

## REA Business Process Modeling Step 5: Attribute Assignment

The fifth step is to assign attributes to each entity in the model and also to assign attributes to any relationships that possess their own attributes. Typically you are provided with a list of attributes the company needs to be able to store; if not, ask someone knowledgeable in the enterprise (i.e., someone familiar with that business process and its information needs) to determine what attributes need to be assigned. Attribute assignment is a very important step. To correctly assign attributes to entities and relationships, you must understand what information the attribute is supposed to communicate, and you must understand exactly what thing in reality each entity symbol and each relationship symbol represents, and at what level of detail the data exist. This may seem like an easy task, and for some entities it is quite simple. For other entities and for some relationships it takes considerable thought. Many system designers do not include attributes on ER models, because it is difficult to fit them into a crowded diagram, and because it seems like effort is duplicated when the ER model is converted into relational tables and the attributes are assigned into the tables. Although it may seem tedious to place the attributes twice, once attaching them to the entities and relationships and next listing them as columns in the appropriate tables, we believe the attributes are a necessary component of the ER model, for two reasons. First, attributes are part of the information that is communicated by an ER model. If they are left off, then that information is not communicated to the user. Second, the process of assigning attributes is best accomplished while formulating the conceptual model because it facilitates understanding of the nature of the entities and relationships. Sometimes in assigning attributes, designers realize they misunderstood which reality an entity set was representing. It is best if these misunderstandings are corrected before the logical level is developed. If it is too difficult to place them on a crowded diagram, they may be listed at the bottom of the diagram, with the name of the entity or relationship to which they apply (notice the grammar format has an advantage here, because it is easy to list as many attributes as an entity or relationship has).

## Entity or Relationship Attribute?

To determine whether an attribute describes an entity or a relationship, isolate whether it is describing just one thing or a combination of things. For example, consider the attribute quantity sold of an inventory item in a sale event. Assume each sale event can involve multiple inventory items and that an inventory item represents a type of inventory (i.e., a model number and description) that can be sold multiple times. Should this entity be assigned to the inventory entity, to the sale entity, or to the stockflow relationship? To answer this question, think about what it describes. Does it describe inventory separately from sale? Could you find a data value for that attribute if you knew which inventory item it was but you didn't know which sale it was related to? That is, if you knew it was Model KXPJ432, but you didn't know whether it was Sale 2, 46, or 79? No, because different quantities may have been sold on each of those sales! So quantity sold is not an attribute of inventory. Does it describe sale separately from inventory? Could you find a data value for that attribute if you knew which sale it was but you didn't know which inventory item was involved? That is, if you knew it was Sale 17 but you didn't know whether it was Model AFLQ127 or Model CLDJ1110? No! So quantity sold is not an attribute of sale. To fill in a data value for the attribute quantity sold, you must know both the item and the sale because it is really describing the relationship between them. Thus it is a relationship attribute, not an entity attribute. Notice that if the attribute of interest was not the quantity of a particular item sold in a sale event, but the total quantity sold of an inventory item throughout the company's history (considering all sale events that have involved that inventory model) then the attribute is an entity attribute and is assigned to inventory. Or if the attribute of interest was the total of all items (of all types) included in a sale event, then it is an entity attribute and is assigned to sale. So you must verify that you understand what data the enterprise wants for each of the attributes on your list.

## Resource Attributes

Resources are usually the most difficult entities to grasp in terms of the underlying reality and what attributes should be used to identify and describe them. Cash is an entity many people who are new to REA modeling have difficulty conceptualizing. When you pictured cash as an entity in thinking about the value system and value chain levels, you probably thought about physical cash—the actual coins and pieces of currency. Most of the time we do not need information about each specific coin and each piece of currency that enters and exits an enterprise; therefore we do not usually represent cash at the specific instance level. Instead, we typically represent cash at an aggregated level, representing characteristics of the accounts in which cash is stored. An enterprise's cash entity often has data attributes such as cash account number, cash account location (e.g., Fourth Street Bank, cash register 42, or secretary's file cabinet drawer in room 144), and cash account type (e.g., checking, savings, money market, petty cash, or cash on hand).

Inventory is another entity that takes some thought, because sometimes instances of the inventory entity set are specifically identified physical items. Other times instances of the inventory entity set are categories into which the physical items are grouped—typically by model or SKU numbers. What determines whether the instances are separate physical items or whether they are categories? If the enterprise does not separately identify each physical unit of inventory then the instances must be categories. For example, consider bags of potato chips at the grocery store. When a bag of potato chips is sold, the cashier scans the UPC code that tells the system what brand and what size package was just scanned. If another bag of chips (of the same brand and size) is scanned, exactly the same information is communicated to the system. There is no way for the system to distinguish between the first physical bag of chips and the second physical bag of chips. Contrast that with personal computers that have serial numbers to separately identify each physical computer. When the serial number is entered into the system, the system knows exactly which physical unit is being sold. Technically the entity that represents category level inventory information should be called Inventory Type and the entity that represents each physical unit of inventory should be called Inventory and there should exist a typification relationship between them. In fact, if an enterprise wants to store data at both levels of detail, that is how the model must be constructed. If an enterprise has no need to separately identify each physical unit of inventory, then often a compromise is made and Inventory Type is substituted for Inventory and used as if it were a resource instead of a resource type.

### Event Attributes

Assignment of attributes to events is usually straightforward. Let's consider the information that is typically needed regarding events. The five Journalism 101 questions—who, what, why, when, and where—are a good representation of what people (and enterprises) want to know about events. The who and why questions are not answered by including attributes to answer them. The who question is answered by the participation relationships between the event and the internal and external agents. The why question is answered by the duality relationship between the event and the causally related opposite event. The what question actually contains two parts. One part is what happened and the other part is what things were affected by the event. The first part is answered by the name of the event and its identifier attribute. The second part is answered by the stockflow relationships between the event and the related resources and sometimes the inclusion of a dollar value attribute. The remaining attributes needed to fill out the whole picture, then, are those that answer the when and the where questions; therefore date and location are often stored as attributes of events. If there is no question as to the when or where for an event set, then these attributes may be excluded. For example, if an enterprise only has one location at which it makes sales, or if the location of a sale doesn't matter for decision-making purposes, then there is no reason to record location as an attribute of sale.

### Agent Attributes

To consider what attributes are likely to be assigned to agents, think about what you typically want to know about people or companies with which you do business. An identifier is needed, of course, to be able to tell one agent from another, especially if two agent instances may have the same name. Assuming you can tell them apart, what else do you need to know? You probably want to know their name and some means of contacting them, such as addresses and telephone numbers. You may also need to keep attributes that tell you something about their qualifications and their performance.

## REA Business Process Modeling Step 6: Participation Cardinality Assignment

The sixth step is to assign participation cardinalities to each relationship in the model. Great care must be taken in assigning cardinalities, as these form some of the business rules and in some cases dictate what data may or may not be able to be entered into the resulting database tables. You may identify the business rules that need to be represented by the cardinalities by examining any narrative description you have and/or by asking someone knowledgeable in the enterprise (notice that you must ask the questions in a "language" they can understand, such as the four questions related to Exhibit 4–3). Business rules are policies and practices the enterprise adopts in its operations. For example, an enterprise's credit policy is a business rule. If they don't offer credit, that policy is represented one way in the cardinalities, whereas if they do offer credit sales that is represented another way. Some people assign cardinalities before they assign attributes. However, cardinality assignment requires a solid understanding of the occurrences within each entity and relationship in the model. Because attribute assignment helps you to verify your understanding of the nature of the entities and relationships and the instances that comprise them, we believe attribute assignment should be completed before cardinalities are assigned.

As with attribute assignment, your assignment of cardinalities is not completely ad hoc. Heuristics exist to guide you; however, keep in mind that heuristics are rules of thumb that *usually* apply, but *don't always* apply. You must carefully consider whether the situation you are modeling is an exception to the heuristic. We have listed some common exceptions along with the heuristics, but other exceptions certainly exist!

### Resource Type–Economic Event (Stockflow) Cardinality Heuristics

If a resource type is substituted for a resource in a stockflow relationship with an economic event, then the general cardinality heuristics are as follows:

$$(0,N) \text{ Resource Type–}(1,N) \text{ Economic Event}$$

The minimum of zero for resource type reflects the common business practice of entering data about resource types before any economic events involving them are recorded. As we see later in this chapter, often the resource type data are entered in conjunction with other events that precede the actual event that causes the resource inflow or outflow. The maximum of many for resource type reflects the fact that resource type is a category level entity and one would expect that if every member of that set were only to be involved a maximum of one time with the set of economic events there would have been no need to represent the entity at the category level.

The minimum of one for economic event reflects the fact that an economic event must involve a resource flow—by definition an economic event either gives or takes something of economic value. The maximum of many for economic event reflects the fact that seldom does an enterprise design its business processes so that each event may involve only one instance of a resource. When an enterprise makes a sale, it would hope at least some of its sales consist of multiple items. When an enterprise purchases merchandise, it would be silly to purchase each item separately, especially if multiple resources are purchased on the same day from the same vendor.

***Common Exception That Changes the One Minimum on Economic Event***   If alternative kinds of resource types could participate in an economic event, then the minimum cardinality for an economic event would change from one to zero. For example, if a purchase could involve a fixed asset or an inventory item (and those are maintained as separate entities) then the participation of purchase with fixed assets would be optional (because the purchase could be of an inventory item) and cash disbursement could be made to an employee or to a supplier or to a creditor (and those are maintained as separate entities). The participation of cash disbursement with an employee would be optional (because it could involve a supplier or creditor instead) and for the same reason, participation with a supplier would be optional and participation with a creditor would be optional.

### *Resource–Economic Event (Stockflow) Cardinality Heuristics*

If a resource entity represents specifically identified resources, the expected cardinality pattern is

$$(0,1) \text{ Resource–}(1,N) \text{ Economic Event}$$

The reasoning for the minimum of zero for resource, the minimum of one for economic event, and the maximum of many for economic event is the same as in the expected cardinality pattern for resource-type–economic event, so we won't repeat that logic here. The only difference between the pattern for stockflow relationships involving resources as opposed to resource types is the expected maximum cardinality. Because resources are specifically identified physical units (as opposed to categories) each can typically be involved in an economic event only one time. Usually the same physical unit of something can be produced or purchased or sold only one time.

***Common Exceptions That Change the One Maximum on Resource***   One exception that changes the maximum of one on resource to a maximum of many occurs when the economic event involves the rental of the resource rather than the permanent transfer of the resource. In this case, what is being exchanged for cash is actually the right to use a resource for a contracted period of time, rather than the resource itself. If an enterprise leases a building from another company, it can rent the same building as part of another economic exchange.

Another exception that changes the maximum of one on resource to a maximum of many occurs when the same resource may be given and taken multiple times. For example, a car dealership that handles both new and used vehicles may sell a car, then acquire the same car when the owner decides to trade it in for another new vehicle, then sell the car to another customer, and eventually reacquire it again. In some such cases an enterprise may decide to assign a different identifier to the resource each time it is reacquired (an argument in favor of this approach is that the condition of the resource is likely different each time) and then the maximum of one would be appropriate. In other cases the history of the specific physical item may be important and the enterprise may choose to keep using the same identifier and specify the maximum cardinality as many.

### Economic Event–Agent (Participation Relationship) Cardinality Heuristics

The general participation cardinality heuristic for agent-event relationships is as follows:

$$(1,1) \text{ Economic Event–}(0,N) \text{ Agent}$$

The minimum of one for the economic event's participation with an agent signifies that most enterprises want to record at least one internal and at least one external agent for each economic event. If we don't know who represented each enterprise involved in the exchange, it is difficult to resolve any future discrepancies about the exchange events.

The maximum of one for the economic event's participation with an internal agent indicates that most enterprises hold one internal agent accountable for (or give them credit for) each economic event. The maximum of one for the economic event's participation with an external agent indicates that most enterprises maintain information about only one external agent involved in a transaction. For example, if two college roommates decide to split the cost of a personal computer for their dorm room, the computer store records the sale as being to one of the roommates. The company can't sell half of a computer! If the two roommates purchase two computers and want the sale split between them, the computer store would typically record two sales, one to each of them. Similarly when an enterprise receives goods, each receipt of goods would come from just one vendor.

The minimum of zero for agents' participation is typical because in most enterprises, data about agents must be entered into the system before they are permitted to participate in any economic events. The maximum of many for agents' participation represents the fact that it would be very unusual to restrict the entire set of agents to participating a maximum of one time each in an event. For example, it would seem completely ridiculous for a company to tell customers they couldn't buy anything more from the company because they've already participated in one sale!

Of course, as with any heuristics there are exceptions. Typical exceptions to the economic event–agent cardinality heuristics are as follows:

**Common Exceptions That Change the One Minimum on Economic Event**   If alternative types of internal agents can process an event, then the minimum cardinality for event would change from one to zero. For example, if a sale could be made by either a salesperson or by a manager (and those are maintained as two separate entities), then the participation of sale with salesperson would be optional (because it could involve a manager instead) and the participation of sale with manager would be optional (because it could involve a salesperson instead).

Similarly if alternate types of external agents could participate in an event, then the minimum cardinality for event would change from one to zero. For example, if a cash disbursement could be made to an employee or to a supplier or to a creditor (and those are maintained as separate entities), then the participation in a cash disbursement with an employee would be optional (because it could involve a supplier or creditor instead) and for the same reason, participation with a supplier would be optional and participation with a creditor would be optional.

**Common Exception That Changes the One Maximum on Economic Event**   If multiple agents share responsibility (or credit) for an economic event then the maximum for the economic event would change to N. For example, if two salespeople assist a customer in selecting the product to buy, and they split the commission resulting from the sale, the sale event has participated in the relationship with salespersons multiple times.

### *Economic Event—Economic Event (Duality Relationship)*
### *Cardinality Heuristics*

Duality relationships typically allow any number of different possible cardinality patterns; thus no heuristic is available. The enterprise's business policies must be examined to determine the correct pattern.

## REA Business Process Modeling Step 7: Validate Model

The final step of constructing an REA model at the business process level is to validate the model with one (or preferably more than one) representative from the enterprise who is knowledgeable about the details and objectives of the business processes being modeled. Validation sessions should result in either confirmation of the model's accuracy or modification of the model. When validating the model with the enterprise representative(s) the REA modeler must take care to be aware of potential miscommunications due to differences in vocabulary. Unfortunately many words have multiple meanings, especially when used in different contexts. When some people talk about a purchase, they may in fact be referring to a purchase order. Informally, that may be okay, but the REA model must be created with strict economic definitions observed, and in those definitions, a purchase does not occur until the title to goods is transferred from the seller to the buyer. At that point a sale occurs for the seller and a purchase occurs for the buyer. When asking enterprise personnel about events, one must be very careful to ask enough questions to ensure that the strict economic definitions are being effectively communicated.

To make sure these steps are clear, next we complete Steps 1 through 6 for the RSWS example. Obviously we can't validate the model with an enterprise representative because it is a fictitious example. The value system and value chain levels for this enterprise are reprinted here as Exhibit 4–5.

### *RSWS Example Step 1*

The economic exchange events identified in the acquisition/payment process bubble on the value chain are acquisition and cash disbursement. We may represent them in diagram or grammar form as follows.

**RSWS Step 1 Result**

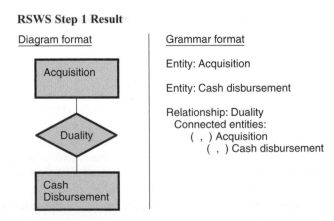

Diagram format

Grammar format

Entity: Acquisition

Entity: Cash disbursement

Relationship: Duality
    Connected entities:
        ( , ) Acquisition
            ( , ) Cash disbursement

**EXHIBIT 4–5**  **Value System and Value Chain Models for Robert Scott Woodwind Shop**

*Value System Level*

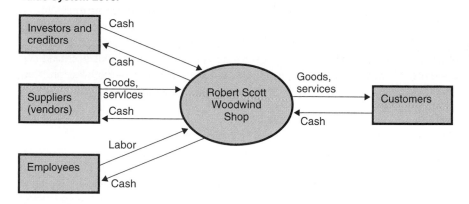

*Value Chain Level*

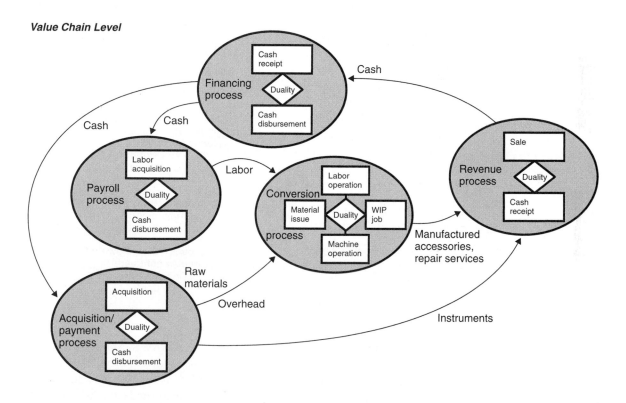

## RSWS Example Step 2

The resource flowing into the acquisition/payment process that gets used up in a decrement event is cash. Therefore we attach the **cash resource** to the cash disbursement decrement event via a stockflow relationship, as illustrated. The resources flowing out of the acquisition cycle and produced by an increment event are instruments, raw materials, and overhead.

At this point we must decide whether the same characteristics will be stored for the resources so we know whether to show each type of resource as separate entities or whether to combine them. In this example, let's say we determine to track the same attributes for instrument inventory and raw materials so we combine them into one entity set. However, we determine that the characteristics of the overhead items/services we acquire are different from the inventory attributes so we create a separate entity set to represent overhead. We create two resource entities, one called inventory and the other called overhead, and link them to the acquisition increment event via two stockflow relationships, as illustrated.

**RSWS Step 2 Result**

Diagram Format

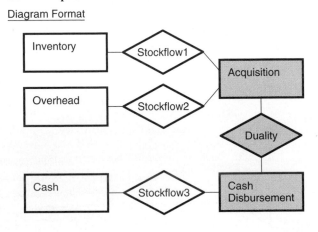

Grammar Format

Entity: Acquisition

Entity: Cash disbursement

**Entity: Cash**

**Entity: Inventory**

**Entity: Overhead**

Relationship: Duality
  Connected entities:
    ( , ) Acquisition
      ( , ) Cash disbursement

**Relationship: Stockflow1**
  **Connected entities:**
    **( , ) Acquisition**
      **( , ) Inventory**

**Relationship: Stockflow2**
  **Connected entities:**
    **( , ) Acquisition**
      **( , ) Overhead**

**Relationship: Stockflow3**
  **Connected entities:**
    **( , ) Cash disbursement**
      **( , ) Cash**

## RSWS Example Steps 3 and 4

In the value system level model, the external agent with which RSWS exchanges cash for goods and services (which inventory and overhead are) is the set of suppliers. Thus we add suppliers as an external agent to our model and we create two participation relationships; one between supplier and acquisition and the other between supplier and cash disbursement.

Neither the value system nor the value chain level identifies internal agents; therefore we must go back and look at the available narrative description for RSWS or ask someone from RSWS who has the appropriate knowledge. The narrative description provided in Chapter 2 is a very high level overview and does not contain enough detail to determine what internal agents apply. Let's say we asked Robert Scott who processes acquisitions and cash disbursements on behalf of RSWS and we receive the following reply: "Johnny Arthur and Cheri Lynn make the acquisitions; Lorie Lisbet, Linda Kay, and Timothy Rob process the cash disbursements—those for acquisitions and all other payments we make. Oh, and Ray Edwards has to approve all checks that are written." Notice that the response we received was at the token level of detail. We want our database to be able to store the token level detail, but we need to form our conceptual model at the type (set) level. We need to know what type-level names we should use to represent the sets to which these individuals belong. In some companies we may not want to distinguish between different employee positions and we may choose simply to attach an entity called Employee to events to represent internal agent participation. Whether that is a good idea depends on whether we want to store the same attributes for all categories of employees. If we need to store different attributes about different sets of employees (i.e., we need different attributes for purchasing agents than we do for accounts payable clerks or managers), then we may choose to represent each category of employee as a separate entity and show relationships between the event and the appropriate employee category agent.

If we represent all employees as a single entity set, we must take care to identify separate relationships to represent different roles involving different individuals with respect to each event. For example, processing cash disbursements is a different role from authorizing them; therefore, if RSWS chooses to maintain one overall entity set for employee, it should create two relationships between the cash disbursement event and the employee agent. Let's assume that RSWS wants to keep its employees in separate sets depending on their positions.

When we interview Robert Scott further, he tells us that Johnny and Cheri are called purchase agents; Lorie, Linda, and Timothy are called accounts payable (A/P) clerks; and Ray is a manager. Therefore we add purchasing agent as an entity and connect it to acquisition via a participation relationship. We add A/P clerk as an entity and connect it to cash disbursement via a participation relationship. And we add manager as an entity and connect it to the cash disbursement via an authorization relationship (to distinguish the role of the manager with respect to the cash disbursement from that of the A/P clerks). We take this opportunity to ask Robert Scott a few more questions, because we know we are going to need more information about the roles these employees are playing to assign cardinalities. To begin, we confirm with Scott that RSWS wants to be able to enter information about employees as soon as they are hired and not wait until after they have participated in an event. His reply, "Of course; in fact, I want your system to make sure no transaction can be entered unless a valid employee is entered as the responsible person. I also want the transaction to be rejected if an invalid product or service is entered for the transaction. Information about products we buy and sell should be entered before any information about the purchases and sales is entered."

We ask Scott whether Johnny and Cheri ever have to work together on a purchase and assume joint responsibility for that purchase or whether each of them processes a separate set of purchases. He replies, "Sometimes Johnny will help Cheri open the boxes and count all the different types of inventory that arrive in one of her incoming shipments, or vice versa, but Cheri signs off on and assumes responsibility for her receiving reports and Johnny signs off on and assumes responsibility for his receiving reports. In fact for all activities that happen at RSWS I want just one employee I can blame if something goes wrong or give credit when something is awesome." We make a note of that and then remember what Scott said earlier about the A/P clerks processing cash disbursements and Ray signing all the checks. He says, "Oh yes, I can see why that seems contrary to what I just said. It really isn't though, because I hold Ray responsible for all payments, and in case we hire additional managers I would hold whichever manager approved a payment responsible for it. But we still need to track which A/P clerk participated in each payment so the personnel department can have that information for evaluation purposes." Based on this interview with Robert Scott, we attach internal and external agents to our model as illustrated.

**RSWS Steps 3 and 4 Result**

Diagram Format

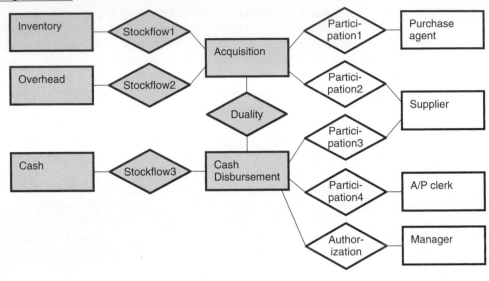

Grammar form at

Entity: Acquisition

Entity: Cash disbursement

Entity: Cash

Entity: Inventory

Entity: Overhead

**Entity: A/P clerk**

**Entity: Manager**

**Entity: Purchase agent**

**Entity: Supplier**

Relationship: Duality
  Connected entities:
    ( , ) Acquisition
      ( , ) Cash disbursement

Relationship: Stockflow1
  Connected entities:
    ( , ) Acquisition
      ( , ) Inventory

Relationship: Stockflow2
  Connected entities:
    ( , ) Acquisition
      ( , ) Overhead

Relationship: Stockflow3
  Connected entities:
    ( , ) Cash Disbursement
      ( , ) Cash

**Relationship: Participation1**
  **Connected entities:**
    **( , ) Acquisition**
      **( , ) Purchase agent**

**Relationship: Participation2**
  **Connected entities:**
    **( , ) Acquisition**
      **( , ) Supplier**

**Relationship: Participation3**
  **Connected entities:**
    **( , ) Cash disbursement**
      **( , ) Supplier**

**Relationship: Participation4**
  **Connected entities:**
    **( , ) Cash disbursement**
      **( , ) A/P clerk**

**Relationship: Authorization**
  **Connected entities:**
    **( , ) Cash disbursement**
      **( , ) Manager**

## RSWS Step 5

This step is to assign attributes to the appropriate entities and relationships in the REA business process model. Assume RSWS has given you the following list of attributes:

- Acquisition ID
- Actual unit cost of an inventory item purchased on an acquisition
- A/P clerk identification number
- Bond rating for an A/P clerk
- Cash account balance
- Cash account number
- Cash disbursement identification number
- Date goods or services were acquired
- Date of cash disbursement
- Description of inventory item
- Description of overhead item
- Dollar amount of a cash disbursement applied to a specific acquisition
- ID code assigned to overhead item
- Identification number for a manager
- List selling price per unit of inventory item
- Location of a cash account
- Manager's highest degree
- Name of A/P clerk
- Name of manager
- Name of purchase agent
- Name of supplier
- Purchase agent identification number
- Purchase authorization limit for a purchase agent
- Quality rating for supplier
- Quantity of an inventory item purchased on an acquisition
- Quantity of an overhead item purchased on an acquisition
- Quantity on hand of inventory item
- SKU number of inventory item
- Standard unit cost of inventory item
- Supplier address
- Supplier number
- Total dollar amount of a cash disbursement
- Total dollar value of an acquisition
- Type of cash account

Table 4–2 illustrates the thought processes needed to assign attributes. In this table, the first column contains the attribute description as given in the list. The second column contains an abbreviation that we can include in our model to save space and avoid crowding. A (PK) is added next to the abbreviation for any attributes we identify as primary keys. The third column contains the name of the entity or relationship to which the attribute should be assigned. (Note: You probably won't do this as a separate step once you understand the process of attribute assignment, but it helps you to follow the logic of assigning attributes.)

**TABLE 4–2**
**Attribute**
**Assignment**

| Attribute description in list | Abbreviation | Assignment |
|---|---|---|
| Acquisition ID | Acq-id (PK) | Acquisition |
| Actual unit cost of an inventory item purchased on an acquisition | Item-unit-cost | Stockflow1 |
| A/P clerk identification number | AP-id (PK) | A/P clerk |
| Bond rating for an A/P clerk | AP-bond | A/P clerk |
| Cash account balance | AcctBal | Cash |
| Cash account number | AcctNum (PK) | Cash |
| Cash disbursement identification number | CD-id (PK) | Cash disbursement |
| Date goods or services were acquired | Acq-date | Acquisition |
| Date of cash disbursement | CD-date | Cash disbursement |
| Description of inventory item | Item-desc | Inventory |
| Description of overhead item | OH-desc | Overhead |
| Dollar amount of a cash disbursement applied to a specific acquisition | CD-acq-applied | Duality |
| ID code assigned to overhead item | OH-id (PK) | Overhead |
| Identification number for a manager | Mgr-id (PK) | Manager |
| List selling price per unit of inventory item | Item-list-price | Inventory |
| Location of a cash account | Acct Loc | Cash |
| Manager's highest degree | Mgr-degree | Manager |
| Name of A/P clerk | AP-name | A/P clerk |
| Name of manager | Mgr-name | Manager |
| Name of purchase agent | PA-name | Purchase agent |
| Name of supplier | Sup-name | Supplier |
| Purchase agent identification number | PA-id (PK) | Purchase agent |
| Purchase authorization limit for a purchase agent | PA-limit | Purchase agent |
| Quality rating for supplier | Sup-rating | Supplier |
| Quantity of an inventory item purchased on an acquisition | Item-qty-purch | Stockflow1 |
| Quantity of an overhead item purchased on an acquisition | Oh-qty-purch | Stockflow2 |
| Quantity on hand of inventory item | Item-qoh | Inventory |
| SKU number of inventory item | Item-SKU (PK) | Inventory |
| Standard unit cost of inventory item | Item-std-cost | Inventory |
| Supplier address | Sup-add | Supplier |
| Supplier number | SupNum (PK) | Supplier |
| Total dollar amount of a cash disbursement | CD-amt | Cash disbursement |
| Total dollar value of an acquisition | Acq-amt | Acquisition |
| Type of cash account | AcctType | Cash |

Next we place each of these attributes in the appropriate place on our ER model and make sure each entity has a primary key attribute and at least one descriptor attribute. If no attributes describing an entity are needed for decision-making purposes (and you are sure the list of attributes given to you was complete), then usually the entity should not be included in your model.

## RSWS Step 5 ER Grammar with Attributes

Entity: Acquisition
**Attributes:  Acq-id**
              **Acq-date**
              **Acq-amt**
**Identifier:  Acq-id**

Entity: Cash disbursement
**Attributes:  CD-id**
              **CD-date**
              **CD-amt**
**Identifier:  CD-id**

Entity: Cash
**Attributes:  AcctNum**
              **AcctType**
              **AcctLoc**
              **AcctBal**
**Identifier:  AcctNum**

Entity: Inventory
**Attributes:  Item-SKU**
              **Item-desc**
              **Item-std-cost**
              **Item-list-price**
              **Item-qoh**
**Identifier:  Item-SKU**

Entity: Overhead
**Attributes:  OH-id**
              **OH-desc**
**Identifier:  OH-id**

Entity: A/P clerk
**Attributes:  AP-id**
              **AP-name**
              **AP-bond**
**Identifier:  AP-id**

Entity: Manager
**Attributes:  Mgr-id**
              **Mgr-name**
              **Mgr-degree**
**Identifier:  Mgr-id**

Entity: Purchase agent
**Attributes:  PA-id**
              **PA-name**
              **PA-limit**
**Identifier:  PA-id**

Entity: Supplier
**Attributes:  SupNum**
              **Sup-name**
              **Sup-add**
              **Sup-rating**
**Identifier:  SupNum**

Relationship: Duality
    Connected entities:
        ( , ) Acquisition
            ( , ) Cash disbursement
**Attributes: CD-acq-applied**

Relationship: Stockflow1
    Connected entities:
    ( , ) Acquisition
        ( , ) Inventory
**Attributes: Item-qty-purch**
              **Item-unit-cost**

Relationship: Stockflow2
    Connected entities:
    ( , ) Acquisition
        ( , ) Overhead
**Attributes: Oh-qty-purch**

Relationship: Stockflow3
    Connected entities:
        ( , ) Cash disbursement
        ( , ) Cash

Relationship: Participation1
    Connected entities:
        ( , ) Acquisition
            ( , ) Purchase agent

Relationship: Participation2
    Connected entities:
        ( , ) Acquisition
            ( , ) Supplier

Relationship: Participation3
    Connected entities:
        ( , ) Cash disbursement
            ( , ) Supplier

Relationship: Participation4
    Connected entities:
        ( , ) Cash disbursement
            ( , ) A/P clerk

Relationship: Authorization
    Connected entities:
        ( , ) Cash disbursement
            ( , ) Manager

**RSWS Step 5 ER Diagram with Attributes**

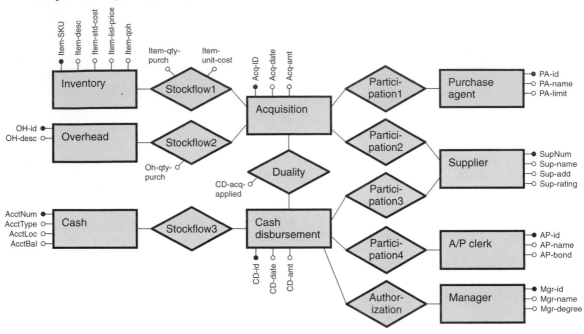

## *RSWS Step 6*

Step 6 assigns cardinalities to the relationships in the REA business process model. We systematically examine each relationship. We know that the instances of the inventory entity set and of the overhead entity set are types rather than tokens. We are reminded of the knowledge that multiple instances of each inventory type and of each overhead type by the quantity-purchased attributes describing each of those entity sets. That knowledge allows us to fill in the maximum cardinality for each of those resource-types in the stockflow1 and stockflow2 relationships as N. We assign zero as the minimum cardinality for each of those because we remember from our interview with Robert Scott that RSWS wants to enter data about resource types before they actually acquire them (following the normal heuristic for stockflow relationships). On the acquisition side of the stockflow1 and stockflow2 relationships, we realize that we have a common heuristic exception for the minimum cardinality. Because we decided to combine acquisitions of inventory and acquisition, yet to maintain them each as separate entity sets, we have a situation where an acquisition can involve alternative resource types. Therefore the participation of an acquisition with either one of those entity sets is optional. An acquisition can involve either inventory or overhead so its participation with inventory cannot be mandatory nor can its participation with overhead be mandatory. When we consider the maximum cardinalities for acquisition in the two stockflow relationships, we realize it is common business sense that an acquisition should be capable of involving multiple types of inventory. We look back at our interview notes and confirm this with Scott's description of Johnny helping Cheri open all the boxes and counting all the types of inventory on one of her incoming shipments. Our cardinalities for the first two stockflow relationships are thus summarized as (0,N) Inventory–(0,N) Acquisition and (0,N) Overhead – (0,N) Acquisition.

Next we look at the stockflow3 relationship between cash and cash disbursement to see if it follows our heuristic. We are confident that we need to establish a cash account before we can make any disbursements out of it and that from one cash account we can make many disbursements. So the (0,N) Resource Type heuristic applies. When we examine the cash disbursement side we realize that a cash disbursement cannot exist without coming from a cash account and since all cash accounts owned by RSWS would be included in this system as members of the cash entity, participation of cash disbursement in the stockflow3 relationship must be mandatory (minimum cardinality = 1). We also realize that if we make disbursement of cash it can only come from one account (maximum cardinality = 1). For example, when we write a check, the check is drawn on just one bank account. If we want to pay a supplier with money from two different checking accounts we must write two checks and that would be considered as two cash disbursements. Our cardinalities for stockflow3 are summarized as (0,N) Cash–(1,1) Cash Disbursement.

Next we evaluate the duality relationship and remember that there is no heuristic for duality relationships. The fact that RSWS has A/P clerks indicates they make purchases on credit (otherwise they wouldn't have accounts payable) so we note the minimum cardinality on acquisition as optional (zero). We are not sure whether an acquisition is ever paid in installment payments (i.e., with multiple cash disbursements) or if they are always paid in full. Similarly, while we know that some cash disbursements are made for expenditures other than acquisitions (for example, to pay employees or to repay loans), we are not sure whether a cash disbursement ever pays for multiple acquisitions. We go to see Robert Scott again and ask him. He tells us RSWS has never made installment payments for any acquisitions and never intends to do so, but that perhaps the system should be set up so that it would be possible. He says RSWS does make payments that combine multiple purchases, though. In his words, "For example, we make a folder for Emersmith and store up the bills for all the purchases we make from Emersmith in a month. At the end of the month we write one check to Emersmith that covers all of those purchases. We do the same thing for each of our other suppliers." Putting all this information together we summarize our duality relationship cardinalities as (0,N) Acquisition–(0,N) Cash Disbursement.

Our participation relationships remain to be examined. We recall our heuristic is (1,1) Economic Event–(0,N) Agent and look for evidence to confirm or refute that heuristic. We recall that Scott told us he wants no transaction to be entered without one person and one person only being identified as the responsible employee. So we know the (1,1) on the Economic Event side is valid for all three of the participation relationships that involve internal agents (participation1, participation4, and participation5). When we consider participation2, between acquisition and supplier, we confirm the (1,1) heuristic for the acquisition side is valid because in RSWS's value system level, there is no alternative external business partner from whom we acquire goods and services. Thus an acquisition must involve a supplier (minimum = 1), and multiple receipts of goods from the same supplier would be considered as multiple acquisitions (maximum = 1). Our examination of participation3 between Cash Disbursement and Supplier reveals a common exception because the value system level model indicates that RSWS makes cash disbursements to external agents other than suppliers. This changes the minimum for cash disbursement to zero. The maximum of one is reasonable because it would not make sense to write one check to two different suppliers. Next we consider the (0,N) Agent heuristic for the five participation relationships. We know the minimum of zero holds true for the internal agent relationships (participation1, participation4, and participation5) because the agent data must exist in our system before any transactions are entered to be able to validate the responsible employee upon entry of the transactions. We also know the maximum of many holds true for all five participation relationships because it is simple common business sense. There is no business reason why an enterprise would want to limit participation in its entire set of a type of economic event to only one time per agent. That would be saying, for example, that once we make a sale to a customer, we could never make another sale to that customer again. Even if that were a reasonable assumption for a small subset of customers, it would be highly unlikely an enterprise would allow no repeat business at all. To evaluate the minimum cardinality for the agent side of the two external agent participation relationships (participation2 and participation3) we consider whether RSWS would enter an acquisition or a cash disbursement to a supplier for which RSWS has not already entered data into the system. We recognize that good business policy would recommend RSWS should have a vendor selection policy that would result in supplier information being entered into the system before any transactions involving them may be entered. We ask Robert Scott whether RSWS has a need to be able to enter supplier information before entering acquisitions or cash disbursements involving that supplier. He confirms that in fact, the vendor selection policy at RSWS requires approval of suppliers prior to engaging in transactions with them. We therefore assign (1,1) Economic Event–(0,N) Agent to participation relationships 1, 2, 4, and 5 and (0,1) Economic Event–(0,N) Agent to participation3. The results of these cardinality assignments are reflected in our completed model as follows:

**RSWS Step 6 Cardinality Assignment in ER Diagram**

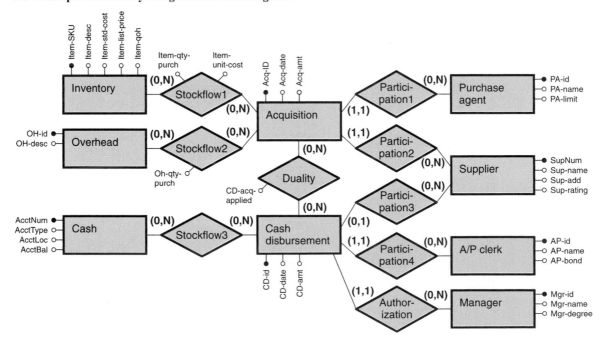

**RSWS Step 6 Cardinality Assignment in ER Grammar**

Entity: Acquisition
Attributes:  Acq-id
         Acq-date
         Acq-amt
Identifier:  Acq-id

Entity: Cash disbursement
Attributes:  CD-id
         CD-date
         CD-amt
Identifier:  CD-id

Entity: Cash
Attributes:  AcctNum
         AcctType
         AcctLoc
         AcctBal
Identifier:  AcctNum

Entity: Inventory
Attributes:  Item-SKU
         Item-desc
         Item-std-cost
         Item-list-price
         Item-qoh
Identifier:  Item-SKU

Entity: Overhead
Attributes:  OH-id
         OH-desc
Identifier:  OH-id

Entity: A/P clerk
Attributes:  AP-id
         AP-name
         AP-bond
Identifier:  AP-id

Entity: Manager
Attributes:  Mgr-id
         Mgr-name
         Mgr-degree
Identifier:  Mgr-id

Entity: Purchase agent
Attributes:  PA-id
         PA-name
         PA-limit
Identifier:  PA-id

Entity: Supplier
Attributes:  SupNum
         Sup-name
         Sup-add
         Sup-rating
Identifier:  SupNum

Relationship: Duality
   Connected entities:
      **(0,N)** Acquisition
      **(0,N)** Cash disbursement
Attributes: CD-acq-applied

Relationship: Stockflow1
   Connected entities:
      **(0,N)** Acquisition
      **(0,N)** Inventory
Attributes: Item-qty-purch
         Item-unit-cost

Relationship: Stockflow2
   Connected entities:
      **(0,N)** Acquisition
      **(0,N)** Overhead
Attributes: Oh-qty-purch

Relationship: Stockflow3
   Connected entities:
      **(1,1)** Cash disbursement
      **(0,N)** Cash

Relationship: Participation1
   Connected entities:
      **(1,1)** Acquisition
      **(0,N)** Purchase agent

Relationship: Participation2
   Connected entities:
      **(1,1)** Acquisition
      **(0,N)** Supplier

Relationship: Participation3
   Connected entities:
      **(0,1)** Cash disbursement
      **(0,N)** Supplier

Relationship: Participation4
   Connected entities:
      **(1,1)** Cash disbursement
      **(0,N)** A/P clerk

Relationship: Authorization
   Connected entities:
      **(1,1)** Cash disbursement
      **(0,N)** Manager

## REA Business Process Level Extensions

The main extension to the core pattern proposed by Geerts and McCarthy (but which still requires further research) is the addition of commitments and relationships involving those commitments. Observation of practice reveals that enterprises typically commit themselves to an economic event before they actually engage in the economic event. For example, a customer makes commitments to receive goods or services and to give cash before actually engaging in the sale and cash receipt events. The extended ontology proposes that each economic event is preceded by a **commitment event,** and that for every commitment event that commits to decrease a resource there is a related commitment event that commits to increase a resource. Those opposite commitment events are related via a **reciprocal** relationship. This relationship is the equivalent of duality but for commitment events instead of for economic events.

Each commitment event also is related to the resource or resource type that it agrees to increase or decrease, and to internal and external agents. The relationship between a commitment event and a resource is called reservation to indicate the purpose of the event to reserve the resource that will be transferred in or out by a future economic event. The relationship between a commitment event and an agent (internal or external) will for purposes of this textbook be called participation. For business processes that involve an exchange with an external business partner (i.e., for all business processes except the conversion process) a bundle of commitments (i.e., an increment commitment event paired with a decrement commitment event) form a **contract** or **mutual commitment event.** A contract commits both enterprises to engage in the future economic events. For example, an accepted customer order commits the seller to transfer the title of goods to the customer and it commits the customer to pay cash to the seller. From the customer's view, this is a purchase and a cash disbursement; from the seller's view this is a sale and a cash receipt. There are reasons beyond the scope of this textbook why both commitments that comprise a contract should be included separately in a business process level REA model. For simplicity sake, in this textbook we are using a simplified version of the model in which only the mutual commitment event is modeled. It is related to the **noncash-related economic event** and to the associated resource or resource type, to the cash resource, and to internal and external agents. The separation of commitment events is most important in the conversion process; in that process the bundled commitments form a schedule rather than a contract and is completely internal to the enterprise. Readers interested in the **extended business process level REA model** for the conversion process may consult Chapter 11. In Exhibit 4–6 we illustrate the simplified extended business process level REA model.

Some academics add another event prior to the commitment/contract event. They differ in what they call this event; for this textbook we call it an **instigation event.** What do you think of when you hear the word *instigator?* For us it brings back memories of a frustrated parent trying to break up a sibling fight saying, "Who's the instigator here?" In other words, "Who started it?" In a business process we often want to know what event started it. Sometimes it may be an internally instigated event such as in the acquisition/payment process when a user department identifies a need for more raw materials and sends a requisition to the purchasing department to ask them to acquire the needed materials. Other times it may be an externally instigated event such as in the sales/collection process when a customer calls to inquire as to availability and pricing for a product or service. Although the instigation event is not officially part of the published REA enterprise ontology, we

**EXHIBIT 4–6**   **Simplified Extended REA Business Process Level Pattern**

Diagram Format

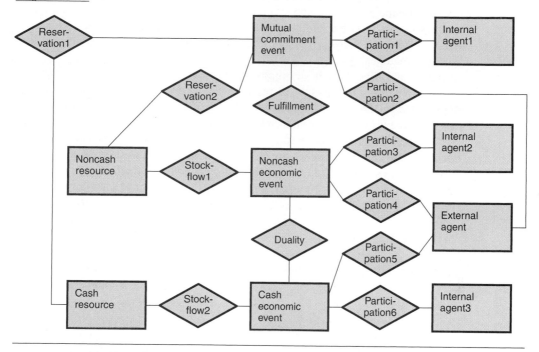

Grammar Format
Entity: Mutual commitment event
Entity: Noncash economic event
Entity: Cash economic event
Entity: Noncash resource
Entity: Cash resource
Entity: External agent
Entity: Internal agent1
Entity: Internal agent2
Entity: Internal agent3

Relationship: Duality
Connected entities:
      Cash economic event
            Noncash economic event
Relationship: Fulfillment
Connected entities:
      Mutual commitment event
            Noncash economic event
Relationship: Reservation1
Connected Entities:
      Mutual commitment event
            Cash resource
Relationship: Reservation2
Connected entities:
      Mutual commitment event
            Noncash resource
Relationship: Stockflow1
Connected entities:
      Noncash economic event
            Noncash resource

Relationship: Stockflow2
Connected entities:
      Cash economic event
            Cash resource
Relationship: Participation1
Connected entities:
      Mutual commitment event
            Internal agent1
Relationship: Participation2
Connected entities:
      Mutual commitment event
            External agent
Relationship: Participation3
Connected entities:
      Noncash economic event
            Internal agent2
Relationship: Participation4
Connected entities:
      Noncash economic event
            External agent
Relationship: Participation5
Connected entities:
      Cash economic event
            External agent
Relationship: Participation6
Connected entities:
      Cash economic event
            Internal agent3

believe many academics have included it in business process level models for most transaction cycles because of its usefulness in economic storytelling. Any good story has a beginning, a middle, and an ending. The instigation event serves as the beginning; the commitment events form the middle; and the economic events conclude the story. In Exhibit
4–7 we show the business process level pattern with instigation events and the corresponding relationships.

Geerts and McCarthy have proposed other extensions to the business process level
model, including selected types of resource-agent relationships and agent-agent relationships. These relationships should be included only when those entities have an association
that is independent of the event in which they have mutual participation. For example, in
the sales/collection process we sometimes need to track information about assignments of
salespeople to customers. When might we need to do that? Consider a company that sends
sales representatives out into the field to call on customers. Each sales representative typically has a territory and customers within a sales representative's territory are assigned to
that sales representative. Other salespeople are not supposed to try to make sales to another

**EXHIBIT 4–7**   **Extended REA Business Process Level Pattern with Instigation Event**

Diagram Format

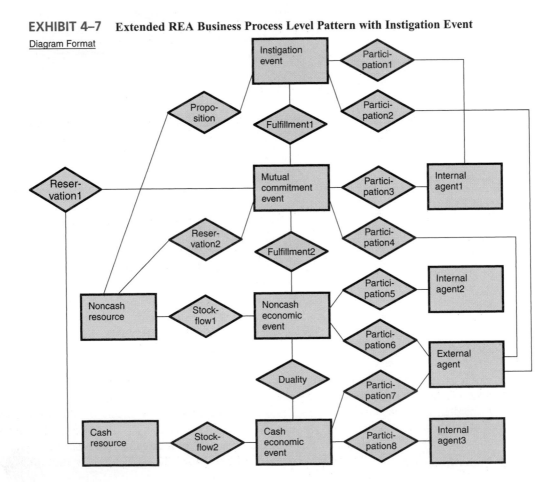

**EXHIBIT 4–7 (continued)**   **Extended REA Business Process Level Pattern with Instigation Event**

Grammar Format

Entity: Instigation event
Entity: Mutual commitment event
Entity: Noncash economic event
Entity: Cash economic event
Entity: Noncash resource
Entity: Cash resource
Entity: External agent
Entity: Internal agent1
Entity: Internal agent2
Entity: Internal agent3

Relationship: Duality
Connected entities:
   Cash economic event
     Noncash economic event
Relationship: Fulfillment1
Connected entities:
   Instigation event
     Mutual commitment event'
Relationship: Fulfillment2
Connected entities:
   Mutual commitment event
     Noncash economic event
Relationship: Proposition
Connected entities:
   Instigation event
     Noncash resource

Relationship: Reservation1
Connected entities:
   Mutual commitment event
     Cash resource
Relationship: Reservation2
Connected entities:
   Mutual commitment event
     Noncash resource
Relationship: Stockflow1
Connected entities:
   Noncash economic event
     Noncash resource
Relationship: Stockflow2
Connected entities:
   Cash economic event
     Cash resource2
Relationship: Participation1
Connected entities:
   Instigation event
     Internal agent1
Relationship: Participation2
Connected entities:
   Instigation event
     External agent
Relationship: Participation3
Connected entities:
   Mutual commitment event
     Internal agent1

Relationship: Participation4
Connected Entities:
   Mutual commitment event
     External agent
Relationship: Participation5
Connected entities:
   Noncash economic event
     Internal agent2
Relationship: Participation6
Connected entities:
   Noncash economic event
     External agent
Relationship: Participation7
Connected entities:
   Cash economic event
     External agent
Relationship: Participation8
Connected entities:
   Cash economic event
     Internal agent3

---

salesperson's customers unless they are specifically asked to help. Such a relationship should not exist if the only relationship between salesperson and customer that is important is their mutual participation in the same sale(s). We can already track that information through the core REA pattern. Similarly sometimes an enterprise may identify a need to track a direct relationship between a resource and an agent who has custody of the resource and is responsible for the resource independently of any event.

In Chapters 8 through 13 we describe additional extensions to the REA enterprise ontology in greater detail. Keep in mind the distinction between operating events, information process events, and decision/management events. **Operating events** are the operating activities performed within business processes to achieve enterprise objectives. This category certainly includes economic exchange events and commitment events. It also includes some instigation events. **Information process events** include three activities: recording data about operating events, maintaining reference data that are important to the organization, and reporting useful information to management and other decision makers. Recording events involve collecting data about operating events and storing the data in a data repository (e.g., a data warehouse, a database, or a file). Maintenance events involve collecting and updating reference data about resources they own, employees they hire, and external parties with whom they do business. The *data repository* formed by recording and maintenance events is used to generate reports for information customers. This third type of information process event, reporting, is the most demanding. Reporting provides information and measurements to support enterprise activities such as planning, controlling, and evaluating everyday tasks and results of operations. Keep in mind that information process events are often the targets of reengineering efforts and, therefore, should not be stored as base objects in an information system. **Decision/management events** are activities in which managers, employees, and external users make decisions about planning, controlling, and evaluating business processes.

Past experience has revealed that students sometimes confuse operating events with information process events. To distinguish these, realize that information process events involve the use of data rather than nondata resources. For example, the delivery of a product to a customer is an example of an operating event; recording data about the delivery and sending a bill to the customer are information process events. The sending of the bill is not what obligates the customer to pay—the transfer of title of goods from the seller to the customer (i.e., the sale event) is what establishes the obligation. Reengineering efforts could eliminate the information process event of sending the bill; therefore, it should not be included in the REA model. Similarly, receiving a payment from a customer for goods and services provided is an operating event; however, recording data about the customer payment is an information process event. A change in the location of a warehouse is an operating event; updating or maintaining the warehouse location in the data repository is an information process event.

The information customer serves as the final arbiter of value. The key to effective information customer support is not the amount of information provided; rather it is the ability to provide accessible, useful, and timely information. You may have the feeling that identifying operating events is like the famous final exam question: Model the universe and give three examples. Where in the world do you draw the line? Our answer to all modeling questions relating to scope is "What does the enterprise need to plan, execute, control, and evaluate?"

## Key Terms and Concepts

Attribute, *53*

Business process, *51*

Cash resource, *71*

Claim, *62*

Commitment event, *82*

Composite attribute, *54*

Concatenated primary key, *54*

Contract, *82*

Decision/management events, *86*

Derivable attribute, *54*

Duality relationship, *56*

Economic event, *62*

Entity, *52*

Extended business process level REA model, *82*

External agent, *64*

Generalization, *55*

Information process event, *85*

Instigation event, *82*

Internal agent, *64*

Maximum participation cardinality, *55*

Minimum participation cardinality, *54*

Mutual commitment event, *82*

Noncash-related economic event, *82*

Operating event, *85*

Participation cardinality, *54*

Primary key attribute, *53*

REA core pattern, *62*

Reciprocal, *82*

Relationship, *52*

Resource, *62*

Resource inflow, *63*

Resource outflow, *63*

Simple attribute, *54*

Static derivable attribute, *54*

Stockflow relationship, *64*

Typification, *55*

Volatile derivable attribute, *54*

# Review Questions

LO4    R1.   Give three examples of each of the three main types of business processes.

LO4    R2.   Describe the relationship between business processes and events.

LO8    R3.   What is an information process? How are information processes triggered?

LO8    R4.   What is the difference between a business process and an information process?

LO8    R5.   How are business and information processes related?

LO8    R6.   Describe three types of information processes.

LO4    R7.   Describe the acquisition/payment process. What are the main activities that make up this process?

LO4    R8.   Describe the sales/collection process. What are the main activities that make up this process?

LO7    R9.   How do you determine the scope of a business process level REA model?

LO7    R10.  List the Journalism 101 questions and explain how they are typically answered in a business process level model.

LO4–LO8    R11.  List and describe the steps in REA business process level modeling.

LO2    R12.  How are maximum cardinalities used when designing enterprise information systems?

LO2    R13.  How are minimum cardinalities used when designing enterprise information systems?

LO1    R14.  Explain the purpose of a primary key attribute.

LO1    R15.  Give some examples of nonkey attributes that would describe the entity customer.

# Multiple Choice Questions

LO1    MC1.  Which of the following is an object that has either a physical or conceptual existence?
   A.  entity
   B.  attribute
   C.  relationship
   D.  cardinality

LO1    MC2.  What is a relationship?
   A.  an entity set
   B.  a characteristic possessed by the primary key of an entity
   C.  an association between entities
   D.  the primary key itself

LO1    MC3.  What term is used to describe a combination of unique key fields?
   A.  concatenated
   B.  composite
   C.  derived
   D.  volatile

LO2    MC4.  Give the minimum and maximum participation cardinalities for an entity that has nonmandatory participation in a relationship and can participate only one time.
   A.  (1,1)
   B.  (1,0)
   C.  (0,1)
   D.  (0,0)

LO2 MC5. Give the minimum and maximum participation cardinalities for an entity that has mandatory participation in a relationship but can participate only one time.
   A. (1,1)
   B. (1,0)
   C. (0,1)
   D. (0,0)

## Discussion Questions

LO2, LO5 D1. If you are trying to assign participation cardinalities to an enterprise's stockflow relationship between purchase and inventory, you would need to ask some questions to a knowledgeable representative of the enterprise. Assuming you have no narrative description to work from, what questions would you ask to get enough information to assign all four cardinalities?

LO2, LO4 D2. If you are trying to assign participation cardinalities to an enterprise's fulfillment relationship between sale order and sale, you would need to ask some questions to a knowledgeable representative of the enterprise. Assuming you have no narrative description to work from, what questions would you ask to get enough information to assign all four cardinalities?

LO2, LO5 D3. What are the heuristic participation cardinalities for a relationship between cash and cash disbursement? Explain each of the four participation cardinalities and identify whether there are any common exceptions to the heuristics.

LO2, LO5 D4. What are the heuristic participation cardinalities for a relationship between sale and inventory, assuming that inventory is mass-produced and tracked at the type level? Explain each of the four participation cardinalities and identify whether there are any common exceptions to the heuristics.

## Applied Learning

LO3 A1. Develop a script for a visit to a doctor's office (based on your past experience or other knowledge about doctors' offices). Next develop a script for a visit to a lawyers' office (based on your past experience or other knowledge about lawyers' offices). Describe the similarities and differences between your two scripts. Is there any identifiable pattern, and if so, what generic label would you assign to it?

LO3 A2. Develop a script for taking a cross-country trip on an airplane (based on your past experience or other knowledge about air travel). Next develop a script for taking a crosscountry trip on a train or bus (based on your past experience or other knowledge about train or bus travel). Describe the similarities and differences between your two scripts. Is there any identifiable pattern, and if so, what generic label would you assign to it?

LO1–LO8 A3. Bowerkate Corporation sells handcrafted surfboards to customers through its network of company salespeople. Each surfboard is given a unique identification number and a suggested selling price when finished. Upon employment each salesperson is immediately assigned to service a separate group of customers. When customer data are initially entered into Bowerkate's information system, the customer is immediately assigned to a salesperson. Each sale can include one or more surfboards and can be paid for in any of three ways: (1) immediately in cash, (2) on the 15th of the following month, or (3) over the course of six months. No more than one salesperson participates in making a particular sale. A salesperson may negotiate with a customer and agree on a selling price for any surfboard that is lower than that surfboard's suggested selling price, especially if the customer is a high-volume customer or if that surfboard is a slow seller (i.e., it has been in stock for a long time). Although the vast majority of cash receipts come from customers (any particular cash receipt would be from only one customer) for sales, some cash receipts come from other sources (e.g., bank loans). Every cash receipt is processed by exactly one of Bowerkate's several cashiers and is deposited into one of Bowerkate's bank accounts. Information about surfboards, employees, and customers often needs to be entered into the database before any transactions involving them have occurred. The following data items (attributes) are of interest to potential users of this model:

surfboard-id#
customer-name
salesperson-name
cash-receipt-total-amount
location-of-cash-account
sale-number
cash-receipt-amount-applied-
to-a-sale
cash-account-number
customer-number
actual-selling-price-for-a-
surfboard
salesperson-commission-rate

cash-account-balance
qty-of-items-sold-on-a-particular-invoice
cashier-name
description-of-surfboard
customer-accounts-receivable-balance
salesperson-number

cashier-ID-number
cash-account-type
suggested-selling-price-for-a-surfboard

sale-total-amount
remittance-advice-number

Note: Salesperson commission rate is determined per contractual arrangement with each salesperson and for a particular salesperson it is the same percentage rate no matter what items he or she sells.

### Required:

Create an REA model (in either BNF Grammar format or in ER diagram format) for Bowerkate Corporation's revenue cycle as just described. Be sure to include all relevant entities, relationships, attributes, and participation cardinalities.

## Answers to Multiple Choice Questions

MC1. A; MC2. C; MC3. A; MC4. C; MC5. A.

# Chapter **Five**

# Task Level Modeling

**LEARNING OBJECTIVES**

The objective of this chapter is to introduce some tools for documenting the task level detail of business processes. The task level in REA modeling is the level at which workflow is documented. After studying this chapter you should be able to:

1. Explain the difference between task level and business process level representations for an enterprise
2. Describe and prepare flowcharts describing the documents, data flows, and processes of an enterprise system
3. Describe and prepare data flow diagrams depicting the flow of data through an enterprise system
4. Identify the similarities and differences between system flowcharts and data flow diagrams
5. Describe various kinds of physical media, file types, and processing methods used in information systems

## INTRODUCTION

In Chapter 2 we defined tasks as the individual steps involved in accomplishing events in an enterprise. The events themselves are actually tasks; however, many tasks should not be represented as events. Tasks for which measurements are either not feasible or not cost effective should not be represented as events. Tasks that are activities that may be changed or eliminated should not serve as foundational elements in an enterprise information system database. The purpose of task level modeling is not to design a database; instead it is to document the flow of data through an enterprise. Tasks that are included in the **workflow** for an enterprise are not represented as base objects in the enterprise database (except for the tasks that are also events). Data captured as a result of tasks may be included in the tables as attributes, and data needed to accomplish tasks can be retrieved from the database via queries.

Pattern discovery at the task level is not as straightforward as at the value system, value chain, and business process levels. Although there are best practices for how certain activities can be accomplished in enterprises, workflow can include steps or activities that can be reengineered away without substantively changing the nature of the enterprise. Tasks also can occur in various sequences for different enterprises (or for different areas within an enterprise) and the sequencing must be represented in task level models. Recall that for the other levels, the models did not represent a sequencing of events, but merely relationships between them. A sale may come before a cash receipt, or vice versa; the order does not matter for establishing the architecture of the enterprise system's core database as long as one can be traced to the other. For the task level, sequencing is important, as enterprises need to document details about the procedural aspects of the business activities and corresponding data entry into and information retrieval from the information system.

The purpose of developing the business process level REA model is to design the enterprise database. Any events, or activities that make up those events, that could be reengineered away without changing the overall nature of the enterprise normally should not be included as core elements of the enterprise database. This avoids the need to substantially alter the enterprise database every time workflow is changed. However, firms must document those events and activities as part of the enterprise's system documentation. An example of task level modeling as compared to business process level modeling may help you to understand the difference.

Jayvision, Inc., is an enterprise that creates video games for children. In its acquisition/payment process, Jayvision used to have the following procedures:

- A department supervisor identified or confirmed the need to acquire a particular product or service, and submitted a requisition form to the purchasing department through the company mail.
- The purchasing department opened the mail, approved (or disapproved) the requisitions and sorted the approved requisitions into piles according to the type of products and services needed. Disapproved requisitions were returned to the department supervisor with an explanation of why the requisitions were denied.
- The purchasing department identified appropriate vendors for the requested products and services. Often this entailed searching the catalogs of established vendors to determine pricing and availability; sometimes the purchasing agent contacted the vendor's sales representative to obtain details about the products and services; sometimes the purchasing agent needed to prepare a request for quote or to issue requests for competitive bids from potential suppliers.
- Once appropriate vendors were selected, the purchasing department prepared purchase orders (based on one or more purchase requisitions) and mailed or faxed them to the vendors. A copy of the purchase order was sent to the accounts payable department, where it was filed in a temporary file in vendor number order awaiting further processing.
- The receiving department for Jayvision received products. Upon receipt a clerk manually counted the products and filled out a receiving report listing the product identification number, quantity received, and a note describing the condition of the items. A copy of the receiving report was sent to the accounts payable department where it was filed in a temporary file in vendor number order awaiting further processing.
- Services were received by various departments; upon receipt of a service, the appropriate department supervisor filled out a "receiving report" for services, including a description of the services received and the dates on which they were received. A copy of the report was sent to the accounts payable department where it was filed in a temporary file in vendor number order awaiting further processing.

- The accounts payable department for Jayvision received vendor invoices in the mail. For each vendor invoice received, an accounts payable clerk retrieved the purchase order and receiving report copies for that vendor. The clerk verified that each line item amount on the vendor invoice represented the correct amount for a product or service that had been both ordered and received. The clerk also double-checked the invoice for mathematical accuracy. If everything was deemed okay, the accounts payable clerk wrote a check to the vendor for the amount of the invoice and forwarded the check with its underlying documentation to the controller. The controller signed the check and gave it to an accounting clerk to copy and send to the vendor. The copy was filed along with the supporting documentation in a permanent file in the accounting department.

Jayvision recently reengineered its acquisition/payment workflow. The new procedures are described as follows:

- A department supervisor identifies or confirms the need to acquire a particular product or service, and enters requisition data into the enterprise database. This entry triggers an electronic notification that is sent to the purchasing department.

- Upon receipt of the electronic notification, the purchasing department examines and approves (or disapproves) the requisitions. Notices regarding disapproved requisitions are electronically sent to the department supervisor with an explanation of why the requisitions were denied.

- The purchasing department identifies appropriate vendors for the requested products and services. Often this entails searching the catalogs of established vendors to determine pricing and availability; sometimes the purchasing agent contacts the vendor's sales representative to obtain details about the products and services; sometimes the purchasing agent needs to prepare a request for quote or to issue requests for competitive bids from potential suppliers.

- Once appropriate vendors are selected, purchase order data are entered into the enterprise data and purchase order forms are electronically generated and are either e-mailed or printed and faxed to the vendors.

- The receiving department for Jayvision receives products. Upon receipt a clerk checks the enterprise database to verify an order had been placed for the vendor from whom the goods were received. The clerk manually counts the products and enters the appropriate receipt data into the enterprise database.

- Services are received by various departments; upon receipt of a service, the appropriate department supervisor enters receiving report data into the enterprise database.

- Each day the enterprise database's interface displays a list (based on the purchase order and purchase data in the database) of the unpaid purchases (receipts of products and services) that are due within three business days. The accounts payable clerk reviews for accuracy each electronic payment suggested by the enterprise database interface. The electronic payments approved by the clerk are submitted to the vendors' bank accounts and recorded in the enterprise database.

The business process level pattern in the old and reengineered acquisition/payment cycles are identical; however the steps to accomplish the workflow associated with the events in the pattern changed significantly. Both the old and the new cycles included need identification (purchase requisition) as an instigator event, ordering of goods or services (purchase order) as a commitment or contract event, receipt of goods (purchase) as an economic increment event, and payment of cash (cash disbursement) as an economic decrement event. Thus the database design is the same under both workflow scenarios. However, the documentation of the document processing and data flows is quite different for the two scenarios. In this chapter you learn how to create this documentation.

Many different types of documentation may be used to represent tasks, including flowcharts, data flow diagrams, process models, and narrative descriptions. This chapter presents two tools used to document tasks: **system flowcharts** and **data flow diagrams.**

# SYSTEM FLOWCHARTING

Enterprises need to document details about workflow—what happens, in what order, and what details are captured, maintained, and reported by the information system. These details may be documented using a variety of different methods. One obviously possible method to use is a narrative description of all the steps in the workflow. Indeed, many companies do create such narratives. However, such narratives are typically voluminous and can be time-consuming to use to find information about a process. System flowcharts are used to graphically document information systems. Pages of narrative describing system processes and data/document flows can be succinctly summarized using flowcharts. System flowcharts focus on the physical aspects of information flows and processes. This chapter presents the rudiments of this tool to help you develop the skills needed to prepare new flowcharts and to interpret existing flowcharts.

Flowcharts are used to describe an entire information system, or some portion thereof. The system flowcharts discussed in this chapter are sometimes called document flowcharts because they illustrate the data flows of the enterprise and how the data flows are processed. Since many of the data flows are contained on documents, document processing typically makes up a large portion of the flowcharts. The entire information system is made up of a series of input, process, and output activities. The inputs and outputs may be paper documents or electronic data and the processes may be manual or computerized. The outputs from the various processes may be used for decision-making purposes or they may serve as inputs to other processes (or both). System flowcharts may be created manually, either freehand or with the help of a plastic flowchart template—a stencil that allows users to trace the outline of the various symbols used in flowcharts. System flowcharts also may be prepared using one of several software packages designed for that purpose. Even word processing software packages often contain **flowcharting symbols** among their drawing tools.

## The Basic Elements of System Flowcharts

System flowcharts consist of three simple graphical elements combined to represent various types of physical information flows and processes:

1. Symbols
2. Flow lines
3. Areas of responsibility

The documents and processes of information systems can be illustrated by linking various symbols together as shown in Exhibit 5–1. Compare the following explanation of the process with its flowchart before we discuss the detailed conventions for preparing flowcharts.

Exhibit 5–1 illustrates possible document flows for processing employee expense reimbursements for an enterprise. Employees in various departments throughout the enterprise spend their own money for expenses such as business-related travel, supplies, and so forth. They then request reimbursement for those expenditures. Employees prepare requests for reimbursement, which they submit along with supporting receipts and documentation justifying the necessity of their expenditure to the Payables department. Payables clerks check the request for accuracy and agreement with the support documents. They also verify whether the support documents are approved by the employee's supervisor and adequately justify the need for the expenditure. The payables clerks then key the approved reimbursement request data to magnetic tape using a key-to-tape encoding machine. The approved reimbursement requests are sent to the payables supervisor who puts them into a temporary file in numeric order. The magnetic tape is sent to the data processing department where it is used as input to a computerized process that generates the reimbursement checks and updates the enterprise database for the expenses and cash disbursement data. The enterprise database is stored on disk. The checks are prepared in duplicate (the copy does not look like a real check; it contains only the check stub information). The check and copy are sent to the payables supervisor. The supervisor pulls the appropriate reimbursement request and support documentation for each check from the temporary file, double checks everything for accuracy, and signs the check. The check is sent to the employee, the check copy is attached to the request and support documents and is filed in a permanent file in employee number order.

Flowcharting symbols and methods can vary widely across professionals and organizations. There is no one set of generally accepted flowcharting principles and symbols. The **flowcharting conventions** and symbols we present in this chapter are representative of those most commonly used.

## Flowcharting Element 1: Symbols

A variety of symbols represent the physical aspects of the document/data flows and processes of an information system. Since flowcharts illustrate the physical features of a system, there are various symbols in each category. For example, there are at least four storage symbols, and the one chosen depends on the physical characteristics of the storage medium (e.g., whether it is a paper file, a disk file, or a tape file). The following describes some of the more frequently used symbols in flowcharting.

### *Input-Process-Output*

Properly constructed system flowcharts are simply related "input-process-output" clusters strung together, with defined starting and stopping points. In system flowcharts, a process is defined as an activity that uses or alters an input to produce an output. An output from one process may be used as input to the next process. Exhibit 5–2 illustrates the typical input, output, and process symbols. Most of the symbols used to illustrate inputs also are used to represent outputs. For example, a document (symbol *B*) may be the output of one process and the input for another process. Similarly, a magnetic tape file (symbol *J*) or a disk file (symbol *I*) may serve as either input or output or both.

**EXHIBIT 5–1** **Example System Flowchart**

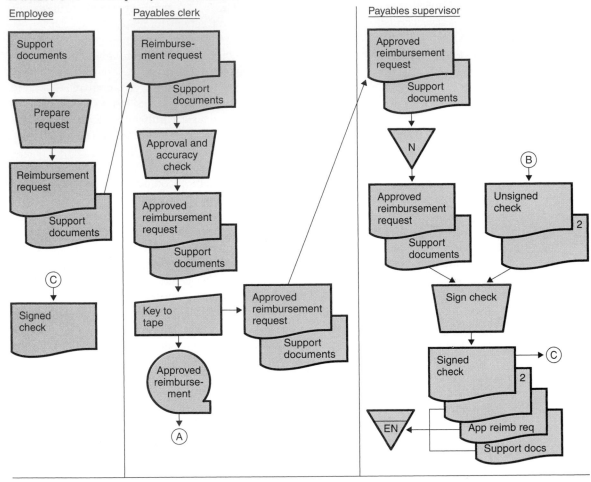

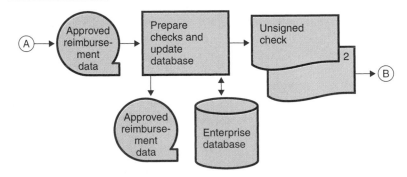

**EXHIBIT 5–2**   **Flowchart Symbols**

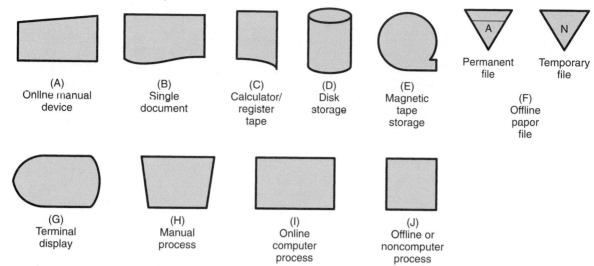

**(A)**
Onllne manual
device

**(B)**
Single
document

**(C)**
Calculator/
register
tape

**(D)**
Disk
storage

**(E)**
Magnetic
tape
storage

Permanent
file

Temporary
file

**(F)**
Offline
papor
file

**(G)**
Terminal
display

**(H)**
Manual
process

**(I)**
Online
computer
process

**(J)**
Offline or
noncomputer
process

### On-line Manual Input Device (Keyboard or Touch-Terminal)

Symbol *A* in Exhibit 5–2 illustrates an online manual device that describes the entry of data into a computer through an on-line keyboard or touch-terminal. When this symbol and the computerized process symbol are used together, they are considered to comprise a single process for the purpose of *input-process-output* logic. That is, there must be some input (such as a document) to the keying/computer process and there must be an output from the keying/computer process (such as a report or an updated masterfile).

### Input/Output Symbols: Paper Documents

Paper documents (symbol *B* in Exhibit 5–2) are used as inputs and as outputs of processes in system flowcharts. The document symbol is one of the most commonly used symbols in system flowcharts, and it has variations that are not illustrated in Exhibit 5–2. Exhibit 5–3 depicts the different symbols commonly used to represent documents (e.g., checks, invoices, and reports) that exist in an information system. The name of the document is entered on the symbol's face (see symbol *A* in Exhibit 5–3). A single document symbol is used to represent one or more documents of the same type; for example, a batch of 100 remittance advices is represented with the single document symbol, provided there is only one copy of each remittance advice. Multiple copies of a document are typically illustrated as staggered symbols for each copy of the document (see symbol *B* in Exhibit 5–3). Each copy is numbered in the top right corner. The numbers may be arranged in whatever sequence best suits the flow of documents from that point in the flowchart. This method easily allows thc flowchart designer to communicate the separate flows of the different copies of the document; for example, one copy of a sale invoice may be sent to the customer, another copy sent to the accounts receivable department, and a third copy filed away. If copies of two (or more) different documents move together in a flowchart, they are illustrated as staggered symbols for each different document with the appropriate copy of the document

**EXHIBIT 5–3    Flowchart Symbols: Documents**

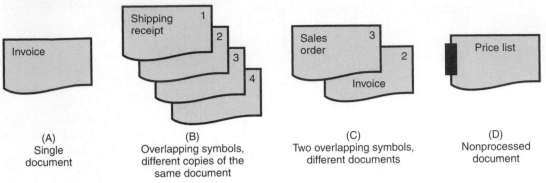

| (A) | (B) | (C) | (D) |
|---|---|---|---|
| Single document | Overlapping symbols, different copies of the same document | Two overlapping symbols, different documents | Nonprocessed document |

noted (if any) (see symbol *C* in Exhibit 5–3). A document used to store reference information, such as a price list or tax table, as opposed to a document that is processed, such as a check or invoice, is often distinguished by darkening the left edge of the symbol (see symbol *D* in Exhibit 5–3).

### Input/Output Symbols: Calculator/Register Tapes

Symbol *C* in Exhibit 5–2 represents printouts of calculations made on a calculator, adding machine, or cash register. These are most often outputs of a manual process, but once they are processed they also can be used as inputs to other processes, such as reconciliations between the manual calculations and the computations of a computer process.

### Input/Output Symbols: Files Containing Stored Data

Files of stored data may be used as input to processes or as output from processes. Computerized processes typically use and produce data stored on disk (symbol *D* in Exhibit 5–2) or on magnetic tape (symbol *E* in Exhibit 5–2). A description of the file contents is entered on the face of the symbol (e.g., "Customer MasterFile" or "Cash Disbursements transaction file"). Examples of disk storage with which you are probably familiar include hard disks, floppy disks, CDs, and DVDs. Examples of magnetic tape storage with which you are probably familiar are audiocassette tapes and VHS videotapes. Some computer systems, especially older mainframe systems, have tape drives instead of disk drives and while you may not have seen or used such hardware, the tape media has many of the same characteristics as the audiocassette tapes and VHS videotapes you have seen and used.

Computerized processes sometimes use and produce data stored in paper files, and of course manual processes can only use and produce manual off-line stored data. Symbol *F* in Exhibit 5–2 represents any storage of paper documents (e.g., file cabinet, safe, cardboard box, or shelves). Two types of off-line storage files exist—temporary and permanent. A temporary file is a storage device for documents that will be involved in subsequent processing. A horizontal line across the top of the file symbol often indicates a permanent file. The method of document order or organization is denoted using an abbreviation such as *A* (alphanumeric), *N* (numeric), or *C* (chronological). Whenever abbreviations or codes are used, you should place a legend on your flowchart to assist readers.

### Input/Output Symbols: Terminal Display

The terminal display symbol (symbol *G* in Exhibit 5–3) illustrates a computer monitor or terminal display. It is often used in conjunction with the on-line computer-device symbol to show data being entered into a computer process using an on-line terminal. Alternatively it may be used to illustrate output from a computer process that is only seen on a computer screen, such as an error message.

### Process Symbols

Different symbols represent processes according to the level of automation included in the processes. The manual-process symbol (symbol *H* in Exhibit 5–2) indicates an operation that is primarily manual (such as completing forms, verifying amounts, or making calculations with a manual calculator). Manual operations most often are used to process documents. There are two machine-processing symbols: one for on-line computer processing (see symbol *I* in Exhibit 5–2) and one for off-line processing or processing performed by a machine other than a computer, such as an optical character reader (see symbol *J* in Exhibit 5–2). A description of the operation is entered on the face of the symbol.

The input-process-output symbols on a system flowchart are supplemented with other symbols that depict the flow of data throughout the system. These other symbols are illustrated in Exhibit 5–4.

### Terminal or System Exit/Entry

The terminal symbol indicates the beginning or ending point of the process represented on a flowchart, and also displays system entry or exit of data (see symbols *A* and *B* in

**EXHIBIT 5–4**   **More Flowchart Symbols**

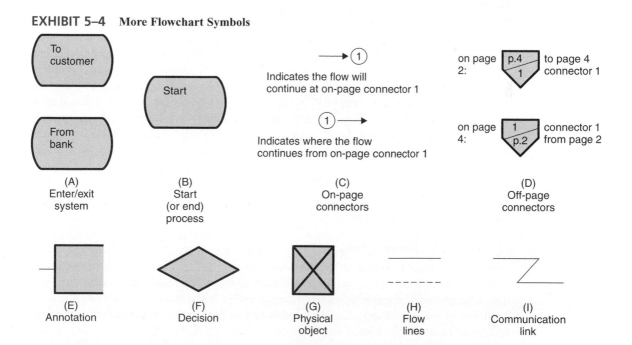

Exhibit 5–4). If the flowchart begins at the top left corner of a page, there is no need to include a start symbol, because the default starting point for a flowchart is the top-left corner.

### On-Page Connector

On-page connectors allow document flows to be bridged within a single page of the flowchart. The use of on-page connectors allows a document to be shown flowing from one position on a page to a distant location on the page without drawing a line across the entire page. Each connector is numbered within a page to enable the reader to know exactly where to continue reading. An arrow pointing to a connector identifies the other connector on the same page where the document flow continues. An arrow pointing away from the connector identifies the connector from which the flow is continuing (see the symbols labeled *C* in Exhibit 5–4).

### Off-Page Connector

Rarely do entire system flowcharts fit on a single page. Off-page connectors are used to connect multiple pages of a document flowchart. The use of off-page connectors is similar to on-page connectors, except they illustrate the continuance of the data flow on another page of the flowchart. Shown within the off-page connector symbol is the page number to which the flow continues (or from which the flow came) and a connector number (see the symbols labeled *D* in Exhibit 5–4).

### Annotation

The annotation symbol includes important supplementary information or explanations that are difficult to describe graphically within the flowchart itself (see symbol *E* in Exhibit 5–4). Use annotations sparingly.

### Decision

Sometimes in a system, the course of action depends on making a decision or choice. For example, if a clerk's task is to review a document for completeness, if the document is complete, the clerk files the document. On the other hand, if the document is incomplete, the clerk sends the document back to the user department. A decision symbol (see symbol *F* in Exhibit 5–4) displays the decision, and a description of the decision can be included in the symbol (e.g., "Is document complete?"). Two labeled **flow lines** exit from the decision symbol to illustrate the indicated course of action. In this case, a line labeled with *yes* (yes the document is complete) would lead to a paper off-line file, while a line labeled *no* (no the document is not complete) would show the document flowing back to the user department.

### Physical (Nondocument) Objects

Symbol *G* in Exhibit 5–4 denotes any physical object that may accompany a document flow (e.g., merchandise, supplies, and fixed assets).

## Flowcharting Element 2: Flow Lines

Flow lines connect the symbols on the document flowchart. A solid line indicates actual physical flow of a document or object. A dotted or dashed line indicates flow of information rather than the physical document (see symbol *H* in Exhibit 5–4). For example, if information is verbally obtained, either in person or on the telephone, the data flow is represented with a dotted or dashed line.

Arrows are used when the document or information flow is not left to right or top to bottom. The assumed flow of documents and information is from top to bottom and from left to right. As long as this flow is followed, arrows are not required. Arrows must be used when there is a counterflow. However, there is nothing wrong with using arrows on all flow lines, and such use eliminates any potential confusion.

Some flowcharts also display communication link symbols (see symbol *J* in Exhibit 5–4). This symbol is used when telephone lines, microwave towers, or satellite transmitters transfer data, particularly when the transfer is from one computer directly to another computer.

## Flowcharting Element 3: Area of Responsibility

**Areas of responsibility** are displayed to enable the flowchart reader to clearly identify changes in responsibility as the documents flow through the system. They are represented on flowcharts by segmenting and labeling columns (see Exhibit 5–1).

Areas of responsibility may be departments, sections within a department, or individual employees within a department. Judgment must be used in choosing the level of subdivision that one column should represent. For example, in a small company one or more pages might represent the billing department.

# PREPARATION CONVENTIONS

Several techniques have been developed to guide the preparation of a flowchart. The main objective of these techniques is to enhance the readability, and thereby enable the validation, of the flowchart.

## Left to Right, Top to Bottom

You have been reading this page from top to bottom and from left to right. A flowchart is most easily understood if you follow the same convention. Therefore, when preparing a document flowchart, begin in the upper left-hand corner and work from left to right and from top to bottom.

## All Documents Must Have an Origin and Termination

A flowchart must clearly indicate where a document is introduced into a system and where it is permanently filed or leaves a system. Each copy of a document must flow to:

1. A permanent file symbol
2. A symbol denoting an exit from the system
3. An off-page connector

Following this convention ensures that the progress of every document has been observed and documented from cradle to grave. Whenever the final destination of a document is unknown, use an annotation symbol to indicate that additional investigation is required.

## Keep Flowcharts Uncluttered

A flowchart is an important analytical and design tool; however, great amounts of detail reduce a flowchart's ability to communicate. For this reason, to the extent possible, observe the following rules:

1. Place areas of responsibility with the most frequent interchange adjacent to each other to avoid long arrows.
2. Enter narrative on charts only within symbols.
3. Avoid explaining with narrative what is already adequately described by the flowchart itself.

## Make Sure the Progress of a Document Is Clear

Diagram a document before and after a process is performed, when entering or leaving a file, and on entering or leaving a page. Also, if a document is altered (e.g., updated, signed, or approved), change the name of the document to indicate its current status. For example, notice in Exhibit 5–1 the flow of the reimbursement request. The manual process "Prepare reimbursement request" creates it. It is sent to the payables clerk where it is approved. The name is changed accordingly to approved reimbursement request. After further processing, it is eventually filed in a permanent file. Similarly, notice the flow of the check. The computerized process in the data processing department generates the check, which at that point is unsigned. Copies 1 and 2 are sent to the payables supervisor, who performs a manual double-check and signing process. The signed check is sent to the employee and the copy, along with the underlying request and support documents, is filed in a permanent file.

## Make Sure Your Flowchart Is Complete: Represent Each Input, Processing, Output, and Storage Step

When flowcharting a process, make sure you include all the major steps in the process. Remember that systems are simply a combination of inputs, processing, outputs, and storage of data.

# SYSTEM FLOWCHART SUMMARY

Following the preceding instructions can guide the development of an effective flowchart for analyzing an information process or system. The flowchart is one of the easier types of documentation for information customers and management to understand. Often, auditors use system and **document/procedure flowcharts** to understand business and systems controls in an environment.

To test whether you are beginning to understand how to read and prepare flowcharts, go back to Exhibit 5–1, and write a short narrative of the process. Compare your narrative to the narrative provided earlier in this chapter to see how accurately you read the flowchart.

Although many individuals and organizations still use flowcharts, their usefulness is limited. The primary weakness of the flowchart is that it is tied to physical information flows and system characteristics that hide the procedural essence of the system. Some flowcharts are full of data and processing artifacts because they are tied to an outdated information technology. Therefore, any effort to propose a new system that takes advantage of current information technology requires the conceptual aspects of the system to be documented and designed. Data flow diagrams are a useful tool for documenting the conceptual aspects of an information system.

# FILE TYPES, MEDIA, AND PROCESSING METHODS

Because system flowcharts reflect the physical media on which data are stored and the automation level of each process, they are difficult to prepare or to interpret without adequate understanding of some features of the common physical media, file types, and tools involved in the information processes. Therefore this section provides a description of some common file types, media on which files are stored, and some common processing methods.

## File Types

Files store data and processing instructions. Each file is named and saved on a storage medium such as a hard disk or magnetic tape. An example of a file is a word processing document created using Microsoft Word or WordPerfect. The two types of files computer users use most often are executable files and data files. *Executable files* are also called program or application files, and they usually have an .exe extension. *Data files* are used to store anything from transaction data to business reference data to a word processing or graphics document. Often files are referred to by their type or content. Types of data files used in most enterprise systems include master files, transaction files, history files, reference files, and suspense files.

*Master files* contain balance data or the status of an entity at a point in time. Examples of master files in enterprise systems are customer, employee, inventory, fixed asset, and supplier master files (to name a few). Master files do not contain event or activity data, but they typically contain balances updated by such data. For example, a customer master file may contain an accounts receivable balance field that is updated by sales and cash receipt activity data. *Transaction files* contain activity data used to update the balances on master files. Examples of transaction files in enterprise systems are cash disbursement, cash receipt, payroll, purchase, and sales transaction files (to name a few). When a transaction file is used to update a master file, the transaction file is said to "run against" the master file.

*History files* or *archive files,* as the names suggest, contain inactive past or historical data. Examples of history files include data files from years past that are no longer subject to updates. History files are distinguished from *backup files,* which are copies of files created in case the files are destroyed. At least one backup file should be stored at a location other than the location of original files. Then a disaster such as a fire or flood that could potentially damage or destroy the original would not affect the backup files. *Reference files* contain referential data such as tax rate schedules or customer price lists. *Suspense files* are files of data that are awaiting some action to complete their processing. Examples include records identified as incomplete or erroneous that need correction and reentry for processing (e.g., a payment by a customer who is not listed in the customer master file or a journal entry that doesn't balance).

## Media

Data for most enterprises are stored on media that fall into three categories: paper, magnetic tape, and disk. Each of these media types was discussed earlier in this chapter; however, a more detailed discussion of them can help you understand some of the associated processing issues. Paper is the most common form of media used in enterprises. Source documents (documents that contain details about transactions) are inputs for many information processes, and paper reports are produced as outputs for many information processes. Paper is the media type most people prefer to use. Although increasingly people are asked to read output screens, reports, and even textbooks on computer monitors, most people still prefer to have the files printed out and to read hardcopy. Although paper has many advantages, including ease of use and lack of dependence on electricity, it also has many disadvantages such as bulk (for storage), lack of search and automated processing capability, and susceptibility to destruction (although all media types may be easily destroyed, backup copies to mitigate inadvertent destruction are more easily made with nonpaper media).

Magnetic tape stores data from source documents and reports in a format that is computer readable. As noted earlier, if you have used audiocassettes of music, or videocassettes of movies, then you have used magnetic tape media. One important feature of magnetic tape media is that data are stored sequentially and may be accessed only sequentially. Sequential storage implies that records are stored one after another in some order (chronologically, by account number, or alphabetically). Retrieving data in a sequential file requires that all data be read in sequential order to find a particular record. For example, suppose you purchase an audiocassette containing songs performed by your favorite recording artist. The songs are stored sequentially (one after another) on the tape. To listen to your favorite song, you must fast forward or rewind (searching the songs one after another) to sequentially access the desired song—there is no faster access option. Enterprises use magnetic tape cartridges and open reel tapes to store transaction and report data and those files require sequential storage and access of data.

Disk technology is increasingly replacing magnetic tape as the preferred media, both for personal audiovisual needs and for enterprise processing applications. Examples of disk technology include hard disks, floppy disks, and Zip disks on computers, and compact disks and DVDs for computers and personal audiovisual needs. From an information processing standpoint, the primary advantage of disk-based storage over magnetic tape storage is the random storage and direct access capability of disk technology. Random storage allows information to be stored in any order on the disk device; in fact a file need not be stored in its entirety in a single location on a disk—part of it may be stored in one location and part of it in another location, although processing is more efficient if files are not fragmented in that manner. Direct access allows each record to be retrieved without reading all the records that precede it in the file. The computer maintains an index of the location of each record, thus allowing the computer to retrieve any record requested by the user regardless of its physical position in a file. There is no need to sequentially search part or all of the other records stored on the storage device. Suppose that instead of purchasing a cassette tape of songs performed by your favorite recording artist you purchased a CD containing those songs. With the CD player you can choose your favorite song from the index and listen to it without having to listen to or fast-forward through the other songs on the CD.

The most obvious distinction between these media types for system flowcharting is that different symbols represent them. However, there are other distinctions. One distinction that must be made is whether updates are made to the same physical file or whether a new file must be created that merges the original data with the updates. If a master file is stored on magnetic tape, updates may not be made to the same physical medium but rather a new magnetic tape must be used and data read from the old master file and the transaction file containing the updates and the updated records rewritten onto the new master file. The reason the updates may not be written directly to the old master file is that they may take up a different amount of space, and could potentially destroy existing data. For example, if you taped four 30-minute television shows on a VCR tape and you want to replace one of those shows with a 60-minute television show, you couldn't do that without destroying one of the other 30-minute television shows. To clarify this even further, suppose the four shows on your tape were episodes of *Gilligan's Island, Seinfeld, I Love Lucy,* and *Cheers.* Further suppose you wanted to keep only the episodes of *Gilligan's Island* and *I Love Lucy,* and you wanted to record a one-hour episode of *Matlock.* So you have a two-hour tape and you want to end up with two hours' worth of shows, deleting two 30-minute episodes and replacing them with one 60-minute episode. If you positioned the tape so that it begins recording where *Seinfeld* starts, you would end up replacing *I Love Lucy* instead of replacing *Cheers*. There is no way to tell the tape to skip over the *I Love Lucy* episode when it comes to it and then start recording again.

Contrast that with the updating of a master file stored on disk. Updates may be written directly to the disk, because it doesn't matter where the data are physically located on the disk. As long as space is available for all the needed data, if you update a customer street address that was 123 Pine St. to 12345 Appleyard Ave. (notice the new address is longer) it will realize the allotted space is not big enough and will add a pointer to a new location on the disk that has adequate space. The logical view (what the user sees when the computer displays these data) does not show that data are stored in fragments, but physically data are stored in that manner. If the data are stored in too many fragments, processing efficiency may decrease; that is why you may get an error message on your personal computer occasionally suggesting that you defrag your hard disk drive. The defrag process rearranges the physical locations of data on the drive to make processing more efficient.

## Processing Methods

The timing of processing reveals the point at which activity data are posted to update the master files. Therefore the processing method determines the timeliness of the data stored in master files. Processing is often identified by type: batch, online, real-time, or report-time processing.

*Batch processing* accumulates transaction data for a period of time to collect a *batch,* or group, of transaction data. Then all of the transactions in the file are posted to the master file in one processing run. Therefore, processing (i.e., updating of the master file) occurs after a group of transaction data is collected. Processing involves merging the data in the transaction file with the current master data to create a *new, updated* master file. Thus, with batch processing, transaction data may not be entered in the computer system until some time after a business activity occurs, and master files may be updated even later. The only time the master file is accurate and up-to-date is immediately after a batch of transaction data has been processed.

*Online processing* means the computer-input device is connected to the CPU so that master files are updated as transaction data are entered. *Real-time* denotes immediate response to an information user; transaction data are entered and processed to update the relevant master files and a response is provided to the person conducting the business event fast enough to affect the outcome of the event. Although they sound similar, online and real-time processing can differ. Real-time processing updates master files as a business activity occurs, while online processing updates master files whenever transaction data are entered (which may *not* be when a business activity occurs). Real-time processing generally requires an online input device.

*Report-time processing* means the data used to generate the requested report are processed as the report is created. Report-time processing is a term used primarily in event-driven systems and it is similar to real-time updating. Most event data are stored in a detailed or disaggregated form and the relevant data are selected and processed; any master files are updated as the information customer's report is generated.

Due to the sequential access limitations of tape, tape storage media always use batch processing. Disk storage media can handle batch, online, or real-time processing.

# DATA FLOW DIAGRAMS

A second documentation tool is the data flow diagram (DFD). Data flow diagramming symbols have a variety of system analysis purposes, including graphically displaying the logical flows of data through a process. Unlike flowcharts, which represent the physical components of an information system, data flow diagrams provide a more conceptual, non-physical display of the movement of data through a system. Like flowcharts, they represent flow of data; however, they disregard such things as organizational units, the computer on which the data are processed, and the media on which the data are stored. The movement of data across offices or departments within a particular system environment is not represented.

Categories of data flow diagrams include:

- Data flow diagrams of the current physical system
- Data flow diagrams of the current logical system
- Data flow diagrams of the new or proposed logical system
- Data flow diagrams of the new proposed physical system

Both logical and physical diagrams use the same set of symbols. The logical diagrams show the conceptual flow of data without including any references to the physical characteristics of the system. The physical diagrams, on the other hand, include labels that describe physical attributes of the system, such as labeling worker or job titles, department names, and the names or descriptions of the technology used to process and store the data.

# DATA FLOW DIAGRAM SYMBOLS

Data flow diagrams include four **data flow diagram symbols:** process, data inflow sources and outflow sinks (destinations), data stores, and data flow lines. Like flowcharting, there are variations on some of the symbols. For example, two standard symbol sets were developed by Gane and Sarson[1] and DeMarco and Yourdon[2] (see Exhibit 5–5). We use the DeMarco and Yourdon symbols in this text.

## Process

Circles are used to represent processes that transform data inflows into information outflows (see symbol *A* in Exhibit 5–5).[3] The circle contains two labels. The first label is a process number (explained later) and the second is a process name.

## Data Sources and Sinks

Rectangles (or squares) represent data (inflow) sources and (information outflow) sinks (see symbol *B* in Exhibit 5–5). The rectangle is labeled with the name of the data source or sink/destination (e.g., customer, vendors, government agency). The sources and sinks

---

[1]C. Gane and T. Sarson, *Structured Systems Analysis* (Englewood Cliffs, NJ: Prentice-Hall, 1979).

[2]T. DeMarco, *Structured Analysis and Systems Specifications* (Englewood Cliffs, NJ: Prentice-Hall, 1979), and E. Yourdon and L. Constantine, *Structured Design* (Englewood Cliffs, NJ: Prentice-Hall, 1979).

[3]Some use rectangular boxes with rounded corners.

**EXHIBIT 5–5   Data Flow Diagram Symbols**

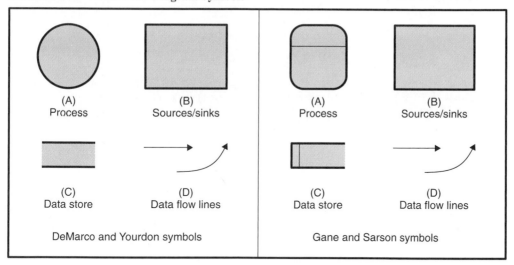

play an important role in the data flow diagram. The sources and sinks are agents external to (i.e., outside the scope of) the system represented on the diagram. They delineate the boundaries of the system.

## Data Stores

Two parallel straight lines are used to display a store or collection of data (see symbol *C* in Exhibit 5–5).[4] Some people refer to data stores as data at rest. A description of the data store contents is entered on the symbol. Data stores are used anytime it is necessary to store the output from a process before sending it on to the next process.

## Data Flow Lines

Data flow lines display the route of data inflow and information outflow (see symbol *D* in Exhibit 5–5). They can be straight or curved lines. The data flow is generally labeled with the name of the data (e.g., a customer order, a bill, a financial analysis) and the arrow indicates the direction of the data flow.

# CONSTRAINTS

As with any documentation tool, some conventions should be followed. The following data flow diagramming rules are recommended by Hoffer, George, and Valacich. Exhibit 5–6 graphically displays several of the rules. We use these rules in this text.

## General Rules

1. All processes should have unique names. If two data flow lines (or data stores) have the same label, they should both refer to the exact same data flow (or data store).

[4]Some use a rectangular box that is open at one end.

**EXHIBIT 5–6** **Data Flow Diagramming Rules**

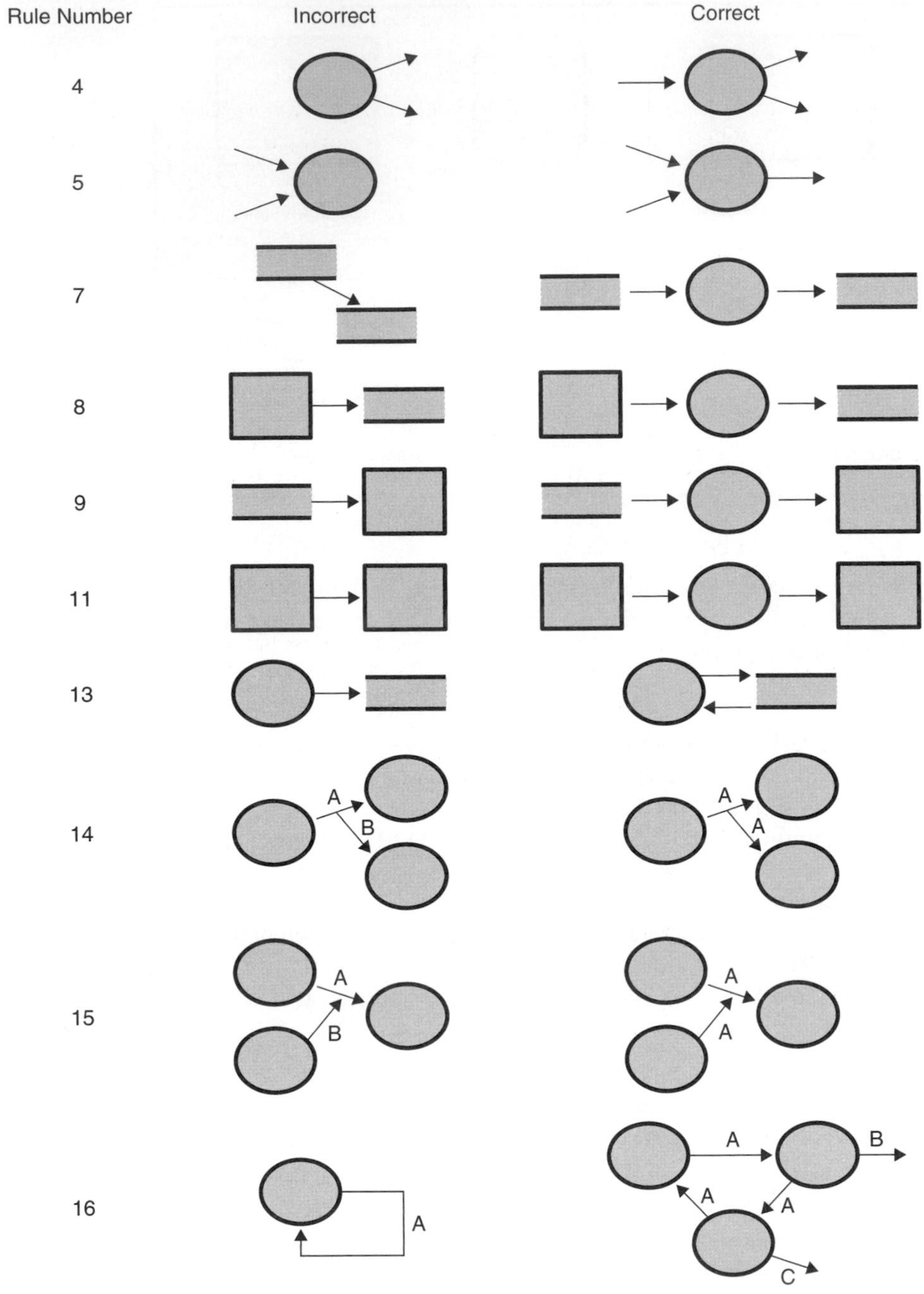

*Source:* J. Hoffer, J. George, and J. Valacich, *Modern Systems Analysis and Design* (Reading, MA: Benjamin/Cummings, 1996), p. 321.

2. The inputs to a process should differ from the outputs of a process.
3. Any single DFD should not have more than about seven processes.

## Process

4. No process can have only outputs. (This would imply that the process is making information from nothing.) If an object has only outputs, then it must be a source.
5. No process can have only inputs. (This is referred to as a black hole.) If an object has only inputs, then it must be a sink.
6. A process has a verb phrase label.

## Data Store

7. Data cannot move directly from one data store to another data store. Data must be moved by a process.
8. Data cannot move directly from an outside source to a data store. Data must be moved by a process that receives data from the source and places the data in the data store.
9. Data cannot move directly to an outside sink from a data store. Data must be moved by a process.
10. A data store has a noun phrase label.

## Source/Sink

11. Data cannot move directly from a source to a sink. It must be moved by a process if the data are of any concern to the system. If data flow directly from a source to a sink (and do not involve processing) then they are outside the scope of the system and are not shown on the system DFD.
12. A source/sink has a noun phrase label.

## Data Flow

13. A data flow has only one direction between symbols. It may flow in both directions between a process and a data store to show a read before an update. To effectively show a read before an update, draw two separate arrows because the two steps (reading and updating) occur at separate times.
14. A fork in a data flow means that exactly the same data go from a common location to two or more different processes, data stores, or sources/sinks. (This usually indicates different copies of the same data going to different locations.)
15. A join in a data flow means that exactly the same data come from any of two or more different processes, data stores, or sources/sinks, to a common location.
16. A data flow cannot go directly back to the same process it leaves. There must be at least one other process that handles the data flow, produces some other data flow, and returns the original data flow to the originating process.
17. A data flow to a data store means update (i.e., delete, add, or change).
18. A data flow from a data store means retrieve or use.
19. A data flow has a noun phrase label. More than one data flow noun phrase can appear on a single arrow as long as all of the flows on the same arrow move together as one package.

**EXHIBIT 5–7**
**Context Level**
**DFD**

## LEVELS OF DATA FLOW DIAGRAMS

Data flow diagrams are divided into levels to keep their size and complexity manageable.

### Context Diagram

The highest level of data flow diagrams is the **context diagram.** Refer to Exhibit 5–7 for a context diagram of a sample sales/collection system. A single system is represented on a context diagram and it provides the scope of the system being represented. The system under investigation is identified in a process symbol in the center of the diagram labeled with a 0. Sources and sinks (destinations) of data and information are also shown. Thus, the context diagram shows one process (representing the entire system) and the sources/sinks that represent the boundaries of the system. The data flow lines into the process represent the input data to the system (provided by sources) and the data flow lines from the process represent the output information from the system (going to the sinks).

### Subsequent Level DFDs

The process identified in the context diagram is divided into the more detailed processes performed within the system. The next level under the context diagram is called **level-zero DFD** and depicts only the very high-level processes of the system. Each of the level-zero processes may be subdivided into more detailed processes in subsequent levels of DFDs. The act of dividing each process on a data flow diagram into more detailed subprocesses is referred to as **decomposition.** When you have decomposed the system processes into the most detailed levels (referred to as the lowest-level DFDs), the resulting DFDs are called **primitive DFDs.**[5]

Each process in a level-zero DFD is labeled sequentially, with a #.0. For example, if a level-zero DFD includes four processes that comprise the system represented in a context diagram, the processes on the level-zero DFD are labeled as 1.0, 2.0, 3.0, and 4.0. The .0 identifies this as the level-zero DFD. For example, Exhibit 5–8 is a level-zero DFD of the context diagram represented in Exhibit 5–7. It shows that the sample sales/collection system has three main high-level process categories:

- Process customer orders (labeled as 1.0).
- Process deliveries to customers (labeled as 2.0).
- Process payments from customers (labeled as 3.0)

[5]Refer to page 335 of J. Hoffer, J. George, and J. Valacich, *Modern Systems Analysis and Design* (Reading, MA: Benjamin/Cummings, 1996), for a list of rules on determining when the primitive DFD level is achieved. This text is also a good source for advanced data flow diagramming concepts and rules.

**EXHIBIT 5–8**
**Level-Zero**
**DFD**

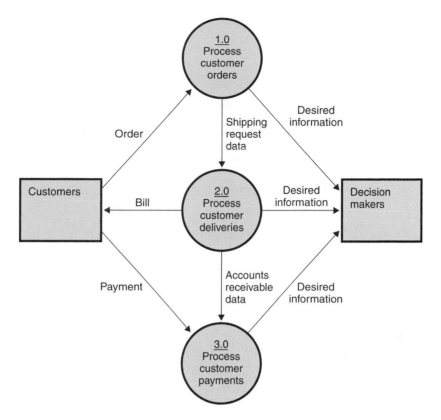

Suppose you wanted to show more detail about the processes represented on Exhibit 5–8. You could create a level-one DFD for each process. Exhibit 5–9 provides a sample level-one DFD for process 1.0 of Exhibit 5–8. It shows that "Process customer order" is made up of two processes: "approve and record customer order data" and "generate information about orders." The two processes are labeled as 1.1 and 1.2, respectively. The first digit refers to the corresponding level-zero process number. The second digit refers to the assigned level-one process number. Notice that you can omit the source/sink symbols (in this case customer and decision makers) on more detailed, lower-level DFDs. In addition, notice that the level-one DFD has the same system input and output data flows as the corresponding level-zero DFD. When such related DFDs are consistent in showing inputs and outflows, they are said to be **balanced DFDs.**

Exhibit 5–10 shows a level-two DFD. It shows that the "approve and record customer order data" process shown in Exhibit 5–10 is comprised of four subprocesses ("1.1.1 receive order data from customer," "1.1.2 check customer status," "1.1.3 check inventory availability," and "1.1.4 record order data"). As noted earlier, additional levels of detail could be provided in subsequent levels of DFDs. For example, if "check customer status" is complex and there are several subprocesses required to complete this process, process 1.1.2 could be divided into subprocesses on a level-three DFD, labeled as 1.1.2.1, 1.1.2.2, 1.1.2.3, and so on.

**EXHIBIT 5-9**
**Level-One**
**DFD**

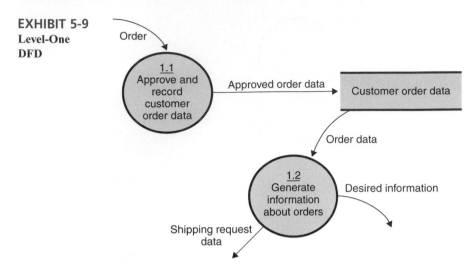

**EXHIBIT 5–10    Level-Two DFD**

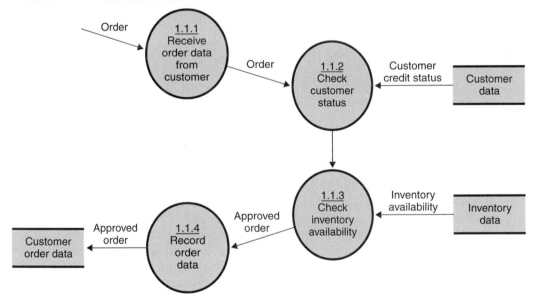

# COMPARING FLOWCHARTS AND DATA FLOW DIAGRAMS

As noted earlier, a primary difference between data flow diagrams and flowcharts is the representation of the physical and logical characteristics of a system. Flowcharts are biased toward representing the physical characteristics of the system, while data flow diagrams can omit the physical system attributes. To illustrate this difference, suppose you wanted to document the data flows in the following manual system scenario: A supervisor in the factory collects the time cards from workers in her department and reviews the calculation

**EXHIBIT 5–11**   **Payroll DFD versus System Flowchart**

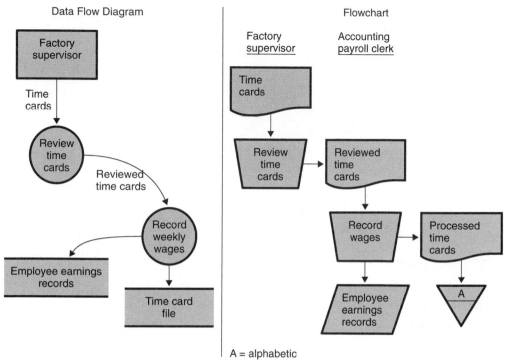

of total hours for the week. She sends the time cards to accounting payroll, where a clerk uses them to record weekly wages in the individual employee earnings record files, then files the time cards alphabetically.

Exhibit 5–11 displays flowchart and data flow diagram documentation segments of this activity. Now suppose the activity remains constant, except that the accounting payroll department automates its process using magnetic tape.

Exhibit 5–12 displays updated flowchart and data flow diagram documentation segments that reflect this change. Notice that the DFD did not change from Exhibit 5–11 to Exhibit 5–12. That is because the conceptual flow of data did not change from the first scenario to the second scenario. The only change was in the physical characteristics of the devices used to route and store the data.

Now suppose everything still remains constant, except that the accounting payroll department decides to upgrade to magnetic disks (examine Exhibit 5–13).

Compare Exhibit 5–13 to Exhibit 5–12 and you see that once again the DFD is identical because the conceptual data flows remained the same. The flowchart changed a second time to reflect the changes in the physical components of the information system. This example should demonstrate to you that data flow diagrams provide more stable documentation of the underlying data flows and processes in the system. Although not as detailed, the data flow diagram helps the reader focus on information, rather than technology. On the other hand, system flowcharts tell the reader exactly what physical components are used for various purposes in the information system.

**EXHIBIT 5–12 Updated Payroll DFD and System Flowcharts**

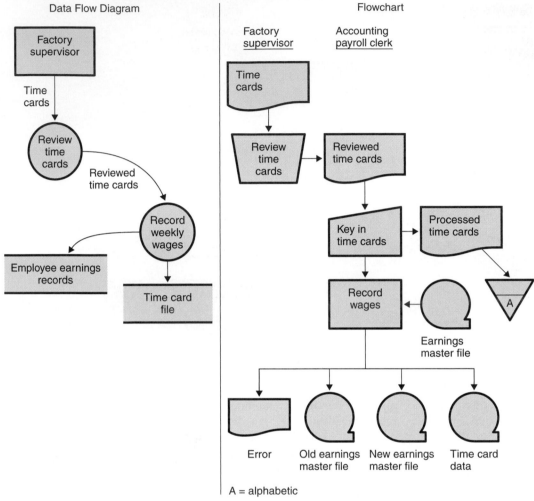

## CONCLUDING COMMENTS

This chapter has presented an overview of both flowcharting and data flow diagramming. Some organizations and consultants have developed their own diagramming techniques. Whether you use flowcharting, data flow diagrams, or a proprietary diagramming tool is really a matter of choice and what you are trying to analyze or design. Diagramming tools combine the efficiency of graphics and rigor of rules to communicate the nature of the process being modeled. It is important for analysts to develop the skills to both read and create documentation of information and business processes using tools such as flowcharts and data flow diagrams.

**EXHIBIT 5–13   Second Update to Payroll DFD and System Flowcharts**

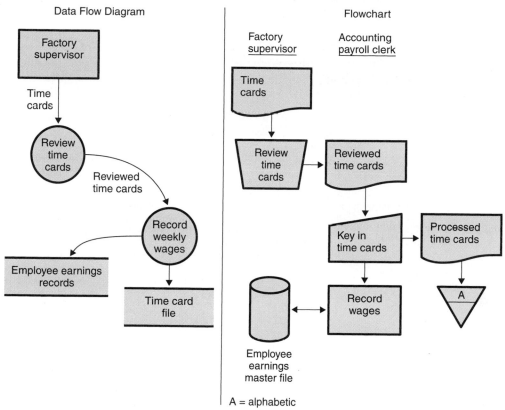

Data Flow Diagram

Flowchart

A = alphabetic

## Key Terms and Concepts

Areas of responsibility, *101*

Balanced DFD, *111*

Context diagram, *110*

Data flow diagram, *94*

Data flow diagram
symbols, *106*

Decomposition, *110*

Document/procedure
flowcharts, *102*

Flowcharting
conventions, *95*

Flowcharting symbols, *94*

Flow lines, *100*

Level-zero DFD, *110*

Primitive DFD, *110*

System flowchart, *94*

Workflow, *91*

## Review Questions

LO2   R1.   Draw the flowcharting symbols and describe the use of each.

LO2   R2.   What are the important flowcharting conventions or techniques you should follow to make a flowchart easier to understand?

LO2   R3.   When should you use an overlapping document symbol instead of a single document symbol in a system flowchart?

LO5    R4. What is the difference between online processing and real-time processing? Can processing be both online and real-time? Can processing be online without being real-time?

LO3    R5. Draw the data flow diagram symbols and describe the use of each.

LO3    R6. List and explain the various levels of data flow diagrams.

LO3    R7. What are the important conventions or techniques you should follow when drawing a data flow diagram?

## Multiple Choice Questions

LO3, LO4    MC1. Of the following representations, which has a primary purpose of illustrating the logical flow of data in a system?
    A. System flowchart
    B. REA business process level entity-relationship diagram
    C. Data flow diagram
    D. All of the above

LO2    MC2. Which symbol should be used in a system flowchart to represent a check that is sent to a supplier?
    A.
    B.
    C.
    D.

LO3    MC3. Which symbol should be used in a data flow diagram to represent a check that is sent to a supplier?
    A.
    B.
    C.
    D.

LO5    MC4. Which type of medium typically requires sequential storage and sequential access?
    A. Zip disk
    B. Paper document
    C. Open-reel tape
    D. CD-ROM

LO5    MC5. Which type of file contains batches of current source activity data?
    A. Transaction file
    B. Master file
    C. Archive file
    D. Reference file

## Discussion Questions

LO4    D1. Explain the difference(s) between data flow diagrams and flowcharts. Which do you think is easier to prepare? Why? Which do you think is easier to interpret? Why?

LO1    D2. Explain the difference(s) between task level and business process level models in the REA ontology.

LO4   D3.   What are the advantages and disadvantages of a system flowchart as compared to a narrative description of an enterprise system's documents, processes, and data flows?

## Applied Learning

LO2   A1.   Develop a system flowchart to represent the acquisition/payment tasks for Jayvision, Inc., as described in the first scenario in this chapter. Next develop a system flowchart to represent the acquisition/payment tasks for Jayvision as described in the second scenario in this chapter. How are they similar? How are they different?

LO3   A2.   Develop a data flow diagram to represent the acquisition/payment tasks for Jayvision, Inc., as described in the first scenario in this chapter. Next develop a data flow diagram to represent the acquisition/payment tasks for Jayvision as described in the second scenario in this chapter. How are they similar? How are they different?

LO2   A3.   Working as a team, visit a local enterprise and flowchart a source document (e.g., a customer order, sales invoice, or purchases order) from origination to its final destination. Also, flowchart a task performed by one of the organization's clerks. In class, exchange your team's flowchart with another team and write a narrative of their flowchart. Prepare a written or verbal critique of how well the other team interpreted the flowchart your team prepared.

LO2, LO3   A4.   The following describes the process to execute a credit sale at Willie's Furniture Store. Sales clerks assist customers in locating and pricing merchandise. A sales clerk prepares a sales invoice with an original and three copies. If the merchandise on an invoice is priced differently than the list price, the price change must be approved with a signature by the sales manager. Copy 3 of the sales invoice is filed by the salesperson in a salesperson file.

The salesperson walks the customer and the remaining copies of the invoice to the credit approval department where the invoice is checked for mathematical errors by a clerk. The credit manager evaluates the credit standing of the customer, approves or rejects the application based on standard company policy, and marks "credit sale" on the invoice along with the results of the credit evaluation. Invoice copy 2 of credit approved sales is given to the customer. The credit approval department keeps the original copy of the invoice in their files (filed numerically) and sends the other copy to shipping.

The shipping department uses their copy as a guide to pull merchandise and deliver it to the customer. The customer is asked to sign the invoice copy as evidence of delivery. The delivery person files the invoice copy by date.

### Required:

a. Prepare a document/procedure flowchart for the process just described.

b. Prepare a logical data flow diagram for this process.

LO2, LO3   A5.   Motor Building Industry (MBI) Incorporated develops and manufactures natural-gas powered motors. Capital tools are the larger, more-prominent assets of the organization. Because of their long life and significant value, considerable attention is devoted to their acquisition and use. The following procedures are used in acquiring capital tools for MBI Inc.

A capital tool is defined as any individual item that costs over $10,000. Capital tools must be requested by a department manager and reviewed and approved by the capital tool planning committee. The department manager prepares a purchase request and a copy (which is filed numerically) and sends the original copy to the planning committee. The planning committee reviews all purchase requests and decides whether to approve the tool request. The committee remits disapproved purchase requests to the requesting manager and forwards approved purchase requests to MBI's purchasing department.

Approved capital tools are purchased by the purchasing department manager. Using the approved purchase request, a purchasing agent prepares a purchase order and a copy for each order. The original is filed numerically and the copy is sent to MBI's receiving department. Each tool is assigned to only one purchasing agent, and the assignment is made according to the vendor from whom the tool is intended to be purchased. Several vendors are assigned to each purchasing agent to establish a personal relationship with the vendor and secure a more favorable price because of their knowledge of the vendor.

Receiving clerks at the dock receive the tools, inspect them, match the tool to a purchase order, complete a receiving report, and route the tool to the department that originally requested it. Receiving clerks send the receiving report to the treasury department and file a copy alphabetically. Purchase orders are filed numerically. Occasionally, tools are received that were never ordered. Even though the number of these items is relatively small, sorting them out and returning them occupies a major portion of the receiving clerk's time.

The treasury department is informed of capital tools received by the receiving report. They pay vendors monthly for the items invoiced by the vendor during the month. An elaborate matching process is required to verify that the price paid is the same as the price negotiated by the purchasing agent.

### Required:

a. Prepare a context diagram for the system.

b. Prepare individual data flow diagrams to represent each of the following: record purchase, maintain buyers, and prepare approved but not yet purchased report. You can omit process numbers for this exercise.

c. Prepare a flowchart of MBI's tool acquisition process (excluding the payment process).

LO2, LO3  A6.  The Warehouse Club is a small merchandise discount store that sells everything from grocery items to automotive parts. The Warehouse Club is able to secure low prices by buying in bulk and by operating out of a leased warehouse. In addition, only paid members are allowed to shop at a Warehouse Club location. The following is a description of the yearly member renewal process.

At or near the first day of each month, an accounts receivable clerk queries the membership database to identify those whose membership expires during the following month. For example, on January 1 a query is executed to identify memberships that expire during February. A membership renewal list is printed for use in preparing individual invoices and for documentation.

Using the computer and the membership renewal list, an accounts receivable clerk prepares an individual invoice for each member. This process automatically updates accounts receivable records. The computer prints two copies of the invoice. The original invoice is sent to the customer and the invoice copy is stored numerically in a filing cabinet. The membership list is also stored in a filing cabinet, but is filed according to the date.

When payment checks are received they are immediately processed. First, a copy is made and stored alphabetically in customer files. Next, account receivable records are updated and customers are given another year of shopping privileges. Finally at the end of the day, checks are endorsed and deposited in the bank.

### Required:

a. Prepare a flowchart of this process.

b. Prepare a logical data flow diagram for this process.

LO2, LO3   A7.   Convenient Computing Associates (CCA) operates a mail-order operation and sells a vast array of computer products and accessories. The following is a description of Convenient Computing's collection process:

The policy of CCA is to collect all accounts receivable as quickly as possible. CCA encourages prompt payment by sending reminder statements at the end of each month and calling customers whose balance is more than 30 days past due.

On the last working day of the month, the accounts receivable clerk prints a statement for each customer showing the balance due on the account. Statements are automatically generated by a computer which maintains the accounts receivable files and records. The original statement is mailed to the customer and a copy of the statement is filed alphabetically according to customers' last names.

On the 15th and the last day of the month, the accounts receivable clerk prints an open accounts receivable aging report by customer. The clerk calls the customer on all invoices more than 30 days past due. The purpose of the call is to verify the accuracy of the invoice data. If the information is correct, a polite reminder is given to encourage prompt payment. The open receivable report is marked with the clerk's initials and the date the call was made, and filed by date when all calls are complete.

### Required:

a. Prepare a flowchart of this process.

b. Prepare a logical data flow diagram for this process.

LO2   A8.   Wiltex Research is a company that performs energy research on a contract basis for major oil and chemical companies. The following narrative describes the process to acquire materials for research projects.

A project manager determines the materials needed for a project and purchases them from a vendor. The project manager completes a purchase order for each type of material. A catalog price is used, or the vendor is contacted by telephone to determine the price. The purchase order has an original and two copies.

The project manager sends the purchase order to the project supervisor for approval or disapproval. The project manager writes approved or disapproved on the purchase order, signs it, and returns it to the project manager. The project manager sends the original copy of approved purchase orders to the vendor; sends Copy 1 to the accounting clerk; and files Copy 2 in a permanent project file (ordered numerically by project number). Disapproved purchase orders are thrown out by the project manager.

The accounting clerk files Copy 1 in a temporary file (numeric by PO number).

The project manager receives and inspects materials sent from the vendor and compares them to the packing slip. The packing slip is sent to the accounting clerk as evidence that the materials have been received. The accounting clerk matches the packing slip with Copy 1 of the purchase order and prepares a check (which has an original and one copy).

The check is attached to the packing slip and Copy 1 of the purchase order is sent to the project supervisor for a signature. Once signed, the entire set of documents is returned to the accounting clerk who sends the original copy of the check to the vendor, and files the copy of the check with the supporting documentation attached to it in a permanent file (ordered numerically by check number).

### Required:

Prepare a flowchart of this process.

## Answers to Multiple Choice Questions

MC1. C; MC2. A; MC3. B; MC4. C; MC5. A.

# Chapter **Six**

# Relational Database Design: Converting Conceptual REA Models to Relational Databases*

## LEARNING OBJECTIVES

The primary objective of this chapter is to describe a procedure for converting a conceptual business process level REA model into a logical relational database model and then into a physical Microsoft Access database implementation. This process involves a relatively straightforward set of rules that could even be programmed as an algorithm so that a computer could accomplish the conversion. This chapter also discusses data entry issues. After studying this chapter, you should be able to

1. Convert a conceptual business process level REA model into a logical relational model
2. Convert a logical relational model into a physical implementation using Microsoft Access
3. Explain the difference between conceptual, logical, and physical database models
4. Enter transaction data into a relational database
5. Interpret a physical database implementation in Microsoft Access to determine what the underlying logical model must have been
6. Interpret a logical relational model to determine what the underlying conceptual model must have been
7. Recognize and implement various application level controls to facilitate the integrity of data entered into a relational database

## INTRODUCTION

Before we introduce any topics in this chapter, we want to emphasize that the REA enterprise ontology and the conceptual models that are developed using this ontology are completely

*Much of the material on converting conceptual models into relational database tables is based on classroom materials prepared by Professor William E. McCarthy at Michigan State University.

independent of any particular database software package and of any particular logical database model. The models developed using the techniques discussed in Chapter 4 may be converted into object-oriented databases, into **relational databases,** or into programming language constructs that are not databases of a specified type.

Three models are typically developed in database design. One type is a **conceptual database model** that is independent of any hardware, software, or even any type of software. The models we developed in Chapter 4 are conceptual models. In database design, conceptual models are converted into **logical models** once the type of database to be used has been determined. Logical models are the second type of model; they are independent of any particular software package, but may be implemented only by using a software package of a certain category. Examples of logical database models include relational, object-oriented, hierarchical, network, and others. Once a conceptual model is converted to a relational logical format, it can no longer be implemented in object-oriented, hierarchical, network, or other software. Rather it is limited to one of many relational database software packages. Similarly, if a conceptual model is converted into an object-oriented format, it can no longer be implemented in non-object-oriented software but may be implemented in a variety of object-oriented software packages. The third type of model used in database design is the **physical database model.** Such a model is created based on the particular database software package in which the database is implemented and is therefore dependent on the software choice.

Because most enterprises use relational database software of some kind, and because most universities make relational database software available to students, we have chosen to focus only on the relational database logical model. For the physical database model we illustrate the concepts discussed in this chapter using Microsoft Access 2002 because of its wide availability both in academia and in practice and because of its ease of use. Please understand that the constructs discussed also apply to other relational database software packages such as SQL Server, Oracle, FoxPro, Paradox and others.

# CONVERTING CONCEPTUAL MODELS INTO RELATIONAL LOGICAL MODELS

To understand the rules for converting a conceptual data model into a relational logical model, you must first understand the structure of the **relational model.** The relational model was developed by Codd and is based on set theory and predicate logic.[1] The primary construct in the relational model is the relation, which is a two-dimensional storage structure (i.e., a storage structure with **rows** and **columns**) more commonly referred to as a table. Each table in the relational model represents either an entity or a relationship between entities. The columns in a relational database table are formally called the table **intension, schema,** or **fields,** and they represent the **attributes** of the entity or relationship set. The rows in a relational database table are formally called the table **extension, tuples,** or **records,** and they represent the specific instances that are members of the entity or relationship set. The order of columns in a table does not matter, nor does the order in which

---

[1]E. F. Codd, "Derivability, Redundancy, and Consistency of Relations Stored in Large Data Banks," *IBM Research Report* RJ599, August 19, 1969; and "A Relational Model of Data for Large Shared Data Banks," *CACM* 13, no. 6 (June 1970), republished in *Milestones of Research: Selected Papers 1958–1982, CACM* 25th Anniversary Issue, *CACM* 26, no. 1 (January 1983).

rows appear. This is because the tables are created in such a way that the rows and columns may be sorted as desired through the use of queries. For this to be possible, one requirement is that all **data values** in a column must conform to the same data format (e.g., date, text, currency). Another requirement is that each cell in a **relational table** (a row-column intersection) can contain only one value. We discuss this requirement further later in this chapter.

The tables in a relational database are linked to each other through primary and foreign keys. Recall from Chapter 4 that a **primary key attribute** consists of one or more characteristics of an entity that uniquely and universally identify each instance of the entity set. A **foreign key** is the primary key of an entity table that is "posted" (added as another column) into another entity table to represent a relationship between those entities.

Exhibit 6–1 illustrates an example of a foreign key attribute. Salesperson ID is the primary key of the Salesperson table, and is posted into the Sale table to establish a link between the Sale and Salesperson tables. Notice that the name of the attribute in the table in which it is the primary key is not required to match the name of the attribute in the table in which it is the foreign key. There is, however, a requirement called **referential integrity** that says a value for a foreign key attribute must either be null (blank) or match one of the data values in the table in which the attribute is a primary key. In the examples in Exhibit 6–1, example (a) meets referential integrity because each value for salesperson in the Sale table is either blank or it matches a data value from the Salesperson table. Example (b) in Exhibit 6–1 violates referential integrity because it includes a data value for a salesperson in the Sale table for salesperson 234567, but there is no salesperson 234567 in the Salesperson table.

Referential integrity is only one principle to which relational databases must adhere. Another important principle is that of **entity integrity.** Entity integrity says that a primary key of a relational table must not contain a **null value** (which in effect would mean it did not have a value at all). This guarantees the uniqueness of entities and enables proper referencing of primary key values by foreign key values. As an example, consider the common practice of many enterprises that use telephone numbers as identifiers for their customers. Among the

**EXHIBIT 6–1**  **Foreign Key Examples**

(a) Meets referential integrity principle

(b) Violates referential integrity principle

**Sale**

| SaleID | Date | Amount | Salesperson |
|---|---|---|---|
| 061401A | 6/14 | $4,218 | 123456 |
| 061401B | 6/14 | $6,437 | 654321 |
| 061501A | 6/15 | $1,112 | 654321 |
| 061501B | 6/15 | $3,300 | |
| 061501C | 6/15 | $1,776 | |

**Salesperson**

| SalespersonID | Name | Telephone |
|---|---|---|
| 123456 | Fred | 555-0063 |
| 654321 | Francis | 555-0007 |

**Sale**

| SaleID | Date | Amount | Salesperson |
|---|---|---|---|
| 061401A | 6/14 | $4,218 | 123456 |
| 061401B | 6/14 | $6,437 | 654321 |
| 061501A | 6/15 | $1,112 | 654321 |
| 061501B | 6/15 | $3,300 | |
| 061501C | 6/15 | $1,776 | 234567 |

**Salesperson**

| SalespersonID | Name | Telephone |
|---|---|---|
| 123456 | Fred | 555-0063 |
| 654321 | Francis | 555-0007 |

issues associated with this practice is the problem that some customers may not have telephone numbers. If a customer, Joe Smith, does not have a telephone number and telephone number is used as the primary key for the Customer table, the entity integrity principle would prohibit the enterprise from entering a row for Joe Smith in the Customer table.

A third principle to which relational databases must adhere is the **one-fact, one-place rule.** To understand this rule you must understand the definition of a **fact** as the term is used in database design. A fact in database design is the pairing of a candidate key attribute value with another attribute value. A candidate key is an attribute value that could be used as a primary key for some entity (not necessarily for the entity in whose table it exists). Because the facts consist of pairs of actual data values, one must consider the likely data entry possibilities to ensure that each fact will appear only one time. That is, facts are found in the extension (rows) of the database tables.

Consider the following Sale table, and examine each of its attributes. What attributes are candidate keys? Are any other attributes paired with a candidate key for which duplicate data are expected?

**Sale**

| SaleID | Date | Amount | CustomerID | CustomerName | CustomerAddress |
|--------|------|--------|------------|--------------|-----------------|
| 8532 | Oct. 2 | $13 | C422 | Andy | 456 Pine St. |
| 9352 | Oct. 14 | $14 | C821 | Jennifer | 987 Forest St. |
| 10215 | Oct. 27 | $20 | C363 | Arlie | 321 Beech St. |
| 14332 | Nov. 5 | $18 | C422 | Andy | 456 Pine St. |
| 17421 | Nov. 16 | $22 | C363 | Arlie | 321 Beech St. |

The two attributes that are candidate keys are SaleID (which in fact is the primary key for this table) and CustomerID, which would be the logical primary key to use for an entity set of all customers. Next examine the data in the table to see if there are any duplicate combinations of candidate keys and other attribute values. Each SaleID is unique, so there is no duplication of facts containing that attribute. However, values for CustomerID are not unique. To determine whether one fact is in multiple places we must examine whether the repeated CustomerIDs are associated with the same data values for another attribute (remember the definition of a fact is a pairing of a candidate key data value with another attribute data value). Inspection of the data reveals that every time C422 is listed as the CustomerID, Andy is listed as the customer name and 456 Pine St. is the customer address. Similarly, each time C363 is listed as the CustomerID, Arlie is listed as the customer name and 321 Beech St. is the customer address. Therefore the one-fact, one-place rule is violated in this table.

Another violation of the one-fact, one-place rule occurs when multiple facts are stored in one place. This phenomenon is commonly known as a **repeating group.** Consider the following table:

**Employee**

| EmployeeID | Name | Office | Degree Earned |
|------------|------|--------|---------------|
| 1 | Tony | Cleveland | BS,MBA |
| 2 | Emily | New York | BA,MBA,PhD |
| 3 | Leigh | Birmingham | BA |

Because employees may have earned multiple degrees, the placement of the Degree Earned attribute in the Employee table creates multiple facts in the same row. That is, there are multiple pairings of a candidate key (EmployeeID) and another attribute (Degree Earned) in at least one row. Similarly if we tried to store any other attribute (telephone number or vehicle owned) for which an employee may have multiple values, we would end up with a repeating group. To be able to retrieve and manipulate data in accordance with set theory and predicate logic, the relational model does not allow repeating groups. Therefore the preceding Employee table is not a relational table.

If we follow prescribed steps for converting a conceptual entity-relationship model into relational tables, most violations of the one-fact, one-place rule can be avoided. We present these steps and then demonstrate their application.

Step 1: Create a separate table to represent each entity in the conceptual model.

    1A: Each attribute of the entity becomes a column in the relational table.

    1B: Each instance (member) of the entity set will become a row in the relational table.

Step 2: Create a separate table to represent each many-to-many relationship in the conceptual model; that is, those relationships for which the maximum participation cardinalities are both many. (The primary key from each entity in the relationship is posted into the relationship table and the combination of those keys becomes a **concatenated primary key** for the relationship table.)

Step 3: For relationships that have a participation **cardinality pattern** of (1,1)–(1,1) consider whether the conceptual model has correctly represented the underlying reality as two separate entities or whether they should in fact be collapsed into one entity. If they are best represented as two separate entities, then follow steps 3A and 3B.

    3A: The primary key of one of the entities is posted into the related entity's table as a foreign key.

    3B: It typically does not matter which entity's primary key is posted into the other entity's table, but do not post both.

Step 4: For any of the remaining relationships that have (1,1) participation by one of the entities, post the related entity's primary key into the (1,1) entity's table as a foreign key.

When Step 4 is completed, the only remaining relationships should have (0,1) participation by one or both of the entities. These relationships take a bit more consideration to determine the best representation in relational tables. In theory, separate tables should be created to represent each of these relationships. However, for practical purposes, posted foreign keys may be used to represent many of these relationships. The decision is based on a concept called **load.** Load indicates how many data values for an attribute are expected to be non-null. A high load indicates most of the values are expected to be non-null (that is good). A low load means not very many of the values are expected to be non-null (that is bad). A goal of efficient database design is to avoid null values as much as possible, while creating as few separate tables as possible. If posting a foreign key from a related entity into a (0,1) entity will result in most data values being non-null, it is most efficient to post the foreign key rather than creating a separate table. If posting a foreign key from a related entity into a (0,1) entity will result in most data values being null, it is most efficient to create a separate table

**EXHIBIT 6–2**
**Customer-Sale**
**Relationship**
**Conceptual**
**Model**
**in Diagram**
**and Grammar**
**Formats**

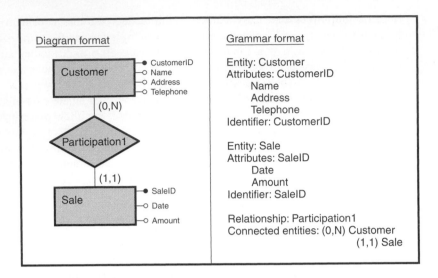

Diagram format

Customer
● CustomerID
○ Name
○ Address
○ Telephone

(0,N)

Participation1

(1,1)

Sale
● SaleID
○ Date
○ Amount

Grammar format

Entity: Customer
Attributes: CustomerID
     Name
     Address
     Telephone
Identifier: CustomerID

Entity: Sale
Attributes: SaleID
     Date
     Amount
Identifier: SaleID

Relationship: Participation1
Connected entities: (0,N) Customer
                    (1,1) Sale

to represent the relationship and post the primary keys of the related entities into the relationship table to form a concatenated primary key. Thus step 5 is stated as

Step 5:  For the remaining relationships that have (0,1) participation by one or both of the entities, consider load.

   5A:  Post the related entity's primary key into the (0,1) entity's table as a foreign key for any of the relationships for which that results in high load.

   5B:  Create a separate table for any of the relationships for which posting a foreign key results in low load.

These five steps are derived from three overall goals: One is to avoid **redundancy** (repeating groups), the second is to avoid null values, and the third is to create a minimal database (one that has as few tables as possible). Redundancy avoidance is crucial in relational database design—a table that contains redundancy is not relational and most relational database software packages will prevent entry of redundant data. The most critical rule for avoiding redundancy in converting a relationship in a conceptual model into relational format is to only allow posting of foreign keys into tables of entities that have a maximum participation of 1 in the relationship being converted. That is because by definition of the cardinalities, if the entity can participate in the relationship multiple times, then there would potentially be multiple values of a foreign key to post into the entity's table. Consider the conceptual model shown in Exhibit 6–2.

Our rules require that we create tables to represent the entities Customer and Sale, as follows:

| Customer | | | | Sale | | |
|---|---|---|---|---|---|---|
| CustomerID | Name | Address | Telephone | SaleID | Date | Amount |

Before following the remaining rules to complete this example, consider the (0,N) next to the customer entity, which communicates the reality that a customer may exist without participating in a sale (the 0 minimum) and that a customer may participate in many sales (the N maximum). If SaleID were posted as a foreign key in the Customer table, redundancy would result because by definition of the N maximum cardinality, the foreign key attribute could take on multiple values. The result would be a non-relational table. To avoid causing redundancy via the table implementation, do not post a foreign key into an entity table that has a maximum cardinality of N with respect to relationship with the foreign key's entity.

If SaleID were posted as a foreign key in the Customer table, null values would also exist in the Customer table, because by definition of the 0 minimum cardinality a customer can exist without a related sale. That leads us to the second goal: avoiding null values. To avoid null values in foreign key fields, post foreign keys only into tables of entities that have mandatory participation in the relationship of interest (i.e., a 1 minimum).

Examine the possibility of posting the primary key from the Customer entity table into the Sale entity table as a foreign key. The (1,1) next to Sale reveals that a sale cannot exist in this enterprise's database without involving a customer, and that a sale involves no more than one customer. Therefore if CustomerID is posted into the Sale table, it will not contain any null values (because of the one minimum) and it will not contain multiple values (because of the one maximum). The general rule to follow, then, is to post foreign keys into entities that have maximum participation of one and mandatory minimum participation in the relationships. Steps 2 through 5 are all derived from this general rule.

Once you realize that posting into a N maximum will (by definition of the cardinality) cause redundancy, Step 2 should be clear to you. Recall that Step 2 says to make separate tables for all many-to-many relationships. Many-to-many relationships are those for which the maximum participation cardinalities of both entities in the relationship are N. The following cardinality patterns are all many-to-many relationships: (0,N)–(0,N); (0,N)–(1,N); (1,N)–(0,N); and (1,N)–(1,N). To make sure Step 2 is clear; consider the relationship for students' declaration of academic majors shown in Exhibit 6–3. The conceptual model for this relationship communicates the information that a student can exist in the database

**EXHIBIT 6–3**
**Student-Major**
**Relationship**
**Conceptual**
**Model**
**in Diagram**
**and Grammar**
**Formats**

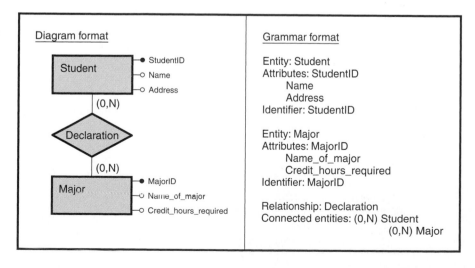

Diagram format

Student
- StudentID
- Name
- Address

(0,N)

Declaration

(0,N)

Major
- MajorID
- Name_of_major
- Credit_hours_required

Grammar format

Entity: Student
Attributes: StudentID
    Name
    Address
Identifier: StudentID

Entity: Major
Attributes: MajorID
    Name_of_major
    Credit_hours_required
Identifier: MajorID

Relationship: Declaration
Connected entities: (0,N) Student
    (0,N) Major

before declaring any major (minimum participation is 0) and that a student can declare multiple majors (maximum participation is N). It also communicates the information that a major can exist in the database before any students have declared it (minimum participation is 0) and that a major can be declared by multiple students (maximum participation is N).

Following Step 1, we create a table to represent the set of students, and another table to represent the set of majors. We have entered data into these tables to help illustrate the example.

**Student**

| StudentID | Name | Address |
|---|---|---|
| 1 | Tony | Cleveland |
| 2 | Emily | New York |
| 3 | Leigh | Birmingham |
| 4 | Abe | Illinois |

**Major**

| MajorID | Name_of_Major | Credit_Hours_Required |
|---|---|---|
| 1110 | Accounting | 183 |
| 1221 | MIS | 180 |
| 1342 | Finance | 180 |
| 2104 | Nuclear Physics | 190 |

The following set of declarations is consistent with the cardinalities:

- Tony is double-majoring in accounting and finance.
- Emily is double-majoring in accounting and MIS.
- Leigh is majoring in finance.
- Abe has not declared a major.

Notice what happens if we post MajorID into the Student table:

**Student**

| StudentID | Name | Address | MajorID |
|---|---|---|---|
| 1 | Tony | Cleveland | 1110, 1342 |
| 2 | Emily | New York | 1110, 1221 |
| 3 | Leigh | Birmingham | 1342 |
| 4 | Abe | Illinois | |

The repeating groups in MajorID represent multiple facts in one place and cause the table to be nonrelational, so we can't do that! Similarly, if we post StudentID into the Major table:

**Major**

| MajorID | Name_of_Major | Credit_Hours_Required | StudentID |
|---|---|---|---|
| 1110 | Accounting | 183 | 1, 2 |
| 1221 | MIS | 180 | 2 |
| 1342 | Finance | 180 | 1, 3 |
| 2104 | Nuclear Physics | 190 | |

The repeating groups in StudentID represent multiple facts in one place and cause the table to be non-relational, so we can't do that. Notice that it does not matter what minimum cardinalities existed for either entity. Even if there were mandatory participation for both student and major such that Abe had declared a major in nuclear physics, the repeating groups problem still exists. The correct table representation for this relationship is as follows:

**Student**

| StudentID | Name | Address |
|-----------|------|---------|
| 1 | Tony | Cleveland |
| 2 | Emily | New York |
| 3 | Leigh | Birmingham |
| 4 | Abe | Illinois |

**Major**

| MajorID | Name_of_Major | Credit_Hours_Required |
|---------|---------------|-----------------------|
| 1110 | Accounting | 183 |
| 1221 | MIS | 180 |
| 1342 | Finance | 180 |
| 2104 | Nuclear Physics | 190 |

**Declaration**

| StudentID | MajorID |
|-----------|---------|
| 1 | 1110 |
| 1 | 1342 |
| 2 | 1110 |
| 2 | 1221 |
| 3 | 1342 |

Next, let's examine Step 3 more closely. Step 3 applies to relationships with the cardinality pattern (1,1)–(1,1). The first part of the step says to consider whether the two entities are conceptually separate or whether they should be combined. Consider an enterprise that earns its revenue by setting up hot-dog stands between the hours of 11:00 A.M. and 2:00 P.M. each day that classes are in session on college campuses. The enterprise places its stands in areas where many students are likely to be walking, and likely to be hungry because no alternative food vendors are nearby. The enterprise sells hot dogs, lemonade, chips, fruit, and cookies. All sales are made on a cash basis. The food and the cash change hands simultaneously. Therefore a sale doesn't exist without a related cash receipt, and the sale only involves one cash receipt since it must be paid in full. So sale has a (1,1) participation in the relationship. Next we have to make a rather bold assumption that sales are the only source of cash for this enterprise (that is, they haven't borrowed money or obtained contributed cash from its owners). That is probably not realistic, but is within the realm of possibility as the owners could have contributed the equipment as capital instead of cash, and the enterprise could have purchased its initial inventory on credit, and then generated enough cash flow from sales to pay for the purchases and make new purchases. If we accept that possibility as the reality for this enterprise, the minimum participation of cash receipt in its relationship with sale is 1 (mandatory). It also seems reasonable to assume maximum participation of cash receipt in its relationship with sale is 1; that says that a cash receipt applies to only one sale. In this scenario, if we receive cash from a customer for a hot dog and lemonade, the cash receipt applies only to that sale.

You might be wondering whether the maximum of 1 on Sale is valid if a boyfriend and girlfriend approach the stand and the boyfriend pays for both their lunches. The hotdog vendor would view that as one sale and one cash receipt, with the boyfriend as the customer. Assume that this is a reasonable (1,1) Sale–(1,1) Cash Receipt relationship. Next it must be determined whether these two entities are conceptually separate (in the context of this enterprise) or whether they should be combined into one entity. To make this determination we must consider the future of this enterprise, allowing for reasonable possible growth, as well as the present circumstances. If we determine this enterprise will never sell lunches on credit and will never obtain cash from a source other than sales, it may be reasonable to combine them into a single entity. If we determine that someday they might obtain cash from other sources, then we should maintain them as separate entities and create separate tables for them. Note that we may determine through this analysis that our chosen cardinality pattern is not the most appropriate choice and we may decide to change the minimum cardinality of cash receipt to optional, in case in the future the enterprise wants to allow cash receipts from loans and owner contributions. If we decide to keep the entities separate, and to keep the cardinality pattern (1,1)–(1,1) then we can post a key from either entity into the other entity's table to establish the relationship in the tables. Consider the following tables, and information about the relationship.

**Sale**

| SaleID | Date | Amount |
|--------|------|--------|
| S1 | 6/5 | $4.25 |
| S2 | 6/5 | $3.75 |

**CashReceipt**

| ReceiptID | Date | Amount |
|-----------|------|--------|
| CR1 | 6/5 | $4.25 |
| CR2 | 6/5 | $3.75 |

CR1 paid for S1 and CR2 paid for S2.

Given the relationship information (notice that the relationship information is consistent with the cardinalities) we can see that if ReceiptID is posted from the CashReceipt table as a foreign key in the Sale table, it would be fine. We would have no repeating group problem and no facts stored in multiple places. Similarly we could post SaleID from the Sale table as a foreign key in the CashReceipt table without any problem. However, we must choose one or the other. If we post both foreign keys, we have created one fact (a pairing of a candidate key attribute with another attribute) in multiple places (in this case, in two different tables). Our recommendation for this particular situation is to post the ReceiptID into the Sale table because that allows the most flexibility in case of future changes in the enterprise. Thus our recommended solution is as follows:

**Sale**

| SaleID | Date | Amount | ReceiptID |
|--------|------|--------|-----------|
| S1 | 6/5 | $4.25 | CR1 |
| S2 | 6/5 | $3.75 | CR2 |

**CashReceipt**

| ReceiptID | Date | Amount |
|-----------|------|--------|
| CR1 | 6/5 | $4.25 |
| CR2 | 6/5 | $3.75 |

From these examples, Step 4 is probably clearer to you now than when we first introduced it. This step says that any remaining relationships that have (1,1) participation by one of the entities should be represented in the tables by posting the related entity's primary key into the (1,1) entity's table as a foreign key. This step covers relationships with the following cardinality patterns: (0,N)–(1,1); (1,N)–(1,1); (0,1)–(1,1); (1,1)–(0,N); (1,1)–(1,N); and (1,1)–(0,1). There is no need to make separate tables to represent any of these relationships, because posting a foreign key into an entity table with (1,1) participation guarantees that no repeating groups or null values will result. Because fewer tables make database querying easier, it is best to avoid making separate tables whenever possible.

Let's revisit the example that was presented in Exhibit 6–2, with the (0,N) Customer–(1,1) Sale relationship. Say that Frank was the customer for sale 1 and Amy was the customer for sale 2, and Frank liked what he bought in sale 1 so much that he came back the next day and bought more. That scenario fits with the cardinality pattern given. We have one customer (Dean) who exists without participating in a sale, and we have one customer (Frank) who participates in multiple sales. And sale involves one and only one customer. We can't post SaleID into Customer because it will cause a repeating group, but we can post CustomerID into Sale.

**Customer**

| CustomerID | Name | Address | Telephone | SaleID |
|------------|------|---------|-----------|--------|
| C1 | Frank | Dover | 555-9999 | S1, S3 |
| C2 | Dean | Amherst | 555-8888 | |
| C3 | Amy | Chicago | 555-7777 | S2 |

**Sale**

| SaleID | Date | Amount | CustomerID |
|--------|------|--------|------------|
| S1 | 5/21 | $40.00 | C1 |
| S2 | 5/22 | $30.00 | C3 |
| S3 | 5/22 | $80.00 | C1 |

Once again, it doesn't matter what the cardinalities are on the entity that is related to the (1,1) entity; we will always have an acceptable relational table if we post a foreign key into the table of an entity that has (1,1) participation in the relationship.

We have saved the most difficult relationships for last. Once you learn Steps 1 through 4, you will be able to apply them quickly and easily, because there is very little subjectivity involved. For Step 5 you will have to be more careful. Still, once you understand the logic to use, this step will also become straightforward.

Step 5 provides guidance for establishing relationships in tables to represent the following cardinality patterns: (0,N)–(0,1); (1,N)–(0,1); (0,1)–(0,N); (0,1)–(1,N); and (0,1)–(0,1). For each of these cardinality patterns the general rule for maximum cardinalities prohibits posting a foreign key into the table of the entity that has (1,N) or (0,N) participation in the relationship. The general rule for maximum cardinalities cannot be broken, because it will cause redundancy in the form of repeating groups. The general rule for minimum cardinalities suggests you shouldn't post a foreign key into the table of the entity that has (0,1) participation in the relationship because it will create null values in the database. Null values are undesirable because they waste space in the database (there is space reserved for the values even though they are not there). To avoid creating redundancy and to avoid creating null values, then, we would need to create separate tables to establish each of these relationships. However, creating separate tables takes up valuable space in the database, and it also makes querying more complicated. So for these cardinality patterns we need to determine which is the least wasteful of space in the database. To make that determination we evaluate a concept called load. Load refers to the number of non-null data values for an attribute. If most of the data values are non-null, the attribute is said to have a high load, or to be highly loaded. If most of the data values are null, the attribute is said to have a low load. This concept applies to any attribute, but for Step 5 we are only interested in load for potential foreign key attributes. The decision we need to make is whether posting into a (0,1) entity's table will result in more wasted space than the space creating a separate table would consume. If posting a foreign key into the (0,1) entity's table would result in only a few null values, that would waste less space than creating a separate table would take. However, if posting a foreign key would result in mostly null values, then a separate table would take less space than the posted foreign key would waste.

Consider the following example. After an enterprise makes purchases, it either pays for the merchandise (with a separate check written for each purchase) or it returns the merchandise to the vendor. The enterprise rarely returns the merchandise; most of the time the merchandise received is satisfactory and the enterprise pays for it. On average 98 out of 100 purchases are paid for and 2 out of 100 purchases result in a purchase return. Sometimes the company will return two purchases made from the same vendor as a single return. Therefore, for this company, a purchase may exist without a related purchase return (minimum 0) and may result in no more than one return (maximum 1). However a purchase return may not exist without a related purchase (minimum 1) and may result from more than one purchase (maximum N). Also, a purchase may exist without a related cash disbursement (minimum 0) and it may result in no more than one cash disbursement (maximum 1). A cash disbursement may exist without a related purchase (in inquiring of the company you discovered that approximately two-thirds of the company's checks are written for employee salaries, dividends, or loan repayments) (minimum 0) and a cash disbursement pays at most for one purchase (maximum 1). This scenario encompasses two relationships of interest for discussing load: the relationship between Purchase and Cash Disbursement and the relationship between Purchase and Purchase Return. Exhibit 6–4 presents the conceptual models of these relationships.

**EXHIBIT 6–4**    **Relationships for Evaluating Load**

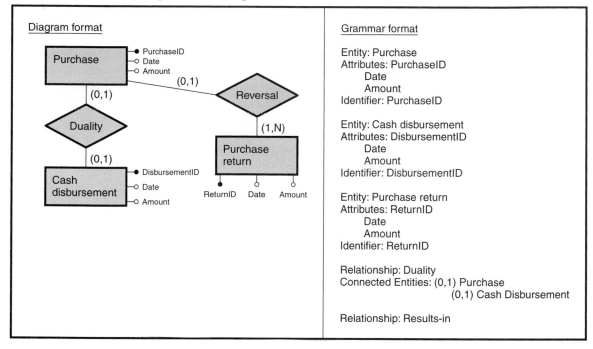

Diagram format

Grammar format

Entity: Purchase
Attributes: PurchaseID
    Date
    Amount
Identifier: PurchaseID

Entity: Cash disbursement
Attributes: DisbursementID
    Date
    Amount
Identifier: DisbursementID

Entity: Purchase return
Attributes: ReturnID
    Date
    Amount
Identifier: ReturnID

Relationship: Duality
Connected Entities: (0,1) Purchase
                      (0,1) Cash Disbursement

Relationship: Results-in

Following Step 1, we create a separate table for each of the entities:

**Purchase**

| PurchaseID | Date | Amount |
|---|---|---|

**Cash Disbursement**

| DisbursementID | Date | Amount |
|---|---|---|

**Purchase Return**

| ReturnID | Date | Amount |
|---|---|---|

Next we examine the conceptual model to determine whether any of the relationships have cardinality patterns for which guidance is provided in Steps 2 through 4. There are none. Therefore we follow the guidance for Step 5 for each of the two relationships. First we examine the *duality* relationship. Because the cardinality pattern is (0,1)–(0,1) the maximum cardinality rule would allow us to post in either direction. That is, we could post PurchaseID into the Cash Disbursement table or we could post DisbursementID into the Purchase table. However, if neither posting results in high load, we should make a separate table to avoid wasting space. We must examine the likely load if we post in each direction and then determine the most efficient solution. First let's examine what is likely to happen if we post PurchaseID into the Cash Disbursement table. We know from the information given to us previously that approximately two-thirds of the checks the company writes are for nonpurchase transactions such as employee salaries, dividends, loan repayments. That means if we post PurchaseID into the Cash Disbursement table, only one-third of the data values will be non-null. That is not a high load, so let's look at the next alternative of posting DisbursementID into the Purchase table. The information we were given revealed that the company pays for 98 out of 100 purchases. It does not matter that the payment is not made immediately; you are concerned with how many of the attribute's data values will eventually be non-null; 98 percent is a high load, so the best solution for this relationship is to post the DisbursementID into the Purchase table. The Purchase table will be changed to

**Purchase**

| PurchaseID | Date | Amount | DisbursementID |
|------------|------|--------|----------------|

The Cash Disbursement and Purchase Return tables remain as shown on the previous page. In the Purchase table, for 2 out of every 100 records, DisbursementID will be blank (null) thus there are only two wasted cells of space for every 100 purchase records. If we had chosen to post PurchaseID into Cash Disbursement, we would have had approximately 66 wasted cells of space for every 100 cash disbursement records. If we had chosen to create a separate table to represent the relationship, we would have added a table as follows:

**Duality**

| PurchaseID | DisbursementID |
|------------|----------------|

For every 100 purchases, there will be 98 records added to this relationship table, as opposed to filling in 98 data values in the DisbursementID field in the Purchase table. This latter approach thus wastes 98 cells of space for every 100 purchase records (the PurchaseID is entered 98 times more in this example than in the **posted key** example). This analysis leads us to believe the DisbursementID posted into the Purchase table is the best solution.

Next we examine the Reversal relationship. Because the cardinality pattern is (0,1) Purchase–(1,N) Purchase Return, the only alternatives we need to compare are that of posting Purchase Return into Purchase versus creating a separate table. The maximum cardinality rule prohibits us from posting PurchaseID into Purchase Return since by definition a purchase return may have resulted from more than one purchase and would cause a repeating group. The information we were given revealed that 2 out of 100 purchases end up being returned. That is a very low load, so if we post ReturnID into the Purchase table nearly all the data values for that attribute will be null. That approach would waste 98 cells of space for every 100 purchase records. The best solution in this case is to create a separate table to represent the Reversal relationship. The relationship table will be established as follows (in addition to the original Purchase and Purchase Return tables):

**Reversal**

| PurchaseID | ReturnID |
|---|---|

For every 100 records entered in the Purchase table, 2 records will be added to this table. This approach in effect wastes only two cells of space for every 100 purchase transactions (because the PurchaseID is entered two more times than in the posted key example). Thus for the Reversal relationship, the separate table is the best approach for establishing the relationship in relational table form.

# RELATIONSHIP ATTRIBUTE PLACEMENT

As you are representing conceptual model relationships in the relational tables, you may wonder where you should place attributes of relationships. Most of the time relationships that have attributes of their own are many-to-many relationships. Recall that separate tables must be created to represent many-to-many relationships. The relationship attributes for many-to-many relationships must be placed in the relationship table; otherwise redundancy occurs. Consider the relationship between Student and Course shown in Exhibit 6–5.

Our first rule requires that we make a separate table for Student and a separate table for Course. Our cardinality-based conversion rules require that a separate table be created to represent the Takes relationship. Exhibit 6–6 displays the initial table structures.

If the attribute Grade earned were placed in the Student table, what would happen when data are entered for the grades earned by Mildred in ACG 611 and in MIS 650? There would be only one cell available to hold two data values. If the attribute were placed in the Course table, what would happen when data are entered for the grades earned by Mildred

**EXHIBIT 6–5**
**Student-**
**Course**
**Relationship**
**Conceptual**
**Model**
**in Diagram**
**and Grammar**
**Formats**

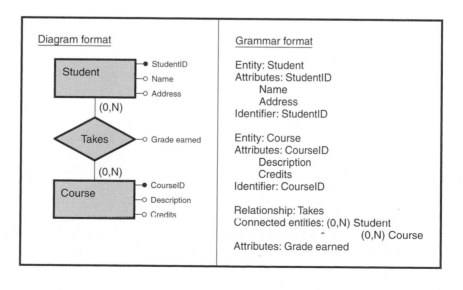

Diagram format

Student — • StudentID
— ○ Name
— ○ Address

(0,N)

Takes — ○ Grade earned

(0,N)

Course — • CourseID
— ○ Description
— ○ Credits

Grammar format

Entity: Student
Attributes: StudentID
  Name
  Address
Identifier: StudentID

Entity: Course
Attributes: CourseID
  Description
  Credits
Identifier: CourseID

Relationship: Takes
Connected entities: (0,N) Student
  (0,N) Course
Attributes: Grade earned

**EXHIBIT 6–6**
**Relational Tables for Student-Takes-Course Model**

**Student**

| StudentID | Name | Address |
|---|---|---|
| 999888 | Mildred | 123 Almanac St. |
| 888777 | Kent | 456 Market Dr. |
| 777666 | Candace | 789 Harriet Ave. |

**Course**

| CourseID | Description | Credits |
|---|---|---|
| ACG611 | Advanced AIS | 3 |
| FIN642 | Financial Markets | 3 |
| MIS650 | IT Management | 3 |

**Takes**

| StudentID | CourseID | Grade Earned |
|---|---|---|
| 999888 | ACG611 | B |
| 999888 | MIS650 | A– |
| 888777 | MIS650 | B+ |

and Kent in MIS 650? Again, there would be only one cell available to hold two data values. The correct placement of the attribute is in the Takes table.

Sometimes a relationship that has an attribute may not be a many-to-many relationship. Consider the following situation:

> An enterprise manufactures and sells inventory items that are specifically identified and tracked via serial numbers. The enterprise deals only with new inventory items—that is, it never repurchases and sells the same inventory item again. The enterprise does not sell anything except these individually identified inventory items. A sale may involve multiple items. The enterprise expects to sell every item that it manufactures. Attributes the enterprise needs to include in its database include the inventory's ItemID, description, and date manufactured; the sale number, date, and dollar amount; and the actual sale price for an inventory item on a sale transaction.

A conceptual model to represent this reality is displayed in Exhibit 6–7.

To convert this model into relational table format, the first step is to create a table for each entity. Next, because the cardinality pattern fits the rules for Step 5, a decision must be made as to whether load would be high enough to justify posting the primary key from the Sale table into the Inventory table as a primary key. Because the enterprise expects all inventory items to eventually be sold, any null values are expected to be temporary and load should be very high. If the relationship is represented with a foreign key, though, what becomes of the relationship attribute? It gets posted along with the foreign key. In this example, although actual sale price describes the relationship—because it can't be determined without knowing both the item and the sale—it doesn't cause any redundancy problem if it is posted into the Inventory table, and the null values that occur for any items that have not yet been sold are only temporarily null. In Exhibit 6–8 we illustrate this table design.

**EXHIBIT 6–7**
**Specific Inventory-Sale Conceptual Model in Diagram and Grammar Formats**

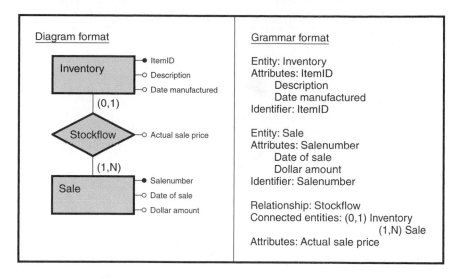

Diagram format

Grammar format

Entity: Inventory
Attributes: ItemID
 Description
 Date manufactured
Identifier: ItemID

Entity: Sale
Attributes: Salenumber
 Date of sale
 Dollar amount
Identifier: Salenumber

Relationship: Stockflow
Connected entities: (0,1) Inventory
 (1,N) Sale
Attributes: Actual sale price

**EXHIBIT 6–8**
**Relational Tables for (0,1) Inventory— (1,N) Sale Example**

**Inventory**

| ItemID | Description | Date Manufactured | Salenumber | Actual Sale Price |
|--------|-------------|-------------------|------------|-------------------|
| I1 | Big blue item | 9/24/05 | 1 | $450 |
| I2 | Triangle green item | 9/25/05 | 1 | $375 |
| I3 | Small square item | 9/26/05 | | |
| I4 | Medium pink item | 9/27/05 | 2 | $500 |

**Sale**

| Salenumber | Date | Dollar Amount |
|------------|------|---------------|
| S1 | 10/12/05 | $825 |
| S2 | 10/15/05 | $500 |

# PHYSICAL IMPLEMENTATION OF RELATIONAL MODEL IN MICROSOFT ACCESS

Once the relational tables are established on paper, forming a logical model, the model may be implemented into physical form using a particular database software package. Microsoft Access is used in this chapter to demonstrate the conversion of a logical model to a physical model. Keep in mind that the procedures are similar but not exactly the same with other relational database software packages. This chapter does not provide you with comprehensive assistance on every aspect of Access. Instead it provides you with an introduction to creating tables in Access and communicating information to Access about the links between the tables (i.e., telling Access which primary keys are posted into other tables as foreign keys or as parts of concatenated primary keys). If you need additional Access instructions, you may use the electronic help facility provided in Access or use an Access reference manual. To get to

**EXHIBIT 6–9**
**Finding Help in Microsoft Access**

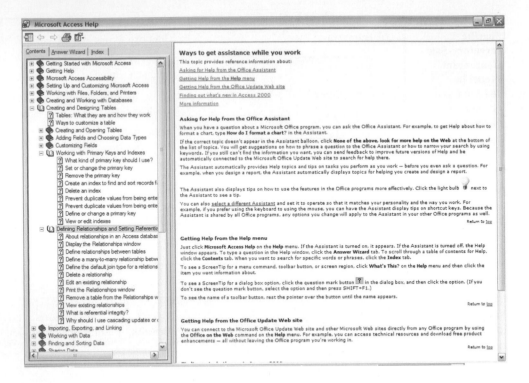

the appropriate area of the help facility, once Access is open, click on Help in the top menu bar, then click on the Contents tab. The areas within help that you are most likely to need for this chapter are under the category Creating and Designing Tables (see Exhibit 6–9) and include Creating and Opening Tables, Adding Fields and Choosing Data Types, Working with Primary Keys and Indexes, and Defining Relationships and Setting Referential Integrity Options. See Exhibit 6–9 to see what this Help Screen looks like.

## Creating and Working with Databases

To enter tables in Microsoft Access, you must create a database file in which to store the tables. For those of you who have used other Microsoft software products, notice that this is different from some of those products. In Microsoft Word or Excel, you may begin creating content in a blank document or spreadsheet and then save it to a file later. Microsoft Access requires you to create a file (and name it) before entering any tables or data. Additions and changes are then automatically saved as Microsoft Access accepts them.

When you start Microsoft Access, a window appears in which you specify whether you want to create a new database using a blank database or a database wizard, or whether you want to open an existing database. (See Exhibit 6–10.)

When you are using Microsoft Access in conjunction with materials in this textbook, do not use any wizards. These wizards have certain defaults built into them. To effectively use the wizards you must understand all the defaults they use and you must know when and how to override them. We do not cover any of that in this book, so we caution you not to use wizards at all, or to use them at your own risk.

**EXHIBIT 6–10**
**Create a**
**Database Using**
**Blank Access**
**Database**

**EXHIBIT 6–11**
**Creating or**
**Opening a**
**Database File**

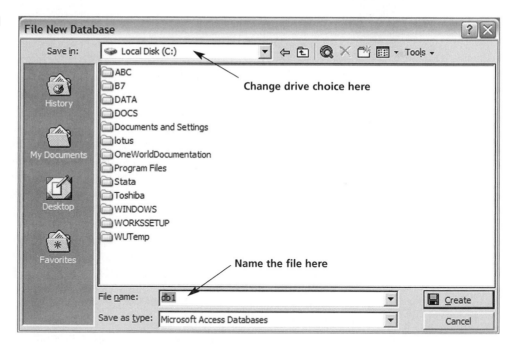

Once you tell Access to open a blank database, you are required to name the database before you can enter any tables or data into it. You may choose to store your database on any of your computer drives. To specify the disk drive on which you want your database to be stored, change the Save in location to your drive choice. Note that to get back to your database the next time you want to use it, you will open an existing database, click on more files and change the Look in location to the same drive choice. See Exhibit 6–11.

**EXHIBIT 6–12**
**Microsoft**
**Access**
**Database**
**Window**

When you create or open an existing database, Microsoft Access displays the Database Window. This is a container for objects stored in the database, including tables, queries, forms, reports, pages, macros, and modules. For this chapter we focus only on tables.

To create a new table, select the table object by clicking on Tables in the left menu bar. (See Exhibit 6–12.) Notice that you have the options of creating a table in **design view,** by using a wizard, or by entering data. If you use design view you have control over all choices that need to be made during table creation.

To open an existing table, make sure Tables is selected as the object type in the left menu bar. A list of all available tables appears; simply double-click on the object you want to open. In Exhibit 6–12 there are no existing tables, so the only choice is to create one.

To begin, double-click on Create table in Design view. This displays a screen with two sections, as shown in Exhibit 6–13.

Section 1 shows the overall layout of the table. The fields (attributes) of the table are listed on the left; in the middle column you can choose the appropriate **data type** for each field (e.g., text, currency, date, or number). The right column provides space for the table designer to write a description of what that field represents. The description may be left blank, and we suspect in most databases most of the descriptions are left blank because, unfortunately, people generally don't take the time or see the need for documenting their system design.

In Section 2 (the field properties panel) you may set additional properties for each field, such as the field size, customized format, default value (the value to be used if the user doesn't enter a value), validation rules, or a specification as to whether the field is required

**EXHIBIT 6–13**

Microsoft
Access Table
Design View

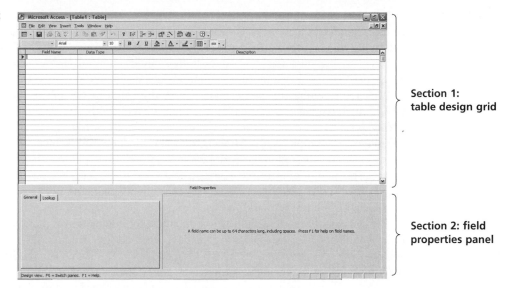

Section 1:
table design grid

Section 2: field
properties panel

to contain data (or whether it's okay for it to have blank values). The panel in Section 2 changes based on which field the cursor is pointed to in Section 1. That is because the field properties for one field can be different from the properties for a different field.

We will work through two examples to give you some experience with creating physical implementations in Access of relational logical models. You may want to work through these examples on a computer as you read the rest of this chapter. (If you have not been working along up to this point, catch yourself up by creating a new blank database, then creating a new table so that your screen resembles Exhibit 6–13). The first model we will implement is the logical model illustrated in Exhibit 6–1(a). This model consists of two tables: Sale and Salesperson.

### Example 1: Creating and Connecting Entity Tables

To create the Sale table, enter the four fields (SaleID, Date, Amount, and Salesperson) in the left column. You may have noticed that Access set a default data type as Text. Move to the middle column and change each data type to its appropriate value. Click on the arrowhead next to Text and a popup list of choices will appear. A good rule of thumb to use when determining appropriate data types is if it isn't a date, and you don't need to be able to perform calculations with it, then set it as text; if you do need to perform calculations with it, then set it as currency if it is a dollar value and as a number if it is not a dollar value. That rule is obviously simplified, but it works well for most situations. For our example, we will specify SaleID as Text, Date as Date, Amount as Currency, and Salesperson as Text. Notice the field properties panel changes as you click from one field to the next in the top section, but don't change anything in the field properties section yet. You may wonder why we used Text for Salesperson, when all the data values we have are numeric. Go back to the rule of thumb. Are we likely to need to calculate anything based on the salesperson ID? No. And it is possible that someday we may start adding letters into our salesperson IDs, so we are better off specifying the type as text.

Now let's think about the field properties section, but without going into detail on most of these settings. One thing you need to be aware of with respect to field properties (and data type, which is also a **field property**) is that if the properties of two fields are different, then Access considers the values in those fields to be different even if the content is the same. Why is that important? Think about posted foreign keys. In our example, the identification number for salesperson is a field in both of our tables. In the Salesperson table (which we haven't yet made) it is the primary key. In the Sale table (which we are currently creating) it is a foreign key. Now, recall from earlier in this chapter the referential integrity principle that relational databases are supposed to meet. That principle said for a data value entered in the Salesperson field in the Sale table to be acceptable, it must either be blank or it must match exactly a data value in the SalespersonID field in the Salesperson table. This means we must be very careful with changing field properties, especially for fields that are primary and foreign keys.

For learning the basics in this textbook, our recommendation is that the only field properties you change for any fields are the data type and the "Required?" field property that specifies whether data entry in the field is mandatory. The data entry requirement property for a field determines whether null values are allowed or not. Therefore you must know something about the enterprise's business rules to make this decision. This is especially important for foreign keys, as in many cases the cardinalities are manifestations of business rules and the degrees of cardinalities are reflected in foreign key postings. For the Exhibit 6–1 example, we did not start with a conceptual model so we don't immediately know cardinality information. But we can figure out the cardinalities from the information given. We know that Sale's participation in the relationship is (0,1). How do we know this? We have null values for Salesperson in the Sale table, so that indicates a sale can exist without a related salesperson (minimum = 0). And because Salesperson is posted into Sale as a foreign key, it cannot have more than one value (maximum = 1). Do we know Salesperson's participation cardinalities for this relationship? From the data in these tables we note that we currently have no salespeople in our database who do not yet have a related sale. But common sense would tell us that we need to enter new salespeople in our database when they are hired, at which point we would not have expected them to have already made a sale. So we assume the minimum is 0. We know for sure that the maximum is N, because we have a salesperson who has made multiple sales (Francis). In our example, then, neither entity has mandatory participation in the relationship, so we need not change the requirement property to yes for any of the fields. [To test your understanding: What if we determined that a sale cannot exist without a salesperson and we change the minimum cardinality on Sale in its relationship with Salesperson to 1? Then in the Sale table we would need to set the **required data entry** property of the Salesperson field to Yes.]

Getting back to our example from Exhibit 6–1 (with no mandatory participation), we have no need to change any field properties other than the data types, which we already changed. At this point, your table design should look like Exhibit 6–14 (ignore the arrows until you read the next paragraph).

Next we need to communicate to Access which field is the primary key of the Sale table. In our case it is the SaleID. To give this information to Access, we must highlight the SaleID field (click on the small gray box to the immediate left of the field) and then click on the icon that looks like a small key. The arrows on Exhibit 6–14 show you how. Once you do this, you will notice a small key symbol appear in the gray box to the immediate

**EXHIBIT 6–14**
**Sale Table**
**Design**

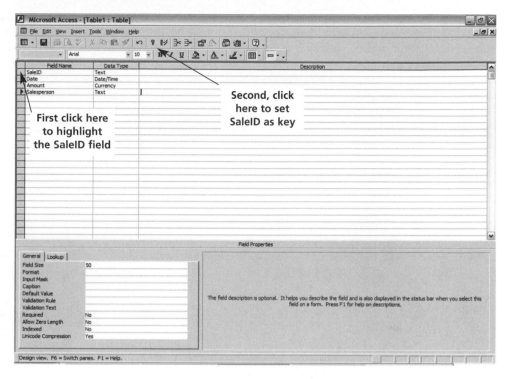

left of the SaleID field. For the moment, we are finished with the Sale table's design, so we need to save the table. You may either choose File, Save from the top menu bar, or click on the icon with the diskette symbol on it. Name the table Sale and then close the table. You will notice that your **database window** now contains a table object called Sale.

Next create the Salesperson table, following similar steps. From the database window, double-click on Create table in Design view. Enter the three fields: SalespersonID, Name, and Telephone. None of these are dates, and none are fields that would likely be part of a calculation, so don't change the data type or any field properties. Set SalespersonID as the primary key. Save the table, giving it the name Salesperson, and close the table. Your database window should now resemble Exhibit 6–15.

Did you notice that we left out one very important piece of information in what we communicated to Access in designing these tables? No, we are not talking about the entry of data values into the tables, although that certainly also needs to be done. We are talking about needing to specify to Access how the tables are linked together. At this point, Access understands that we have a table representing an entity called Sale and Access understands that we have a table representing an entity called Salesperson, but it doesn't have a clue that there is a relationship between Sale and Salesperson. Recall that we established that relationship in our logical model by posting Salesperson as a foreign key into the Sale table. But we have done nothing to differentiate that attribute from any of the other attributes in the Sale table. To Access it looks like just another attribute. We could, of course, type "foreign key from Salesperson table" in the description area for that field (and for system

**EXHIBIT 6–15**

**Database
Window
after Designing
Sale and
Salesperson
Tables**

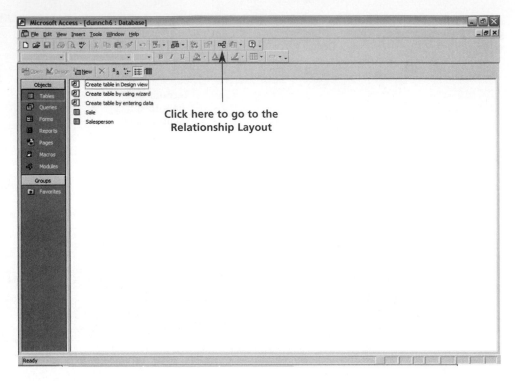

documentation purposes that is a very good thing to do). However, Access doesn't understand natural language and doesn't do any processing based on information in description cells. The way to communicate foreign keys (and composite primary keys that are formed from posting two different entities' primary keys into a relationship table) to Access is by establishing a relationship between the two tables. To do this, go to Access's "Relationship Layout" by clicking on the icon that has three boxes connected by two lines (see arrow in Exhibit 6–15).

The screen that initially appears when you open the **relationship layout** is the Show Table window (see Exhibit 6–16). This screen only appears if there are no tables already in the relationship layout.

Highlight both tables and add them to the layout by clicking Add after they are both highlighted. Then close the Show Table window (but leave the relationship layout window open). Your relationship layout should look like Exhibit 6–17.

Note that you may move a table around on the layout by clicking on its titlebar and dragging it to the desired location. Sometimes you may also resize the table windows within the layout if you want to see all the fields. Next you need to explain to Access that you posted a foreign key. To do this, start with your cursor on SalespersonID in the Salesperson table. Click and drag the cursor to Salesperson in the Sale table. Make sure you drag to the matching field!

When you drop the primary key onto the matching foreign key to which you dragged it, Access will display an "Edit Relationships" window, as shown in Exhibit 6–18.

This window allows you to verify that you are establishing the relationship between the

**EXHIBIT 6–16**
Show Table
Window

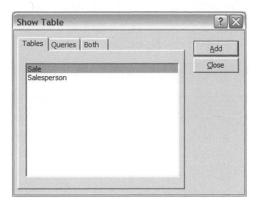

**EXHIBIT 6–17**
Relationship
Layout
with Tables
Added

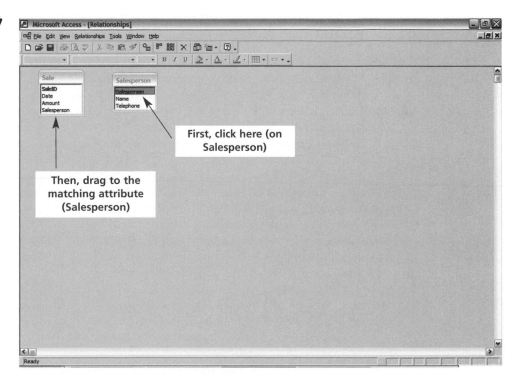

correct two attributes (the attribute that is the primary key in one table and the attribute that is the posted foreign key value in the other table). This window also allows you to **enforce referential integrity** by clicking on the check box next to that phrase. Remember that principle? Note that Microsoft Access does not require that this principle be enforced. That tells you that Access allows you to create databases that are not fully relational. This can cause serious problems with querying if users are not well-trained and very careful. For purposes of this textbook, always enforce referential integrity. You also have the option of setting updates in the primary key field to cascade to also update the related field, and

**EXHIBIT 6–18**
Edit
Relationships
Window

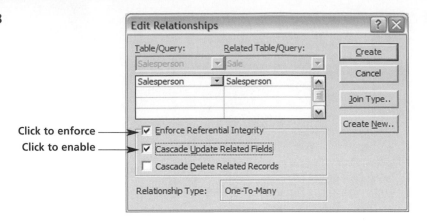

of setting deletions of the record that is represented by the primary key to cascade to also delete records in which it was a participant. The first option is usually a good option, because if you change a customer ID you want it to be changed in all appropriate places. The second option is very dangerous, because you don't want to unintentionally lose data that you may later need.

One important note regarding cascade updates: Many people get the false impression that enabling this option causes data entry of new primary key values to automatically become entered into the related foreign key fields. That cannot happen, because Access doesn't have any way of knowing which particular records in the table in which the foreign key is posted are related to the record in the table from which the foreign key is posted until the data are actually entered. In our sales-salesperson example, when we enter records into the Sale table, Access can't possibly know which salesperson made the sale unless we tell it which one made the sale by entering the value of the foreign key. Notice that simply adding a salesperson to the Salesperson table does not inform Access as to which sales the salesperson has made and will make in the future. However, once you have created a link between the fields themselves by establishing the relationship, enabling cascade updates, and entering common data into the primary and foreign key fields, if you were to decide to renumber salesperson 123456 to be 1234560, when you change that primary key data value in the Salesperson table, the change will flow through and change all the foreign key values that are 123456 to 1234560.

After enforcing referential integrity and enabling cascade updates, click on "Create" to establish the relationship. The relationship layout appears, and now displays the relationship you just created, as shown in Exhibit 6–19.

Although the relationship layout resembles an entity-relationship diagram, it is not! Remember, the only purpose for the relationship layout is to communicate to Access information about posted key relationships. Because decisions about posting keys to implement relationships are made based on cardinalities, there are some resemblances between an ER diagram and the Access relationship layout notation. Notice that when you created the relationship between Sale and Salesperson, some notation appeared on the relationship. A 1 appears beside the SalespersonID in the Salesperson table and an infinity sign appears beside the Salesperson in the Sale table. The 1 beside SalespersonID in the Salesperson table

**EXHIBIT 6–19**
Relationship
Layout

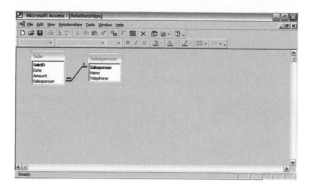

simply means that a particular data value for that attribute (e.g., Salesperson 654321) can appear in that table a maximum of one time. That makes sense given that it is the primary key and a primary key cannot have duplicate values! The infinity sign beside Salesperson in the Sale table indicates that a particular data value for that attribute can appear in that table multiple times (e.g., Salesperson 654321 made multiple sales and can appear in the Sale table multiple times).

### *Example 2: Creating and Connecting Relationship Tables to Entity Tables*

The second example demonstrates the physical implementation of the tables from Exhibit 6–6 that resulted from the many-to-many conceptual model relationship between Student and Course. To begin, create a new blank database following the steps in Exhibits 6–10 and 6–11. Following the same basic procedure that was illustrated in Exhibits 6–12 through 6–14, add two new tables in design view. One should be named Student, and should include the following fields: StudentID (text, primary key), Name (text), Address (text). The other should be named Course, and should include the following fields: CourseID (text, primary key), Description (text), and Credits (number). Next, create another new table in design view and include the following fields: StudentID (text), CourseID (text), and Grade earned (text). For this third table a primary key needs to be specified, but in this example it is a concatenated primary key made up of both StudentID and CourseID. To represent this in Access, click on the gray box immediately to the left of Student ID. Hold the shift key and click on the gray box immediately to the left of Course ID. If you did this correctly, the rows for those two fields are now highlighted. With those rows highlighted, click on the icon that looks like a key. Keys should appear in the gray boxes next to the field names as illustrated in Exhibit 6–20.

Name the table Takes. Next add the Student, Course, and Takes tables to the relationship layout following the same basic procedure used in Exhibit 6–16. Recall that the relationship layout is used to inform Access as to the existence of primary keys that are posted into other tables either as foreign keys or as parts of concatenated primary keys. Therefore you need to tell Access you posted the primary keys from Student and Course into the Takes table to form its concatenated primary key. To do this you simply click on StudentID in the Student table and drag the cursor to StudentID in the Takes table, similar to what was done in Exhibit 6–17. When you release the mouse, the Edit Relationships window appears, as it did in Exhibit 6–18. Check the appropriate boxes to enforce referential integrity and enable

**EXHIBIT 6–20**
Specifying a
Concatenated
Primary Key
in Microsoft
Access

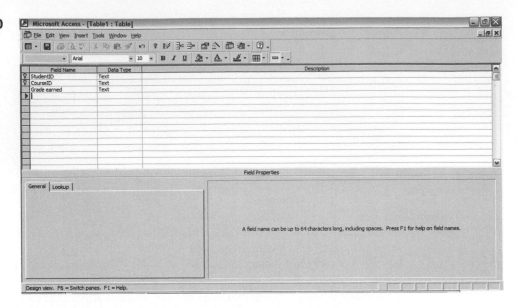

cascade updates, similar to what you did for Exhibit 6–18. Click on OK. A join line should appear connecting StudentID in the Student table to StudentID in the Takes table. Next click on CourseID in the Course table and drag the cursor to CourseID in the Takes table and check the boxes in the Edit Relationships window to enforce referential integrity and enable cascade updates. Your relationship layout should resemble Exhibit 6–21.

## Deleting Existing Relationships

What if you make a mistake and create a relationship you didn't really want? Open the relationship layout. Single-click the line for the relationship you want to delete *(make sure it's highlighted),* and then press the delete key. Notice that you must delete the relationship itself, not just one table that was part of the relationship. If you delete a table from the relationship layout (by selecting the table and pressing the delete key) the relationship will appear to be gone. However, if you click on Relationships on the top menu bar and then Show All you will see that the relationship was retained in Access's memory. Similarly, if you are frustrated with your layout and decide you want to start over, you may notice an icon that looks like a red X that is the Clear Layout icon. Beware! The layout will be cleared, but all the relationships are still in Access's memory so you have not deleted them. As soon as you click on Relationships, Show All they will be back. If you want to delete relationships from your layout you must highlight each relationship and press the delete key. Access will ask you if you really want to permanently delete the relationship, to which you would reply yes. If Access didn't ask you that question, then you didn't delete the relationship!

## Entering Data into Microsoft Access Tables

Once all of your tables are created and you have verified that the relationship layout correctly communicates the posted key information, you are ready to begin entering data into the tables. Two views exist for entering data into a table: **datasheet view** and form view.

**EXHIBIT 6–21**
**Relationship Table Linked to Two Entity Tables**

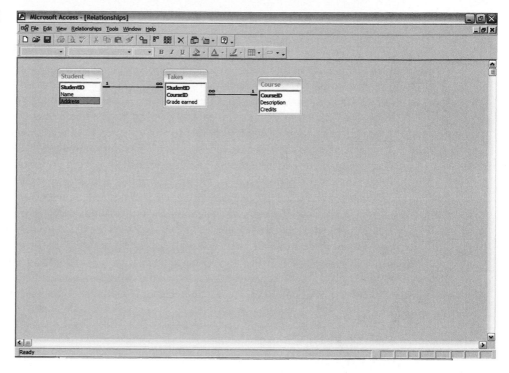

We only discuss datasheet view in this chapter; that is the standard row-column format that most people are used to, and which is available in most relational database packages.

Enter the appropriate data records, using the TAB key to move between fields. You can also use the mouse to move the cursor to a desired field or record. As you tab out of one record to another record, the software automatically saves the record, displaying an error message if it was unable to save the record because of a data entry problem (such as violations of referential integrity). Often, you may see a pencil icon in the left, gray column. The pencil indicates the current record (the one being pointed to in memory). After you finish adding records, choose File, Close from the main menu. Experiment with the arrow keys at the bottom of the table window. They allow you to view different fields and records. Don't worry about entering data in alpha or numeric order. The computer sorts the data via the primary key attribute field.

Keep in mind that if you have enforced referential integrity (as you should have) and established mandatory data entry for appropriate fields (e.g., foreign keys posted into a (1,1) entity table), you must be careful about the order in which you enter the data. Consider the cardinalities in your underlying conceptual model and picture the company's reality in your mind. Think about what order the data would be entered in real life. Generally information about resources and agents is input to corporate databases before any transactions involving them occur. So you should enter your resource and agent data before you enter your event data and relationship data. If you encounter error messages while you are entering data, pay attention to them and try to figure out whether you are entering the data incorrectly or whether you have a flaw in your table design or in your relationship layout that needs to be fixed before you proceed with data entry.

# CONCLUDING COMMENTS

In this chapter you have learned how to take a conceptual representation (on paper) of an enterprise's reality and convert it, first into a logical set of relational tables (on paper) and then into a physical implementation of relational tables using Microsoft Access software. You also learned how to enter data into the tables. In the next chapter, you will learn something about what you can do with data after it has been entered into a relational database. For it is in the querying capabilities that the real power of the relational database is found. When you start on that chapter, please do not forget all that you learned in this chapter. A solid understanding of table design is foundational for a solid understanding of querying. A solid understanding of querying is foundational for retrieval of valid data, which in turn is crucial for sound decision making. Perhaps it is now becoming clear to you (if it wasn't already clear) why all enterprise system users (that is, anyone who might someday form an ad hoc query of a relational database) must understand the basics of relational database design. Hopefully seeing the translation of the conceptual models into an actual working database has helped clarify some of the concepts that we covered in Chapters 2 through 4 by making them more concrete. You may find it worthwhile to go back and reread those chapters now that you have a better understanding of the end result.

## Key Terms and Concepts

### General Terms and Concepts

Attribute, *122*
Cardinality pattern, *125*
Column, *122*
Concatenated primary key, *125*
Conceptual database model, *122*
Data value, *123*
Entity integrity, *123*
Extension, *122*
Fact, *124*

Field, *122*
Foreign key, *123*
Intension, *122*
Load (high and low), *125*
Logical model, *122*
Null value, *123*
One-fact, one-place role, *124*
Physical database model, *122*
Posted key, *134*

Primary key attribute, *123*
Record, *122*
Redundancy, *126*
Referential integrity, *123*
Relational database, *122*
Relational model, *122*
Relational table, *123*
Repeating group, *124*
Row, *122*
Schema, *122*
Tuple, *122*

### Microsoft Access Terms and Concepts

Data type (field property), *140*
Database window, *143*
Datasheet view, *148*

Design view, *140*
Enforce referential integrity, *145*

Field property, *142*
Relationship layout, *144*
Required data entry (field property), *142*

## Review Questions

LO4  R1.  What type of data does each record in an event table contain?

LO4  R2.  What type of data does each record in a resource table contain?

LO4    R3.    What type of data does each record in an agent table contain?

LO1    R4.    What is the purpose of a foreign key?

LO1    R5.    Does every table in a relational database contain a foreign key? Explain.

LO4    R6.    What tables are needed to perform a recording information process?

LO4    R7.    What tables are needed to perform a maintenance information process?

LO3    R8.    What are the differences between conceptual, logical, and physical database models?

LO7    R9.    What is referential integrity, and how do you enforce referential integrity in Microsoft Access?

LO7    R10.    What does it mean to set a field property to require data entry? Is that the same thing as referential integrity? If not, what is the purpose for setting a field property to require data entry?

## Multiple Choice Questions

LO3    MC1.    Which of the following is not a typically developed database design?
A. Physical
B. Logical
C. Canonical
D. Conceptual

LO1    MC2.    A relational table has a row with data but a missing primary key; this violates:
A. Referential integrity
B. Entity integrity
C. One-fact, one-place
D. No violation

LO2    MC3.    What is the name of an attribute stored as a formula to allow data computations?
A. Trojans
B. Independent contributors
C. Triggers
D. Participants

LO1    MC4.    Load indicates:
A. The capacity of the database
B. The dollar amounts of the data
C. Null values
D. How many data values for an attribute are expected to be non-null

LO1    MC5.    Creating separate tables to represent relationships helps to avoid:
A. Redundancy
B. Non-null values
C. Null values
D. Both A and C above.

## Discussion Questions

LO1    D1.    Say you are trying to create relational database tables to implement a conceptual model that has a relationship (0,1) Sale–duality–(0,N) Cash Receipt. You have created a table for Sale and a table for Cash Receipt. You are considering whether to post a foreign key from Cash Receipt into Sale. You have the following information available. Explain whether each of these statements adds to the knowledge you already had and how each affects your decision as to whether to post the foreign key. If you decide not to post a foreign key from Cash receipt into Sale, what other choices do you have for implementing this relationship in the relational tables?

- Nearly all of this enterprise's sales are made on credit.
- The enterprise very rarely has any bad debts resulting from sales.
- Nearly all of this enterprise's cash receipts apply to sales.

LO1 D2. In creating relational tables we have three objectives. Explain what these objectives are, and how we attempt to meet them in converting a conceptual model into relational tables. Do any of these objectives contradict each other, and if so, to which do we give precedence?

LO1 D3. Explain the rule used to create relational database tables from a conceptual model relationship that has the cardinality pattern (0,N)–(0,N). How should the relationship be implemented and why does it need to be implemented that way? Does the rule differ if either or both of the minimum cardinalities are changed to 1?

LO1 D4. Explain the rule used to create relational database tables from a conceptual model relationship that has the cardinality pattern (0,N)–(1,1). How should the relationship be implemented and why is it best implemented that way? Are there any other choices for implementing the relationship? What if the pattern is changed to (1,N)–(1,1);

**EXHIBIT 6–22**

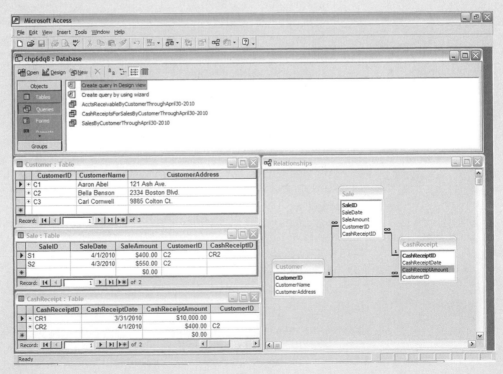

would you implement the relationship differently? What if the cardinality pattern is (1,1)–(0,N) or (1,1)–(1,N)?

LO1   D5. What should be your first consideration if you encounter a relationship with a cardinality pattern (1,1)–(1,1) and why? What choices do you have for implementing the relationship into relational tables and how will you decide which is the most appropriate implementation?

LO2   D6. When creating a physical relational database implementation, what should you do with derivable attributes? Does your answer differ for static derivable attributes versus volatile derivable attributes? Does the particular database software being used affect your choice? Explain.

LO4   D7. Is the following statement true or false? Explain your answer: "Recording an event only involves adding one record to an event table."

LO5, LO6   D8. Inspect the physical database components implemented in Microsoft Access as displayed in Exhibit 6–22. Construct the likely underlying logical and conceptual models.

LO6   D9. Inspect the following logical relational database tables. Construct the likely underlying conceptual model.

**Library Book Loan Event**

| LoanID | Date | Time |
|--------|------|------|
| L1 | 1/21/2010 | 8:32 |
| L2 | 1/21/2010 | 8:37 |
| L3 | 1/21/2010 | 8:48 |

**Library Book Renewal Event**

| RenewID | Date | Time |
|---------|------|------|
| R1 | 2/7/2010 | 9:10 |
| R2 | 2/8/2010 | 8:20 |
| R3 | 2/28/2010 | 12:40 |

**Loan-Renewal**

| LoanID | RenewID |
|--------|---------|
| L1 | R1 |
| L1 | R3 |
| L3 | R2 |

LO6   D10. Inspect the following logical relational database tables. Assuming the tables were created correctly and that entered data are complete and accurate, what must have been the minimum and maximum participation cardinalities of the Inventory Type entity in the Stockflow relationship?

**Inventory Type**

| ItemID | Description | Unit Cost |
|--------|-------------|-----------|
| I1 | Heart pin | $4.59 |
| I2 | Topaz ring | $22.35 |
| I3 | Diamond pendant | $332.50 |

**Stockflow**

| ItemID | SaleID | Quantity Sold |
|--------|--------|---------------|
| I1 | S1 | 20 |
| I2 | S1 | 5 |
| I2 | S2 | 10 |

# Applied Learning

LO4   A1. Use the following partial database tables to answer the required questions:

## Sales Event Table

| Sales Event # | Date | Terms | Salesperson ID | Customer ID |
|---|---|---|---|---|
| 1 | 11/5 | 2 10, net 30 | 2 | 2543 |
| 2 | 11/5 | 2 10, net 30 | 4 | 635 |
| 3 | 11/5 | COD | 6 | 1845 |

## Sale-Inventory Table

| Sale Event # | Inventory Item # | Inventory Quantity | Price each |
|---|---|---|---|
| 1 | 876 | 10 | 1.25 |
| 1 | 674 | 8 | 0.875 |
| 1 | 451 | 30 | 0.995 |
| 2 | 887 | 54 | 1.475 |
| 2 | 513 | 188 | 0.525 |
| 3 | 736 | 36 | 24.995 |
| 3 | 001 | 58 | 7.875 |
| 3 | 302 | 16 | 8.00 |
| 3 | 224 | 114 | 8.75 |

## Salesperson Table

| Salesperson ID | Last Name | First Name |
|---|---|---|
| 2 | Cleaves | Mateen |
| 4 | Warrick | Peter |
| 6 | Peterson | Morris |
| 8 | Janakowski | Sebastian |

## Cashier Table

| Cashier ID | Last Name | First Name |
|---|---|---|
| 1 | Weinke | Chris |
| 2 | Outzen | Marcus |

## Cash Receipts Event Table

| Cash Receipt # | Date | Check # | Cashier ID | Sales Event # | Customer ID | Cash Account # | Amount Received |
|---|---|---|---|---|---|---|---|
| 1001 | 11/6 | 11097 | 1 | 2 | 635 | 110146758 | $ 178.35 |

## Customer Table

| Customer ID | Last Name | First Name | Address | City | State | Zip |
|---|---|---|---|---|---|---|
| 101 | Conrad | Chris | 5629 Longfellow Dr. | Paragould | AK | 65323 |
| 183 | Anderson | Paul | 674 Sunderland Lane | Sioux City | IA | 63126 |
| 635 | Padgham | Donna | 1264 Algonquin Road | Mason | MI | 48854 |
| 1845 | Oliver | Andrew | 8512 Bonita Dr. | Clearwater | FL | 33051 |
| 2543 | Cook | Carol | 536 Secondary Ave. | Fremont | CA | 75518 |

**Cash Table**

| Cash # | Type of Account | Bank Name |
|---|---|---|
| 110146758 | Regular checking | North First |
| 1203948102 | Payroll checking account | Credit Grantors |

**Inventory Table**

| Inventory Item # | Description |
|---|---|
| 001 | XL T-shirt |
| 224 | XL Sweatshirt |
| 302 | XXL T-shirt |
| 451 | Felt pennant |
| 513 | Ping-pong ball |
| 674 | Golf ball |
| 736 | XL Polo shirt |
| 876 | Bumper sticker |
| 887 | Foam football |

## Required:

a. What events, resources, and agents must have been included in the underlying conceptual model from which these relational tables were designed?

b. Identify the primary key of each table.

c. Identify each foreign key in the database.

d. List the resources and agents involved in Sale event 2.

e. List the resources and agents involved in Cash Receipt 1001.

f. Suppose you wanted to generate an invoice (bill) for customer 2543 that lists the customer name and address, the salesperson name, and all other information about the sale, including the items sold. Which tables contain the data you will need to generate the invoice?

g. Suppose you wanted to generate a report listing each customer name and the amount due from each customer. Which tables contain the data you need to generate the report?

h. Explain why "total sales amount" did not need to be included as an attribute in the sales table. What are the pros and cons associated with leaving this attribute out of the database tables?

i. If you need to record the following sale:

Sale event 4; on 11/10; COD terms; Salesperson 2; Customer 101; 30 units of item 887, for a total of $44.25.

What tables would you use? How many records would you add or modify in the tables?

j. If you need to maintain your records to reflect a change in Donna Padgham's last name and address, what tables would you use? How many records would you add or modify in the tables.

k. If you need to record the following cash receipt:

Cash receipt 1002; on 11/10; from customer 2543 to pay off sale event 1; in the amount of $49.35 deposited into cash account 110146758

What tables would you use? How many records would you add or modify in the tables?

LO1, LO2, LO3  **A2.** Tom owns a small recreational trailer business in a suburban community located close to the mountains. The community is relatively small but growing at a fast rate. Tom's business is growing, not because of his effective sales style and personality, but due to the growth of the community. Tom's competition thus far has been nearly nonexistent, but as the area grows he expects to encounter increasing competition.

Tom sells mostly trailers for vacationing and camping. When customers arrive on Tom's lot, they are greeted by a salesperson. The salesperson may show the customers the trailers on the lot, but the salesperson need not be present during the entire showing. Depending on customer preference, the salesperson either takes the customer on a tour or allows the customer to freely roam the lot, inspecting trailers at leisure.

Since recreational trailers are fairly large-ticket items, customers often leave the lot without making a purchase, only to return another day after making the decision to purchase a trailer. When a customer decides to make a purchase, the salesperson initiates a series of procedures to properly document the order and sale transaction. First, the salesperson determines the model of the selected trailer and offers the customer a list of options that correspond to the particular model. The customer may (1) purchase a trailer off the lot with no added features, (2) purchase a trailer off the lot with additional features, or (3) special order a trailer that is not currently on the lot.

In most cases, customers do not pay cash for their trailers. If, however, the customer pays cash, a simple sales contract is prepared and the customer drives off with a trailer. The majority of the customers use an installment method of purchase. Before an installment purchase is authorized, the customer's credit must be verified to determine creditworthiness.

With an installment purchase, an installment agreement is prepared in addition to the sales contract. Tom has arranged financing through a local bank for all installment sales. When an installment sale is made, the bank sends Tom a lump sum payment equal to the price of the trailer. Instead of making payment to Tom, customers pay the bank plus interest. In either case, Tom receives a lump sum payment for each trailer sold, whether that lump sum comes from the customer or from the bank. If multiple customers finance trailer purchases on the same day, the bank issues one payment to Tom for the combined total.

Once the credit is approved, the customer can take delivery of the trailer. This involves a delivery person inspecting and cleaning the trailer. The customer may pick up the trailer or have the delivery person tow it to the customer's home.

### Required:

Tom's Trailer Sales has identified the following events of interest: Customer Looks at Trailers; Customer Orders Trailer; Deliver Trailer; and Receive Payment.

a. What business process is described?

b. What resource flows (in and out) exist in the value chain with respect to this business process?

c. For each resource inflow to this process in the value chain, identify the economic event that uses it up, and for each resource outflow from this process in the value chain, identify the economic event that produces it.

d. Create an REA business process level model for this business process; make sure to include attributes and cardinalities. Use judgment to determine at least two attributes for each entity. List any assumptions you make to determine cardinalities for which the narrative is inconclusive.

e. Convert your conceptual model from part (d) into relational database tables.

f. Create a physical implementation of your relational database tables using Microsoft Access (or an alternative database software package of your instructor's choice).

LO1, LO2, LO3, LO4, LO7

A3. Look at the REA business process level conceptual model for Happy Thoughts Gift Shop (HTGS), in both diagram and grammar formats. This model is incomplete to keep the project manageable in a short time frame, but contains enough entities and relationships to give you valuable practice creating logical and physical level models. Please do not add any additional entities, relationships, or attributes to the model.

## Happy Thoughts Gift Shop Conceptual Model

### Diagram format

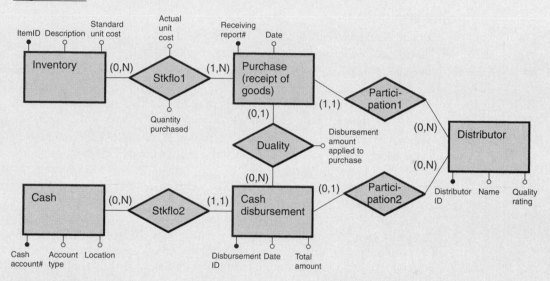

### Grammar format

Entity: Cash
Attributes: Cash account#
   Account type
   Location
Identifier: Cash account#
Entity: Cash disbursement
Attributes: Disbursement ID
   Date
   Total amount
Identifier: Disbursement ID
Entity: Distributor
Attributes: Distributor ID
   Name
   Quality rating
Identifier: Distributor ID
Entity: Inventory
Attributes: Item ID
   Description
   Standard unit cost
Identifier: Item ID

Entity: Purchase (receipt of goods)
Attributes: Receiving report#
   Date
Identifier: Receiving report#
Relationship: Duality
Connected entities: (0,1) Purchase
               (0,N) Cash disbursement
Attributes: Disbursement amount applied to purchase
Relationship: Participation1
Connected entities: (1,1) Purchase
               (0,N) Distributor
Relationship: Participation2
Connected entities: (0,1) Cash disbursement
               (0,N) Distributor
Relationship: Stockflow1
Connected entities:  (0,N) Inventory
               (1,N) Purchase (receipt of goods)
Attributes: Quantity purchased
   Actual Unit cost
Relationship: Stockflow2
Connected entities:  (0,N) Cash
               (1,1) Cash disbursement

Along with the conceptual model (in whichever format you prefer) you also need to know the following information:

HTGS eventually pays for 99 percent of its purchases; only very rarely does HTGS return merchandise to a distributor.

HTGS hires a payroll specialty firm (WKP, which stands for We Know Payroll) to handle writing paychecks to employees. Thus HTGS writes one check per month to WKP to cover the employees' gross pay plus WKP's processing fees. Occasionally HTGS also writes checks for other things such as loan repayments and general and administrative service acquisitions; however, most of its cash disbursements (approximately 85 out of every 100 checks) apply to purchases of inventory from distributors.

## Required:

a. Convert the conceptual model into a logical level model using the relational model. (That is, prepare relational table structures on paper)

b. Create a new database in Microsoft Access that has your first and last name followed by proj1 as the name of the database (e.g., abelincolnproj1 for a student named Abe Lincoln). Access will add the "mdb" file extension that indicates the file is a Microsoft database file. It is always a good idea to make backups of your work.

c. Add each of the tables from your relational solution for HTGS to the database, defining the data types for each field and identifying the primary key(s) for each table. For foreign keys, enter "foreign key from _____table" (filling in the name of the table from which it was posted) into the field's description field. This is not required by Access but is a project requirement to ensure your understanding of the foreign keys (and it is a good habit to start for documentation purposes). For each foreign key field, if the related minimum cardinality requires mandatory participation, make sure that the field requirement is "yes" (not "no" which is the default). For example, a (0,N) Salesperson–(1,1) Sale relationship implemented with SalespersonID posted into the Sale table. SalespersonID is a foreign key in the Sale table, and the participation of Sale with respect to that foreign key is mandatory. That is, we cannot enter data about a sale without specifying which salesperson was responsible for that sale. In that case, SalespersonID must be set for required data entry = "yes".

d. Create and save the relationship layout for the database, including all tables in the database (this should be done after you have entered all of the tables from requirement (c). Set referential integrity and cascade updates (but not cascade deletes) on all relationships.

e. Make up data to enter into the database tables. Each table must have at least 3 records and you must enter data that are internally consistent and that conform to the minimum and maximum cardinalities. For *internal consistency,* you need to make sure the data make sense when viewed as a whole. For example, if you indicate that cash receipt #478 applied to sale #1764, and sale #1764 was made to customer #2, then cash receipt #478 should also be indicated as coming from customer #2. For the *minimum cardinalities,* if there is optional participation (for example, a salesperson can be entered into the database before any transactions occur) you need to have data reflect this (e.g., a row for a salesperson in the Salesperson table that is not included in any of the rows in the Sale table—in other words, create a salesperson that hasn't yet made a sale). If participation is mandatory (such as a sale has to have a customer) you need to have data reflect this (every sale record has a customer associated with it). If you followed the instructions in requirement (c) and specified such fields as required, Access will force you to enter a data value for those mandatory cases that involved foreign keys. However, for mandatory participation in relationships that are implemented with separate tables, you will need to enter the data appropriately and will get no warning from Access. For the *maximum cardinalities,* your data should illustrate either "at most one" or "at most many" participation. For example, say relationship between sale and inventory is such that one invoice can include multiple inventory stock numbers and one inventory stock number may be included on multiple sale invoices. Your database should illustrate that at least one of your sales must include multiple inventory items, and at least one of your inventory item numbers must be sold more than once. Note that in some cases conforming to the maximum cardinalities may require you to enter more than three records in a table.

f. Turn in the relational table structures you created on paper in requirement (a) and turn in the Access database file you created in requirements (b) through (e).

## Answers to Multiple Choice Questions

MC1. C; MC2. B; MC3. C; MC4. D; MC5. D.

# Chapter **Seven**

# Information Retrieval from Relational Databases

## LEARNING OBJECTIVES

The objective of this chapter is to illustrate the means by which information can be retrieved (via querying) from relational databases to meet demands for enterprise decisions. After studying this chapter you should be able to:

1. Identify and explain the purpose of the three primary relational algebra operators
2. Identify and explain the primary components of a Structured Query Language (SQL) query statement
3. Identify the relational algebra operations achieved by a given SQL statement
4. Create a SQL statement to retrieve requested information from a relational database
5. Examine a SQL statement and the tables to which it will be applied and identify the query result
6. Find errors in a SQL statement
7. Create a Microsoft Access Query By Example (QBE) to retrieve information from relational tables
8. Examine a Microsoft Access QBE query and the tables to which it applies and identify the query result
9. Find errors in a Microsoft Access QBE query

## INTRODUCTION

In Chapter 6 we discussed the need for sound database design as a necessity for valid **information retrieval.** In this chapter we discuss querying logic and skills that are also necessary for valid information retrieval. If a database is not designed correctly, information retrieved from it may be meaningless; however, an enterprise database may be perfectly designed and still produce meaningless information if it is retrieved incorrectly. Two philosophies for providing information to decision makers are prevalent in practice. One approach has information systems professionals predetermine what information users need from the database. Then the IS professionals create queries and build interfaces that allow the users to run the queries without knowing any specifics of how they are constructed. The other approach does not presuppose what information a user may need but instead allows users to **query** the database in an ad hoc fashion. This approach requires users to be trained in whatever querying language is used for the database software in which the enterprise database is implemented. Of course, these approaches may be combined by some enterprises so that an interface is created to allow retrieval of some predetermined types of information and **ad hoc querying** is allowed for other information needs.

The need for learning how to retrieve information from relational databases for those who desire to become information systems professionals is obvious. However, the need is equally great for anyone who may perform ad hoc querying of a database to support their decision making, or for anyone who may evaluate the integrity of information retrieved from an enterprise database. In short, all business professionals should be versed in the techniques of relational database querying. This chapter includes a three-pronged approach to database querying. First some elements of **relational algebra** are discussed to lay the foundation of the underlying logical procedures in querying. Relational algebra is part of the relational database model and therefore is based on set theory and predicate logic. The second prong discussed is **Structured Query Language (SQL),** which is a querying language shared by many relational database software packages. The third prong discussed is **Query By Example (QBE),** which is a type of query interface intended to be more point-and-click in nature and to require less user expertise. This chapter illustrates the QBE version used in Microsoft Access. Different relational database software packages have slightly different QBE interfaces; however, familiarity with the Microsoft Access QBE interface should help you to also understand QBE interfaces in other relational database software.

# QUERYING RELATIONAL DATABASES

Enterprises need information in many formats to support different types of decisions. Much of the information is derived from the same underlying data, but those data must be aggregated in various ways. For example, the marketing manager for the southeast region of an enterprise may need to know last month's sales dollar value for the southeast region. That same marketing manager may also need to know what last month's sales quantity was for a particular product or product line in the southeast region. The accountant for the enterprise needs to know last month's total sales for the entire enterprise to report on the income statement. These three pieces of information are based on the same underlying data—that is, the disaggregated sales data which include sale dates, locations, products sold, cash receipts received in exchange, and internal and external participating agents.

Because data are stored in a format different from that format in which they need to be retrieved, it takes a certain skill set to be able to effectively query a database. Several ingredients are necessary for good information retrieval. First, the database itself must have been well designed. If the tables are not fully relational, if the tables are incompletely specified, or if the conceptual model has not been correctly converted into relational format, querying will be difficult or even impossible. Second, the query designer must have a thorough knowledge of the database table structures and of the nature of the data in the tables. To understand the database table structures, the query designer must have some basic knowledge of database design. Third, the query designer must completely understand the desired output—that is, the information actually needed to support the decision of interest. Fourth, the query designer must have good logic and reasoning skills. Fifth, the query designer must know the querying language used to retrieve information from the enterprise's database. Several querying language choices exist, but not all of them are available for every database package. We discuss three of the prevalent choices next.

# RELATIONAL ALGEBRA

When the relational database model was initially created, Codd specified relational algebra as a language for retrieving data from the tables.[1] Because the tables were created in conformance with set theory and predicate logic, it makes sense that the means for retrieving data from the tables is also based on set theory and predicate logic.

Many relational algebra operators are used to allow complete manipulation of relational database tables; however, most basic queries are covered by three of these operators: **PROJECT, SELECT,** and **JOIN.** In applying these operators, we discuss horizontal and vertical subsets of tables. Rows form the horizontal part of a relational table; columns form the vertical part of a table. Therefore a horizontal subset is a part of the table that includes only some of the table's rows (but includes all the columns). A vertical subset is a part of the table that includes only some of the table's columns (but includes all the rows). PROJECT (pronounced prō-JĔCT') is an operator that retrieves a **vertical subset of a table.** The SELECT operator retrieves a **horizontal subset of a table.** The JOIN operator is the most powerful of the relational algebra operators, allowing us to combine separate but related tables by linking them on their common attributes.

The following tables give examples of each of the relational algebra operators.

**Employee**

| EmplD | SocialSec# | LastName | FirstName | Street Address | Pay Rate | Telephone | DeptID |
|-------|-----------|----------|-----------|----------------|----------|-----------|--------|
| E1 | 123345678 | Adams | Anita | 144 Apple St. | $10 | 555-1234 | D4 |
| E2 | 234456789 | Boston | Benjamin | 255 Banana Rd. | $12 | 555-2345 | D2 |
| E3 | 345567890 | Crabb | Charlie | 366 Cherry Ave. | $14 | 555-3456 | D2 |
| E4 | 456678901 | Davis | Deborah | 477 Dip Dr. | $32 | 555-4567 | D1 |
| E5 | 567789101 | Engler | Edward | 588 Eggplant St. | $11 | 555-5678 | D4 |
| E6 | 678891012 | Folkert | Fawn | 699 Fruity Ave. | $23 | 555-6789 | D3 |

**Department**

| DepartmentID | Name |
|--------------|------|
| D1 | Executive Management |
| D2 | Accounting |
| D3 | Information Systems |
| D4 | Operations |

[1]E. F. Codd, "Derivability, Redundancy, and Consistency of Relations Stored in Large Data Banks," *IBM Research Report* RJ599, August 19, 1969; and "A Relational Model of Data for Large Shared Data Banks," *CACM* 13, no. 6 (June 1970), republished in *Milestones of Research: Selected Papers 1958–1982, CACM* 25th Anniversary Issue, vol. 26, no. 1 (January 1983).

| Training Courses | | |
|---|---|---|
| CourseID | Description | Length |
| AC1 | Accounting Fundamentals | 2 days |
| AC2 | Chart of Accounts | 5 days |
| IS1 | Basic Information Systems | 5 days |
| IS2 | Database Design | 5 days |
| MD100 | ERP Systems | 10 days |

| Employee Takes Course | | |
|---|---|---|
| EmplID | CourseID | DateTaken |
| E3 | AC1 | May 1–2 |
| E3 | AC2 | June 24–28 |
| E6 | IS1 | June 24–28 |
| E6 | IS2 | July 8–12 |
| E4 | AC1 | Oct 14–15 |

## PROJECT Example

Imagine the enterprise wants to create an emergency phone tree—a list of employee names and their telephone numbers. The first step is to determine which table or tables contain the attributes that need to be accessed by the user. Only one table is needed—the Employee table. However, the enterprise does not want to simply print out the employee table because they do not want sensitive information such as social security numbers and pay rates to be included on the phone tree; they only want the names and phone numbers to appear. Therefore they need a vertical subset of the Employee table. A relational algebra query that makes use of a PROJECT provides the requested information:

PROJECT Employee Over (LastName, FirstName, Telephone) Giving Answer

This command tells the database software package to list a vertical subset of the Employee table, with that subset consisting of the three columns that contain the last name, first name, and telephone, and to present that subset in a new view called Answer. The result of this relational algebra operation is:

| Answer | | |
|---|---|---|
| LastName | FirstName | Telephone |
| Adams | Anita | 555-1234 |
| Boston | Benjamin | 555-2345 |
| Crabb | Charlie | 555-3456 |
| Davis | Deborah | 555-4567 |
| Engler | Edward | 555-5678 |
| Folkert | Fawn | 555-6789 |

## SELECT Example

Imagine this has been a difficult economic year for the enterprise, especially in terms of cash flow, and as a result the enterprise has decided to give cost-of-living raises to only those employees whose current pay rate is less than $15 per hour. Since only the payroll department personnel are going to see the information, there is no need to leave out any attributes from the query result. Therefore they need a horizontal subset of the Employee table, filtering out those employees who make $15 or more per hour. A relational algebra query that makes use of a SELECT will provide the requested information:

SELECT Employee Where PayRate <15 Giving Answer

This command tells the database software package to list a horizontal subset of the Employee table, with that subset consisting of the employees for which the PayRate data value is less than 15, and to present that subset in a new view called Answer. The result of this relational algebra operation is:

**Answer**

| EmpID | SocialSec# | LastName | FirstName | Street Address | Pay Rate | Telephone | DeptID |
|-------|-----------|----------|-----------|----------------|----------|-----------|--------|
| E1 | 123345678 | Adams | Anita | 144 Apple St. | $10 | 555-1234 | D4 |
| E2 | 234456789 | Boston | Benjamin | 255 Banana Rd. | $12 | 555-2345 | D2 |
| E3 | 345567890 | Crabb | Charlie | 366 Cherry Ave. | $14 | 555-3456 | D2 |
| E5 | 567789101 | Engler | Edward | 588 Eggplant St. | $11 | 555-5678 | D4 |

## JOIN Examples

A JOIN combines two or more tables on the basis of a common attribute. Recall from Chapter 6 that relationships between entities are represented in relational database tables by posting attributes from some tables into other tables (e.g., by posting a foreign key into another table, or by creating a concatenated primary key by posting keys from two different tables to form a new table). Joins are used to establish these links between tables for querying purposes when information from two or more related tables is needed to answer a question or create a report.

Two types of joins are of interest for most enterprise queries. One is called an **inner join** or an **equi-join.** This type of join combines the tables together, keeping only those rows for which the data values of the common attribute match exactly. Note that the JOIN operator in relational algebra retains all attributes of both tables. Performing a PROJECT operation on the answer then eliminates unwanted columns.

Imagine the enterprise wants to prepare a list of employees and the names of the departments to which they are assigned. Most of the information needed for this query is available in the Employee table; however, to obtain the names of the departments, the Department table is also needed. Begin with a JOIN relational algebra command as follows:

JOIN Employee Department Where Employee.DeptID=Department.DepartmentID
Giving Answer

The result of this command is:

**Answer**

| EmpID | SocialSec# | Last Name | First Name | Street Address | Pay Rate | Telephone | DeptID | Depart-mentID | Name |
|-------|-----------|-----------|------------|----------------|----------|-----------|--------|---------------|------|
| E1 | 123345678 | Adams | Anita | 144 Apple St. | $10 | 555-1234 | D4 | D4 | Operations |
| E2 | 234456789 | Boston | Benjamin | 255 Banana Rd. | $12 | 555-2345 | D2 | D2 | Accounting |
| E3 | 345567890 | Crabb | Charlie | 366 Cherry Ave. | $14 | 555-3456 | D2 | D2 | Accounting |
| E4 | 456678901 | Davis | Deborah | 477 Dip Dr. | $32 | 555-4567 | D1 | D1 | Executive Management |
| E5 | 567789101 | Engler | Edward | 588 Eggplant St. | $11 | 555-5678 | D4 | D4 | Operations |
| E6 | 678891012 | Folkert | Fawn | 699 Fruity Ave. | $23 | 555-6789 | D3 | D3 | Information Systems |

To filter out all columns other than the employee names and department names (if those were the only attributes needed) a PROJECT command can be issued as follows:

PROJECT Answer Over (LastName, FirstName, Name) Giving Answer2

The result of this command is:

**Answer2**

| LastName | FirstName | Name |
|----------|-----------|------|
| Adams | Anita | Operations |
| Boston | Benjamin | Accounting |
| Crabb | Charlie | Accounting |
| Davis | Deborah | Executive Management |
| Engler | Edward | Operations |
| Folkert | Fawn | Information Systems |

For this example, an inner join yielded complete information because all employees are assigned to departments, and all departments have at least one employee assigned to them.

Sometimes an inner join leaves out some information that is important for a given decision. Using the example tables given, imagine the enterprise wants a list of the employee names and the IDs and descriptions of each training course each employee has completed. The data needed to satisfy this information need are located in the Employee and Training Courses tables. However, the table that establishes the relationship between these entities is also needed in completing the query because that is where the common attributes between Employee and Training Course are located. In other words, there are no common attributes in the Employee and Training Course tables. However, the Employee and Employee Takes Course tables contain a common attribute (EmplID), and the Training Course and Employee Takes Course tables contain a common attribute (CourseID). Thus we need to perform two join operations as follows:

JOIN Employee Employee_Takes_Course Where
Employee.EmpID=Employee_Takes_Course.EmplID Giving Answer

JOIN Answer Training_Course Where Answer.CourseID=Training_Course.CourseID
Giving Answer2

The result of the first JOIN is

**Answer**

| EmpID | SocialSec# | Last Name | First Name | Street Address | Pay Rate | Telephone | DeptID | EmplID | Course ID | Date Taken |
|-------|-----------|-----------|------------|----------------|----------|-----------|--------|--------|-----------|------------|
| E3 | 345567890 | Crabb | Charlie | 366 Cherry Ave. | $14 | 555-3456 | D2 | E3 | AC1 | May 1–2 |
| E3 | 345567890 | Crabb | Charlie | 366 Cherry Ave. | $14 | 555-3456 | D2 | E3 | AC2 | June 24–28 |
| E4 | 456678901 | Davis | Deborah | 477 Dip Dr. | $32 | 555-4567 | D1 | E4 | AC1 | Oct 14–15 |
| E6 | 678891012 | Folkert | Fawn | 699 Fruity Ave. | $23 | 555-6789 | D3 | E6 | IS1 | June 24–28 |
| E6 | 678891012 | Folkert | Fawn | 699 Fruity Ave. | $23 | 555-6789 | D3 | E6 | IS2 | July 8–12 |

The result of the second JOIN is

**Answer2**

| EmpID | SocialSec# | Last Name | First Name | Street Address | Pay Rate | Telephone | DeptID | EmplID | CourseID | Date Taken |
|-------|------------|-----------|------------|----------------|----------|-----------|--------|--------|----------|------------|
| E3 | 345567890 | Crabb | Charlie | 366 Cherry Ave. | $14 | 555-3456 | D2 | E3 | AC1 | May 1–2 |
| E3 | 345567890 | Crabb | Charlie | 366 Cherry Ave. | $14 | 555-3456 | D2 | E3 | AC2 | June 24–28 |
| E4 | 456678901 | Davis | Deborah | 477 Dip Dr. | $32 | 555-4567 | D1 | E4 | AC1 | Oct 14–15 |
| E6 | 678891012 | Folkert | Fawn | 699 Fruity Ave. | $23 | 555-6789 | D3 | E6 | IS1 | June 24–28 |
| E6 | 678891012 | Folkert | Fawn | 699 Fruity Ave. | $23 | 555-6789 | D3 | E6 | IS2 | July 8–12 |

**Answer2 (continued—part of same Answer2 table)**

| CourseID | Description | Length |
|----------|-------------|--------|
| AC1 | Accounting Fundamentals | 2 days |
| AC2 | Chart of Accounts | 5 days |
| AC1 | Accounting Fundamentals | 2 days |
| IS1 | Basic Information Systems | 5 days |
| IS2 | Database Design | 5 days |

Next we need to perform a PROJECT operation to eliminate the duplicate columns and to filter out any columns that are not needed based on the information request, as follows:

PROJECT Answer2 Over (LastName, FirstName, CourseID, Description) Giving Answer3

The result of this command is:

**Answer3**

| LastName | FirstName | CourseID | Description |
|----------|-----------|----------|-------------|
| Crabb | Charlie | AC1 | Accounting Fundamentals |
| Crabb | Charlie | AC2 | Chart of Accounts |
| Davis | Deborah | AC1 | Accounting Fundamentals |
| Folkert | Fawn | IS1 | Basic Information Systems |
| Folkert | Fawn | IS2 | Database Design |

Examine closely the Answer3 result to determine whether this list meets our information need; it contains employee names and the course ID and description of courses they have taken. If we only want a list of employees that have taken firm-offered training courses, then our need is met. However, what if we want all our employees included on this list, with blanks left next to those who have not yet taken a firm-offered training course? Then our need was not met, because three of our employees (Anita Adams, Benjamin Boston, and Edward Engler) do not appear in Answer3. Let's backtrack to figure out when and why they were deleted. Notice that they did not appear in Answer2 either. Indeed, they were eliminated when the first JOIN of Employee and Employee Takes Course was performed, because their employee IDs did not appear in the Employee Takes Course table and the

JOIN was an inner join. To include all the employees in our answer, we must perform a different type of join. An **outer join** keeps unmatched records and pairs them with null values. A full outer join keeps unmatched records from both sides, and the final answer (with the projection done) would look as follows:

**Answer3 (result of full outer joins and projection)**

| LastName | FirstName | CourseID | Description |
|----------|-----------|----------|-------------|
| Adams | Anita | | |
| Boston | Benjamin | | |
| Crabb | Charlie | AC1 | Accounting Fundamentals |
| Crabb | Charlie | AC2 | Chart of Accounts |
| Davis | Deborah | AC1 | Accounting Fundamentals |
| Engler | Edward | | |
| Folkert | Fawn | IS1 | Basic Information Systems |
| Folkert | Fawn | IS2 | Database Design |
| | | MD100 | ERP Systems |

A right outer join keeps unmatched records from the second table listed in the join and eliminates unmatched records from the first table in the join. The answer for our example with a right outer join is:

**Answer3 (result of right outer join and projection)**

| LastName | FirstName | CourseID | Description |
|----------|-----------|----------|-------------|
| Crabb | Charlie | AC1 | Accounting Fundamentals |
| Crabb | Charlie | AC2 | Chart of Accounts |
| Davis | Deborah | AC1 | Accounting Fundamentals |
| Folkert | Fawn | IS1 | Basic Information Systems |
| Folkert | Fawn | IS2 | Database Design |
| | | MD100 | ERP Systems |

A left outer join keeps unmatched records from the first table listed in the join and eliminates unmatched records from the second table in the join. The answer for our example with a left outer join is:

**Answer3 (result of left outer join and projection)**

| LastName | FirstName | CourseID | Description |
|----------|-----------|----------|-------------|
| Adams | Anita | | |
| Boston | Benjamin | | |
| Crabb | Charlie | AC1 | Accounting Fundamentals |
| Crabb | Charlie | AC2 | Chart of Accounts |
| Davis | Deborah | AC1 | Accounting Fundamentals |
| Engler | Edward | | |
| Folkert | Fawn | IS1 | Basic Information Systems |
| Folkert | Fawn | IS2 | Database Design |

Which of these answers best satisfies the information need we were trying to meet? The left outer join provides a list of all employees (whether or not they have taken a training course) and for those who have taken training courses, it lists the training courses taken.

Therefore for this information need, the left outer join provided the best solution. For other information needs, an inner join, or a right outer join, or a full outer join may provide the best data. The best answer depends on the question being asked!

# STRUCTURED QUERY LANGUAGE

Although relational algebra was developed as part of the relational model, it is not the most commonly used **data manipulation language** today. One weakness of relational algebra is that each operator must be accomplished in a separate query. That is, a projection and a selection are not accomplished in the same query; two queries need to be executed to accomplish the two operations. Structured Query Language (SQL) was developed to enable the performance of multiple operations in a single query. It was also believed that use of a standard format for every query would simplify the task of query development, which had proven to be very difficult for many users. For relational algebra, users must learn different **syntax** for each of the various relational algebra operators (including the three we have discussed as well as several others). In SQL, every information retrieval query follows a structured, predefined syntax as follows:

SELECT *attribute name(s)*
FROM *table name(s)*
WHERE *condition criteria is met;*

Note that the semicolon at the end of the SQL statement is very important if the system you are using allows more than one SQL statement to be executed in the same call to a database server, because it communicates to the database software that the end of the query statement has been reached. If that is left off, the query will not be executed. Most current relational database software packages automatically put the semicolon at the end of the statement to help avoid the syntax error that may occur when it is missing. For some queries not every component in this syntax is necessary, and for other queries additional components must be included, but in general every SQL statement must conform to this format. Although most companies and most database software packages do not make direct use of relational algebra syntax, it is helpful when you are deriving queries to consider the three major relational algebra operators and determine how you will accomplish those in either SQL or QBE. To begin we examine how the selection, projection, and join operators are achieved in SQL.

The first component of each SQL statement (that is, the SELECT component) specifies which attribute(s) are to be included in the answer to the query. Recall that attributes are the columns of the table(s). Thus this component of the SQL statement accomplishes the projection relational algebra operator. The second component of each SQL statement (that is, the FROM component) specifies the tables that contain the data to include in the answer. If there is just one table, this component of the SQL statement simply identifies which table it is. If multiple tables are needed to meet the information request, this component helps to achieve the relational algebra JOIN operation (but does not achieve the join without the next component). The third component of the SQL statement can serve two purposes. In combination with the FROM component, it helps to achieve the relational algebra JOIN by specifying the fields for which the two joined tables should have equal values. Alternatively (or additionally) the WHERE component specifies criteria to be met by records in

**TABLE 7–1**
Correspondence
of Relational
Algebra
Operators and
SQL Statement
Components

| Relational Algebra Operator | SQL Statement Component(s) |
|---|---|
| PROJECT | SELECT attribute name(s) |
| SELECT | WHERE criteria are met |
| JOIN | FROM table names |
| | WHERE posted key field data values match |

order to be included in the answer. Thus the WHERE component of an SQL statement accomplishes the relational algebra selection operator. Table 7–1 summarizes the SQL statement components—**SELECT-FROM-WHERE**—that correspond to each of the relational algebra operators.

Next we use SQL to demonstrate the same queries that we formulated earlier.

## PROJECT Example

The first query generated a list of employees' names and phone numbers to be used for an emergency phone tree. The query required a projection operator only. In SQL the query is stated as follows:

SELECT LastName, FirstName, Telephone

FROM Employee;

Notice that when we are not trying to accomplish a relational algebra JOIN nor a relational algebra SELECT operator, there are no criteria to be met and thus there is no WHERE component to the statement.

## SELECT Example

The second query we formulated with relational algebra was the list of employees (including all attributes) whose pay rate is less than $15 per hour. This query required the relational algebra selection operator but no projection or join operators. The SQL statement for this query is as follows:

SELECT *

FROM Employee

WHERE PayRate <15.00;

Note that the asterisk (*) is a wildcard symbol and simply tells the database software package to include all attributes in the query result.

## Combining SELECT and PROJECT in SQL

Notice that it is very easy to combine a relational algebra selection operator with a projection operator in a single SQL statement. Say you wanted to retrieve the names and telephone numbers of the employees whose pay rate is less than $15 so you could call those employees to tell them they are getting a cost-of-living raise. The following SQL statement accomplishes everything the previous two statements did.

SELECT LastName, FirstName, Telephone

FROM Employee

WHERE PayRate <15.00;

# JOIN Examples

Next let's examine how to accomplish the information request for a list of all employees and the names of the departments to which they are assigned. We begin with a SQL statement that accomplishes only the JOIN operation (that is equivalent to the first relational algebra JOIN statement). The SQL statement is as follows:

SELECT *

FROM Employee, Department

WHERE Employee.DeptID=Department.DepartmentID;

In our relational algebra example of this query, we had to execute a second query to accomplish the PROJECT operation. Our SQL statement may be revised slightly to accomplish both the JOIN and the PROJECT in just one query as follows:

SELECT LastName, FirstName, Name

FROM Employee, Department

WHERE Employee.DeptID=Department.DepartmentID;

Keep in mind that the latter query replaces the former query. Whereas in relational algebra we must use two separate queries to accomplish the two separate operations, in SQL we combined them into just one query.

To specify that a JOIN needs to be an outer join (to retrieve all records from a table for which no match is available in the joined table), the syntax needs to be varied slightly. The outer join must be specified as a **Left Join** or a **Right Join** in the From clause of your SQL statement. Whether you use a left or right outer join depends on the order in which you list the tables in your SQL statement. Assume for our employees and departments example we want the list to include the DeptName in our answer, and we want the names of all departments even if they do not have any employees assigned to them. Our statement should be formulated as follows:

SELECT DeptName, LastName, FirstName, Name

FROM Department LeftJoin Employee

On Department.DepartmentID=Employee.DeptID;

The following Right Join statement would accomplish exactly the same thing:

SELECT DeptName, LastName, FirstName, Name

FROM Employee RightJoin Department

On Department.DepartmentID=Employee.DeptID;

Some other clauses are needed to accomplish many queries for decision-making purposes. For example, we need to be able to calculate amounts based on fields in our database. You may recall from Chapter 4 that it is undesirable to store any derivable attributes for which the value will change upon the entry of new data. For example, "Quantity on Hand" as an attribute in an Inventory table has a value that needs to be increased every time a purchase is made of an inventory item and decreased every time a sale is made of an inventory item. Unless the database is capable of using a concept called triggers, which is like storing a formula instead of a value in the table's cell, it is preferable not to store this as an attribute in the Inventory table, but instead to create a query we can run whenever we need an updated value for this field. Therefore we need to be able to create formulas within our queries to calculate such values.

## Using Mathematical, Special Comparison, and Logical Operators in SQL Queries

Mathematical **comparison operators** are sometimes needed as criteria by which data values are selected for inclusion in a query result. Examples of mathematical comparison operators include:

| | |
|---|---|
| = | equal to |
| < | less than |
| > | greater than |
| <= | less than or equal to |
| >= | greater than or equal to |
| <> | not equal to (in some software this is denoted as !=) |

These comparison operators may be applied to any type of field. For date fields, dates that are earlier in time are considered to be "less than" dates that are later in time. For example, April 1, 1980, is less than June 1, 1980. Most database software packages are able to compare and to perform calculations with date fields because they store the Julian date rather than the text format of the date. The Julian date is the value assigned to a date based on a continuous count assignment to days on the Julian calendar starting January 1, 4713 B.C.E. (before common era). That date is assigned a Julian value of 1. Today's Julian date value (depending on when you are reading this) is likely somewhere in the 2.5 to 3 million range. For text fields, earlier letters in the alphabet are considered to be less than later letters in the alphabet. For example, *apple* is less than *banana*. Because comparison operators assist in isolating certain rows (i.e., relational algebra's selection operation) they are included in the WHERE clause of an SQL statement. The query used earlier as an example accomplishing a SELECT in SQL (SELECT * FROM Employee WHERE PayRate < 15.00;) used a mathematical comparison operator.

BETWEEN is a special comparison operator that identifies instances within a certain range of values. The endpoints of the range are included. Use of a BETWEEN operator is equivalent to using a combination of less than or equal to with greater than or equal to. For example, a query to include all sales for the month of June 2005 in its answer could be constructed using WHERE SaleDate >=6/1/2005 AND SaleDate <=6/30/2005, or it could be constructed using WHERE SaleDate BETWEEN 6/1/2005 and 6/30/2005.

IS NULL is a special comparison operator that identifies instances for which an attribute value does not exist. EXISTS is a special comparison operator that identifies instances for which an attribute value does exist.

Queries may include **logical operators,** also known as Boolean search operators, such as AND, OR, and NOT. The AND operator accomplishes a set intersection; an answer to a query connecting two criteria by an AND will contain only the instances that meet both criteria. The OR operator accomplishes a set union; an answer to a query connecting two criteria by an OR contains all instances that meet at least one of the criteria. The NOT operator identifies instances that do not meet one or more conditions.

## Using Calculations and Aggregation Functions in SQL Queries

There are two types of calculations we may need in queries. One type of calculation performs **mathematical operations** within a particular column of data values, such as a computation of the average or sum of a set of values. Calculations within a column are **aggregation functions,** and several are standard in SQL. To compute the average of a column in a query, you would simply add AVG in front of the field name in the SELECT clause of the SQL statement. For example, if we wanted to compute the average payrate for all of our employees, we could specify:

SELECT AVG(PayRate)
FROM Employee;

Other aggregation functions that are applied the same way include SUM (to add a column), MAX (to find the largest value in a column), MIN (to find the smallest value in a column), and COUNT (to tell how many data values are in a column).

When we use aggregation functions in querying, we may not always want aggregate results for the table in its entirety. Sometimes we want aggregate results for certain combinations of rows in the table. For example, we may want to calculate total sales for each date, or we may want to know total purchase amount for each vendor. SQL offers a component called **GROUP BY** that may be added after the WHERE component of a SQL statement to achieve this subtotaling. Whatever field(s) the query is asked to group by will be grouped together and any aggregation function that is used will be applied to the subgroups rather than to the entire table. Examine the following Sale table.

**Sale**

| SaleID | Date | Amount | Customer |
|--------|----------|----------|----------|
| S108 | April 26 | $432.00 | C76 |
| S109 | April 26 | $118.00 | C83 |
| S110 | April 27 | $625.00 | C19 |
| S111 | April 28 | $375.00 | C38 |
| S112 | April 28 | $864.00 | C76 |

If you wanted to calculate total sales separately for each date, you will need to GROUP BY date. The query is formulated as follows:

SELECT Date, SUM(Amount)
FROM Sale
GROUP BY Date;

The answer that results from this query is:

**SalesByDate**

| Date | SumofAmount |
|----------|-------------|
| April 26 | $550.00 |
| April 27 | $625.00 |
| April 28 | $1,239.00 |

If instead, you wanted to calculate total sales separately for each customer, you will need to GROUP BY customer. The query is formulated as follows:

SELECT Customer, SUM(Amount)
FROM Sale
GROUP BY Customer;

The answer that results from this query is:

**SalesByCustomer**

| Customer | SumofAmount |
|----------|-------------|
| C19 | $625.00 |
| C38 | $375.00 |
| C76 | $1,296.00 |
| C83 | $118.00 |

The other type of calculation needed in some queries is a calculation that computes a mathematical function using data values from two fields in a record. Examine the following table that represents a stockflow relationship between Sale and Inventory.

**Stockflow**

| ItemID | SaleID | QtySold | UnitSellPrice |
|--------|--------|---------|---------------|
| I1 | S108 | 10 | $25.00 |
| I1 | S109 | 4 | $25.00 |
| I1 | S111 | 15 | $25.00 |
| I2 | S108 | 10 | $15.00 |
| I2 | S112 | 41 | $14.00 |
| I3 | S108 | 4 | $8.00 |
| I3 | S109 | 2 | $9.00 |
| I3 | S112 | 29 | $10.00 |
| I5 | S110 | 25 | $25.00 |

To calculate the sale line extension for a stockflow record, a new field must be created and defined as the product of QtySold and UnitSellPrice. The query is formulated as follows:

```
SELECT QtySold*UnitSellPrice As SaleLineExtension
FROM Stockflow;
```

## QUERY BY EXAMPLE IN MICROSOFT ACCESS

Much of the ad hoc querying that is done to support enterprise decision making is done by users who are not trained in SQL. Although most relational database software can run queries that are created in SQL form, most packages also offer an interface intended to make querying have more of a point-and-click feel. Such an interface is called Query By Example (QBE) because it has the user provide an example of what they want the answer to their query to look like. The user doesn't need to learn SQL code to generate many useful queries. However, it is very important to understand exactly what the different elements of the QBE interface accomplish when developing a query. If you do not ask the correct question, you will not get the correct answer! Query By Example can seem easier than it really is. Think about this: the less you understand the language of a person (or computer software) to whom you are asking a question, the more likely you are to make a mistake in asking that question. You may understand what you are trying to ask, but if you cannot adequately communicate the question to the database software, you will not get the answer you need. The dangerous thing is that you may not even realize the answer is incorrect! Of course that warning is also true for users querying with SQL, but our own anecdotal experience leads us to believe QBE is more likely than SQL to cause a false sense of security for untrained users. Most users who are trained in SQL are instructed to test their query construction before relying on the result, whereas many QBE users do not receive such instruction.

Because we are using Microsoft Access as our physical implementation software, next we examine some elements of querying with the QBE interface in Access. Note that Access also offers a **SQL view** in which users can directly enter queries in SQL form, so if you are comfortable with SQL you may choose to bypass the QBE interface.

To create a new query in Microsoft Access, you first need to open a database. It is important for you to have a solid understanding of both the design and content of the tables from which you are trying to retrieve information before you create any queries. The overall approach to Querying By Example in Access is as follows

1. Select the table(s) and/or query(ies) that contain the fields that eventually need to appear in the query result, and establish any joins that are needed (make sure to use the appropriate join type).
2. Drag the fields that need to be manipulated or that need to appear in the query result into the **query grid** in the lower half of the query design view.
3. Complete whatever steps are needed to develop the answer
   a. Set criteria to filter out irrelevant records.
   b. Use aggregation functions within fields for which such calculations are appropriate OR create calculated fields using standard mathematical operators.
   c. Apply any other needed functions such as Group By or Sort.

Keep in mind that you may need to accomplish your end result with a series of queries that build on each other. Generally you will end up with a wrong answer if you mix calculated fields (which perform mathematical calculations involving multiple columns) and aggregation functions (which summarize within a column). Access doesn't know which to do first, the **vertical calculations** or the **horizontal calculations** and if the query runs at all, it may create an answer that includes every possible combination of everything. It is best to create one query that applies the aggregation functions and then create a new query (using the first query as the starting object) that accomplishes the horizontal calculations, or vice versa, depending on the query demands.

## Familiarization with Database

To allow a comparison and contrast with relational algebra and SQL, we use the same queries introduced earlier for discussing QBE. The database we use therefore consists of the same tables we used earlier in the chapter. We display them here in Microsoft Access as Exhibit 7–1 so you can see that we are using the same data. We also provide the Access data file in case you want to follow along on a computer as you read.

To display each of these tables on the screen simultaneously we simply opened each one in datasheet view and resized the table windows so they would fit on the screen. We next display the **relationship layout** as Exhibit 7–2 so you can familiarize yourself with the relationships between tables that are formed by the use of posted keys.

**EXHIBIT 7–1** Tables in Microsoft Access

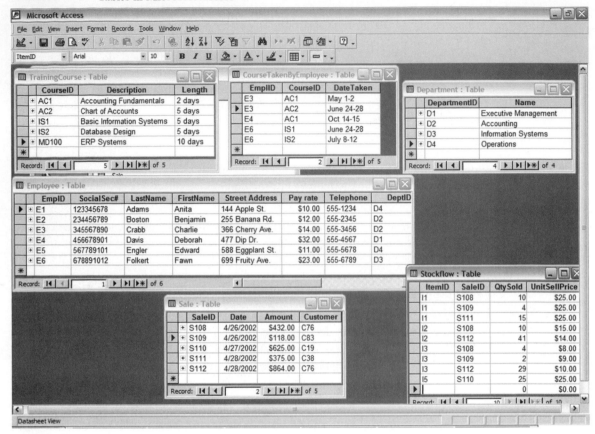

**EXHIBIT 7–2**
**Relationship
Layout
for Employee
Example
Tables**

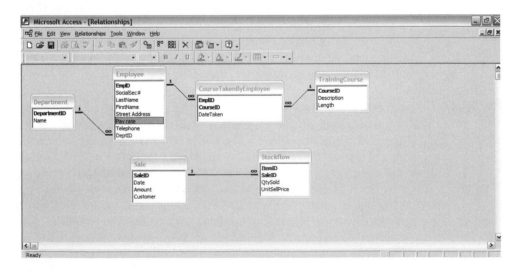

**EXHIBIT 7–3** **Design View of Employee and Related Tables**

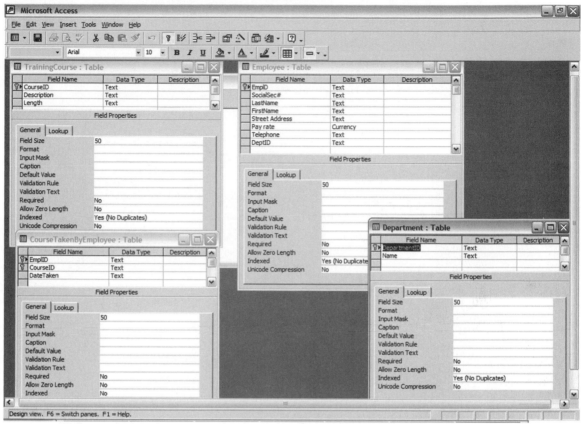

Please note that this is not intended to be a complete database. Only the tables necessary to illustrate the query examples are included. It is important for you to familiarize yourself with each table's design. The table design view for the Employee and related tables that are used for most of the queries are displayed as Exhibit 7–3.

It is more informative to look at the **design view** within Microsoft Access itself, because the field properties panel may be different for each field, and you can see those differences only by clicking on each field and then examining the field properties panel. From the upper panel you can see the data type, which in many cases is all you need to know about each field when using it in a query. Knowing the data type is important because you can use most mathematical functions only on number and currency fields; you can also perform limited mathematical functions on date fields, for example to compute the difference between two dates or between a stored date and the current date. The latter is useful for calculating information such as the number of days an invoice is past due; the former is useful for calculating information such as the average delivery time for a particular vendor. You must be familiar with the structure of the database tables you are querying.

**EXHIBIT 7–4**
**Starting a New**
**Query**

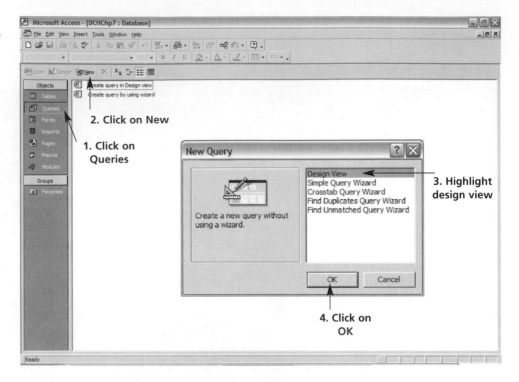

**EXHIBIT 7–5**
**Show Table**
**Window**

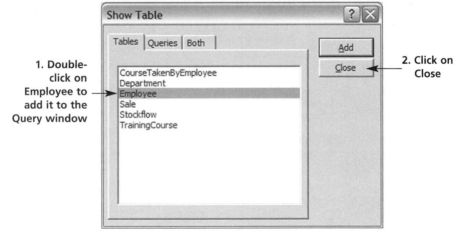

## Starting a Query and Adding the Appropriate Tables and/or Queries

In the database window, click the Query button and choose New. Microsoft Access will then display the New Query dialog box (see Exhibit 7–4). Choose design view (do not use query wizards without having a complete understanding of the assumptions the wizards make).

Microsoft Access displays the Show Table window, which displays a list of tables and queries in your database. The default is to show the tables; if you want to base a query on an existing query, you can click on either the Queries or the Both tab. Exhibit 7–5 illus-

**EXHIBIT 7–6**
**Query Window**

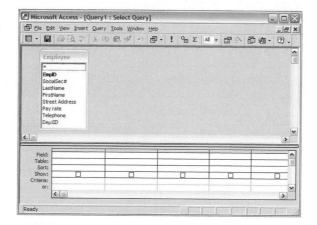

trates the Show Table window. To include tables in the query, either double-click on each table name or click each name and click the Add button. To select multiple tables and add them simultaneously, press the Ctrl key while you click on the table names and when all the chosen table names are highlighted, click on Add. When all appropriate tables and/or queries are added to the **query window,** click on Close. For our first query (generate a list of employees' names and phone numbers to be used for an emergency phone tree) we only need the Employee table, so simply double-click on Employee, then click on Close.

Resize the Query window and the Employee table window that appear so you can see all the fields in the Employee table and still see the lower panel of the query window as shown in Exhibit 7–6. To resize windows, simply click and drag on the edges or corners.

The next step is to add field names from the table to the query grid. This can be accomplished either by clicking the field name(s) and dragging them down to the grid or by double-clicking each field name to add it to the grid. For our query we need only the names and phone numbers for the emergency phone tree. Therefore we add LastName, First-Name, and Telephone to the query grid as illustrated in Exhibit 7–7.

Because our query only needed to accomplish a PROJECT relational algebra operation, our query is complete. To see the results of the query, we can either click on the icon that looks like an exclamation mark (!), or switch to **datasheet view** (either click on the datasheet toolbar button or select View, Datasheet). A query's answer in Microsoft Access is not actually a table, but is called a **dynaset.** A dynaset looks and behaves like a table but is not actually stored as a table—it is generated as a view each time the query is run. The dynaset resulting from your query will appear. If new data that affect the query result are added to the database, the next time the query is run, the dynaset will reflect the addition of the new data. The answer to our first query is shown in Exhibit 7–8.

Once we are certain our query is executing properly, we need to save the query so it can be run again in the future. To save the query, either click on the Save icon (it looks like a diskette) or click on File, Save. That will bring up a Save As window into which you can type a meaningful name for your query and click on OK. See Exhibit 7–9.

Our second query (a list of all attributes of employees whose hourly pay rate is less than $15) accomplishes the relational algebra SELECT operator. To begin, create a new query and add the Employee table to the query window following the same steps illustrated in

**EXHIBIT 7–7**

Employee
Phone Tree
Query Design

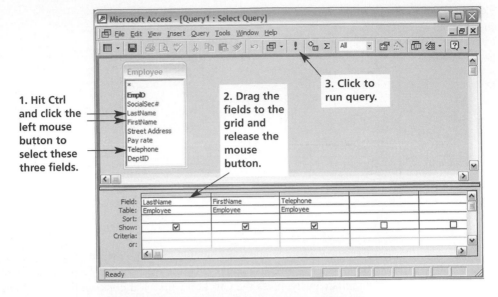

1. Hit Ctrl and click the left mouse button to select these three fields.

2. Drag the fields to the grid and release the mouse button.

3. Click to run query.

**EXHIBIT 7–8**

Employee
Phone Tree
Query Result

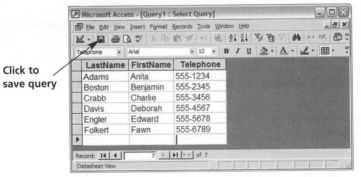

Click to save query

| LastName | FirstName | Telephone |
|----------|-----------|-----------|
| Adams | Anita | 555-1234 |
| Boston | Benjamin | 555-2345 |
| Crabb | Charlie | 555-3456 |
| Davis | Deborah | 555-4567 |
| Engler | Edward | 555-5678 |
| Folkert | Fawn | 555-6789 |

**EXHIBIT 7–9**

Save As
Window

1. Type meaningful query name here

Query Name: EmployeePhoneTreeList

2. Click OK

Exhibits 7–4 through 7–6. The next step is to add all the fields from the Employee table into the query grid. Next it is time to specify the criteria by which the horizontal subset is to be defined. In this example, the field for which the criterion needs to be specified is PayRate, and the criterion is <15. The query grid includes a line labeled Criterion on which to enter the logical operator expression. Criteria should be entered on the same line in the appropriate fields for any query that includes the logical operator AND. Criteria should be entered in the Criteria line for one of the appropriate fields and on the Or line for the other appropriate field for a query that includes the logical operator OR.

**EXHIBIT
7–10(a)
Employees
with PayRate
<15 Query
Design**

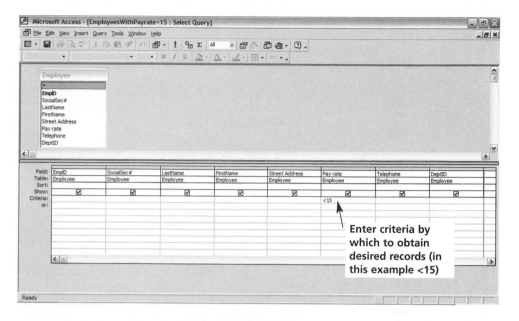

**EXHIBIT
7–10(b)
Employees
with PayRate
<15 Query
Result**

| EmpID | SocialSec# | LastName | FirstName | Street Address | Pay rate | Telephone | DeptID |
|-------|------------|----------|-----------|----------------|----------|-----------|--------|
| E1 | 123345678 | Adams | Anita | 144 Apple St. | $10.00 | 555-1234 | D4 |
| E2 | 234456789 | Boston | Benjamin | 255 Banana Rd. | $12.00 | 555-2345 | D2 |
| E3 | 345567890 | Crabb | Charlie | 366 Cherry Ave. | $14.00 | 555-3456 | D2 |
| E5 | 567789101 | Engler | Edward | 588 Eggplant St. | $11.00 | 555-5678 | D4 |

Record: ⏮ ◀   5   ▶ ⏭ ▶✳ of 5

Datasheet View

Exhibit 7–10(a) illustrates the appropriate design for this query, and Exhibit 7–10(b) shows the resulting dynaset.

The third query we looked at in relational algebra and SQL was one in which we wanted a list of employees and the names of the departments to which they are assigned. This query required a JOIN relational algebra operator as well as a PROJECT to narrow down the answer to only include the employee name and department name columns. In SQL we were able to combine those two operators into one query. In QBE we are also able to accomplish both operators with a single query. To formulate this query in QBE, follow the steps in Exhibits 7–4 through 7–6 adding both the Employee and the Department tables to the query window. Then add the LastName and FirstName fields from the Employee table and add the Name field from the Department table to the query window. Exhibit 7–11 shows the result of these steps. Notice that a join line automatically appeared between Employee and Department, linking the DepartmentID field in the Department table with the DeptID field in the Employee table. This line represents the join that was established in the relationship layout as Access's means for knowing that DeptID in the Employee table is a posted foreign key from the Department table. Exhibit 7–12 shows the result of this query.

**EXHIBIT 7–11**
**Employee and Department JOIN Query Design**

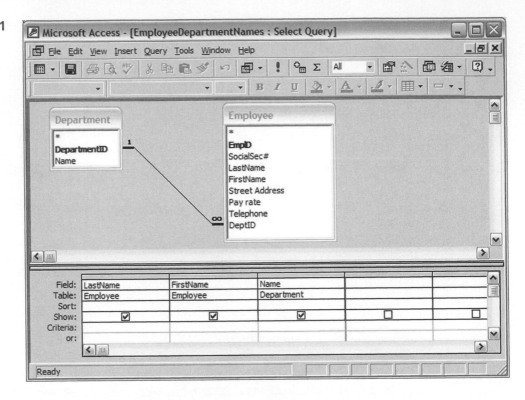

**EXHIBIT 7–12**
**Employee and Department JOIN Query Result**

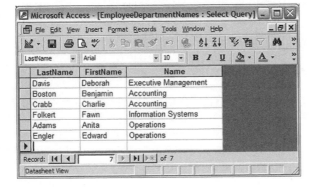

The fourth query we examined previously in this chapter was the list of all employees and the training courses they have taken. To formulate this query in QBE follow the steps in Exhibits 7–4 through 7–6, adding the Employee, CourseTakenByEmployee, and TrainingCourse tables to the query window. The joins established in the relationship layout appear in the query window (between the EmplID fields in the Employee and CourseTakenByEmployee tables and between the CourseID fields in the CourseTakenByEmployee and TrainingCourse tables). Next add the appropriate field names to the query grid (last name, first name, course ID, course name). At this point your query design should resemble Exhibit 7–13(a).

**EXHIBIT
7–13(a)
Initial Query
Design
Employees
and Courses
Taken**

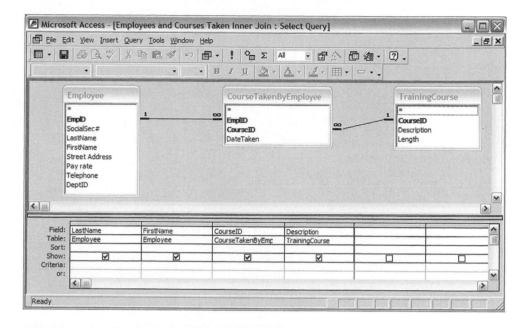

**EXHIBIT
7–13(b)
Result
of Initial
Query Design
Employees
and Courses
Taken**

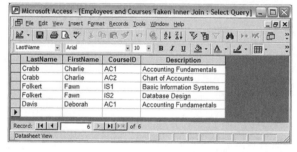

Running this query results in the dynaset shown in Exhibit 7–13(b). What does this answer tell you about the type of join Access uses by default? It must be an inner join, because only those employees who have actually taken courses show up in our answer.

To include ALL employees in the list, showing a blank for those who have not taken any training courses, the join types must be changed. To change the join types, go back to the query design and double-click on the join line between Employee and CourseTakenByEmployee. A **Join Properties window** will appear similar to the one shown in Exhibit 7–14. This confirms the join was established as an inner join, as it says "Only include rows where the joined fields from both tables are equal." This needs to be changed to "Include ALL records from Employee and only those records from CourseTakenByEmployee where the joined fields are equal." Notice that with Access's QBE you don't specify inner join, left join, or right join—you simply choose the option that describes what you are trying to accomplish.

Once you have chosen the appropriate option, click on OK. Next change the join type for the join between CourseTakenByEmployee and TrainingCourse to include all records from CourseTakenByEmployee and only those records from TrainingCourse where the

**EXHIBIT 7–14**
**Join Properties**
**Window**

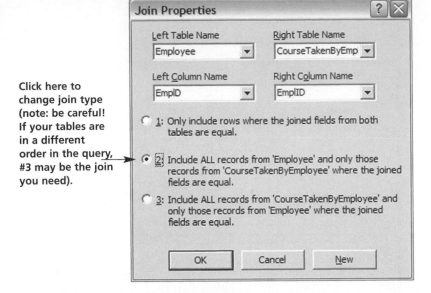

Click here to
change join type
(note: be careful!
If your tables are
in a different
order in the query,
#3 may be the join
you need).

**EXHIBIT 7–15**
**Revised Join**
**Lines**

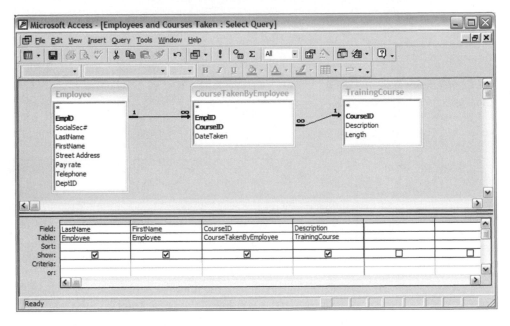

joined fields are equal. Notice that the join lines change to arrows, as illustrated in Exhibit 7–15. The arrows point from the table for which all records will be included and toward the table for which the records whose joined fields are equal will be included. When you run the query again, your answer should resemble Exhibit 7–16.

The fifth query we examined earlier was to calculate the average pay rate for our employees. This query requires an aggregation function called AVG. In QBE aggregation func-

**EXHIBIT 7–16**
**Result
of Revised
Query Design
Employees
and Courses
Taken**

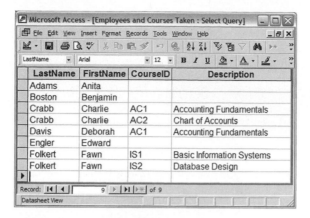

**EXHIBIT
7–17(a)**
**Average
PayRate Query
Design**

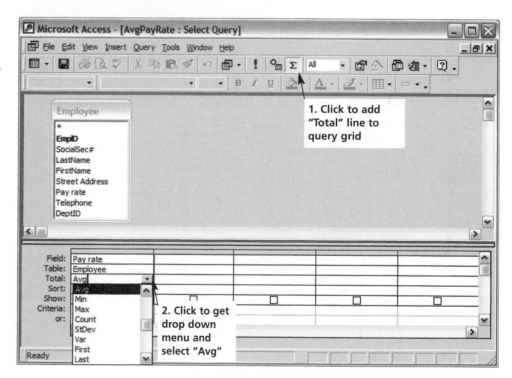

tions may be added to the query grid by clicking on an icon that looks like a summation symbol. When that icon is clicked, a Total line is added to the query grid. When this line is added, it defaults to a Group By aggregation. If you click on Group By, a drop down menu appears from which you can select Avg. Exhibit 7–17(a) illustrates the appropriate query design, and Exhibit 7–17(b) illustrates the query result.

The sixth query we examined earlier in this chapter calculated total sales separately for each date. In QBE this query is accomplished by adding the Sale table to the query window, dragging the date and amount fields to the query grid, adding the Total line to the

**EXHIBIT
7–17(b)**
**Average Pay
Rate Query
Result**

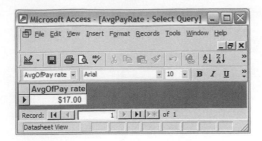

**EXHIBIT
7–18(a)**
**Total Sales
by Date Query
Design**

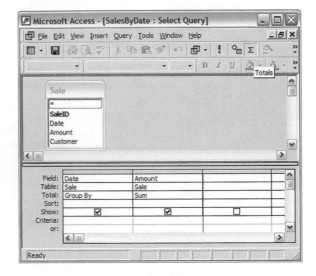

**EXHIBIT
7–18(b)**
**Total Sales
by Date Query
Result**

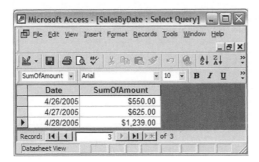

query grid, and setting the Total line to Group By for the Date field and to Sum for the Amount field. This query design is illustrated in Exhibit 7–18(a) and the result is displayed in Exhibit 7–18(b).

If instead, you wanted to calculate total sales separately for each customer, you would need to drag the Customer and Amount fields to the query grid, GROUP BY Customer and SUM Amount. It is important when you are using aggregation functions that you only drag the fields to the query grid that actually participate in an aggregation. If you drag the Date,

**EXHIBIT 7–19**
**SaleLineExtens**
**ion Query—**
**Using the**
**Expression**
**Builder**

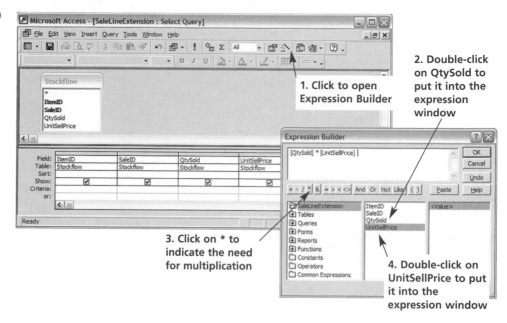

1. Click to open
Expression Builder

2. Double-click
on QtySold to
put it into the
expression
window

3. Click on * to
indicate the need
for multiplication

4. Double-click on
UnitSellPrice to put
it into the
expression window

Customer, and Amount fields, it is going to first group by Date and then group by Customer (or vice versa depending which field is listed first). This will not give you the sum you want!

The final query we examined earlier required a calculation of quantity sold multiplied by the unit sales price to compute a sale line extension for a stockflow record. To accomplish this query in QBE, add the Stockflow table to the query window. Drag all the fields to the query grid. Save the query as SaleLineExtension. Saving the query with fields in the query grid makes those fields available for manipulation in an Access tool called the **Expression Builder.** With the cursor in the next available blank field in the query grid, click on the icon that looks like a magic wand, as illustrated in Exhibit 7–19. Once the Expression Builder is open, double-click on the QtySold field to place it in the expression window. Then click on the asterisk symbol for multiplication. Double-click on the UnitSellPrice field to place it into the expression window. The expression tells Access this field should store the multiplication of QtySold and UnitSellPrice. Click on OK to close the Expression Builder. The result of this query appears in Exhibit 7–20.

In the dynaset, the expression is labeled with a generic term *Expr1*. To change this to a more meaningful name, switch back to the query's design view and in the expression's field, highlight the Expr1 and type the more meaningful name, as shown in Exhibit 7–21.

We noted earlier that Access allows query entry via an SQL view as an alternative to the QBE view. Let's enter the SQL statement for the final query directly into Access instead of using the QBE interface as an illustration. Start a new query, and when the **Show Table window** appears, hit close without adding any tables or queries to your query window. In the upper left corner, the SQL with the small down arrow next to it indicates the path to switch to SQL view. Click on the arrow next to SQL to display the SQL view, as shown in Exhibit 7–22.

The SQL view appears with the word SELECT followed by a semicolon. Access knows that every SQL statement begins with the word SELECT and ends with a semicolon. All that is needed is the detail that goes in between. Type the SQL statement in as shown in Exhibit 7–23, then run the query to see the same dynaset that resulted earlier using QBE.

**EXHIBIT 7–20**
**SaleLineItem**
**Extension**
**Query Result**

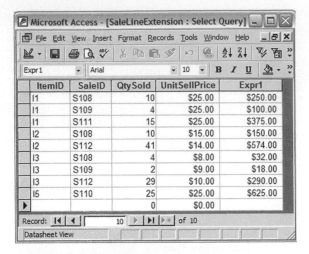

**EXHIBIT 7–21**
**Renaming a**
**Field**

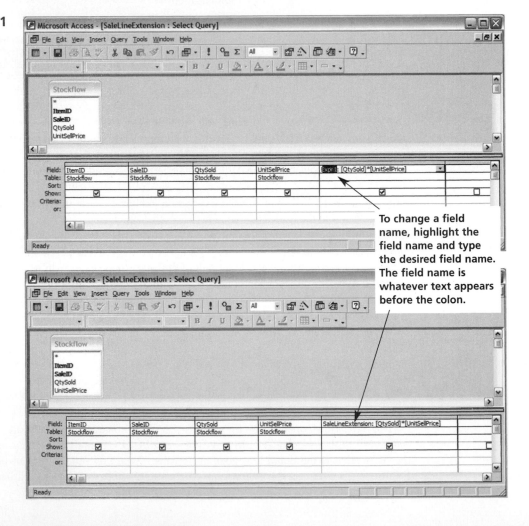

To change a field name, highlight the field name and type the desired field name. The field name is whatever text appears before the colon.

**EXHIBIT 7–22**
**Creating a Query in Microsoft Access SQL View**

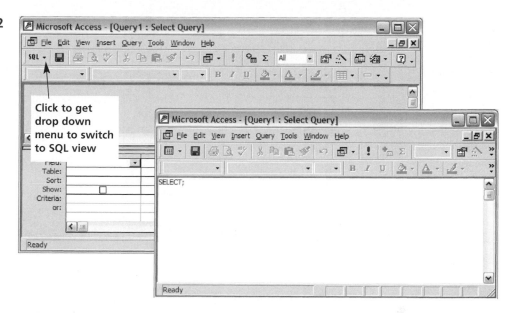

**EXHIBIT 7–23**
**SQL Statement and Resulting Dynaset**

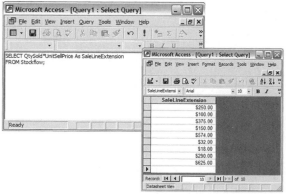

Compare Exhibit 7–23 with Exhibit 7–20; the only difference is the ItemID, SaleID, QtySold, and UnitSellPrice attributes do not appear in Exhibit 7–23. That is because the SQL statement did not specifically ask for those to be included. A slight revision to the SQL statement will cause those fields to appear in the dynaset, as follows:

> SELECT ItemID, SaleID, QtySold, UnitSellPrice, QtySold*UnitSellPrice As SaleLineExtension FROM Stockflow;

## PARAMETER QUERIES

Often users need to reuse ad hoc queries they construct on a regular basis, changing only the date criteria. For example, a marketing manager that wants to know the total sales for a particular inventory item for a week or a month could use the same query with different date constraints. To increase the reusability of queries, Access offers the option of creating parameter queries. Consider a query that specifies a date range as the criteria: BETWEEN 1/1/05 and

**EXHIBIT
7–24(a)**
**Parameter
Query Design**

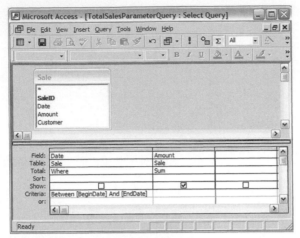

**EXHIBIT
7–24(b)**
**Prompt
for Value for
the [BeginDate]
Parameter**

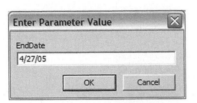

**EXHIBIT
7–24(c)**
**Prompt
for Value for
the [EndDate]
Parameter**

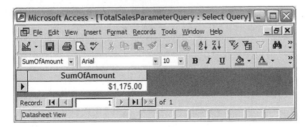

**EXHIBIT
7–24(d)**
**Parameter
Query Result**

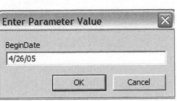

1/31/05. A user who wants to reuse this query in the future for a different date range (e.g. BE-TWEEN 2/1/05 and 2/28/05) must change the design of the query to change the date constraint. A **parameter query** for this situation does not specify the exact dates; instead, it includes parameter names for each date, for example BETWEEN [BeginDate] and [EndDate]. When the query is run, Access realizes that it doesn't know what BeginDate and EndDate are, so Access prompts the user to specify the values of these parameters. This enables the user to change the dates each time the query is run without changing the design of the query.

Exhibit 7–24(a) illustrates the design of a parameter query. Access's syntax for parameters requires that they be enclosed in square brackets. Parts (b), (c), and (d) of Exhibit 7–24 show the prompts for the parameter values and the final query result.

# CONCLUDING COMMENTS

Querying provides the power of the relational database model. Once you unlock the mystery of query construction, whether you prefer SQL or QBE, you can tap into the wealth of information that is at your fingertips in a well-designed relational database. Enterprises today typically store vast amounts of data in relational databases that can be retrieved in a variety of different formats for different decision-making purposes. To ensure the information retrieved is valid, users should be well versed in relational database design, semantic query logic, and the syntax of the particular query language used. This chapter is intended to provide you with only a cursory introduction to querying in SQL and Microsoft Access's QBE. To become proficient at querying, you must practice and learn through trial and error. The automated help facility in Microsoft Access contains more examples of queries and will help you to solidify your understanding of the query window, QBE grid, Expression Builder, and other syntactic features of Microsoft Access QBE. If you do an Internet search using a search engine such as www.google.com and keywords *SQL tutorial* you will find several tutorial sites that provide help with understanding SQL syntax. Note, however, that you won't find solutions for the semantic nature of queries you need to formulate. Rather, you must first figure out where the desired information is in your database and determine how to get that information (thinking about this in terms of the relational algebra operators can be very helpful). We strongly recommend using a pencil and a calculator (or exporting data to a spreadsheet) to figure solutions out manually before attempting to create a query in Microsoft Access. That ensures that you understand the logic of the query before enveloping the logic into the syntax of either QBE or SQL, and it also gives you some check figures to use in determining whether the query is functioning as planned. Comprehensive testing of queries that are intended to be reused is crucial to ensure they will work for different dates (if date constraints are included), and after new data are entered into the database. In each of the business process chapters in this textbook (Chapters 8–13) we discuss information needs and provide some details about the semantic query logic needed to develop some commonly needed figures for management decision making, including many financial statement line items.

# Key Terms and Concepts

## General Terms and Concepts

Ad hoc querying, *162*

Aggregation functions, *173*

Comparison operator, *172*

Data manipulation language, *169*

Equi-join, *165*

GROUP BY, *173*

Horizontal calculation, *175*

Horizontal subset of a table, *163*

Information retrieval, *161*

Inner join, *165*

JOIN (in relational algebra), *163*

Left Join, *171*

Logical operator, *172*

Mathematical operation, *172*

Outer join, *168*

PROJECT (in relational algebra), *163*

Query, *162*

Query By Example (QBE), *162*

Relational algebra, *162*

Right Join, *171*

SELECT (in relational algebra), *163*

SELECT-FROM-WHERE (in SQL), *170*

Structured Query Language (SQL), *162*

Syntax, *169*

Vertical calculation, *175*

Vertical subset of a table, *163*

**Microsoft Access Terms and Concepts**

| | | |
|---|---|---|
| Datasheet view, *179* | Join Properties | Query window, *179* |
| Design view, *177* | window, *183* | Relationship layout, *175* |
| Dynaset, *179* | Parameter query, *190* | Show Table window, *187* |
| Expression Builder, *187* | Query grid, *175* | SQL view, *175* |

## Review Questions

LO1   **R1.** Which of the relational algebra operators is needed to retrieve a vertical subset (i.e., a subset of columns) from a relational database table?

LO1   **R2.** Which of the relational algebra operators is needed to retrieve a horizontal subset (i.e., a subset of rows) from a relational database table?

LO1   **R3.** Which of the relational algebra operators is needed to combine two tables together in a query?

LO2   **R4.** What is the standard format of an SQL query statement?

LO3   **R5.** Which component of an SQL statement accomplishes a relational algebra SELECT operation?

LO3   **R6.** Which component of an SQL statement accomplishes a relational algebra PROJECT operation?

LO3   **R7.** Which components of an SQL statement accomplish a relational algebra JOIN operation?

LO7   **R8.** What is the advantage to creating a query that includes a date constraint as a parameter query?

LO4, LO7   **R9.** What is the difference between an aggregation (vertical calculation) and a horizontal calculation?

LO4, LO7   **R10.** Give an example of a query for which you would need to use a left join instead of an inner join.

## Multiple Choice Questions

LO7   **MC1.** A query's answer in Microsoft Access is referred to as a:
     A. PROJECT
     B. Dynaset
     C. Dataset
     D. None of the above

LO7   **MC2.** In Microsoft Access, the displayed links of all tables can be viewed in the:
     A. Elements display
     B. Table design
     C. Relationship layout
     D. QBE interface

LO4   **MC3.** What does the asterisk (*) mean in SQL?
     A. Include all attributes
     B. Modify attribute
     C. Delete attribute
     D. None of the above

LO7   MC4.  QBE is an acronym for:
A. Query Before Example
B. Query By Excellence
C. Query By E-mail
D. Query By Example

LO4–LO9   MC5.  You have 200 distributors in your vendor table. Of these 200 distributors, approximately 40 are potential sources from whom no purchases have yet been made. You need a report that provides the DistributorID, Name, and the total purchase dollar amounts made during a specified time period. The report needs to include each of the 200 distributors, with zero balances appearing for the vendors from whom no purchases have been made. Assume the table structures appear in your database layout as follows:

| Purchase | Distributor |
| --- | --- |
| PurchaseNumber | DistributorID |
| Date | Name |
| DollarAmount | Address |
| Cash DisbursementID | Phone |
| VendorID | QualityRating |

What type of join do you need between the Distributor and Purchase tables for the query on which this report will be based?
A.  Inner join
B.  Full outer join
C.  Left outer join
D.  Right outer join

## Discussion Questions

LO1, LO2, LO3   D1.  What are the advantages (and/or disadvantages) of SQL compared to relational algebra?

LO2, LO7   D2.  What are the advantages (and/or disadvantages) of QBE compared to SQL?

LO5, LO6, LO8, LO9   D3.  Explain why a poor database design results in information retrieval problems.

LO5, LO6, LO8, LO9   D4.  Explain how incorrect information retrieval results may be obtained from even a perfectly designed database.

LO4   D5.  Create a query in SQL that will list the last name, first name, and telephone number for all the customers who live in Florida. States are entered in the database using their two digit postal abbreviation (Florida is FL). The customer table structure (field types are noted) follows:

**Customer**

| CustomerID | LastName | FirstName | Telephone | City | State | CreditLimit | AcctsReceivableBalance |
| --- | --- | --- | --- | --- | --- | --- | --- |
| Text | Text | Text | Text | Text | Text | Currency | Currency |

LO5   D6.  You have three tables in your relational database: Student, Course, and TakenBy.

**Student**

| StudentID | Name | Address |
|-----------|------|---------|
| S1 | Angelo Ramon | 8892 Sandhurst |
| S2 | Chloe Zenker | 1262 Gingersnap |
| S3 | Harold George | 1495 Colorado |

**Course**

| CourseID | Description | No. Credits |
|----------|-------------|-------------|
| C1 | Economics | 3 |
| C2 | Finance | 3 |
| C3 | Marketing | 3 |

**TakenBy**

| StudentID | CourseID | Semester | GradeEarned |
|-----------|----------|----------|-------------|
| S1 | C1 | Sp2010 | A |
| S1 | C3 | Sp2010 | B+ |
| S1 | C2 | Fa2010 | A− |
| S2 | C1 | Sp2010 | B |
| S2 | C2 | Fa2010 | A |
| S2 | C3 | Fa2010 | A |
| S3 | C1 | Fa2010 | A |
| S3 | C2 | Fa2010 | B+ |

What information will result from the following SQL query applied to this relational database?

> SELECT StudentID, Name
> FROM Student, TakenBy
> WHERE Student.StudentID=TakenBy.StudentID AND CourseID=C1 AND GradeEarned=A;

LO6    D7. You have three tables in your relational database: Movie, Star, and RolePlayed.

**Movie**

| MovieID | Title | Rating |
|---------|-------|--------|
| M1 | Castaway | PG-13 |
| M2 | You've Got Mail | PG |
| M3 | City of Angels | PG-13 |

**Star**

| StarID | Name | YearBirth |
|--------|------|-----------|
| St1 | Tom Hanks | 1956 |
| St2 | Meg Ryan | 1961 |
| St3 | Nicolas Cage | 1964 |

**RolePlayed**

| MovieID | StarID | CharacterName |
|---------|--------|---------------|
| M1 | St1 | Chuck Noland |
| M2 | St1 | Joe Fox |
| M2 | St2 | Kathleen Kelly |
| M3 | St2 | Maggie Rice |
| M3 | St3 | Seth |

If the goal is to retrieve the title and rating of each movie in which Meg Ryan played a role, what errors, if any, exist in the following SQL statement?

SELECT *

FROM RolePlayed

WHERE StarID="Meg Ryan";

LO8  D8. You have two tables in your relational database: Loan and Lender as illustrated in Exhibit 7–25 below. What information will result from the QBE query applied to the relational database tables in Exhibit 7–25?

**EXHIBIT 7–25**

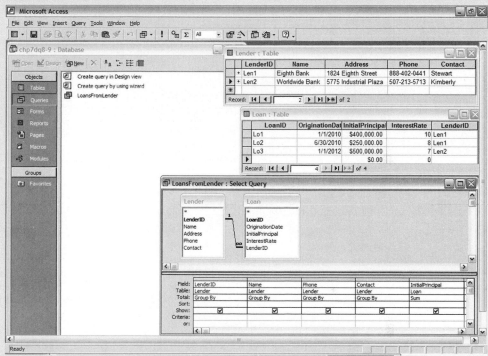

LO9  D9. Inspect the StockflowSale-Inventory table and related QBE query in Exhibit 7–26. What errors, if any, exist in the QBE query if the goal of the query is to calculate the total sales dollar value for each inventory item?

**EXHIBIT 7–26**

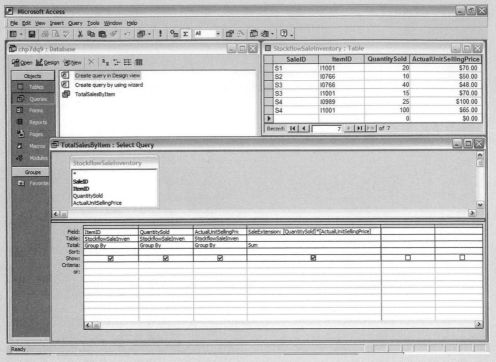

# Applied Learning

LO3, LO8 **A1.** This applied learning assignment is based on the table structures for Friendly Public Library (FPL). The table structures and underlying conceptual model for FPL are illustrated in Exhibits 7–27 and 7–28. These exhibits do not represent the entire database for FPL but include enough information for you to develop the queries they need. Like most public libraries, FPL lends different types of media (e.g., books, journals, maps, and videos) to patrons at no cost. Different types of media may be borrowed for various lengths of time; some media types are noncirculating and may only be used in the library. FPL created a database in which to store some of its information, but FPL has not yet created any queries. For each of the following scenarios you are asked to create a query (or set of queries) to meet the information need identified by FPL. Your instructor will provide you with the electronic database file in Microsoft Access. You may use SQL view or QBE for each of the queries. For each query, print out the query design (use Alt-PrintScreen to copy the query design and then paste it into a word processing application) and also print out the query result (you can use the File, Print menu to print the result). Be sure to label the printouts and put your name on your assignment.

a. Marketing wants to know whether more children's fiction books are checked out during the month of July than during the month of September. To determine this, Marketing has requested that you create a query that calculates the number of children's fiction books checked out during July and another query that calculates the number

**EXHIBIT 7–27    FPL Table Structures***

**Media Type**

| TypeCode | CategoryDescription | CheckoutPeriod |
| --- | --- | --- |

**Media**

| ItemID | Title | Author | Publisher | YearPublished | DateAcquired | MediaType[FK] |
| --- | --- | --- | --- | --- | --- | --- |

**Library Staff**

| EmpID | Name | Address | City | State | Zip | Phone | WH | SocSec# | BankAcct# |
| --- | --- | --- | --- | --- | --- | --- | --- | --- | --- |

**Patron**

| PatronID | Name | Address | City | State | Zip | Phone | PatronType[FK] |
| --- | --- | --- | --- | --- | --- | --- | --- |

**Loan (Checkout)**

| LoanID | Date | Patron[FK] | LibraryStaff[FK] |
| --- | --- | --- | --- |

**Loan-Media**

| LoanID | ItemID | DateDue | DateReturned |
| --- | --- | --- | --- |

**Patron Type**

| TypeCode | Description | AgeCriteria |
| --- | --- | --- |

*Primary keys are double-underlined; foreign keys are indicated with FK; WH = withholdings

of children's fiction books checked out during September so that Marketing can compare the totals. Can you think of a third query to make the comparison for Marketing so they don't have to make the comparison manually?

b. Payroll has decided that all library employees must be paid via direct deposit. Until now direct deposit has been available to employees but was not required. Payroll needs a list of all library employees for whom no direct deposit information is on file to prepare a memorandum to send to those employees. The list should include the employee ID, name, address, and telephone number for each employee for whom direct deposit information is missing.

c. Operations is concerned that the library is running short on space in its public access areas. Therefore, Operations wants to move all library holdings that are of a certain age and that have not been checked out recently into a basement storage area. Those items will be kept for some length of time and those that are not requested by any patrons during that time will be sold, discarded, or given away. Items in the basement that are requested by patrons will be moved to the main public access areas. Operations anticipates the need to identify items to be moved to the basement storage area several times a year; therefore they request that the queries you write be ones they can reuse with their choice of specified dates (for age of item and for how recently an item has been checked out).

d. Circulation needs to send out overdue notices each day to patrons whose media have not been returned by the due date. Write a query or set of queries Circulation can use

**EXHIBIT 7–28** **FPL Conceptual Model**

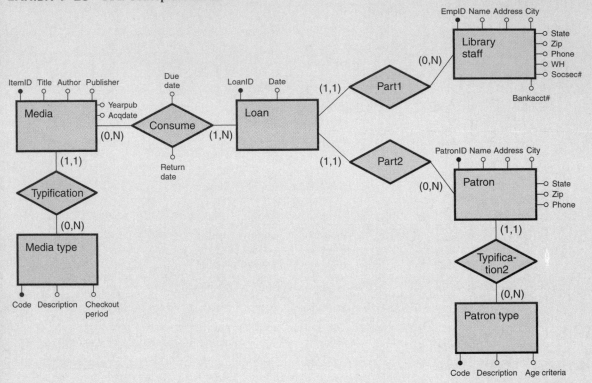

each day to identify the patron name, address, city, state, zip, and media title(s) for each overdue item. Obviously it needs to be a query (set) that can be reused each day, with the ability to specify the date(s) involved.

e. What is another information need you can think of for which some area of FPL may need a query or set of queries developed? Develop a query or query set that satisfies the information need you identified.

# Answers to Multiple Choice Questions

MC1. B; MC2. C; MC3. A; MC4. D; MC5. A.

# Chapter **Eight**

# The Sales/Collection Business Process

## LEARNING OBJECTIVES

The objective of this chapter is to encourage an in-depth understanding of the sales/collection business process, with a focus on the modeling of this transaction cycle with the REA enterprise ontology and querying to meet information needs for this cycle. After studying this chapter you should be able to:

1. Identify activities and documents common to sales/collection business processes for various enterprises
2. Recognize similarities and differences between different types of revenue-generating enterprises
3. Identify the components of the REA ontology in the sales/collection business process
4. Explain how the sales/collection business process fits into an enterprise's value system
5. Explain how the sales/collection business process fits into an enterprise's value chain
6. Create a REA business process level model for an enterprise's sales/collection business process
7. Identify common information needs within the sales/collection process
8. Create queries to meet common information needs in the sales/collection process

## INTRODUCTION

The **sales/collection business process** is sometimes called the revenue transaction cycle or the order to cash mega-process; therefore, you must look past the labels an enterprise assigns to its various activities and examine the substance to identify the sales/collection process for a given enterprise. This chapter is the first of several in this module that examine business processes in detail. Each of these chapters discusses how the transaction cycle of interest fits into the value system and value chain levels for various enterprises. The REA business process level design pattern is then discussed, as well as the task activities that typically occur, the risks and internal controls associated with those activities, the information needs that arise within the business process, and the development of specific queries using Microsoft Access to meet some of the identified information needs.

# SALES/COLLECTION BUSINESS PROCESS IN AN ENTERPRISE VALUE SYSTEM

As you analyze and model a business process, you must clearly understand its purpose and objectives. You must realize how the business process fits into the value system of the enterprise as a whole. At the value system level, the sales/collection process is the point of contact between the customer and the enterprise. Goods and/or services flow from the enterprise to the customer; cash flows from the customer to the enterprise, as highlighted in Exhibit 8–1.

From the value system we surmise that to exchange goods and services for cash with the customers, we must attract customers, then help those customers select goods and services, deliver the goods and services requested, and collect payments for the goods and services. Generating revenue is the key to achieving growth and profitability. Enterprises can produce an abundance of goods and create a variety of services, but the real test of value is whether someone will pay a price that covers the cost of goods and services and provide the enterprise with an acceptable return on invested funds.

# SALES/COLLECTION BUSINESS PROCESS IN ENTERPRISE VALUE CHAINS

The value chain reveals interfaces between the sales/collection process and other business processes. Exhibit 8–2 illustrates the typical value chains for manufacturing enterprises; for merchandising enterprises such as retail stores, wholesale distributors, and rental agencies; and for service-provision enterprises. Goods and services are made available to an enterprise's revenue process as a result of the conversion, acquisition/payment, and payroll processes; the revenue process turns those goods and services into cash, which is made available to the financing process. To turn the goods and services into cash, the revenue process must include at least one economic event that transfers out the goods and services (i.e., a decrement event) and at least one economic event that transfers in the cash (i.e., an increment event).

**EXHIBIT 8–1**

**Sales/Collection Process in an Enterprise Value System**

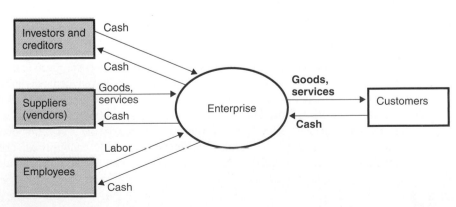

**EXHIBIT 8–2**   **Sales/Collection Process in the Value Chain**

Partial Value Chain for Manufacturers

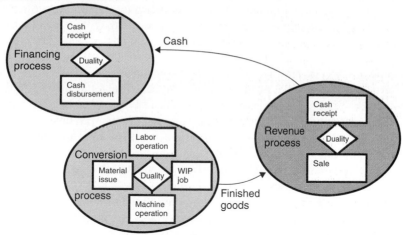

For Wholesale or Retail Distributors and Rental Agencies

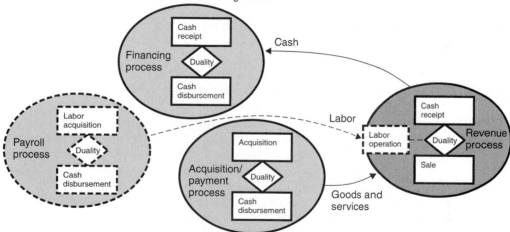

Partial Value Chain for Service Providers

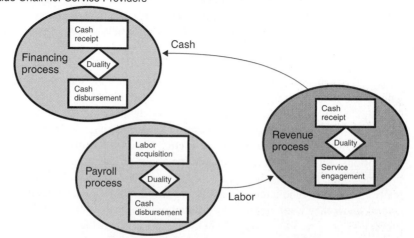

Although labor operations exist in every enterprise's revenue process (i.e., sales representatives and other employees perform labor in executing revenue cycle events) in most enterprises they are not explicitly tracked and matched to the revenue-generating activity. Instead the labor cost is simply aggregated into a number called selling, general, and administrative expenses. Service providers are a notable exception. Because labor is in essence the **inventory** service providers sell, it usually becomes cost-beneficial for them to track and measure details of labor operations. Other enterprises for which labor operations are an important component of the revenue-generating activities may also track labor operations. For example, a furniture store that provides delivery service to customers who purchase the furniture may want to track the labor details associated with delivering the furniture. Or a restaurant that offers food delivery to customers' front doors may want to track the labor details associated with delivering the food. For enterprises that have determined a benefit in excess of the cost of tracking labor operations in their revenue cycles, a link between the payroll process and the revenue process should be materialized and accompanied by a labor operation event that participates in the duality relationship, as shown by dotted lines in Exhibit 8–2.

# SALES/COLLECTION BUSINESS PROCESS LEVEL REA MODELS

Recall that the extended REA ontology described in Chapter 4 and illustrated in Exhibit 8–3 identifies the pattern underlying each transaction cycle, which consists of **instigation events, mutual commitment events,** economic exchange events, resources, agents, types, and various relationships such as stockflow, duality, fulfillment, reservation, proposition, and participation. In this section we describe the extended REA ontology components specific to the sales/collection business process, noting differences for different types of enterprises (e.g. merchandiser versus manufacturer or service provider).

The *REA* pattern aids in analyzing business processes and events by highlighting the *what* (the resources involved in the event) and the *who* (the internal and external agents) of each event. Notice that the *where* and the *when* are often stored as attributes of each event. The events, agents, and resources involved in the sales/collection process vary somewhat from enterprise to enterprise. The general pattern discussed in this chapter can be easily adapted and applied to meet the exact requirements of any enterprise (e.g., nonprofit or governmental agencies, wholesalers, bartering arrangements, catalog sales, cash sales, retailers, service providers, prepaid sale activities, or manufacturers).

## Instigation Events (Marketing Events, Customer Inquiries)

Instigation events may be internally instigated (i.e., by the enterprise) or externally instigated (i.e., by an external business partner of the enterprise). The sales/collection process is instigated by the attraction of a customer's decision to buy the enterprise's goods or services. In an effort to influence customer decision making, an enterprise plans, executes, and evaluates a variety of **marketing events** (e.g., **sales calls,** advertising campaigns, or promotions) intended to inform customers about products and/or services and hopefully influence them to trigger the sales/collection process. Therefore marketing efforts are typically considered to be internally generated instigation events. Conversely, sometimes customers know they want a particular product or service and they search for a source for that product or service. They may call an enterprise to see if the product or service they need

**EXHIBIT 8–3**   **Sales/Collection Extended REA Ontology Database Design Pattern**

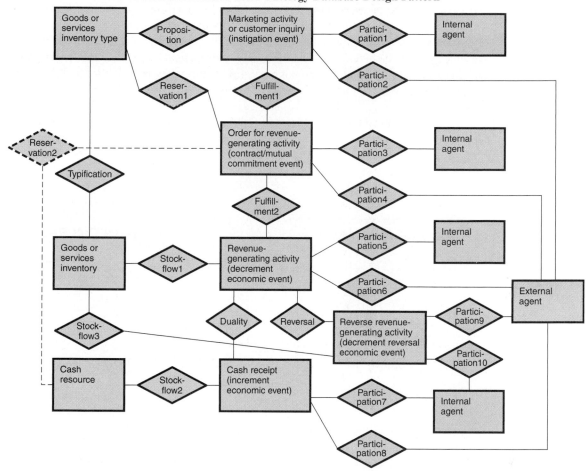

Note 1: Reservation2 is shown with dashed lines to indicate that it is often excluded from the model because the revenue-generating activity (decrement economic event) is often a more reliable cash flow budget factor than is the mutual commitment event.

Note 2: Goods or services inventory may be excluded for enterprises for which it is not cost effective to use specific identification; if so, stockflow1 and stockflow2 should connect to the goods or services inventory type entity. In other cases, the mutual commitment event may specify an instance of goods or services inventory; if so, reservation1 should connect to the goods or services inventory entity.

Note 3: This diagram does not attempt to differentiate internal agents for the various events; for some enterprises one category of employees may participate in all these events; for others there may be several different categories of employees involved.

is available, without having participated in a marketing event. Such customer inquiries are externally generated instigation events. Quotes or bids may be provided to the customer as part of instigation events.

Agents involved in instigation events usually are sales/marketing personnel or customer service representatives (internal agents) and customers (external agents). Typically there is no need to specifically identify a good or service for purposes of instigation events; all that is needed is information about the type of good or service promoted. Of course, some enterprises have atypical or unusual circumstances and may therefore involve different agents and/or may require specific identification of goods and services being marketed.

Attributes of instigation events that should be captured typically include the date, time, and location of the event, and the duration of the customer contact. The instigation event data should also be able to be linked to data regarding the related sales and marketing or customer service personnel, the customer, and the types of goods or services that were presented to the customer. Data regarding sales call instigation events are often captured on a sales call form such as that in Exhibit 8–4. This form may be either a paper document or part of a software application interface. In either case, similar data are captured and stored.

The set of relational tables illustrated in Exhibit 8–5 correspond to Exhibit 8–3's entity-relationship representation of the sales call event, the relationships in which it participates (proposition, fulfillment1, participation1, and participation2), and the related entities **(in-**

**EXHIBIT 8–4**
**Sales Call Report**

**Your Source Company**
*Your Source for Everything You Need*
123 Main St.
Anytown, USA 12345

**Sales Call Report**

No. ___42___

| Salesperson name | Jimmy Vitale | | Salesperson # | E23 |
| --- | --- | --- | --- | --- |
| Customer name | Needmore Stuff | | Customer # | C2323 |

| Sales call location | Needmore Stuff warehouse |
| --- | --- |

| Date | 5/4/2010 | Start time | 9:12 a.m. | End time | 10:00 a.m. |
| --- | --- | --- | --- | --- | --- |

| Customer representative called on | Sarah Gibson |
| --- | --- |
| What is this person's position? | Procurement supervisor |

**What products/services were presented at this sales call?**

Big stuff (Item BIS1)
Little stuff (Item LIS1)
Huge stuff (Item HUS1)
Tiny stuff (Item TIS1)

Did a sale order result from this sales call?  Yes ☒  Order Number ___14___  No ☐

**If yes, what products/services were ordered by the customer?**

TIS1
LIS1



**Follow-up comments (e.g., customer reaction to products, other notes):**

Customer likes small things! Had no interest at all in big or huge stuff, don't bother presenting again. The smaller the better!

## EXHIBIT 8–5 Relational Tables Encompassing Sales Call Event

### Sales Call (Instigation) Event

| Sales Call ID | Date | StartTime | EndTime | Location | SalesRepIDFK | CustomerIDFK |
|---|---|---|---|---|---|---|
| 42 | 5/4/2010 | 9:12 a.m. | 10:00 a.m. | Customer | E23 | C2323 |

### Proposition Relationship

| Sales Call ID | Item ID | Customer Reaction to Product |
|---|---|---|
| 42 | BIS1 | Negative |
| 42 | LIS1 | Positive |
| 42 | HUS1 | Negative |
| 42 | TIS1 | Positive |

### Sales Representative (Internal Agent)

| Sales Rep ID | Name | Address | Telephone | DateOfBirth |
|---|---|---|---|---|
| E23 | Jimmy Vitale | 425 ConAir Drive | 555-5678 | Aug 18, 1962 |

### Customer (External Agent)

| Customer ID | Name | Address | Telephone | Credit Rating |
|---|---|---|---|---|
| C2323 | Needmore Stuff | 86906 Enterprise Court | 555-8989 | A+ |

### Inventory Type (Resource Type)

| Item ID | Description | UnitOfMeasure | Standard Cost | List Price |
|---|---|---|---|---|
| BIS1 | Big Stuff | Each | $20.00 | $50.00 |
| HUS1 | Huge Stuff | Each | $30.00 | $70.00 |
| LIS1 | Little Stuff | Box of 6 | $36.00 | $72.00 |
| TIS1 | Tiny Stuff | Box of 12 | $48.00 | $96.00 |

### Sale Order (Mutual Commitment) Event

| Sale Order ID | Order Date | Date Needed | Total Dollar Amt | Sales Tax | Shipping Charge | Sales CallIDFK | Sales RepIDFK | Customer IDFK |
|---|---|---|---|---|---|---|---|---|
| 14 | 5/4/2010 | 5/7/2010 | $1,100.00 | $0 | $0 | 42 | E23 | C2323 |

Note: Fulfillment1 relationship is implemented with Sales Call ID posted into Sale Order table. Participation1 relationship is implemented with Sales Rep ID posted into Sales Call table. Participation2 relationship is implemented with Customer ID posted into Sales Call table. Customer reaction to product is included as an attribute in the proposition table because it is intended to measure the reaction to the product on a particular sales call. It is assumed that the customer could react differently to the same product on a different sale. In essence, customer reaction to a product on a sales call is an attribute of a ternary relationship; however, since the ternary relationship is not represented, and since each sales call involves a maximum of one customer, the proposition table is the best place to store this attribute.

ventory type, sales order, sales representative, and customer). Other possible tables could be derived depending on the relationship cardinalities. Data from the form in Exhibit 8–4 have been entered into the database tables; however, some of these data (e.g., inventory and customer information) would already have existed in the database tables before the sales call data were added to the tables, so all that is added regarding those objects is the relationship information so they can be linked to the event. The sale order data would normally be entered upon processing of the order; we are assuming the sales order generated at the sales call was processed immediately. More detail about the order event is provided in the next section.

# Mutual Commitment Events (Customer Orders, Rentals, Service Agreements)

A mutual commitment event exists if the enterprise and an external business partner have each agreed to exchange resources at a defined future time. In the sales/collection process the most common mutual commitment events are **customer orders,** rental agreements, and service agreements. A mutual commitment doesn't always happen at a discrete point in time; often it involves a series of activities. Typically a customer (the external agent) places an order with the enterprise for goods or services (the resource). Typically there is no need to specifically identify goods or services for mutual commitment events; rather information about the type of good or service promised to the customer is sufficient. Sales or customer service representatives and/or order entry clerks (internal agents) assist the customer and collect the order data. The enterprise determines whether to commit by checking the availability of requested goods or services, verifying all price and date information, and contacting the customer if necessary to adjust pricing or dates promised. The enterprise also determines whether to extend credit to the customer; therefore a credit manager also may serve as an internal agent.

These determinations are important because the enterprise does not want to commit unless it is confident both parties can fulfill their parts of the sales transaction (i.e., the enterprise must have the ability to fill the order and the customer must have the ability to make payment). Once the customer's order is approved, it becomes an accepted sale order and is considered a mutual commitment. Ideally an enterprise wants to be able to trace each sale order (mutual commitment event) to a sales call or other instigation event. Sometimes it is impossible to determine which marketing efforts led to commitments for an enterprise; in such cases the fulfillment1 relationship is typically not materialized. For other enterprises, commitments typically occur only as part of marketing events; for example, vacation ownership, or time-share, sales. In those rare cases, the commitment and instigation events may be collapsed into a single entity. Linking the marketing efforts to the commitment event provides valuable information to evaluate marketing effectiveness, so enterprises should consider the feasibility and cost of materializing this link.

Attributes of mutual commitment events that typically should be captured include the date, time, and dollar amount of the order; the date by which the customer needs the goods or services delivered; the delivery method to be used (e.g., Federal Express, UPS, or customer pick-up); the desired location of the delivery; and the payment terms. The order data should also be able to be linked to data regarding the related resources, agents, and **economic decrement events,** and, if possible, to the related instigation event. Data regarding sale order commitment events are often captured on a sale order form such as that shown in Exhibit 8–6. This form may be either a paper document or part of a software application interface that is used to update the enterprise database. For many enterprises, the data for sales orders are obtained from a customer purchase order form, commonly referred to as a customer order. The primary difference between a customer order and a sale order is that the customer order is in the customer's format, whereas the sale order is in the seller's format.

The set of relational tables in Exhibit 8–7 correspond to Exhibit 8-3's entity-relationship representation of the sales order event and the relationships in which it participates (reser-

**EXHIBIT 8–6**    Sale Order

| **Your Source Company** | **Sale Order** |
|---|---|

*Your Source for Everything You Need*
123 Main St.
Anytown, USA 12345

ORDER NO:    14
DATE    5/4/2010

| Ordered by: | Ship to: |
|---|---|
| Sarah Gibson | Needmore Stuff |
| | 86906 Enterprise Dr. |
| | Anytown, USA 12345 |
| | |

| SALESPERSON | P.O. NUMBER | EST. SHIP DATE | TO SHIP VIA | TERMS |
|---|---|---|---|---|
| E23 | Verbal | 5/5/2010 | FedEx | N/30 |

| QUANTITY | STOCK # | DESCRIPTION | UNIT PRICE | AMOUNT |
|---|---|---|---|---|
| 2 | LIS1 | Little Stuff, box of 6 | $70.00 | $ 140.00 |
| 10 | TIS1 | Tiny Stuff, box of 12 | $96.00 | $ 960.00 |

| | |
|---|---|
| SUBTOTAL | $1,100.00 |
| SALES TAX | 0 |
| SHIPPING & HANDLING | 0 |
| ORDER TOTAL | $1,100.00 |

vation, fulfillment1, fulfillment2, participation3, and participation4). Other possible tables could be derived, depending on the relationship cardinalities. Data from the form in Exhibit 8–6 have been entered into the database tables; however, some of these data would already have existed in the database tables (e.g., the customer and inventory information) before the sales order data were added to the tables.

Similar types of data are captured on similar forms (again, either in electronic interfaces or on paper documents) for other mutual commitment events such as service agreements and rental contracts. Exhibit 8–8 shows a service agreement; note the similarities in the types of data captured regarding the service agreement and the sale order events. Similar data would also be captured for rental agreements.

## Economic Decrement Event (Sale, Shipment, Rental, or Service Engagement)

The economic decrement event in the sales/collection process may take on one of several labels because it represents the revenue generating activity, which can take various forms. The revenue generating activity is the decrement event; resources made available to the

## EXHIBIT 8–7 Relational Tables Encompassing Sales Order Event

### Sale Order (Mutual Commitment) Event

| Sale Order ID | Order Date | Date Needed | Total Dollar Amt | Sales Tax | Shipping Charge | Sales CallIDFK | Sales RepIDFK | Customer IDFK |
|---|---|---|---|---|---|---|---|---|
| 14 | 5/4/2010 | 5/7/2010 | $1,100.00 | $0 | $0 | 42 | E23 | C2323 |

### Sales Call (Instigation) Event

| Sales Call ID | Date | StartTime | EndTime | Location | SalesRepIDFK | CustomerIDFK |
|---|---|---|---|---|---|---|
| 42 | 5/4/2010 | 9:12 a.m. | 10:00 a.m. | Customer | E23 | C2323 |

### Reservation Relationship

| Sales Order ID | Item ID | Quantity Ordered | Quoted Unit Price |
|---|---|---|---|
| 14 | LIS1 | 2 | 70.00 |
| 14 | TIS1 | 10 | 96.00 |

### Sales Representative (Internal Agent)

| Sales Rep ID | Name | Address | Telephone | DateOfBirth |
|---|---|---|---|---|
| E23 | Jimmy Vitale | 425 ConAir Drive | 555-5678 | Aug 18, 1962 |

### Customer (External Agent)

| Customer ID | Name | Address | Telephone | Credit Rating |
|---|---|---|---|---|
| C2323 | Needmore Stuff | 86906 Enterprise Court | 555-8989 | A+ |

### Inventory Type (Resource Type)

| Item ID | Description | UnitOfMeasure | Standard Cost | List Price |
|---|---|---|---|---|
| BIS1 | Big Stuff | Each | $20.00 | $50.00 |
| HUS1 | Huge Stuff | Each | $30.00 | $70.00 |
| LIS1 | Little Stuff | Box of 6 | $36.00 | $72.00 |
| TIS1 | Tiny Stuff | Box of 12 | $48.00 | $96.00 |

### Fulfillment2 Relationship

| Sales Order ID | Sale ID |
|---|---|

Note: Participation3 relationship is implemented with Sales Rep ID posted into Sales Order table. Participation4 relationship is implemented with Customer ID posted into Sales Order table. Fulfillment1 relationship is implemented with Sales Call ID posted into Sales Order table. Fulfillment2 data are not yet entered, assuming a time lag between order and shipment.

revenue cycle by the acquisition and/or conversion cycles must be given or used up in exchange for the resource (usually cash) received from external partners. Usually the enterprise gives up goods, services, or the temporary use of goods. If the revenue generating activity involves the sale of merchandise, the event may be called *Sale, Delivery,* or *Shipment* depending in part on whether the customer is on-site to accept possession of the goods or whether the enterprise must deliver or ship the goods to the customer. The important con-

**EXHIBIT 8–8**   **Service Agreement**

**Your Source Company**
*Your Source for Everything You Need*
123 Main St.
Anytown, USA 12345

**Repair Service Order**

ORDER NO: _____

DATE _____

**Ordered by:**

**Ship to:**

| SALESPERSON | P.O. NUMBER | ESTIMATED COMPLETION DATE | TO SHIP VIA | TERMS |
|---|---|---|---|---|
| | | | | |

Parts and supplies

| QUANTITY | STOCK # | DESCRIPTION | UNIT PRICE | AMOUNT |
|---|---|---|---|---|
| | | | | |
| | | | SUBTOTAL | |

Labor charges

| HOURS | SERVICE TYPE | DESCRIPTION | REPAIR PERSON | HOURLY RATE | AMOUNT |
|---|---|---|---|---|---|
| | | | | | |
| | | | | SUBTOTAL | |
| | | | | SALES TAX | |
| | | | | SHIPPING & HANDLING | |
| | | | | TOTAL DUE | |

**THANK YOU FOR YOUR BUSINESS!**

sideration is that a decrement event that represents the sale of goods must represent the point at which title to the merchandise transfers from the seller to the buyer. If title has not transferred, then no decrement has occurred and the sale event cannot be materialized.

If the enterprise sells services rather than goods, then the resource given up to the customers is a set of employee services, making those services unavailable to provide to someone else. Such a decrement event is usually called ***Service Engagement*** or something that more specifically describes the kinds of services performed by the enterprise, such as *Repair Service, Audit Engagement,* or *Consultation.* In the case of enterprises that rent merchandise to customers, the economic decrement event is usually called ***Rental.*** The rental event does not involve the transfer of title of goods, but instead involves a transfer of the right to use goods for an agreed upon length of time. The rental event begins when the right to temporary possession of the goods transfers from the lessor to the lessee and ends when possession of the goods transfers back from the lessee to the lessor.

Economic decrement events in the revenue cycle do not always happen at discrete points in time; rather they are often made up of a series of workflow activities. Once a mutual commitment is made, the enterprise's fulfillment of that commitment is accomplished by the tasks that make up the economic decrement event. For enterprises that sell or rent merchandise that must be shipped to the customer location, these tasks include picking the inventory from the warehouse, packing the inventory into boxes, and shipping the boxes to the customer via a common carrier. The rental event also includes receiving the returned merchandise, inspecting it, and returning it to the warehouse. Economic decrement events for service enterprises generally require active involvement of trained employees who perform the services. The enterprise must identify the requirements of the services to be rendered and select an individual or group of individuals to perform the services. Services may be provided over an extended period of time by a variety of people.

Some enterprises may have multiple revenue generating activities. For example, some enterprises ship finished products to customers and also provide services. Some enterprises may have various combinations for different customers. For example, a computer manufacturer may serve one customer by shipping a new computer and letting the customer install it and handle all conversion. For another customer, the enterprise may deliver the computer, assist with installation, and convert existing applications for processing on the new computer. Yet another customer may request that enterprise to repair a computer that the enterprise had previously sold to the customer. The different events may need to be recorded as separate entities in the REA business process level model, or they may be combined into one economic decrement event entity. The appropriate representation depends on the data captured regarding each different decrement event. If different attributes are needed for the types of decrements, usually they should be represented as separate event entities, each participating in the duality relationship with the appropriate **economic increment event.**

Several documents often are prepared in conjunction with the activities that comprise the economic decrement event: **picking slips, packing slips, bills of lading,** and **sales invoices.** A picking slip is a document that identifies the goods taken out of the warehouse and made available to be shipped (see Exhibit 8–9). Other names for this document include pick ticket, picking ticket, pick list, and picking list.

Often a picking slip is initially prepared by the sale order clerk and sent to the warehouse to authorize an inventory clerk to "pick" the goods out of the warehouse; the inventory clerk then completes the picking slip. Sometimes the pick ticket is actually a copy of the sales order with the cost column replaced by a "quantity picked" column (picking list copies may be designed to accomplish this without having to fill out separate documents). The inventory clerk notes the quantities of each item picked, notes any stockout problems, and signs the form to indicate the transfer of custody of those goods to the shipping area.

A packing slip (sometimes called a packing list) is a document that identifies the goods that have been shipped to a customer (see Exhibit 8–10). Often the packing slip is a copy of the picking slip on which a shipping clerk fills in the quantities of each item packed, notes any discrepancies from the picking slip, and signs to indicate transfer of custody of the goods to a common carrier.

**EXHIBIT 8–9**   **Picking List**

| | |
|---|---|
| **Your Source Company** | PICKING TICKET:   15 |
| *Your Source for Everything You Need* | Clerk ID   137 |
| 123 Main St. | |
| Anytown, USA 12345 | |

**Order Number:** 14          **Order Date:** 5/4/2010          **Warehouse:** WH1

| **Sold To:**  Needmore Stuff | **Ship To:**  Needmore Stuff |
|---|---|
| 86906 Enterprise Dr. | 86906 Enterprise Dr. |
| Anytown, USA 12345 | Anytown, USA 12345 |
| | |

| CUST NUMBER | P.O. NUMBER | TERMS | REP NUMBER |
|---|---|---|---|
| C2323 | Verbal | n/30 | E23 |

| SHIP VIA | DATE-TO-SHIP | | |
|---|---|---|---|
| FedEx | 5/5/2010 | | |

| ITEM ID | DESCRIPTION | QTY ORDERED | QTY PICKED |
|---|---|---|---|
| LIS1 | Little Stuff, box of 6 | 2 | 2 |
| TIS1 | Tiny Stuff, box of 12 | 10 | 10 |

| LINE ITEMS | TOTAL QUANTITY | |
|---|---|---|
| 2 | 12 | |

The bill of lading also indicates transfer of custody of goods from the enterprise to a common carrier; however, it contains different data from the packing slip. Rather than documenting details about each type of item shipped and the quantities of those items, the bill of lading documents details about how many boxes made up the shipment and the dimensions and/or weight of those boxes. See the bill of lading in Exhibit 8–11.

Sales invoices (electronic or paper) communicate to customers that the enterprise has fulfilled its commitment and requests the customer to remit payment to fulfill its commitment. If the customer already paid for the merchandise, the invoice indicates that no balance is due. Exhibit 8–12 shows a sales invoice.

Exhibit 8–13 shows the relational tables that correspond to Exhibit 8–3's entity-relationship representation of the sale event, the relationships in which it participates (stockflow1, fulfillment2, duality, reversal, participation5, and participation6), and the related resource type entities. Other possible tables could be derived, depending on the relationship cardinalities. Some of the data from the forms in Exhibits 8–9 through 8–12 have been entered into the database tables. Other data from those forms could be added to the tables as well (if the attributes are added to the appropriate tables). Some of the data entered in the tables did not come directly from those forms but would already have existed in the database tables based on earlier activities of the enterprise.

**EXHIBIT 8–10    Packing List**

**Your Source Company**
*Your Source for Everything You Need*
123 Main St.
Anytown, USA 12345

PACKING LIST:    15

Clerk ID    137

If there are any questions about this shipment,
contact our sales department (999) 555-3333

| Needmore Stuff | YOUR PURCHASE ORDER NUMBER |
|---|---|
| 86906 Enterprise Dr. | Verbal |
| Anytown, USA 12345 | |
| **Contact:** Sarah Gibson | **No. Items Ordered:** 2 |

| WAREHOUSE LOCATION | YOUR SOURCE PART NO. | FILL QUANTITY | ITEM DESCRIPTION | YOUR LINE | YOU ORDERED | WE SHIPPED |
|---|---|---|---|---|---|---|
| WH1 | LIS1 | 2 | Little Stuff | 1 | 2 | 2 |
| WH1 | TIS1 | 10 | Tiny Stuff | 2 | 10 | 10 |

Creating separate documents for the picking, packing, and shipment of inventory and for customer billing is not a requirement of any enterprise information system, nor is it required that those activities be separated into four tasks. An interface to an enterprisewide information system may make approved sale order data available on the company intranet and the shipping function may be integrated with the warehousing function. Thus, an inventory clerk may view the approved order details; pick, pack, and ship the goods; and transmit an electronic invoice to the customer's information system all in one task, with no need to document transfers of custody (i.e., the picking and packing) because custody did not change until the goods were shipped to the customer.

Relationships in which the economic decrement event participates typically include a **fulfillment relationship** (enabling the enterprise to trace which mutual commitment event the decrement fulfilled), a **duality relationship** (allowing the enterprise to trace a related economic increment that represents the other part of the exchange), a **stockflow relationship** (to trace the resource or resource type that was given up in the decrement event), **participation relationships** with the internal and external agents, and occasionally a **reversal relationship** (allowing the enterprise to trace sale returns to the original sales for which they reversed the economic effect).

Internal agents typically associated with economic decrement events via participation relationships include salespeople, shipping clerks, delivery clerks, and engagement personnel. External agents typically associated with economic decrement events via participation relationships include transportation suppliers (such as UPS or Federal Express) and customers. The resources typically associated with the economic decrement event via stockflow relationships in the revenue cycle are usually *inventory, inventory type,* or *service type.* Most manufacturers and merchandisers do not specifically identify inventory, so the resource that participates in the stockflow relationship is usually *inventory type.* For

**EXHIBIT 8–11   Bill of Lading**

| UNIFORM STRAIGHT BILL OF LADING — Domestic | Document No. ___15___ |
|---|---|

**Your Source Company**
*Your Source for Everything You Need*
123 Main St.
Anytown, USA 12345

Shipper s No. ____14789B____
Carrier s No. ____8796801____
Date ____5/5/2010____

____Federal Express____
(Name of Carrier)

Route:                                                                 Vehicle Number:

| No. shipping units | Kinds of Packaging, Description of Articles, Special Marks and Exceptions | Weight (Subject to Correction) | Rate | Charges (for Carrier use only) |
|---|---|---|---|---|
| 1 | Box, stuff | 15 lbs. | 1.14 | |
| | | | | |
| | | | | |
| | | | | |
| | | | | |
| | | | | |

| REMIT C.O.D. TO: N/A ADDRESS | COD Amt:$ 0.00 | C.O.D. FEE: $N/A PREPAID ☐ COLLECT☐ |
|---|---|---|

Note — Where the rate is dependent on value, shippers are required to state specifically in writing the agreed or declared value of the property.
The agreed or declared value of the property is hereby specifically stated by the shipper to be not exceeding.

$ _1,200.00_____ per _box_____

Subject to Section 7 of the conditions, if this shipment is to be delivered to the consignee without recourse on the consignor, the consignor shall sign the following statement:
The carrier shall not make delivery of this shipment without payment of freight and all other lawful charges.

_____
(Signature of Consignor)

Total Charges $ 17.10

FREIGHT CHARGES
Check Appropriate Box:
☐ Freight prepaid
☒ Bill to shipper
☐ Collect

Received subject to the classifications and tariffs in effect on the date of the issue of this Bill of Lading, the property described above in apparent good order, except as noted (contents and condition of contents)

Shipping Clerk ID: 137

those enterprises that do specifically identify inventory items, the resource in the stockflow relationship is *inventory*. For service providers, the resource involved in the stockflow relationship is usually *service type*.

## Economic Increment Event (Cash Receipt)

Cash receipts are economic increment events that increase the enterprise's cash balance. Cash receipts may take the form of checks, currency, or coins—anything that can be deposited into a cash account held either in a bank or on hand in petty cash. Notice that if a customer pays with a credit card, the enterprise has not yet received cash; the cash receipt does not occur until the credit card company pays the enterprise. In the latter case, the cash

**EXHIBIT 8–12** **Sales Invoice**

**Your Source Company**
*Your Source for Everything You Need*
123 Main St.
Anytown, USA 12345

**Sale Invoice**

INVOICE NO: ___12___

DATE ___5/5/2010___

**Sold To:**

Needmore Stuff
86906 Enterprise Dr.
Anytown, USA 12345

**Ship To:**

Needmore Stuff
86906 Enterprise Dr.
Anytown, USA 12345

| SALESPERSON | P.O. NUMBER | S.O. NUMBER | DATE SHIPPED | SHIPPED VIA | TERMS |
|---|---|---|---|---|---|
| E23 | Verbal | 14 | 5/5/2010 | FedEx | N/30 |

| QUANTITY | STOCK # | DESCRIPTION | UNIT PRICE | AMOUNT |
|---|---|---|---|---|
| 2 | LIS1 | Little Stuff, box of 6 | $70.00 | $ 140.00 |
| 10 | TIS1 | Tiny Stuff, box of 12 | $96.00 | $ 960.00 |
| | | SUBTOTAL | | $1,100.00 |
| | | SALES TAX | | 0 |
| | | SHIPPING & HANDLING | | 0 |
| | | **TOTAL DUE** | | $1,100.00 |

Make all checks payable to: Your Source Company

**THANK YOU FOR YOUR BUSINESS!**

receipt must be connected to two external agents—the customer, whose accounts receivable balance will be decreased as a result of the cash receipt, and the credit card company, from whom the cash was literally received.

**Cash receipts** may occur at various times during the sales/collection process. Some cash receipts may occur as orders are placed (i.e., a prepayment); other cash receipts may occur at the point of sale or upon delivery of goods or services; still other cash receipts may occur days or weeks after sales take place. The receipt of cash is a custodial function. Two documents are typically involved in task activities that comprise the cash receipt event: **remittance advices** and **deposit slips.** When payment is received, cashiers, accounts receivable clerks, or other company employees (internal agents) verify the payment information is correctly recorded on a remittance advice. A remittance advice is a document (usually the portion of a customer invoice or **customer statement** that says "return this stub with payment") that advises the enterprise the customer is remitting payment. In Exhibit 8–14 we show a customer statement with a detachable remittance advice.

**EXHIBIT 8–13**   **Sample Relational Tables Encompassing Sale Event**

**Sale Order (Mutual Commitment) Event**

| Sale Order ID | Order Date | Date Needed | Total Dollar Amt | Sales Tax | Shipping Charge | Sales CallID FK | Sales RepID FK | Customer ID FK |
|---|---|---|---|---|---|---|---|---|
| 14 | 5/4/2010 | 5/7/2010 | $1,100.00 | $0 | $0 | 42 | E23 | C2323 |

**Sale (Economic Decrement) Event**

| Sale ID | Date | PickListID | PackListID | BOL# | Sales RepID FK | CustomerID FK | CashReceiptID FK |
|---|---|---|---|---|---|---|---|
| 12 | 5/5/2010 | 15 | 15 | 15 | E23 | C2323 | |

**Stockflow1 Relationship**

| Sale ID | Item ID | Quantity Sold | Actual Unit Price |
|---|---|---|---|
| 12 | LIS1 | 2 | 70.00 |
| 12 | TIS1 | 10 | 96.00 |

**Sales Representative (Internal Agent)**

| Sales Rep ID | Name | Address | Telephone | DateOfBirth |
|---|---|---|---|---|
| E23 | Jimmy Vitale | 425 ConAir Drive | 555-5678 | Aug 18, 1962 |

**Shipping Clerk (Internal Agent)**

| Shipping Clerk ID | Name | Address | Telephone | DateOfBirth |
|---|---|---|---|---|
| E41 | Amy Milano | 8892 Eddy Ave. | 555-9557 | January 3, 1964 |

**Customer (External Agent)**

| Customer ID | Name | Address | Telephone | Credit Rating |
|---|---|---|---|---|
| C2323 | Needmore Stuff | 86906 Enterprise Court | 555-8989 | A+ |

**Inventory Type (Resource Type)**

| Item ID | Description | UnitOfMeasure | Standard Cost | List Price |
|---|---|---|---|---|
| BIS1 | Big Stuff | Each | $20.00 | $50.00 |
| HUS1 | Huge Stuff | Each | $30.00 | $70.00 |
| LIS1 | Little Stuff | Box of 6 | $36.00 | $72.00 |
| TIS1 | Tiny Stuff | Box of 12 | $48.00 | $96.00 |

**Fulfillment2 Relationship**

| Sale Order ID | Sale ID |
|---|---|
| 14 | 12 |

Continued

A deposit slip is promptly prepared summarizing all payments for a prescribed time period (usually a day); the deposit slip and payments are deposited into one of the enterprise's bank accounts. Due to the risk of loss, cash should be deposited at least daily, all employers who have access to cash should be bonded, and two employees should verify cash transactions. In

**EXHIBIT 8–13** (Concluded)

| Cash Receipt (Economic Increment) Event | | | | | |
|---|---|---|---|---|---|
| **CashReceiptID** | **Date** | **DollarAmount** | **CashAccountID**FK | **CustomerID**FK | **CashierID**FK |
| RA20 | 5/19/2010 | $1,100.00 | Ca123501 | C2323 | E111 |

| Sale Return (Economic Decrement Reversal) Event | | | | | |
|---|---|---|---|---|---|
| **Sale Return ID** | **Date** | **$Amount** | **SalesRepID**FK | **CustomerID**FK | **SaleID**FK |

Note: Participation5 relationship is implemented with Sales Rep ID posted into Sale table. Participation6 relationship is implemented with Customer ID posted into Sale table. Duality relationship is implemented with Cash Receipt ID posted into Sale table. Cash receipt data are not yet entered, assuming a time lag between shipment and cash receipt. Reversal relationship is implemented with Sale ID posted into Sales Return table. Return data are not yet entered, assuming a time lag between shipment and sale return.

**EXHIBIT 8–14** **Customer Statement with Remittance Advice**

**Your Source Company**
*Your Source for Everything You Need*
123 Main St.
Anytown, USA 12345

PAGE
1

**STATEMENT**

Needmore Stuff
86906 Enterprise Dr.
Anytown, USA 12345

| DATE | CUSTOMER NUMBER |
|---|---|
| 5/19/2010 | C2323 |

**TERMS:** N/30

PAGE
1

**REMITTANCE ADVICE #** 20

| DATE | CUSTOMER NUMBER |
|---|---|
| | C2323 |

← PLEASE DETACH HERE AND RETURN THIS STUB WITH YOUR REMITTANCE
**TO:** Your Source Company
123 Main St.
Anytown, USA 12345

| INVOICE NUMBER | DATE | CURRENT | PAST 1–30 | PAST 31–60 | PAST 61–90 | PAST 91–120 | INVOICE NUMBER | AMOUNT APPLIED |
|---|---|---|---|---|---|---|---|---|
| 12 | 5/5/2010 | 1,100.00 | | | | | 12 | $ 960.00 |

| TOTAL DUE | | TOTAL CURRENT | TOTAL PAST 1–30 | TOTAL PAST 31–60 | TOTAL PAST 61–90 | TOTAL PAST 91–120 | TOTAL DUE | TOTAL REMITTED |
|---|---|---|---|---|---|---|---|---|
| $1,100.00 | | $1,100.00 | $0 | $0 | $0 | $0 | $1,100.00 | $ 960.00 |

REVIEWED BY _____

addition to having customers mail or bring payments directly to the business, an enterprise can use the *lockbox method* or **electronic funds transfers** to collect customer payments. When the lockbox method is used, customers mail their checks to a post office address, and for a fee, a bank will pick up, total, and directly deposit the funds into the company's account. In such situations the post office serves as an external agent. The bank then sends a copy of the deposit information and the remittance advices to the company. Electronic funds transfers reduce human involvement with cash by having customers electronically transfer funds from their bank accounts directly to the company's bank account. The form of payment is incidental to the occurrence of the event.

Attributes captured regarding cash receipts usually include a cash receipt identifier (such as a unique remittance advice number), date, amount received, customer identification, employee identification (such as employees who count and deposit the cash), the account number where the cash is deposited, the location of payment (such as mail, or in person at the main office), and the check number of the payment. Some enterprises link payments to specific invoices, while others simply apply payments to the outstanding balance.

Enterprise systems should include the ability to record a cash receipt without linking it to a specific customer. For example, suppose someone sends a check but neglects to send the remittance advice and the name on the check does not correspond to the name of any existing customer account. The enterprise should be able to deposit the funds and tag the transaction as "unapplied cash" (a cash payment that was received but was not posted to a customer's receivable balance). If this occurs, the system should generate a listing of "unapplied cash" transactions and, as with all errors, they should be investigated and corrected as soon as possible. The enterprise system should also allow enterprises to choose how they want to link customer payments to customer accounts. Two methods include specific invoice and balance forward. As the name implies, the specific invoice method involves matching payments to specific sales invoices. When enterprises use a balance forward approach, they apply payments to a customer's total liability, rather than any specific invoice.

In Exhibit 8–15 we show a set of relational tables that correspond to Exhibit 8–3's entity-relationship representation of the cash receipt event and the revenue cycle relationships in which it participates (duality, stockflow2, participation7, and participation8). Other possible tables could be derived, depending on the relationship cardinalities. Additional tables are also likely necessary to correspond to relationships in which the cash receipt event participates in other transaction cycles such as financing. The tables in Exhibit 8–15 are only those typically applicable to the sales/collection process.

## Economic Decrement Reversal Event (Sales Returns and Sales Allowances)

Unfortunately, goods are not always acceptable to customers for various reasons. Perhaps the goods do not meet quality standards represented in the sale agreement or the product specifications of the customer; or perhaps the customer's needs changed while the goods were in transit. Three options are available to handle disagreements like these: The enterprise may allow the customer to keep the product and receive an adjustment or allowance in the price, or the enterprise may allow the customer to return the product and decrease the customer's account receivable or issue a cash refund. Alternatively the enterprise may take a no returns—all sales final approach. If returns are allowed, the returned products are the resources involved in the **sales return** event. Although the return increases the inventory resource, the return is inherently different from an economic increment event such as

**EXHIBIT 8–15** **Relational Tables Encompassing Cash Receipt Event**

**Cash Receipt (Economic Increment) Event**

| CashReceiptID | Date | DollarAmount | CashAccountID<sup>FK</sup> | CustomerID<sup>FK</sup> | CashierID<sup>FK</sup> |
|---|---|---|---|---|---|
| RA20 | 5/19/2010 | $960.00 | Ca123501 | C2323 | E111 |

**Sale (Economic Decrement) Event**

| Sale ID | Date | PickListID | PackListID | BOL# | SalesRepID<sup>FK</sup> | CustomerID<sup>FK</sup> | CashReceiptID<sup>FK</sup> |
|---|---|---|---|---|---|---|---|
| 12 | 5/5/2010 | 15 | 15 | 15 | E23 | C2323 | RA20 |

**Cashier (Internal Agent)**

| CashierID | Name | Address | Telephone | DateOfBirth |
|---|---|---|---|---|
| E111 | Missy Witherspoon | 1710 Crestwood Dr. | 555-9392 | May 11, 1960 |

**Customer (External Agent)**

| Customer ID | Name | Address | Telephone | Credit Rating |
|---|---|---|---|---|
| C2323 | Needmore Stuff | 86906 Enterprise Court | 555-8989 | A+ |

**Cash (Resource Type)**

| CashAccountID | AccountType | Location |
|---|---|---|
| Ca123501 | Checking | 1st Local Bank |

Note: Participation7 relationship is implemented with Cashier ID posted into Cash Receipt table. Participation8 relationship is implemented with Customer ID posted into Cash Receipt table. Duality relationship is implemented with Cash Receipt ID posted into Sale table. Stockflow relationship is implemented with Cash Account ID posted into Cash Receipt table.

a purchase. In effect, the return reverses the sale event, which was an economic decrement event. Therefore we call this an **economic decrement reversal event.** If the goods were specifically identified upon sale, they should be specifically identified upon return; if they were measured and recorded at the type level upon sale, they should be measured in that same manner for the return. Typically the customer is the external agent involved in the return event (a common carrier may also need to be linked as an external agent) and a sales manager serves as the internal agent.

Attributes typically captured regarding sales returns include an identifier for the event, the return date, and the dollar amount of the return. Links should also be available to attributes of related agents and merchandise inventory. Several documents may be used in workflow tasks that make up the sales return event, such as return authorizations, receiving reports, and credit memos. The return authorization is a document that gives permission for the customer to return merchandise and is typically prepared in response to a customer's request to return goods through the mail or via a common carrier. In retail stores a modified document combines the customer request and store authorization; it indicates what inventory items were returned. Receiving reports are completed by inventory or receiving clerks when returned goods are received from customers. The receiving report lists the items and the quantities and condition of each item received. If the customer already paid for the mer-

**EXHIBIT 8–16   Sales Return Authorization**

**Your Source Company**
*Your Source for Everything You Need*
123 Main St.
Anytown, USA 12345

**RETURN
AUTHORIZATION**   __1__

DATE   __5/12/2010__

Customer No.  __C2323__

Address:        86069 Enterprise Dr.
                Anytown, USA 12345

For clarification contact

   Name    __Sarah Gibson__

   Phone   __555-8989__

All returns must be clean, in salable condition, and shipped prepaid. Thank you for your cooperation.

Customer Return Request No.   __3__

Date of Request   __5/9/2010__

RETURN CODES:

**A**  OVERSTOCK

**B**  DAMAGED

**C**  DEFECTIVE

**D**  WRONG PRODUCT
       BILLED & SHIPPED

**E**  CORRECT PRODUCT
       BILLED BUT WRONG
       PRODUCT SHIPPED

**F**  OTHER

☐ Cash Refund - Please

☒ Credit to Account - Please

| ITEM ID | DESCRIPTION | RETURN CODE | INVOICE NO. | QTY. RETURNED | UNIT PRICE | EXTENSION |
|---------|-------------|-------------|-------------|---------------|------------|-----------|
| LIS1    | Little Stuff | F – too big | 12 | 2 | 70.00 | $140.00 |
|         |             |             |             |               |            |           |
|         |             |             |             |               |            |           |
|         |             |             |             |               | TOTAL      |           |

chandise, the enterprise issues a cash refund. Because the cash refund reverses the cash receipt event, which is an economic increment event, we call the refund an **economic increment reversal event.** The **credit memorandum** (also called **credit memo**) is an internal document used to communicate to the accounting department that a journal entry needs to be made with a credit to the customer's account receivable. A copy may also be sent to the customer to confirm that she was given credit. Exhibits 8–16 through 8–18 illustrate a sales return authorization, receiving report, and credit memorandum.

Exhibit 8–19 shows a set of relational tables that correspond to Exhibit 8–3's entity-relationship representation of the sales return event and the relationships in which it participates (reversal, stockflow3, participation9, and participation10). Other possible tables could be derived, depending on the relationship cardinalities.

**EXHIBIT 8–17    Receiving Report**

| **Your Source Company** | | **RECEIVING REPORT** | |
|---|---|---|---|
| *Your Source for Everything You Need*<br>123 Main St.<br>Anytown, USA 12345 | | NO. ___25___ | |

| DATE    **5/12/2010** | | PURCH ORD NO./SALE<br>RETURN AUTH NO. | **SR1** |
|---|---|---|---|
| RECEIVED FROM    Needmore Stuff | | PREPAID<br>10 | |
| ADDRESS    86906 Enterprise Dr.<br>Anytown, USA 12345 | | COLLECT | |
| FREIGHT CARRIER<br>**Federal Express** | | FREIGHT BILL NO.<br>**FE78901256** | |

| | QUANTITY | ITEM NO | DESCRIPTION |
|---|---|---|---|
| 1. | 2 | LIS1 | Little Stuff |
| 2. | | | |
| 3. | | | |
| 4. | | | |
| 5. | | | |
| 6. | | | |
| 7. | | | |
| 8. | | | |
| 9. | | | |

REMARKS: CONDITIONS, ETC.
    Perfect condition

| RECEIVED BY<br>E111 | DELIVERED TO<br>E23 |
|---|---|

BE SURE TO<br>MAKE THIS RECORD<br>ACCURATE AND COMPLETE

# INFORMATION NEEDS AND MEASURES IN THE SALES/COLLECTION PROCESS

Information from the sales/collection process can provide decision-making support for many information customers. An information customer is someone who needs information. Information needs fit into the following categories:

- Internal users need information about internal phenomena.
- Internal users need information about external phenomena.
- External users need information about internal phenomena.
- External users need information about external phenomena.

**EXHIBIT 8–18** Credit Memorandum

**Your Source Company**
*Your Source for Everything You Need*
123 Main St.
Anytown, USA 12345

**CREDIT MEMO**

NO. ___1___

CREDIT TO ___Needmore Stuff___

DATE ___5/19/2010___

CUSTOMER
ACCUNT NO. ___C2323___

| RETURN AUTH NO. | INVOICE NO. | | INVOICE DATE | RECEIVING REPORT NO. | |
|---|---|---|---|---|---|
| SR1 | 12 | | 5/5/2010 | 25 | |
| ITEM NUMBER | DESCRIPTION | | QUANTITY | PRICE EACH | AMOUNT |
| LIS1 | Little Stuff | | 2 | 70.00 | 140.00 |
| | | | | | |
| | | | | | |
| | | | | | |
| | | | | **TOTAL CREDIT** | 140. 00 |

You must present this copy when applying to future orders.

APPLY ON FUTURE ORDER ONLY ☐
REFUND BY CHECK ☐
CREDIT ACCOUNT ☒

Prepared by
___Elmore Kirk___
Credit Manager Emp# ___16___

Within each of these categories, users need information at different levels of detail. We next analyze each of the entities and relationships in the business process level pattern to give some ideas about the queries that may be needed to satisfy information needs regarding these objects for internal and external users. The queries presented are not a comprehensive set of queries (there are simply too many potentially useful queries to list them all). However, the set provided should provide you guidance for creating similar queries to satisfy similar information needs. To describe example queries needed in the sales/collection process we use the database tables in Exhibit 8–20.

## Resource Queries in the Sales/Collection Process

Internal and external users may need information regarding an enterprise resource or resource type. The resources and resource types most commonly present in the sales/collection process are inventory (specifically identified inventory, inventory types, or service types) and cash. For each resource, users may need any of the following:

- Detailed status information at one or more points in time for each resource instance.
- Detailed status information at one or more points in time for only those resource instances meeting specified criteria.

**EXHIBIT 8–19**   **Relational Tables Encompassing Sales Return Event**

**Sales Return (Economic Decrement Reversal) Event**

| Sale ReturnID | Date | Dollar Amount | Receiving ReportNo. | Credit Memo# | Credit MgrID | SaleID<sup>FK</sup> | CustomerID<sup>FK</sup> | Receiving ClerkID<sup>FK</sup> |
|---|---|---|---|---|---|---|---|---|
| SR1 | 5/12/2010 | $140.00 | RR25 | 1 | E16 | 12 | C2323 | E247 |

**Sale (Economic Decrement) Event**

| Sale ID | Date | PickListID | PackListID | BOL# | SalesRepID<sup>FK</sup> | CustomerID<sup>FK</sup> | CashReceiptID<sup>FK</sup> |
|---|---|---|---|---|---|---|---|
| 12 | 5/5/2010 | 15 | 15 | 15 | E23 | C2323 | RA20 |

**Receiving Clerk (Internal Agent)**

| ClerkID | Name | Address | Telephone | DateOfBirth |
|---|---|---|---|---|
| E247 | Kenneth Barki | 4312 Monticello Dr. | 556-4891 | April 14, 1945 |

**Customer (External Agent)**

| Customer ID | Name | Address | Telephone | Credit Rating |
|---|---|---|---|---|
| C2323 | Needmore Stuff | 86906 Enterprise Court | 555-8989 | A+ |

**Stockflow3 Relationship**

| Sale Return ID | Item ID | Quantity Returned | Actual Unit Price | Condition of Goods | Reason Returned |
|---|---|---|---|---|---|
| 12 | LIS1 | 2 | 70.00 | Perfect | Too big |

**Inventory Type (Resource Type)**

| Item ID | Description | UnitOfMeasure | Standard Cost | List Price |
|---|---|---|---|---|
| BIS1 | Big Stuff | Each | $20.00 | $50.00 |
| HUS1 | Huge Stuff | Each | $30.00 | $70.00 |
| LIS1 | Little Stuff | Box of 6 | $36.00 | $72.00 |
| TIS1 | Tiny Stuff | Box of 12 | $48.00 | $96.00 |

Note: Participation9 relationship is implemented with Customer ID posted into Sales Return table. Participation10 relationship is implemented with Clerk ID posted into Sales Return table. Reversal relationship is implemented with Sale ID posted into Sales Return table.

- Summarized status information at one or more points in time for all resource instances.
- Summarized status information at one or more points in time for only those resource instances meeting specified criteria.

With regard to each of the above, users may need to know all characteristics of the instances in the answer set, or they may need only a subset of the characteristics. Information regarding inventory and cash that may be needed by internal users (such as salespeople) and by external users (such as customers) includes:

- A list of each inventory item or item type offered for sale by an enterprise.
- A list of all inventory items or item types that possess certain characteristics (e.g., all books, real estate listings with lake frontage, toys with selling prices within a

**EXHIBIT 8–20**   **Sales/Collection Process Database Tables for Queries**

**Cash (Resource Type)**

| CashAccountID | AccountType | Location | DateAccountEstablished |
|---|---|---|---|
| Ca123501 | Checking | 1st Local Bank | April 1, 2010 |
| Ca789125 | Savings | 1st Local Bank | April 1, 2010 |
| Ca351235 | Petty | Onsite—Cashier Desk drawer | April 15, 2010 |
| Ca351327 | Petty | Onsite—CEO Assistant's File Cabinet | April 22, 2010 |

**Inventory Type (Resource Type)**

| Item ID | Description | UnitOfMeasure | Standard Cost | List Price |
|---|---|---|---|---|
| BIS1 | Big Stuff | Each | $20.00 | $50.00 |
| HUS1 | Huge Stuff | Each | $30.00 | $70.00 |
| LIS1 | Little Stuff | Box of 6 | $36.00 | $72.00 |
| MIN1 | Miniature Stuff | Box of 24 | $56.00 | $110.00 |
| TIS1 | Tiny Stuff | Box of 12 | $48.00 | $96.00 |
| TTP12 | Tiara | Each | $10.00 | $25.00 |

**Sales Call (Instigation) Event**

| Sales Call ID | Date | StartTime | EndTime | Location | SalesRepID[FK] | CustomerID[FK] |
|---|---|---|---|---|---|---|
| 42 | 5/4/2010 | 9:12 a.m. | 10:00 a.m. | Customer | E23 | C2323 |
| 43 | 5/4/2010 | 9:27 a.m. | 10:35 a.m. | Ours | E26 | C4731 |
| 44 | 5/5/2010 | 10:30 a.m. | 11:15 a.m. | Customer | E23 | C6125 |

**Sale Order (Mutual Commitment) Event**

| Sale Order ID | Order Date | Date Needed | Dollar Total | Sales Tax | Shipping Charge | Sales CallID[FK] | Sales RepID[FK] | Customer ID[FK] | |
|---|---|---|---|---|---|---|---|---|---|
| 14 | 5/4/2010 | 5/7/2010 | $1,100.00 | $0 | $0 | 42 | E23 | C2323 | |
| 15 | 5/4/2010 | 5/12/2010 | $3,050.00 | $0 | $0 | 43 | E26 | C4731 | |
| 16 | 5/6/2010 | 5/9/2010 | $4,305.00 | $0 | $0 | 42 | E23 | C2323 | |
| 17 | 5/8/2010 | 5/17/2010 | $8,280.00 | $0 | $0 | 43 | E26 | C4731 | Continued |

certain range, video games in GameBoy Advance format, and preventive dental care services).

- Quantity on hand of an inventory item type as of a specified date.
- Total cost value of inventory on hand as of a specified date.
- A list of all cash accounts owned by an enterprise as of a specified date.
- Balance in a specific cash account as of a specified date.
- Total balance in all cash accounts as of a specified date.

Whether the information needed by a user is detailed or summarized, whether it involves one or more instances, and whether it includes one or more characteristics of the resource(s), resource queries within the sales/collection process typically only require one table. Notice that some of the information needs listed above do not fall completely within

**EXHIBIT 8–20**   **(Continued)**

**Sale (Economic Decrement) Event**

| Sale ID | Date | Dollar Total | Pick ListID | Pack ListID | BOL# | Sales RepIDFK | CustomerIDFK | Cash ReceiptIDFK |
|---|---|---|---|---|---|---|---|---|
| 12 | 5/5/2010 | $1,100.00 | 15 | 15 | 15 | E23 | C2323 | RA20 |
| 13 | 5/7/2010 | $3,050.00 | 16 | 16 | 16 | E26 | C4731 | RA21 |
| 14 | 5/8/2010 | $2,100.00 | 17 | 17 | 17 | E23 | C2323 | RA20 |
| 15 | 5/10/2010 | $2,205.00 | 18 | 18 | 18 | E23 | C2323 | |

**Cash Receipt (Economic Increment) Event**

| CashReceiptID | Date | Dollar Total | CashAccountIDFK | CustomerIDFK | CashierIDFK |
|---|---|---|---|---|---|
| RA20 | 5/19/2010 | $3,060.00 | Ca123501 | C2323 | E111 |
| RA21 | 5/24/2010 | $3,050.00 | Ca123501 | C4731 | E111 |
| RA22 | 5/31/2010 | $25,000.00 | Ca123501 | | E111 |

**Sales Return (Economic Decrement Reversal) Event**

| Sale ReturnID | Date | Dollar Amount | Receiving ReportNo. | Credit Memo# | Credit MgrID | SaleIDFK | CustomerIDFK | Receiving ClerkIDFK |
|---|---|---|---|---|---|---|---|---|
| SR1 | 5/12/2010 | $140.00 | RR25 | 1 | E16 | 12 | C2323 | E247 |

**Customer (External Agent)**

| Customer ID | Name | Address | Telephone | Credit Rating |
|---|---|---|---|---|
| C2323 | Needmore Stuff | 86906 Enterprise Court | 555-8989 | A+ |
| C2831 | Targeted One | 41352 Price Ln. | 555-1771 | B+ |
| C4731 | Gottahave Moore | 1207 Emperor Dr. | 555-5688 | B |
| C6125 | Don't Wantmuch | 3421 Carradine St. | 555-9098 | A+ |

**Cashier (Internal Agent)**

| CashierID | Name | Address | Telephone | DateOfBirth | |
|---|---|---|---|---|---|
| E111 | Missy Witherspoon | 1710 Crestwood Dr. | 555-9392 | May 11, 1960 | |
| E222 | Eponine Eldridge | 1003 Zenker Dr. | 555-9099 | July 29, 1972 | Continued |

the sales/collection process and therefore cannot be provided by single-table queries unless the database allows the storage of volatile derivable attributes (triggers) as described in Chapter 6. For example, calculation of quantity on hand of inventory requires the use of quantities purchased of inventory along with the quantities sold of inventory. Purchased quantities are part of the acquisition/payment process and quantities sold are part of the sales/collection process. Therefore, unless quantity on hand is stored as a triggered update field attribute in the inventory table, the query will be complex and involve tables from multiple business processes. Similarly, calculation of the total cash balance requires the use of cash receipts from multiple business processes (primarily financing and sales/collection) and the use of cash disbursements from multiple business processes (primarily from acquisition/payment, payroll, and financing). Therefore unless the balance of each

**EXHIBIT 8–20   (Continued)**

**Receiving Clerk (Internal Agent)**

| ClerkID | Name | Address | Telephone | DateOfBirth |
|---------|------|---------|-----------|-------------|
| E247 | Kenneth Barki | 4312 Monticello Dr. | 556-4891 | April 14, 1945 |
| E251 | Rita Barki | 4312 Monticello Dr. | 556-4891 | May 22, 1948 |

**Sales Representative (Internal Agent)**

| Sales Rep ID | Name | Address | Telephone | DateOfBirth |
|--------------|------|---------|-----------|-------------|
| E23 | Jimmy Vitale | 425 ConAir Drive | 555-5678 | Aug 18, 1962 |
| E26 | Cyndie North | 122 Front St. | 555-6353 | Apr 4, 1961 |
| E30 | Wayland Stindt | 3506 Carthan St. | 555-0621 | Dec 29, 1973 |

**Proposition Relationship (Sales Call–Inventory)**

| Sales Call ID | Item ID | Customer Reaction to Product |
|---------------|---------|------------------------------|
| 42 | BIS1 | Negative |
| 42 | LIS1 | Positive |
| 42 | HUS1 | Negative |
| 42 | TIS1 | Positive |
| 42 | MIN1 | Undecided |
| 43 | BIS1 | Positive |
| 43 | LIS1 | Undecided |
| 43 | HUS1 | Positive |
| 43 | TIS1 | Negative |
| 43 | MIN1 | Negative |
| 44 | BIS1 | Negative |
| 44 | LIS1 | Negative |
| 44 | HUS1 | Negative |
| 44 | TIS1 | Negative |
| 44 | MIN1 | Negative |

Continued

cash account is stored as a triggered update field in the cash resource type table, the query will involve multiple tables from multiple business processes. Queries that involve multiple tables from multiple business processes are discussed in Chapter 10 (View Integration and Implementation Compromises) since an understanding of how the business process models are integrated and the resulting tables are derived is useful for understanding the query design. For Chapter 8 we focus on the single-table resource queries per the earlier list that are found within the sales/collection process.

A list of each inventory item or item type offered for sale by an enterprise is a query that can be answered using a single-table query of the inventory or inventory type table. The structured query language code for this query based on the tables in Exhibit 8–20 is

SELECT * FROM InventoryType:

The asterisk (*) is a wild card that indicates all characteristics of the inventory type are to be included in the answer. There is no WHERE clause because all instances of inventory type are to be included. Notice that since there is no selection of certain instances nor any

**EXHIBIT 8–20** (Concluded)

**Reservation Relationship (Sale Order–Inventory)**

| Sales Order ID | Item ID | Quantity Ordered | Quoted Unit Price |
|---|---|---|---|
| 14 | LIS1 | 2 | 70.00 |
| 14 | TIS1 | 10 | 96.00 |
| 15 | BIS1 | 40 | 60.00 |
| 15 | HUS1 | 13 | 50.00 |
| 16 | MIN1 | 41 | 105.00 |
| 17 | LIS1 | 120 | 69.00 |

**Fulfillment2 Relationship (Sale Order–Sale)**

| Sale Order ID | Sale ID |
|---|---|
| 14 | 12 |
| 15 | 13 |
| 16 | 14 |
| 16 | 15 |

**Stockflow1 Relationship (Sale–Inventory)**

| Sale ID | Item ID | Quantity Sold | Actual Unit Price |
|---|---|---|---|
| 12 | LIS1 | 2 | 70.00 |
| 12 | TIS1 | 10 | 96.00 |
| 13 | BIS1 | 40 | 60.00 |
| 13 | HUS1 | 13 | 50.00 |
| 14 | MIN1 | 20 | 105.00 |
| 15 | MIN1 | 21 | 105.00 |

**Stockflow3 Relationship (Sale Return–Inventory)**

| Sale Return ID | Item ID | Quantity Returned | Actual Unit Price | Condition of Goods | Reason Returned |
|---|---|---|---|---|---|
| 12 | LIS1 | 2 | 70.00 | Perfect | Too big |

projection of certain characteristics, the answer is simply a listing of the inventory type table. In Microsoft Access, therefore, the information can be obtained by simply opening the inventory type table in datasheet view. Or a query could be constructed with SQL as noted above; the same query in Query-By-Example (QBE) format is displayed in Exhibit 8–21, along with the query result.

This single-table query could easily be revised to list only the inventory item types that possess certain characteristics, such as those with list selling prices less than $70 or those with each as a unit of measure. The query also could provide only selected characteristics; for example, when providing inventory information to customers, perhaps the enterprise doesn't want to include the standard cost information. To meet any of these information needs, queries could be constructed that are similar to the following query that lists only the description, unit of measure, and list price of those items that have list prices less than $70. The SQL code for this query using the tables from Exhibit 8–20 is

**EXHIBIT 8–21**   **Microsoft Access QBE View of Query to List Each Inventory Item Type for Sale**

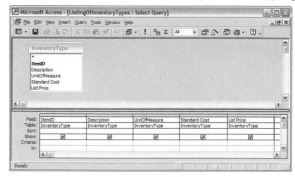

**EXHIBIT 8–22**   **Query to List Selected Characteristics of Items with List Price < $70.00**

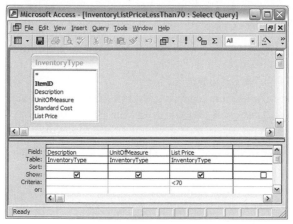

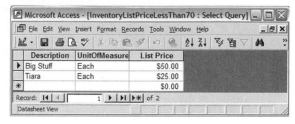

SELECT Description, UnitOfMeasure, ListPrice

FROM InventoryType

WHERE ListPrice < 70;

The Microsoft Access QBE and query results are illustrated in Exhibit 8–22.

To obtain a list of cash accounts owned by the enterprise as of a certain date, such as April 20, 2010, a similar single-table query would be constructed with SQL code as follows:

SELECT *

FROM Cash

WHERE DateAccountEstablished < April 20, 2010;

Please realize that to use this SQL statement you need to format the date according to the required syntax of the software you are using. For example, in Microsoft Access the WHERE clause syntax is WHERE DateAccountEstablished <#4/20/2010#. In Microsoft Access QBE if you enter the date constraint as <4/20/2010, Microsoft Access automatically inserts the #'s in the appropriate places.

**EXHIBIT 8–23    QBE and Result for List of Cash Accounts as of April 20, 2010**

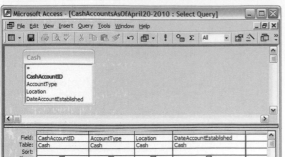

Exhibit 8–23 illustrates this query in Microsoft Access QBE format, along with its result.

## Event Queries in the Sales/Collection Process

Internal and external users may need information regarding events. The most common events in the sales/collection process are sales calls, sale orders, sales, cash receipts, and sale returns. For each of these types of events, users may need any of the following:

- Detailed information about each event instance (i.e., what happened, when did it happen, where did it happen, and so on)
- Detailed information about each event instance that meets specified criteria (e.g., events of a specified type that occurred during a specified time period or that occurred at a specified location)
- Summarized information for all instances of an event type for a specified time period (e.g., total of the event instances during a specified time period)
- Summarized information for only those instances of an event type for a specified time period that meet specific criteria (e.g., average dollar value of the event instances for a specified location during a specified time period)

With regard to each of the above, users may need to know all characteristics of the instances in the answer set, or they may need only a subset of the characteristics. Information regarding sales calls, sale orders, sales, cash receipts, and sale returns that may be needed by internal users (such as salespeople) and by external users (such as customers) includes (among many other possibilities):

- Location of a sales call
- Total number of sales calls, sale orders, or sales that occurred at a specified location or during a specified time period
- Total dollar amount for a specific sale order, sale, cash receipt, or sale return
- Total or average dollar amount of all sale orders, sales, cash receipts, or sale returns for one or more specified time periods

**EXHIBIT 8–24**  Query and Result for Date and Location of Sales Call 44

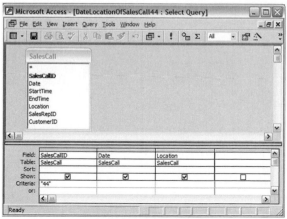 

- Total or average dollar amount of sale orders, sales, cash receipts, or sale returns in a specific location for one or more specified time periods
- Sales tax applicable to a specified sale event
- Shipper's tracking number for a shipment sale event
- Date a sale event occurred
- Length of a sales call (end time minus start time)

Using the tables from Exhibit 8–20, next we create some example queries for similar information needs. For one query a user wants to know the date and location of sales call 44. The SQL code for such a query is

SELECT SalesCallID, Date, Location
FROM SalesCall
WHERE SalesCallID=44;

For Microsoft Access, the QBE and resulting solution are illustrated in Exhibit 8–24.

An event query with a vertical aggregation that can be constructed from the tables in Exhibit 8–20 is the total sales dollar amount for a specified time period. Say the accountants need that figure for the income statement they are preparing for the week May 1–7, 2010. The SQL code for this query is

SELECT Sum(DollarTotal)
FROM Sale
WHERE Date BETWEEN 5/1/2010 AND 5/7/2010;

The Microsoft Access QBE and result are displayed in Exhibit 8–25.

## Agent Queries in the Sales/Collection Process

Internal and external users may need information regarding an internal or external agent or agent type. The internal agents most commonly present in the sales/collection process are salespersons, credit managers, inventory clerks, cashiers, and service-providing employees

**EXHIBIT 8–25** **Microsoft Access QBE and Result for Total Sales May 1–7, 2010**

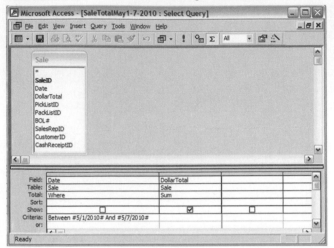

(such as consultants, medical care providers, and waitresses). The external agents most commonly present in the sales/collection process are customers or clients. For each agent or agent type, users may need any of the following:

- Detailed status information at one or more points in time for each agent instance
- Detailed status information at one or more points in time for only those agent instances meeting specified criteria
- Summarized status information at one or more points in time for all agent instances
- Summarized status information at one or more points in time for only those agent instances meeting specified criteria

With regard to each of the above, users may need to know all characteristics of the instances in the answer set, or they may need only a subset of the characteristics. Information regarding various types of employees and customers that may be needed by internal users (such as supervisors and salespeople) and by external users (such as customers) includes:

- A list of all salespeople, cashiers, inventory clerks, or credit managers for an enterprise
- A list of all employees that possess certain characteristics (e.g., all waiters and waitresses who are at least 21 years old, all staff auditors who have passed the CPA exam, or all salespeople whose pay is commission-based)

An example agent query that can be constructed using the tables in Exhibit 8–20 is one that identifies and lists all attributes of all customers with at least an A credit rating. The SQL code is

```
SELECT *
FROM Customer
WHERE CreditRating ="A" or CreditRating="A+";
```

**EXHIBIT 8–26** **Microsoft Access QBE and Result for Customer Credit Rating A or A+**

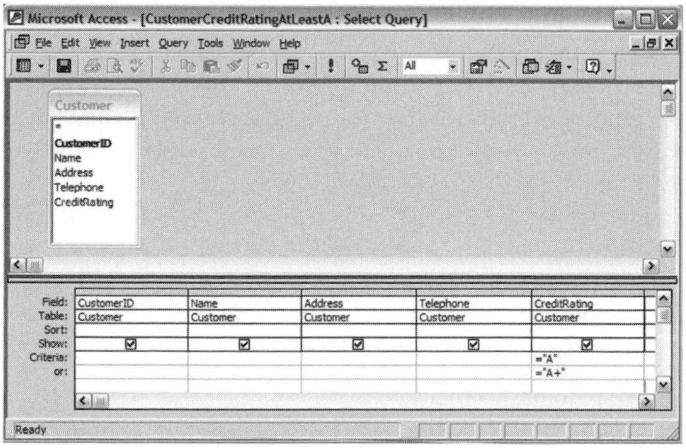

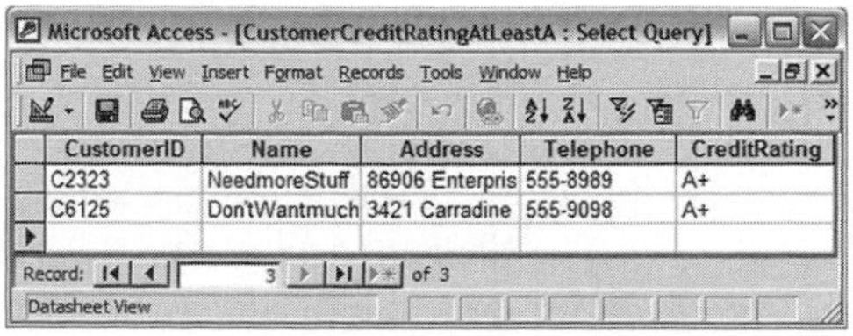

The Microsoft Access QBE and query result are displayed in Exhibit 8–26.

# RELATIONSHIP QUERIES IN THE SALES/COLLECTION PROCESS

Although resource, event, and agent queries satisfy some information needs, many information needs can be satisfied only by combining information about resources, events, and/or agents. For example, for an event it is not always sufficient to know only what happened (and when and where) but also what resources were affected by or involved in the event, who was affected by or involved in the event, why did the event occur (e.g., what other events led to the event) or what was the result of the event (what subsequent events occurred)? Therefore let's examine each relationship in the REA business process pattern to study what types of queries help to satisfy information needs arising from these relationships.

## Duality Relationship Queries in the Sales/Collection Process

Duality relationships represent exchanges comprised of two or more events. Some types of information needs with respect to duality relationships in general are

- Identification as to whether a specified exchange is completed.
- Identification of completed exchanges for a specified time period.
- Identification of incomplete exchanges for a specified time period.
- Calculation of the amount of claims, such as prepaid expenses, payables, unearned revenues, or receivables, either in total or for a specified exchange event.
- Calculation of the total or average length of the timing differences between the events involved in one or more exchanges.

In the sales/collection process the most common economic increment and economic decrement events that participate in duality relationships are sales (or service engagements), cash receipts, and sale returns. If a sale (decrement) occurs without corresponding cash receipts (increments) or sale returns (decrement reversals) that total the sale amount, then there exists a claim that is typically called accounts receivable. The sales invoices that represent the sales for which cash receipts have not yet occurred are called open sales invoices. If a cash receipt (increment) occurs without corresponding sales (decrements) that total the cash receipt amount, then there exists a claim that is typically called deferred revenue. If a sale return (decrement reversal) occurs without corresponding sales (decrements) that total the sale return amount, then there is an error because something that never happened cannot be reversed. For example, some information needs for which queries can be created using the duality relationship in the sales/collection process are

- Calculation of the outstanding receivable balance for a sale (or service engagement) invoice.
- Creation of an **open sales invoice file** (a list of open sales invoices).
- Calculation of total accounts receivable at a point in time.
- Calculation of prepaid revenue at a point in time.
- Aging of accounts receivable.
- Calculation of the average number of days it takes to collect receivables.

Using the tables in Exhibit 8–20 we can construct a query to calculate the total dollar amount of accounts receivable on a particular date (we call it the balance sheet date because accounts receivable is a line item on an enterprise's balance sheet). Consider the information needed for such a query. Accounts receivable is calculated as the total dollar amount of all sales minus any cash receipts applicable to those sales and minus any sales returns. The calculation should only include those events that occurred during the time period up to and including the balance sheet date. For example, if a sale for $1,000 occurred on June 29, then $200 of the merchandise was returned on July 6 and the customer paid the remaining $800 on July 15, then as of June 30 accounts receivable for the sale was $1,000; as of July 7, accounts receivable for the sale was $800; and as of July 31 accounts receivable for the sale was $0. If the dates are not properly constrained or if the information is not linked together correctly in constructing the query, the result may be incorrect. Notice that there is no beginning date constraint; even if the sale took place last year, if it was not returned nor was cash received to settle the receivable, then it is still receivable. When bad debts are important, an enterprise may need to add an event entity to the conceptual model for bad debt writeoffs that would also be subtracted from sales in calculating accounts receivable.

Procedures for computing accounts receivable in aggregate are generally as follows:

1. Calculate total sales dollar value through the balance sheet date by using the sale table.
2. Calculate total cash receipts that applied to sales, for which the cash receipts occurred before or on the balance sheet date, using the duality relationship to isolate only those cash receipts that applied to sales because the cash receipt table includes other cash receipts from financing or purchase returns).
   a. If the duality relationship is represented with a separate table, join the cash receipt table to the duality table, establish the constraint on the cash receipt date, and sum the cash receipt amounts.
   b. If duality is represented with the cash receipt identifier posted as a foreign key in the sale table, then join the cash receipt table to the sale table and establish the constraint on the cash receipt date. Then, in another query, sum the cash receipt

amounts. (Note: Do not combine these steps into one query because any cash receipt that paid for multiple sales will be counted multiple times in the sum and your query result will be incorrect.)

3. Calculate total sale returns that occurred through the balance sheet date, using the sale return table.

4. Subtract the amounts calculated in steps 2 and 3 from the amount calculated in step 1.

These procedures cannot be accomplished in a single query because steps 1 through 3 each involves vertical aggregations based on different tables and step 4 involves a horizontal calculation using those results. Multiple strategies exist to formulate the queries needed to generate this accounts receivable figure; the queries shown in Exhibit 8–27 are one possibility.

The number of queries it took to generate accounts receivable may dismay you. Especially when you realize that you would need to change the design of the accounts receivable queries when you need to generate accounts receivable for a different date, such as June 30. The reason the queries are not seamlessly reusable is because the May 31, 2010, date was hard-wired into the queries. Fear not! A relatively simple tweak may be made to the May 31 queries that will enable any user to generate an accounts receivable figure as of any date without having to change the query design. This is done through the use of parameter queries, which were briefly discussed in Chapter 7. Exhibit 8–28 illustrates each of the queries from Exhibit 8–27 for which changes in the date constraint were made to remove the hard-wired 5/31/2010 values and insert in their places a variable name "bsdate" (for balance sheet date). As long as the same variable name is used in all related queries, when the user runs the final query (AcctsReceivableFinal), the user will only have to enter the balance sheet date one time and that date will be plugged into all the related sub-queries.

**EXHIBIT 8–27**   **Queries to Calculate Accounts Receivable as of May 31, 2010**
Query Step 1: Total Sales Through May 31, 2010

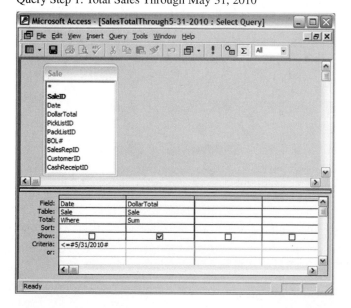

## EXHIBIT 8–27 (Continued)

Query Step 2a: Identify Cash Receipts Applicable to Sales Received Through May 31, 2010

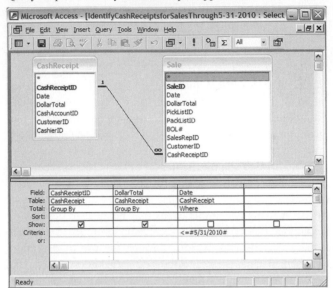

Query Step 2b: Sum Cash Receipts Applicable to Sales Received Through May 31, 2010

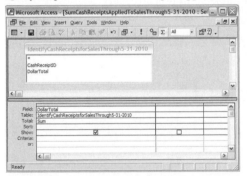

Query Step 3: Total Sale Returns Through May 31, 2010

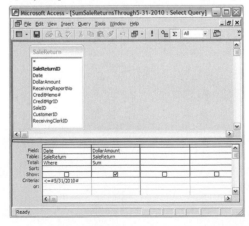

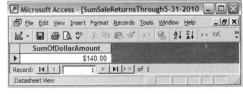

**EXHIBIT 8–27** (Concluded)

Query Step 4: Calculate Query 1 Result–Query 2 Result–Query 3 Result

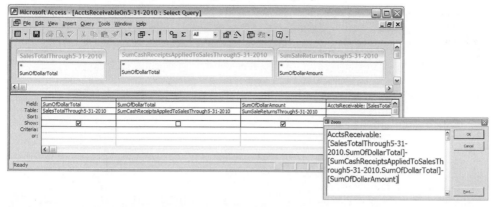

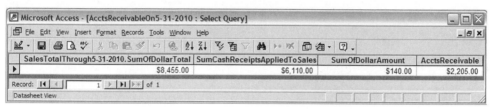

**EXHIBIT 8–28** **AcctReceivable Parameter Queries**

Query Step 1

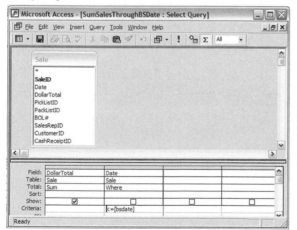

Query Step 2a

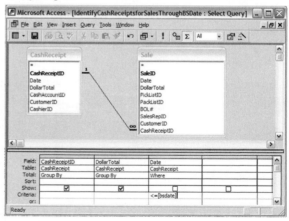

When developing queries, you must test them adequately; for example, by entering different dates to ensure a query works for various time periods. If a different date is entered into the query illustrated in Exhibit 8–28, it does not work correctly. Exhibit 8–29 displays the result obtained for the balance sheet date of May 15, 2010.

The problem is that no cash receipts were applied to sales up to 5/15/2010. Therefore a null value exists for the field SumCashReceiptsForSales. Microsoft Access can't use a null value in

## EXHIBIT 8–28 (Concluded)

Query Step 2b

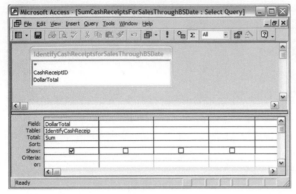

Query Step 3

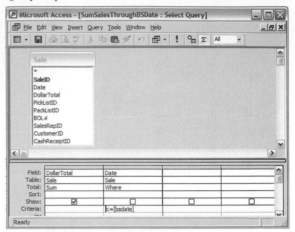

Query Step 4

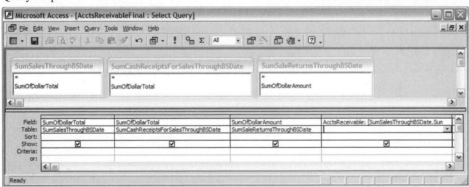

A user who runs the query "AcctsReceivableFinal" will see:

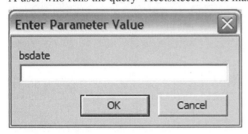

A user entering 5/31/2010 in the box as bsdate will see:

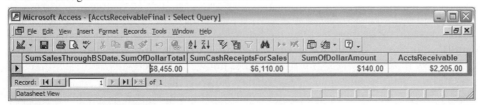

**EXHIBIT 8–29**
**Result of Previous Query with May 15, 2010, Balance Sheet Date**

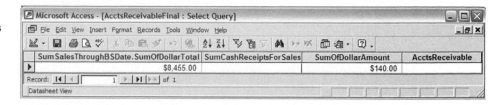

**EXHIBIT 8–30** **Query Step 4 Revised to Include Nz (Null-to-Zero) Function**

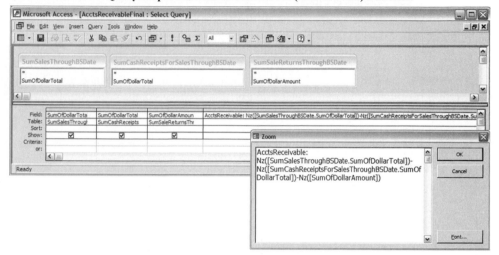

Result for May 15, 2010, Balance Sheet Date

a calculation, so the AcctsReceivable field displays as null also. To fix this, a function called Nz (null-to-zero) must be inserted into the calculation for any field that is at risk for having a null value. The null-to-zero does not actually change a null value to a zero; it simply treats the field as if it were zero. Nz must be applied separately to each field, not applied to the overall calculation, otherwise it will evaluate whether the entire calculation is null and if so, treat it as zero. Exhibit 8–30 illustrates the use of Nz in the calculation for the final query step of Exhibit 8–28 and the resulting answer when the query is run for the balance sheet date May 15, 2010.

## Stockflow Relationship Queries in the Sales/Collection Process

Stockflow relationships represent associations between economic increment or decrement events and the resources that are increased or decreased by those events. Therefore stockflow relationships are commonly used in queries to satisfy information needs about the effect of economic events on resources or about the resources involved in events. Some common information needs are

- What resources or resource types were increased or decreased by an economic event?
- What quantity of a resource or resource type was increased or decreased by an economic event?
- What dollar value of a resource or resource type was increased or decreased by an economic event?
- When did an event increase or decrease a specific resource or resource type?
- Where did an event increase or decrease a specific resource or resource type?

Such information needs can require detailed descriptions of particular transactions or they may require aggregations such as sums or averages. The preceding types of information may be used as part of a trend analysis to project future events and their expected effects on resources or resource types, and/or they may be compared to similar information for competitors to gauge the level of competitive advantage (or disadvantage) the enterprise may have.

Within the sales/collection process, some common information needs of these types are

- Which inventory types were decreased by a specific sale event?
- What quantity of each inventory type was decreased by a specific sale event?
- Which inventory types were increased by a sale return event?
- What quantity of each inventory type was increased by a specific sale return event?
- What selling price was charged for an inventory type on a specific sale event?
- What selling price was granted as credit for an inventory type on a specific sale return event?
- What was the total dollar value of sales for a specified time period? (Note: If the total sale amount is stored in the sale event table, then it is not necessary to use the stockflow relationship to meet this information need.)
- What is the average dollar value of sales of a specified inventory type for a specified time period?

Assume a marketing manager has requested two reports of sales dollars by inventory item to see which inventory items have generated the most sales and the least. The first report covers the week of May 1–7, 2010, and the second report covers the week of May 8–14, 2010. In each report, the manager wants the ItemID, the item description, and the total sales dollar amount. How would you construct a query from the tables in Exhibit 8–20 to meet the manager's need?

Begin by examining the tables to see which tables you need. Because this query combines information about sales and inventory, you need to look at the stockflow relationship and related entities and determine which of the database tables represent those constructs. Then examine those tables to see which contain the relevant information. In this case the Sale, InventoryType, and StockflowSaleInventory tables contain the desired information. Exhibit 8–31 displays the Microsoft Access QBE and result. The query is constructed as a parameter query so that the same query may be run for each week.

Examine the results in Exhibit 8–31. Carefully compare them to each other and to the InventoryType table in Exhibit 8–20. Do these reports meet the marketing manager's need? No. What is the problem? Although the reports adequately identify the item with the highest dollar sales (Big Stuff for May 1–7 and Miniature Stuff for May 8–14), they do not display the items with lowest dollar sales, which are in fact those items that haven't sold at all. The reason for this is the equi-join between InventoryType and StockflowSaleInventory. The

**EXHIBIT 8–31   Queries to Determine Dollar Value Sold of Each Inventory Item**

Query Step 1 Join Tables, Constrain Dates, and Extend Sale Amounts

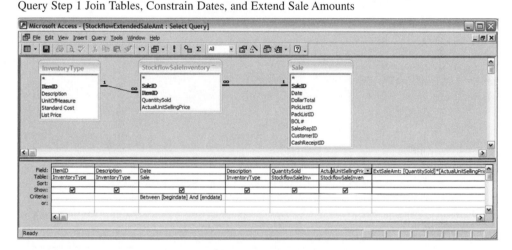

Query Step 2 Sum Extended Sale Amounts for Each Item

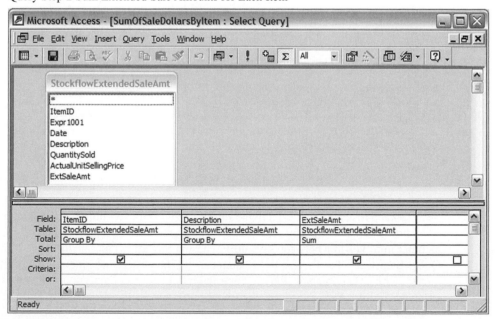

**EXHIBIT 8–31** (Concluded)

Result for May 1–7, 2010

Result for May 8–14, 2010

**EXHIBIT 8–32** **Queries to Identify Highest and Lowest Selling Inventory**

Query Step 1 Constrain Dates and Calculate Extended Sale Amounts for Inventory Sales

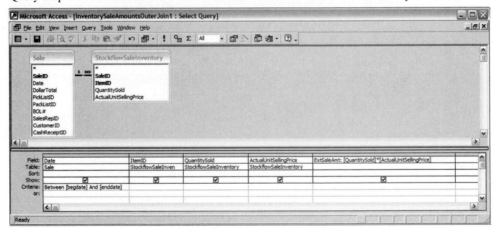

equi-join results in a solution that only includes instances with matching values in both ta-bles. To keep instances that exist in the InventoryType table without matching values in the StockflowSaleInventory table, the join type between those two tables must be changed to an outer join. The join between InventoryType and StockflowSaleInventory as shown in the Query Step 1 panel of Exhibit 8–31 cannot simply be changed to an outer join because the query includes three tables, thus making the outer join too ambiguous for Access to un-derstand. Exhibit 8–32 illustrates the revised query steps that better satisfy the marketing manager's information need.

**EXHIBIT 8–32**   **(Concluded)**
Query Step 2 Join Extended Sale Amounts for Inventory That Was Sold to Inventory Type Table

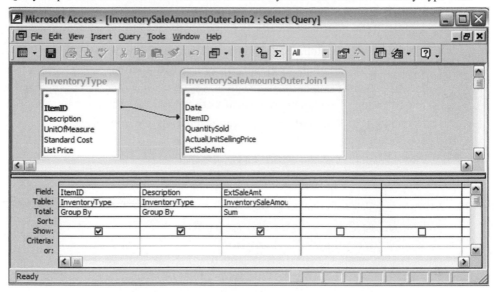

Result for May 1–7, 2010

Result for May 8–14, 2010

# Fulfillment Relationship Queries in the Sales/Collection Process

Fulfillment relationships are similar to duality relationships in that both relationships represent associations between events. Whereas duality relationships associate two or more economic events, fulfillment relationships either represent associations between economic events and the commitments that led to the economic events or they represent associations between commitment events and the instigation events that led to the commitments. Therefore some of the information needs to be satisfied with fulfillment relationships include:

- Identification of unfulfilled commitments or instigation events.
- Identification of fulfilled commitments or instigation events.
- Identification of commitment events that were not preceded by instigation events, or identification of economic events that were not preceded by commitment events.
- Calculation of length of time between instigation and commitment events or between commitment and economic events.

**EXHIBIT 8–33**
**Calculation of Days to Fill Sale Orders**

Query Step 1 Calculate Number of Days to Fill Each Sale Order for Orders Accepted in May

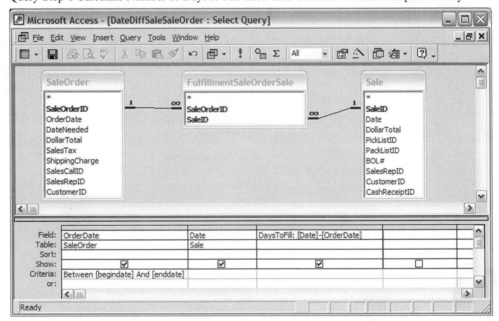

Result of Query Step 1

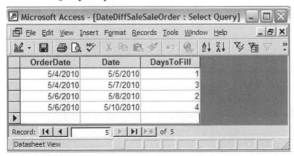

- Identification of causes of commitments and/or of economic events.
- Identification of results of instigations and/or of commitment events.

In the sales/collection process the most common instigation events are sales calls; the most common commitment events that fulfill the sales calls are sale orders (or service engagement contracts); and the most common economic decrement events that fulfill the sale orders are sales (or service engagements). If a sales call occurs without a corresponding sale order, the sales call is unfulfilled. If a sale order occurs without a corresponding sale, the sale order is unfulfilled. A list of unfilled sale orders is called an **open sales order file.** Some example information needs for which queries can be created using the fulfillment relationships in the sales/collection process are:

- Creation of an open sales order file.
- Identification of successful sales calls (i.e., those sales calls that resulted in orders)
- Calculation of number of average days the enterprise takes to fill sale orders for a given time period.

Using the tables in Exhibit 8–20, a query can be constructed to calculate the number of days the enterprise took to fill each sale order, and a further query can be constructed to calculate the average number of days the enterprise takes to fill sale orders for that time period. Exhibit 8–33 illustrates the queries needed to satisfy these information needs. Note that if the date fields had not been designed as Date/Time fields, they could not be subtracted to calculate the number of days to fill the order.

**EXHIBIT 8–33**
**(Concluded)**

Query Step 2 Calculate Average of Days to Fill Orders

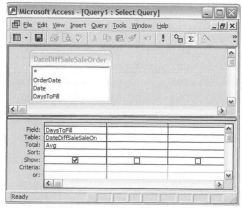

Result of Query Step 2

## Proposition Relationship Queries in the Sales/Collection Process

**Proposition relationships** represent associations between instigation events and the resources the events propose to increase or decrease. Therefore proposition relationships are commonly used in queries to satisfy information needs about the proposed effect of instigation events on resources or the resources involved in instigation events. Some common information needs are

- What resources or resource types does the instigation event propose to increase or decrease?
- What quantity of a resource or resource type is the proposed increase or decrease for an instigation event?
- When did an instigation event propose to increase or decrease a specific resource or resource type?

Within the sales/collection process, the most common instigation events are sales calls, and the most common resource involved in a sales call is inventory type. Some common information within the sales/collection process are

- Which inventory types were presented as part of a sales call event?
- What selling price was proposed for an inventory type in a specific sales call event?
- What was the reaction to each inventory type presented in a specific sales call event?
- Have any inventory types never been presented in any sales call event?
- How many different types of inventory were presented in a specific sales call event?

Using the tables in Exhibit 8–20, a query can be constructed to identify which (if any) inventory items have never received a positive customer reaction during a sales call. Exhibit 8–34 displays the query needed to satisfy this information need.

## Reservation Relationship Queries in the Sales/Collection Process

**Reservation relationships** represent associations between commitment events and the resources the events are committing to increase or decrease. Therefore reservation relationships are commonly used in queries to satisfy information needs about the eventual effect of commitment events on resources or the resources involved in commitment events. Some common information needs are

- What resources or resource types is a commitment event agreeing to increase or decrease?
- What quantity of a resource or resource type is a commitment event agreeing to increase or decrease?
- What dollar value of a resource or resource type is a commitment event agreeing to increase or decrease?
- When did an event commit to increase or decrease a specific resource or resource type?
- Where did an event commit to increase or decrease a specific resource or resource type?

Within the sales/collection process, the most common commitment events are sale orders and the most common resource associated with commitment events is inventory type. Some common information needs of these types within the sales/collection process are

**EXHIBIT 8–34**
**Queries to Identify Inventory Items with No Positive Customer Reactions**

Query Step 1 Identify Items in Sales Calls with Positive Reactions

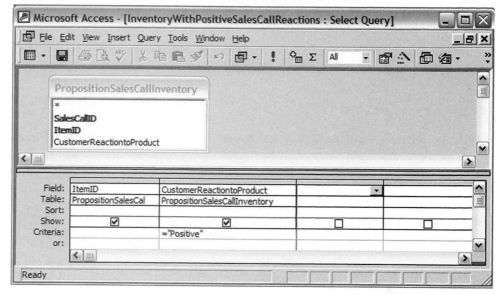

Query Step 2 Outer Join InventoryType to Positive Reactions, Identify Those without Positives

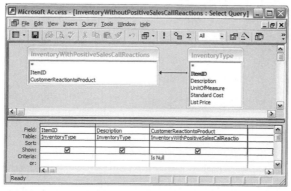

Result

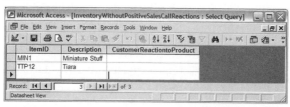

- Which inventory types does a specific commitment event agree to decrease?
- What quantity of each inventory type does a specific commitment event agree to decrease?
- What selling price was quoted for each inventory type in a specific commitment event?

- What was the total dollar value of sale orders for a specified time period? (Note: If the total dollar amount is stored in the sale order event table, then it is not necessary to use the reservation relationship to meet this information need.)
- What is the average dollar value of sale orders of a specified inventory type for a specified time period?

Because these queries are very similar to the examples already illustrated for the proposition and stockflow relationship queries, no additional examples are displayed in detail.

## Participation Relationship Queries in the Sales/Collection Process

Participation relationships represent associations between various events and the agents who participate in the events. Therefore participation relationships are commonly used in queries to satisfy information needs for identification of which agents participated in events or the events in which agents have participated. Any common information needs on this list could be required for either internal or external agents:

- Which agents participated in a specified event?
- In how many events of a specified type has a specified agent participated?
- What is the total dollar value of events of a specific type in which a specified agent has participated for a specified time period?
- When did a specified event in which a specified agent participated occur?
- Where did a specified event in which a specified agent participated occur?

Within the sales/collection process, some common information needs of these types are

- To which customer was a specific sale made?
- By which salesperson was a specific sale order accepted?
- How many sales calls did a specified salesperson make during a specified time period?
- What is the total (or average) dollar amount of sales made by each salesperson during a specified time period?
- When was a specified shipment sent to a specified customer?
- Where did a specified sales call to a specified customer take place?

Using the database tables in Exhibit 8–20, a query can be constructed to calculate the number of sales calls made by each salesperson for a specified time period. The tables needed are SalesCall and Salesperson, since the relevant participation relationship is implemented with SalespersonID posted as a foreign key in the SalesCall table. Exhibit 8–35 displays the query.

You may be wondering why the query in Exhibit 8–35 was constructed in two steps rather than combining both steps into one. If both steps are combined, any sales representative who has not made any sales calls during the time period identified by the date constraints will not appear in the solution at all; thus E30 Wyland Stindt does not appear on the list. Try it!

## Queries Requiring Multiple Relationships in the Sales/Collection Process

Sometimes information that crosses multiple relationships must be retrieved to satisfy an information need. For example, a query that requires information about both a resource and an agent that were involved in an economic event needs to use both a stockflow rela-

**EXHIBIT 8–35**
**Query for Number of Sales Calls Made by Each Salesperson for a Time Period**

Query Step 1 Constrain Dates on Sales Calls

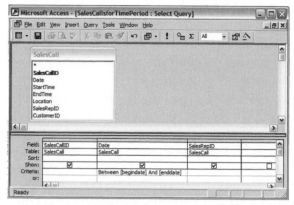

Query Step 2 Join Sales Calls to Sales Representatives and Count Sales Calls Made by Each

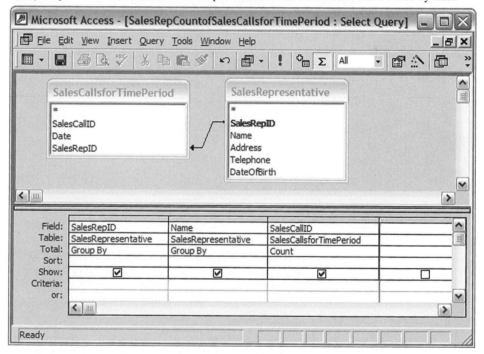

Result for May 1–15, 2010

tionship and a participation relationship. These types of queries are the most complicated to construct, and yet are typically the most powerful tools for meeting information needs. Within the sales/collection process, some common information needs that require use of multiple relationships are

- Which sale orders have been partially filled? (Requires stockflow, reservation, and fulfillment-sale-order-sale relationships.)
- What is the total dollar value of accounts receivable for a specified customer at a point in time? (Requires duality, participation-customer-sale, and participation-customer-cash-receipt relationships.)
- What inventory types have been presented to a specified customer in sales calls during a specified time period? (Requires proposition and participation-customer-sales-call relationships.)
- Which salesperson presented a specified inventory type to a specified customer? (Requires proposition, participation-customer-sales-call, and participation-salesperson-sales-call relationships.)
- What is the total dollar amount of sales of a specified inventory type that have been made to customers in a specified region? (Requires stockflow and participation-customer-sale relationships.)
- In what region have sales calls involving a specified inventory type been the most successful? (Requires proposition, fulfillment-sales-call-sale-order, and reservation relationships.)

In the discussion of fulfillment relationship queries, a query was constructed to calculate the average number of days an enterprise had taken to fill sale orders (revisit Exhibit 8–33). That query has one weakness; it does not distinguish a filled sale order from a partially filled sale order. As long as the enterprise has sent something from a customer's order to the customer, it counts the order as having been filled for purposes of calculating the days it took to fill the order. When the remainder of the order is filled, that sale date is also factored into the calculation of days to fill the order; in the average calculation it is as if the two parts of the order that are shipped separately are two different orders with the same order date. Over a reasonably long time frame, this distinction is not usually crucial so the query shown in Exhibit 8–33 may be useful. If, however, the firm does not want to count an order as filled until it is *completely* filled, or if the firm wants to determine which sale orders have been only partially filled, additional relationship information is needed.

Using the database tables in Exhibit 8–20, a query can be constructed to determine which sale orders have been only partially filled. This query requires information from the sale order event, reservation relationship, fulfillment relationship, sale event, and stockflow relationship. The data needed regarding the sale order event are the order ID (to link to the reservation and fulfillment relationships) and the date on which the order was placed. The data needed regarding the sale event are the sale ID (to link to the fulfillment and stockflow relationships) and the date on which the sale occurred. In a previous query we saw that it is useful to complete date constraints as a preliminary step in queries that join multiple items together, as it helps to prevent filtering out records that should be included in an answer. The first two steps of the query demonstrated in Exhibit 8–36 therefore isolate the sale orders through a user-specified date and isolate the sales through a user-specified

**EXHIBIT 8–36**
**Query
to Identify
Partially Filled
Sale Orders**

Query Step 1 Constrain Sale Order Date to Have Occurred up to User-Specified Ending Date

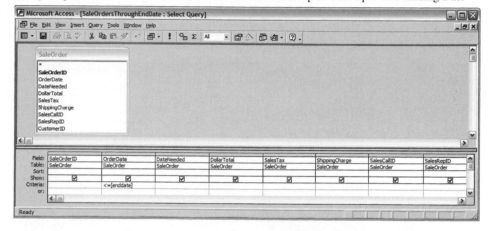

Query Step 2 Constrain Sale Date to Have Occurred up to User-Specified Ending Date

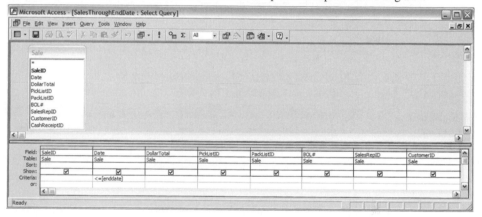

date. In fact, to aid ad hoc querying it is probably useful to create two separate queries for each event in a database, one that keeps all attributes of the event and constrains the event date to have occurred before or on a user-specified date and one that keeps all attributes of the event and constrains the event date to have occurred between user-specified beginning and ending dates.

The third step joins the date-constrained sale orders to the reservation relationship, thereby date constraining the reservation relationship. The fourth step joins the date-constrained sales to the stockflow relationship table, thereby date constraining the stock-flow relationship. The fifth step joins the date-constrained reservation result to the fulfillment relationship table to add the related sale ID to each reservation record; similarly, the sixth step joins the date-constrained stockflow result to the fulfillment relationship table to add the related sale order ID to each stockflow record. The seventh step joins the results from steps 5 and 6 together based on sale ID, sale order ID, and inventory item ID. The quantity sold field is summed so that if multiple sales applied to the same sale order the

**EXHIBIT 8–36**
**(Continued)**

Query Step 3 Join Date-Constrained Sale Orders with Reservation Relationship to Identify Quantities of Items Ordered (in Effect Date Constraining the Reservation Relationship)

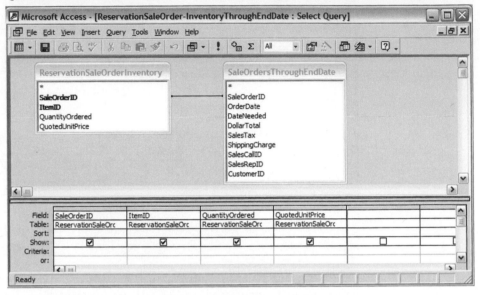

Query Step 4 Join Date-Constrained Sales with Stockflow Relationship to Identify Quantities of Items Sold (in Effect Date Constraining the Stockflow Relationship)

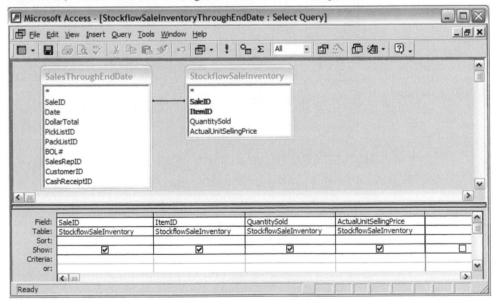

total sold can be compared to the quantity ordered. The final step subtracts that total sold from the quantity ordered to calculate the unfilled quantity of each item on sale orders that have been at least partially filled. This series of query steps does not include sale orders that have not been filled at all; additional steps would be needed to include those in the an-

**EXHIBIT 8–36**
**(Continued)**

Query Step 5 Join Date-Constrained Reservation with Fulfillment to Link Sale Orders to Sale IDs

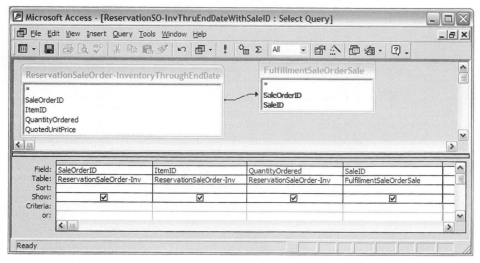

Query 6 Join Date-Constrained Stockflow with Fulfillment to Link Sales with Sale Order IDs

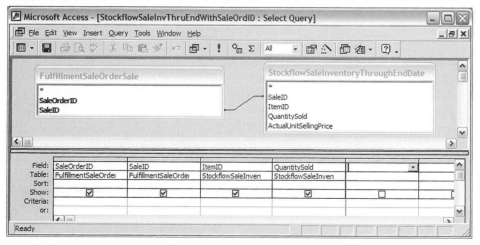

swer. As you can see, queries that involve multiple relationships can become quite complex. It is important to organize your thinking and not combine too many steps.

## CONCLUDING COMMENTS

This chapter presented an overview of the activities in the sales/collection process and discussed the extended REA pattern as it is applied to this process, including similarities and differences in the pattern for enterprises with different types of revenue-generating activities. Whether an enterprise sells hot dogs at a small stand outside a university library, or

**EXHIBIT 8–36**
**(Concluded)**

Query 7 Join ReservationWithSaleIDs to StockflowWithSaleOrderIDs, Linking Sale ID, Sale Order ID, and Item ID; Group by Sale Order ID; Sum Quantities Sold

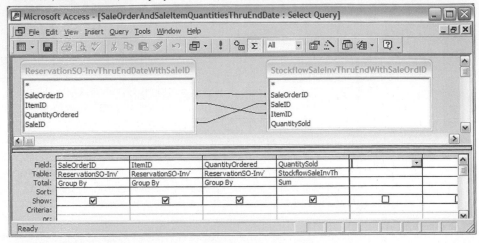

Query 8 Use SaleOrderAndSaleItemQuantites Result and Subtract Sum of Quantity Sold from Quantity Ordered to Get Unfilled Quantities of Partially Filled Sale Orders

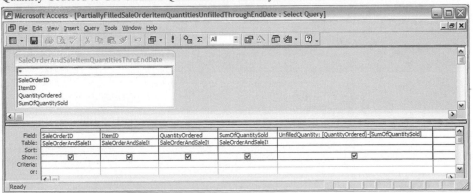

Result for Query Run with 5/8/2010 as End Date

sells custom-made computers via orders placed on the Internet, whether it sells dental services, insurance, or some combination of products and services, the enterprise's events very likely fit the REA pattern. The event labels for an enterprise may be different than those used in this textbook; therefore the concepts learned here cannot be routinely applied with rote memorization. The key for discovering the pattern fit for a specific enterprise is to think about the nature of the events and particularly the resources affected by them. It helps many people to think first at the value system level—what resources does the enterprise exchange with its customers? Next think at the value chain level—what resources are provided to the revenue cycle by the enterprise's various types of acquisition/payment cycles, what resources does the revenue cycle provide to other cycles such as financing, and most importantly what exchange is made? Once you are confident you are thinking effectively about resources and events that are part of the revenue process and you have identified the economic increment and decrement events that comprise the duality relationship, then it should be relatively easy to determine the commitment events and instigation events that led to each economic event, and to connect resources, internal agents, and external agents to each event as needed. Finally, consider whether extra relationships such as custody, assignment, or typification, as discussed in Chapter 6, apply, or even whether some extra relationships apply that are unique to the enterprise you are modeling. As long as the foundation of the system database is consistent with REA, extra constructs usually may be added without compromising the advantages the pattern provides for automated reasoning and interenterprise integration.

Documents often used in the sales/collection process were illustrated and example database tables were generated. Some example information needs and queries to satisfy them were presented. Those presented represent only a small fraction of the many different information needs that enterprises have on a daily basis. One goal of this chapter is to enable students who one day may be faced with meeting someone's information needs to think creatively and generate queries to meet those information needs. The database tables presented in this chapter are not comprehensive. Database tables in real-world enterprise system applications such as PeopleSoft, Oracle Applications, or SAP have dozens (sometimes even hundreds) of attributes. Examination of the attributes available in an enterprise system database is a critical step in developing queries that report values of those attributes in the format needed by a user.

## Key Terms and Concepts

Bill of lading, *210*
Cash receipt, *214*
Credit memorandum or credit memo, *219*
Customer order, *206*
Customer statement, *214*
Deposit slip, *214*
Duality relationship, *212*
Economic decrement event, *206*
Economic decrement reversal event, *218*
Economic increment event, *210*

Economic increment reversal event, *219*
Electronic funds transfer, *217*
Fulfillment relationship, *212*
Instigation event, *202*
Inventory, *202*
Inventory type, *204–205*
Marketing event, *202*
Mutual commitment event, *202*
Open sales invoice file, *232*
Open sales order file, *243*

Packing slip, *210*
Participation relationship, *212*
Picking slip, *210*
Proposition relationship, *244*
Remittance advice, *214*
Rental, *209*
Reservation relationship, *244*
Reversal relationship, *212*
Sales call, *202*
Sales/collection business process, *199*

Sales invoice, *210*                Sales return, *217*                Service type, *212*
Sales order, *205*                Service engagement, *209*            Stockflow relationship, *212*

# Review Questions

LO1    R1.   List three objectives of the sales/collection process.

LO5    R2.   How is the sales/collection process related to the conversion process, the acquisition payment process, and the financing process?

LO1, LO7    R3.   What is the difference between a customer order and a sales order?

LO1, LO7    R4.   Explain the difference between a sales order and a sales invoice.

LO1    R5.   What is an electronic funds transfer?

LO7, LO8    R6.   What is an open sales order? In a database designed using the REA ontology, how can open sales orders be identified?

LO7, LO8    R7.   What is an open sales invoice? In a database designed using the REA ontology, how can open sales invoices be identified?

LO7, LO8    R8.   During which event should an enterprise recognize revenue for an FOB shipping point sales transaction: Sale Order, Shipment, or Cash Receipt? Explain your response.

LO3, LO6    R9.   Identify typical resources, internal agents, and external agents associated with each of the following business events:
a. Sales call or similar instigation event.
b. Sales order or similar mutual commitment event.
c. Sale, shipment, and/or service engagement or other economic decrement event.
d. Cash receipt or other economic increment event.
e. Sale return or other economic decrement reversal event.

# Multiple Choice Questions

LO1    MC1.   Which document is typically associated with the activities involved in the sales return event?
A. Receiving report
B. Sales order
C. Sales call report
D. Sales invoice

LO4    MC2.   The revenue cycle represents the point of contact between the enterprise and which set of external business partners?
A. Investors and creditors
B. Suppliers
C. Customers
D. Employees

LO5    MC3.   The resource made available by the sales/collection process to the finance process in a typical enterprise value chain is:
A. Inventory
B. Property, plant, and equipment
C. Labor
D. Cash

LO6    MC4. Which of the following entities are usually paired in a stockflow relationship in the sales/collection process?

      A. Sales call and inventory
      B. Cash and cash receipt
      C. Sales order and inventory
      D. Sales order and sale

LO6    MC5. Which of the following events should reflect the point in time at which title to goods transferred from the enterprise to a customer?

      A. Sales call
      B. Sales order
      C. Sale
      D. Cash receipt
      E. Sales return

## Discussion Questions

LO7    D1. Describe at least two sales/collection process information needs for each of the following:

      a. Management
      b. Marketing
      c. Finance and accounting
      d. Human resource
      e. Production

LO2, LO4, LO6    D2. Consider the following enterprise: Online Sheet Music (OSM) is a company that provides a website from which customers can identify sheet music they want to buy for piano, guitar, and other musical instruments. Customers can view ratings provided by other customers, read summaries provided by sheet music publishers, and locate pricing information. When customers order sheet music, they place their orders via OSM. However, OSM does not take possession of any sheet music and hold it as inventory. Rather, OSM orders the sheet music from the appropriate sheet music publishers and arranges for the sheet music to be shipped directly from the publishers to the customers. The customers pay OSM for the sheet music, and OSM pays the publishers a portion of the proceeds from the customers, keeping the excess as revenues.

      a. How does the enterprise value system level REA model for OSM differ from that illustrated in Exhibit 8–1? That is, what resources are provided by OSM to the customers? What resources are received in exchange? And what resources are provided by OSM to the publishers and what resources are received in exchange? Does your answer depend on whether OSM ever accepts legal title to the sheet music even though OSM never physically possesses the inventory?

      b. How does the business process level REA model for OSM's sales/collection process differ from that illustrated in Exhibit 8–3? Does the pattern change? Or is the difference merely in the labeling of some of the resources, agents, events, and relationships?

LO8    D3. What entities and/or relationships most likely need to be included in a query to calculate the accounts receivable balance for each customer? Assume the balance is not stored as a volatile derivable attribute in the customer table.

# Applied Learning

LO6    A1.    Quandrax Computers is a store that buys computer components for low prices, assembles the components into computers, and then sells the computers at high prices. Each computer is assigned a unique identification number, and computers that have common configurations are categorized into types (e.g., Longitude is a laptop that is easily networked and is recommended for businesses; Element is a desktop that is intended for home and small businesses). Categories can be entered into the database before any computers in the categories are actually assembled. The computer components are purchased from wholesalers. One of Quandrax's purchasing agents submits an order to the wholesaler that has listed a given component for sale. If the order is accepted, one of Quandrax's inventory clerks receives the items. Multiple orders accepted by the same supplier may be consolidated into one purchase. Orders are accepted in their entirety or not at all. Nearly all of Quandrax's orders are accepted. Sometimes the incorrect components are delivered to Quandrax and Quandrax has to return them to the appropriate supplier. Sometimes Quandrax returns components to suppliers for other reasons, such as the result of a change in planned production of a certain category of computers. Only about 10 percent of Quandrax's purchased components are returned to suppliers, and any return would result from only one purchase.

When payment is due for a purchase, one of Quandrax's cashiers issues one check for payment in full for the items on that purchase. Sometimes if multiple purchases have been made from the same supplier within a short time, Quandrax pays for those purchases with just one check. One of Quandrax's managers is required to not only authorize all purchase orders greater than $5,000 but also sign all checks (including checks written for expenditures other than purchases of computer components). Quandrax needs to keep track of the managers' participation in these events as well as the participation of other employees in these events. In physically implementing the conceptual model into the database tables, Quandrax wants to combine all employee types into just one table. This means Quandrax would keep the separate employee entities on the E-R diagram, but make just one employee table to represent all of the employee entities, then post keys or make relationship tables as necessary to implement all relationships of employees to the relevant events.

All sales are handled via mail or e-mail, as Quandrax does not have any showrooms. Quandrax assigns salespeople to its large corporate customers and the salespeople take sample computers to the customer locations to demonstrate features as part of their sales calls. Only a small percentage of Quandrax's sales calls result in orders, and sometimes a salesperson might need to make several sales calls to the same customer to obtain one order from that customer. Orders also result from customers surfing the Internet and seeing descriptions of the computers on Quandrax's website. These customers are not assigned to specific salespeople; Quandrax only tracks the salesperson that actually took the order. Some of Quandrax's salespeople are hired to handle just such orders and as such are not assigned specifically to any customers.

If a customer orders multiple computers on one sale order and some of the computers are immediately available whereas the others are not yet assembled, Quandrax ships the available computers right away and then ships the remainder of the order when the rest of the computers are assembled. Sometimes Quandrax combines computers from multiple sale orders into a single shipment. For example, once a customer ordered 10 computers and the next day decided that wouldn't be enough so he ordered 4 more. Quandrax shipped all 14 computers in one shipment. Quandrax only accepts checks for its sales of computers; customers can pay for multiple sales with a single check, but no partial payments are accepted. Each sale transaction is tracked by a shipment ID; an invoice is sent to the customer that is due within 10 days, with no discounts allowed. Quandrax does not allow any sale returns; that is, all sales are final. Cash receipts are never split between two cash accounts; rather each receipt is assigned to one of Quandrax's cash accounts by one of Quandrax's cashiers. Quandrax also receives cash from other activities, such as loans, so the database must allow for that. Suppliers, employees, and customers need to be entered into the database before any transactions involving them occur.

The following attributes are of interest to Quandrax. Some of them are related to the acquisition/payment cycle (we will use this scenario again in Chapter 10 and you will need them then). The attributes that are related to the sales/collection process must be included in your solution. Do not add attributes to the list. Use the boldface attribute abbreviations in parentheses next to the attributes in the list. List any assumptions you make, along with the reasons behind your assumptions (i.e., state what you think is vague in the problem, say what you are going to assume to clear up the ambiguity, and make a case for that assumption).

Purchase Order Number **(PO#)**

Supplier ID **(SuppID)**

Employee ID **(EmpID)**

Purchase Order Date **(PODate)**

Purchase Date **(PurchDate)**

Location of cash account **(Ca-Loc)**

Cash Account Number **(CashAcct#)**

Name of supplier **(SupName)**

Receiving Report Number **(RR#)**

Computer Category ID code **(Cat-ID)**

Component ID code **(CompoID)**

Cash Disbursement Date **(CD-Date)**

Name of employee **(EmpName)**

Purchase return ID **(PR-ID)**

Cash Disbursement Number **(CD#)**

Sale Order ID **(SO-ID)**

Shipment ID **(Ship-ID)**

Date of sales call **(SC-Date)**

Customer check number **(CR-Chk#)**

Sales Call ID **(SC-ID)**

Cash Receipt ID **(CR-ID)**

Customer ID **(Cust-ID)**

Date of cash receipt **(CR-Date)**

Name of customer **(Cust-Name)**

Total sale dollar amount **(Sale-Amt)**

Type of employee **(EmpType)**

Date of sale order **(SO-Date)**

Date of purchase return **(PR-Date)**

Dollar amount of cash receipt **(CR-Amt)**

Current balance of cash account **(AcctBal)**

Shipping address for a customer **(Cust-Ship)**

Date of sale/shipment of computers **(Ship-Date)**

Description of a computer category **(Cat-Desc)**

Computer component description **(Comp-desc)**

Total dollar amount of a cash disbursement **(CD-Amt)**

Standard cost for a computer component **(Std-Cost)**

Quantity of a computer component returned **(Qty-Ret)**

Type of supplier (i.e., wholesaler or individual) **(SupType)**

Identification number for a finished computer **(CompuID)**

Quantity of a computer component ordered on purchase order **(Qty-Ord)**

Proposed selling price for a type of computer on a sales call **(Prop-SP)**

Ordered cost for a computer component on a purchase order **(PO-Unit-Cost)**

Suggested selling price for computers [hint: by category] **(List-price)**

Date assembly was completed for a finished computer **(Assemb-Date)**

Quoted selling price for each item on a sale order **(Ord-SP)**

Actual selling price for a particular finished computer **(Act-SP)**

Quantity of a computer component received on a purchase **(Qty-Rec)**

Actual cost of a computer component on a particular purchase **(Item-Unit-Cost)**

### Required:

Create a business process level REA model (in either grammar or diagram format) for Quandrax Computers' sales/collection process. Be sure to include all relevant entities, relationships, attributes, and participation cardinalities.

## Answers to Multiple Choice Questions

MC1. A; MC2. C; MC3. D; MC4. B; MC5. C.

# Chapter **Nine**

# The Acquisition/Payment Business Process

### LEARNING OBJECTIVES

The objective of this chapter is to encourage an in-depth understanding of the acquisition/payment business process, with a focus on the modeling of this transaction cycle with the REA enterprise ontology and querying to meet information needs for this cycle. After studying this chapter you should be able to:

1. Identify activities and documents common to acquisition/payment business processes for various enterprises
2. Identify the components of the REA ontology in the acquisition/payment business process
3. Explain how the acquisition/payment business process fits into an enterprise's value system
4. Explain how the acquisition/payment business process fits into an enterprise's value chain
5. Create a REA business process level model for an enterprise's acquisition/payment business process
6. Identify common information needs within the acquisition/payment process
7. Create queries to meet common information needs in the acquisition/payment process

## INTRODUCTION

The **acquisition/payment business process** is sometimes also called the expenditures transaction cycle or the procure to pay mega-process; therefore you must look past the labels an enterprise assigns to its various activities and examine the substance to identify the acquisition/payment process for a given enterprise. In this chapter we discuss how the acquisition/payment transaction cycle fits into the value system and value chain levels. We then discuss the REA business process level design pattern for various enterprises, as well as the task activities that typically occur and the information needs that arise within the business process.

# ACQUISITION/PAYMENT BUSINESS PROCESS IN AN ENTERPRISE VALUE SYSTEM

The acquisition/payment transaction cycle includes the activities associated with buying, maintaining, and paying for goods and services needed by enterprises. This includes acquiring raw materials, component parts, and other resources contained in finished products or services. It also includes acquiring, and paying for, a variety of other goods and services (e.g., utilities, supplies, insurance, repairs, maintenance, research, development, professional and legal services, and property, plant, and equipment). Processes that are special cases of the acquisition/payment process but that are typically considered separate business processes include the human resources business process (acquisition of and payment for employee labor) and the financing business process (acquisition and repayment of financial capital). We discuss these processes separately in Chapters 12 and 13.

In this chapter we discuss the strategy, objectives, and nature of the acquisition/payment process. You may recognize that many of the activities in this business process are essentially the same activities as we examined in the sales/collection process only viewed from the perspective of the buyer rather than the seller. Therefore you may want to read or reread Chapter 8 and consider the similarities and differences in those activities from the buyer's perspective versus the seller's perspective.

As you analyze and model a business process, you must clearly understand its purpose and objectives. You must realize how the business process fits into the value system and enterprise value chain. At the value system level, the acquisition/payment process is the point of contact between the enterprise and its suppliers (vendors). The enterprise gives cash to the suppliers in exchange for goods and services as highlighted in Exhibit 9–1.

The value chain reveals interfaces between the acquisition/payment process and other business processes. Exhibit 9–2 illustrates the typical value chain interfaces.

The overall objective of the acquisition/payment process is to provide needed resources for the enterprise's other business processes when they are needed. This objective can be broken into several subgoals:

- **Purchase** items from reliable vendors.
- Purchase high-quality items, or at least items of the desired quality.

**EXHIBIT 9–1**
**Acquisition/
Payment
Process in the
Enterprise
Value System**

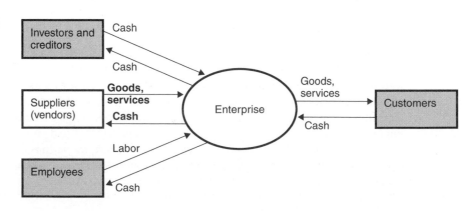

**EXHIBIT 9–2    Acquisition/Payment Process in the Value Chain**

Partial Value Chain for Manufacturers

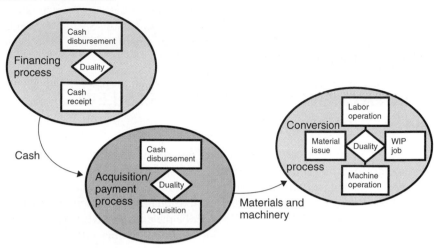

Partial Value Chain for Nonmanufacturers

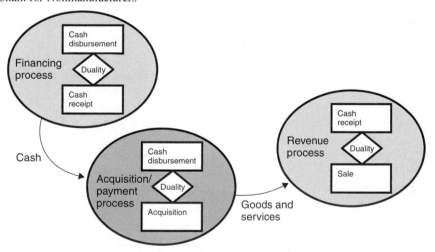

- Obtain the desired items at the best possible price.
- Purchase only those items that are properly authorized and are for legitimate company purposes.
- Have resources available and in useful condition when they are needed by the company.
- Receive only those items ordered, and receive all the items ordered.
- Control items received so they are not lost, stolen, or broken.
- Pay for the items received in a timely manner to the appropriate party.

Organizations can acquire a variety of goods and services. These include **inventory,** supplies, various services, utilities, or property, plant, and equipment. We begin our discussion of the acquisition/payment process by reviewing some of its more common events. Two important reminders before we begin the discussion: First, because we discuss the activities in a sequential fashion, it may seem that the acquisition/payment process is linear. That is not necessarily true. Increasingly, business processes and the activities that comprise those processes are dynamic, rather than linear and static. Second, remember that the activities in this process are linked to activities in other processes. We are concentrating on one process at a time to simplify our analysis.

# ACQUISITION/PAYMENT BUSINESS PROCESS LEVEL REA MODELS

Recall that the extended REA ontology described in Chapter 4 and illustrated in Exhibit 9–3 identifies the pattern underlying each transaction cycle, which consists of **instigation events, mutual commitment events,** economic exchange events, resources, agents, types, and various relationships such as stockflow, duality, fulfillment, reservation, proposition, and participation. In this section we describe the extended REA ontology components specific to the acquisition/payment business process, noting differences for types of enterprises (e.g., a merchandiser versus a manufacturer or service provider).

The *REA* pattern aids in analyzing business processes and events by highlighting the *what* (the resources involved in the event) and the *who* (the internal and external agents) of each event. Notice that the *where* and the *when* often are stored as attributes of each event. The events, agents, and resources involved in the acquisition/payment process vary somewhat from enterprise to enterprise. The general pattern discussed in this chapter easily can be adapted and applied to meet the exact requirements of any enterprise. Multiple instances of the pattern may also be used for an enterprise. For example, if the enterprise separately tracks acquisitions of inventory, acquisitions of general and administrative supplies and services, and acquisitions of operating assets (such as land, buildings, machinery, or equipment) the enterprise may create three patterns similar to the one shown in Exhibit 9–3 with different labels to indicate the differences in the resource, event, and agent names. In Exhibit 9–4 we show the pattern to illustrate the purchase of operating assets. A similar copy could be constructed to illustrate the purchase of general and administrative supplies and services.

## Instigation Events—Need Identification and Request for Goods/Services

The acquisition/payment process responds to an authorized individual's (internal agent's) requests for goods or services (resources) that are approved for use by the company. Various supervisors identify the need for goods and services by monitoring enterprise activities such as production levels, sales levels, capital improvement plans, capital budgets, sales forecasts, trends, and projections. This monitoring of levels, forecasts, and needs is a critical component of the purchasing process, and the information system should help by providing accurate, timely, and well-controlled information. Once supervisors or other authorized individuals identify a need for goods, they communicate that need to an authorized buyer (internal purchasing agent) via a **purchase requisition.** Thus the instigation event in the acquisition/payment cycle often is labeled the purchase requisition event.

Agents involved in instigation events in the acquisition/payment process usually are department supervisors (internal agents who initiate the requisition) and purchasing repre-

**EXHIBIT 9–3** **Acquisition/Payment Extended REA Ontology Database Design Pattern**

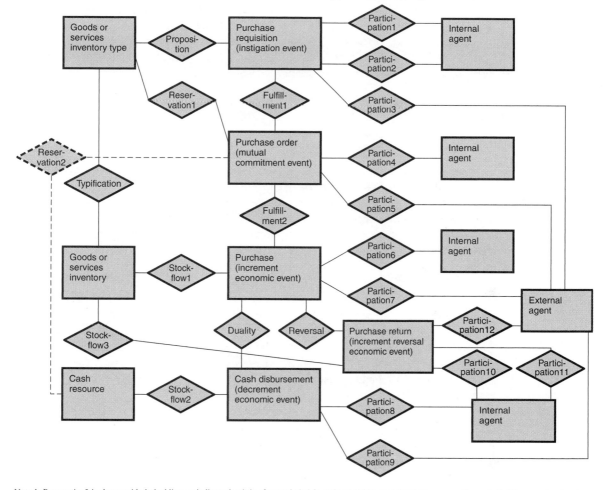

Note 1: Reservation2 is shown with dashed lines to indicate that it is often excluded from the model because the revenue-generating activity (decrement economic event) is often a more reliable cash flow budget factor than is the mutual commitment event.

Note 2: Goods or services inventory may be excluded for enterprises for which it is not cost effective to use specific identification; if so, Stockflow1 and Stockflow2 should connect to the Goods or Services Inventory Type entity. In other cases, the mutual commitment event may specify an instance of goods or services inventory; if so, Reservation1 should connect to the Goods or Services Inventory entity.

Note 3: This diagram does not attempt to differentiate internal agents for the various types of events; for some enterprises one category of employee may participate in all these events; for others there may be several different categories of employees involved.

Note 4: Participation relationships 1 and 2 reflect the reality that one internal agent (typically a department supervisor) will initiate the purchase requisition and another internal agent (often a purchasing agent) processes the purchase requisition. Therefore the set of all internal agents plays two different roles with respect to the event and each role must be tracked via a separate relationship. Similarly participation relationships 10 and 11 indicate that one internal agent (again a department supervisor) authorizes a purchase return and another (often a shipping clerk) processes the return. Other events may also involve multiple internal agents in different roles (e.g., if one employee prepares the cash disbursements and another employee signs them); they should also participate in multiple participation relationships.

sentatives (internal agents who process or deny the requisition). Requisitions may include a recommended vendor for the requested goods or services; these data may be tracked in the database and represented via the participation3 relationship shown in Exhibit 9–3. Typically there is no need to specifically identify a good or service for purposes of instigation events; all that is needed is information about the type of good or service requested. Of

**EXHIBIT 9–4** **Business Process Level Pattern for Operating Assets Acquisition**

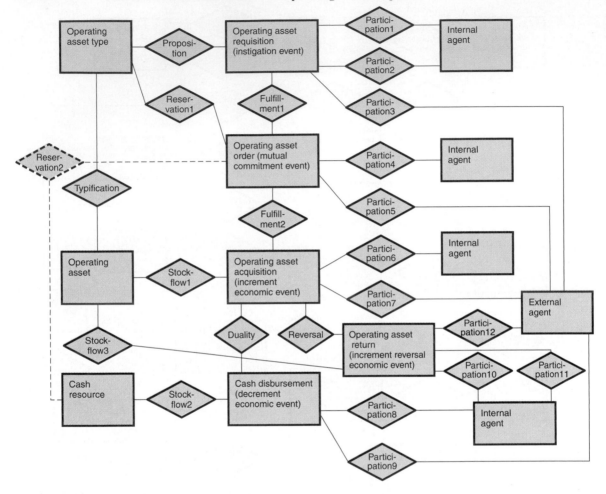

course, some enterprises have atypical or unusual circumstances and may therefore involve different agents and/or may require specific identification of requested goods and services.

Attributes of instigation events that typically should be captured include the date and time of the event. The instigation event data should also be able to be linked to data regarding the related employees, requested vendor (if one is specified), and the types of requested goods or services. Data regarding purchase requisition instigation events are often captured on a purchase requisition form such as that shown in Exhibit 9–5. This form may be either a paper document or part of a software application interface. In either case, similar data are captured and stored.

The set of relational tables illustrated in Exhibit 9–6 correspond to Exhibit 9–3's entity-relationship representation of the purchase requisition event, the relationships in which it participates (proposition, fulfillment1, participation1, participation2, and participation3), and the related entities (**inventory type, purchase order,** department supervisor, purchasing agent, and supplier). Other possible tables could be derived depending on the relationship cardinalities. Data from the form in Exhibit 9–5 have been entered into the database

**EXHIBIT 9–5**   **Purchase Requisition**

| **Your Source Company**<br>*Your Source for Everything You Need*<br>123 Main St.<br>Anytown, USA 12345 | **PURCHASE REQUISITION**<br>NO: ___R17___ |
| --- | --- |

| Date prepared:<br>4/20/2010 | Prepared by:<br>E12 | | Suggested Vendor:<br>V7 |
| --- | --- | --- | --- |
| Deliver To:<br>    Product Warehouse | | Attention:   Patrick<br>                  Wellesley | Date Needed:<br>           5/2/2010 |

| Item<br>Number | Quantity | Description | Price/Unit |
| --- | --- | --- | --- |
| BIS1 | 100 | Big Stuff | $20.00 |
| LIS1 | 200 | Little Stuff | $36.00 |
| HUS1 | 100 | Huge Stuff | $30.00 |
| TIS1 | 300 | Tiny Stuff | $48.00 |

Reason Needed:
      To meet customer demand for these products.

| Approved by:<br>        E5 | Department:<br>          Sales | Date Approved:<br>    4/22/2010 | |
| --- | --- | --- | --- |

tables; however, some of these data (e.g., inventory and supplier information) would have existed already in the database tables before the requisition data were added to the tables so all that is added regarding those objects is the relationship information that links them to the event. New data that would be entered as a result of the purchase requisition event are shown in color.

## Mutual Commitment Events (Purchase Orders, Rental Agreements, Service Agreements)

A mutual commitment event exists if the enterprise and an external business partner have each agreed to exchange resources at a defined future time. In the acquisition/payment process the most common mutual commitment events are purchase orders, rental agreements, and service agreements. A mutual commitment event doesn't always happen at a discrete point in time; often it involves a series of activities. Typically a purchase agent (the internal agent) places an order on behalf of the enterprise with a supplier (the external agent) for goods or services (the resource). There is usually no need to specifically identify goods or services for mutual commitment events; rather, information about the type of good or service ordered from the supplier is sufficient. The enterprise determines whether to commit by checking the availability of funds to pay for the goods or services, checking the vendor's availability of needed goods or services, obtaining vendor references if the vendor is not already on the approved vendor list, verifying all price and date information, and contacting the supplier if necessary to adjust pricing or dates needed. These determinations are important because the enterprise does not want to commit unless it is confident both parties can fulfill their parts of the purchase transaction (i.e., the supplier must have the ability to fill the order and the enterprise must have the ability to make payment).

**EXHIBIT 9–6**   **Relational Tables Encompassing Purchase Requisition Event**

**Purchase Requisition (Instigation) Event**

| RequisitionID | Date | Maximum Budget for This Purchase | Date Needed | SuperID[FK] | Purch AgentID[FK] | Recommended SupplierID[FK] |
|---|---|---|---|---|---|---|
| R17 | 4/22/2010 | $30,000.00 | 5/2/2010 | E5 | E12 | V7 |

**Proposition Relationship**

| Requisition ID | Item ID | Quantity Needed | Estimated Unit Cost |
|---|---|---|---|
| R17 | BIS1 | 100 | $20.00 |
| R17 | LIS1 | 200 | $36.00 |
| R17 | HUS1 | 150 | $30.00 |
| R17 | TIS1 | 300 | $48.00 |

**Department Supervisor (Internal Agent)**

| Super ID | Name | Address | Telephone | DateOfBirth |
|---|---|---|---|---|
| E5 | Patrick Wellesley | 53125 Fenton Dr. | 555-1112 | March 4, 1958 |

**Purchasing Agent (Internal Agent)**

| PurchaseAgent ID | Name | Address | Telephone | DateOfBirth |
|---|---|---|---|---|
| E12 | Joy Berwick | 1237 Kirkland Ave. | 555-8914 | July 14, 1960 |

**Supplier (External Agent)**

| Supplier ID | Name | Address | Telephone | Performance Rating |
|---|---|---|---|---|
| V7 | Joe's Favorite Vendor | 89056 Ransom Hwy. | 555-7655 | Excellent |

**Inventory Type (Resource Type)**

| Item ID | Description | UnitOfMeasure | Standard Cost | List Price |
|---|---|---|---|---|
| BIS1 | Big Stuff | Each | $20.00 | $50.00 |
| HUS1 | Huge Stuff | Each | $30.00 | $70.00 |
| LIS1 | Little Stuff | Box of 6 | $36.00 | $72.00 |
| TIS1 | Tiny Stuff | Box of 12 | $48.00 | $96.00 |

**Purchase Order (Mutual Commitment) Event**

| Purchase Order ID | PO Date | Date Promised | Total Dollar Amt | Purchase RequisitionID[FK] | Purchase AgentIDFK | SupplierID[FK] |
|---|---|---|---|---|---|---|
| | | | | | | |

Note: Fulfillment1 relationship is implemented with RequisitionID posted into Purchase Order table. Participation1 relationship is implemented with SupervisorID posted into Requisition table. Participation2 relationship is implemented with PurchaseAgentID posted into Requisition table. Participation3 relationship is implemented with suggested SupplierID posted into Requisition table. Fulfillment1 data are not yet entered, assuming a time lag between requisition and order.

Attributes of mutual commitment events that typically should be captured include the date, time, and dollar amount of the order; the date by which the enterprise needs the goods or services delivered; the delivery method to be used (e.g., Federal Express, UPS, or customer pick-up), the desired location of the delivery; and the payment terms. The order data

**EXHIBIT 9–7**    Purchase Order

**Your Source Company**
*Your Source for Everything You Need*
123 Main St.
Anytown, USA 12345

**Purchase Order**

NO:    16

This number must appear on all related
correspondence, shipping papers, and invoices.

**To:**    Joe's Favorite Vendor
89056 Ransom Hwy.
Metro Village, USA 54321

**Ship To:**    Your Source Company
123 Main St.
Anytown, USA 12345

| P.O. DATE | REQUISITION # | REQUISITIONER | SHIP VIA | F.O.B. POINT | TERMS |
|-----------|---------------|---------------|----------|--------------|-------|
| 4/24/2010 | R17 | E5 | UPS | Shipping | N/30 |

| QTY | UNIT | ITEM NO. | DESCRIPTION | UNIT PRICE | AMOUNT |
|-----|------|----------|-------------|------------|--------|
| 100 | Each | BIS1 | Big Stuff | $20.00 | $2,000.00 |
| 150 | Each | HUS1 | Huge Stuff | $29.00 | $4,350.00 |
| 200 | Box/6 | LIS1 | Little Stuff | $35.50 | $7,100.00 |
| 300 | Box/12 | TIS1 | Tiny Stuff | $50.00 | $15,000.00 |

1. Please send two copies of your invoice.

2. Enter this order in accordance with the prices, terms, delivery method, and specifications listed above.

3. Please notify us immediately if you are unable to ship as specified.

4. Send all correspondence to:
Purchasing Manager
Your Source Company
123 Main St., Anytown, USA 12345

| | |
|---|---|
| SUBTOTAL | $28,450.00 |
| SALES TAX | $0.00 |
| SHIPPING & HANDLING | $0.00 |
| OTHER | $0.00 |
| **TOTAL** | **$28,450.00** |

Authorized by:    *Joy Berwick*    E12        Date:    4/24/2010

also should be linked to data regarding the related resources, agents, and **economic increment events,** and to the related instigation event. Data regarding purchase order commitment events are often captured on a purchase order form such as that shown in Exhibit 9–7. This form may be either a paper document or part of a software application interface used to update the enterprise database.

Data from the form in Exhibit 9–7 have been entered into the database tables in Exhibit 9–8; however, some of these data (e.g., inventory and supplier information) would already have existed in the database tables before the purchase order data were entered. The only data added regarding those objects are the relationship information that links them to the purchase order event. The new data entered to record the mutual commitment event are shown in color.

The set of relational tables in Exhibit 9–8 correspond to Exhibit 9–3's entity-relationship representation of the purchase order event and the relationships in which it participates (reservation1, fulfullment1, fulfillment2, participation4, and participation5). Other possible tables could be derived, depending on the relationship cardinalities.

**EXHIBIT 9–8    Relational Tables Encompassing Purchase Order Event**

**Purchase Order (Mutual Commitment) Event**

| Purchase Order ID | PO Date | Date Promised | Total Dollar Amt | Purchase RequisitionID^FK | Purchase AgentID^FK | SupplierID^FK |
|---|---|---|---|---|---|---|
| PO16 | 4/24/2010 | 5/2/2010 | $28,450.00 | R17 | E12 | V7 |

**Purchase Requisition (Instigation) Event**

| RequisitionID | Date | Maximum Budget for This Purchase | Date Needed | SuperID^FK | Purch AgentID^FK | Recommended SupplierID^FK |
|---|---|---|---|---|---|---|
| R17 | 4/22/2010 | $30,000.00 | 5/2/2010 | E5 | E12 | V7 |

**Reservation1 Relationship**

| Purchase Order ID | Item ID | Quantity Needed | Quoted Unit Cost |
|---|---|---|---|
| PO16 | BIS1 | 100 | $20.00 |
| PO16 | LIS1 | 200 | $35.50 |
| PO16 | HUS1 | 150 | $29.00 |
| PO16 | TIS1 | 300 | $50.00 |

**Purchasing Agent (Internal Agent)**

| Purchase Agent ID | Name | Address | Telephone | DateOfBirth |
|---|---|---|---|---|
| E12 | Joy Berwick | 1237 Kirkland Ave. | 555-8914 | July 14, 1960 |

**Supplier (External Agent)**

| Supplier ID | Name | Address | Telephone | Performance Rating |
|---|---|---|---|---|
| V7 | Joe's Favorite Vendor | 89056 Ransom Hwy. | 555-7655 | Excellent |

**Inventory Type (Resource Type)**

| Item ID | Description | UnitOfMeasure | Standard Cost | List Price |
|---|---|---|---|---|
| BIS1 | Big Stuff | Each | $20.00 | $50.00 |
| HUS1 | Huge Stuff | Each | $30.00 | $70.00 |
| LIS1 | Little Stuff | Box of 6 | $36.00 | $72.00 |
| TIS1 | Tiny Stuff | Box of 12 | $48.00 | $96.00 |

**Fulfillment2 Relationship**

| Purchase Order ID | Receiving Report ID |
|---|---|

Note: Participation4 relationship is implemented with PurchAgent ID posted into Purchase Order table. Participation5 relationship is implemented with Supplier ID posted into Purchase Order table. Fulfillment1 relationship is implemented with Requisition ID posted into Purchase Order table. Fulfillment2 data are not yet entered, assuming a time lag between order and receipt of goods.

Similar types of data are captured on similar forms (again, either in electronic interfaces or on paper documents) for other mutual commitment events such as service agreements and rental contracts. Similar types of data are captured regarding the service and rental agreements as are captured for the purchase order events.

# Economic Increment Event (Purchase [Receipt of Goods], Rental, or Service Acquisition)

The economic increment event in the acquisition/payment process may take on one of several labels to represent the various resources acquired. Typically if goods are being acquired, the increment event is called *Acquisition, Purchase,* or *Receipt of Goods.* If the resource acquired is a temporary right to use goods, the event is usually called *Rental.* A rental acquisition begins when the right to temporary possession of the goods transfers from the supplier to the enterprise and ends when possession of the goods transfers back from the enterprise to the supplier. When services or utilities are acquired, the label is often *Service Acquisition* or *General and Administrative Service Acquisition.* Whatever label is used, the important consideration is that an increment event must represent the point at which benefit was received by the enterprise. It is at this point that a liability is incurred (unless the acquisition was prepaid). Enterprises usually purchase several types of resources (e.g., inventory, operating assets, and general and administrative services) and therefore must decide for database design purposes whether to combine the different acquisitions into one acquisition event entity (attached to multiple different resource entities) or to create separate patterns as illustrated in Exhibits 9–3 and 9–4, with different event entities and different resource entities. The decision to combine or separate acquisitions of different resources usually depends on whether different attributes need to be captured for the different acquisitions. If different attributes are needed for the different increments, usually they should be represented as separate event entities, each participating in a **duality relationship** with the appropriate **economic decrement event.** If the same attributes are captured for acquisitions of inventory, operating assets, and service types (and especially if the same sequentially numbered documents or interface screens are used), then they may be combined into a common acquisition event.

A **receiving report** is the primary document prepared by the enterprise in conjunction with the economic increment event. Receiving reports are completed by inventory or receiving clerks when goods or services are received from suppliers. Receiving reports similar to Exhibit 9–9 list the items and the quantities and condition of each item received. If a document is to be used to represent an acquisition event, the receiving report is the most representative choice because it indicates the point at which benefit was received by the enterprise. Many companies do not record acquisitions until they receive **vendor invoices** similar to the one in Exhibit 9–10. Data captured on vendor invoices may provide additional details of the acquisition; however, such data usually can be stored as nonkey attributes of the acquisition event entity. Enterprises that assign a nondocument-related primary key to the acquisition event, or that assign the receiving report number as the primary key of the acquisition event, can record acquisition data upon receipt of goods and services rather than waiting for the vendor invoice to arrive several days or even weeks later. In general, it is unwise for the enterprise to use an externally prepared document as a base object in its system when an internally prepared alternative is available.

Relationships in which the economic increment event in the acquisition/payment process participates typically include a **fulfillment relationship** (enabling the enterprise to trace which mutual commitment event the increment fulfilled), a duality relationship (allowing the enterprise to trace a related economic decrement that represents the other part of the exchange), a **stockflow relationship** (to trace the resource or resource type received in the decrement event), **participation relationships** with the internal and external agents,

**EXHIBIT 9–9** Receiving Report

| | | | |
|---|---|---|---|
| **Your Source Company** | | | **RECEIVING REPORT** |

*Your Source for Everything You Need*
123 Main St.
Anytown, USA 12345

NO: ___18___

| DATE | **4/30/2010** | PURCH ORD NO./SALE RETURN AUTH NO. | **PO16** |
|---|---|---|---|
| RECEIVED FROM | Joe's Favorite Vendor | | PREPAID |
| | | | XX |
| ADDRESS | 89056 Ransom Hwy. Metro Village, USA 54321 | | COLLECT |

| FREIGHT CARRIER | FREIGHT BILL NO. |
|---|---|
| **UPS** | **XYAT31253** |

| | QUANTITY | ITEM NO | DESCRIPTION |
|---|---|---|---|
| 1. | 100 | BIS1 | Big Stuff |
| 2. | 200 | LIS1 | Little Stuff |
| 3. | 150 | HUS1 | Huge Stuff |
| 4. | 300 | TIS1 | Tiny Stuff |
| 5. | | | |
| 6. | | | |
| 7. | | | |
| 8. | | | |
| 9. | | | |

REMARKS: CONDITIONS, ETC.
   Perfect condition

| RECEIVED BY | DELIVERED TO |
|---|---|
| E111 | E5 |

BE SURE TO
MAKE THIS RECORD
ACCURATE AND COMPLETE

and occasionally a **reversal relationship** (allowing the enterprise to trace **purchase returns** to the original acquisitions for which they reversed the economic effect).

Internal agents typically associated with economic increment events via participation relationships include purchase agents and receiving clerks. External agents typically associated with economic increment events via participation relationships include suppliers, common carriers (such as UPS or Federal Express), and credit card companies. The resources typically associated with the economic increment event via stockflow relationships in the acquisition cycle are usually *inventory, inventory type, service type, supply type,* or *operating asset.* Most manufacturers and merchandisers do not specifically identify inventory, so the resource that participates in the stockflow1 relationship for inventory acquisition is usually *inventory type.* For those enterprises that do specifically identify inventory items, the resource in the stockflow1 relationship is *inventory.* For general and ad-

**EXHIBIT 9–10**   **Vendor Invoice**

---

**Invoice**

NO: ____4167____

DATE: ____5/3/2010____

**Joe's Favorite Vendor**
*Let us be your favorite too!*
89056 Ransom Hwy.
Metro Village, USA 54321

**Sold To:**

Your Source Company
123 Main St.
Anytown, USA 12345

**Ship To:**

same

| P.O. NUMBER | SALESPERSON | PACKING LIST# | DATE SHIPPED | SHIPPED VIA | TERMS |
|---|---|---|---|---|---|
| 16 | Veronica | 4199 | 4/27/2010 | UPS | N/30 |

| QUANTITY | STOCK # | DESCRIPTION | UNIT PRICE | AMOUNT |
|---|---|---|---|---|
| 100 | BIS1 | Big Stuff | $20.00 | $2,000.00 |
| 200 | LIS1 | Little Stuff | $35.50 | $7,100.00 |
| 150 | HUS1 | Huge Stuff | $29.00 | $4,350.00 |
| 300 | TIS1 | Tiny Stuff | $50.00 | $15,000.00 |

|  |  |
|---|---|
| SUBTOTAL | $28,450.00 |
| SALES TAX | 0 |
| SHIPPING & HANDLING | 0 |
| **TOTAL DUE** | $28,450.00 |

Make all checks payable to: Joe's Favorite Vendor
Please make sure your account number is on all correspondence and checks.

**THANK YOU!**

---

ministrative service acquisitions, the resource involved in the stockflow1 relationship is usually *service type.* For supply acquisitions the associated resource is usually *supply type,* and for operating asset acquisitions the associated resource is usually *operating asset* (note that typically operating assets are specifically identified).

The set of relational tables in Exhibit 9–11 correspond to Exhibit 9–3's entity-relationship representation of the inventory acquisition event and the relationships in which it participates (stockflow1, fulfillment2, participation6, participation7, duality, and reversal). Other possible tables could be derived, depending on the relationship cardinalities. Data from the forms in Exhibits 9–9 and 9–10 have been entered into the database tables; however, some of these data (e.g., inventory and supplier information) would already have existed in the database tables before the purchase data were added to the tables so all that is added regarding those objects is the relationship information that links them to the purchase event. The new data to be added upon receipt of goods are shown in color. The additional data to be entered upon receipt of the vendor invoice are shown in another color.

**EXHIBIT 9–11    Relational Tables Encompassing Purchase Event**

**Purchase (Economic Increment) Event**

| Receiving ReportID | Date | Dollar Amount | Receiving ClerkID<sup>FK</sup> | SupplierID<sup>FK</sup> | Vendor Invoice# | Invoice Amount | Cash DisbID<sup>FK</sup> |
|---|---|---|---|---|---|---|---|
| RR18 | 4/30/2010 | $28,450.00 | E111 | V7 | VI4167 | $28,450.00 | |

**Purchase Order (Mutual Commitment) Event**

| Purchase Order ID | PO Date | Date Promised | Total Dollar Amt | Purchase RequisitionID<sup>FK</sup> | Purchase AgentID<sup>FK</sup> | SupplierID<sup>FK</sup> |
|---|---|---|---|---|---|---|
| PO16 | 4/24/2010 | 5/2/2010 | $28,450.00 | R17 | E12 | V7 |

**Stockflow1 Relationship**

| Receiving Report ID | Item ID | Quantity Received | Actual Unit Cost |
|---|---|---|---|
| RR18 | BIS1 | 100 | $20.00 |
| RR18 | LIS1 | 200 | $35.50 |
| RR18 | HUS1 | 150 | $29.00 |
| RR18 | TIS1 | 300 | $50.00 |

**Receiving Clerk (Internal Agent)**

| Receiving Clerk ID | Name | Address | Telephone | DateOfBirth |
|---|---|---|---|---|
| E111 | Kendall Galligan | 1235 Germandy Dr. | 555-6812 | December 12, 1970 |

**Supplier (External Agent)**

| Supplier ID | Name | Address | Telephone | Performance Rating |
|---|---|---|---|---|
| V7 | Joe's Favorite Vendor | 89056 Ransom Hwy. | 555-7655 | Excellent |

**Inventory Type (Resource Type)**

| Item ID | Description | UnitOfMeasure | Standard Cost | List Price |
|---|---|---|---|---|
| BIS1 | Big Stuff | Each | $20.00 | $50.00 |
| HUS1 | Huge Stuff | Each | $30.00 | $70.00 |
| LIS1 | Little Stuff | Box of 6 | $36.00 | $72.00 |
| TIS1 | Tiny Stuff | Box of 12 | $48.00 | $96.00 |

**Fulfillment2 Relationship**

| Purchase Order ID | Receiving Report ID |
|---|---|
| PO16 | RR18 |

**Purchase Return (Economic Increment Reversal) Event**

| Purchase ReturnID | Date | Dollar Amount | Packing Slip# | Debit Memo# | Receiving ReportID<sup>FK</sup> | SupplierID<sup>FK</sup> | Dept SuperID<sup>FK</sup> | Shipping ClerkID<sup>FK</sup> |
|---|---|---|---|---|---|---|---|---|
| | | | | | | | | |

Note: Participation6 relationship is implemented with PurchAgent ID posted into Purchase table. Participation7 relationship is implemented with Supplier ID posted into Purchase table. Reversal relationship is implemented with Receiving Report ID posted into Purchase Return table. Duality and reversal relationship data are not yet entered, assuming a time lag between Purchase and either Cash Disbursements or Purchase Returns. Purchase dollar amount is derived using quantities received and actual unit costs in the stockflow relationship (actual unit costs typically equal the "committed to" unit costs in the reservation relationship, but could be adjusted per supplier acknowledgment).

## Economic Decrement Event (Cash Disbursement)

**Cash disbursements** are economic decrement events that decrease the enterprise's cash balance. Cash disbursements may be made via paper **check,** debit card, electronic funds transfer, or cash payment. Notice that if the enterprise uses a credit card to pay a supplier, the enterprise has not yet disbursed cash; the cash disbursement does not occur until the enterprise pays the credit card company. In the latter case, the cash disbursement must be connected to two external agents —the supplier, whose accounts payable balance decreases as a result of tendering the credit card, and the credit card company, to whom the cash was literally paid.

Cash disbursements may occur at various times during the acquisition/payment process. Some cash disbursements may be made as orders are placed (i.e., prepayments); other cash disbursements may occur at the point of acquisition or upon pickup of goods or services; still other cash disbursements may occur days or weeks after acquisitions take place. The disbursement of cash is a custodial function; therefore, employees assigned responsibility for this event should not have additional authorization or recording responsibilities. Several documents are typically involved in task activities that comprise the cash disbursement event: **disbursement vouchers,** vendor invoices, purchase orders, and receiving reports. Two of the main concerns in the acquisition/payment process are for enterprises to ensure they do not receive goods or services they did not order, and more importantly to ensure they do not disburse cash for goods or services that they did not receive. To address these concerns, many enterprises prepare disbursement vouchers to authorize cash disbursements, using the purchase orders, receiving reports, and vendor invoices as support documentation. In Exhibit

**EXHIBIT 9–12**   **Disbursement Voucher**

**Your Source Company**
*Your Source for Everything You Need*
123 Main St.
Anytown, USA 12345

**Disbursement Voucher**

NO:  __40__

**Date Prepared:**  5/25/2010
**Authorized by:**  E36

**Vendor Number:**  V7
**Remit Payment To:**
  Joe's Favorite Vendor
  89056 Ransom Hwy.
  Metro Village, USA 54321

| VENDOR INVOICE | | INVOICE AMOUNT | RETURNS & ALLOWANCES | DISCOUNT | NET PAYMENT AMOUNT | SUPPORT DOCUMENTS EXAMINED BY |
|---|---|---|---|---|---|---|
| NUMBER | DATE | | | | | |
| 4167 | 5/2/2010 | $28,450.00 | $0.00 | $0.00 | $28,450.00 | DJB |
| | | | | | | |
| | | | | | | |
| | | | | | | |
| **PAYMENT TOTALS:** | | $28,450.00 | $0.00 | $0.00 | $28,450.00 | |

| CHECK NUMBER: | 41235 |
|---|---|
| CASH ACCOUNT#: | Ca123501 |

**EXHIBIT 9–13** **Relational Tables Encompassing Cash Disbursement Event**

**Cash Disbursement (Economic Decrement) Event**

| Disb Voucher ID | Voucher Date | Dollar Amount | Check Number | Cash AccountIDFK | A/P ClerkIDFK | SupplierIDFK |
|---|---|---|---|---|---|---|
| 40 | 5/25/2010 | $28,450.00 | 41235 | Ca123501 | E36 | V7 |

**Cash (Resource Type)**

| CashAccountID | AccountType | Location |
|---|---|---|
| Ca123501 | Checking | 1st Local Bank |

**Purchase (Economic Increment) Event**

| Receiving ReportID | Date | Dollar Amount | Receiving ClerkIDFK | SupplierIDFK | Vendor Invoice# | Invoice Amount | Cash DisbIDFK |
|---|---|---|---|---|---|---|---|
| RR18 | 4/30/2010 | $28,450.00 | E111 | V7 | VI4167 | $28,450.00 | 40 |

**Accounts Payable Clerk (Internal Agent)**

| A/P Clerk ID | Name | Address | Telephone | DateOfBirth |
|---|---|---|---|---|
| E36 | Diane Bowersox | 9115 Wolfgang Court | 555-7244 | September 15, 1963 |

**Supplier (External Agent)**

| Supplier ID | Name | Address | Telephone | Performance Rating |
|---|---|---|---|---|
| V7 | Joe's Favorite Vendor | 89056 Ransom Hwy. | 555-7655 | Excellent |

Note: Stockflow2 relationship is implemented with Cash AccountID posted into Cash Disbursement table. Participation8 relationship is implemented with A/P Clerk ID posted into Cash Disbursement table. Participation9 relationship is implemented with Supplier ID posted into Cash Disbursement table. Duality relationship is implemented with Cash Disbursement ID posted into Purchase table.

9–12 we illustrate a disbursement voucher. The comparison of the vendor invoice with the purchase orders and receiving reports to ensure the enterprise is paying only for goods and services ordered and received is commonly known as the three-way match.

Some enterprises have reengineered the workflow in the acquisition/payment process in a manner similar to Ford Motor Company as described in Chapter 1. Ford implemented an integrated automated system that completely eliminated the vendor invoices and disbursement vouchers. Rather than having an individual employee perform the three-way match after the events had occurred, Ford's information system matched the purchase to the purchase order as the receipt of goods occurred. Payment was then automatically generated based on the quantities received and the contractual costs per the purchase order commitment event.

Attributes captured regarding cash disbursements usually include a cash disbursement identifier (such as a disbursement voucher number), date, amount paid, supplier identification, employee identification (such as employees who write the checks), the account number from which the cash is disbursed, and the check number of the payment. Exhibit 9–13 shows a set of relational tables that correspond to Exhibit 9–3's entity-relationship representation of the cash disbursement event and the acquisition cycle relationships in which it participates (duality, stockflow2, participation8, and participation9). Other possible tables could be derived, depending on the relationship cardinalities. Additional tables are likely necessary to correspond to relationships in which the cash disbursement event participates in other transaction cycles such as financing and payroll. The tables shown in Exhibit 9–13 are applicable to the acquisition/payment process. Data from the form in Exhibit 9–12 have been entered into the database tables; however, some of these data (e.g., purchase, cash, and supplier information) would already have existed in the database tables before the cash disbursement data were added to the tables so all that is added regarding those objects is the relationship information that links them to the cash disbursement event. The new data to be added for the cash disbursement event are shown in color.

## Economic Increment Reversal Event (Purchase Returns and Allowances)

If goods and services received do not meet the identified needs, the enterprise may decide to reverse the increment event by returning the goods or requesting an allowance for the unsatisfactory services. For purchase return events, the returned products are the associated resources. Although a purchase return event decreases the inventory resource, the return is inherently different from an economic decrement event such as a sale. Because the return in effect reverses the purchase event, we call purchase return an **economic increment reversal event.** If the goods were specifically identified upon acquisition, they should be specifically identified upon return; if they were measured and recorded at the type level upon acquisition, they should be measured in that same manner for the return. Typically the supplier is the external agent involved in the return event (a common carrier also may need to be linked as an external agent), a department supervisor authorizes the purchase return as an internal agent, and a shipping clerk processes the purchase return as an internal agent.

Attributes typically captured regarding purchase returns include an identifier for the event, the return date, and the dollar amount of the return. Links also should be available to attributes of related agents and merchandise inventory. Several documents may be used in workflow tasks that make up the purchase return event: requests to return goods, packing slips, bills of lading, and debit memos. A **request to return goods** notifies a supplier of the enterprise's dissatisfaction with goods and asks permission to return those goods instead of paying for them (or in exchange for a refund). In response, the enterprise receives return authorization information from the supplier (in various formats, such as a paper document, an e-mail, or a phone call). Inventory or shipping clerks complete packing slips to document the details of each return of goods to suppliers. If the goods are returned via common carriers, bills of lading usually are also prepared. Packing slips list the items and quantities of each item returned; bills of lading list the number and dimensions of boxes in which the returned goods are packed. If a cash refund is received it reverses the cash disbursement event, which is an economic decrement. Therefore we call the cash refund an **economic decrement reversal event. Debit memorandums** (also called debit memos) are internal documents used to communicate the need for a journal entry to debit (decrease) the enterprise's accounts payable balance for that supplier. Such a document is unnecessary in an enterprise system that eliminates journals and ledgers. In Exhibits 9–14 through 9–16 we illustrate a request to return, packing slip, and debit memorandum.

Exhibit 9–17 shows a set of relational tables that correspond to Exhibit 9–3's entity-relationship representation of the purchase return event and the relationships in which it participates (reversal, stockflow3, participation10, participation 11, and participation12). Other possible tables could be derived, depending on the relationship cardinalities. Data from the forms in Exhibits 9–14 through 9–16 have been entered into the database tables; however, inventory, purchase, and supplier information already would have existed in the

**EXHIBIT 9–14** Request to Return Goods to Supplier

## REQUEST TO RETURN FROM ⟶

**Your Source Company**
*Your Source for Everything You Need*
123 Main St.
Anytown, USA 12345

Ret. Request No. ___3___
Date of Request _____

VENDOR:

All returns will be clean, in salable condition, and shipped prepaid. A prompt reply will be greatly appreciated. Thank you for your cooperation.

RETURN CODES:

☐ Cash Refund - Please

☒ Credit to Account - Please

**A** OVERSTOCK
**B** DAMAGED
**C** DEFECTIVE
**D** WRONG PRODUCT BILLED & SHIPPED
**E** CORRECT PRODUCT BILLED BUT WRONG PRODUCT SHIPPED
**F** OTHER

**FOR CLARIFICATION CONTACT**

Account No. _____

Name ___Patrick Wellesley___

Request by _____

Phone ___555-3333___

| DEPT. | QUAN. REQ. | PRODUCT NUMBER | DESCRIPTION | RETURN CODE | INVOICE NO. | QUAN. RET. | LIST PRICE | COST OR DISC. | EXTENSION |
|-------|-----------|----------------|-------------|-------------|-------------|------------|------------|---------------|-----------|
| Sales | 48 | TTP12 | Tiara | C | 48592 | 48 | | $10.00 | $480.00 |
| | | | | | | | | | |
| | | | | | | | | | |
| | | | | | | | | | |
| | | | | | | | | | |
| | | | | | | | | | |
| | | | | | | | | TOTAL | $480.00 |

*Patrick Wellesley, Es*
**Return Authorized by**

**EXHIBIT 9–15   Packing List**

| | |
|---|---|
| **Your Source Company** | **RETURNS PACKING LIST** __22__ |
| *Your Source for Everything You Need* | Clerk ID __137__ |
| 123 Main St. | |
| Anytown, USA 12345 | |

If there are any questions about this shipment, contact our sales department (999) 555-3333

| Trina's Trinkets | **RETURN AUTHORIZATION NUMBER:** 485 |
|---|---|
| 1612 Myway Rd. | **ORIGINAL PURCHASE NUMBER:** RR25 |
| Hinterland, USA 23456 | |
| **Contact:** Trina Weeble | |

| PART NUMBER | QUANTITY RETURNED | UNIT OF MEASURE | ITEM DESCRIPTION |
|---|---|---|---|
| TTP12 | 48 | each | Tiara, faux gold with inlaid baubles |

**EXHIBIT 9–16   Debit Memorandum**

| | |
|---|---|
| **Your Source Company** | **DEBIT MEMO** |
| *Your Source for Everything You Need* | NO: __3__ |
| 123 Main St. | |
| Anytown, USA 12345 | |

| DEBIT TO | Trina's Trinkets | DATE | 5/22/2010 |
|---|---|---|---|

SUPPLIER ACCOUNT NO. __V90__

| RETURN AUTH NO. | INVOICE NO. | INVOICE DATE | PURCHASE ID | |
|---|---|---|---|---|
| 485 | 48592 | 5/15/20xx | RR25 | |
| ITEM NUMBER | DESCRIPTION | QUANTITY | PRICE EACH | AMOUNT |
| TTP12 | Tiara | 48 | 10.00 | 480.00 |
| | | | | |
| | | | **TOTAL DEBIT** | 480. 00 |

database tables before the purchase return data were added to the tables so all that is added regarding those objects is the relationship information that links them to the purchase return event. The new data to be added upon return of goods are shown in color.

**EXHIBIT 9–17   Relational Tables Encompassing Purchase Return Event**

**Purchase Return (Economic Increment Reversal) Event**

| Purchase ReturnID | Date | Dollar Amount | Packing Slip# | Debit Memo# | Receiving ReportID<sup>FK</sup> | SupplierID<sup>FK</sup> | Dept SuperID<sup>FK</sup> | Shipping ClerkID<sup>FK</sup> |
|---|---|---|---|---|---|---|---|---|
| PR3 | 5/17/2010 | $480.00 | 22 | 3 | RR25 | V90 | E5 | E41 |

**Purchase (Economic Increment) Event**

| Receiving ReportID | Date | Dollar Amount | Receiving ClerkID<sup>FK</sup> | SupplierID<sup>FK</sup> | Vendor Invoice# | Invoice Amount | Cash DisbID<sup>FK</sup> |
|---|---|---|---|---|---|---|---|
| RR18 | 4/30/2010 | $28,450.00 | E111 | V7 | VI4167 | $28,450.00 | 40 |
| RR25 | 5/12/2010 | $480.00 | E111 | V90 | 48592 | $480.00 | |

**Stockflow3 Relationship**

| Purchase Return ID | Item ID | Quantity Returned | Actual Unit Cost |
|---|---|---|---|
| PR3 | TTP12 | 48 | $10.00 |

**Shipping Clerk (Internal Agent)**

| Shipping Clerk ID | Name | Address | Telephone | DateOfBirth |
|---|---|---|---|---|
| E41 | Amy Milano | 8892 Eddy Ave. | 555-9557 | January 3, 1964 |

**Department Supervisor (Internal Agent)**

| DeptSupervisorID | Name | Address | Telephone | DateOfBirth |
|---|---|---|---|---|
| E5 | Patrick Wellesley | 53125 Fenton Dr. | 555-1112 | March 4, 1958 |

**Supplier (External Agent)**

| Supplier ID | Name | Address | Telephone | Performance Rating |
|---|---|---|---|---|
| V7 | Joe's Favorite Vendor | 89056 Ransom Hwy. | 555-7655 | Excellent |
| V90 | Trina's Trinkets | 1612 Myway R. | 555-2424 | Very Good |

**Inventory Type (Resource Type)**

| Item ID | Description | UnitOfMeasure | Standard Cost | List Price |
|---|---|---|---|---|
| BIS1 | Big Stuff | Each | $20.00 | $50.00 |
| HUS1 | Huge Stuff | Each | $30.00 | $70.00 |
| LIS1 | Little Stuff | Box of 6 | $36.00 | $72.00 |
| TIS1 | Tiny Stuff | Box of 12 | $48.00 | $96.00 |
| TTP12 | Tiara | Each | $10.00 | $25.00 |

Note: Participation10 relationship is implemented with Dept Supervisor ID posted into Purchase Return table. Participation11 relationship is implemented with Shipping Clerk ID posted into Purchase Return table. Participation12 relationship is implemented with Supplier ID posted into Purchase Return table. Reversal relationship is implemented with Purchase ID posted into Purchase Return table.

# INFORMATION NEEDS AND MEASURES IN THE ACQUISITION/PAYMENT PROCESS

Information from the acquisition/payment process can provide decision-making support for many information customers. An information customer is someone who needs information; they fit into the following categories:

- Internal users need information about internal phenomena.
- Internal users need information about external phenomena.
- External users need information about internal phenomena.
- External users need information about external phenomena.

Within each of these categories, various users need information at different levels of detail. We next analyze each of the entities and relationships in the business process level pattern to give some idea of the types of queries that may be needed to satisfy information needs for internal and external users regarding these objects. The queries presented are not a comprehensive set of queries; there are simply too many potentially useful queries to list them all. The set provided should guide you in creating similar queries to satisfy similar information needs. To describe example queries needed in the acquisition/payment process we use the database tables shown in Exhibit 9–18.

## Resource Queries in the Acquisition/Payment Process

Internal and external users may need information regarding an enterprise resource or resource type. The resources and resource types most commonly present in the acquisition/payment process are inventory (specifically identified inventory, inventory types, or service types), cash, and operating assets such as supplies, property, plant, and equipment. To make effective acquisition decisions, enterprise department supervisors and purchasing department personnel must obtain information about products and services available from external suppliers, including information about features, availability, safety, and prices. They also need to compare that information to existing products and services and to the needs that those products and services are fulfilling. For each resource, users may need any of the following:

- Detailed status information at one or more points in time for each resource instance.
- Detailed status information at one or more points in time for only those resource instances meeting specified criteria.
- Summarized status information at one or more points in time for all resource instances.
- Summarized status information at one or more points in time for only those resource instances meeting specified criteria.

With regard to each of these, users may need to know all characteristics of the instances in the answer set, or they may need only a subset of the characteristics. Information regarding inventory and cash that may be needed by internal users (such as purchasing agents) and by external users (such as suppliers) includes the same list as we noted in the sales/collection process.

- A list of each inventory item or item type normally stocked by an enterprise.
- A list of all inventory items or item types that possess certain characteristics; examples include all books, real estate listings with lake frontage, toys with selling prices within

**EXHIBIT 9–18   Acquisition/Payment Process Database Tables for Queries**

**Operating Assets (Resource)**

| Asset TagID | Description | AcqDate | AcqCost | Asset Category | Estimated LifeYrs | Estimated Salvage | IRSListed Property |
|---|---|---|---|---|---|---|---|
| OA1 | Building | 4/1/2010 | $200,000.00 | Buildings | 40 | $20,000.00 | No |
| OA2 | Property | 4/1/2010 | $300,000.00 | Land | 0 | $0.00 | No |
| OA3 | Executive desk | 4/10/2010 | $2,000.00 | Furniture | 10 | $200.00 | No |
| OA4 | Manager desk | 4/10/2010 | $1,500.00 | Furniture | 10 | $100.00 | No |
| OA5 | Manager desk | 4/10/2010 | $1,500.00 | Furniture | 10 | $100.00 | No |
| OA6 | Administrator desk | 4/10/2010 | $1,000.00 | Furniture | 10 | $100.00 | No |
| OA7 | Administrator desk | 4/10/2010 | $1,000.00 | Furniture | 10 | $100.00 | No |
| OA8 | Executive desk chair | 4/10/2010 | $500.00 | Furniture | 7 | $50.00 | No |
| OA9 | Manager task chair | 4/10/2010 | $350.00 | Furniture | 7 | $50.00 | No |
| OA10 | Manager task chair | 4/10/2010 | $350.00 | Furniture | 7 | $50.00 | No |
| OA11 | Task chair | 4/10/2010 | $175.00 | Furniture | 7 | $25.00 | No |
| OA12 | Task chair | 4/10/2010 | $175.00 | Furniture | 7 | $25.00 | No |
| OA13 | Task chair | 4/10/2010 | $175.00 | Furniture | 7 | $25.00 | No |
| OA14 | Task chair | 4/10/2010 | $175.00 | Furniture | 7 | $25.00 | No |
| OA15 | Toshiba tecra | 4/15/2010 | $3,000.00 | Computers | 5 | $300.00 | Yes |
| OA16 | Dell optima desktop | 4/15/2010 | $2,000.00 | Computers | 5 | $200.00 | Yes |
| OA17 | Dell optima desktop | 4/15/2010 | $2,000.00 | Computers | 5 | $200.00 | Yes |
| OA18 | Dell optima desktop | 4/15/2010 | $2,000.00 | Computers | 5 | $200.00 | Yes |
| OA19 | Warehouse shelving | 4/16/2010 | $10,000.00 | Fixtures | 40 | $0.00 | No |
| OA20 | Fax machine | 4/17/2010 | $400.00 | Comm Equip | 3 | $0.00 | Yes |

**Cash (Resource Type)**

| CashAccountID | AccountType | Location | DateAccountEstablished |
|---|---|---|---|
| Ca123501 | Checking | 1st Local Bank | April 1, 2010 |
| Ca789125 | Savings | 1st Local Bank | April 1, 2010 |
| Ca351235 | Petty | Onsite—Cashier desk drawer | April 15, 2010 |
| Ca351327 | Petty | Onsite—CEO assistant's file cabinet | April 22, 2010 |

**Inventory Type (Resource Type)**

| Item ID | Description | UnitOfMeasure | Standard Cost | List Price | |
|---|---|---|---|---|---|
| BIS1 | Big Stuff | Each | $20.00 | $50.00 | |
| HUS1 | Huge Stuff | Each | $30.00 | $70.00 | |
| LIS1 | Little Stuff | Box of 6 | $36.00 | $72.00 | |
| MIN1 | Miniature Stuff | Box of 24 | $56.00 | $110.00 | |
| TIS1 | Tiny Stuff | Box of 12 | $48.00 | $96.00 | |
| TTP12 | Tiara | Each | $10.00 | $25.00 | *Continued* |

**EXHIBIT 9–18**   **(Continued)**

### Purchase Requisition (Instigation) Event

| Purch ReqID | Date | Maximum Budget for This Purchase | Date Needed | SuperID_FK | Purch AgentID_FK | Recommended SupplierID_FK |
|---|---|---|---|---|---|---|
| R17 | 4/22/2010 | $30,000 | 5/2/2010 | E5 | E12 | V7 |
| R18 | 5/5/2010 | | 5/23/2010 | E5 | E12 | V14 |
| R19 | 5/6/2010 | | 5/20/2010 | E5 | E12 | V7 |
| R20 | 5/15/2010 | | 5/25/2010 | E5 | E12 | |
| R21 | 5/18/2010 | | 5/26/2010 | E5 | E12 | V7 |

### Purchase Order (Mutual Commitment) Event

| Purchase OrderID | OrderDate | DateNeeded | DollarTotal | Purchase ReqID_FK | Purchase AgentID_FK | Supplier ID_FK |
|---|---|---|---|---|---|---|
| PO16 | 4/24/2010 | 5/2/2010 | $28,450.00 | R17 | E12 | V7 |
| PO17 | 5/5/2010 | 5/8/2010 | | R18 | E12 | V14 |
| PO18 | 5/5/2010 | 5/12/2010 | | R18 | E12 | V90 |
| PO19 | 5/6/2010 | 5/10/2010 | | R19 | E12 | V14 |
| PO20 | 5/6/2010 | 5/24/2010 | | R19 | E12 | V7 |
| PO21 | 5/16/2010 | 5/24/2010 | | R20 | E12 | V14 |

### Purchase (Economic Increment) Event

| Receiving ReportID | Date | Dollar Amount | Receiving ClerkID_FK | SupplierID_FK | Vendor Invoice# | Invoice Amount | Cash DisbID_FK |
|---|---|---|---|---|---|---|---|
| RR18 | 4/30/2010 | $28,450.00 | E111 | V7 | VI4167 | $28,450.00 | 40 |
| RR19 | 5/8/2010 | $1,100.00 | E111 | V14 | 821536 | $1,100.00 | |
| RR21 | 5/10/2010 | $3,240.00 | E111 | V14 | 821983 | $3,240.00 | |
| RR22 | 5/12/2010 | $2,000.00 | E111 | V7 | VI5213 | $2,000.00 | |
| RR25 | 5/12/2010 | $480.00 | E111 | V90 | 312353 | $480.00 | |

### Cash Disbursement (Economic Decrement) Event

| DisbVoucherID | VoucherDate | DollarAmount | CheckNo. | CashAcctID_FK | APClerkID_FK | PayeeID_FK |
|---|---|---|---|---|---|---|
| 39 | 5/15/2010 | $746.57 | 41234 | Ca123501 | E36 | E23 |
| 40 | 5/25/2010 | $28,450.00 | 41235 | Ca123501 | E36 | V7 |
| 41 | 5/29/2010 | $398.12 | 41236 | Ca123501 | E36 | E41 |

### Purchase Return (Economic Increment Reversal) Event

| Purchase ReturnID | Date | Dollar Amount | Packing Slip# | Debit Memo# | Receiving ReportID_FK | SupplierID_FK | Dept SuperID_FK | Shipping ClerkID_FK |
|---|---|---|---|---|---|---|---|---|
| PR3 | 5/17/2010 | $480.00 | 22 | 3 | RR25 | V90 | E5 | E41 |

### Supplier (External Agent)

| SupplierID | Name | Address | Telephone | PerformanceRating |
|---|---|---|---|---|
| V7 | Joe's Favorite Vendor | 89056 Ransom Hwy. | 555-7655 | Excellent |
| V14 | Reliable Rudy's | 34125 Michigan Ave. | 555-1199 | Very Good |
| V90 | Trina's Trinkets | 1612 Myway Rd. | 555-2424 | Very Good |

*Continued*

## EXHIBIT 9–18 (Continued)

### Shipping Clerk (Internal Agent)

| ShippingClerkID | Name | Address | Telephone | DateOfBirth |
|---|---|---|---|---|
| E41 | Amy Milano | 8892 Eddy Ave. | 555-9557 | January 3, 1964 |

### Department Supervisor (Internal Agent)

| DeptSupervisorID | Name | Address | Telephone | DateOfBirth |
|---|---|---|---|---|
| E5 | Patrick Wellesley | 53125 Fenton Dr. | 555-1112 | March 4, 1958 |

### Accounts Payable Clerk (Internal Agent)

| APClerkID | Name | Address | Telephone | DateOfBirth |
|---|---|---|---|---|
| E36 | Diane Bowersox | 9115 Wolfgang Ct. | 555-7244 | September 15, 1963 |

### Receiving Clerk (Internal Agent)

| ClerkID | Name | Address | Telephone | DateOfBirth |
|---|---|---|---|---|
| E247 | Kenneth Barki | 4312 Monticello Dr. | 556-4891 | April 14, 1945 |
| E251 | Rita Barki | 4312 Monticello Dr. | 556-4891 | May 22, 1948 |

### Proposition Relationship (Purchase Requisition–Inventory Type)

| PurchReqID | Item ID | QuantityNeeded | EstimatedUnitCost |
|---|---|---|---|
| R17 | BIS1 | 100 | $20.00 |
| R17 | LIS1 | 200 | $36.00 |
| R17 | HUS1 | 150 | $30.00 |
| R17 | TIS1 | 300 | $48.00 |
| R18 | MIN1 | 20 | $56.00 |
| R18 | TTP12 | 20 | $10.00 |
| R19 | MIN1 | 60 | $56.00 |
| R19 | BIS1 | 100 | $20.00 |
| R20 | TTP12 | 20 | $10.00 |
| R21 | LIS1 | 200 | $36.00 |

### Reservation Relationship (Purchase Order–Inventory Type)

| PurchOrderID | ItemID | QuantityOrdered | QuotedUnitPrice |
|---|---|---|---|
| PO16 | BIS1 | 100 | $20.00 |
| PO16 | LIS1 | 200 | $35.50 |
| PO16 | HUS1 | 150 | $29.00 |
| PO16 | TIS1 | 300 | $50.00 |
| PO17 | MIN1 | 20 | $55.00 |
| PO18 | TTP12 | 20 | $10.00 |
| PO19 | MIN1 | 60 | $54.00 |
| PO20 | BIS1 | 100 | $20.00 |
| PO21 | TTP12 | 20 | $11.00 |

*Continued*

**EXHIBIT 9–18**  (Concluded)

**Fulfillment2 Relationship (Purchase Order–Purchase)**

| PurchaseOrderID | PurchaseID |
| --- | --- |
| PO16 | RR18 |
| PO17 | RR19 |
| PO18 | RR25 |
| PO19 | RR21 |
| PO20 | RR22 |

**Stockflow1 Relationship (Purchase–Inventory Type)**

| PurchaseID | ItemID | PurchaseQuantity | ActualUnitCost |
| --- | --- | --- | --- |
| RR18 | BIS1 | 100 | $20.00 |
| RR18 | LIS1 | 200 | $35.50 |
| RR18 | HUS1 | 150 | $29.00 |
| RR18 | TIS1 | 300 | $50.00 |
| RR19 | MIN1 | 20 | $55.00 |
| RR21 | MIN1 | 60 | $54.00 |
| RR22 | BIS1 | 100 | $20.00 |
| RR25 | TTP12 | 48 | $10.00 |

**Stockflow3 Relationship (Purchase Return–Inventory Type)**

| PurchReturnID | Item ID | QuantityReturned | ActualUnitCost |
| --- | --- | --- | --- |
| PR3 | TTP12 | 48 | $10.00 |

a certain range, video games in GameBoy Advance format, and preventive dental care services.

- Quantity on hand of an inventory item type as of a specified date.
- Total cost value of inventory on hand as of a specified date.
- A list of all cash accounts owned by an enterprise as of a specified date.
- Balance in a specific cash account as of a specified date.
- Total balance in all cash accounts as of a specified date.

Similar information can be retrieved regarding operating assets such as supplies, land, buildings, furniture, vehicles, and machinery; for example:

- A list of general and administrative supply and service types for which the enterprise maintains descriptive data.
- A list of fixed assets owned by an enterprise.
- Book value of a depreciable fixed asset owned by an enterprise on a specified date.
- Average age of an enterprise's machinery on a specified date.

Whether the information needed by a user is detailed or summarized, whether it involves one or more instances, and whether it includes one or more characteristics of the resources, resource queries within the acquisition/payment process typically require only one table. As noted in the sales/collection process discussion, some of the information needs—for example,

**EXHIBIT 9–19**
**QBE to List Each Fixed Asset Owned on 5/31/2010**

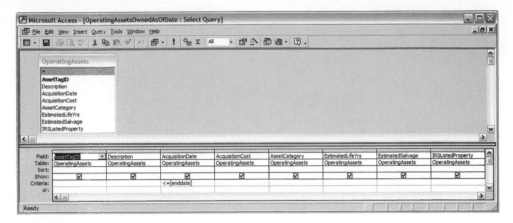

Notice the query is a parameter query so the user will see the following window when running the query:

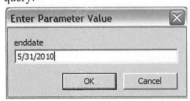

The Query Yields the Following Result

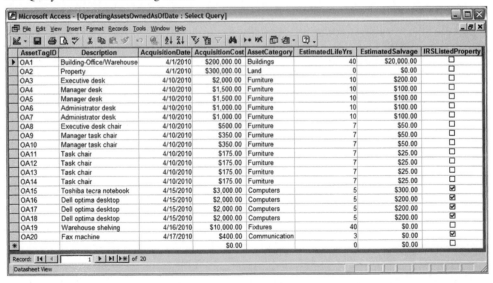

inventory quantity on hand and cash balance—do not fall completely within the acquisition/payment process and therefore cannot be provided by single-table queries unless the database allows the storage of volatile derivable attributes (triggers) as described in Chapter 6. Queries that involve multiple tables from multiple business processes are discussed in Chapter 10 since an understanding of how the business process models are integrated and the resulting tables are derived is useful for understanding the query design. For Chapter 9 we focus on the single-table resource queries that are found within the acquisition/payment process.

A list of each fixed asset owned by an enterprise on May 31, 2010, is a query that can be answered using a single-table query of the fixed assets table. The structured query language code for this query based on the tables in Exhibit 9–18 is

> SELECT *
> FROM OperatingAssets
> WHERE AcquisitionDate <= 5/31/2010;

The same query in Query-By-Example (QBE) format in Microsoft Access is displayed in Exhibit 9–19, along with the query result.

You may wonder why the resource table for operating assets includes the characteristic, acquisition date, as that characteristic may be more appropriately assigned to the relationship between purchase and operating asset. Because the operating assets are each specifically identified and the same asset is not purchased multiple times, there is no design disadvantage to including the characteristic in the asset table. There are query advantages (as in the previous example) to including acquisition date in the asset table; therefore it has been placed in the asset table.

The single-table query in Exhibit 9–19 could easily be revised to list only the fixed assets that possess certain characteristics; for instance, those with estimated salvage values greater than $200 or those classified as listed property by the Internal Revenue Service. To meet information needs such as these, queries could be constructed that are similar to the following query that lists the asset tag ID, description, acquisition date, acquisition cost, estimated useful life in years, and estimated salvage value of all computers owned by the enterprise on May 1, 2010, based on the tables in Exhibit 9–18. The SQL code for this query is

> SELECT AssetTagID, Description, AcquisitionDate, AcquisitionCost,
> EstimatedLifeYrs, EstimatedSalvage
> FROM OperatingAssets
> WHERE AssetCategory=Computers AND AcquisitionDate<=5/1/2010;

The Microsoft Access QBE and query results are illustrated in Exhibit 9–20. Notice the query in Exhibit 9–20 is established as a parameter query. Also notice the asset category field is included in the query grid to set the criteria but it does not appear in the answer because the "Show" box is not checked. Finally, notice to establish the AND logic for the criteria (thereby including only those records in the answer that meet both criteria), both criteria (acquisitiondate<=[enddate] and assetcategory="computers") are listed on the same line of the query grid. If they were listed on separate lines, the logic to combine the criteria would become OR and any records that meet either criteria would be included in the answer.

## Event Queries in the Acquisition/Payment Process

Internal and external users may need information regarding events. The most common events in the acquisition/payment process are purchase requisitions, purchase orders, purchases, cash disbursements, and purchase returns. For each of these types of events, users may need any of the following:

- Detailed information about each event instance, such as what happened, when did it happen, where did it happen?

**EXHIBIT 9–20** **Query to List Selected Characteristics of Computers Owned as of 5/1/2010**

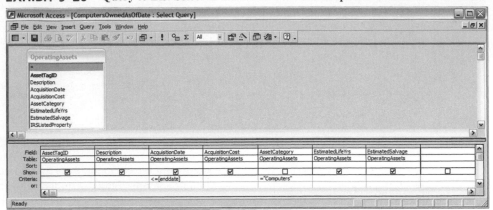

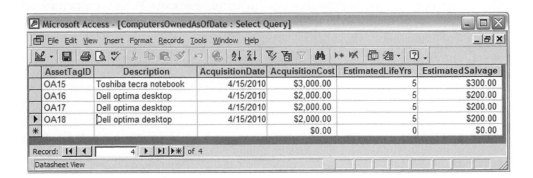

- Detailed information about each event instance that meets specified criteria; for example, events of a specified type that occurred during a specified time period or that occurred at a specified location.
- Summarized information for all instances of an event type for a specified time period such as the total event instances during a specified time period.
- Summarized information for a specified time period for only those instances of an event type that meet specific criteria; for example, the average dollar value of the event instances for a specified location during a specific time period.

With regard to each of these queries, users may need to know all characteristics of the instances in the answer set, or they may need only a subset of the characteristics. Information regarding the various types of acquisition/payment events that may be needed by internal users (such as purchasing agents) and by external users (such as suppliers) includes (among many other possibilities):

- Total number of purchase orders made during a specified time period.
- Total dollar amount for a specific purchase order, general and administrative service and supplies acquisition, operating asset acquisition, inventory acquisition, cash disbursement, or purchase return.

- Total or average dollar amount of all acquisition/payment events of a specified type for one or more specified time periods.
- Seller's tracking number for an expected purchase event.
- Date a purchase event occurred.

Using the tables from Exhibit 9–18, next we create some example queries for similar information needs. For one query a user wants to know the date and dollar amount of purchase order 18. The SQL code for such a query is

SELECT PurchOrderID, OrderDate, DollarTotal
FROM PurchaseOrder
WHERE PurchOrderID=PO18;

For Microsoft Access, the QBE and resulting solution are illustrated in Exhibit 9–21. Notice that the query illustrated in Exhibit 9–21 is not set up as a parameter query; therefore, if a user wants to find the date and dollar total for PO19 next, either this query must be revised or a new query must be created. Of course, since this is a relatively simple, one-table query, the user may choose to simply view the purchase order event table and find the date and dollar total of purchase order 19.

## Agent Queries in the Acquisition/Payment Process

Internal and external users may need information regarding an internal or external agent or agent type. The internal agents most commonly present in the acquisition/payment process are purchase agents, accounts payable clerks, inventory clerks (may be separated into receiving and shipping), and supervisors. The external agents most commonly present in the acquisition/payment process are suppliers or vendors. For each agent or agent type, users may need any of the following:

- Detailed status information at one or more points in time for each agent instance.
- Detailed status information at one or more points in time for only those agent instances meeting specified criteria.
- Summarized status information at one or more points in time for all agent instances.
- Summarized status information at one or more points in time for only those agent instances meeting specified criteria.

With regard to these information needs, users may need to know all characteristics of the instances in the answer set, or they may need only a subset of the characteristics. Information regarding various employees and suppliers that may be needed by internal users (such as supervisors and purchase agents) and by external users (such as suppliers) includes:

- A list of all purchase agents, accounts payable clerks, inventory clerks, or supervisors for an enterprise.
- A list of employees that possess certain characteristics (e.g., all accounts payable clerks whose honesty is insured under a specified minimum fidelity bond).
- A list of employees that live in a specified city or state.
- A list of all employee names and telephone numbers for an emergency phone tree.

**EXHIBIT 9–21    Query and Result for Date and Dollar Amount of Purchase Order No. 18**

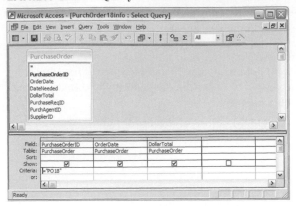

An example agent query that can be constructed using the tables in Exhibit 9–18 is one that identifies and lists all attributes of all suppliers with a performance rating of Very Good. The SQL code is

SELECT *
FROM Supplier
WHERE PerformanceRating="Very Good";

The Microsoft Access QBE and query result are displayed in Exhibit 9–22.

# RELATIONSHIP QUERIES IN THE ACQUISITION/ PAYMENT PROCESS

Although resource, event, and agent queries satisfy some information needs, many information needs can be satisfied only by combining information about resources, events, and/or agents. For example, for an event it is not always sufficient to know only what happened (and when and where) but also what resources were affected by or involved in the event, who was affected by or involved in the event, why did the event occur (e.g., what other events led to the event), or what was the result of the event (what subsequent events occurred)? Therefore let's examine each relationship in the REA business process pattern to study what types of queries help to satisfy information needs arising from these relationships.

## Duality Relationship Queries in the Acquisition/Payment Process

Duality relationships represent exchanges comprised of two or more events. Some types of information needs with respect to duality relationships in general are

- Identification as to whether a specified exchange is completed.
- Identification of completed exchanges for a specified time period.
- Identification of incomplete exchanges for a specified time period.
- Calculation of the amount of claims; for example, prepaid expenses, payables, unearned revenues, or receivables, either in total or for a specified exchange event.

**EXHIBIT 9–22    QBE and Result for Supplier Performance Rating of Very Good**

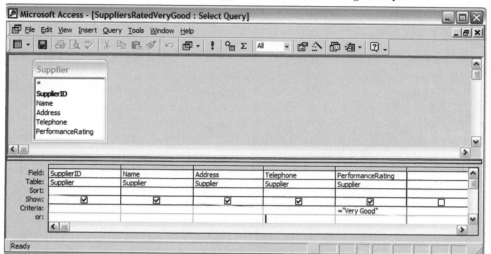

- Calculation of the total or average length of the timing differences between the events involved in one or more exchanges.

In the acquisition/payment process the most common economic increment and economic decrement events that participate in duality relationships are purchases (acquisitions), cash disbursements, and purchase returns. If a purchase (increment) occurs without corresponding cash disbursements (decrements) or purchase returns (increment reversals) that total the purchase amount, there exists a claim typically called accounts payable. If a cash disbursement (decrement) occurs without corresponding purchases (increments) that total the cash disbursement amount, there exists a claim typically called prepaid expense. If a purchase return (increment reversal) occurs without corresponding purchases (increments) that total the purchase return amount, then there is an error because something that never happened cannot be reversed. Some information needs for which queries can be created using the duality relationship in the acquisition/payment process are

- Calculation of the outstanding payable balance for a purchase.
- Calculation of total accounts payable at a point in time.

- Calculation of prepaid expenses at a point in time.
- Aging of accounts payable.
- Calculation of the average number of days it takes to pay vendor invoices.

Using the tables in Exhibit 9–18 we can construct a query to calculate the total dollar amount of accounts payable on a particular date. We call it the balance sheet date because accounts payable is a line item on an enterprise's balance sheet. Consider the information needed for such a query. Accounts payable is calculated as the total dollar amount of all acquisitions minus any cash disbursements applicable to those purchases and minus any purchase returns. The calculation should include only those events that occurred during the time period up to and including the balance sheet date. For example, if a purchase for $3,000 occurred on June 29, then $600 of the merchandise was returned on July 6 and the customer paid the remaining $2,400 on July 15, then as of June 30 accounts payable for the purchase was $3,000; as of July 7, accounts payable for the purchase was $2,400; and as of July 31 accounts payable for the purchase was $0. If the dates are not properly constrained or if the information is not linked together correctly in constructing the query, the result may be incorrect. Notice that there is no beginning date constraint; even if the purchase took place last year, if it was not returned or paid for, then it is still payable.

Procedures for computing accounts payable in aggregate are generally as follows:

Determine what kinds of acquisitions are represented in your database (except for employee services) and for each kind of acquisition follow these steps:

1. Determine which table contains the acquisition date and dollar amount (usually these are found in the acquisition event table).
2. Sum the acquisition amount through the balance sheet date (with no beginning date constraint).
3. Determine which tables contain the cash disbursements that applied to those acquisitions and calculate the applicable cash disbursements total. To determine this, examine the duality relationship.
   a. When the duality relationship is represented with a separate table, join the duality table to the cash disbursement table, establish the ending date constraint on the cash disbursement date field (with no beginning date constraint), and sum the cash disbursement amount applied to the acquisition.
   b. When the duality relationship is represented with the cash disbursement identifier posted as a foreign key into the acquisition table, join the cash disbursement table to the acquisition table, establish the ending date constraint on the cash disbursement date field (with no beginning date constraint), and sum the cash disbursement amounts.
4. Calculate total purchase returns that occurred through the balance sheet date, using the purchase returns table.
5. Subtract the results of steps 3 and 4 from the result of step 2 to get accounts payable as of the balance sheet date.

These procedures cannot be accomplished in a single query because steps 1 through 4 each involves vertical aggregations based on different tables and step 5 involves a horizontal

**EXHIBIT 9–23   Queries to Calculate Accounts Payable for Purchases as of May 31, 2010**

Query Steps 1 and 2: Determine Acquisition Types and Sum Acquisition Dollar Amounts Through May 31, 2010. For the partial database table set given, purchases of inventory are the only acquisitions for which enough detail is given to compute accounts payable.

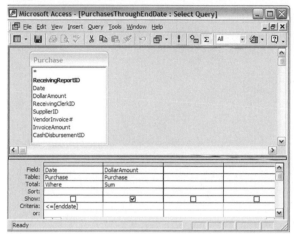

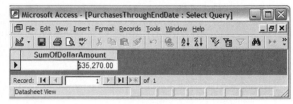

Query Step 3a: Identify Cash Disbursements Applicable to Purchases Paid Through May 31, 2010

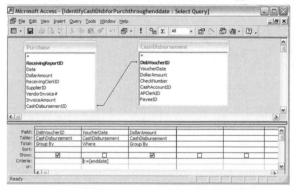

Query Step 3b: Sum Cash Disbursements Applicable to Purchases Paid Through May 31, 2010

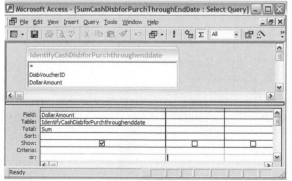

*Continued*

## EXHIBIT 9–23 (Concluded)

Query Step 4: Calculate Total Purchase Returns Through May 31, 2010

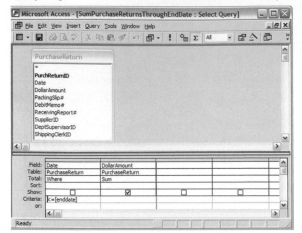

Query Step 5: Calculate Query 2 Result–Query 3 Result–Query 4 Result

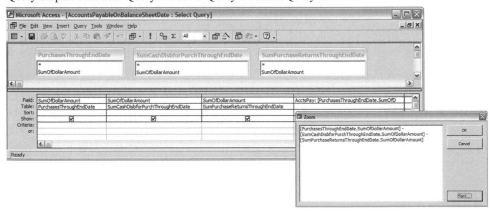

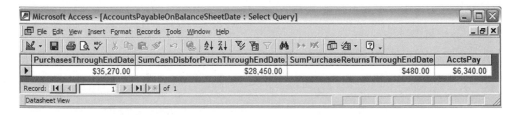

calculation using those results. Multiple strategies exist to formulate the queries needed to generate this accounts payable figure. Exhibit 9–23 outlines a set of queries to calculate accounts payable for inventory acquisitions for the tables in Exhibit 9–18. Additional queries would be needed to calculate accounts payable for operating asset purchases and general and administrative supply and service acquisitions (notice that the partial set of tables in Exhibit 9–18 does not include the detail of those acquisitions).

**EXHIBIT 9–24**  **Result of Accounts Payable Query for May 8, 2010**

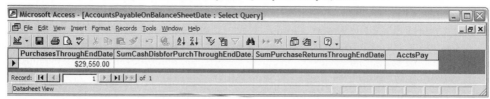

**EXHIBIT 9–25**  **Accounts Payable Query Step 5 Revised to Include Nz (Null-to-Zero) Function**

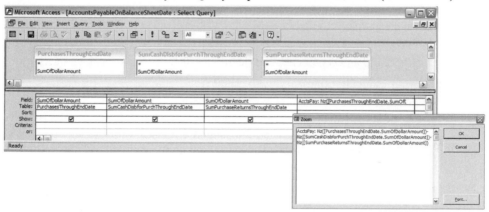

Result for May 8, 2010, Balance Sheet Date

The query steps illustrated in Exhibit 9–23 work adequately for the date 5/31/2010 because purchases, applicable cash disbursements, and applicable purchase returns had all occurred by that date. However, if the query is run for an earlier date such as May 8, 2010, the query produces the nonsense result shown in Exhibit 9–24.

Although purchases had occurred through May 8, no payments nor purchase returns had occurred. Microsoft Access cannot compute a balance for accounts payable in such a scenario without further instructions from the query developer about how to handle the null values. In Exhibit 9–25 we first show the revised expression that requests Microsoft Access to treat null values for any of the three fields used in the expression as if they were zeros; second, we show the result when the revised query is run to calculate accounts payable on May 8, 2010.

## Stockflow Relationship Queries in the Acquisition/Payment Process

Stockflow relationships represent associations between economic increment or decrement events and the resources that are increased or decreased by those events. Therefore stockflow relationships are commonly used in queries to satisfy information needs as to the effect of economic events on resources or as to the resources involved in events. Some common information needs are

- What resources or resource types were increased or decreased by an economic event?
- What quantity of a resource or resource type was increased or decreased by an economic event?
- What dollar value of a resource or resource type was increased or decreased by an economic event?
- When did an event increase or decrease a specific resource or resource type?
- Where did an event increase or decrease a specific resource or resource type?

Such information needs can require detailed descriptions of particular transactions or they may require aggregations such as sums or averages. The preceding information may be used as part of a trend analysis to project future events and their expected effects on resources or resource types, and/or they may be compared to similar information for competitors to gauge the level of competitive advantage (or disadvantage) the enterprise may have.

Within the acquisition/payment process, some common information needs of these types are

- Which inventory types were increased by a specific purchase event?
- What quantity of each inventory type was increased by a specific purchase event?
- Which inventory types were decreased by a purchase return event?
- What quantity of each inventory type was decreased by a specific purchase return event?
- What unit cost was charged for an inventory type on a specific purchase event?
- What unit cost was granted as credit for an inventory type on a specific purchase return event?
- What was the total dollar value of purchases for a specified time period? (Note: If the total purchase dollar amount is stored in the purchase event table, then it is not necessary to use the stockflow relationship to meet this information need.)
- What is the average dollar value of purchases of a specified inventory type for a specified time period?

Enterprises commonly need to calculate the weighted average unit cost of inventory items purchased during a specified time period. Such a query involves the stockflow relationship between purchase and inventory. The weighted average unit cost of an item is calculated as the total purchase dollar amount for that item during the time period divided by the total quantity purchased of that item during the time period. The general procedures for determining weighted average unit cost for each inventory item during a time period are as follows:

1. Determine which table contains the purchase date attribute (usually this is in the table that represents the purchase economic event).
2. Determine which table contains the purchase quantities and actual unit cost information (usually these attributes are in the table that represents the stockflow relationship between purchase and inventory).

3. Join the tables together, set the date constraints (beginning and ending dates for desired time period), and multiply the quantities purchased by the actual unit costs to get the total purchase line-item amounts.

4. Group the result from step 3 by inventory item and sum the purchase quantity and the total purchase line-item dollar amount.

5. Start with the result from step 4 and, still grouping by inventory item, divide the sum of the total purchase line item by the sum of the total purchased quantity.

Exhibit 9–26 displays the Microsoft Access QBE and result for the queries to provide the requested information for the weighted average unit cost for inventory types purchased in a specified time period. The query is constructed as a parameter query so that the query may be run for alternative time periods.

## Fulfillment Relationship Queries in the Acquisition/Payment Process

Fulfillment relationships are similar to duality relationships in that both represent associations between events. Whereas duality relationships associate two or more economic events, fulfillment relationships represent either associations between economic events and the commitments that led to the economic events or associations between commitment events and the instigation events that led to the commitments. Therefore, some of the information needs to be satisfied with fulfillment relationships include

- Identification of unfulfilled commitments or instigation events.
- Identification of fulfilled commitments or instigation events.
- Identification of commitment events that were not preceded by instigation events, or identification of economic events that were not preceded by commitment events.
- Calculation of length of time between instigation and commitment events or between commitment and economic events.
- Identification of causes of commitments and/or of economic events.
- Identification of results of instigations and/or of commitment events.

In the acquisition/payment process the most common instigation events are purchase requisitions; the most common commitment events that fulfill the purchase requisitions are purchase orders; and the most common economic decrement events that fulfill the purchase orders are purchases. If a purchase requisition occurs without a corresponding purchase order, the purchase requisition is unfulfilled. An unfulfilled purchase requisition is called an **open purchase requisition.** If a purchase order occurs without a corresponding purchase, the purchase order is unfulfilled. A list of unfulfilled purchase orders is called an **open purchase order file.** Some information needs for which queries can be created using the fulfillment relationships in the acquisition/payment process are:

- Creation of an open purchase order file.
- Identification of filled purchase requisitions (i.e., those purchase requisitions that resulted in purchase orders).
- Calculation of average number of days the enterprise takes to fill purchase requisitions for a given time period.
- Identification of the purchase order that corresponds to a purchase.

**EXHIBIT 9–26** **Queries to Determine Weighted Average Unit Cost of Inventory Types**

Join Purchase and Stockflow Tables, Constrain Purchase Date, and Calculate Line-Item Extensions

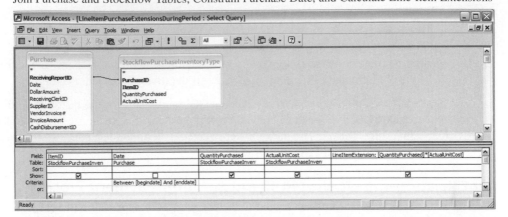

Sum Purchase Quantities and Line-Item Extensions for Each Item ID

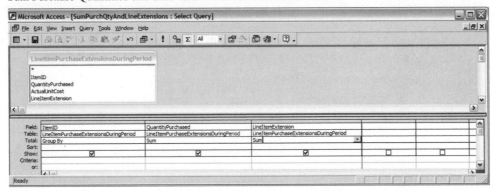

Divide Total Line-Item Extensions by Total Purchase Quantities for Each Item ID

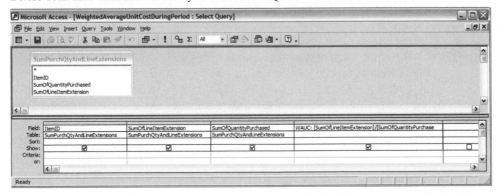

Using the tables in Exhibit 9–18, a query can be constructed to calculate the average number of days the enterprise took to fill each purchase requisition. Exhibit 9–27 illustrates the queries needed to satisfy this information need. Note that if the date fields had not been designed as Date/Time fields, they could not be subtracted to calculate the number of days to fill the requisition.

**EXHIBIT 9–26**   (Concluded)

Result for May 1–31, 2010

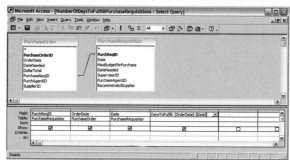

**EXHIBIT 9–27**

**Calculation of Average Number of Days to Fulfill Purchase Requisitions**

Calculate Raw Number of Days to Fulfill Each Purchase Requisition

Calculate the Average of the Number of Days to Fulfill Each Purchase Requisition

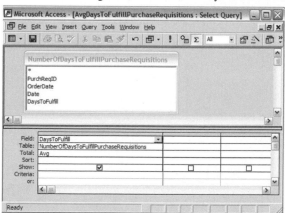

Result

## Proposition Relationship Queries in the Acquisition/Payment Process

**Proposition relationships** represent associations between instigation events and the resources the events propose to increase or decrease. Therefore proposition relationships are commonly used in queries to satisfy information needs as to the proposed effect of instigation events on resources or as to the resources involved in instigation events. Some common information needs are

- What resources or resource types does the instigation event propose to increase or decrease?
- What quantity of a resource or resource type is the proposed increase or decrease for an instigation event?
- When did an instigation event propose to increase or decrease a specific resource or resource type?

Within the acquisition/payment process, the most common instigation events are purchase requisitions, and the most common resource involved in a purchase requisition is inventory type. Some common information needs within the acquisition/payment process are

- Which inventory types were identified as needed in a purchase requisition event?
- What unit cost was estimated for an inventory type in a specific purchase requisition event?
- How many times has a specified inventory type been requisitioned during a time period?
- How many types of inventory were requisitioned in a specific purchase requisition event?

Using the tables in Exhibit 9–18, a query can be constructed to identify the number of times during May in which the item MIN1 has been requisitioned. Exhibit 9–28 displays the query needed to satisfy this information need.

**EXHIBIT 9–28**
**Query
to Calculate
the Number
of Times
During May
2010 in Which
MIN1 Has
Been
Requisitioned**

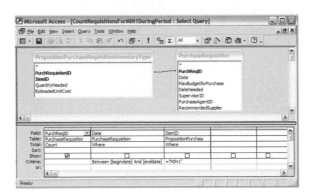

Result

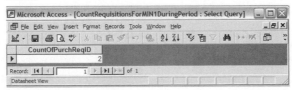

## Reservation Relationship Queries in the Acquisition/Payment Process

**Reservation relationships** represent associations between commitment events and the resources the events are committing to increase or decrease. Therefore reservation relationships are commonly used in queries to satisfy information needs as to the eventual effect of commitment events on resources or as to the resources involved in commitment events. Some common information needs are

- What resources or resource types is a commitment event agreeing to increase or decrease?
- What quantity of a resource or resource type is a commitment event agreeing to increase or decrease?
- What dollar value of a resource or resource type is a commitment event agreeing to increase or decrease?
- When did an event commit to increase or decrease a specific resource or resource type?
- Where did an event commit to increase or decrease a specific resource or resource type?

Within the acquisition/payment process, the most common commitment events are purchase orders and the most common resource associated with commitment events is inventory type. Some common information needs of these types within the acquisition/payment process are

- Which inventory types does a specific commitment event agree to increase?
- What quantity of each inventory type does a specific commitment event agree to increase?
- What unit cost was quoted for each inventory type in a specific commitment event?
- What was the total dollar value of purchase orders for a specified time period? (Note: If total dollar amount is stored in the purchase order event table, then it is not necessary to use the reservation relationship to meet this information need.)
- What is the average dollar value of purchase orders of a specified inventory type for a specified time period?

Because these queries are very similar to the examples already illustrated for the proposition and stockflow relationship queries, no additional examples are displayed in detail.

## Participation Relationship Queries in the Acquisition/Payment Process

Participation relationships represent associations between various events and the agents who participate in the events. Therefore participation relationships are commonly used in queries to satisfy information needs to identify which agents participated in events or as to the events in which agents have participated. Some common information needs are (any on this list could be needed for either internal agents or external agents)

- Which agent(s) participated in a specified event?
- In how many events of a specified type has a specified agent participated?
- What is the total dollar value of events of a specified type in which a specified agent has participated for a specified time period?
- When did a specified event in which a specified agent participated occur?
- Where did a specified event in which a specified agent participated occur?

**EXHIBIT 9–29**
**Query for Date and Receiving Clerk Associated with a Specified Purchase**

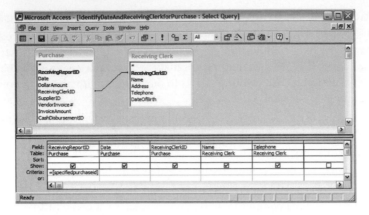

Result for Purchase RR18

Within the acquisition/payment process, some common information needs of these types are

- From which supplier was a specific purchase made?
- By which purchase agent was a specific purchase order placed?
- How many purchase orders did a specified purchase agent make during a specified time period?
- What is the total or average dollar amount of purchases made by each purchasing agent during a specified time period?
- When was a specified purchase received, and by which receiving clerk (include clerk's ID, name, and telephone number)?
- To which supplier have the most purchase returns been made?

Using the database tables in Exhibit 9–18, a query can be constructed to identify when a specified purchase was received and by which receiving clerk. The tables needed are Purchase and Receiving Clerk, since the relevant participation relationship is implemented with Receiving-ClerkID posted as a foreign key in the Purchase table. See the query in Exhibit 9–29.

## Queries Requiring Multiple Relationships in the Acquisition/Payment Process

Sometimes information that crosses multiple relationships must be retrieved to satisfy an information need. For example, a query that requires information about both a resource and an agent that were involved in an economic event will need to use both a stockflow relationship and a participation relationship. These types of queries are the most complicated to construct, and yet are typically the most powerful tools for meeting information needs. Within the acquisition/payment process, some common information needs that require use of multiple relationships are:

- Which purchase orders have been partially filled? (requires stockflow, reservation, and fulfillment-purchaseorder-purchase relationships)
- What is the total dollar value of accounts payable for a specified supplier at a point in time? (requires duality, participation-supplier-purchase, and participation-supplier-cash-disbursement relationships)
- On which requisitions has a specified vendor been the recommended supplier? (requires proposition and participation-purchaserequisition-supplier relationships)
- Which purchase agent ordered a specified inventory type from a specified supplier? (requires reservation, participation-supplier-purchaseorder, and participation-purchaseagent-purchaseorder relationships)
- What is the total dollar amount of purchases of a specified inventory type that have been made from suppliers in a specified region? (requires stockflow-purchase-inventory and participation-supplier-purchase relationships)

The procedures for calculating individual supplier payable balances are similar to those for calculating total accounts payable; however, they are slightly more complicated by the addition of the participation relationships. The general procedures are as follows:

Determine what kinds of acquisitions are represented in your database (except for employee services) and for each kind of acquisition follow these steps:

1. Determine which tables contain the acquisition date, dollar amount, and related supplier (usually these are found in the acquisition event table). Group by supplier, and sum the acquisition amount through the balance sheet date (with no beginning date constraint).
2. Determine which tables contain the cash disbursements that applied to those acquisitions. To determine this, examine the duality-purchase-cashdisbursement relationship.
   a. When the duality relationship is represented with a separate table, join the duality table to the cash disbursement table, establish the ending date constraint on the cash disbursement date field (with no beginning date constraint), group by supplier, and sum the cash disbursement amount applied to the acquisition.
   b. When the duality relationship is represented with the cash disbursement identifier posted as a foreign key into the acquisition table, join the cash disbursement table to the acquisition table, establish the ending date constraint on the cash disbursement date field (with no beginning date constraint), group by supplier, and sum the cash disbursement amounts.
3. Determine which tables contain purchase returns that applied to those acquisitions. To determine this, examine the duality-purchase-purchasereturn relationship
   a. When the purchase-purchasereturn relationship is represented with a separate table, join the purchase return table to the acquisition table, establish the ending date constraint on the purchase return table date field (with no beginning date constraint), group by supplier, and sum the purchase return amount applied to the acquisition.
   b. When the purchase-purchasereturn relationship is represented with purchase ID posted as a foreign key in the purchase return table, establish the ending date constraint on the purchase return table date field (with no beginning date constraint), group by supplier, and sum the purchase return amount applied to the acquisition.
4. Subtract the results of steps 2 and 3 from the result of step 1 to get accounts payable for each supplier as of the balance sheet date.

## EXHIBIT 9–30   QBE to Calculate Accounts Payable Balances for Each Supplier

Constrain Purchase Date and Sum Purchase Dollar
Amount for Each Vendor

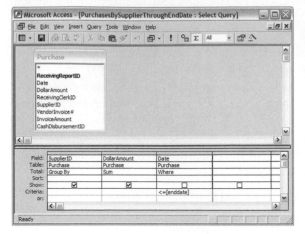

Join Purchase and Cash Disbursement Tables and
Constrain Cash Disbursement Date

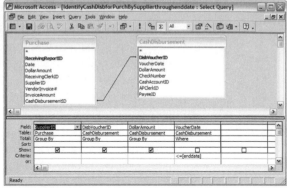

Sum the Cash Disbursements by Supplier

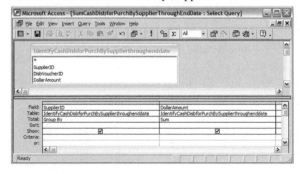

Join Purchase and Purchase Return Tables; Constrain
Purchase Return Date

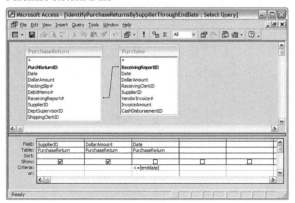

Sum Purchase Returns by Supplier

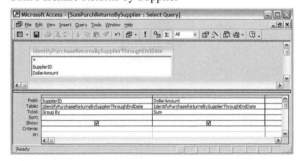

*Continued*

**EXHIBIT 9–30**   **(Concluded)**

Combine Purchases and Purchase Returns by Supplier to Get Unreturned Purchases

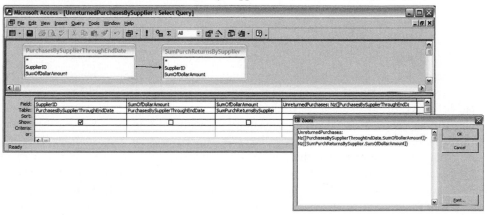

Combine Unreturned Purchases and Cash Disbursements by Supplier to Get
Unpaid Purchases

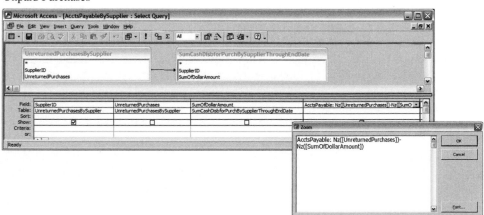

(Note: The last two query steps cannot be combined into a single query step because outer joins are
needed to include purchases from suppliers to whom neither payments nor returns have been made.
Inclusion of two outer joins in the same query is too ambiguous for Microsoft Access to evaluate.)

Result for May 31, 2010

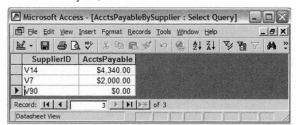

Exhibit 9–30 illustrates a set of queries to calculate accounts payable balances on a specified date for each individual supplier based on the database tables in Exhibit 9–18.

# CONCLUDING COMMENTS

This chapter presented an overview of the activities in the acquisition/payment process and discussed the extended REA pattern as it is applied to this process, including similarities and differences in the pattern for different acquisitions. Whether an enterprise acquires general and administrative services, inventory, operating assets, or supplies, the enterprise's acquisition/payment events very likely fit the REA pattern. The event labels for an enterprise may be different than those used in this textbook; therefore the concepts learned here cannot be routinely applied with rote memorization. The key for discovering the pattern fit for a specific enterprise is to think about the nature of the events and particularly the resources affected by them. It helps many people to think first at the value system level—what resources does the enterprise exchange with its customers. Second, think at the value chain level—what resources need to be provided to the revenue cycle and to the conversion cycle. Those resources need to be acquired and paid for, so identifying them yields guidance as to how many instances of the acquisition/payment process pattern template are applicable for an enterprise. Does the enterprise only need to purchase inventory? Or must it also purchase operating assets and services? Once you are confident you are thinking effectively about resources and events that are part of the acquisition/payment process and you have identified the economic increment and decrement events that comprise the duality relationship, it should be relatively easy to determine the commitment events and instigation events that led to each economic event, and to connect resources, internal agents, and external agents to each event as needed. Finally, consider whether extra relationships such as custody, assignment, and typification—as discussed in Chapter 6—apply, or even whether some extra relationships apply that are unique to the enterprise you are modeling. As long as the foundation of the system database is consistent with REA, usually extra constructs may be added without compromising the advantages the pattern provides for automated reasoning and interenterprise integration.

Documents that are used often in the acquisition/payment process were illustrated and example database tables were generated. Some information needs and queries to satisfy them were presented. Those presented represent only a small fraction of the many information needs that enterprises have on a daily basis; one goal of this chapter is to enable students who may one day be faced with meeting someone's information needs to be able to think creatively and generate queries to meet those information needs. The database tables presented in this chapter are not comprehensive. Database tables in real-world enterprise system applications such as PeopleSoft, Oracle Applications, or SAP have dozens (sometimes even hundreds) of attributes. Examination of the attributes available in an enterprise system database is a critical step in developing queries that report values of those attributes in the format needed by a user.

# Key Terms and Concepts

Acquisition/payment
business process, *259*
Cash disbursement, *273*
Check, *273*
Debit memorandum, *275*
Disbursement voucher, *273*
Duality relationship, *269*
Economic decrement
event, *269*
Economic decrement
reversal event, *275*
Economic increment
event, *267*
Economic increment
reversal event, *275*

Fulfillment
relationship, *269*
Instigation event, *262*
Inventory, *261*
Inventory type, *264*
Mutual commitment
event, *262*
Open purchase order
file, *295*
Open purchase
requisition, *295*
Participation
relationship, *269*
Proposition
relationship, *298*

Purchase, *260*
Purchase order, *264*
Purchase requisition, *262*
Purchase return, *270*
Receiving report, *269*
Request to return goods, *275*
Reservation
relationship, *299*
Reversal relationship, *270*
Stockflow
relationship, *269*
Vendor invoice, *269*

# Review Questions

LO1   R1.  List eight objectives of the acquisition/payment process.

LO4   R2.  How is the acquisition/payment process related to the conversion process, the sales/collection process, the human resource process, and the financing process?

LO1, LO7   R3.  What is the difference between a purchase requisition and a purchase order?

LO7   R4.  What is an open purchase order?

LO1, LO7   R5.  Which is the most appropriate time to record a purchase and the corresponding liability: upon the receipt of goods or upon the receipt of a vendor's invoice? Explain your response.

LO2, LO5   R6.  Identify the resources, internal agents, and external agents associated with each of the following business events:

    a.  Purchase requisition (instigation) event

    b.  Purchase order for goods/services (mutual commitment) event

    c.  Receipt of goods/services (economic increment) event

    d.  Cash disbursement (economic decrement) event

    e.  Purchase return (economic increment reversal) event

LO7   R7.  Which relationships should you examine if you want to create a query to calculate accounts payable?

LO1, LO2   R8.  What does a participation relationship between a purchase requisition and a vendor usually represent?

LO1, LO2   R9.  Do most companies keep track of operating assets (e.g., property and equipment) at the individual instance level or at the type level? Why?

# Multiple Choice Questions

LO1, LO6   MC1.  Which document is most closely associated with the activities involved in the purchase return event?
   A.  Packing list
   B.  Purchase order
   C.  Purchase requisition
   D.  Vendor invoice

LO3   MC2.  The acquisition/payment process represents the point of contact between the enterprise and which set of external business partners?
   A.  Investors and creditors
   B.  Suppliers
   C.  Customers
   D.  Employees

LO4   MC3.  The resource made available by the finance process to the acquisition/payment process in a typical enterprise value chain is:
   A.  Inventory
   B.  Property, plant, and equipment
   C.  Labor
   D.  Cash

LO2, LO5   MC4.  Which of the following entities are usually paired in a stockflow relationship in the acquisition/payment process?
   A.  Purchase requisition and inventory type
   B.  Purchase and inventory type
   C.  Purchase order and inventory type
   D.  Purchase order and purchase

LO1, LO2   MC5.  Which of the following events should reflect the point in time at which title to goods transferred from a supplier to the enterprise in the acquisition/payment process?
   A.  Purchase requisition
   B.  Purchase order
   C.  Purchase
   D.  Cash disbursement
   E.  Purchase return

# Discussion Questions

LO5   D1.  The tables in Exhibit 9–18 do not portray the design for storage of acquisitions of resources other than inventory (e.g., operating assets or general and administrative service types). If the enterprise determined that the attributes that need to be stored for operating asset acquisitions are the acquisition ID, date, and dollar total (and foreign keys from related cash disbursements, suppliers, and receiving clerks) what design alternatives should the enterprise consider for storing the operating asset acquisition information?

LO6   D2.  Describe at least two acquisition/payment process information needs for each of the following:

a.  Management
b.  Marketing
c.  Finance and accounting
d.  Human resource
e.  Production

LO6, LO7   D3.  What entities and/or relationships most likely need to be included in a query to portray the unfilled purchase orders made by each purchasing agent?

# Applied Learning

LO5   A1.  Quandrax Computers is a store that buys computer components for low prices, assembles the components into computers, and then sells the computers at high prices. Each computer is assigned a unique identification number, and computers that have common configurations are categorized into types (e.g., Longitude is a laptop that is easily networked and is recommended for businesses; Element is a desktop that is intended for home and small businesses). Categories can be entered into the database before any computers in the categories are actually assembled. The computer components are purchased from wholesalers. One of Quandrax's purchasing agents submits an order to the wholesaler that has listed a given component for sale. If the order is accepted, one of Quandrax's inventory clerks receives the items. Multiple orders accepted by the same supplier may be consolidated into one purchase. Orders are accepted in their entirety or not at all. Nearly all of Quandrax's orders are accepted. Sometimes the incorrect components are delivered to Quandrax and Quandrax has to return them to the appropriate supplier. Sometimes Quandrax returns components to suppliers for other reasons, such as the result of a change in planned production of a certain category of computers. Only about 10 percent of Quandrax's purchased components are returned to suppliers, and any return would result from only one purchase.

When payment is due for a purchase, one of Quandrax's cashiers issues one check for payment in full for the items on that purchase. Sometimes if multiple purchases have been made from the same supplier within a short time, Quandrax pays for those purchases with just one check. One of Quandrax's managers is required to not only authorize all purchase orders greater than $5,000 but also to sign all checks (including checks written for expenditures other than purchases of computer components). Quandrax needs to keep track of the managers' participation in these events as well as the participation of other employees in these events. In physically implementing the conceptual model into the database tables, Quandrax wants to combine all employee types into just one table. This means Quandrax would keep the separate employee entities on the E-R diagram, but make just one employee table to represent all of the employee entities, then post keys or make relationship tables as necessary to implement all relationships of employees to the relevant events.

All sales are handled via mail or e-mail, as Quandrax does not have any showrooms. Quandrax assigns salespeople to its large corporate customers and the salespeople take sample computers to the customer locations to demonstrate features as part of their sales calls. Only a small percentage of Quandrax's sales calls result in orders, and sometimes a salesperson might need to make several sales calls to the same customer to obtain one order from that customer. Orders also result from customers surfing the Internet and seeing descriptions of the computers on Quandrax's website. These customers are not assigned to specific salespeople; Quandrax only tracks the salesperson that actually took the order. Some of Quandrax's salespeople are hired to handle just such orders and as such are not assigned specifically to any customers.

If a customer orders multiple computers on one sale order and some of the computers are immediately available whereas the others are not yet assembled, Quandrax ships the available computers right away and then ships the remainder of the order when the rest of the computers are assembled. Sometimes Quandrax combines computers from multiple sale orders into a single shipment. For example, once a customer ordered 10 computers and the next day decided that wouldn't be enough so he ordered 4 more. Quandrax shipped all 14 computers in one shipment. Quandrax only accepts checks for its sales of computers; customers can pay for multiple sales with a single check, but no partial payments are accepted. Each sale transaction is tracked by a shipment ID; an invoice is sent to the customer that is due within 10 days, with no discounts allowed. Quandrax does not allow any sale returns; that is, all sales are final. Cash receipts are never split between two cash accounts; rather each receipt is assigned to one of Quandrax's cash accounts by one of Quandrax's cashiers. Quandrax also receives cash from other activities such as loans, so the database must allow for that. Suppliers, employees, and customers need to be entered into the database before any transactions involving them occur.

The following attributes are of interest to Quandrax; some are related to the sales/collection cycle. The attributes that are related to the acquisition/payment process must be included in your solution. Do not add attributes to the list. Use the boldface attribute abbreviations in parentheses next to the attributes in the list. List any assumptions you make, along with the reasons behind your assumptions (i.e., state what you think is vague in the problem, say what you are going to assume to clear up the ambiguity, and make a case for that assumption).

| | |
|---|---|
| Purchase Order Number **(PO#)** | Purchase return ID **(PR-ID)** |
| Supplier ID **(SuppID)** | Cash Disbursement Number **(CD#)** |
| Employee ID **(EmpID)** | Sale Order ID **(SO-ID)** |
| Purchase Order Date **(PODate)** | Shipment ID **(Ship-ID)** |
| Purchase Date **(PurchDate)** | Date of sales call **(SC-Date)** |
| Location of cash account **(Ca-Loc)** | Customer check number **(CR-Chk#)** |
| Cash Account Number **(CashAcct#)** | Sales Call ID **(SC-ID)** |
| Name of supplier **(SupName)** | Cash Receipt ID **(CR-ID)** |
| Receiving Report Number **(RR#)** | Customer ID **(Cust-ID)** |
| Computer Category ID code **(Cat-ID)** | Date of cash receipt **(CR-Date)** |
| Component ID code **(CompoID)** | Name of Customer **(Cust-Name)** |
| Cash Disbursement Date **(CD-Date)** | Total sale dollar amount **(Sale-Amt)** |
| Name of employee **(EmpName)** | Type of employee **(EmpType)** |

Date of sale order **(SO-Date)**

Date of purchase return **(PR-Date)**

Dollar amount of cash receipt **(CR-Amt)**

Current balance of cash account **(AcctBal)**

Shipping address for a customer **(Cust-Ship)**

Date of sale/shipment of computers **(Ship-Date)**

Description of a computer category **(Cat-Desc)**

Computer component description **(Comp-desc)**

Total dollar amount of a cash disbursement **(CD-Amt)**

Standard cost for a computer component **(Std-Cost)**

Quantity of a computer component returned **(Qty-Ret)**

Type of supplier (wholesaler or individual) **(SupType)**

Identification number for a finished computer **(CompuID)**

Quantity of a computer component ordered on purchase order **(Qty-Ord)**

Proposed selling price for a type of computer on a sales call **(Prop-SP)**

Ordered cost for a computer component on a purchase order **(PO-Unit-Cost)**

Suggested selling price for computers [hint: by category] **(List-price)**

Date assembly was completed for a finished computer **(Assemb-Date)**

Quoted selling price for each item on a sale order **(Ord-SP)**

Actual selling price for a particular finished computer **(Act-SP)**

Quantity of a computer component received on a purchase **(Qty-Rec)**

Actual cost of a computer component on a particular purchase **(Item-Unit-Cost)**

### Required

Create a business process level REA model (in either grammar or diagram format) for Quandrax Computers' acquisition/payment process. Be sure to include all relevant entities, relationships, attributes, and participation cardinalities.

## Answers to Multiple Choice Questions

MC1. A; MC2. B; MC3. D; MC4. B; MC5. C.

# Chapter **Ten**

# View Integration and Implementation Compromises

### LEARNING OBJECTIVES

One objective of this chapter is to explain how to unite the business process level REA models for multiple transaction cycles. A second objective is to explain implementation compromises commonly made at each step in conceptual modeling and database design. A final objective of this chapter is to demonstrate retrieval of information from multiple integrated business processes. After studying this chapter you should be able to

1. Identify the steps needed to integrate multiple business process level REA models
2. Complete an integration of two or more business process level REA conceptual models
3. Identify and create common conceptual level, logical level, and physical level implementation compromises
4. Explain common reasons for compromising implementations
5. Identify information needs that require information from multiple tables in multiple business processes
6. Create queries to satisfy information needs that require information from multiple business processes

## INTRODUCTION

Recall from Chapter 2 that one of the reasons we create models of information systems is to control complexity. We initially create business process level models separately for each transaction cycle because each cycle presents a manageable set of events and related resources and agents. The creating of separate models for different portions of a system is called **view modeling.** To create a database that can serve as the foundation for an integrated enterprisewide information system, however, the separate views must be integrated to form a comprehensive model. Although we introduced the conversion of a conceptual model to a logical model, followed by the implementation into a physical database as if those steps would be part of each separate transaction cycle analysis, in fact the separate conceptual models for each business process view should be integrated before the conversion to the logical and physical levels occurs. This step is called **view integration.**

Once a comprehensive conceptual model is created, the entire model is converted into a logical level model and is implemented into a physical level database software package. During the conceptual modeling, logical modeling, and implementation phases, compromises must often be made based on practical limitations of technology and measurement tools. In this chapter we explain some of those compromises and reasons for making such compromises.

One goal of relational database design is to store enterprise data in such a way that it may be retrieved in various formats to satisfy diverse **information needs.** Some information needs require data from multiple business processes. Retrieval of such information requires understanding of the integrated design of the relational tables.[1]

# VIEW INTEGRATION

When you use the full REA ontology as a foundation for designing an enterprisewide database, the first step is to consider the enterprise in the context of its external business partners and to create a value system level model. The second step is to consider the resource flows among the transaction cycles within the enterprise and to create a value chain level model. Identifying the resource flows at the value chain level helps to identify the points of integration of the transaction cycles and therefore also helps to identify points of integration for the conceptual models of those transaction cycles.

View integration may be used in the normal course of database design for a single enterprise; alternatively it may be used to consolidate separate databases as a result of a corporate merger, acquisition, or other forms of business consolidation. Whether in the original design phase for a single enterprise or in the consolidation of separate databases, view integration involves three basic steps:

1. Identify the common entities in two views.
2. Merge the common entities, resolving any **entity conflicts** and performing a set union of their attributes.
3. Examine each relationship and resolve any **relationship conflicts.**

Conceptual models are integrated based on their common entities. The resources that flow from one business process to another are common entities to those business processes; sometimes the processes also share common agent or event entities. One entity conflict is **name conflict;** this occurs when the same entity included in different conceptual models

---

[1]Much of the material in this chapter is based on S. R. Rockwell and W. E. McCarthy, "REACH: Automated Database Design Integrating First-Order Theories, Reconstructive Expertise, and Implementation Heuristics for Accounting Information Systems," *International Journal of Intelligent Systems in Accounting, Finance & Management* 8, no. 3 (1999), pp. 181–197; and on C. Batini, S. Ceri, and S. B. Navathe, *Conceptual Database Design: An Entity-Relationship Approach* (Redwood City, CA:The Benjamin/Cummings Publishing Company, 1992).

is not labeled identically. Often different people on the same design team separately model the different views and may use synonymous labels. A person who models the different views at different times may use **synonyms** for the same entity. For example, the entity set representing disbursements of cash may be labeled *payment* in the financing process and it may be labeled *cash disbursement* (or some other synonym) in the payroll process. Another type of name conflict occurs when conceptually different entities are given the same label. For example, say, two enterprises merged operations and need to merge their databases. One enterprise labeled its sale order entity (mutual commitment event) as Sales. The other enterprise labeled its sale entity (economic event) as Sales. That is a case of a **homonym**—the same word to represent two different things.

**Attribute conflict** exists if different attributes have been identified as important for describing the same entity in various views. The most extreme attribute conflict exists when different attributes are assigned as primary key identifiers for the same entities. Perhaps one designer assigned a unique identifier called Employee ID as the primary key for the Employee entity, and another entity used social security number for the same purpose. Other attribute conflicts include overlapping but nonidentical sets of attributes assigned to the same entity set in different cycles. For example, a person who modeled *Inventory Type* in the acquisition/payment process may have included the attributes *item ID, description, unit of measure,* and *standard unit cost* as attributes. A different person who modeled *Inventory Type* in the sales/collection process may have included *item ID, description, unit of measure,* and *list selling price* as attributes. All necessary attributes of an entity set needed for all business processes in which that entity set occurs should be included in an enterprisewide database. To resolve entity and attribute name conflicts, choose a common label for each common entity, choose the most appropriate primary key, and perform a set union of the attributes needed for the different cycles. Once the entity sets that are shared by the views to be integrated are identified, relabeled, and assigned the complete set of attributes, the relationships must be examined and relabeled if necessary to see if relationship name conflicts or relationship structure conflicts exist. Each relationship should have a unique name to avoid any possible confusion in communications about relationships in the database. Relationship name conflicts are resolved in the same way as entity and attribute name conflicts. Relationship structure conflicts exist when the same relationship is assigned different cardinalities in multiple views.

Exhibits 10–1 through 10–5 illustrate the process of view integration. Exhibits 10–1 and 10–2 show separate view models for the revenue and acquisition cycles of a company that sells custom-made surfboards. Exhibit 10–3 reorganizes the conceptual models to align the shared entities. Exhibit 10–4 illustrates the merging of the models with the set union of attributes for each shared entity. This exhibit also illustrates that when an entity participates in multiple relationships and it isn't convenient to place the relationships close to each other, a copy of the entity may be portrayed with a diagonal slash in the bottom right corner of the entity and no attributes attached to the entity. A person who sees an entity illustrated in such a manner should look elsewhere on the diagram to see the details of that entity set. Exhibit 10–5 illustrates the relabeling of the relationships so each relationship has a unique name. The result is an integrated conceptual model containing the core events, resources, and agents for a revenue and an acquisition cycle of a small enterprise.

**EXHIBIT 10–1**  Revenue Cycle View

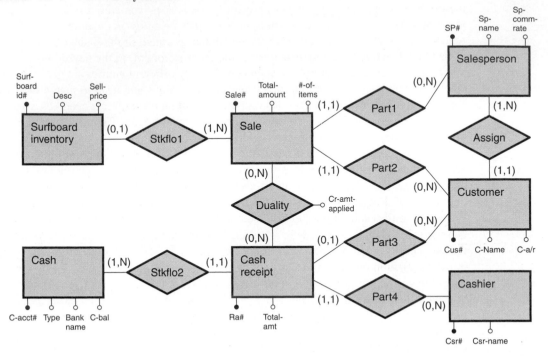

**EXHIBIT 10–2**  Acquisition Cycle View

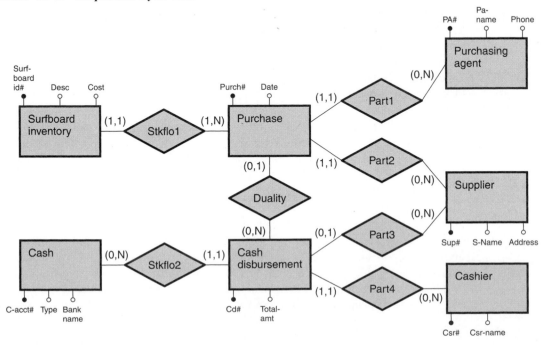

**EXHIBIT 10–3** View Integration Step 1—Identify the Common Entities

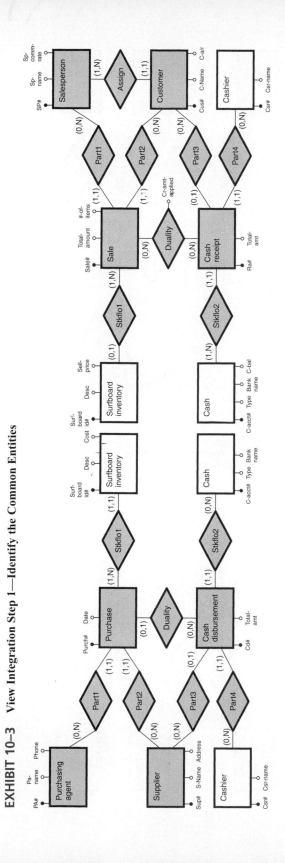

**EXHIBIT 10–4   View Integration Step 2—Merge on Common Entities**

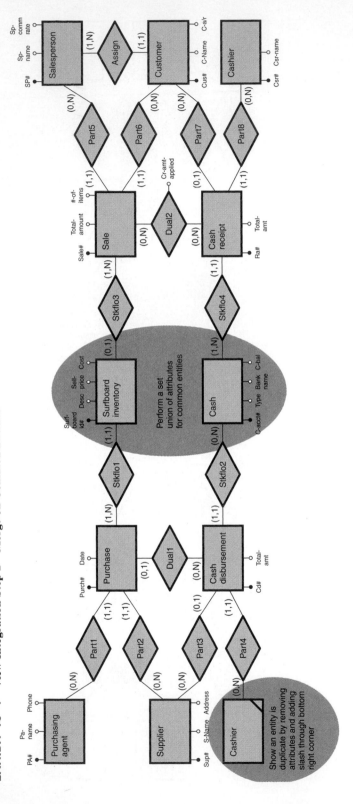

**EXHIBIT 10–5** View Integration Step 3—Resolve Relationship Name Conflicts

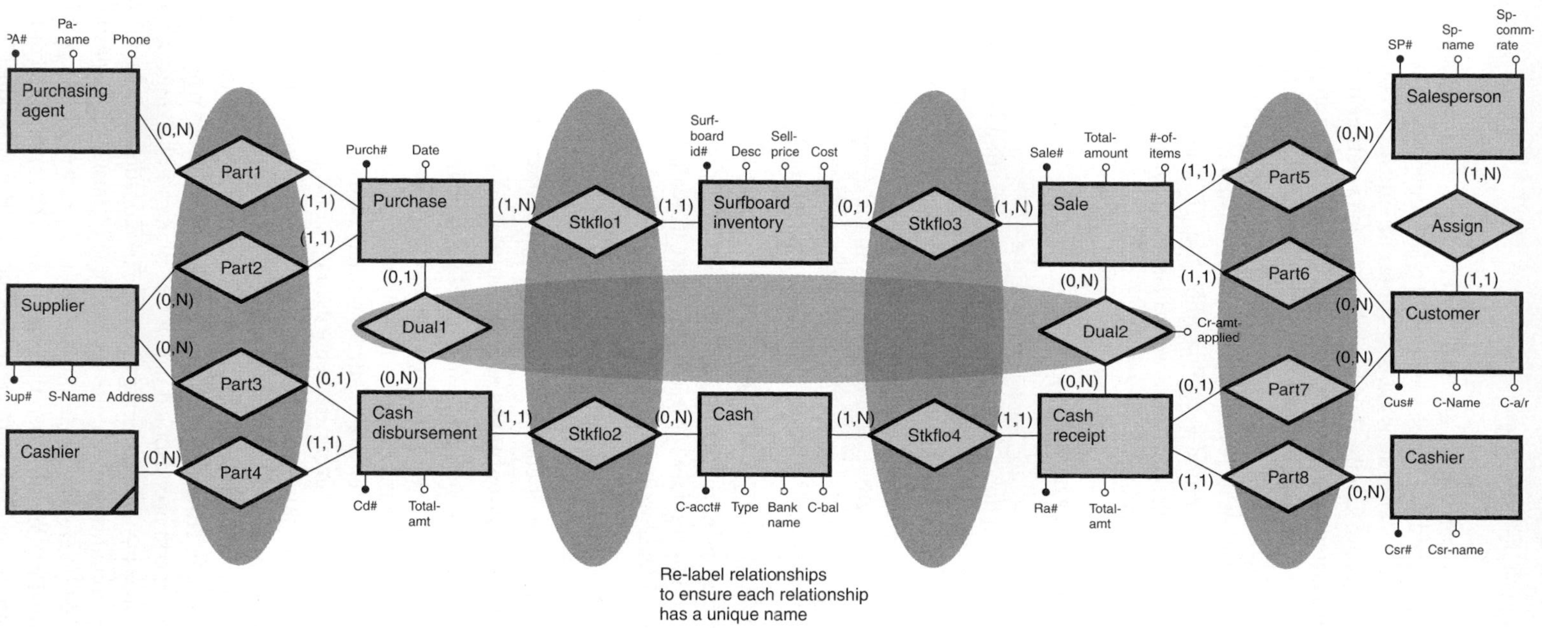

You may recall the ER grammar format that was introduced in Chapter 4. Consider how that format facilitates some aspects of view integration. Reorganization of the physical diagram layout is not an issue, and **copies of entities** become unnecessary, as entities and relationships are simply alphabetized and each relationship that contains an entity as one of its connected entities refers back to the same entity in the alphabetized list. Of course the steps involving identification of common entities, resolution of entity conflicts, resolution of attribute conflicts, and resolution of relationship conflicts are still necessary and the grammar does not necessarily provide any advantage over the diagram format. Although overall view integration is facilitated by the ER grammar format, the diagram format facilitates other tasks. Therefore we are not recommending one format versus the other; we are merely identifying possible strengths of each format.

# IMPLEMENTATION COMPROMISE

An ideal information system is a model of perfection—it is what the information system would be if we could make it everything we desire. Unfortunately such an information system is not usually achievable; compromises must be made due to practical considerations, insufficient measurement techniques, and other constraints. In this section we discuss some common **implementation compromises** in the design of enterprisewide databases. Some of the implementation compromises we discuss are made at the conceptual level, some are made at the logical level, and some are made at the physical implementation level.

## Conceptual Level Modeling Compromises

**Conceptual level modeling compromises** occur anytime we determine we cannot completely and accurately represent an object in reality. Common compromises made at the conceptual level include

- Exclusion of an entity or relationship because of inadequate measurement mechanisms or because no decision need exists for those data.
- Consolidation of conceptually congruent entities.
- **Materialization of tasks as event entities.**

It is only practical to include measurable and definable phenomena in a conceptual model from which a database will be designed. Often we can identify the existence of phenomena that we cannot measure; it is an implementation compromise to exclude those objects from the conceptual model. For example, we may be aware that in an enterprise's revenue cycle, many different resources are being used up in the process of generating revenue. Fixed assets such as the storefront display room, the warehouse, the shelving within those facilities, equipment such as cash registers, supplies such as cash register tape, pens, and staplers, and the labor of sales personnel and support staff are consumed to varying degrees within the revenue cycle. However, trying to measure the extent to which each of those resources (and possibly others) is consumed within that cycle is a challenge. Until cost-effective means for directly measuring and tracing the resources consumed to the resources acquired as a result, the conceptual model for the revenue cycle must be compromised to exclude those immeasurable items. The cost of those resources may still be tracked via the acquisition cycle conceptual model; however, those costs must be represented only as period expenses rather than directly matched to the revenues they helped to produce.

In other cases measurement mechanisms may exist, but no decision need exists and therefore an enterprise may decide to exclude an entity or relationship. For example, if an enterprise has only one purchasing agent, and intends to always have only one purchasing agent, then there is no need to track which internal agent is responsible for purchases. Or if an enterprise sells merchandise only to cash customers and has no need to track information about individual customers, the enterprise could choose not to materialize an entity for customer data. Sometimes an enterprise chooses not to implement all the relationships called for by the REA pattern. For example, an enterprise may make a declarative/procedural trade-off, whereby it decides to exclude the declarative duality relationship between purchase and cash disbursement because the enterprise determines no need to apply payments directly to individual purchases and by procedurally tracing purchases and cash disbursements each to the related vendor, the enterprise may be able to determine accounts payable by vendor (though not by purchase).

In some enterprises, certain pairs or groups of events always occur simultaneously. Such events are called **conceptually congruent events.** The practical compromise is to collapse, or consolidate, the entities, for conceptually congruent events. For example, consider Only Gas, a gas station/convenience store that sells only gasoline. Only Gas sells gasoline for cash—no credit cards, checks, or sales on account are permitted. Only Gas's procedures are as follows:

- Customers are required to bring their car keys and driver's licenses to the cashier's window, which is conveniently located adjacent to the gas pumps.
- Cashiers unlock the appropriate pumps, enabling the customers to pump gas.
- Customers pump gas into vehicles or containers, then return to the cashier's window; pay for the gas, retrieve their car keys and driver's licenses, and drive away.

These activities encompass multiple events within the sales/collection process, including the sale order, sale, and cash receipt. There is no identifiable need to separate these events for Only Gas, because they are conceptually congruent. That is, each occurrence of a sale order is automatically accompanied by an occurrence of sale and an occurrence of cash receipt. Another way of looking at this is that the cardinality pattern is

Sale Order (1,1)–(1,1) Sale (1,1)–(1,1) Cash Receipt.

A sale order would not be entered into Only Gas's system without also entering exactly one sale and exactly one cash receipt. This allows the entities to be collapsed (consolidated) into a single entity in the conceptual model. Therefore instead of the normal conceptual model reflecting

the compromised conceptual model could be portrayed as follows:

```
┌──────────┐
│  Cash    │
│  sale    │
└──────────┘
```

We make a simplifying assumption here that Only Gas does not have cash receipts from other sources such as loans. If that assumption were invalid, there may be a need to separate the cash receipt event; however, sale order and sale could still be collapsed into a single entity, as follows:

The consolidation of conceptually congruent events simplifies the conceptual model as compared to the full REA ontology pattern. Another type of implementation compromise—modeling tasks as entities—increases the complexity of the conceptual model. Recall from earlier chapters that workflow tasks that comprise an event may involve preparation of multiple documents. For example, the sale event as described in Chapter 8 may sometimes involve picking, packing, and shipping of inventory and may involve preparation of as many as four documents: picking slip, packing list, bill of lading, and sale invoice. Or the purchase requisition event as described in Chapter 9 may involve requesting quotes or bids from potential vendors to help determine the one with whom to place a purchase order. Some companies may determine they have a need to keep the attributes from each of these tasks separate from each other rather than combining them into the event they comprise. Therefore a company may choose to model the requests for quotes and the receipt of quotes from vendors as events between the purchase requisition and purchase order as follows:

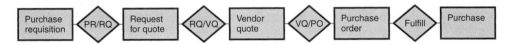

Because the enterprise also would need to track each resource and agent involved with each of these activities, the complexity added to the conceptual model may be burdensome. Also, if workflow changes in the future, the database design will need to change. Enterprises should exercise caution in determining whether to materialize tasks as entities; in general it is not recommended. To make the determination, enterprises should consider what is needed to plan, control, execute, and evaluate its activities and employees. If the attributes can be stored and retrieved effectively for the needed decisions using the standard REA template, then the standard template should be used. If the attributes cannot be stored and retrieved effectively in the standard template for an enterprise, then separate entities should be created in which to store the task attributes.

## Logical Level Modeling Compromises

Compromises are also made at the logical level. In fact, the procedures recommended in Chapter 6 for posting a foreign key for appropriate cardinality patterns that would result in a high **load** are a **logical level implementation compromise.** A theoretically pure relational database should never allow a **null value** in a table. To be completely consistent with the relational model theory, Chapter 6's step 5 should require relationships that have cardinality patterns of (0,1)–(0,1); (0,1)–(0,N); (0,1)–(1,N); (0,N)–(0,1); and (1,N)–(0,1) to be implemented with separate tables. Such an implementation would avoid the possibility of null values. The trade-off is the increased complexity of queries that involve multiple tables. Because queries often focus on relationships, relationships that are implemented with

amount for Sale 1 is computed, it does not change as additional sales are added to the enterprise system. If the total sale dollar amount is stored as an attribute in the Sale event table, it simplifies all additional queries the enterprise needs that include total sales dollar amounts as components (e.g., accounts receivable or total sales by salesperson).

Another physical implementation compromise is that of event activity roll-up. This compromise recognizes that enterprise databases exist in a finite storage space and also recognizes that the larger the size of the database, the less efficient querying becomes. A benefit of enterprise information systems founded on enterprisewide databases is the ability to produce financial statements without actually closing the books. This is sometimes called a **virtual close.** The disadvantage of never closing the books is the uncontrolled growth of the database—the database may quickly grow too large for optimized, proficient querying. One means of controlling that growth is to wait until such a time as event history detail is not needed and then roll that data up into a single event occurrence. In Exhibit 10–8 we illustrate event history roll-up.

**EXHIBIT 10–7**
**Combination of Entity Sets Without Generalization**

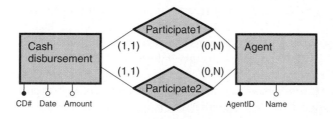

**EXHIBIT 10–8**
**Event History Roll-up**

**Sale—Original Table**

| SaleID | Date | Amount | Customer | Salesperson |
|--------|------|--------|----------|-------------|
| S1 | 1/1 | $400.00 | C23 | SP4 |
| S2 | 1/1 | $450.00 | C17 | SP2 |
| S3 | 1/5 | $875.00 | C46 | SP3 |
| S4 | 1/5 | $125.00 | C72 | SP4 |
| S5 | 1/6 | $350.00 | C14 | SP3 |
| S6 | 1/7 | $500.00 | C17 | SP2 |
| S7 | 1/8 | $700.00 | C46 | SP3 |

**Sale Table with Event History Rolled Up**

| SaleID | Date | Amount | Customer | Salesperson |
|--------|------|--------|----------|-------------|
| SR1 | 1/1 | #3,400.00 | C0 | SP0 |

SR1 represents the set of sales 1 through 7.
C0 is set up as a dummy customer.
SP0 is set up as a dummy salesperson.

# INFORMATION NEEDS THAT REQUIRE DATA FROM MULTIPLE BUSINESS PROCESSES

Consideration of the value system and value chain levels of the REA ontology reveals that resources typically are the objects on which business process model views are integrated. Information needs that involve multiple business processes are therefore likely to be focused on resources. Exhibit 10–9 portrays a partial set of database tables for the revenue and acquisition cycles of an enterprise. These tables are useful for illustrating some example queries that require integration of information from multiple business processes.

Many of the information needs that involve both the revenue cycle and the acquisition cycle involve cash and inventory, resources shared by those business processes. The calculations of cash balances (either for one or more specific accounts or for the total balance of all cash accounts) are typically affected by all the transaction cycles except the conversion process. In a database these accounts are usually represented in a cash entity table; however, the balance is a derivable attribute that is not stored unless the software is capable of triggers. Therefore a set of queries is needed to calculate the total cash receipts through the date for which the balance is needed; then to calculate the total cash disbursements through the date for which the balance is needed; and finally to subtract the total cash disbursements from the total cash receipts. If the cash receipt amounts and the cash disbursement amounts are stored as attributes in the cash receipt and cash disbursement tables, respectively, the querying is quite simple. If the company only stores amounts in duality relationship tables, then all the appropriate duality tables need to be joined to the cash receipt and disbursement event tables to apply the **date constraints** and get the totals. Most companies recognize the value of storing the amount field in the cash receipt and disbursement event tables, so we consider that case and ignore the more complicated possibility. The process for querying to provide the cash balance on a specified date is typically as follows.

1. Determine which table contains the cash receipt date (usually this is in the table that represents the cash receipt event) and make sure the same table also contains the cash receipt amount field.
2. Determine which table contains the cash disbursement date (usually this is in the table that represents the cash disbursement event) and make sure the same table also contains the cash disbursement amount field.
3. Create a query that establishes the ending date constraint (with no beginning date constraint) and **sum** the dollar amount field in the cash receipt event table (or other table identified in step 1).
4. Create a query that establishes the ending date constraint (with no beginning date constraint) and sum the dollar amount field in the cash disbursement event table (or other table identified in step 2).
5. Create a query that subtracts the total in step 4 from the total in step 3.

Exhibit 10–10 depicts a set of **queries by example (QBE)** to generate the cash balance for the enterprise represented in the tables in Exhibit 10–9.

Several needs for inventory-related information require integration of data from multiple business processes. Examples include calculations of the quantity on hand for inventory on a specified date, calculations of the dollar cost value of inventory on hand on a specified date, and calculations of the dollar cost value of inventory that was sold during a

**EXHIBIT 10–9** Database Tables for Integrated Revenue and Acquisition Cycles

## Operating Assets (Resource)

| Asset TagID | Description | AcqDate | AcqCost | Asset Category | Estimated LifeYrs | Estimated Salvage | IRSListed Property |
|---|---|---|---|---|---|---|---|
| OA1 | Building | 4/1/2010 | $200,000.00 | Buildings | 40 | $20,000.00 | No |
| OA2 | Property | 4/1/2010 | $300,000.00 | Land | 0 | $0.00 | No |
| OA3 | Executive desk | 4/10/2010 | $2,000.00 | Furniture | 10 | $200.00 | No |
| OA4 | Manager desk | 4/10/2010 | $1,500.00 | Furniture | 10 | $100.00 | No |
| OA5 | Manager desk | 4/10/2010 | $1,500.00 | Furniture | 10 | $100.00 | No |
| OA6 | Administrator desk | 4/10/2010 | $1,000.00 | Furniture | 10 | $100.00 | No |
| OA7 | Administrator desk | 4/10/2010 | $1,000.00 | Furniture | 10 | $100.00 | No |
| OA8 | Executive desk chair | 4/10/2010 | $500.00 | Furniture | 7 | $50.00 | No |
| OA9 | Manager task chair | 4/10/2010 | $350.00 | Furniture | 7 | $50.00 | No |
| OA10 | Manager task chair | 4/10/2010 | $350.00 | Furniture | 7 | $50.00 | No |
| OA11 | Task chair | 4/10/2010 | $175.00 | Furniture | 7 | $25.00 | No |
| OA12 | Task chair | 4/10/2010 | $175.00 | Furniture | 7 | $25.00 | No |
| OA13 | Task chair | 4/10/2010 | $175.00 | Furniture | 7 | $25.00 | No |
| OA14 | Task chair | 4/10/2010 | $175.00 | Furniture | 7 | $25.00 | No |
| OA15 | Toshiba tecra | 4/15/2010 | $3,000.00 | Computers | 5 | $300.00 | Yes |
| OA16 | Dell optima desktop | 4/15/2010 | $2,000.00 | Computers | 5 | $200.00 | Yes |
| OA17 | Dell optima desktop | 4/15/2010 | $2,000.00 | Computers | 5 | $200.00 | Yes |
| OA18 | Dell optima desktop | 4/15/2010 | $2,000.00 | Computers | 5 | $200.00 | Yes |
| OA19 | Warehouse shelving | 4/16/2010 | $10,000.00 | Fixtures | 40 | $0.00 | No |
| OA20 | Fax machine | 4/17/2010 | $400.00 | Comm Equip | 3 | $0.00 | Yes |

## Cash (Resource Type)

| CashAccountID | AccountType | Location | DateAccountEstablished |
|---|---|---|---|
| Ca123501 | Checking | 1st Local Bank | April 1, 2010 |
| Ca789125 | Savings | 1st Local Bank | April 1, 2010 |
| Ca351235 | Petty | Onsite—Cashier desk drawer | April 15, 2010 |
| Ca351327 | Petty | Onsite—CEO assistant's file cabinet | April 22, 201 |

## Inventory Type (Resource Type)

| Item ID | Description | UnitOfMeasure | Standard Cost | List Price |
|---|---|---|---|---|
| BIS1 | Big Stuff | Each | $20.00 | $50.00 |
| HUS1 | Huge Stuff | Each | $30.00 | $70.00 |
| LIS1 | Little Stuff | Box of 6 | $36.00 | $72.00 |
| MIN1 | Miniature Stuff | Box of 24 | $56.00 | $110.00 |
| TIS1 | Tiny Stuff | Box of 12 | $48.00 | $96.00 |
| TTP12 | Tiara | Each | $10.00 | $25.00 |

## Purchase Requisition (Instigation) Event

| Purch ReqID | Date | Maximum Budget for This Purchase | Date Needed | SuperIDFK | Purch AgentIDFK | Recommended SupplierIDFK |
|---|---|---|---|---|---|---|
| R17 | 4/22/2010 | $30,000.00 | 5/2/2010 | E5 | E12 | V7 |
| R18 | 5/5/2010 | $1,400.00 | 5/23/2010 | E5 | E12 | V14 |
| R19 | 5/6/2010 | $5,500.00 | 5/20/2010 | E5 | E12 | V7 |
| R20 | 5/15/2010 | $200.00 | 5/25/2010 | E5 | E12 | |
| R21 | 5/18/2010 | $7,500.00 | 5/26/2010 | E5 | E12 | V7 |

## EXHIBIT 10–9   (Continued)

**Purchase Order (Mutual Commitment) Event**

| Purchase OrderID | OrderDate | DateNeeded | Dollar Total | Purchase ReqID<sup>FK</sup> | Purchase AgentID<sup>FK</sup> | Supplier ID<sup>FK</sup> |
|---|---|---|---|---|---|---|
| PO16 | 4/24/2010 | 5/2/2010 | $28,450.00 | R17 | E12 | V7 |
| PO17 | 5/5/2010 | 5/8/2010 | $1,100.00 | R18 | E12 | V14 |
| PO18 | 5/5/2010 | 5/12/2010 | $200.00 | R18 | E12 | V90 |
| PO19 | 5/6/2010 | 5/10/2010 | $3,240.00 | R19 | E12 | V14 |
| PO20 | 5/6/2010 | 5/24/2010 | $2,000.00 | R19 | E12 | V7 |
| PO21 | 5/16/2010 | 5/24/2010 | $220.00 | R20 | E12 | V14 |

**Purchase (Economic Increment) Event**

| Receiving ReportID | Date | Dollar Amount | Receiving ClerkID<sup>FK</sup> | SupplierID<sup>FK</sup> | Vendor Invoice# | Invoice Amount | Cash DisbID<sup>FK</sup> |
|---|---|---|---|---|---|---|---|
| RR18 | 4/30/2010 | $28,450.00 | E111 | V7 | VI4167 | $28,450.00 | 40 |
| RR19 | 5/8/2010 | $1,100.00 | E111 | V14 | 821536 | $1,100.00 | |
| RR21 | 5/10/2010 | $3,240.00 | E111 | V14 | 821983 | $3,240.00 | |
| RR22 | 5/12/2010 | $2,000.00 | E111 | V7 | VI5213 | $2,000.00 | |
| RR25 | 5/12/2010 | $480.00 | E111 | V90 | 312353 | $480.00 | |

**Cash Disbursement (Economic Decrement) Event**

| DisbVoucherID | VoucherDate | DollarAmount | CheckNbr | CashAcctID<sup>FK</sup> | APClerkID<sup>FK</sup> | PayeeID<sup>FK</sup> |
|---|---|---|---|---|---|---|
| 39 | 5/15/2010 | $746.57 | 41234 | Ca123501 | E36 | E23 |
| 40 | 5/25/2010 | $28,450.00 | 41235 | Ca123501 | E36 | V7 |
| 41 | 5/29/2010 | $398.12 | 41236 | Ca123501 | E36 | E41 |

**Purchase Return (Economic Increment Reversal) Event**

| Purchase ReturnID | Date | Dollar Amount | Packing Slip# | Debit Memo# | Receiving ReportID<sup>FK</sup> | SupplierID<sup>FK</sup> | Dept SuperID<sup>FK</sup> | Shipping ClerkID<sup>FK</sup> |
|---|---|---|---|---|---|---|---|---|
| PR3 | 5/17/2010 | $480.00 | 22 | 3 | RR25 | V90 | E5 | E41 |

**Sales Call (Instigation) Event**

| Sales Call ID | Date | StartTime | EndTime | Location | SalesRepID<sup>FK</sup> | CustomerID<sup>FK</sup> |
|---|---|---|---|---|---|---|
| 42 | 5/4/2010 | 9:12 a.m. | 10:00 a.m. | Customer | E23 | C2323 |
| 43 | 5/4/2010 | 9:27 a.m. | 10:35 a.m. | Ours | E26 | C4731 |
| 44 | 5/5/2010 | 10:30 a.m. | 11:15 a.m. | Customer | E23 | C6125 |

**Sale Order (Mutual Commitment) Event**

| Sale Order ID | Order Date | Date Needed | Dollar Total | Sales Tax | Shipping Charge | Sales CallID<sup>FK</sup> | Sales RepID<sup>FK</sup> | Customer ID<sup>FK</sup> |
|---|---|---|---|---|---|---|---|---|
| 14 | 5/4/2010 | 5/7/2010 | $1,100.00 | $0 | $0 | 42 | E23 | C2323 |
| 15 | 5/4/2010 | 5/12/2010 | $3,050.00 | $0 | $0 | 43 | E26 | C4731 |
| 16 | 5/6/2010 | 5/9/2010 | $4,305.00 | $0 | $0 | 42 | E23 | C2323 |
| 17 | 5/8/2010 | 5/17/2010 | $8,280.00 | $0 | $0 | 43 | E26 | C4731 |

**EXHIBIT 10–9**  (Continued)

### Sale (Economic Decrement) Event

| Sale ID | Date | Dollar Total | PickListID | PackListID | BOL# | SalesRepID^FK | CustomerID^FK | CashReceiptID^FK |
|---------|------|--------------|------------|------------|------|---------------|---------------|------------------|
| 12 | 5/5/2010 | $1,100.00 | 15 | 15 | 15 | E23 | C2323 | RA20 |
| 13 | 5/7/2010 | $3,050.00 | 16 | 16 | 16 | E26 | C4731 | RA21 |
| 14 | 5/8/2010 | $2,100.00 | 17 | 17 | 17 | E23 | C2323 | RA20 |
| 15 | 5/10/2010 | $2,205.00 | 18 | 18 | 18 | E23 | C2323 | |

### Cash Receipt (Economic Increment) Event

| CashReceiptID | Date | Dollar Total | CashAccountID^FK | CustomerID^FK | CashierID^FK |
|---------------|------|--------------|------------------|---------------|--------------|
| RA20 | 5/19/2010 | $3,060.00 | Ca123501 | C2323 | E111 |
| RA21 | 5/24/2010 | $3,050.00 | Ca123501 | C4731 | E111 |
| RA22 | 5/31/2010 | $25,000.00 | Ca123501 | | E111 |

### Sales Return (Economic Decrement Reversal) Event

| Sale ReturnID | Date | Dollar Amount | Receiving ReportNo. | Credit Memo# | Credit MgrID | SaleID^FK | CustomerID^FK | Receiving ClerkID^FK |
|---------------|------|---------------|---------------------|--------------|--------------|-----------|---------------|----------------------|
| SR1 | 5/12/2010 | $140.00 | RR25 | 1 | E16 | 12 | C2323 | E247 |

### Employee (Internal Agent)

| EmployeeID | Name | Address | Telephone | DateOfBirth | EmployeeType |
|------------|------|---------|-----------|-------------|--------------|
| E41 | Amy Milano | 8892 Eddy Ave. | 555-9557 | January 3, 1964 | Shipping Clerk |
| E5 | Patrick Wellesley | 53125 Fenton Dr. | 555-1112 | March 4, 1958 | Supervisor |
| E36 | Diane Bowersox | 9115 Wolfgang Ct. | 555-7244 | September 15, 1963 | Accounts Payable Clerk |
| E247 | Kenneth Barki | 4312 Monticello Dr. | 556-4891 | April 14, 1945 | Receiving Clerk |
| E251 | Rita Barki | 4312 Monticello Dr. | 556-4891 | May 22, 1948 | Receiving Clerk |
| E111 | Missy Witherspoon | 1710 Crestwood Dr. | 555-9392 | May 11, 1960 | Cashier |
| E222 | Eponine Eldridge | 1003 Zenker Dr. | 555-9099 | July 29, 1972 | Cashier |
| E23 | Jimmy Vitale | 425 ConAir Drive | 555-5678 | Aug 18, 1962 | Sales Representative |
| E26 | Cyndie North | 122 Front St. | 555-6353 | Apr 4, 1961 | Sales Representative |
| E30 | Wayland Stindt | 3506 Carthan St. | 555-0621 | December 29, 1973 | Sales Representative |

### Supplier (External Agent)

| SupplierID | Name | Address | Telephone | PerformanceRating |
|------------|------|---------|-----------|-------------------|
| V7 | Joe's Favorite Vendor | 89056 Ransom Hwy. | 555-7655 | Excellent |
| V14 | Reliable Rudy's | 34125 Michigan Ave. | 555-1199 | Very Good |
| V90 | Trina's Trinkets | 1612 Myway Rd. | 555-2424 | Very Good |

### Customer (External Agent)

| Customer ID | Name | Address | Telephone | Credit Rating |
|-------------|------|---------|-----------|---------------|
| C2323 | Needmore Stuff | 86906 Enterprise Court | 555-8989 | A+ |
| C2831 | Targeted One | 41352 Price Ln. | 555-1771 | B+ |
| C4731 | Gottahave Moore | 1207 Emperor Dr. | 555-5688 | B |
| C6125 | Don't Wantmuch | 3421 Carradine St. | 555-9098 | A+ |

**EXHIBIT 10–9**
(Continued)

### Proposition Relationship (Purchase Requisition–Inventory Type)

| PurchReqID | Item ID | QuantityNeeded | EstimatedUnitCost |
|---|---|---|---|
| R17 | BIS1 | 100 | $20.00 |
| R17 | LIS1 | 200 | $36.00 |
| R17 | HUS1 | 150 | $30.00 |
| R17 | TIS1 | 300 | $48.00 |
| R18 | MIN1 | 20 | $56.00 |
| R18 | TTP12 | 20 | $10.00 |
| R19 | MIN1 | 60 | $56.00 |
| R19 | BIS1 | 100 | $20.00 |
| R20 | TTP12 | 20 | $10.00 |
| R21 | LIS1 | 200 | $36.00 |

### Reservation Relationship (Purchase Order–Inventory Type)

| PurchOrderID | ItemID | QuantityOrdered | QuotedUnitPrice |
|---|---|---|---|
| PO16 | BIS1 | 100 | $20.00 |
| PO16 | LIS1 | 200 | $35.50 |
| PO16 | HUS1 | 150 | $29.00 |
| PO16 | TIS1 | 300 | $50.00 |
| PO17 | MIN1 | 20 | $55.00 |
| PO18 | TTP12 | 20 | $10.00 |
| PO19 | MIN1 | 60 | $54.00 |
| PO20 | BIS1 | 100 | $20.00 |
| PO21 | TTP12 | 20 | $11.00 |

### Fulfillment Relationship (Purchase Order–Purchase)

| PurchaseOrderID | PurchaseID |
|---|---|
| PO16 | RR18 |
| PO17 | RR19 |
| PO18 | RR25 |
| PO19 | RR21 |
| PO20 | RR22 |

### Stockflow Relationship (Purchase–Inventory Type)

| PurchaseID | ItemID | PurchaseQuantity | ActualUnitCost |
|---|---|---|---|
| RR18 | BIS1 | 100 | $20.00 |
| RR18 | LIS1 | 200 | $35.50 |
| RR18 | HUS1 | 150 | $29.00 |
| RR18 | TIS1 | 300 | $50.00 |
| RR19 | MIN1 | 20 | $55.00 |
| RR21 | MIN1 | 60 | $54.00 |
| RR22 | BIS1 | 100 | $20.00 |
| RR25 | TTP12 | 48 | $10.00 |

**EXHIBIT 10–9**
**(Continued)**

### Stockflow Relationship (Purchase Return–Inventory Type)

| PurchReturnID | Item ID | QuantityReturned | ActualUnitCost |
|---|---|---|---|
| PR3 | TTP12 | 48 | $10.00 |

### Proposition Relationship (Sales Call–Inventory)

| Sales Call ID | Item ID | Customer Reaction to Product |
|---|---|---|
| 42 | BIS1 | Negative |
| 42 | LIS1 | Positive |
| 42 | HUS1 | Negative |
| 42 | TIS1 | Positive |
| 42 | MIN1 | Undecided |
| 43 | BIS1 | Positive |
| 43 | LIS1 | Undecided |
| 43 | HUS1 | Positive |
| 43 | TIS1 | Negative |
| 43 | MIN1 | Negative |
| 44 | BIS1 | Negative |
| 44 | LIS1 | Negative |
| 44 | HUS1 | Negative |
| 44 | TIS | Negative |
| 44 | MIN1 | Negative |

### Reservation Relationship (Sale Order–Inventory)

| Sales Order ID | Item ID | Quantity Ordered | Quoted Unit Price |
|---|---|---|---|
| 14 | LIS1 | 2 | 70.00 |
| 14 | TIS1 | 10 | 96.00 |
| 15 | BIS1 | 40 | 60.00 |
| 15 | HUS1 | 13 | 50.00 |
| 16 | MIN1 | 41 | 105.00 |
| 17 | LIS1 | 120 | 69.00 |

### Fulfillment Relationship (Sale Order–Sale)

| Sale Order ID | Sale ID |
|---|---|
| 14 | 12 |
| 15 | 13 |
| 16 | 14 |
| 16 | 15 |

### Stockflow Relationship (Sale–Inventory)

| Sale ID | Item ID | Quantity Sold | Actual Unit Price |
|---|---|---|---|
| 12 | LIS1 | 2 | 70.00 |
| 12 | TIS1 | 10 | 96.00 |
| 13 | BIS1 | 40 | 60.00 |
| 13 | HUS1 | 13 | 50.00 |
| 14 | MIN1 | 20 | 105.00 |
| 15 | MIN1 | 21 | 105.00 |

**EXHIBIT 10–9**
**(Concluded)**

| Stockflow Relationship (Sale Return–Inventory) | | | | | |
|---|---|---|---|---|---|
| Sale Return ID | Item ID | Quantity Returned | Actual Unit Price | Condition of Goods | Reason Returned |
| 12 | LIS1 | 2 | 70.00 | Perfect | Too big |

**EXHIBIT 10–10**  **QBE to Calculate Cash Balance on a Specified Date**

Sum Dollar Amounts of All Cash Receipts Through Ending Date (No Beginning Date Constraint)

Sum Dollar Amounts of All Cash Disbursements Through Ending Date (No Beginning Date Constraint)

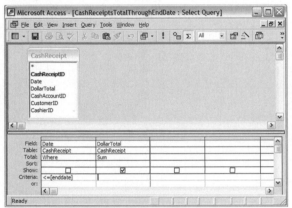

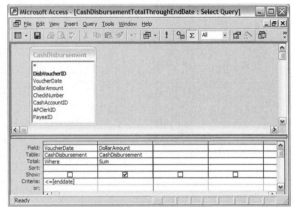

Subtract Sum of Cash Disbursements from the Sum of Cash Receipts to Get Total Ending Balance

Result as of May 31, 2010

specified time period. Of these three examples the simplest is calculation of the quantity on hand of each inventory item. Exhibit 10–11 demonstrates queries to calculate quantity on hand of each inventory item based on the enterprise database tables in Exhibit 10–9. The more complicated examples are described later in this chapter.

Quantity on hand consists of quantities purchased minus quantities returned minus quantities sold through a specified ending date (with no beginning date constraint). Notice the similarity to the calculation of cash balance, which was the amount of cash receipts minus the amount of cash disbursements through a specified date. The pattern for both calculations is balance equals inflows minus outflows. An important difference between the queries in Exhibit 10–10 for the total cash balance and the queries to be developed for the quantity on hand of each inventory item is the fact that the latter requires a separate balance for each item whereas for the cash query we did not compute a separate balance for each cash account (although that certainly is another information need of most enterprises).

**EXHIBIT 10–11   QBE to Calculate Quantities on Hand for Inventory Types**

Steps 1, 2, and 7: Constrain Purchase Date; Sum Quantities Purchased for Each Inventory Type

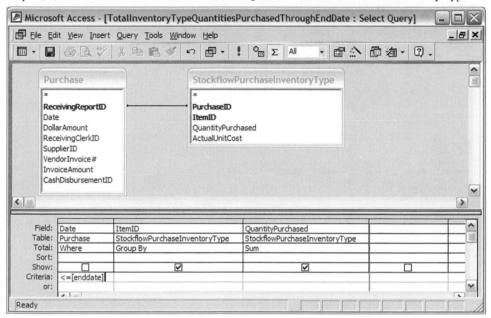

Steps 3, 4, and 8: Constrain Purchase Return Date; Sum Quantities Returned by Inventory Type

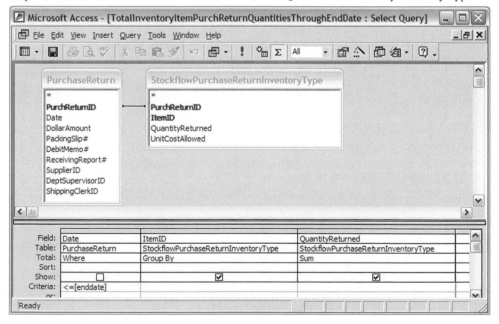

**EXHIBIT 10–11**
**(Concluded)**

Steps 5, 6, and 9: Constrain Sale Date; Sum Quantities Sold for Each Inventory Type

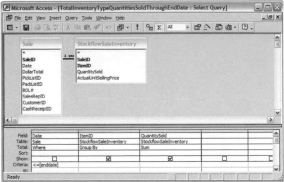

Step 10: Join Quantities Purchased and Returned to Compute Unreturned Purchase Quantities

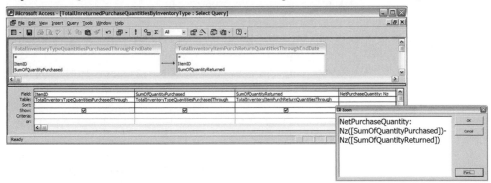

Step 11: Join Net Purchase Quantities and Quantities Sold to Calculate Quantity on Hand

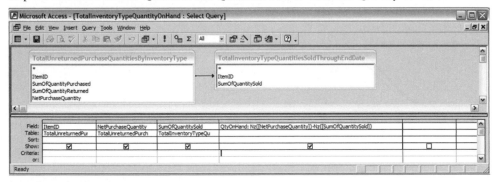

Result for May 31, 2010

| ItemID | NetPurchaseQuantity | SumOfQuantitySold | QtyOnHand |
|--------|---------------------|-------------------|-----------|
| BIS1 | 200 | 40 | 160 |
| HUS1 | 150 | 13 | 137 |
| LIS1 | 200 | 2 | 198 |
| MIN1 | 80 | 41 | 39 |
| TIS1 | 300 | 10 | 290 |
| TP12 | 0 | | 0 |

The procedures for calculating inventory item quantities on hand typically are as follows:

1. Determine which table contains the purchase date attribute (usually this is in the table that represents the purchase economic event).

2. Determine which table contains the purchase quantity attribute and the item ID (usually this is in the table that represents the stockflow relationship between the purchase economic event and the inventory resource).

3. Determine which table contains the purchase return date attribute (usually this is in the table that represents the purchase return economic event).

4. Determine which table contains the quantity returned attribute and the item ID (usually this is in the table that represents the stockflow relationship between the purchase return economic event and the inventory resource).

5. Determine which table contains the sale date attribute (usually this is in the table that represents the sale economic event).

6. Determine which table contains the quantity sold attribute and the item ID (usually this is in the table that represents the stockflow relationship between the sale economic event and the inventory resource).

7. **Join** the tables identified in steps 1 and 2, **group by** inventory item, set the ending date constraint (with no beginning date constraint), and sum the quantity purchased to get the total quantity purchased per inventory item. Make sure to include the inventory item identifier attribute in the query result to provide a means for linking to the result in step 8.

8. Join the tables identified in steps 3 and 4, group by inventory item, set the ending date constraint (with no beginning date constraint), and sum the quantity returned to get the total quantity returned per inventory item. Make sure to include the inventory item identifier attribute in the query result to provide a means for linking to the result in step 7.

9. Join the tables identified in steps 5 and 6, group by inventory item, set the ending date constraint (with no beginning date constraint), and sum the quantity sold to get the total quantity sold per inventory item. Make sure to include the inventory item identifier attribute in the query result to provide a means for linking to the results in steps 7 and 8.

10. Join the results from steps 7 and 8. Change the join type to include all records from the total quantity purchased query and the matches from the total quantity returned query. The **null to zero (Nz) function** is necessary in the calculation to subtract the total quantity returned from the total quantity purchased. For example, this calculation expression would look something like this (depending on the query's variable names):

$$Nz(SumPurchaseQty) - Nz(SumQtyReturned).$$

This formula results in the unreturned purchase quantities for each item.

11. Join the results from step 9 with the results from step 10. Change the join type to include all records from the total unreturned quantities purchased query and the matches from the total quantity sold query. The null to zero (Nz) function is

needed in the calculation to subtract the total quantity sold from the total unreturned purchase quantity. For example, this calculation expression would look something like this (depending on the query's variable names):

$$\text{Nz(SumUnreturnedPurchaseQty)} - \text{Nz(SumSaleQty)}$$

This query result yields the total quantity on hand separately for each inventory item.

Once the quantities on hand of inventory types are calculated on a specified date, an enterprise also may want to assign cost values to those inventory types. Various cost assumptions may be used to assign costs to inventory types, including weighted average unit cost, first-in-first-out (FIFO), and last-in-first-out (LIFO). The assignment of costs based on FIFO or LIFO entails the writing of program code that is too complex for this textbook. The assignment of weighted average unit costs to inventory types on hand is less complex and can be accomplished without extensive program code, as demonstrated in Exhibit

**EXHIBIT 10–12   QBE to Assign Weighted Average Costs to Inventory Types on Hand**
Steps 1, 2, and 3: Constrain Purchase End Date, Calculate Purchase Line Extensions

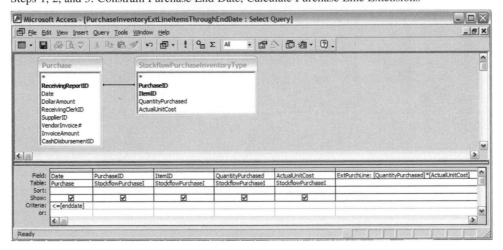

Step 4: Sum Purchase Quantities and Purchase Line Extensions

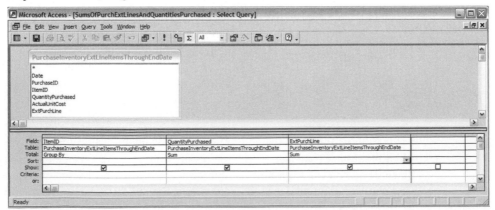

**EXHIBIT 10–12**   **(Concluded)**

Step 5: Divide Total Purchase Line Extensions by Quantities to Get Weighted Average Unit Costs

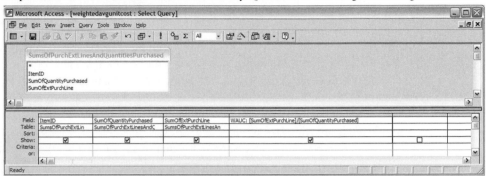

Step 6: Combine Weighted Average Costs with Quantities
on Hand to Get Inventory Cost by Item

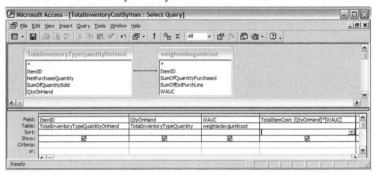

Result for May 31, 2010

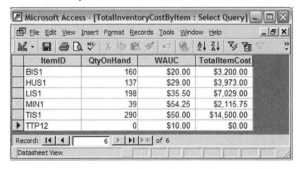

| ItemID | QtyOnHand | WAUC | TotalItemCost |
|--------|-----------|------|---------------|
| BIS1 | 160 | $20.00 | $3,200.00 |
| HUS1 | 137 | $29.00 | $3,973.00 |
| LIS1 | 198 | $35.50 | $7,029.00 |
| MIN1 | 39 | $54.25 | $2,115.75 |
| TIS1 | 290 | $50.00 | $14,500.00 |
| TTP12 | 0 | $10.00 | $0.00 |

Record: 6 of 6

10–12. The overall steps to compute weighted average costs for inventory types and to assign them to the quantities on hand are as follows:

1. Determine which table contains the purchase date attribute (usually this is in the table that represents the purchase economic event).

2. Determine which table contains the purchase quantities and unit cost information (usually these attributes are in the table that represents the stockflow relationship between purchase and inventory type).

3. Join the tables together, set the ending date constraint (with no beginning date constraint), and, if necessary, multiply the quantities purchased by the actual unit costs to get the total purchase line-item amount.

4. Group the result from step 3 by inventory ID and sum the purchase quantity and the total purchase line-item amount. (Note: if the total purchase line-item amount is a stored attribute you may combine steps 3 and 4 into a single query.)

5. Start with the result from step 4 and, still grouping by inventory ID, divide the sum of the total purchase line item by the sum of the total purchased quantity to get the weighted average unit cost for each inventory type.

6. Combine the result from step 5 with the quantities on hand of inventory type (result of step 11 in Exhibit 10–11) to get the cost value of each inventory type on hand.

If the enterprise needs the total dollar cost value of all inventory items on hand as of a specified date, then the result from step 6 of Exhibit 10–12 may be summed as illustrated in Exhibit 10–13.

A difficult issue associated with the queries demonstrated in Exhibits 10–12 and 10–13, depending on the needs the information is intended to address, is that the aggregation of all purchases up to the ending date results in the inclusion of relatively old costs. For some decision needs that may be fine; but other decision needs may require consideration of only the more recent costs. Alternative means for computing weighted average unit costs may be employed to allocate the costs differently; for this textbook we only illustrate the simplest approach.

Cost of goods sold is a line item on enterprise income statements that is similar to the calculation of the dollar value of inventory on hand. Whereas the calculation of inventory on hand applies an assumed cost value to the quantities of inventory types on hand; the cal-

**EXHIBIT 10–13**
**QBE**
**to Calculate**
**Total Inventory**
**Cost Value on a**
**Specified Date**

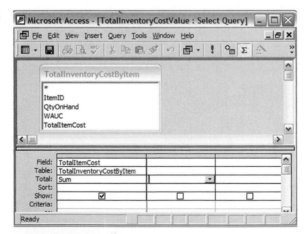

Result for May 31, 2010

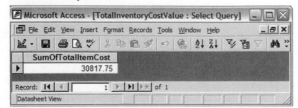

culation of cost of goods sold applies an assumed cost value to the quantities of inventory types sold during a specified time period. The total cost value of inventory on hand appears as a line item on enterprise balance sheets. The same cost value assumption must be used in calculating inventory on the balance sheet and cost of goods sold on the income statement. Therefore, if weighted average unit cost is used as the costing assumption for inventory, it must also be used for cost of goods sold.

The overall procedures needed to calculate cost of goods sold are as follows:

1. Determine which table contains the sale date attribute; usually this is in the table that represents the sale economic event.

2. Determine which table contains the sale quantities; usually this is in the table that represents the stockflow relationship between sale and inventory.

3. Join the tables together, set date constraints for the beginning and ending of the income statement period, group by inventory ID, and sum the quantity sold.

4. Join a weighted average unit cost query result as found in Exhibits 10–12 and 10–13 (conceptually this is a list of inventory items and the weighted-average cost for each item) to the result from COGS step 3 (conceptually this is a list of all inventory items that have been sold and the total quantity sold of each item). Multiply the quantity sold by the weighted average unit cost; this will give you the total weighted average cost separated by inventory items.

5. Create a final query that sums the weighted average cost per inventory item sold to get the total COGS for the income statement.

Exhibit 10–14 illustrates the QBE for queries following these procedures.

**EXHIBIT 10–14**
**QBE for Cost of Goods Sold**

Steps 1, 2, 3: Constrain Sale Date (Begin and End); Group by Inventory ID and Sum Sale Quantity

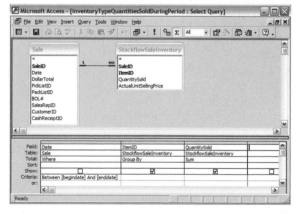

Step 4: Multiply Quantities Sold by Weighted Average Unit Cost to Get COGS by Item

**EXHIBIT 10–14**
**(Concluded)**

Step 5: Sum COGS by Item to Get Total Cost of Goods Sold

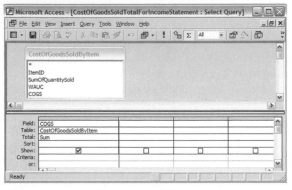

Result for May 1–May 31, 2010

# CONCLUDING COMMENTS

View integration is required to merge multiple conceptual models to form a single model used as a blueprint for an enterprisewide database. View integration is a part of the normal database design process, merging views from related business processes. View integration may also result from merging two different databases as a result of a corporate merger, acquisition, or other business consolidation. As the conceptual models are created and integrated, some compromises may be made due to inadequate measurement techniques, practical considerations, and other constraints. When the integrated conceptual model is converted into a logical model, more compromises may be made. And as the logical model is transformed into a physical implementation, still more compromises may be made. Once the final integrated database is designed; information retrieval also may require data from multiple business processes. Queries to retrieve such information typically involve data from multiple entities and multiple relationships, and inherently are more complex than single-table and single-relationship queries.

## Key Terms and Concepts

| | | |
|---|---|---|
| Attribute conflict, *313* | Conceptual level | Conceptually congruent |
| Combined entity key | modeling | events, *319* |
| posting, *321* | compromises, *318* | Copies of entities, *318* |

Date constraint, *324*
Derivable attribute, *321*
Entity conflict, *312*
Event activity roll-up, *321*
Group by, *333*
Homonym, *313*
Implementation
compromise, *318*
Information need, *312*
Join, *333*
Load, *320*

Logical level
implementation
compromise, *320*
Materialization of tasks as
event entities, *318*
Name conflict, *312*
Null to zero (Nz) function
(in Microsoft Access), *333*
Null value, *320*
Physical level
compromises, *321*

Query, *321*
Query by example
(QBE), *324*
Relationship conflict, *312*
Sum, *324*
Synonym, *313*
View integration, *312*
View modeling, *311*
Virtual close, *323*

## Review Questions

LO1    R1.  What three basic steps are involved in view integration?

LO1, LO2, LO3    R2.  What are two types of entity name conflicts that must be resolved when identifying common entities in multiple business process conceptual models?

LO, LO2, LO3    R3.  In view integration, what is attribute conflict and how is it resolved?

LO3    R4.  List and describe three conceptual level implementation compromises.

LO3    R5.  List and describe three logical level implementation compromises.

LO3    R6.  List and describe two physical level implementation compromises.

LO2    R7.  Explain what aspects of view integration may be easier with the ER grammar format than with the ER diagram format.

LO2, LO3    R8.  What notation is used in a conceptual model in diagram format to represent a duplicate copy of an entity set that is already used elsewhere in the model?

## Multiple Choice Questions

LO3    MC1.  Which of the following is a conceptual level implementation compromise?
  A.  Consolidation of congruent event entities
  B.  Combined entity key posting
  C.  Event history roll-up
  D.  Storage of derivable attributes

LO3    MC2.  At what levels may implementation compromises be made?
  A.  Conceptual
  B.  Logical
  C.  Physical
  D.  All of the above

LO2    MC3.  Which of the following is typically an integration point between the sales/collection and acquisition/payment processes for a wholesale distributor?
  A.  Salesperson
  B.  Supplier
  C.  Inventory
  D.  Sale order

LO5     MC4.  What resources are involved in most information needs that encompass both the revenue and acquisition cycles?
   A.  Raw materials inventory and finished goods inventory
   B.  Operating assets and salespeople
   C.  Merchandise (or finished goods) inventory and cash
   D.  Cash and cashiers

LO5, LO6     MC5.  Which of the following financial statement line items cannot be calculated in queries that involve only a single business process, but instead require data from multiple business processes?
   A.  Sales on the income statement
   B.  Cost of goods sold on the income statement
   C.  Accounts receivable on the balance sheet
   D.  Rent expense on the income statement

# Discussion Questions

LO2     D1.  An enterprise's financing cycle model includes a cash entity with the attributes cash account number, account type, and account balance. The same enterprise's payroll cycle model includes a cash entity with the attributes cash account ID, cash account type, and cash account location.
   a.  If the enterprise integrates the financing and payroll views, how many cash entities should the integrated view include?
   b.  What attributes should the integrated model include for the cash entities?
   c.  What questions do you need to ask (or what assumptions do you need to make) to determine the answer to question (b)?

LO3     D2.  Examine the relational database tables in Exhibit 10–9. Compare them to the relational database tables in Exhibits 8–20 and 9–18 from Chapters 8 and 9. What difference do you notice that could be considered an implementation compromise?

LO3, LO4     D3.  A relationship between cash receipt and customer for an enterprise has cardinalities (0,1) cash receipt–(0,N) customer. The enterprise creates a cash receipt table and a customer table to represent the entities. To represent the relationship, the enterprise posts the primary key of the customer entity table into the cash receipt entity table. Why is this considered an implementation compromise, and at what level (conceptual, logical, or physical) is it an implementation compromise?

LO4     D4.  Why might a company decide to roll up its cash disbursement event activity? Is this an implementation compromise? If so, does the compromise occur at the conceptual, logical, or physical level?

LO3, LO4     D5.  Glorious Bea Enterprises (GBE) receives cash from various external business partners, including investors, creditors, customers, and suppliers. GBE wants to store information about all external business partners in a single database table. Describe the conceptual, logical, and physical level implementation compromises GBE needs to make.

# Applied Learning

LO2     A1.  Quandrax Computers is a store that buys computer components for low prices, assembles the components into computers, and then sells the computers at high prices.

Each computer is assigned a unique identification number, and computers that have common configurations are categorized into types (e.g., Longitude is a laptop that is easily networked and is recommended for businesses; Element is a desktop that is intended for home and small businesses). Categories can be entered into the database before any computers in the categories are actually assembled. The computer components are purchased from wholesalers. One of Quandrax's purchasing agents submits an order to the wholesaler that has listed a given component for sale. If the order is accepted, one of Quandrax's inventory clerks receives the items. Multiple orders accepted by the same supplier may be consolidated into one purchase. Orders are accepted in their entirety or not at all. Nearly all of Quandrax's orders are accepted. Sometimes the incorrect components are delivered to Quandrax and Quandrax has to return them to the appropriate supplier. Sometimes Quandrax returns components to suppliers for other reasons, such as the result of a change in planned production of a certain category of computers. Only about 10 percent of Quandrax's purchased components are returned to suppliers, and any return would result from only one purchase.

When payment is due for a purchase, one of Quandrax's cashiers issues one check for payment in full for the items on that purchase. Sometimes if multiple purchases have been made from the same supplier within a short time, Quandrax pays for those purchases with just one check. One of Quandrax's managers is required to not only authorize all purchase orders greater than $5,000 but also sign all checks (including checks written for expenditures other than purchases of computer components). Quandrax needs to keep track of the managers' participation in these events as well as the participation of other employees in these events. In physically implementing the conceptual model into the database tables, Quandrax wants to combine all employee types into just one table. This means Quandrax would keep the separate employee entities on the E-R diagram, but make just one employee table to represent all of the employee entities, then post keys or make relationship tables as necessary to implement all relationships of employees to the relevant events.

All sales are handled via mail or e-mail, as Quandrax does not have any showrooms. Quandrax assigns salespeople to its large corporate customers and the salespeople take sample computers to the customer locations to demonstrate features as part of their sales calls. Only a small percentage of Quandrax's sales calls result in orders, and sometimes a salesperson might need to make several sales calls to the same customer to obtain one order from that customer. Orders also result from customers surfing the Internet and seeing descriptions of the computers on Quandrax's website. These customers are not assigned to specific salespeople; Quandrax only tracks the salesperson that actually took the order. Some of Quandrax's salespeople are hired to handle just such orders and as such are not assigned specifically to any customers.

If a customer orders multiple computers on one sale order and some of the computers are immediately available whereas the others are not yet assembled, Quandrax ships the available computers right away and then ships the remainder of the order when the rest of the computers are assembled. Sometimes Quandrax combines computers from multiple sale orders into a single shipment. For example, once a customer ordered 10 computers and the next day decided that wouldn't be enough so he ordered 4 more. Quandrax shipped all 14 computers in one shipment. Quandrax only accepts checks for its sales of computers; customers can pay for multiple sales with a single check, but no partial payments are accepted. Each sale transaction is tracked by a shipment ID; an invoice is sent to the customer that is due within 10 days, with no discounts allowed. Quandrax does not allow any sale returns, that is, all sales are final. Cash receipts are never split between two cash accounts; rather each receipt is assigned to one of Quandrax's cash accounts by one of Quandrax's cashiers. Quandrax also receives cash from other activities such as loans, so the database must allow for that. Suppliers, employees, and customers need to be entered into the database before any transactions involving them occur.

The following attributes are of interest to Quandrax; some are related to the acquisition/payment cycle. The attributes that are related to the sales/collection process must be included in your solution. Do not add attributes to the list. Use the boldface attribute abbreviations in parentheses next to the attributes in the list. List any assumptions you make, along with the reasons behind your assumptions (i.e., state what you think is vague in the problem, say what you are going to assume to clear up the ambiguity, and make a case for that assumption).

Purchase Order Number (**PO#**)

Supplier ID (**SuppID**)

Employee ID (**EmpID**)

Purchase Order Date (**PODate**)

Purchase Date (**PurchDate**)

Location of cash account (**Ca-Loc**)

Cash Account Number (**CashAcct#**)

Name of supplier (**SupName**)

Receiving Report Number (**RR#**)

Computer Category ID code (**Cat-ID**)

Component ID code (**CompoID**)

Cash Disbursement Date (**CD-Date**)

Name of employee (**EmpName**)

Purchase return ID (**PR-ID**)

Cash Disbursement Number (**CD#**)

Sale Order ID (**SO-ID**)

Shipment ID (**Ship-ID**)

Date of sales call (**SC-Date**)

Customer check number (**CR-Chk#**)

Sales Call ID (**SC-ID**)

Cash Receipt ID (**CR-ID**)

Customer ID (**Cust-ID**)

Date of cash receipt (**CR-Date**)

Name of Customer (**Cust-Name**)

Total sale dollar amount (**Sale-Amt**)

Type of employee (**EmpType**)

Date of sale order (**SO-Date**)

Date of purchase return (**PR-Date**)

Dollar amount of cash receipt (**CR-Amt**)

Current balance of cash account (**AcctBal**)

Shipping address for a customer (**Cust-Ship**)

Date of sale/shipment of computers (**Ship-Date**)

Description of a computer category (**Cat-Desc**)

Computer component description (**Comp-desc**)

Total dollar amount of a cash disbursement (**CD-Amt**)

Standard cost for a computer component (**Std-Cost**)

Quantity of a computer component returned (**Qty-Ret**)

Type of supplier (i.e., wholesaler or individual) (**SupType**)

Identification number for a finished computer (**CompuID**)

Quantity of a computer component ordered on purchase order (**Qty-Ord**)

Proposed selling price for a type of computer on a sales call (**Prop-SP**)

Ordered cost for a computer component on a purchase order (**PO-Unit-Cost**)

Suggested selling price for computers [hint: by category] (**List-price**)

Date assembly was completed for a finished computer (**Assemb-Date**)

Quoted selling price for each item on a sale order (**Ord-SP**)

Actual selling price for a particular finished computer (**Act-SP**)

Quantity of a computer component received on a purchase (**Qty-Rec**)

Actual cost of a computer component on a particular purchase (**Item-Unit-Cost**)

**Required**

   a. Create a business process level REA model (in either grammar or diagram format) for Quandrax Computers' sales/collection process. Be sure to include all relevant entities, relationships, attributes, and participation cardinalities. (If you completed applied learning problem 8–1 you may use the solution you already created for that problem).

   b. Create a business process level REA model (in either grammar or diagram format) for Quandrax Computers' acquisition/payment process. Be sure to include all relevant entities, relationships, attributes, and participation cardinalities. (If you completed applied learning problem 9–1 you may use the solution you already created for that problem).

   c. Integrate the views created in steps (a) and (b) into a single conceptual model.

   d. Convert the conceptual model into a logical set of relational database tables.

   e. Identify implementation compromises (if any) made at the conceptual and logical levels.

## Answers to Multiple Choice Questions

MC1. A; MC2. D; MC3. C; MC4. C; MC5. B.

# Chapter **Eleven**

# The Conversion
# Business Process

**LEARNING OBJECTIVES**

The objectives of this chapter are to introduce the conversion business process, to discuss the REA ontology representation of conversion processes, and to describe some of the typical information needs in the conversion business process. After studying this chapter you should be able to:

1. Identify the activities and documents common to most conversion business processes
2. Recognize similarities and differences between various types of conversion processes
3. Explain the various components of the REA ontology in the conversion business process
4. Create a REA business process level model for an enterprise's conversion process
5. Identify common information needs within the conversion process
6. Create database queries to retrieve conversion process information from a relational database

## CONVERSION BUSINESS PROCESS IN AN ENTERPRISE VALUE SYSTEM

The **conversion process** includes the business events associated with converting raw inputs such as materials, labor, machinery, and other fixed assets into finished outputs. Most of the time the conversion process involves the manufacture or production of **finished goods,** so it is sometimes called the manufacturing process or the production process. As you analyze and model a business process, you must clearly understand its purpose and objectives. You will better understand this process if you can base your understanding on some personal experience. Have you ever been involved in a conversion cycle? Perhaps you do not have experience in the manufacturing process of a corporation or other business entity; however, most people have participated in the production of some type of finished product. Have you ever cooked, made crafts, created something on a computer,

345

written a story, or made lemonade? If so, then you have some real life experience with conversion cycle activities. In this chapter we use the example of baking cookies to demonstrate many of the concepts.[1] If you have never baked cookies, we recommend you find a recipe and bake a batch of your favorite cookies before reading the rest of this chapter!

It may seem to you that the conversion processes for most firms will be different because the products they produce are so different. Indeed, the specific workflow tasks vary greatly among enterprises. However, the REA business process level pattern underlies virtually all conversion processes. In analyzing the conversion process for an enterprise, begin by realizing how the conversion process fits into the value system of the enterprise as a whole. At the value system level, the conversion process is completely inside the enterprise bubble (see Exhibit 11–1). It is an internal business process that typically does not provide a point of contact with any external agents. Although an enterprise may need information from external agents or may need to provide information to external agents regarding the conversion process, keep in mind that the value system level depicts *resource* flows, *not* information flows. Typically any resource flows between the enterprise and the external agents are part of either the acquisition/payment or the revenue processes that interface with the conversion process.

The value chain reveals interfaces between the conversion process and other business processes. Exhibit 11–2 illustrates the typical value chain interfaces for manufacturers. Materials and machinery are made available to the conversion process as a result of the acquisition/payment process. Labor is made available to the conversion process as a result of the human resource process. The conversion process turns those inputs (materials, machinery, and labor) into finished products, which are made available to the revenue process. To convert the materials, machinery, and labor into finished goods, the conversion process must include economic events that use up those inputs and an economic event that produces the finished products.

# CONVERSION BUSINESS PROCESS LEVEL REA MODELS

Conversion processes can be broadly categorized into two types: batch processes and continuous processes. Batch processes involve the production of an established number of

**EXHIBIT 11–1**
**Conversion
Process in the
Enterprise
Value System**

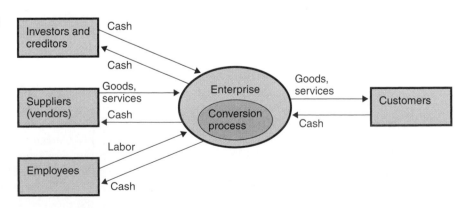

[1]We thank Julie Smith David of Arizona State University for the idea of using cookie baking to illustrate conversion cycle concepts.

**EXHIBIT 11–2   Conversion Process in the Value Chain**

Partial Value Chain

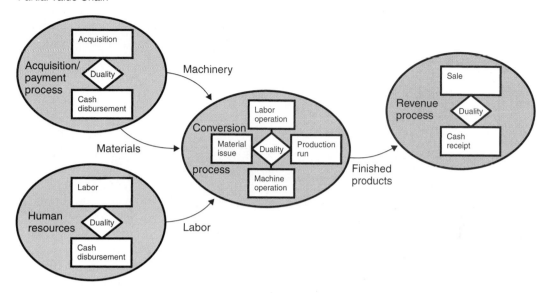

product units, or they may involve a particular job such as a car repair, the printing of a customized wedding invitation, or a consulting engagement. Continuous processes produce a homogeneous product somewhat continuously. Examples include the production of cement, petroleum products, flour, beer, and steel. The main difference between batch processes and continuous processes is that for batch processes, natural starting and ending points exist for assigning costs to the **production run,** whereas for continuous processes, artificial starting and ending points must be created for cost assignment purposes. Usually these start and end points are arbitrarily chosen boundaries of a time period. That period may span minutes, hours, days, weeks, or even months, depending on the nature of the enterprise's conversion process. Presumably the time periods should be chosen such that they are long enough to include the production of at least one identifiable resource. For example, the time period used for the **economic increment event** for an agricultural crop may be designated as the growing season, whereas an hour may be deemed an appropriate time period for a production run of breakfast cereal. Once the production run event is determined as either a batch, job, or time period, cost assignment is relatively straightforward. The assignment of manufacturing costs to units produced is an averaging process; you simply divide the manufacturing costs (accumulated either by job, batch, or time period) by the number of units produced in that job, batch, or time period.

We begin our detailed discussion of the conversion process by reviewing some of its more common events in the context of cookie baking. While a wide variety of workflow activities may be included in a conversion process, and as a result the task level modeling will vary accordingly, a pattern exists into which the activities can be categorized for data storage and for data exchange purposes for most, if not all, enterprises.

Recall that the REA pattern captures data to answer the who, what, where, when, why questions regarding a transaction cycle. Answers to the when and where questions are

**EXHIBIT 11–3**   **Conversion Cycle Core REA Pattern**

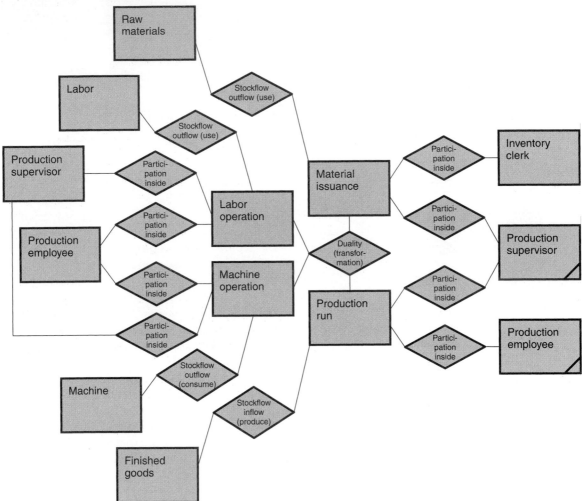

typically stored as attributes, unless the location is also a resource; for example, a particular manufacturing plant, or a particular machine. Answers to the who, what, and why questions are provided by the relationships captured in the core REA pattern as illustrated for the conversion cycle in Exhibit 11–3. The **participation relationships** identify the who for each event, and the stockflow relationships indicate the what for each event. The **duality relationship** reveals why the enterprise engages in the economic events of the cycle.

The core REA pattern for the conversion cycle consists of the same components as the core pattern for the sales/collection and acquisition/payment processes. Recall that the core REA pattern for those cycles contains economic increment events paired by duality with **economic decrement events.** Each economic event is linked to the resource or resource type that the event increases or decreases, and each economic event is linked to at least one initiator agent (who may be internal or external) and at least one responsible agent (who is typically internal). In the conversion cycle instead of only two paired economic exchange events, typically four economic events are tracked in detail. Three of these events are economic decrement events that represent the using up of the machinery, labor, and **raw materials.** The fourth event is the economic increment event—the production run that produces the finished goods.

The duality relationship in the conversion cycle is slightly different from the duality relationships in the sales/collection and acquisition/payment processes. In the revenue and acquisition cycles, duality usually represents a transfer-type exchange of one or more resources for one or more different resources. That is, the enterprise trades one or more resources for another resource. Usually one of the resources is cash and the other resource is a noncash resource such as raw materials or finished goods inventory. Such a relationship is a **transfer duality relationship.** In the conversion process, the duality relationship represents a transformation-type exchange of noncash resources. That is, the enterprise transforms raw input resources into a finished good resource. The relationship is therefore called a **transformation duality relationship.** Note that there is no requirement that only two economic events be paired in a duality relationship in the revenue and acquisition cycles; in fact, both of those cycles also include **labor operations** that use up the labor resource. Activities in those cycles also may use up fixed assets, **equipment,** utilities, and so forth. However, the use of labor and fixed assets is typically not tracked at the same level of detail in those cycles as in the conversion cycle, because labor and fixed assets are usually immaterial compared to the primary economic decrement event and because the necessary measurement tools and techniques are usually cost prohibitive. In the conversion process, the labor and **machine operation** costs often exceed the costs of the raw materials; it is cost beneficial, and in fact crucial, to measure them.

As in the acquisition and revenue cycles, the core REA pattern has been extended to include commitment events and additional relationships such as reservation, reciprocal, executes (fulfillment), linkage, and custody. Exhibit 11–4 illustrates the extended conversion cycle pattern for the business process level of the REA enterprise ontology.

As in the acquisition and revenue cycles, the specific labels on the resources, events, and agents differ depending on the nature of the enterprise's conversion cycle. Exhibit 11–5 illustrates labels that could be used for an enterprise whose conversion cycle involves cookie baking.

## Economic Increment Event: Production Run

The center of the pattern is made up of the duality relationship and the events that participate in that relationship. The event that usually leaps to mind when contemplating the conversion process is the production run (sometimes called work-in-process job), because that is the event that actually increases the quantity of a finished good. In other words, the production run is the event that is intended to achieve the overall objective of the conversion process—the production of a finished product resource. In Exhibit 11–5, the cookie batch is the economic increment event—that is, the production run event that produces finished cookies. Data typically captured regarding production run events are an assigned identifier for the event, the date/time the event started, and the date/time the event ended. Data also are recorded regarding what resources and agents are involved.

The relational tables in Exhibit 11–6 illustrate some of the data attributes that may be captured with respect to the cookie batch event and its related resources and agents. The

**EXHIBIT 11–4**  **Extended REA Conversion Cycle Business Process Level Pattern**

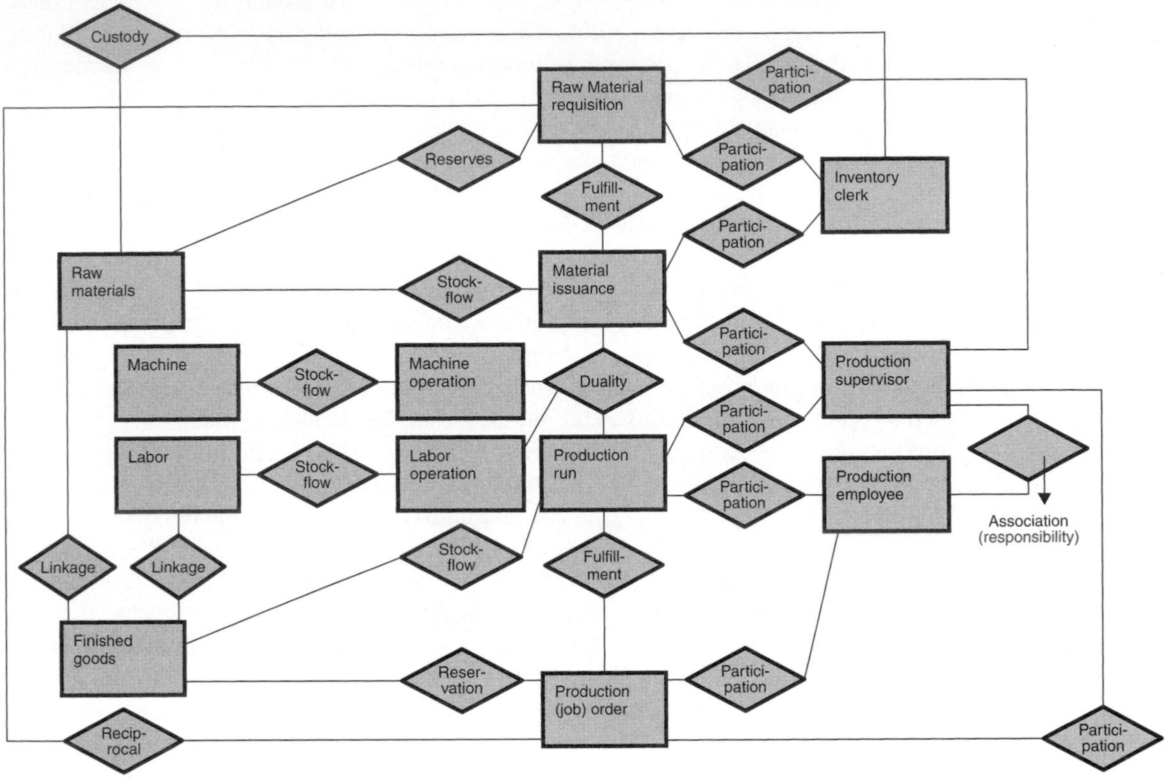

Note: Links from machine operation to production supervisor and to production employee and from labor operation to production supervisor and to production employee have been omitted to increase readability of the diagram. Those relationships should also be included. Similarly there may exist machinery requisitions and labor requisitions as commitments to the machine operation and labor operation events.

cookie batch table stores the event data that pertain to each batch as a whole—when it started, when it ended, how many cookies the batch was supposed to produce as well as how many cookies the batch actually did produce, and the supervisor in charge of the batch. The finished cookies table stores the resource data that describe the finished cookies. The resources are not individually identified (e.g., with a separate identification number for each physical cookie) but instead are identified at the type or category level; that is, each separate kind of cookie is assigned a different identification code. For some enterprises, each physical product may need to be specifically identified with a serial number. In that case, both a finished resource entity and a resource-type entity need to be included in the conceptual model. We discuss such a situation later in the chapter.

The stockflow table stores the data needed to identify which type of cookie was produced in each cookie batch. The baking supervisor table stores data that describe supervisors, such as their names and phone numbers. The participation relationship between baking supervisor and cookie batch is not represented with a separate table, but is traceable via a posted foreign key of supervisor ID in the cookie batch table. The baking employee table stores data that describe **production employees,** such as their names, phone num-

**EXHIBIT 11–5   Cookie Baking Conversion Business Process Level Model**

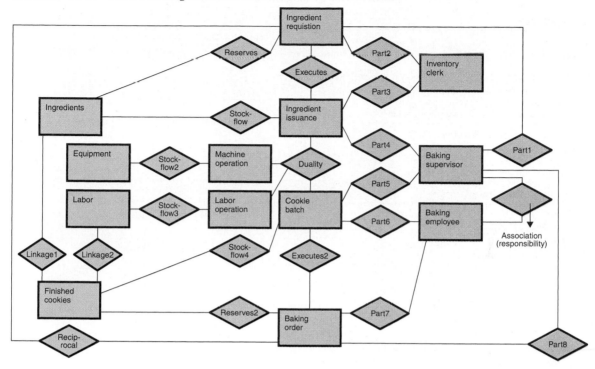

bers, and which supervisor is assigned responsibility for them. The participation-cookiebatch-bakingemployee table represents the relationship between baking employees and cookie batches, enabling users to identify which employees worked on each separate cookie batch.

In this example, we can see that Larry, Moe, and Curly baked 40 frosted sugar cookies with candy sprinkles under the supervison of Ricky. They started on July 15, 2010, at 6:30 A.M and finished that same day at 7:15 A.M. Fred and Ethel baked 48 snickerdoodles under the supervision of Lucy. They also started on July 15, 2010, at 6:30 A.M.; however, they took longer to finish their batch, ending at 7:37 A.M.

## Economic Decrement Event: Material Issuance

The cookie batch event also is involved in the duality relationship, which as noted earlier, identifies what economic decrement events the enterprise must engage in such that the economic increment event can occur. In other words, it identifies what the enterprise needed to use up to produce the finished cookies. One economic decrement event that typically exists is the using up of raw materials in the production process. Those raw materials are usually transformed into finished goods and lose their own identity and nature in the process. Such an event is given a label such as materials issuance and the stockflow relationship between the issuance event and the raw materials is specified as a **use stockflow relationship.** In the cookie-baking

## EXHIBIT 11–6   Relational Database Tables Encompassing Cookie Batch Event

**CookieBatch**

| BatchID | StartTime | CompletionTime | Scheduled Quantity | Actual Quantity | SupervisorID |
|---------|-----------|----------------|---------------------|------------------|--------------|
| WJ1 | 7/15/2010 6:30:00 AM | 7/15/2010 7:15:00 AM | 40 | 40 | S2 |
| WJ2 | 7/15/2010 6:30:00 AM | 7/15/2010 7:37:00 AM | 48 | 48 | S1 |

**StockflowCookieBatch-FinishedCookieType**

| BatchID | FinishedCookieTypeID |
|---------|----------------------|
| WJ1 | FSCS |
| WJ2 | SN |

**FinishedCookieType**

| CookieID | Description | UnitsPerPackage | ListPrice |
|----------|-------------|-----------------|-----------|
| CC | Chocolate chip plain | 12 | $2.99 |
| CCP | Chocolate chip with pecans | 12 | $2.99 |
| FSCS | Frosted sugar cookies with candy sprinkles | 10 | $3.59 |
| M | Molasses | 12 | $3.29 |
| OR | Oatmeal raisin | 12 | $2.99 |
| PB | Peanut butter | 12 | $2.99 |
| SC | Sugar cookies plain | 12 | $2.99 |
| SN | Snickerdoodles | 12 | $3.59 |

**BakingSupervisor**

| SupervisorID | SupervisorName | SupervisorPhone |
|--------------|----------------|-----------------|
| S1 | Lucy | 1-1234 |
| S2 | Ricky | 1-4321 |

**Baking Employee**

| EmployeeID | EmployeeName | EmployeePhone | SupervisorID |
|------------|--------------|---------------|--------------|
| PE1 | Fred | 1-6789 | S2 |
| PE2 | Ethel | 1-9876 | S2 |
| PE3 | Larry | 1-7698 | S1 |
| PE4 | Moe | 1-6798 | S1 |
| PE5 | Curly | 1-8796 | S1 |

**ParticipationCookieBatchBakingEmployee**

| BatchID | EmployeeID |
|---------|------------|
| WJ1 | PE3 |
| WJ1 | PE4 |
| WJ1 | PE5 |
| WJ2 | PE1 |
| WJ2 | PE2 |

**EXHIBIT 11–7**
**Move Ticket**
**Document**

**Move Ticket No.** _____

Batch number _____

Move date: _____

Moved from: _____          Taken by: _____

Moved to: _____          Received by: _____

Production order number: _____

example, the label ingredient issuance has been used for the materials issuance event. Data typically captured regarding material issuance events are an assigned identifier for the issuance, the date/time of the issuance, and the location of the issuance. Data also are recorded about which resources and agents are involved and the underlying production order.

A **move ticket** typically is used to document the actual use of raw materials (i.e., the materials issuance event); sometimes the move ticket number is used to identify the event instead of an assigned identifier. See Exhibit 11–7 for a move ticket document.

The relational tables in Exhibit 11–8 illustrate some of the data attributes that may be captured with respect to the ingredient issuance event and its relationships with ingredients, inventory clerks, supervisors, and the cookie batch event. The duality table identifies which ingredient issuances apply to which cookie batches. The ingredient issuance table stores the event data that pertain to each issuance, such as when and where it occurred, who authorized it (supervisor), and who executed it (inventory clerk). In the example shown, the participation relationships between baking supervisor and ingredient issuance and between inventory clerk and ingredient issuance are not represented by separate tables, but are traceable via posted foreign keys of supervisor ID and employee ID in the ingredient issuance table.

The ingredients table stores the resource data that describe the types of ingredients available for use in the production process. As with the finished cookies, the ingredients are not individually identified but instead are identified at the type or category level (i.e., each separate kind of ingredient is assigned a different identification code). The stockflow table stores the data needed to identify which type of ingredient (and how much of each) was actually issued in each ingredient issuance event.

In this example, we can see that Ted and Alice issued several different ingredients to Ricky and to Lucy for the frosted sugar cookie and snickerdoodle cookie batches on July 15, 2005, between 6:20 and 6:30 A.M. Each of the ingredients was issued to the workcenter where the initial work involving the ingredients was to take place.

## Economic Decrement Event: Labor Operation

Notice that in this example, for simplicity's sake the duality relationship is represented in three separate duality tables: one that links the cookie batch to the related material issuances, one that links the cookie batch to the related labor operations, and one that links the cookie batch to the related machine operations. Alternatively, one duality table could have been created to link all four economic events together.

The labor operation event is an economic decrement event that represents the performance of a particular activity in the conversion process by a production employee, thereby using up

**EXHIBIT 11–8** **Relational Database Tables Encompassing Ingredient Issuance Event**

**DualityCookieBatch-IngredientIssuance**

| BatchID | IngredientIssuanceID |
|---------|----------------------|
| WJ1 | RMI4238 |
| WJ1 | RMI4239 |
| WJ1 | RMI4240 |
| WJ2 | RMI4241 |
| WJ2 | RMI4242 |
| WJ1 | RMI4243 |
| WJ2 | RMI4244 |
| WJ1 | RMI4245 |
| WJ2 | RMI4246 |

**IngredientIssuance**

| IngredientIssuanceID | IssuanceTime | Location | InventoryClerkID | SupervisorID |
|----------------------|--------------|----------|------------------|--------------|
| RMI4238 | 7/15/2010 6:20:00 AM | WorkcenterA | IC1 | S2 |
| RMI4239 | 7/15/2010 6:22:00 AM | WorkcenterB | IC2 | S2 |
| RMI4240 | 7/15/2010 6:24:00 AM | WorkcenterC | IC2 | S2 |
| RMI4241 | 7/15/2010 6:28:00 AM | WorkcenterD | IC1 | S1 |
| RMI4242 | 7/15/2010 6:26:00 AM | WorkcenterE | IC2 | S1 |
| RMI4243 | 7/15/2010 6:29:00 AM | WorkcenterC | IC1 | S2 |
| RMI4244 | 7/15/2010 6:29:30 AM | WorkcenterE | IC1 | S1 |
| RMI4245 | 7/15/2010 6:29:00 AM | WorkcenterC | IC2 | S2 |
| RMI4246 | 7/15/2010 6:29:30 AM | WorkcenterE | IC2 | S1 |

**StockflowIssuanceofIngredients**

| IngredientID | IssuanceID | QuantityIssued | UnitOfMeasure |
|--------------|------------|----------------|---------------|
| WS | RMI4238 | 5 | cups |
| FL | RMI4238 | 7 | cups |
| EG | RMI4239 | 4 | each |
| SH | RMI4239 | 2 | cups |
| VN | RMI4239 | 3 | teaspoons |
| SL | RMI4238 | 2 | teaspoons |
| CS | RMI4240 | 1 | cup |
| WS | RMI4241 | 6 | cups |
| FL | RMI4241 | 8 | cups |
| EG | RMI4242 | 4 | each |
| SH | RMI4242 | 3 | cups |
| VN | RMI4242 | 4 | teaspoons |
| SL | RMI4241 | 2 | teaspoons |
| CN | RMI4241 | 1 | cup |
| PK | RMI4243 | 4 | each |
| PK | RMI4244 | 4 | each |
| ILFS | RMI4245 | 4 | each |
| ILSN | RMI4246 | 4 | each |

*(Continued)*

**EXHIBIT 11–8** (Concluded)

**Ingredients**

| IngredientID | Description | UnitOfMeasure | StandardCostPerUnitOfMeasure |
|---|---|---|---|
| WS | White sugar | 50 lb bag | $10.00 |
| EG | Eggs, large AA grade | 2 dozen carton | $1.29 |
| FL | Flour, white sifted | 100 lb bag | $20.00 |
| VN | Vanilla, pure | 1 liter bottle | $20.00 |
| SL | Salt, iodized | 5 lb bag | $1.00 |
| PB | Peanut butter | 10 lb jar | $8.37 |
| CN | Cinnamon | 16 oz tin | $3.29 |
| CM | Chocolate morsels | 10 lb bag | $19.49 |
| PE | Pecans | 2 lb bag | $5.32 |
| SH | Shortening | 10 lb can | $12.10 |
| CS | Candy sprinkles | 1 lb tin | $3.18 |
| BU | Butter | 10 lb box | $3.98 |
| BS | Brown sugar | 50 lb bag | $9.47 |
| PK | Plastic container | each | $0.12 |
| ILFS | Ingredient label—frosted sugar | each | $0.01 |
| ILSN | Ingredient label—snickerdoodle | each | $0.01 |

**InventoryClerk**

| InventoryClerkID | ClerkName | ClerkPhone |
|---|---|---|
| IC1 | Ted | 1-5678 |
| IC2 | Alice | 1-8765 |

**Baking Supervisor**

| SupervisorID | SupervisorName | SupervisorPhone |
|---|---|---|
| S1 | Lucy | 1-1234 |
| S2 | Ricky | 1-4321 |

the resource of that person's labor. Many people often are confused about the difference between labor (also called **labor type**) and labor operation. Labor is a resource-type entity set that represents a list of the types of labor that can be performed in labor operations. Labor operations are the actual using up of the available labor. Data typically captured to describe labor types are the description and standard or budget information such as the standard hourly cost of each type of labor. Data typically captured to describe labor operations are the starting and ending date/time of the labor operation events and the total elapsed time of each labor operation. Keep in mind that data regarding labor types and labor operations can be captured and stored only if measurement techniques exist and are cost effective. In the acquisition and revenue cycle, labor operations and labor types are typically not measured and recorded. In the conversion process, labor operations are often measured and recorded—but not always.

When they are measured and recorded, labor operations usually are documented on **job time tickets** or time track forms that indicate the starting and stopping times for the labor operations and provide descriptions of the labor operations on a specific date by a specific employee. The job time ticket or time track number serves as an identifier for the labor operation event. See Exhibit 11–9 for a job time ticket.

**EXHIBIT 11–9**
**Job Time**
**Ticket Form**

| Job time ticket no. _____ | | | | | |
|---|---|---|---|---|---|
| Employee ID _____ | | Name _____ | | Date _____ | |
| Start time | Stop time | Total time | Rate | Total amount | Job number |
|  |  |  |  |  |  |
| Approved by _____ | | | | | |
| | | Department Supervisor | | | |

The relational tables in Exhibit 11–10 illustrate some of the data attributes that may be captured about the labor operations event and its relationships with labor, baking employees, baking supervisors, and the cookie batch event. The duality table identifies which labor operations apply to which cookie batches. The labor operations table stores the event data that pertain to each labor operation, such as when it began and ended, who authorized it (supervisor), and who executed it (employee). The labor table stores the resource data that describe the types of labor available for use in the production process. The stockflow table stores the data needed to identify which type of labor (and how much of each) was actually used in each labor operation event.

The participation relationship between baking supervisor and labor operation is not represented with a separate table, but is traceable via a posted foreign key of supervisor ID in the labor operations table. Similarly, the participation relationship between baking employee and labor operations is represented with the employee ID posted as a foreign key in the labor operations table.

In this example, we can see that to make the frosted sugar cookies, Larry took 10 minutes to mix the dry ingredients while Moe took 12 minutes to mix the moist ingredients. Curly took 5 minutes to combine the dry and moist ingredients. Larry took 5 minutes to form the cookie dough into cookies and put them onto a cookie sheet. Curly took 1 minute to put the cookie sheet into the oven and set the timer. Twelve minutes later, Curly took the cookies out of the oven. Four and a half minutes later Larry took 4 minutes to frost the cookies, then Moe took 1 minute to add candy sprinkles and Curly took 2 minutes to package the final cookies.

Meanwhile, to bake the snickerdoodles, Fred took 10 minutes to mix the dry ingredients while Ethel took 10 minutes to mix the moist ingredients. Ethel then took 5 minutes to combine the dry and moist ingredients and then she took 2 minutes to form the dough and put the cookies onto the cookie sheet. Fred took 1 minute to put the cookies into the oven and set the timer. Twelve minutes later Fred took 30 seconds to take the cookies out of the oven. Nearly 35 minutes later, Ethel took 2 minutes to package the finished cookies. Notice that one of the things the tables don't show us is the reason for significant gaps in time—for example, why did they wait 35 minutes to package the cookies? It turns out that Fred thought Ethel had packaged them already, whereas Ethel thought that was Fred's responsibility. Lucy

**EXHIBIT 11–10**  Relational Database Tables Encompassing Labor Operation Event

**DualityCookieBatch-LaborOperation**

| BatchID | LaborOperationID |
|---------|------------------|
| WJ1 | LO21 |
| WJ1 | LO22 |
| WJ1 | LO23 |
| WJ1 | LO24 |
| WJ1 | LO25 |
| WJ1 | LO26 |
| WJ1 | LO28 |
| WJ1 | LO29 |
| WJ2 | LO30 |
| WJ2 | LO33 |
| WJ2 | LO34 |
| WJ2 | LO35 |
| WJ2 | LO36 |

**Labor Operation**

| LaborOperationID | StartTime | EndTime | EmployeeID | SupervisorID |
|------------------|-----------|---------|------------|--------------|
| LO21 | 7/15/2010 6:30:00 AM | 7/15/2010 6:40:00 AM | PE3 | S2 |
| LO22 | 7/15/2010 6:30:00 AM | 7/15/2010 6:40:00 AM | PE4 | S2 |
| LO23 | 7/15/2010 6:40:00 AM | 7/15/2010 6:45:00 AM | PE5 | S2 |
| LO24 | 7/15/2010 6:45:00 AM | 7/15/2010 6:50:00 AM | PE3 | S2 |
| LO25 | 7/15/2010 6:50:00 AM | 7/15/2010 6:51:00 AM | PE5 | S2 |
| LO26 | 7/15/2010 7:03:00 AM | 7/15/2010 7:03:30 AM | PF5 | S2 |
| LO27 | 7/15/2010 7:08:00 AM | 7/15/2010 7:12:00 AM | PE3 | S2 |
| LO28 | 7/15/2010 7:12:00 AM | 7/15/2010 7:13:00 AM | PE4 | S2 |
| LO29 | 7/15/2010 7:13:00 AM | 7/15/2010 7:15:00 AM | PE5 | S2 |
| LO30 | 7/15/2010 6:30:00 AM | 7/15/2010 6:40:00 AM | PE1 | S1 |
| LO31 | 7/15/2010 6:30:00 AM | 7/15/2010 6:40:00 AM | PE2 | S1 |
| LO32 | 7/15/2010 6:40:00 AM | 7/15/2010 6:45:00 AM | PE2 | S1 |
| LO33 | 7/15/2010 6:45:00 AM | 7/15/2010 6:47:00 AM | PE2 | S1 |
| LO34 | 7/15/2010 6:47:00 AM | 7/15/2010 6:48:00 AM | PE1 | S1 |
| LO35 | 7/15/2010 7:00:00 AM | 7/15/2010 7:00:30 AM | PE1 | S1 |
| LO36 | 7/15/2010 7:35:00 AM | 7/15/2010 7:37:00 AM | PE2 | S1 |

**Baking Employee**

| EmployeeID | EmployeeName | EmployeePhone | SupervisorID | |
|------------|--------------|---------------|--------------|---|
| PE1 | Fred | 1-6789 | S2 | |
| PE2 | Ethel | 1-9876 | S2 | |
| PE3 | Larry | 1-7698 | S1 | |
| PE4 | Moe | 1-6798 | S1 | |
| PE5 | Curly | 1-8796 | S1 | *(Continued)* |

was in a comic mood and had been keeping them so well entertained that it wasn't until Ricky came in to gloat to Lucy that his crew had already finished their cookies even though they had the harder cookies to make (harder in that they involved more labor operations).

**EXHIBIT 11–10**

**(Concluded)**

**Labor Type**

| LaborTypeID | Description |
| --- | --- |
| L1 | Mix dry ingredients |
| L2 | Mix moist ingredients |
| L3 | Combine dry and moist ingredients |
| L4 | Add morsels to mixed dough |
| L5 | Add nuts to mixed dough |
| L6 | Form dough into cookies |
| L7 | Put cookies onto cookie sheet |
| L8 | Put cookie sheet into oven |
| L9 | Set cookie timer |
| L10 | Take cookie sheet out of oven |
| L11 | Frost cookies |
| L12 | Sprinkle cookies |
| L13 | Package cookies |

**StockflowLaborTypeinLaborOperation**

| LaborTypeID | LaborOperationID |
| --- | --- |
| L1 | LO21 |
| L2 | LO22 |
| L3 | LO23 |
| L6 | LO24 |
| L7 | LO24 |
| L8 | LO25 |
| L9 | LO25 |
| L10 | LO26 |
| L11 | LO27 |
| L12 | LO28 |
| L13 | LO29 |
| L1 | LO30 |
| L2 | LO31 |
| L3 | LO32 |
| L7 | LO33 |
| L8 | LO34 |
| L9 | LO34 |
| L10 | LO35 |
| L13 | LO36 |

## Economic Decrement Event: Machine Operation

Along with using up materials and labor, conversion processes also often use up machinery and equipment. An economic decrement event called machine operation is included in the REA enterprise ontology to capture the consumption of a portion of the machine's useful life. The machine operation event is slightly different in nature from the material issuance and labor operation economic decrement events, in that the machinery typically still exists in its original form (although with some added wear and tear) after the machine operation occurs. In contrast, the material issuance and labor operation events result in the materials and available labor being completely used up—they no longer exist in their original form but have been transformed into finished goods. Nevertheless, part of the machine's useful life has been consumed and represents a resource decrease that in some cases is cost-beneficial to measure and record. Although machine operations could be tracked using a separate document similar to a job time ticket, usually machine operations are only tracked on the production run cost sheet.

The relational tables in Exhibit 11–11 illustrate some of the data attributes that may be captured with respect to the machine operation event and its relationships with equipment, baking employees, baking supervisors, and the cookie batch event. The duality table identifies which machine operations apply to which cookie batches. The machine operation table stores the event data that pertain to each machine operation, such as when it began and ended, who authorized it (supervisor), and who executed it (employee). The equipment table stores the resource data that describe the equipment available for use in the production process. Each piece of equipment or machine is specifically identified with a unique ID; that is, this is a token-level entity set rather than a type-level entity set. Specific identification of fixed assets allows the tracking of cost allocation in accordance with generally accepted accounting principles. The stockflow table stores the data needed to identify which equipment was actually used in each machine operation event. The equipment does not get completely used up in the machine operation; rather, it is partially consumed. Thus the stockflow relationship is called a **consume stockflow**. The same piece of equipment can thus be used in multiple machine operations.

The participation relationships between baking supervisor and machine operation and between baking employee and machine operation are not represented with separate tables, but are traceable via posted foreign keys of supervisor ID and employee ID in the machine operations table.

In this example, we can see that the sugar cookie production run (batch) required three machine operations (notice that we are using the term *machine* loosely—to represent any fixed asset used in production; some enterprises may prefer to only track consumption of fixed assets that exceed a certain cost value). The first was a measure and mix operation that partially consumed a heavy duty mixer and measuring device set. The second was a baking operation that partially consumed a cookie sheet and an oven. The third was a finishing operation that partially consumed frosting utensils. The snickerdoodle batch required only two machine operations. The first was a measure and mix operation that partially consumed a heavy duty mixer and a measuring device set. The second was a baking operation that partially consumed a cookie sheet and an oven.

## Commitment to Economic Increment Event: Production Order

The discussion thus far has centered on the core economic exchange pattern in the REA ontology at the business process level. We next discuss the extension of the pattern to include commitment events and related resource and agent relationships. In the conversion cycle the commitments that make up a mutual commitment event are typically not bundled together into a single event as they are in the revenue and acquisition processes. Therefore in the conversion process, one event commits to an economic decrement event and another event commits to an economic increment event. In theory each economic event is preceded by a commitment to that event. The production order event is the event that represents the enterprise's commitment to engage in a production run. That is, the production order is the commitment to an economic increment event that will increase the finished goods resource. Production

**EXHIBIT 11–11** Relational Database Tables Encompassing Machine Operation Event

**DualityCookieBatchMachineOperation**

| BatchID | MachineOperationID |
|---------|--------------------|
| WJ1 | MO12 |
| WJ1 | MO13 |
| WJ1 | MO14 |
| WJ2 | MO15 |
| WJ2 | MO16 |

**Machine Operation**

| MachineOperationID | StartTime | EndTime | EmployeeID | SupervisorID |
|--------------------|-----------|---------|------------|--------------|
| MO12 | 7/15/2010 6:30:00 AM | 7/15/2010 6:45:00 AM | PE5 | S2 |
| MO13 | 7/15/2010 6:51:00 AM | 7/15/2010 7:03:00 AM | PE5 | S2 |
| MO14 | 7/15/2010 7:08:00 AM | 7/15/2010 7:12:00 AM | PE3 | S2 |
| MO15 | 7/15/2010 6:30:00 AM | 7/15/2010 6:45:00 AM | PE2 | S1 |
| MO16 | 7/15/2010 6:40:00 AM | 7/15/2010 7:00:00 AM | PE2 | S1 |

**Equipment**

| FixedAssetID | Description | Acquisition Date | Cost | Estimated LifeYears | Estimated SalvageValue |
|--------------|-------------|------------------|------|---------------------|------------------------|
| FA1 | Oven | 1/3/2010 | $400.00 | 10 | $50.00 |
| FA2 | Oven | 4/2/2009 | $500.00 | 3 | $100.00 |
| FA3 | Heavy duty mixer | 3/17/2009 | $150.00 | 3 | $0.00 |
| FA4 | Measuring device set | 2/16/2009 | $80.00 | 5 | $10.00 |
| FA5 | Cookie sheet | 2/18/2009 | $10.00 | 3 | $0.00 |
| FA6 | Cookie sheet | 1/3/2010 | $15.00 | 3 | $0.00 |
| FA7 | Frosting utensils | 1/3/2010 | $10.00 | 5 | $0.00 |
| FA8 | Heavy duty mixer | 2/15/2010 | $170.00 | 3 | $0.00 |
| FA9 | Measuring device set | 2/15/2010 | $75.00 | 5 | $10.00 |

**StockflowEquipmentinMachineOperation**

| FixedAssetID | MachineOperationID |
|--------------|--------------------|
| FA1 | MO13 |
| FA2 | MO16 |
| FA3 | MO12 |
| FA4 | MO12 |
| FA5 | MO13 |
| FA6 | MO16 |
| FA7 | MO14 |
| FA8 | MO15 |
| FA9 | MO15 |

*(Continued)*

order information is typically captured on a document (or data entry screen) that is called a production order. See the **production order document** in Exhibit 11–12.

The relational tables in Exhibit 11–13 illustrate some of the data attributes that may be captured with respect to the **production order event** (in this example it is called a baking

**EXHIBIT 11–12**
**Production Order**

| Production Order No. _____ | | | | | | | |
|---|---|---|---|---|---|---|---|
| Date _____ | | Product number _____ | | Description _____ | | | |
| Approved by: _____ | | Deliver to: _____ | | Begin date: _____ | | Complete by: _____ | |
| Work center | Operation | Quantity completed | Labor type description | Start date | Time | End date | Time |
| | | | | | | | |
| | | | | | | | |
| | | | | | | | |
| | | | | | | | |
| | | | | | | | |

order) and its relationships with finished cookies, baking employees, baking supervisors, and the cookie batch event. The duality table identifies which machine operations apply to which cookie batches. The production order table stores the event data that pertain to each production order, such as the order date, the requested completion date, and who authorized it (supervisor). The finished cookies table stores the resource data that describe the finished goods the production order is committing to increase. Notice that this is the same finished cookie table that was described in relationship to the production run economic increment event. The reservation table stores the data needed to identify how many of each finished cookie type are going to be produced when the production order is fulfilled.

We can see in this example that baking order PO1 committed the company to produce 40 frosted sugar cookies and called for Larry, Moe, and Curly to be the baking employees and for Ricky to be the supervisor for the job. Cookie batch WJ1 fulfilled baking order PO1; tracing back to the tables in Exhibit 11–6 reveals that WJ1 produced all 40 frosted sugar cookies. We also can see that baking order PO2 committed the company to produce 44 snickerdoodles and called for Fred and Ethel to be the baking employees and for Lucy to be the supervisor for the job. Cookie batch WJ2 fulfilled baking order PO2; tracing back to the tables in Exhibit 11–6 reveals that WJ2 produced 48 snickerdoodles, more than needed. Whether that is good or bad depends on the company policy. We might suspect that 48 were produced because the recipe for the company (which we discuss later in the **linkage relationships** section) is designed to make multiples of 12, and the snickerdoodles are typically packaged by the dozen.

## Commitment to Economic Decrement Event: Materials Requisition

Theoretically every economic decrement event should be related to a corresponding commitment for that decrement. The only commitment for an economic decrement in the example given is the raw material requisition event. Because the word *requisition* may bring to your mind a purchase requisition (an instigation event in the acquisition/payment process as described in Chapter 10), we must point out that a material requisition is not the

**EXHIBIT 11–13** Relational Database Tables Encompassing Baking Order Event

**BakingOrder**

| BakingOrderID | BakingOrderDateTime | RequestedCompletion | SupervisorID |
|---|---|---|---|
| PO1 | 7/14/2010 4:30:00 PM | 7/15/2010 8:00:00 AM | S2 |
| PO2 | 7/14/2010 4:31:30 PM | 7/15/2010 8:00:00 AM | S1 |
| PO3 | 7/15/2010 4:45:00 PM | 7/16/2010 8:00:00 AM | S1 |
| PO4 | 7/15/2010 4:46:00 PM | 7/16/2010 8:00:00 AM | S1 |
| PO5 | 7/15/2010 4:50:00 PM | 7/16/2010 8:00:00 AM | S2 |

**ReservationBakingOrderFinishedCookieType**

| CookieID | BakingOrderID | QuantityReserved |
|---|---|---|
| FSCS | PO1 | 40 |
| SN | PO2 | 44 |

**FinishedCookieType**

| CookieID | Description | UnitsPerPackage | ListPrice |
|---|---|---|---|
| CC | Chocolate chip plain | 12 | $2.99 |
| CCP | Chocolate chip with pecans | 12 | $2.99 |
| FSCS | Frosted sugar cookies with candy sprinkles | 10 | $3.59 |
| M | Molasses | 12 | $3.29 |
| OR | Oatmeal raisin | 12 | $2.99 |
| PB | Peanut butter | 12 | $2.99 |
| SC | Sugar cookies plain | 12 | $2.99 |
| SN | Snickerdoodles | 12 | $3.59 |

**BakingSupervisor**

| SupervisorID | SupervisorName | SupervisorPhone |
|---|---|---|
| S1 | Lucy | 1-1234 |
| S2 | Ricky | 1-4321 |

**ParticipationBakingEmployeeScheduledForBakingOrder**

| EmployeeID | ProductionOrderID |
|---|---|
| PE1 | PO2 |
| PE2 | PO2 |
| PE3 | PO1 |
| PE4 | PO1 |
| PE5 | PO1 |

**BakingEmployee**

| EmployeeID | EmployeeName | EmployeePhone | SupervisorID |
|---|---|---|---|
| PE1 | Fred | 1-6789 | S2 |
| PE2 | Ethel | 1-9876 | S2 |
| PE3 | Larry | 1-7698 | S1 |
| PE4 | Moe | 1-6798 | S1 |
| PE5 | Curly | 1-8796 | S1 |

*(Continued)*

**EXHIBIT 11–13**  (Concluded)

| CookieBatchFulfillsBakingOrder | |
|---|---|
| **BatchID** | **BakingOrderID** |
| WJ1 | PO1 |
| WJ2 | PO2 |

**EXHIBIT 11–14**
**Materials**
**Requisition**

**Materials Requisition No.** _____

| Date _____ | | Production order number _____ | | |
|---|---|---|---|---|
| Approved by _____ | | Deliver to _____ | | |
| Material ID | Description | Quantity | Unit cost | Total cost |
|  |  |  |  |  |
|  |  |  |  |  |
|  |  |  |  |  |

same thing as a purchase requisition. A materials requisition (sometimes called a **raw materials requisition**) is a commitment event whereby the inventory clerk or warehouse supervisor commits to the **production supervisor** to transfer materials from the materials warehouse to the production floor. A materials requisition assumes the raw materials are available within the enterprise, and is reserving them for use. In contrast, warehouse personnel initiate purchase requisitions to indicate the need to acquire the raw materials from an external source. Thus, if a materials requisition is initiated for which insufficient materials are on hand in the warehouse, this will likely trigger a purchase requisition and thereby instigate events in the acquisition/payment process. However, the raw materials requisition event occurs within the conversion cycle and the purchase requisition event occurs within the acquisition/payment cycle. Data captured regarding raw materials requisitions typically include the date/time of requisition and information about the resources and agents involved in the event. Each requisition is assigned a unique identifier. Requisition data are typically captured on a document or data entry screen called a materials requisition. See the material requisition form in Exhibit 11–14.

The relational tables in Exhibit 11–15 illustrate some of the data attributes that may be captured with respect to the materials requisition event (in this example it is called an ingredient requisition) and its relationships with ingredients, inventory clerks, baking supervisors, and the production order event. The executes or **fulfillment relationship** identifies which ingredient issuances fulfill which ingredient requisitions. The ingredient requisition

**EXHIBIT 11–15** **Relational Database Tables Encompassing Ingredient Requisition Event**

**IngredientRequisition**

| RequisitionID | RequisitionDate | SupervisorID | BakingOrderID |
|---|---|---|---|
| 1002 | 7/14/2010 4:35:00 PM | S2 | PO1 |
| 1003 | 7/14/2010 4:35:30 PM | S1 | PO2 |

**Baking Supervisor**

| SupervisorID | SupervisorName | SupervisorPhone |
|---|---|---|
| S1 | Lucy | 1-1234 |
| S2 | Ricky | 1-4321 |

**ParticipationInventoryClerkIngredientRequisition**

| InventoryClerkID | IngredientRequisitionID |
|---|---|
| IC1 | 1002 |
| IC1 | 1003 |
| IC2 | 1002 |
| IC2 | 1003 |

**Inventory Clerk**

| InventoryClerkID | ClerkName | ClerkPhone |
|---|---|---|
| IC1 | Ted | 1-5678 |
| IC2 | Alice | 1-8765 |

**ReservationIngredientRequisitionIngredients**

| IngredientID | IngredientRequisitionID | QuantityReserved | Unit of Measure |
|---|---|---|---|
| CN | 1003 | 0.5 | cup |
| CS | 1002 | 1 | cup |
| EG | 1002 | 4 | each |
| EG | 1003 | 4 | each |
| FL | 1002 | 8 | cups |
| FL | 1003 | 6 | cups |
| ILFS | 1002 | 4 | each |
| ILSN | 1003 | 4 | each |
| PK | 1002 | 4 | each |
| PK | 1003 | 4 | each |
| SH | 1002 | 2.67 | cups |
| SH | 1003 | 1.75 | cups |
| SL | 1002 | 2 | teaspoons |
| SL | 1003 | 1.75 | teaspoons |
| VN | 1002 | 4 | teaspoons |
| VN | 1003 | 2.75 | teaspoons |
| WS | 1002 | 6 | cups |
| WS | 1003 | 4.66 | cups |

*(Continued)*

table stores the event data that pertain to each ingredient requisition, such as the requisition date, the requested completion date, and who authorized it (supervisor). The ingredients table in Exhibit 11–15 is the same one shown in Exhibit 11–8; it stores the resource

**EXHIBIT 11–15** (Concluded)

| IngredientIssuanceFulfillsIngredientRequisition | |
| --- | --- |
| IngredientIssuanceID | IngredientRequisitionID |
| RMI4238 | 1003 |
| RMI4239 | 1003 |
| RMI4240 | 1002 |
| RMI4241 | 1002 |
| RMI4242 | 1002 |
| RMI4243 | 1002 |
| RMI4244 | 1003 |
| RMI4245 | 1002 |
| RMI4246 | 1003 |

data that describe the ingredients that are available for reservation by the ingredient requisition. The **reservation relationship** table depicts which ingredients the ingredient requisition is committing to decrease.

We can see in Exhibit 11–15 that ingredient requisition 1002 reserves the ingredients needed for the 40 frosted sugar cookies per baking order PO1, and requisition 1003 reserves the ingredients needed for the 44 snickerdoodles per baking order PO2. We can see that the ingredient issuances fulfilled the ingredient requisitions; a close examination reveals that more ingredients were issued for the snickerdoodles than were requisitioned. The issuance amounts were sufficient to make 48 cookies rather than 44 cookies.

## Custody Relationship

Companies often give custody of materials (and possibly finished goods) to a set of inventory clerks to protect the goods from theft or other misappropriation. Exhibit 11–4 includes a custody relationship between raw materials and inventory clerk; however, the example shown in Exhibit 11–5 does not include any custody relationships. Custody relationships should only be included in a business process level REA model if there is a direct relationship between raw materials or finished goods and an internal agent. That relationship must exist independently of their mutual participation in an event such that it would need to be tracked separately from the relationships that connect the resource and the agent to the common event. In other words, if all you need to know is which inventory clerk issued which raw materials in an issuance event, there is no need for a custody relationship—you can already determine that information from the stockflow relationship and the participation relationship. However, if some types of materials are assigned to one set of inventory clerks for security and other types of materials are assigned to another set of inventory clerks, and you need to track which clerks are responsible for a material, then you need a custody relationship.

## Association (Responsibility) Relationship

Association relationships exist when there is a need to track a direct relationship between two types of agents. As with custody, such a relationship must be independent of their mutual participation in a common event. Association relationships vary depending on the types of agents that are being connected. Relationships between an internal and an external agent (such as the salesperson to customer relationship in the revenue cycle) are called

**EXHIBIT 11–16** Relational Database Tables for Association (Responsibility) Relationship

**Baking Supervisor**

| SupervisorID | SupervisorName | SupervisorPhone |
|---|---|---|
| S1 | Lucy | 1-1234 |
| S2 | Ricky | 1-4321 |

**Baking Employee**

| EmployeeID | EmployeeName | EmployeePhone | SupervisorID |
|---|---|---|---|
| PE1 | Fred | 1-6789 | S2 |
| PE2 | Ethel | 1-9876 | S2 |
| PE3 | Larry | 1-7698 | S1 |
| PE4 | Moe | 1-6798 | S1 |
| PE5 | Curly | 1-8796 | S1 |

assignment relationships. In the conversion cycle the most common association relationship is between two internal agents and represents the fact that one type of internal agent is in charge of, or is responsible for, the other type of internal agent. Such an association is called a responsibility relationship. In Exhibit 11–5 a responsibility relationship is depicted between the baking supervisors and the baking employees. Exhibit 11–16 illustrates the relational tables that include the responsibility relationship. In this case a foreign key of supervisor ID is posted into the baking employee table to represent the relationship. These tables indicate that Lucy is responsible for Larry, Moe, and Curly, and that Ricky is responsible for Fred and Ethel. You may notice that for WJ1, Ricky supervised Larry, Moe, and Curly and for WJ2, Lucy supervised Fred and Ethel. This may seem disturbing to you given the association relationship; however, remember that the association relationship is independent of the agents' mutual participation in a cookie batch event. Ricky and Lucy can share information about the employees' performance; the responsibility relationship indicates that Lucy will officially evaluate Larry, Moe, and Curly and that Ricky will officially evaluate Fred and Ethel.

## Reciprocal Relationship

The **reciprocal relationship** in Exhibit 11–4 is the equivalent of duality only for the commitment events instead of for the economic events. The commitment for an economic increment event must be accompanied by a commitment for an economic decrement event to reflect the inherent nature of give and take in business processes. Production orders (the commitment to the economic increment event) triggers the requisitioning of materials (the commitment to one of the economic decrement events). If commitments to the labor operation and machine operations had been tracked, they would also be participants in the reciprocal link. The reciprocal relationship represents a schedule of what is to be produced and what will need to be used and consumed in the production. In Exhibit 11–5 a reciprocal relationship is depicted between the ingredient requisition and the baking order events. Exhibit 11–17 illustrates the relational tables that include the reciprocal relationship. In this case a foreign key of baking order ID is posted into the ingredient requisition table to represent the relationship. These tables indicate that requisition 1002 is related to baking order PO1 and requisition 1003 is related to baking order PO2.

**EXHIBIT 11–17**   Relational Database Tables for Reciprocal Relationship

**IngredientRequisition**

| RequisitionID | RequisitionDate | SupervisorID | BakingOrderID |
|---|---|---|---|
| 1002 | 7/14/2010 4:35:00 PM | S2 | PO1 |
| 1003 | 7/14/2010 4:35:30 PM | S1 | PO2 |
| 1004 | 7/15/2010 4:50:00 PM | S1 | PO3 |
| 1005 | 7/15/2010 4:51:00 PM | S1 | PO4 |
| 1006 | 7/15/2010 4:55:00 PM | S2 | PO5 |

**BakingOrder**

| BakingOrderID | BakingOrderDateTime | RequestedCompletion | SupervisorID |
|---|---|---|---|
| PO1 | 7/14/2010 4:30:00 PM | 7/15/2010 8:00:00 AM | S2 |
| PO2 | 7/14/2010 4:31:30 PM | 7/15/2010 8:00:00 AM | S1 |
| PO3 | 7/15/2010 4:45:00 PM | 7/16/2010 8:00:00 AM | S1 |
| PO4 | 7/15/2010 4:46:00 PM | 7/16/2010 8:00:00 AM | S1 |
| PO5 | 7/15/2010 4:50:00 PM | 7/16/2010 8:00:00 AM | S2 |

**EXHIBIT 11–18**
**Bill**
**of Materials**

| Bill of Materials _____ | | |
|---|---|---|
| Product ID _____ | | Standard batch quantity _____ |
| Product description _____ | | |
| **Material ID** | **Material description** | **Quantity needed** |
| | | |
| | | |
| | | |
| | | |
| | | |

## Linkage Relationships

The linkage relationships in Exhibit 11–4 and in Exhibit 11–5 provide a means for identifying the materials of which a finished good is composed and the types of labor needed to produce a finished good. Information about the linkage relationship between the materials and a finished good is often captured on a **bill of materials.** We show a bill of materials in Exhibit 11–18.

Information about the linkage relationship between labor types and finished goods is usually captured on an **operations list.** See an operations list document in Exhibit 11–19.

The relational tables shown in Exhibit 11–20 illustrate some of the attributes often stored with respect to the linkage relationships between raw materials and finished goods

**EXHIBIT 11–19**
**Operations List**

Operations List _____

Product ID _____                          Standard batch quantity _____

Description _____

| Work center | Labor type | Description | Standard time/unit | |
|---|---|---|---|---|
| | | | Setup | Processing |
| | | | | |
| | | | | |
| | | | | |
| | | | | |

**EXHIBIT 11–20    Relational Database Tables Encompassing the Linkage Relationships**

**LinkageIngredientsNeededForFinishedCookies**

| CookieTypeID | IngredientID | QuantityNeeded | UnitOfMeasure | CookieBatchSize |
|---|---|---|---|---|
| FSCS | CS | 0.25 | cup | 10 |
| FSCS | EG | 1 | each | 10 |
| FSCS | FL | 1.75 | cups | 10 |
| FSCS | ILFS | 1 | each | 10 |
| FSCS | PK | 1 | each | 10 |
| FSCS | SH | 0.5 | cup | 10 |
| FSCS | SL | 0.5 | teaspoon | 10 |
| FSCS | VN | 0.75 | teaspoon | 10 |
| FSCS | WS | 1 | cup | 10 |
| SN | CN | 3 | teaspoons | 12 |
| SN | EG | 1 | each | 12 |
| SN | FL | 1.5 | cups | 12 |
| SN | ILSN | 1 | each | 12 |
| SN | PK | 1 | each | 12 |
| SN | SH | 0.67 | cup | 12 |
| SN | SL | 0.5 | teaspoon | 12 |
| SN | VN | 1 | teaspoon | 12 |
| SN | WS | 1.5 | cups | 12  *(Continued)* |

and between labor and finished goods. Such information provides standards against which actual commitments and production may be compared for variance analyses and performance evaluations. The bills of materials and operations lists are typically used in the planning stages of the conversion process for made-to-stock finished goods. These documents are used to help in preparing the production order document that represents the commitment to the economic increment event.

**EXHIBIT 11–20**   (Continued)

**Ingredient**

| IngredientID | Description | UnitOfMeasure | StandardCostPerUnitOfMeasure |
|---|---|---|---|
| BS | Brown sugar | 50 lb bag | $9.47 |
| BU | Butter | 10 lb box | $3.98 |
| CM | Chocolate morsels | 10 lb bag | $19.49 |
| CN | Cinnamon | 16 oz tin | $3.29 |
| CS | Candy sprinkles | 1 lb tin | $3.18 |
| EG | Eggs, large AA grade | 2 dozen carton | $1.29 |
| FL | Flour, white sifted | 100 lb bag | $20.00 |
| ILFS | Ingredient label—frosted sugar | each | $0.01 |
| ILSN | Ingredient label—snickerdoodle | each | $0.01 |
| PB | Peanut butter | 10 lb jar | $8.37 |
| PE | Pecans | 2 lb bag | $5.32 |
| PK | Plastic container | each | $0.12 |
| SH | Shortening | 10 lb can | $12.10 |
| SL | Salt, iodized | 5 lb bag | $1.00 |
| VN | Vanilla, pure | 1 liter bottle | $20.00 |
| WS | White sugar | 50 lb bag | $10.00 |

**Finished Cookie Type**

| CookieID | Description | UnitsPerPackage | ListPrice | |
|---|---|---|---|---|
| CC | Chocolate chip plain | 12 | $2.99 | |
| CCP | Chocolate chip with pecans | 12 | $2.99 | |
| FSCS | Frosted sugar cookies with candy sprinkles | 10 | $3.59 | |
| M | Molasses | 12 | $3.29 | |
| OR | Oatmeal raisin | 12 | $2.99 | |
| PB | Peanut butter | 12 | $2.99 | |
| SC | Sugar cookies plain | 12 | $2.99 | |
| SN | Snickerdoodles | 12 | $3.59 | *(Continued)* |

In the linkage1 relationship table we can see the quantity of each ingredient needed to make a batch of 20 frosted sugar cookies and the quantity of each ingredient needed to make a batch of 24 snickerdoodles. The batch size used for the materials linkage relationship is an arbitrary choice depending on the needs of the enterprise. Some enterprises attempt to list the quantity needed to produce a single unit of the finished product. Such an approach would require us to divide each of the quantities in the linkage1 table by 20 for the frosted sugar cookies and by 24 for the snickerdoodles. Keeping the measurement at such a fine level of detail may not always be practical or useful. How do you divide an egg by 20 or 24? The linkage2 labor type relationship does not indicate a particular quantity of labor for each finished cookie type. However, such an attribute could be added as a standard to which actual labor use could be compared. If a quantity (e.g., number of minutes) of each labor type is indicated, a batch size also would need to be included similar to that shown for the linkage1 relationship table. In this example it was determined that although you could double the quantity of materials needed for a batch size that was twice as big and get a valid measure, you couldn't double the number of minutes for each labor type for a double-sized

**EXHIBIT 11–20** (Concluded)

**LaborType**

| LaborTypeID | Description |
| --- | --- |
| L1 | Mix dry ingredients |
| L10 | Take cookie sheet out of oven |
| L11 | Frost cookies |
| L12 | Sprinkle cookies |
| L13 | Package cookies |
| L2 | Mix moist ingredients |
| L3 | Combine dry and moist ingredients |
| L4 | Add morsels to mixed dough |
| L5 | Add nuts to mixed dough |
| L6 | Form dough into cookies |
| L7 | Put cookies onto cookie sheet |
| L8 | Put cookie sheet into oven |
| L9 | Set cookie timer |

**LinkageLaborNeededForFinishedCookieType**

| CookieTypeID | LaborTypeID |
| --- | --- |
| FSCS | L1 |
| FSCS | L10 |
| FSCS | L11 |
| FSCS | L12 |
| FSCS | L13 |
| FSCS | L2 |
| FSCS | L3 |
| FSCS | L6 |
| FSCS | L7 |
| FSCS | L8 |
| FSCS | L9 |
| SN | L1 |
| SN | L10 |
| SN | L13 |
| SN | L2 |
| SN | L3 |
| SN | L7 |
| SN | L8 |
| SN | L9 |

batch and get a meaningful number; therefore the attributes were not captured. In other words, if it takes 4 minutes to mix the dry ingredients (1 cup of white sugar, 1¾ cups of flour, and a ½ teaspoon of salt) to make a batch of 10 cookies, it will likely not take 16 minutes to mix the dry ingredients (4 cups of white sugar, 7 cups of flour, and 2 teaspoons of salt) to make a batch of 40 cookies. To help you make sense of the linkage relationships you can think of them as the two parts of a recipe. Recipes in a cookbook typically contain a list of the ingredients along with the quantities needed to make an identified quantity of a food dish. Recipes also include a list of steps needed to prepare the food dish.

# INFORMATION NEEDS AND MEASURES IN THE CONVERSION PROCESS

The most common information customers for the conversion process include top management, production personnel, accountants, and auditors. Typically no external information customers are directly associated with the conversion process. Results of the conversion process are summarized indirectly in various line items on financial statements prepared by accountants and made available to the public.

We next analyze each of the entities and relationships in the conversion process pattern to provide some ideas about the types of queries that satisfy information needs in the conversion process. The queries presented are not a comprehensive set of queries as there are simply too many potential queries to list them all; however, the set provided should guide you when creating similar types of queries. To describe example queries needed in the conversion process we use the database tables in Exhibits 11–6, 11–8, 11–10, 11–11, 11–13, 11–15, 11–16, 11–17, and 11–20.

## Resource Queries in the Conversion Process

The most common resources and resource types in the conversion process are raw materials inventory, labor type, machinery, and finished goods inventory. For each resource, users may need any of the following:

- Detailed status information at one or more points in time for each resource instance.
- Detailed status information at one or more points in time for only those resource instances meeting specified criteria.
- Summarized status information at one or more points in time for all resource instances.
- Summarized status information at one or more points in time for only those resource instances meeting specified criteria.

With regard to each of the above, users may need to know all characteristics of the instances in the answer set, or they may need only a subset of the characteristics.

Raw materials and finished goods inventory may be tracked at the type level and/or may be specifically identified; therefore, queries may be needed at either of those levels of detail. Labor is typically tracked only at the type level. Machinery and other operating assets are usually specifically identified, but may also be tracked at the category level. For example, most enterprises assign an identification tag to each operating asset that has a cost value exceeding a certain threshold; however, they also keep track of the category to which the asset belongs (i.e., furniture, computer equipment, or office equipment). Since the raw materials and machinery resources in the conversion process are the same as those acquired in the acquisition/payment process and the finished goods resources in the conversion process is the same as the inventory resources in the revenue process, any query that focuses solely on a resource table will be very similar to the resource queries displayed in Exhibits 8–21 and 8–22 in Chapter 8, and in Exhibits 9–19 and 9–20 in Chapter 9.

## Event Queries in the Conversion Process

Users may need information regarding events. The most common events in the conversion process are materials requisitions, materials issuances, labor operations, machine operations, production orders, and production runs. For each of these events, users may need any of the following:

- Detailed information about each event instance (i.e., what happened, when did it begin and end, at which workstation did it occur).
- Detailed information about each event instance that meets specified criteria (e.g., specific events that occurred during a specified time period or at a specified workstation).
- Summarized information for all instances of an event type for a specified time period (e.g., total of the event instances during a specified time period).
- Summarized information for only those instances of an event type for a specified time period that meet specified criteria (e.g., average dollar value of the event instances for a specified location during a specified time period).

Among many other possibilities, some information needs in the conversion process regarding events are

- Length of a specific production run (end time minus start time).
- Average length of the production runs within a specified time period.
- Total number of production runs that occurred at a specified plant or workstation or during a specified time period.
- Date and/or time an issuance of materials occurred.

From the event tables in the cookie manufacturing example (IngredientRequisition, BakingOrder, CookieBatch, IngredientIssuance, LaborOperation, and MachineOperation) some of the many specific queries that may be developed are

- *How long did it take to produce a specific batch of cookies?* Using the CookieBatch table, calculate the difference between the start time and the completion time for a specified batch.
- *Count the number of ingredient issuances that were made to Workcenter E.* Using the IngredientIssuance table, use the Count function to count the issuances for which the Location field is WorkcenterE.
- *When did the most recent ingredient requisition take place?* Using the IngredientRequisition table, use the Max function to identify the largest (most recent) date in the RequisitionDate field.
- *Which baking orders are requested for completion on a particular day?* Using the BakingOrder table, specify the desired day as a criterion by which to select the corresponding orders.
- *How many machine operations took longer than 14 minutes to complete?* Using the MachineOperation table, create an expression to calculate the difference in start and end times and then use the expression as a criterion by which to select the corresponding machine operations.

A caution before you try to do each of these example queries in Microsoft Access: The queries that involve calculations with date/time fields may not provide meaningful results because of the complexities of formatting the results; to make them meaningful involves use of Visual Basic code that is beyond the scope of most courses for which this textbook is appropriate. Therefore you may not want to try the queries that involve date/time calculations.

## Agent Queries in the Conversion Process

Because the conversion process does not typically involve external agents, the agent queries center on various types of employees. The employees commonly involved in conversion processes are production supervisors, production workers, and inventory clerks. Queries may be needed to obtain any of the following:

- Detailed status information at one or more points in time for each employee.
- Detailed status information at one or more points in time for each employee who meets specified criteria.
- Summarized status information at one or more points in time for all employees.
- Summarized status information at one or more points in time for all employees who meet specified criteria.

Because the agent tables in the cookie manufacturing example (BakingSupervisor, BakingEmployee, and InventoryClerk) only include employee IDs, names, and telephone numbers, not many queries can be constructed other than a list of employees and their telephone numbers. A complete database would typically include many other attributes of employees that could provide useful information for decision makers.

### *Relationship Queries*

Combining information from various resource, event, and agent tables in accordance with the relationships in which they participate can provide much richer data than single table queries. We next discuss queries based on the various types of relationships in the conversion process.

## Duality Relationship Queries in the Conversion Process

As explained earlier, duality relationships in conversion processes represent transformations rather than exchanges. Raw inputs are not exchanged for finished goods; rather they are converted into finished goods. The duality relationship connects **raw material issuances,** machine operations, and labor operations that use up the inputs to the production runs that produce the finished goods. Information needs with respect to duality relationships in conversion processes include (among other possibilities):

- Identification of labor operations related to one or more specified production runs.
- Identification of machine operations related to one or more specified production runs.
- Identification of raw material issuances related to one or more specified production runs.
- Calculation of the time taken for a labor (or machine) operation as a percentage of a complete production run.
- Count of the number of raw material issuances (or labor operations or machine operations) related to a specified production run.

For the cookie manufacturing example, duality queries could investigate

- Which labor operations (or machine operations or ingredient issuances) related to batch WJ1 and which related to batch WJ2?
- How many ingredient issuances were associated with each cookie batch?

- How much of the total production time for batch WJ1 consisted of machine operations and how much of the time consisted of labor operations?

As noted earlier, queries that calculate differences in date/time fields are very difficult to create successfully in Microsoft Access so we do not recommend you try the last query.

## Stockflow Relationship Queries in the Conversion Process

Stockflow relationships in the conversion process represent the use or consumption of input resources by economic decrement events and the production of finished good resources by economic increment events. Therefore stockflow relationships commonly are used in queries to identify the effect of economic events on resources or to identify the resources used up or produced by the economic events. Some common information needs that can be addressed by stockflow relationships in general are

- What resources or resource types were increased or decreased by an economic event?
- What quantity of a resource or resource type was increased or decreased by an economic event?
- What dollar value of a resource or resource type was increased or decreased by an economic event?
- When did an event increase or decrease a specific resource or resource type?
- Where did an event increase or decrease a specific resource or resource type?

These information needs may be addressed at a detailed level or they may be aggregated for groups of events and/or resources/resource types. The information may be used in isolation or used as part of a trend analysis to project future events and their expected effects on resources or resource types. Within the conversion process, some common stockflow information needs (among many other possibilities) are

- Which raw material types were decreased by a material issuance?
- What quantity of each raw material inventory type was decreased by a material issuance?
- What types of labor were used in a labor operation?
- What equipment was used (and/or for how long) in a machine operation?
- What finished goods were produced by a production run?
- What quantity of each finished good was produced by a production run?
- What is the standard unit cost of the raw materials used by a material issuance?

In the cookie manufacturing example, questions such as the following could be answered via stockflow relationship queries:

- *How long did it take to sprinkle the cookies in labor operation 28?* Because this involves a date/time calculation, you should not attempt this in Microsoft Access.

- *How many frosted sugar cookies with candy sprinkles were produced on July 15, 2010, and in which batches?* Join finished cookie type table to duality cookie batch-cookie type table using cookie type ID to determine which batches were for frosted sugar cookies with candy sprinkles. Join duality cookie batch-cookie type table to cookie batch table using batch ID, constrain date = 7/15/2010 and sum the actual quantity produced.

- *What kind of cookies were produced in batch WJ1?* Join finished cookie type table to duality batch-cookie type table using cookie type ID. Enter criteria =WJ1 in batch ID field and display the batch ID, cookie type ID, and cookie type description.
- *How many machine operations were necessary to make cookie batch WJ1?* Join machine operations table to DualityCookieBatchMachineOperation table; set criteria for batch ID − WJ1 and count the machine operations ID field.

## Fulfillment Queries in the Conversion Process

Fulfillment relationships in the conversion process represent associations between the production order and production run (the production run fulfills the production order) and between the materials (or labor or equipment) requisition and the materials issuance (or labor or machine operation). Fulfillment relationship queries in the conversion process in general include:

- Identification of unfilled commitment events (production orders for which production runs have not yet occurred, materials requisitions for which materials issuances have not yet occurred, and so on.)
- Identification of filled commitment events (production orders for which production runs have occurred, or materials requisitions for which materials issuances have occurred).
- Identification of economic events for which commitments were not made (production runs that were not ordered or material issuances that were not requisitioned).
- Calculation of length of time between commitment events and economic events (the length of time between production order and production run or between material requisition and material issuance).
- Identification of causes for economic events (which production order led to a production run or which material requisition led to a material issuance).
- Identification of results of commitment events (which production run fulfilled a production order or which material issuance fulfilled a material requisition).

In the cookie manufacturing example, questions such as the following could be answered via fulfillment relationship queries:

- *Has baking order PO4 been fulfilled?* Join BakingOrder table to CookieBatch table with an outer join keeping all baking orders; include bakingorder ID from BakingOrder table and batch ID from CookieBatch table; set criteria to select baking order =PO4.
- *Have any ingredient issuances occurred that were not related to ingredient requisitions?* Join IngredientIssuance table to IngredientIssuanceFulfillsIngredientRequisition table with an outer join keeping all ingredient issuances; include issuance ID from IngredientIssuance table and ingredient requisition number from IngredientIssuanceFulfillsIngredientRequisition table; set criteria to select null ingredient requisitions.
- *What is the average length of time between baking orders and cookie batches for this company?* Because this involves a date/time calculation, do not attempt this in Microsoft Access.
- *What baking order triggered cookie batch WJ2?* Join CookieBatch table to CookieBatchFulfillsBakingOrder table using cookie batch ID; include baking order ID; set criteria to select batch ID =WJ2.

## Reservation Queries in the Conversion Process

Reservation relationships in the conversion process represent associations between commitment events such as production orders and materials requisitions and the resources those events are committing to increase or decrease. Therefore reservation relationships are commonly used in queries to satisfy information needs as to the eventual effect of commitment events on resources or as to the resources involved in commitment events. Some common information needs in the conversion process are

- What finished good or finished good type is a production order agreeing to produce?
- What quantity of a finished good or finished good type is a production order agreeing to produce?
- What is the dollar value of the finished good or finished good type a production order is agreeing to produce?
- When did a production order commit to produce a specific finished good or finished good type?
- What material or material type is a materials requisition agreeing to use up?
- What quantity of each material type is a materials requisition agreeing to use up?
- What is the standard or actual unit cost for each material a materials requisition is agreeing to use up?
- When did a materials requisition commit to using up a material or material type?

In the cookie manufacturing example, questions such as the following could be answered via reservation relationship queries:

- *What kind of cookies is baking order PO5 agreeing to produce and when are they scheduled to be produced?* Join the ReservationBakingOrderFinishedCookie table to the FinishedCookieType and to the BakingOrder tables to see that PO5 is agreeing to produce molasses cookies by July 16, 2010, at 8:00 A.M.
- *How many peanut butter cookies are scheduled to be produced on July 16, 2010, and which production order represents the agreement to produce them?* Join ReservationBakingOrderFinishedCookie table to the FinishedCookieType and to the BakingOrder tables to determine that PO4 has scheduled 36 peanut butter cookies for production.
- *What are the descriptions of the ingredients scheduled to be used up by ingredient requisition 1002?* Join Ingredients table to ReservationIngredientRequisitionIngredient. Enter criteria =1002 in IngredientRequisitionID field and display the ingredient description.

## Participation Queries in the Conversion Process

Participation relationships in the conversion cycle typically represent the associations between production orders, materials requisitions, material issuances, machine operations, labor operations, and production runs and the employees who authorize those events (typically supervisors) and the employees who accomplish the events (typically production workers or inventory clerks). Therefore participation relationships are commonly used in queries to satisfy information needs to identify employees who participated in events or the events in which specified employees participated. Some common information needs are

- Which production supervisor authorized a machine operation?
- By how many production orders has a production employee been scheduled to work?

- How long did a production employee take to perform a labor operation?
- How many production orders have been authorized by a specific production supervisor?
- Which inventory clerk accomplished a materials issuance?

In the cookie manufacturing example, questions such as the following could be answered via participation relationship queries:

- *What is the name of the supervisor who authorized machine operation MO13?* Join the MachineOperation table to the BakingSupervisor table; enter criterion =MO13 in the MachineOperationID field and display the supervisor name field.
- *What are the names of the employees who were scheduled on baking order PO2?* Join the ParticipationBakingOrderBakingEmployee table to the BakingEmployee table; enter criterion =PO2 in the baking order ID field and display the employee name field.
- *What are the names and phone numbers of the inventory clerks who processed ingredient issuances RMI4240–RMI4245?* Join the IngredientIssuance table to the InventoryClerk table; enter criteria BETWEEN RMI4240 and RMI4245 in the ingredient issuance ID field and display the ClerkName and ClerkPhone fields.
- *How many production runs has Lucy supervised?* Join the CookieBatch table to the BakingSupervisor table; enter criterion =Lucy in the supervisor name field; enter aggregate function COUNT in the BatchID field.

## Linkage Queries in the Conversion Process

Linkage relationships in the conversion cycle typically represent the associations between finished goods and raw materials and also between finished goods and labor type. As described earlier, the information content within the linkage between finished goods and raw materials is often captured by enterprises on bill of materials documents, and the information content within the linkage between finished goods and labor types is often captured on operations list documents. Therefore queries encompassing the linkage relationships ask the same kind of questions that could be answered from one of those documents. Some examples are

- What raw materials are needed to produce a finished good or finished good type?
- What quantity of each raw material is needed to produce a finished good or finished good type?
- Which finished goods contain a specified raw material or a specified labor type?
- What labor types are needed to produce a finished good or finished good type?

In the cookie manufacturing example, questions such as the following could be answered via linkage relationship queries:

- *How much white sugar is needed to make a batch of snickerdoodles?* Join the FinishedCookieType, Ingredients, and Linkage tables; enter criteria =Snickerdoodles in the finished cookie type description field and =white sugar in the ingredient description field; display the quantity needed and unit of measure fields.
- *Which finished cookie types contain brown sugar?* Join the FinishedCookieType, Ingredients, and LinkageIngredientsInCookieType tables; enter criterion =brown sugar in the ingredient description field; display the finished cookie type description field.

- *Which finished cookie types require the labor type frost cookies?* Join the Finished-CookieType, LaborType, and LinkageLaborTypeNeededForFinishedCookieType tables; enter criterion =Frost cookies in labor type description field; display the finished cookie type description field.

## CONCLUDING COMMENTS

This chapter presented an overview of the activities in the conversion process and discussed the extended REA pattern as it applies to this process. Whether enterprises produce cereal, video games, furniture, or some other resource, the REA pattern for the necessary components of their conversion processes will be similar to each other. Designing an information system that supports the complexities and intricacies of a conversion process requires a careful analysis and a detailed understanding of the objectives of the process. Traditionally, organizations have generated multiple systems to support the conversion process. In fact, organizations often develop financial accounting systems and a variety of separate cost/managerial accounting systems. By using the REA ontology to design an integrated enterprise information system, organizations can derive financial statement information and other information needed to support a variety of programs (including activity-based costing, quality management, just-in-time inventories, and material requirements planning).

## Key Terms and Concepts

Bill of materials, *367*
Consume stockflow, *359*
Conversion process, *345*
Duality relationship, *348*
Economic decrement event, *348*
Economic increment event, *347*
Equipment, *349*
Finished goods, *345*
Fulfillment relationship, *363*
Job time ticket, *355*
Labor operation, *349*

Labor type, *355*
Linkage relationship, *361*
Machine operation, *349*
Move ticket, *353*
Operations list, *367*
Participation relationship, *348*
Production employee, *350*
Production order document, *360*
Production order event, *360*
Production run, *347*
Production supervisor, *363*

Raw material issuance, *373*
Raw materials, *349*
Raw materials requisition, *363*
Reciprocal relationship, *366*
Reservation relationship, *365*
Transfer duality relationship, *349*
Transformation duality relationship, *349*
Use stockflow relationship, *351*

## Review Questions

LO1    R1. What is the difference between a materials requisition and a purchase requisition?

LO1, LO2    R2. What is the primary objective of the conversion process?

LO3    R3. How is the conversion process related to the financing process, the human resource process, the acquisition/payment process, and the sales/collection process?

LO3  R4.  Identify the resources and agents associated with each of the following events in the conversion process:
  a.  Materials requisition (commitment to decrement)
  b.  Materials issuance (economic decrement)
  c.  Labor operation (economic decrement)
  d.  Machine operation (economic decrement)
  e.  Production order (commitment to increment)
  f.  Production run (economic increment)

LO5  R5.  Describe the information needed by each of the following in performing their role in the conversion process:
  a.  Management
  b.  Payroll
  c.  Accounting
  d.  Personnel

LO6  R6.  On which relationship in the conversion process would you base a query to calculate the time taken for a machine operation as a percentage of a complete production run?

LO6  R7.  What entities and/or relationships should you consider when creating a query to identify the quantity of each ingredient that was decreased by an ingredient issuance?

## Multiple Choice Questions

LO1, LO3  MC1.  Which document typically represents the same phenomena as the linkage relationship between raw materials and finished goods?
  A.  Operations list
  B.  Job time ticket
  C.  Bill of materials
  D.  Move ticket

LO3  MC2.  The conversion process represents the point of contact between the enterprise and which set of external business partners?
  A.  Investors and creditors
  B.  Suppliers
  C.  Customers
  D.  None—it is primarily an internal transaction cycle

LO3  MC3.  The resource typically made available by the conversion process to the sales/collection process in a typical enterprise value chain is
  A.  Raw materials inventory
  B.  Finished goods inventory
  C.  Employee labor
  D.  Cash

LO3  MC4.  Which of the following pairs of entities is typically found in a stockflow relationship in the conversion process?
  A.  Machine operation and machine
  B.  Materials requisition and materials
  C.  Materials requisition and production supervisor
  D.  Production run and production order

LO3   MC5.  Which of the following events reflects the commitment of the enterprise to produce one or more finished goods at a future point in time?

A.  Materials requisition
B.  Materials issuance
C.  Production run
D.  Production order

## Discussion Questions

LO3   D1.  How is the business process level pattern for the conversion cycle similar to the business process pattern for the revenue cycle? How are the two patterns different?

LO3   D2.  Explain the most likely points of integration between the acquisition/payment cycle and the conversion cycle business process level models.

LO2   D3.  Respond whether you agree or disagree with the following statement and explain why. "The conversion cycle business process level model for a company that crochets baby clothes would look very different from the conversion cycle business process level model for an automobile manufacturer, because obviously the steps and activities needed to produce baby clothes are very different from the steps and activities needed to produce automobiles."

LO3   D4.  Respond whether you agree or disagree with the following statement and explain why. "We can't use the REA pattern to model the business process level for the conversion cycle because it doesn't involve any exchanges with external agents."

LO3   D5.  Why are labor operations and labor types often tracked in the conversion process but usually not tracked in the revenue process?

LO2   D6.  How will the relational database table design differ for a company whose production run involves 10 distinct steps versus a company whose production run involves 35 distinct steps?

LO6   D7.  Consider the database tables in Exhibit 11–15. Describe the necessary procedures to construct one or more queries to determine what quantity (and unit of measure) of each ingredient Lucy requisitioned.

## Applied Learning

LO4   A1.  Marvelous Industries (MI) is a company that creates specialty plaques to commemorate marvelous occasions such as the Olympic games, bicentennial celebrations, and victorious athletic teams' seasons. Most of its business centers on victorious athletic teams' seasons at all levels, from professional and college all the way down to preschool. Some of the plaques it creates are requested by customers and are tailored to customer specifications (especially the smaller quantities needed for preschool through high school teams or occasions); most plaques are made to stock specifications and apply to collegiate and professional sports. For example, MI created specialty plaques to commemorate the Florida State University's 1999 football national championship. One plaque featured an image of Peter Warrick reaching to grab a pass in the end zone that was a key touchdown in the championship game. Another plaque featured an image of Coach Bobby Bowden raising the championship trophy in triumph and also included the team schedule and score summary. There were several other styles that included images in various themes such as team in action, star players, posed team, and coach in action.

When MI began doing business, the controller determined through various analyses that it was cost beneficial to purchase all of the raw materials rather than to manufacture them in-house. The raw materials MI starts with include unfinished, unstained plaques in various sizes and shapes, stain, paint, matting and mounting material, prints (images), and finishing varnish. The plaques, stain, paint, matting/mounting materials, and finishing varnish are purchased from wholesalers. Because the nature of the various kinds of raw materials is quite different (thus resulting in different attributes) and they are used in different parts of the production process, MI has chosen to keep each of these categories as different entities. Prints (images) are purchased from various photographers and other sources (or sometimes provided by the customer for customized orders). We omit the design layout process and associated costs in this case for simplicity sake.

MI's manufacturing process has three phases; one production order prepared by a production supervisor initiates and authorizes activities for all three phases. Each phase is primarily manual; although hand tools are used, their cost is so immaterial that their consumption is not tracked. Also, MI wants to track what type of labor is involved for each work in progress job (e.g., stain plaque, paint plaque, cut matting material, mount print, and so on), but does not want to track individual labor operations. In phase one, a plaque preparation supervisor requisitions unfinished plaques from the warehouse to be used in a staining or painting job. An inventory clerk processes the requisition and issues the plaques to the staining or painting job where they are received by the preparation supervisor. The preparation supervisor also requisitions stain and/or paint and these requisitions are processed in the same manner as the unfinished plaque requisitions. The plaques are stained or painted a color appropriate to the theme created in that particular job. Each job consists of the production of multiple copies of the same plaque design. Usually the stain or paint for an athletic team is one of the team colors. For Florida State's championship season many of the plaques were stained with the color garnet; others were painted gold. A preparation supervisor issues the prepared plaques to an assembly supervisor, who receives them into an assembly job. An assembly supervisor requisitions images and any matting and mounting materials needed for the plaque style from the warehouse. An inventory clerk processes the requisition and issues the requested materials to the assembly job where they are received by the assembly supervisor. Assembly production employees complete the assembly job and upon completion an assembly supervisor issues the assembled plaques to a finishing supervisor who receives them into a finishing job. A finishing supervisor requisitions finishing varnish to be used in the finishing job. An inventory clerk processes the requisition and issues the finishing varnish to the finishing job where it is received by the finishing supervisor. Finishing production employees complete the finishing job, after which the finished plaques are transferred to the sales warehouse.

### Required

1. Create a partial value chain that illustrates each of the three phases of the conversion process as if they are separate cycles (i.e., include a separate circle with duality-linked

events in it for each phase and illustrate all resource inputs and outputs). For resources that come from or go to other processes (such as acquisition and sales cycles) draw an arrow in the appropriate direction, label it with the resource name, and note which cycle is its source or destination.

2. Create a business process level REA diagram in entity-relationship format for the preparation phase. Please be sure to label all entities and all relationships, and assign attributes to the entities and relationships from the following list.

3. Create a business process level REA diagram in entity-relationship format for the finishing phase. Please be sure to label all entities and all relationships, and assign attributes to the entities and relationships from the following list.

The following attributes need to be accounted for in your solution

Assembled plaque ID **(AP-ID)**

Assembled plaque issuance ID **(AP-Iss-ID)**

Assembly job number **(Assmb-Job#)**

Color of a prepared plaque **(Pp-color)**

Color of stain or paint **(Color)**

Date of materials requisition **(Date-Req)**

Date production order was prepared **(PO-Date)**

Date/time stamp an assembly job is completed **(Comp-AJ)**

Date/time stamp an assembly job is started **(AJ-Start)**

Date/time stamp a finishing job is completed **(Comp-FJ)**

Date/time stamp a finishing job is started **(FJ-Start)**

Date/time stamp a preparation job is completed **(PJ-Comp)**

Date/time stamp a preparation job is started **(Start-PJ)**

Date/time stamp for issuance of assembled plaques to a finishing job **(AP-Iss-Time)**

Date/time stamp for issuance of finishing varnish to a finishing job **(FV-Iss-Time)**

Date/time stamp for issuance of matting/mounting materials to an assembly job **(MM-Iss-Time)**

Date/time stamp for issuance of unfinished plaques to a preparation job **(UP-Iss-Time)**

Date/time stamp for issuance of images to an assembly job **(Im-Iss-Time)**

Date/time stamp of prepared plaque issuance **(Time-PP-Iss)**

Date/time stamp of stain/paint issuance **(Time-SP-Iss)**

Description of an assembled plaque **(Ap-desc)**

Description of a finished plaque **(Fp-desc)**

Description of a labor type **(LT-Desc)**

Description of matting/mounting material **(MM-Desc)**

Finished plaque ID **(FP-ID)**

Finishing job number **(Fin-Job#)**

Finishing varnish ID **(FV-ID)**

Finishing varnish issuance ID **(FV-Iss-ID)**

Image ID **(Imag-ID)**

Image issuance ID **(Im-Iss-ID)**

Inventory clerk ID **(IC-ID)**

Labor type ID **(LT-ID)**

Luster of finishing varnish **(FV-Luster)**

Materials requisition ID **(Req-ID)**

Matting/Mounting material ID **(MM-ID)**

Matting/mounting material issuance ID **(MM-Iss-ID)**

Name of inventory clerk **(name-ic)**

Name of production employee **(PE-name)**

Name of supervisor **(name-super)**

Preparation job number **(Prep-Job#)**

Prepared plaque ID **(PP-ID)**

Prepared plaque issuance ID **(PP-Iss-ID)**

Production employee ID **(PE-ID)**

Production order ID **(Prod-Ord-ID)**

Quantity of assembled plaques used in a finishing job **(Qty-used-ap)**

Quantity of each unfinished plaque type requested on a requisition **(UP-Qty-Req)**

Quantity of each stain/paint type requested on a requisition **(SP-Qty-Req)**

Quantity of each matting/mounting material type requested on a requisition **(Qty-Req-MM)**

Quantity of finishing varnish type used in a finishing job **(FV-qty-used)**

Quantity of matting/mounting material type used in an assembly job **(MM-qty-used)**

Quantity of prepared plaques used in an assembly job **(Qty-used-pp)**

Quantity of stain/paint used in a preparation job **(Qty-used-sp)**

Quantity of unfinished plaques used in a preparation job **(Qty-used-up)**

Requested completion date for a job on a production order **(Due-Date-PO)**

Shape of a prepared plaque **(Pp-shape)**

Shape of an unfinished plaque **(Shape-up)**

Size of an image **(Im-Size)**

Size of a prepared plaque **(Size-pp)**

Size of an unfinished plaque **(Size-up)**

Stain or paint ID **(SP-ID)**

Stain/paint issuance ID **(SP-Iss-ID)**

Standard cost of a matting/mounting material **(Std-Cost-MM)**

Standard cost of an unfinished plaque **(Std-Cost-up)**

Standard cost per gallon for finishing varnish **(Std-Cost-FV)**

Standard cost per gallon for stain or paint **(Std-Cost-SP)**

Suggested retail price for a finished plaque **(SRP)**

Supervisor ID **(Super-ID)**

Theme for an image (e.g., team in action, posed team) **(Theme)**

Type of wood from which an unfinished plaque is made **(Wood-type)**

Unfinished plaque ID **(UP-ID)**

Unfinished plaque issuance ID **(UP-Iss-ID)**

## Answers to Multiple Choice Questions

MC1. C; MC2. D; MC3. B; MC4. A; MC5. D.

# Chapter **Twelve**

# The Human Resource Business Process

## LEARNING OBJECTIVES

The objectives of this chapter are to introduce the human resource business process, to discuss the REA ontology representation of human resource processes, and to describe some of the typical information needs in the human resource business process. After studying this chapter you should be able to:

1. Identify the activities and documents common to most human resource business processes
2. Explain the various components of the REA ontology in the human resource process
3. Create a REA business process level model for an enterprise's human resource process
4. Identify common information needs that exist within the human resource process
5. Create database queries to retrieve human resource process information from a relational database

## HUMAN RESOURCE BUSINESS PROCESS IN AN ENTERPRISE VALUE SYSTEM

The human resource process (also called the payroll cycle) encompasses all of the activities needed to acquire and pay for **employee** labor. Although the specific workflow activities differ in various enterprises' human resource processes, we discuss the pattern for the information system's base objects that has been identified as common to most payroll cycles. Activities in the human resource process include hiring, **training,** evaluating, terminating, and paying employees for their labor, knowledge, and skills. Often these activities are separated into two subprocesses: personnel and payroll. The personnel function hires, trains, evaluates, and terminates employees. The payroll function disburses payments to employees. In this chapter, we use the terms *human resource process* and *payroll cycle* as synonyms, so please don't confuse payroll cycle with the payroll function that is a subset of the cycle as a whole.

The human resource process is in essence a special case of the acquisition/payment cycle. The personnel function acquires and maintains employee labor and the payroll function pays for employee labor. Because the acquisition of and payment for goods and outside services often results in different information needs than the acquisition of and payment for labor, both with respect to the types of resources acquired and the types of agents from whom they are acquired, the payroll cycle is usually kept separate from the acquisition/payment cycle.

As you analyze and model a business process, you must clearly understand its purpose and objectives. You must realize how the business process fits into the value system and enterprise value chain. At the value system level, the human resource process is the point of contact between the enterprise and its employees. At this point of contact, the employees are external business partners to the enterprise; in other words they are engaging in arm's-length exchanges. Whereas in other business processes we have considered employees as internal agents, in the human resource process the only employees we consider as internal agents are those whose job functions involve processing payroll (and notice that those employees are also members of the external agent employee entity set with respect to their own provision of labor to the enterprise).

At arm's length, the enterprise gives cash to the employees in exchange for the employees' labor as highlighted in Exhibit 12–1. Actually, along with their labor (described as time worked at a particular wage rate), the employees also provide knowledge and skills to the enterprise. However, the enterprise usually does not end up owning the **employees' knowledge and skills** so we must assume measurements of the knowledge and skills are encompassed in the wage rate and time worked. Today many enterprises are attempting to develop techniques for owning employees' skills and knowledge so that those can be separated to some extent from the simple time-worked construct. To accomplish this, enterprises are creating knowledge bases and artificial intelligence based decision support systems in which to store the knowledge and procedural decision-making processes of its most valuable knowledge-intensive employees. Although significant progress has been made in the area of knowledge bases and decision support systems, most information systems still can measure labor acquisition only as time worked.

The value chain reveals interfaces between the payroll process and other business processes. In Exhibit 12–2 we illustrate the typical value chain interfaces.

**EXHIBIT 12–1**
**Human Resource Process in the Enterprise Value System**

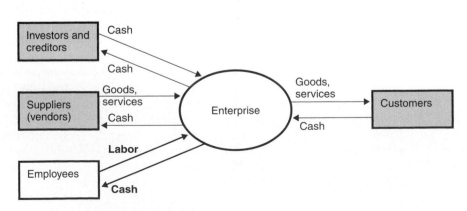

**EXHIBIT 12–2**
**Human Resource Process in the Value Chain**

Partial Value Chain

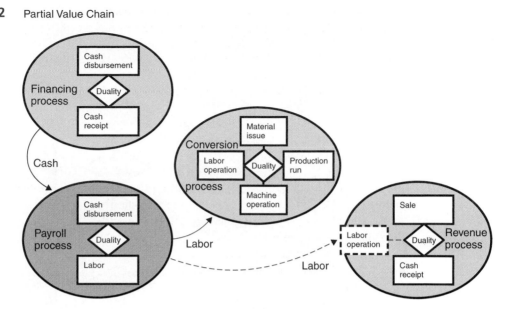

Notice that the solid arrows of Exhibit 12–2 only depict the human resource process making labor available to the conversion process. In many companies the conversion cycle is the only process wherein the use of labor is tracked at a specific enough level to justify including it at the value chain level. If we specifically track labor use in another business process we would similarly show labor as an output of payroll and as an input to the other process. The dashed arrow illustrates the value chain depiction of labor made available to the revenue process in which the specific use of that labor is included as an **economic decrement event.** A similar depiction would be used for labor that is specifically tracked in the acquisition/payment and/or financing processes.

The primary objective of the human resource process is to provide the human labor and expertise the enterprise needs to function efficiently and effectively. Because employees' labor is a valuable asset for many enterprises, it is important to model its acquisition and payment as correctly and completely as possible in a cost effective manner. We begin our business process level discussion of the payroll cycle by reviewing some of its more common events. Two important reminders before we begin the discussion: Because we discuss the activities in a sequential fashion, it may seem that the human resource process is linear. That is not necessarily true. Increasingly, business processes and the activities that comprise those processes are dynamic, rather than linear and static. Also, remember that the activities in this process are linked to and sometimes overlap activities in other processes. We are concentrating on one process at a time to simplify our analysis.

## HUMAN RESOURCE BUSINESS PROCESS LEVEL REA MODELS

Recall that the extended REA ontology described in Chapter 4 and illustrated in Exhibit 12–3 identifies the pattern underlying each transaction cycle, which consists of instigation

**EXHIBIT 12–3** **Payroll Cycle Extended REA Ontology Database Design Pattern**

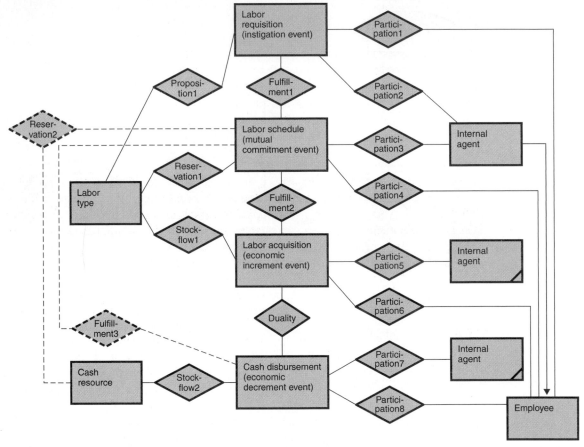

Note 1: This diagram does not attempt to differentiate internal agents for the different events; for some enterprises one category of employee may participate in all these events; for others there may be several different categories of employee involved. For most enterprises, labor requisitions, labor schedules, and labor acquisitions are the responsibility of department supervisors and cash disbursements for labor are the responsibility of payroll clerks.

Note 2: Reservation2 and Fulfillment3 are shown with dashed lines to indicate that they often are excluded from the model because the expenditure-generating activity (i.e., the economic increment event) is often a more reliable cash flow budget factor than is the mutual commitment event.

Note 3: The generalization relationship indicated with the arrow between internal agent and employee indicates the internal agents are a subset of the employee entity.

Note 4: The diagonal slash in the bottom right corner of an entity indicates the entity is a copy of an entity that was already used elsewhere on the diagram. It is used to help avoid crossing too many lines and thereby creating confusion in an entity-relationship diagram).

events, mutual commitment events, economic exchange events, resources, agents, types, and various relationships such as stockflow, duality, fulfillment, reservation, proposition, and participation. In this section we describe the extended REA ontology components specific to the human resource business process.

We remind you that instigation events and the relationships in which they participate (such as proposition) are not part of the published REA ontology. We have added them to the business process level models in this text as a convenient means of fleshing out the complete story of each business process: A proposal is made in the instigation event. The proposal is acted upon and a mutual agreement is reached in the commitment event.

The mutual commitment is fulfilled by the economic events that comprise the exchange of resources. These base objects exist in every cycle for every enterprise; however, it may not be cost effective to measure and store the details of all these phases.

The *REA* pattern aids in analyzing business processes and events by highlighting the *what* (the resources involved in the event) and the *who* (the internal and external agents) of each event. Notice that the *where* and the *when* often are stored as attributes of each event. The events, agents, and resources involved in the human resource process vary somewhat from enterprise to enterprise. The general pattern discussed in this chapter can be adapted easily and applied to meet the exact requirements of any enterprise (e.g., nonprofit or governmental agencies, wholesalers, retailers, service providers, or manufacturers).

## Resources

Human capital is the resource acquired in the human resource process. Human capital is made up of the work employees perform and the knowledge and skills employees use in performing that work. Because human capital is mostly intangible, it is very difficult to measure. Ownership is also difficult to establish, as discussed earlier in this chapter. If we could resolve the ownership and measurement issues, then we would directly represent the human capital resource as an entity in an enterprise's business process level model. Instead, we typically substitute an entity called labor type. The **labor type resource** entity serves as an inventory of the kinds of labor an enterprise may need to acquire and use in its operations. The attributes typically captured to represent labor types include an identifier, a description, and a standard (budgeted) hourly wage rate for that type of labor.

Cash is the resource given in exchange for labor. Cash in the payroll cycle is typically represented by the cash accounts from which **paychecks** are written. Paychecks usually are written from either a regular checking account or an imprest checking account. An imprest checking account normally maintains a zero balance. For example, when the amount of cash disbursements needed for a payroll period is determined, a company that uses an imprest checking account transfers the total amount of the paychecks from one of its regular checking accounts to its imprest account. Paychecks to each specific employee are drawn on the imprest checking account. As time passes, if the imprest account balance is positive, that indicates employees are not all cashing their paychecks. If the imprest account balance becomes negative, a mistake likely occurred. Either situation warrants investigation. Attributes typically captured to represent the set of cash accounts include an identifier, type, description, and location of each account. If financial institutions such as banks or credit unions maintain most of the cash accounts, then the account numbers assigned by the financial institutions also need to be captured. Cash account balance is an example of a volatile derivable attribute for which a stored query may be created and reused for quick retrieval.

## Instigation Events—Need Identification and Request for Labor

Supervisors determine the need for labor by monitoring enterprise growth (or lack thereof), production plans, sales forecasts, employee turnover, and other trends and projections. Identification of a need for labor often is labeled as a labor requisition event as shown in Exhibit 12–3. Labor requests occur on an ongoing basis as part of normal operations and involve identification of the number of hours (or some similar basis) existing employees are needed to provide specific types of labor. The labor requisition event is fulfilled by the scheduling of one or more employees to provide that labor.

**EXHIBIT 12–4**   **Document for Labor Requisition Event: Staffing Plan**

Your Source Company
Staffing Plan ___7___
For Period April 1, 2010–April 7, 2010

Date Plan Approved ___2/24/2010___                                    Approved by ___E5___

| Labor type | Quantity of Labor Needed (in hours) | | | | | | | | Std Wage Rate | Ext. Amount |
|---|---|---|---|---|---|---|---|---|---|---|
| | 4/1 | 4/2 | 4/3 | 4/4 | 4/5 | 4/6 | 4/7 | Total | | |
| CT2 Cashier duties | 16 | 16 | 16 | 16 | 16 | 0 | 0 | 80 | $10.00 | $800.00 |
| US3 Cleaning/janitorial | 8 | 8 | 8 | 8 | 8 | 12 | 0 | 52 | $6.00 | $312.00 |
| AP1 Sales tax preparation | 12 | 12 | 12 | 12 | 12 | 0 | 0 | 60 | $15.00 | $900.00 |
| CT1 Data entry | 12 | 12 | 12 | 12 | 12 | 12 | 12 | 84 | $9.00 | $756.00 |
| Totals | 48 | 48 | 48 | 48 | 48 | 24 | 12 | 276 | | $2,768.00 |

List IDs and names of any requested employees here, as well as for what type of labor

___E23 James Worthwhile for tax preparation___

Agents involved in instigation events in the payroll cycle usually are department supervisors (internal agents who authorize the requisition) and employees (external agents whose skills and knowledge are the subject of the request). As noted earlier, because labor is intangible usually it is measured via categories and is specified as a labor type. Attributes of labor requisitions that typically should be captured include the date and time of the requisition. The requisition event data should be linked to data regarding the related supervisor, requested employees (if any are specified), and the type of labor requested. Documentation of need identification for labor may vary widely. Although theoretically we could expect to see a labor requisition form that looks much like a purchase requisition form as shown in the acquisition/payment cycle chapter, not many enterprises use such forms for routine labor need identification. Indeed, most need for labor is identified by department supervisors who themselves also approve the request based on their own department's **budget.** The most commonly used form of documentation on which a department supervisor may communicate the department's need for labor for a specified time period is a staffing plan that has identified the types and quantities of labor needed but has not assigned specific employees to the **schedule.** Exhibit 12–4 illustrates such a plan.

The set of relational tables illustrated in Exhibit 12–5 correspond to Exhibit 12–3's entity-relationship representation of the labor requisition event, the relationships in which it participates (proposition, fulfillment1, participation1, and participation2), and the related entities (labor type, labor schedule, department supervisor, and employee). Alternative tables could be derived depending on the relationship cardinalities. Data from the form in Exhibit 12–4 have been entered into the database tables; however, some of these data

**EXHIBIT 12–5**  **Relational Tables Encompassing Labor Requisition Event (partial data)**

**LaborRequisition (Instigation) Event**

| LaborReqID | Date | Maximum Budget for Request | Total Estimated Budget Request | Labor Request Period | SuperID<sup>FK</sup> |
|---|---|---|---|---|---|
| LR7 | 2/24/2010 | $3,000.00 | $2,768.00 | 4/1/2010–4/7/2010 | E5 |

**Proposition Relationship**

| LaborReqID | LaborTypeID | Hours Needed | Estimated Hourly Wage |
|---|---|---|---|
| LR7 | CT2 | 80 | $10.00 |
| LR7 | US3 | 52 | $6.00 |
| LR7 | AP1 | 60 | $15.00 |
| LR7 | CT1 | 84 | $9.00 |

**ParticipationLaborRequisitionEmployee (Participation1) Relationship**

| LaborReqID | Requested EmployeeID |
|---|---|
| LR7 | E23 |

**DepartmentSupervisor (Internal Agent)**

| SuperID | Authorized Spending Limit |
|---|---|
| E5 | $425,000 |

**Employee (External Agent)**

| EmpID | Name | Address | Telephone | DateOfBirth | Rating | Position | Type | Wage |
|---|---|---|---|---|---|---|---|---|
| E5 | Patrick Wellesley | 53125 Fenton Dr. | 555-1112 | March 4, 1958 | Excellent | Supervisor | Salary | $35.50 |
| E15 | Donna Davis | 149 Rovetta Dr. | 555-9932 | Feb. 3, 1954 | Superior | Cashier | Hourly | $10.50 |
| E16 | Nancy Hardaway | 271 Rovetta Dr. | 555-2117 | June 11, 1956 | Excellent | Cashier | Hourly | $9.75 |
| E17 | Joe Thompson | 535 Olson St. | 555-2277 | Apr. 24, 1947 | Excellent | Custodian | Hourly | $6.20 |
| E18 | Freda Matthews | 3214 Deerlake St. | 555-1222 | Aug. 6, 1940 | Good | Custodian | Hourly | $5.90 |
| E19 | John Matthews | 3214 Deerlake St. | 555-1222 | Oct. 14, 1940 | Good | Custodian | Hourly | $5.90 |
| E20 | Paula Cosgrove | 5006 Jazz Ct. | 555-5200 | Apr. 18, 1958 | Excellent | Data Entry | Hourly | $8.50 |
| E21 | Rob Fordham | 4444 Zephyr Ln. | 555-4545 | June 4, 1975 | Excellent | Data Entry | Hourly | $9.00 |
| E22 | Francis Johnson | 1261 Mason Dr. | 555-0129 | May 5, 1980 | Good | Data Entry | Hourly | $8.25 |
| E23 | James Worthwhile | 5432 Wadsworth Ln | 555-7777 | Apr. 14, 1964 | Superior | Accountant | Salary | $15.00 |
| E36 | Diane Bowersox | 9115 Wolfgang Ct | 555-7244 | Sept 15, 1963 | Superior | Payroll | Hourly | $8.75 |

**LaborType (Resource Type)**

| Item ID | Description | Standard Hourly Wage |
|---|---|---|
| CT2 | Cashier duties | $10.00 |
| US3 | Clean sales showroom and stockroom | $6.00 |
| AP1 | Prepare quarterly sales tax return | $15.00 |
| CT1 | Enter data for sales transactions | $9.00 |

**LaborSchedule (Mutual Commitment) Event**

| Labor ScheduleID | Date Schedule Approved | Begin Date | End Date | Total Dollar Amt | LaborReqID<sup>FK</sup> | SuperID<sup>FK</sup> |
|---|---|---|---|---|---|---|
| | | | | | | |

Note: Fulfillment1 relationship is implemented with LaborReqID posted into Labor Schedule table. Participation2 relationship is implemented with SuperID posted into Requisition table. Fulfillment1 data are not yet entered, assuming a time lag between requisition and schedule.

(e.g., labor type and employee information) would have existed already in the database tables before the requisition data were added to the tables so only the relationship information that links them to the event is recorded for those objects. New data that would be entered as a result of the labor requisition event are shown in color.

## Mutual Commitment Event (Labor Schedule)

A mutual commitment event exists when an enterprise and an external business partner have each agreed to exchange specified quantities of resources at a defined future time. In the payroll process a labor schedule serves as a mutual commitment event. An employee schedule is typically prepared by a supervisor with inputs from the employee as to when the employee is and is not available to work. This is similar to a purchase agent's preparation of a purchase order with input from a supplier as to the availability of goods or services. The employee schedule represents a commitment by the employee to provide the labor as specified and a commitment by the enterprise to pay the employee the contracted wage rate for the labor provided. If the employee does not work his or her scheduled hours, (as when a supplier doesn't fill a purchase order for goods) the enterprise is not obligated to pay for those hours not worked.

Attributes of labor schedule events that typically should be captured include the date the schedule was approved, the total dollar amount to which the schedule commits, and the time period covered by the schedule (often in the form of a beginning date and an ending date). The labor schedule should also be linked to data regarding the related labor types, employees, supervisor, **labor acquisition event,** and labor requisition event. Data regarding labor schedule events are often captured on a form such as that shown in Exhibit 12–6. This form may be either a paper document, an electronic spreadsheet, or part of a software application interface that is used to update the enterprise database.

The set of relational tables in Exhibit 12–7 correspond to Exhibit 12–3's entity-relationship representation of the labor schedule event and the relationships in which it

**EXHIBIT 12–6** Labor Schedule

Your Source Company
Employee Schedule ___7___
For Period April 1, 2010–April 7, 2010

Date Schedule Approved __3/4/2010_____                Approved by __E5_____

| Empl ID | Name | 4/1/10 | 4/2/10 | 4/3/10 | 4/4/10 | 4/5/10 | 4/6/10 | 4/7/10 | Total hours |
|---------|------|--------|--------|--------|--------|--------|--------|--------|-------------|
| E15 | Donna Davis | 7–4 | 7–4 | 7–4 | 7–4 | 7–4 | | | 40 |
| E16 | Nancy Hardaway | 9–6 | 9–6 | 9–6 | 9–6 | 9–6 | | | 40 |
| E17 | Joe Thompson | 7–4 | 7–4 | 7–4 | 7–4 | 7–4 | | | 40 |
| E18 | Freda Matthews | | | | | | 7–2 | | 6 |
| E19 | John Matthews | | | | | | 7–2 | | 6 |
| E20 | Paula Cosgrove | 9–1 | 9–1 | 9–1 | 9–1 | 9–1 | 9–1 | 9–1 | 28 |
| E21 | Rob Fordham | 8–5 | 8–5 | 8–5 | 8–5 | 8–5 | | | 40 |
| E22 | Francis Johnson | | | | | | 8–5 | 8–5 | 16 |
| E23 | James Worthwhile | 8–8 | 8–8 | 8–8 | 8–8 | 8–8 | | | 60 |

**EXHIBIT 12–7**   **Relational Tables Encompassing Labor Schedule Event (partial data)**

**LaborSchedule (Mutual Commitment) Event**

| Labor ScheduleID | Date Schedule Approved | Begin Date | End Date | Total Dollar Amt | LaborReqID^FK | SuperID^FK |
|---|---|---|---|---|---|---|
| LS7 | 3/4/2010 | 4/1/2010 | 4/7/2010 | $2,758.80 | LR7 | E5 |

**LaborRequisition (Instigation) Event**

| LaborReqID | Date | Maximum Budget for Request | Estimated Budget for Request | Labor Request Period | SuperID^FK |
|---|---|---|---|---|---|
| LR7 | 2/24/2010 | $3,000.00 | $2,768.00 | 4/1/2010–4/7/2010 | E5 |

**ReservationLaborScheduleLaborType (Reservation1) Relationship**

| LaborScheduleID | LaborTypeID | HoursScheduled |
|---|---|---|
| LS7 | CT2 | 80 |
| LS7 | US3 | 52 |
| LS7 | AP1 | 60 |
| LS7 | CT1 | 84 |

**ParticipationLaborScheduleEmployee (Participation4) Relationship**

| LaborScheduleID | Scheduled EmployeeID | Hours Scheduled | Wage Rate |
|---|---|---|---|
| LS7 | E15 | 40 | $10.50 |
| LS7 | E16 | 40 | $9.75 |
| LS7 | E17 | 40 | $6.20 |
| LS7 | E18 | 6 | $5.90 |
| LS7 | E19 | 6 | $5.90 |
| LS7 | E20 | 28 | $8.50 |
| LS7 | E21 | 40 | $9.00 |
| LS7 | E22 | 16 | $8.25 |
| LS7 | E23 | 60 | $15.00 |

**DepartmentSupervisor (Internal Agent)**

| SuperID | Authorized Spending Limit |
|---|---|
| E5 | $425,000 |

*(Continued)*

participates (reservation1, fulfillment1, fulfillment2, participation3, and participation4). Other possible tables could be derived, depending on the relationship cardinalities. Data from the form in Exhibit 12–6 have been entered into the database tables; however, some of these data (e.g., labor type, supervisor, and employee information) would already have existed in the database tables before the labor schedule data were added to the tables so only the relationship information that links them to the labor schedule should be added for those objects. The new data entered to record the labor schedule event are shown in color.

## Economic Increment Event (Labor Acquisition)

Labor acquisition is the primary **economic increment event** in the human resource process. This event represents the provision of labor to an enterprise by an employee. Each

**EXHIBIT 12–7** (Concluded)

**Employee (External Agent)**

| EmpID | Name | Address | Telephone | DateOfBirth | Rating | Position | Type | Wage |
|---|---|---|---|---|---|---|---|---|
| E5 | Patrick Wellesley | 53125 Fenton Dr. | 555-1112 | March 4, 1958 | Excellent | Supervisor | Salary | $35.50 |
| E15 | Donna Davis | 149 Rovetta Dr. | 555-9932 | Feb. 3, 1954 | Superior | Cashier | Hourly | $10.50 |
| E16 | Nancy Hardaway | 271 Rovetta Dr. | 555-2117 | June 11, 1956 | Excellent | Cashier | Hourly | $9.75 |
| E17 | Joe Thompson | 535 Olson St. | 555-2277 | Apr. 24, 1947 | Excellent | Custodian | Hourly | $6.20 |
| E18 | Freda Matthews | 3214 Deerlake St. | 555-1222 | Aug. 6, 1940 | Good | Custodian | Hourly | $5.90 |
| E19 | John Matthews | 3214 Deerlake St. | 555-1222 | Oct. 14, 1940 | Good | Custodian | Hourly | $5.90 |
| E20 | Paula Cosgrove | 5006 Jazz Ct. | 555-5200 | Apr. 18, 1958 | Excellent | Data Entry | Hourly | $8.50 |
| E21 | Rob Fordham | 4444 Zephyr Ln. | 555-4545 | June 4, 1975 | Excellent | Data Entry | Hourly | $9.00 |
| E22 | Francis Johnson | 1261 Mason Dr. | 555-0129 | May 5, 1980 | Good | Data Entry | Hourly | $8.25 |
| E23 | James Worthwhile | 5432 Wadsworth Ln | 555-7777 | Apr. 14, 1964 | Superior | Accountant | Salary | $15.00 |
| E36 | Diane Bowersox | 9115 Wolfgang Ct | 555-7244 | Sept 15, 1963 | Superior | Payroll | Hourly | $8.75 |

**LaborType (Resource Type)**

| Item ID | Description | Standard Hourly Wage |
|---|---|---|
| CT2 | Cashier duties | $10.00 |
| US3 | Clean sales showroom and stockroom | $6.00 |
| AP1 | Prepare quarterly sales tax return | $15.00 |
| CT1 | Enter data for sales transactions | $9.00 |

**FulfillmentLaborAcquisitionLaborSchedule (Fulfillment2) Relationship**

**LaborScheduleID LaborAcquisitionID**

Note: Participation3 relationship is implemented with SuperID posted into the Labor Schedule table. Fulfillment1 relationship is implemented with RequisitionID posted into Labor Schedule table. Fulfillment2 data are not yet entered, assuming a time lag between schedule and labor acquisition.

instance typically covers a time period. The time period may be the same as the enterprise pay period, or each day's time worked by each employee may serve as an instance of the labor acquisition event. Daily (or even more frequent) recording of labor acquisitions allows for a more complete picture of the enterprise on a continual basis because the time lag between the company receiving the benefit of the economic increment event and the recording of that benefit (and the related liability) is minimized.

The primary document prepared by the enterprise in conjunction with the economic increment event is a **timecard.** Timecards may be completed on a daily, weekly, or other basis. Timecards are typically completed by employees and approved by supervisors. Timecards list the times employees started working (punched in) and stopped working (punched out) for each day in the covered time period. In Exhibit 12–8 we illustrate a timecard.

Relationships in which the labor acquisition event in the human resource process participates typically include a **fulfillment relationship** (enabling the enterprise to trace which labor schedule event the acquisition fulfilled), a **duality relationship** (allowing the enterprise to trace the related cash disbursements), a **stockflow relationship** (to trace the labor type that was acquired), and **participation relationships** with the supervisor and employee. Department supervisors are typically associated with labor acquisition events via participa-

**EXHIBIT 12–8**    Timecard

| Time Card #  49 | Pay Period  4/1/2010–4/7/2010 |
|---|---|

Employee ID  E23          Employee Name   James Worthwhile

| Monday  4/1 | | | | Tuesday  4/2 | | | | Wednesday  4/3 | | | | Thursday  4/4 | | | | Friday  4/5 | | | | Saturday  4/6 | | | | Sunday  4/7 | | | |
|---|---|---|---|---|---|---|---|---|---|---|---|---|---|---|---|---|---|---|---|---|---|---|---|---|---|---|---|
| In | Out | In | Out | In | Out | In | Out | In | Out | In | Out | In | Out | In | Out | In | Out | In | Out | In | Out | In | Out | In | Out | In | Out |
| 7 | – | – | 7 | 7 | – | – | 7 | 7 | – | – | 7 | 7 | – | – | 7 | 7 | – | – | 7 | | | | | | | | |
| | | | | | | | | | | | | | | | | | | | | | | | | | | | |
| | | | | | | | | | | | | | | | | | | | | | | | | | | | |

I hereby attest that I worked the hours recorded above.

*James S. Worthwhile*                                   4/5/2010
Employee Signature                                      Date

Approved by   E5        Date:   4/8/2010
Initials   PW

tion (responsibility) relationships. Employees serve as the external agents related to labor acquisition events via participation relationships. Labor type is the resource typically associated with the labor acquisition events via stockflow relationships in the payroll cycle.

The set of relational tables in Exhibit 12–9 correspond to Exhibit 12–3's entity-relationship representation of the purchase event and the relationships in which it participates (stockflow1, fulfillment2, participation5, participation6, and duality). Other possible tables could be derived, depending on the relationship cardinalities. Data from the form in Exhibit 12–8 have been entered into the database tables; however, some of these data (e.g., labor type and employee information) would already have existed in the database tables before the labor acquisition data were added to the tables so only relationship information that links them to the labor acquisition event is added for those objects. The new data to be added upon provision of labor by employees are shown in color.

## Economic Decrement Event (Cash Disbursement)

Cash disbursements are economic decrement events that decrease the enterprise's cash balance. Cash disbursements in the payroll cycle may be made via paper check, electronic funds transfer **(direct deposit),** or cash payment. Most enterprises use either paper checks or direct deposit to pay employees. Paycheck or direct deposit stubs typically contain information such as gross pay, net pay, and the various **withholdings** that make up the difference between gross and net pay (such as income tax, social security, medicare, health insurance premiums, and retirement plan contributions). Exhibit 12–10 illustrates a direct deposit stub.

Cash disbursements may occur at various times during the human resource process. Most enterprises pay employees only after acquiring labor from the employees. Some enterprises do offer advances to employees; those are advance payments for which the employee is obliged either to provide the corresponding labor or to repay the cash with interest. Attributes captured regarding cash disbursements usually include a cash disbursement identifier (such as a disbursement voucher number), date, amount paid, supplier identification (which may be

**EXHIBIT 12–9** **Relational Tables Encompassing Labor Acquisition (partial data)**

**LaborAcquisition (Economic Increment) Event**

| AcquisitionID | BeginDate | EndDate | Total Hours | GrossPay | EmplID<sup>FK</sup> | SuperID<sup>FK</sup> |
|---|---|---|---|---|---|---|
| TC49 | 4/1/2010 | 4/7/2010 | 60 | $900.00 | E23 | E5 |

**LaborSchedule (Mutual Commitment) Event**

| Labor ScheduleID | Date Schedule Approved | Begin Date | End Date | Total Dollar Amt | LaborReqID<sup>FK</sup> | SuperID<sup>FK</sup> |
|---|---|---|---|---|---|---|
| LS7 | 3/4/2010 | 4/1/2010 | 4/7/2010 | $2,758.80 | LR7 | E5 |

**StockflowLaborAcquisitionLaborType (Stockflow1) Relationship**

| AcquisitionID | LT-ID | Hours Worked | Wage |
|---|---|---|---|
| TC49 | AP1 | 60 | $15.00 |

**DualityLaborAcquisitionCashDisb Relationship**

| LaborAcquisitionID | Voucher# | Withholdings Amount |
|---|---|---|

**DepartmentSupervisor (Internal Agent)**

| SuperID | Authorized Spending Limit |
|---|---|
| E5 | $425,000 |

**LaborType (Resource Type)**

| Item ID | Description | Standard Hourly Wage |
|---|---|---|
| CT2 | Cashier duties | $10.00 |
| US3 | Clean sales showroom and stockroom | $6.00 |
| AP1 | Prepare quarterly sales tax return | $15.00 |
| CT1 | Enter data for sales transactions | $9.00 |

**FulfillmentLaborAcquisitionLaborSchedule (Fulfillment2) Relationship**

| LaborScheduleID | LaborAcquisitionID |
|---|---|
| LS7 | TC49 |

**Employee (External Agent)**

| EmplD | Name | Address | Telephone | DateOfBirth | Rating | Position | Type | Wage |
|---|---|---|---|---|---|---|---|---|
| E5 | Patrick Wellesley | 53125 Fenton Dr. | 555-1112 | March 4, 1958 | Excellent | Supervisor | Salary | $35.50 |
| E15 | Donna Davis | 149 Rovetta Dr. | 555-9932 | Feb. 3, 1954 | Superior | Cashier | Hourly | $10.50 |
| E16 | Nancy Hardaway | 271 Rovetta Dr. | 555-2117 | June 11, 1956 | Excellent | Cashier | Hourly | $9.75 |
| E17 | Joe Thompson | 535 Olson St. | 555-2277 | Apr. 24, 1947 | Excellent | Custodian | Hourly | $6.20 |
| E18 | Freda Matthews | 3214 Deerlake St. | 555-1222 | Aug. 6, 1940 | Good | Custodian | Hourly | $5.90 |
| E19 | John Matthews | 3214 Deerlake St. | 555-1222 | Oct. 14, 1940 | Good | Custodian | Hourly | $5.90 |
| E20 | Paula Cosgrove | 5006 Jazz Ct. | 555-5200 | Apr. 18, 1958 | Excellent | Data Entry | Hourly | $8.50 |
| E21 | Rob Fordham | 4444 Zephyr Ln. | 555-4545 | June 4, 1975 | Excellent | Data Entry | Hourly | $9.00 |
| E22 | Francis Johnson | 1261 Mason Dr. | 555-0129 | May 5, 1980 | Good | Data Entry | Hourly | $8.25 |
| E23 | James Worthwhile | 5432 Wadsworth Ln | 555-7777 | Apr. 14, 1964 | Superior | Accountant | Salary | $15.00 |
| E36 | Diane Bowersox | 9115 Wolfgang Ct | 555-7244 | Sept 15, 1963 | Superior | Payroll | Hourly | $8.75 |

Note: Participation5 relationship is implemented with SuperID posted into Labor Acquisition table. Participation6 relationship is implemented with EmplID posted into Labor Acquisition table. Duality data are not yet entered, assuming a time lag between Labor Acquisition and Cash Disbursement.

**EXHIBIT 12–10    Direct Deposit Notification**

| *Your Source Company*<br>Direct Deposit Notification<br><br><br>Employee ID __23__<br>Employee Name<br>_____James Worthwhile_____ | **Time<br>Card**<br>49 | **Gross<br>Pay**<br>$900 | **Income<br>Tax<br>W/H**<br>$180.10 | **FICA<br>W/H**<br>$68.85 | **Medicare<br>W/H**<br>$13.05 | No. __49__<br><br><br><br><br><br>**Net Pay**<br>$638.00 |
|---|---|---|---|---|---|---|

*Your Source Company*                                             No. __49____

                                                   Voucher No. __89_____

                                                        Date __4/14/2010_____

**James S. Worthwhile**

Your net pay has been transmitted electronically (EFT)
to your financial institution according to your instructions.

an employee who supplied labor), employee identification (i.e., employee who wrote the check), the account number from which the cash is disbursed, and the check number of the payment. Exhibit 12–11 shows a set of relational tables that correspond to Exhibit 12–3's entity-relationship representation of the **cash disbursement event** and the payroll cycle relationships in which it participates (duality, stockflow2, participation7, and participation8). Other possible tables could be derived, depending on the relationship cardinalities. As noted in the acquisition/payment cycle chapter, additional tables are necessary to correspond to relationships in which the cash disbursement event participates in other transaction cycles such as acquisition/payment and financing. The tables shown in Exhibit 12–11 are applicable to the human resource process. Data from the form in Exhibit 12–10 have been entered into the database tables; however, some of these data (e.g., labor acquisition, cash, and employee information) would already have existed in the database tables before the cash disbursement data were added to the tables. Only relationship information that links those objects to the cash disbursements is added to the database upon the cash disbursement. The new data to be added for the cash disbursement event are shown in color.

## INFORMATION NEEDS AND MEASURES IN THE HUMAN RESOURCE PROCESS

The most common information customers for the human resource business process include top management, employees, accountants, and auditors. We next analyze each of the entities and relationships in the human resource process pattern to provide some ideas as to the types of queries that may be needed to satisfy information needs in the payroll cycle. The queries presented are not a comprehensive set of queries because there are simply too

**EXHIBIT 12–11**   **Relational Tables Encompassing Cash Disbursement Event (partial data)**

**CashDisbursement (Economic Decrement) Event**

| Disb Voucher ID | Voucher Date | Dollar Amount | Check Number | Cash AccountIDFK | Payroll ClerkIDFK | PayeeIDFK |
|---|---|---|---|---|---|---|
| 88 | 4/14/2010 | $2,028.46 | 40404 | Ca123501 | E36 | Ca987654 |
| 89 | 4/14/2010 | $638.00 | 49 | Ca987654 | E36 | E23 |

**Cash (Resource Type)**

| CashAccountID | AccountType | Location |
|---|---|---|
| Ca123501 | Checking | 1st Local Bank |
| Ca987654 | Imprest checking | 1st Local Bank |

**DualityLaborAcquisitionCashDisb Relationship**

| LaborAcquisitionID | Voucher# | Withholdings Amount |
|---|---|---|
| TC49 | 89 | $262.00 |

**LaborAcquisition (Economic Increment) Event**

| AcquisitionID | BeginDate | EndDate | Total Hours | GrossPay | EmplIDFK | SuperIDFK |
|---|---|---|---|---|---|---|
| TC49 | 4/1/2010 | 4/7/2010 | 60 | $900.00 | E23 | E5 |

**PayrollClerk (Internal Agent)**

| PayrollClerkID | Fidelity Bond Rating |
|---|---|
| E36 | AA |

**Employee (External Agent)**

| EmplID | Name | Address | Telephone | DateOfBirth | Rating | Position | Type | Wage |
|---|---|---|---|---|---|---|---|---|
| E5 | Patrick Wellesley | 53125 Fenton Dr. | 555-1112 | March 4, 1958 | Excellent | Supervisor | Salary | $35.50 |
| E15 | Donna Davis | 149 Rovetta Dr. | 555-9932 | Feb. 3, 1954 | Superior | Cashier | Hourly | $10.50 |
| E16 | Nancy Hardaway | 271 Rovetta Dr. | 555-2117 | June 11, 1956 | Excellent | Cashier | Hourly | $9.75 |
| E17 | Joe Thompson | 535 Olson St. | 555-2277 | Apr. 24, 1947 | Excellent | Custodian | Hourly | $6.20 |
| E18 | Freda Matthews | 3214 Deerlake St. | 555-1222 | Aug. 6, 1940 | Good | Custodian | Hourly | $5.90 |
| E19 | John Matthews | 3214 Deerlake St. | 555-1222 | Oct. 14, 1940 | Good | Custodian | Hourly | $5.90 |
| E20 | Paula Cosgrove | 5006 Jazz Ct. | 555-5200 | Apr. 18, 1958 | Excellent | Data Entry | Hourly | $8.50 |
| E21 | Rob Fordham | 4444 Zephyr Ln. | 555-4545 | June 4, 1975 | Excellent | Data Entry | Hourly | $9.00 |
| E22 | Francis Johnson | 1261 Mason Dr. | 555-0129 | May 5, 1980 | Good | Data Entry | Hourly | $8.25 |
| E23 | James Worthwhile | 5432 Wadsworth Ln | 555-7777 | Apr. 14, 1964 | Superior | Accountant | Salary | $15.00 |
| E36 | Diane Bowersox | 9115 Wolfgang Ct | 555-7244 | Sept 15, 1963 | Superior | Payroll | Hourly | $8.75 |

Note: Stockflow2 is implemented with Cash AccountID posted into Cash Disbursement table. Participation7 is implemented with PayrollClerkID posted into Cash Disbursement table. Participation8 is implemented with PayeeID posted into Cash Disbursement table.

many potential queries to list them all; however, the following set should provide you guidance for creating similar queries. To describe example queries needed in the payroll cycle use the database tables in Exhibits 12–5, 12–7, 12–9, 12–11.

## Resource Queries in the Human Resource Process

Labor type and cash are the resources that most commonly exist in the human resource process. For each resource, users may need any of the following:

- Detailed status information at one or more points in time for each resource instance.
- Detailed status information at one or more points in time for only those resource instances meeting specified criteria.
- Summarized status information at one or more points in time for all resource instances.
- Summarized status information at one or more points in time for only those resource instances meeting specified criteria.

With regard to each list item, users may need to know all characteristics of the instances in the answer set, or they may need only a subset of the characteristics.

Labor is typically tracked only at the type level. Cash is tracked by the accounts in which the cash is stored. Some example queries based on the tables in this chapter are as follows:

- *What are the descriptions for all labor types for the enterprise?* Use the labor type table; display all fields.
- *Which labor types have standard hourly wage rates less than $10?* Use the LaborType table; enter criterion <10 in the StdHourlyWageRate field; display labor type description.
- *Does the enterprise own any **imprest cash accounts?*** Use the Cash table; enter criterion LIKE *imprest* in the AccountType field; display the cash account ID (notice the LIKE command coupled with the wild card * symbols identifies any account type that includes the word *imprest* in the type name).
- *What is the average standard hourly wage rate for all labor types?* Use the LaborType table; apply the AVG aggregation function to the standard hourly wage field.

## Event Queries in the Human Resource Process

Users may need information regarding events. The most common events in the human resource process are labor requisitions, labor schedules, labor acquisitions, and cash disbursements. For each of these types of events, users may need any of the following:

- Detailed information about each event instance.
- Detailed information about each event instance that meets specified criteria.
- Summarized information for all instances of an event type for a specified time period.
- Summarized information for only those instances of an event type for a specified time period that meet specified criteria.

Some example queries to satisfy information needs regarding events in the human resource process are (among many other possibilities) as follows:

- *What is the maximum budget amount for labor requisition LR7?* Using the LaborRequisition table, enter criterion =LR7 in the labor requisition ID field; display the maximum budget for request field.
- *When was labor schedule LS7 approved?* Using the LaborSchedule table, enter criterion =LS7 in the labor schedule ID field; display the date schedule approved field.
- *How many days of labor are included on labor acquisition TC49?* Using the LaborAcquisition table, enter criterion =TC49 in the acquisition ID field; create an expression to subtract the begin date field from the end date field.

- *How many cash disbursements were made on 4/14/2010?* Using the CashDisbursement table, enter criterion =4/14/2010 in the voucher date field; apply COUNT aggregation function to the disbursement voucher ID field.
- *What is the dollar value of wages expense for April 2010?* Using the LaborAcquisition table, enter criteria >=4/1/2010 in begin date field and <=4/30/2010 in the end date field; apply the SUM aggregation function to the gross pay field. *Note:* This query reveals the need for companies to track labor acquisitions at a finer level of detail than in this example. When the desired wages expense period includes only part of the time-card period, it is impossible to isolate the portion of the gross pay applied to the desired wages expense period.

## Agent Queries in the Human Resource Process

The agents commonly involved in human resource processes are the employees from whom labor is acquired, the department supervisors who authorize labor acquisitions, and the **payroll clerks** who generate the paychecks (cash disbursements). Queries may be needed to obtain any of the following:

- Detailed status information at one or more points in time for each employee.
- Detailed status information at one or more points in time for each employee who meets specified criteria.
- Summarized status information at one or more points in time for all employees.
- Summarized status information at one or more points in time for all employees who meet specified criteria.

Some example queries based on the tables in this chapter are as follows:

- *What are the names and positions of the employees who have been rated as excellent?* Using the Employee table, enter criterion =Excellent in the rating field; display the name and position fields.
- *What is the average wage of the data entry employees?* Using the Employee table, enter criterion =Data Entry in the position field; apply the AVG aggregation function to the Wage field.
- *What are the names and birth dates of employees who were born in 1960 or earlier?* Using the Employee table, enter criterion <=12/31/1960 in the date of birth field; display the name and date of birth fields.

### Relationship Queries

Combining information from various resource, event, and agent tables in accordance with the relationships in which they participate can provide much richer data than single table queries. We next discuss queries based on the various types of relationships in the human resource process.

## Duality Relationship Queries in the Human Resource Process

The duality relationship set in the human resource process connects labor acquisitions to cash disbursements, as it represents exchanges of cash for labor. Information needs with respect to duality relationships in the human resource process include (among other possibilities):

- Calculation of the outstanding wages payable balance at a point in time.
- Identification of the labor acquisition for which a cash disbursement was made.
- Identification of cash advances made to employees.
- Identification and calculation of amounts withheld from gross pay amounts for employee and employer payroll-related taxes.

Based on the tables in this chapter, duality queries could investigate

- *Had labor acquisition TC49 been paid for as of 4/10/2010?* Join the LaborAcquisition table to the DualityLaborAcquisitionCashDisb and CashDisbursement tables; enter criteria =TC49 in the acquisition ID field and <=4/10/2010 in the voucher date field.
- *What total dollar amount was withheld from payroll checks during the month of April 2010?* Join the DualityLaborAcquisitionCashDisb table to the CashDisbursement table; enter criteria BETWEEN 4/1/2010 and 4/30/2010 in the cash disbursement dollar amount field; apply the SUM aggregation operator to the cash disbursement dollar amount field.
- *What is the balance of wages payable as of April 30, 2010?* **Query 1:** Wages payable are increased by gross pay amounts that represent the cost of labor acquired. To find the gross pay amounts for labor acquisitions that occurred through April 30, 2010, use the LaborAcquisition table; enter criterion <=4/30/2010 in the end date field; apply the SUM aggregation operator to the gross pay field. **Query 2:** Wages payable are decreased by net pay amounts of paychecks and by withholdings amounts. To find the paycheck and withholdings amounts that occurred through April 30, 2010, join the DualityLaborAcquisitionCashDisb table to the CashDisbursement table; enter criterion <=4/30/2010 in the cash disbursement voucher date; apply the SUM aggregation operator to the cash disbursement dollar amount field and also to the withholdings amount field. **Query 3:** Subtract the two sums calculated in query 2 from the sum calculated in query 1.

## Stockflow Relationship Queries in the Human Resource Process

Stockflow relationships in the human resource process represent the connections between resources labor type and cash and the economic events that increase labor and decrease cash. Some common stockflow information needs in the human resource process (among other possibilities) are

- Which cash account was decreased by a cash disbursement?
- What is the total dollar amount of cash disbursements made from a specified cash account during a time period?
- What quantity of each labor type was acquired by a labor acquisition event?
- How many different labor types were acquired by a labor acquisition event?
- Which labor acquisitions have involved a specified labor type?

Based on the example tables in this chapter, stockflow queries could investigate:

- *What is the total dollar amount of cash disbursements that were made from imprest checking accounts during the month of April 2010?* Join the CashDisbursement table to the Cash table; enter criteria LIKE *imprest* in the account type field and BETWEEN 4/1/2010 and 4/30/2010 in the voucher date field; apply the SUM aggregation operator to the dollar amount field.

- *How many different types of labor were acquired on labor acquisition TC49?* Join the LaborAcquisition table to the StockflowLaborAcquisitionLaborType table; enter criterion =TC49 in the acquisition ID field; apply the COUNT aggregation operator to the labor type field.

## Fulfillment Queries in the Human Resource Process

The fulfillment relationships that are typically materialized in the human resource process represent associations between the labor schedules and labor acquisitions (the acquisitions fulfill the schedules) and between the labor requisitions and labor schedules (the schedules fulfill the requisitions). Fulfillment relationship queries in the human resource process in general include:

- Identification of unfilled commitment events (e.g., schedules for which work has not yet been performed, requisitions for which schedules have not yet been developed).
- Identification of filled commitment events (e.g., schedules for which labor was acquired, labor requisitions for which schedules were developed).
- Identification of economic events for which commitments were not made (e.g., labor acquisitions that were not scheduled).
- Identification of results of commitment events (e.g., which labor acquisitions resulted from a labor schedule, and were there any discrepancies between the scheduled and actual acquisitions).

Based on the example tables in this chapter, questions such as the following could be answered via fulfillment relationship queries in the human resource process:

- *Has baking order PO4 been fulfilled?* Join BakingOrder table to CookieBatch table with an outer join keeping all baking orders; include bakingorder ID from BakingOrder table and batch ID from CookieBatch table; set criteria to select baking order =PO4.
- *Have any ingredient issuances occurred that were not related to ingredient requisitions?* Join IngredientIssuance table to IngredientIssuanceFulfillsIngredientRequisition table with an outer join keeping all ingredient issuances; include issuance ID from IngredientIssuance table and ingredient requisition number from IngredientIssuanceFulfillsIngredientRequisition table; set criteria to select null ingredient requisitions.
- *What is the average length of time between baking orders and cookie batches for this company?* Because this involves a date/time calculation, you should not attempt this in Microsoft Access.
- *What baking order triggered cookie batch WJ2?* Join CookieBatch table to CookieBatchFulfillsBakingOrder table using cookie batch ID; include baking order ID; set criteria to select batch ID =WJ2.

## Reservation Queries in the Human Resource Process

The **reservation relationship** that is typically materialized in the human resource process represents the associations between labor schedules and the types of labor the schedules commit to acquire. Some enterprises also materialize the reservation associations between the labor schedules and the cash the schedules commit to decrease. Therefore reservation relationships in the human resource process commonly are used in queries to satisfy information needs as to the eventual effect of labor schedules on cash or as to the labor types involved in labor schedules. Some common information needs (among many others) in the payroll cycle are

- What labor type or types is a labor schedule agreeing to acquire?
- How many hours of a specified labor type is a labor schedule committing to acquire?
- What is the dollar value of cash reserved by a labor schedule?
- On what dates is a labor schedule committing to acquire a specified labor type?

Based on the example tables in this chapter, questions such as the following could be answered via reservation relationship queries in the payroll cycle:

- *What are the descriptions of the labor types that labor schedule LS7 is committing to acquire?* Join the ReservationLaborScheduleLaborType table to the LaborType table; enter criterion =LS7 in the labor schedule ID field; display the labor type description field.
- *How many hours of cashier duties does labor schedule LS7 commit to acquire?* Join ReservationLaborScheduleLaborType table to the LaborType table; enter criteria LIKE *cashier* in the labor type description field and =LS7 in the labor schedule ID field; display the hours scheduled field.

## Participation Queries in the Human Resource Process

Participation relationships in the payroll cycle typically represent the associations between labor requisitions, labor schedules, labor acquisitions, and cash disbursements and the employees who authorize those events (typically supervisors for labor acquisition and payroll clerks for cash disbursements) and the employees who accomplish those events (typically a generalized employee entity set). Therefore participation relationships are commonly used in queries to satisfy information needs to identify employees who participated in events or as to the events in which specified employees participated. Some common payroll cycle information needs are

- Which department supervisor authorized a labor requisition?
- By how many labor schedules has an employee been scheduled to work?
- How many hours did an employee work on a labor acquisition?
- How many labor schedules has a specific department supervisor authorized?
- Which payroll clerk issued a specific cash disbursement?

Based on the tables in this chapter, questions such as the following could be answered via participation relationship payroll cycle queries:

- *What is the name of the supervisor who authorized labor requisition LR7?* Join the LaborRequisition table to the DepartmentSupervisor and Employee tables; enter criterion =LR7 in the labor requisition ID field and display the supervisor name field.
- *What are the names of the employees who were scheduled on labor schedule LS7?* Join the ParticipationLaborScheduleEmployee table to the Employee table; enter criterion =LS7 in the labor schedule ID field and display the employee name field.

- *Who worked on labor acquisition TC49 and how many hours did the employee work?*
  Join the LaborAcquisition table to the Employee table; enter criterion =TC49 in the acquisition ID field; display the employee name field and the total hours field.

## CONCLUDING COMMENTS

This chapter presented an overview of the activities in the human resource process and discussed the extended REA pattern as it is applied to this process. Information needs associated with the human resource business process were also described in this chapter, although those identified are not a comprehensive list. An enterprise with an enterprise system based on the REA pattern is able to satisfy most (if not all) of the information needs by constructing queries based on its database tables.

## Key Terms and Concepts

Budget, *390*
Cash disbursement
event, *397*
Direct deposit, *395*
Duality relationship, *394*
Economic decrement
event, *387*
Economic increment
event, *393*
Employee, *385*

Employee knowledge and
skills, *386*
Fulfillment
relationship, *394*
Imprest cash account, *399*
Labor acquisition
event, *392*
Labor type resource, *389*
Participation
relationship, *394*

Paycheck, *389*
Payroll clerk, *400*
Reservation
relationship, *402*
Schedule, *390*
Stockflow relationship, *394*
Timecard, *394*
Training, *385*
Withholdings, *395*

## Review Questions

LO1   R1.  What is the primary objective of the human resource process?

LO2   R2.  How is the human resource process related to the conversion process, the sales/collection process, the acquisition/payment process, and the financing process?

LO1   R3.  What is the difference between a timecard in the payroll process and a job time ticket in the conversion process?

LO1   R4.  Which functions in the human resource process are typically thought of as personnel functions, and which functions are typically thought of as payroll functions?

LO2   R5.  Identify the resources, internal agents, external agents, and possible locations associated with each of the following business events in the human resource process:
  a.  Schedule (commitment to increment) event
  b.  Labor acquisition (economic increment) event
  c.  Budget (commitment to decrement) event
  d.  Cash disbursement (economic decrement) event

LO4    R6. Describe the information required by each of the following in performing their role in the human resource process:
a. Management
b. Payroll
c. Accounting
d. Personnel

# Multiple Choice Questions

LO1, LO2    MC1. Which document typically represents the same phenomena as the labor acquisition (economic increment) event?
A. Payroll register
B. Operations list
C. Timecard
D. Schedule

LO2    MC2. The labor acquisition process represents the point of contact between the enterprise and which set of external business partners?
A. Investors and creditors
B. Suppliers
C. Customers
D. Employees

LO2    MC3. The resource made available by the human resource process to the conversion process in a typical enterprise value chain is
A. Inventory
B. Property, plant, and equipment
C. Labor
D. Cash

LO2    MC4. Which of the following entities are usually paired in a stockflow relationship in the human resource process?
A. Labor acquisition and employee
B. Labor type and schedule
C. Cash and cash disbursement
D. Employee and supervisor

LO2    MC5. Which of the following events reflects the commitment of the enterprise to receive an employee's labor for a future time period?
A. Schedule
B. Labor acquisition
C. Cash budget
D. Cash disbursement

# Discussion Questions

LO5    D1. How do you compute the dollar amount of wages payable for financial statement purposes using a database designed with the REA ontology?

LO1    D2. How does training provided to employees affect the resources in the human resource process?

LO5  D3. Consider the tables in Exhibit 12–7. Describe the necessary procedures to construct a query to determine the number of hours for which Freda Matthews is scheduled to work during the first week of April 2010.

LO5  D4. Consider the tables in Exhibit 12–5. Describe the necessary procedures to construct a query to determine the total number of labor hours needed for unfulfilled labor requisitions.

## Applied Learning

LO3  A1.  Customers engage Kravenhall Katering to provide food and beverages at upscale parties. When notified about an upcoming party, one of Kravenhall's supervisors must determine staffing needs. The supervisor records the number of hours required for each type of labor (e.g., cooking a ham, baking a cake, serving food, or bartending) on a staffing plan for the catering job. The supervisor also notes on the staffing plan whether the client has requested any specific employees for the catering job. The supervisor then creates a schedule for the catering job by calling the employees who have the skills needed for each type of labor and verifying their availability and willingness to participate in the catering job for a specified wage rate. The schedule lists each employee and the date and hours the employee will need to work on this job. When the catering job occurs, details of the hours worked by each employee are recorded on a timecard. The supervisor verifies the accuracy of each timecard and sends them to the payroll department. On the 15th and last day of each month, a payroll clerk summarizes each employee's timecards for catering jobs in the current pay period. The clerk calculates gross pay, withholdings, and net pay dollar amounts and enters the payment information into the database. The net pay amounts are transferred to the employees' bank accounts via direct deposit and a pay stub is given to each employee for recordkeeping purposes.

Cash disbursements are tracked via voucher number, since check numbers and direct deposit numbers for different checking accounts may overlap. Kravenhall's cash accounts are all located in banks; Kravenhall has multiple accounts in some banks and single accounts in other banks. For example, Kravenhall has checking, savings, and money market accounts at First Metro Bank and only a certificate of deposit account at Uniontown Bank. Information about banks is only entered into Kravenhall's system after information is entered about the accounts in those banks. Less than half of the payments Kravenhall issues are for payroll; other checks are written to vendors, stockholders, lenders, and so on. Payroll clerks only process payroll payments; employees in various other positions process nonpayroll payments.

After labor type information is entered, Kravenhall needs to determine and enter the various skill types (e.g., baking skill or bartending skill) and the degree of skill level (i.e., high, medium, or low) needed for each type of labor. For example, for the labor type *bake a souffle,* a high degree of baking skill may be needed; whereas for the labor type *bake a cake,* a low degree of baking skill may suffice. To aid in scheduling, Kravenhall wants to be able to look up the degree of each skill type each employee possesses and the means by which the employee acquired the skill (e.g., by taking a class, through experience, or by some other means). Therefore after information about employees is entered into the system, information describing the skill types each employee possesses must also be entered.

**Required:**

a. Prepare an REA business process level model for Kravenhall in ER diagram or grammar format including all relevant entities, relationships, attributes, and participation cardinalities. The following attributes are of interest to Kravenhall and should be included in your solution. Do not add or subtract any attributes.

Payroll clerk ID
Employee ID
Voucher number
Employee schedule ID
Cash account number
Check or direct deposit number
Supervisor ID
Staffing plan number
Labor type description
Bank name
Check or direct deposit amount
Employee name
Standard wage rate for labor type
Timecard date
Maximum number of subordinates allowed for a supervisor
Total scheduled hours for each labor type on an employee schedule
Standard wage rate for a labor type used on a staffing plan
Means by which an employee acquired a skill type
Degree of a skill type possessed by an employee
Estimated wage rate for each labor type on an employee schedule
Bank ID

Check or direct deposit date
Cash account type
Employee phone number
Timecard number
Labor type ID
Date staff plan approved
Bank address
Payroll clerk fidelity bond rating
Employee address
Date employee schedule approved
Skill type ID
Skill type description
Degree of skill type required for a labor type
Requested hours on a staffing plan for each type of labor
Total hours worked by each employee on a timecard
Negotiated wage rate for each employee on an employee schedule
Actual wage rate for an employee on a timecard
Total scheduled hours for each employee on an employee schedule
Amounts withheld from payment for each timecard

b. Convert your REA business process level model into a set of minimal relational table structures.

# Answers to Multiple Choice Questions

MC1. C; MC2. D; MC3. C; MC4. C; MC5. A.

# Chapter **Thirteen**

# The Financing Business Process

## LEARNING OBJECTIVES

The objectives of this chapter are to introduce the financing business process, to discuss the REA ontology representation of financing processes, and to describe some typical information needs in the financing business process. After studying this chapter you should be able to:

1. Identify the activities and documents common to most financing business processes
2. Explain the various components of the REA ontology in the financing process
3. Create a REA business process level model for an enterprise's financing process
4. Identify common information needs that exist within the financing process
5. Create database queries to retrieve financing process information from a relational database

## FINANCING BUSINESS PROCESS IN AN ENTERPRISE VALUE SYSTEM

The financing business process provides the capital resources an enterprise needs to fund all aspects of its operations. A substantial portion of cash is used to fund two of the business processes we have discussed already: the acquisition/payment process and the human resource process. Much of the cash available to the financing process comes from the sales/collection process. However, when insufficient cash is available via the sales/collection process, other financing alternatives are used.

The financing process includes the activities associated with acquiring and paying for the use of cash through various debt and equity financing mechanisms. Activities in the financing process are triggered by an enterprise's need to obtain cash from an external source. The most obvious time of need for external cash is when an enterprise is new, before it has engaged in any operations. However, at other times enterprises may have insufficient internal cash available either because of timing differences between cash outflows and expected cash inflows or because of the need to expand operations or add capacity.

One mechanism for acquiring cash is **debt financing,** whereby the enterprise borrows cash from one or more external business partners for a specified period of time and with the agreement that the enterprise will pay a specified interest rate as well as repayment of the principal balance. Another mechanism for acquiring cash is **equity financing,** whereby the enterprise issues **shares of stock** (that represent the right to share in various ownership interests) in exchange for cash.

The financing process is in essence a special case of the acquisition/payment cycle; in it the enterprise acquires and pays for various types of financing. Because different information needs often exist with respect to the acquisition and payments for cash as compared to the exchange of cash for goods and services, the financing cycle is usually maintained as a separate transaction cycle. In this chapter we discuss the strategy, objectives, and nature of the financing process.

As you analyze and model a business process, you must clearly understand its purpose and objectives. You must realize how the business process fits into the value system and enterprise value chain. At the value system level, the financing process is the point of contact between the enterprise and its **investors** and **creditors.** The enterprise gives cash to its investors and creditors in exchange for cash they previously provided to the enterprise, as highlighted in Exhibit 13–1.

The value chain reveals interfaces between the financing process and other business processes. Exhibit 13–2 illustrates the typical value chain interfaces.

The arrows in Exhibit 13–2 depict the financing process accepting responsibility for cash made available by the revenue process and making cash available to the payroll and general acquisition/payment processes. The payroll process disburses that cash in exchange for acquisition of labor from employees. The general acquisition/payment process disburses that cash in exchange for acquisitions of goods and services from suppliers. Cash received in the revenue process is made available to the financing process wherein it is disbursed to investors and creditors in exchange for the earlier described cash receipts or it is reinvested in the enterprise by being made available to the various acquisition processes.

The primary objective of the financing process is to provide the financial capital the enterprise needs to function efficiently and effectively. The objectives of this process are to have the liquid funds needed to run the enterprise while not letting cash sit idle. Sufficient cash availability enables enterprises to purchase in quantity to obtain more favorable prices

**EXHIBIT 13–1**
**Financing Process in the Enterprise Value System**

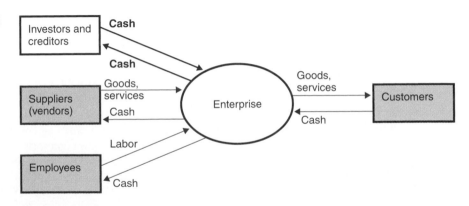

**EXHIBIT 13–2**
**Financing Process in the Value Chain**

Partial Value Chain

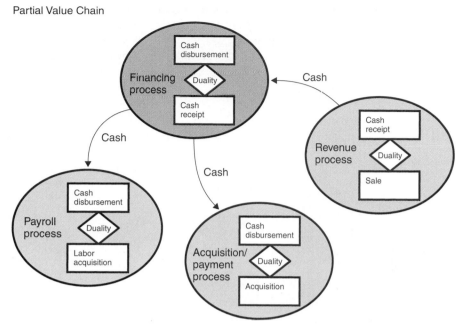

and to take advantage of cash discounts. Having cash available to pay obligations on time and the ability to pay in cash give an organization a great deal of power.

We begin our business process level discussion of the financing cycle by reviewing some of its more common events. Two important reminders before we begin the discussion: Because we discuss the activities in a sequential fashion, it may seem that the financing process is linear. That is not necessarily true. Increasingly, business processes and the activities that comprise those processes are dynamic, rather than linear and static. Although the specific workflow activities differ in various enterprises' financing processes, we discuss the pattern for the information system's base objects that has been identified as common to most financing processes. Also, remember the activities in this process are linked to and sometimes overlap activities in other processes. We are concentrating on one process at a time to simplify our analysis.

# FINANCING BUSINESS PROCESS LEVEL REA MODELS

Recall that the extended REA ontology described in Chapter 4 and illustrated in Exhibit 13–3 identifies the pattern underlying each transaction cycle, which consists of instigation events, mutual **commitment events,** economic exchange events, resources, agents, types, and various relationships such as stockflow, duality, fulfillment, reservation, proposition, and participation. In this section we describe the extended REA ontology components specific to the finance business process.

We remind you that instigation events and the relationships in which they participate (such as proposition) are not part of the published REA ontology. We have added them to the business process level models in this text as a convenient means of fleshing out the

**EXHIBIT 13–3**    **Generic Financing Cycle Extended REA Ontology Database Design Pattern**

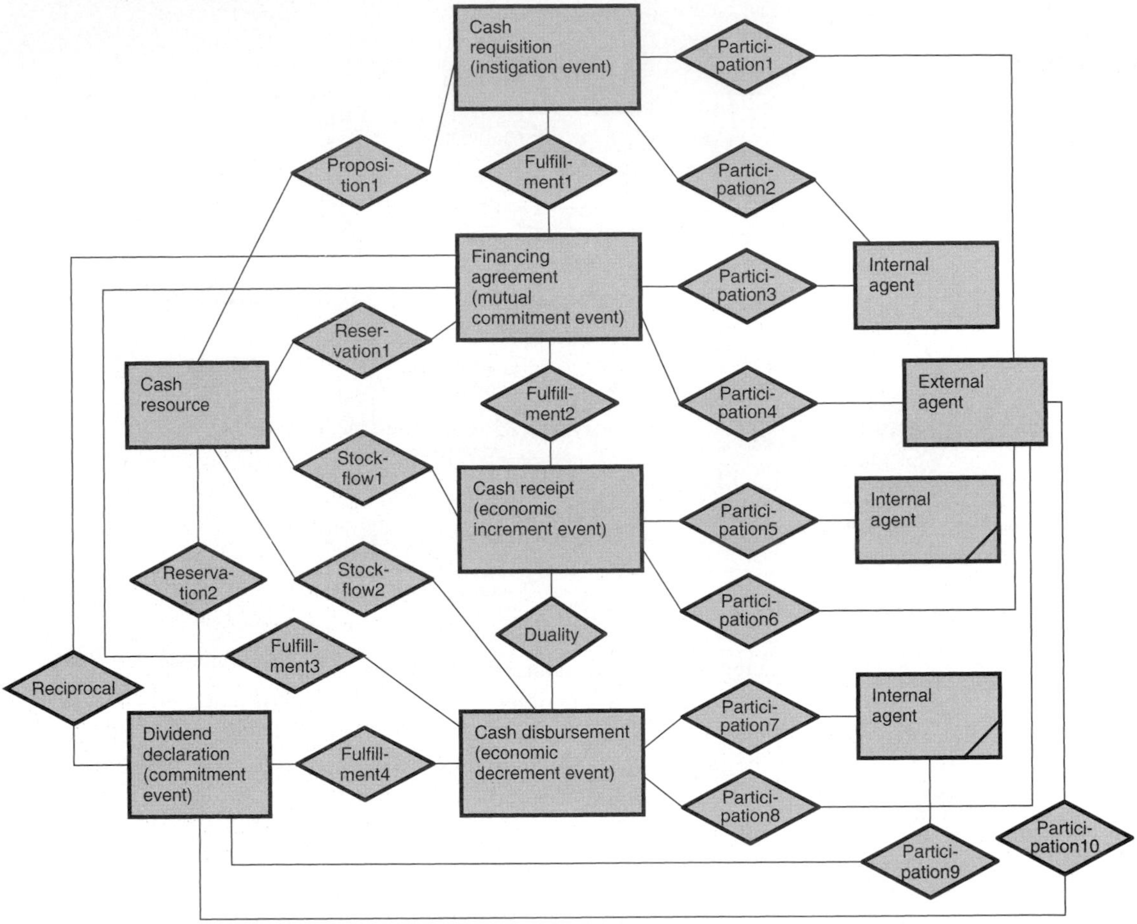

Note 1: This diagram does not attempt to differentiate internal agents for the various types of events; for some enterprises one category of employee may participate in all these events; for others there may be several categories of employees involved. For most enterprises, financing requisitions and financing agreements are the responsibility of financing officers, cash receipts are the responsibility of cashiers, and cash disbursements are the responsibility of accounts payable clerks.
Note 2: The diagonal slash in the bottom right corner of an entity indicates the entity is a copy of an entity that was already used elsewhere on the diagram. It helps avoid crossing too many lines and thereby creating confusion in an entity-relationship diagram.
Note 3: Fulfillment3 relationship applies only to debt financing agreements; Reciprocal relationship and Fulfillment4 relationship apply only to equity financing agreements.

complete story of each business process. A proposal is made in the instigation event. The proposal is acted upon and a mutual agreement is reached in the commitment event. The mutual commitment is fulfilled by the economic events that comprise the exchange of resources. These base objects exist in every cycle for every enterprise; however, it may not be cost-effective to measure and store the details of all these phases.

The *REA* pattern aids in analyzing business processes and events by highlighting the *what* (the resources involved in the event) and the *who* (the internal and external agents) of each event. Notice that the *where* and the *when* are often stored as attributes of each event. The events, agents, and resources involved in the financing process vary somewhat from enterprise to enterprise. The general pattern discussed in this chapter can be easily adapted and applied to meet the exact financing requirements of any enterprise (e.g., nonprofit or governmental agencies, wholesalers, retailers, service providers, or manufacturers).

## Resources

Cash is both the resource acquired and the resource given in the financing process. Cash is represented in an enterprise system as the various stores of cash owned by the enterprise. Bank accounts, petty cash accounts, on-hand cash accounts, and other types of cash accounts are all potential instances of the cash resource for an enterprise. The cash resource is a type entity, because it is normally not practical and cost-effective to identify and represent the serial number of each piece of currency owned by an enterprise; rather the amounts of currency and coin and negotiable cash instruments (such as checks or money orders) are combined into cash accounts of various types such as checking, savings, or petty cash. The attributes typically captured to represent cash accounts include an identifier, a name for the cash account, the type of cash account it is (e.g., savings or checking), the location, an account number assigned by the financial institution in which the account is located (if applicable), and the balance of the account. Because cash account balance is a volatile derivable attribute, it should only be included in a relational database table for cash if the database software allows the use of triggered update fields. Otherwise, a stored query may be created and reused for quick retrieval of the cash account balance attribute.

## Instigation Events—Need Identification and Request for Cash

**Financial officers** typically determine the need for cash by monitoring enterprise growth (or lack thereof), production plans, sales forecasts, employee turnover, and other trends and projections, and creating a **cash flow budget** that incorporates expected cash receipts from the sales/collection and financing processes and expected cash disbursements from the various acquisition/payment processes. Forecasted cash shortfalls result in decisions to acquire cash from external sources via either debt or equity financing. This identification of need for cash is often labeled as a **cash requisition event** as shown in Exhibit 13–3. The cash requisition event is fulfilled by the financing agreement.

Agents involved in instigation events in the financing cycle usually are financial officers (internal agents who authorize the requisitions) and investors/creditors (external agents). Attributes of cash requisitions that typically should be captured include the date, time, and dollar amount of the requisition. The requisition event data should also be linked to data regarding the related financial officer, investor and/or creditor, and the type of financing agreement requested. Documentation of need identification for cash may vary widely. Some enterprises use a cash requisition form that looks much like a purchase requisition form as shown in the acquisition/payment cycle chapter. Others simply issue a memorandum summarizing the need for additional cash and the mechanism by which the enterprise proposes to obtain the cash. In Exhibit 13–4 we illustrate a cash requisition form.

The set of relational tables illustrated in Exhibit 13–5 correspond to Exhibit 13–3's entity-relationship representation of the cash requisition event, the relationships in which it participates (proposition, fulfillment1, participation1, and participation2), and the related entities (cash, financing agreement, financial officer, and proposed investor/creditor). Alternative tables could be derived depending on the relationship cardinalities. Data from the form in Exhibit 13–4 have been entered into the database tables; however, some of these data (e.g., cash account, employee information, and investor/creditor information) would

**EXHIBIT 13–4**   Cash Requisition Document

| YOUR SOURCE COMPANY | | | | |
|---|---|---|---|---|
| **CASH REQUISITION** | | | | No.  3 |
| Date Prepared:<br>4/05/2010 | | Prepared by:<br>E64 | Date Needed:<br>5/2/2010 | Suggested Source:<br>V41 |
| Cash<br>Account | Amount<br>Needed | Reason Needed | | |
| Ca123501 | $1,450,000 | Cash Flow Budget created 4/05/2010 for the fiscal year reveals<br>$1,429,413 cash shortfall due to expansion plans | | |
| Approved by:<br>E62 | | Approval Signature: | | Date Approved:<br>4/15/2010 |

already have existed in the database tables before the requisition data were added to the tables so only the relationship information that links them to the event is recorded for those objects. New data that would be entered as a result of the labor requisition event are shown in color.

## Mutual Commitment Event (Financing Agreement)

A mutual commitment event exists when an enterprise and an external business partner have each agreed to exchange specified quantities of resources at a defined future time. Because debt financing and equity financing are different financing mechanisms, with different information needs resulting from the commitment agreements for each, most enterprises need to separately represent financing agreements involving debt and equity. For debt financing, the mutual commitment is called a loan contract, a promissory note, a mortgage, or a bond certificate. For equity financing, the mutual commitment is typically called a **stock issuance commitment event.** The primary difference between debt financing and equity financing is the specification and timing of the resulting cash inflows and outflows. Debt financing agreements usually specify a determinable dollar amount and timing of the cash inflow (loan proceeds) and of the cash outflows (loan repayments). That is not to say that the exact dollar amounts are certain; in fact, the exact dollar amounts may vary depending on the timing of the cash flows. Equity financing agreements specify a determinable dollar amount and timing of the cash inflow (stock proceeds); however, the cash outflows (dividend payments or stock repurchases) are less certain about both the timing and the dollar amounts. Investors buy enterprise stock (and thus provide cash to the enterprise) with the expectation of getting cash back in the form of dividend payments and capital appreciation so they can sell the stock in the stock market for more than they paid for it.

Attributes of debt financing agreement events that typically should be captured include the agreement date, the total dollar amount to which the agreement commits, the interest rate that applies to the agreement, and the maturity date of the agreement. The debt financing agreement should also be linked to data regarding the cash account into which the proceeds are deposited, the financial officer responsible for the loan, the creditor from which the financing was acquired, the resulting cash receipt and **cash disbursement events,** and the cash requisition event the agreement fulfills. Debt financing agreements are

**EXHIBIT 13–5**  **Relational Tables Encompassing Cash Requisition Event**

**CashRequisition (Instigation) Event**

| CashReqID | Date | Dollar Amount Requested | OfficerID<sup>FK</sup> | Suggested Investor/Creditor<sup>FK</sup> |
|---|---|---|---|---|
| 3 | 4/15/2010 | $1,450,000 | E64 | V41 |

**PropositionCashReqCashAcct (Proposition) Relationship**

| CashReqID | CashAccountID | Amount Needed |
|---|---|---|
| 3 | Ca123501 | $1,450,000 |

**FinancialOfficer (Internal Agent)**

| OfficerID | Authorized Debt Limit |
|---|---|
| E64 | $2,500,000 |

**Investor/Creditor (External Agent)**

| CreditorID | Name | Address | Telephone | Performance Rating |
|---|---|---|---|---|
| V41 | First Chance Bank | 43221 Financial Institute Way | 555-5576 | Excellent |

**Cash (Resource Type)**

| CashAccountID | AccountType | Location |
|---|---|---|
| Ca123501 | Checking | 1<sup>st</sup> Local Bank |

**DebtFinancingAgreement (Mutual Commitment) Event**

| LoanID | LoanDate | MaturityDate | InterestRate | Amount | CashReqID<sup>FK</sup> | CreditorID<sup>FK</sup> | OfficerID<sup>FK</sup> |
|---|---|---|---|---|---|---|---|
| | | | | | | | |

**EquityFinancingAgreement (Mutual Commitment) Event**

| StockID | IssueDate | Type | #shares | Par Value | Amount | CashReqID<sup>FK</sup> | InvestorID<sup>FK</sup> | OfficerID<sup>FK</sup> |
|---|---|---|---|---|---|---|---|---|
| | | | | | | | | |

Note: Fulfillment1 relationship is implemented with CashReqID posted into Debt Financing Agreement table and with CashReqID posted into Equity Financing Agreement table. Participation1 relationship is implemented with Suggested Investor/CreditorID posted into Cash Requisition table. Participation2 relationship is implemented with OfficerID posted into Cash Requisition table. Fulfillment1 data are not yet entered, assuming a time lag between cash requisition and financing agreements.

typically represented on paper as promissory notes or as bond certificates. In Exhibit 13–6 we illustrate a promissory note, and in Exhibit 13–7, a bond certificate.

Attributes of equity financing agreements that typically should be captured include the date the stock was issued, the par value of the stock, the number of shares issued, and the dollar amount for which the stock was issued. Exhibit 13–8 illustrates a share of stock. As mentioned earlier, the shares of stock do not guarantee future cash flows. Preferred stock may indicate a percentage or dollar amount for which preferred shareholders have dividend preference over common shareholders; however that does not guarantee **dividends** will ever be paid to anyone. Therefore the equity financing agreement may not be considered to be a mutual commitment event although the stock carries an implicit commitment on the part of the enterprise. Explicit commitments related to equity financing agreements are called dividend declarations. Enterprises declare (announce) they will pay dividends of a specific amount on a specific date. Dividend declarations are considered to be legal obligations of the enterprise; that is, once a dividend is declared the enterprise is required by law to actually pay the dividend. Dividend declarations are typically represented as

**EXHIBIT 13–6** Promissory Note

---

### *PROMISSORY NOTE*
SAMPLE for illustration purposes only

$450,000                                                          Date: May 1, 2009

For value received, the undersigned Your Source Company (the "Borrower"), at 123 Main St., Anytown, USA 12345, promises to pay to the order of First Chance Bank, (the "Lender"), at 43221 Financial Institute Way, (or at such other place as the Lender may designate in writing) the sum of $450,000.00 with 10% interest payments due on April 30 of each year beginning with April 30, 2010.

The unpaid principal shall be payable in full on April 30, 2029 (the "Due Date").

All payments on this Note shall be applied first in payment of accrued interest and any remainder in payment of principal.

If any payment obligation under this Note is not paid when due, the remaining unpaid principal balance and any accrued interest shall become due immediately at the option of the Lender.

The Borrower reserves the right to prepay this Note (in whole or in part) prior to the Due Date with no prepayment penalty.

If any payment obligation under this Note is not paid when due, the Borrower promises to pay all costs of collection, including reasonable attorney fees, whether or not a lawsuit is commenced as part of the collection process.

If any of the following events of default occur, this Note and any other obligations of the Borrower to the Lender, shall become due immediately, without demand or notice:
1) the failure of the Borrower to pay the principal and any accrued interest in full on or before the Due Date;
2) the death of the Borrower or Lender;
3) the filing of bankruptcy proceedings involving the Borrower as a debtor;
4) the application for the appointment of a receiver for the Borrower;
5) the making of a general assignment for the benefit of the Borrower's creditors;
6) the insolvency of the Borrower;
7) a misrepresentation by the Borrower to the Lender for the purpose of obtaining or extending credit.

If any one or more of the provisions of this Note are determined to be unenforceable, in whole or in part, for any reason, the remaining provisions shall remain fully operative.

All payments of principal and interest on this Note shall be paid in the legal currency of the United States. The Borrower waives presentment for payment, protest, and notice of protest and nonpayment of this Note.

No renewal or extension of this Note, delay in enforcing any right of the Lender under this Note, or assignment by Lender of this Note shall affect the liability or the obligations of the Borrower. All rights of the Lender under this Note are cumulative and may be exercised concurrently or consecutively at the Lender's option.

Signed this  1st  day of  May 2009  , at

Borrower: Your Source Company

By:  Woodrow D. James
     Woodrow D. James, on behalf of Your Source Company

---

commitment events that are related via reciprocal relationships to the equity financing agreement commitment events. Dividend declarations should be linked to data regarding the cash that they reserve for future payment, to the internal and external agents, and to the cash disbursement events that fulfill the commitments.

**EXHIBIT 13–7**   **Bond Certificate**

**EXHIBIT 13–8**   **Stock Certificate**

**EXHIBIT 13–9**   **Relational Tables Encompassing Commitment Event(s)**

**Debt FinancingAgreement (Mutual Commitment) Event**

| LoanID | LoanDate | MaturityDate | InterestRate | Amount | CashReqID[FK] | CreditorID[FK] | OfficerID[FK] |
|--------|----------|--------------|--------------|--------|---------------|----------------|---------------|
| L1 | 5/1/2009 | 4/30/2029 | 10% | $450,000 | 3 | V41 | E64 |

**EquityFinancingAgreement (Commitment) Event**

| StockID | IssueDate | Type | #shares | Par Value | Amount | CashReqID[FK] | InvestorID[FK] | OfficerID[FK] |
|---------|-----------|------|---------|-----------|--------|---------------|----------------|---------------|
| E1 | 5/1/2010 | Common | 50,000 | $4 | $500,000 | 3 | I234 | E64 |
| E2 | 5/1/2010 | Common | 50,000 | $4 | $500,000 | 3 | I235 | E64 |

**ReservationFinanceAgreementCashAcct (Reservation1) Relationship**

| FinanceAgreementID | CashAccountID | Amount Reserved |
|--------------------|---------------|-----------------|
| L1 | Ca123501 | $450,000 |
| E1 | Ca123501 | $500,000 |
| E2 | Ca123501 | $500,000 |

**ReciprocalDivDecEquityFinancing (Reciprocal) Relationship**

| StockID | DividendDeclarationID |
|---------|-----------------------|
| E1 | DD1 |
| E2 | DD1 |

**DividendDeclaration (Commitment) Event**

| DividendDeclarationID | DeclarationDate | DollarAmountperShare | PaymentDate | OfficerID[FK] |
|-----------------------|-----------------|----------------------|-------------|---------------|
| DD1 | 4/30/2011 | $.50 | 5/17/2010 | E64 |

**ParticipationDivDecInvestor (Participation10) Relationship**

| DividendDeclarationID | InvestorID |
|-----------------------|------------|
| DD1 | I234 |
| DD1 | I235 |

*(Continued)*

The set of relational tables in Exhibit 13–9 correspond to Exhibit 13–3's entity-relationship representation of the financing agreement events (with debt financing agreements and equity financing agreements in separate tables), the **dividend declaration commitment event,** and the relationships in which the various commitment events participate (reservation1, reservation2, fulfillment1, fulfillment2, participation3, participation4, participation9, and participation10). Alternative table configurations could be derived from this example, depending on the relationship cardinalities. You may have noticed that the cash requisition in this example had only suggested a creditor as the source of cash. However, apparently the financial officer decided to obtain most of the needed financing via issuance of common stock. Data from the forms in Exhibits 13–6 and 13–8 have been entered into the database tables; however, some of these data (e.g., cash account, financial officer, and investor/creditor information) would already have existed in the database tables before the financing agreement data were added to the tables so only the relationship information that links them to the financing agreement should be added for those objects.

**EXHIBIT 13–9**   (Continued)

**CashRequisition (Instigation) Event**

| CashReqID | Date | Dollar Amount Requested | OfficerIDᶠᴷ | Suggested Investor/Creditorᶠᴷ |
|---|---|---|---|---|
| 3 | 4/15/2009 | $1,450,000 | E64 | V41 |

**FinancialOfficer (Internal Agent)**

| OfficerID | Name | Authorized Debt Limit |
|---|---|---|
| E64 | Donald James | $2,500,000 |

**Investor/Creditor (External Agent)**

| Investor/CreditorID | Name | Address | Telephone | Performance Rating |
|---|---|---|---|---|
| V41 | First Chance Bank | 43221 Financial Institute Way | 555-5576 | Excellent |
| I234 | CREF | 1 Retirement Dr. | 555-9988 | Excellent |
| I235 | Schwarb | 852 Mutual Manor Ct. | 555-7312 | Excellent |

**Cash (Resource Type)**

| CashAccountID | AccountType | Location |
|---|---|---|
| Ca123501 | Checking | 1st Local Bank |

**FulfillmentCashReceiptFinancing (Fulfillment2) Relationship**

| FinancingAgreementID | CashReceiptID |
|---|---|
| | |

**FulfillmentCashDisbDebtFinancing (Fulfillment3) Relationship**

| LoanID | CashDisbursementID | Principal Pmt Amt | Interest Pmt Amt |
|---|---|---|---|
| | | | |

Note: Participation3 relationship is implemented with OfficerID posted into FinancingAgreement tables. Participation4 relationship is implemented with InvestorID posted into EquityFinancingAgreement table and with CreditorID posted into DebtFinancingAgreement table. Participation9 relationship is implemented with OfficerID posted into DividendDeclaration table. Fulfillment1 relationship is implemented with CashReqID posted into FinancingAgreement tables. Fulfillment2, Fulfillment3, and Fulfillment4 data are not yet entered, assuming a possible time lag between commitment events and the resulting cash receipts and cash disbursements. There is also a time lag between the financing agreements and the dividend declaration commitment event; this is indicated via the dates entered and the entry of the later event and relationship data in italic print.

The new data entered to record the financing agreement event are shown in italic. The new data entered to record the dividend declaration that is reciprocally related to the equity finance agreement are shown in italic print.

## Economic Increment Event (Cash Receipt)

Cash receipt is the primary **economic increment event** in the finance process. For debt financing agreements, the **cash receipt event** represents the receipt of the cash proceeds of the loan or bond. For equity financing agreements, the cash receipt event represents the receipt of the cash proceeds of the stock issuance. In both cases, the cash receipt event fulfills the commitment of the investors and creditors to provide cash to the enterprise; at the point of cash receipt, the enterprise has not yet fulfilled its commitment to provide loan repayments or dividend payments to the investors and creditors. As in the sales/collection process, the receipt of cash is a custodial function. The document typically involved in task activities that comprise the cash receipt event in the financing cycle is a deposit slip. When cash from financing is received (usually in the form of checks), internal agents (usually **cashiers**) verify the payment information is correctly recorded on a deposit slip. A copy of the deposit slip is retained by the enterprise and the original is sent with the proceeds to the bank for deposit. In some cases investors and creditors may electronically transfer funds to the enterprise rather than sending checks through the mail. In such cases the investors and creditors may send a direct deposit notification; otherwise the monthly bank statement will serve as notification of the cash receipt.

Relationships in which the cash event in the financing process participates typically include a **fulfillment relationship** (enabling the enterprise to trace which debt or equity financing agreement event the cash receipt fulfilled), a **duality relationship** (allowing the enterprise to trace the related cash disbursements), a **stockflow relationship** (to trace the cash account into which the cash receipt was deposited), and **participation relationships** with internal agents (typically cashiers) and external agents (investors or creditors).

The set of relational tables in Exhibit 13–10 correspond to Exhibit 13–3's entity-relationship representation of the cash receipt event and the relationships in which it participates (stockflow1, fulfillment2, participation5, participation6, and duality). Other possible tables could be derived, depending on the relationship cardinalities. Example data regarding cash receipt events have been entered into the database tables; however, some of these data (e.g., cash account, financing agreement, investor and creditor information, and employee information) would already have existed in the database tables before the cash receipt data were added to the tables so only relationship information that links them to the cash receipt event is added for those objects. The new data to be added upon receipts of cash from financing agreements are printed in color.

## Economic Decrement Event (Cash Disbursement)

Cash disbursements are **economic decrement events** that decrease the enterprise's cash balance. Cash disbursements in the financing cycle are typically made by paper check or **electronic funds transfer** and are made to fulfill the terms of the financing agreement, in exchange for the cash receipts that occurred at a previous point in time. Attributes captured regarding cash disbursements usually include a cash disbursement identifier (such as a disbursement voucher number), date, amount paid, the check number of the payment, payee identification (investor or creditor), employee identification (i.e., employee who wrote the check), the cash account from which the cash is disbursed, and links to the reason for the cash disbursement (i.e., what commitment it is fulfilling and the economic increment event that began the exchange). Exhibit 13–11 shows a set of relational tables that correspond to Exhibit 13–3's entity-relationship representation of the cash disbursement event and the financing cycle relationships in which it participates (duality, fulfillment3, fulfillment4, stockflow2, participation7, and participation8). Alternative table configurations could be derived, depending on the relationship cardinalities. As noted in the acquisition/payment cycle chapter, additional tables are necessary to correspond to relationships in which the cash disbursement event participates in other transaction cycles such as acquisition/payment and payroll. The tables shown in Exhibit 13–10 are applicable to the financing process. Data for cash disbursements applicable to the financing process have been entered into the database tables; however, some of these data (e.g., financing agreements, dividend declaration, cash accounts, investor/creditor information, and employee information) would already have existed in the database tables before the cash disbursement data were added to the tables. Only

**EXHIBIT 13–10** **Relational Tables Encompassing Cash Receipts**

**CashReceipt (Economic Increment) Event**

| CashReceiptID | Date | DollarAmount | CashAccountID[FK] | ExtAgentID[FK] | CashierID[FK] |
|---|---|---|---|---|---|
| RA14 | 5/1/2009 | $450,000 | Ca123501 | V41 | E111 |
| RA15 | 5/1/2010 | $500,000 | Ca123501 | I234 | E111 |
| RA16 | 5/1/2010 | $500,000 | Ca123501 | I235 | E111 |

**FulfillmentCashReceiptFinancingAgreement (Fulfillment2) Relationship**

| FinancingAgreementID | CashReceiptID |
|---|---|
| L1 | RA14 |
| E1 | RA15 |
| E2 | RA16 |

**DebtFinancingAgreement (Mutual Commitment) Event**

| LoanID | LoanDate | MaturityDate | InterestRate | Amount | CashReqID[FK] | CreditorID[FK] | OfficerID[FK] |
|---|---|---|---|---|---|---|---|
| L1 | 5/1/2009 | 4/30/2029 | 10% | $450,000 | 3 | V41 | E64 |

**EquityFinancingAgreement (Mutual Commitment) Event**

| StockID | IssueDate | Type | #shares | Par Value | Amount | CashReqID[FK] | InvestorID[FK] | OfficerID[FK] |
|---|---|---|---|---|---|---|---|---|
| E1 | 5/1/2010 | Common | 50,000 | $4 | $500,000 | 3 | I234 | E64 |
| E2 | 5/1/2010 | Common | 50,000 | $4 | $500,000 | 3 | I235 | E64 |

**Cashier (Internal Agent)**

| CashierID | Name | Address | Telephone | DateOfBirth |
|---|---|---|---|---|
| E111 | Missy Witherspoon | 1710 Crestwood Dr. | 555-9392 | May 11, 1960 |

**Investor/Creditor (External Agent)**

| Investor/CreditorID | Name | Address | Telephone | Performance Rating |
|---|---|---|---|---|
| V41 | First Chance Bank | 43221 Financial Institute Way | 555-5576 | Excellent |
| I234 | CREF | 1 Retirement Dr. | 555-9988 | Excellent |
| I235 | Schwarb | 852 Mutual Manor Ct. | 555-7312 | Excellent |

**Cash (Resource Type)**

| CashAccountID | AccountType | Location |
|---|---|---|
| Ca123501 | Checking | 1st Local Bank |

**DualityCashDisbursementCashReceipt Relationship**

| CashReceipt | CashDisbursementID |
|---|---|

Note: Participation5 relationship are implemented with CashierID posted into CashReceipt table. Participation6 relationship is implemented with ExtAgentID posted into CashReceipt table. Duality data are not yet entered, assuming a time lag between CashReceipt and CashDisbursement.

relationship information that links those objects to the cash disbursements is added to the database upon entry of the cash disbursement. The new data to be added for the cash disbursement event are shown in colored print.

**EXHIBIT 13–11**　**Relational Tables Encompassing Cash Disbursement Event**

**CashDisbursement (Economic Decrement) Event**

| Disb Voucher ID | Voucher Date | Dollar Amount | Check Number | Cash AccountID[FK] | Financing ClerkID[FK] | PayeeID[FK] |
|---|---|---|---|---|---|---|
| 124 | 4/30/2010 | $45,000 | 921 | Ca123501 | E36 | V41 |
| 138 | 5/17/2010 | $25,000 | 935 | Ca123501 | E36 | I234 |
| 139 | 5/17/2010 | $25,000 | 936 | Ca123501 | E36 | I235 |

**DualityCashDisbursementCashReceipt Relationship**

| CashReceipt | CashDisbursementID |
|---|---|
| RA14 | 124 |
| RA15 | 138 |
| RA16 | 139 |

**FulfillmentCashDisbDebtFinancing (Fulfillment3) Relationship**

| LoanID | CashDisbursementID | PrincipalPaid | InterestPaid |
|---|---|---|---|
| L1 | 124 | $0 | $45,000 |

**FulfillmentCashDisbEquityFinancing (Fulfillment4) Relationship**

| DividendDeclarationID | CashDisbursementID |
|---|---|
| DD1 | 138 |
| DD1 | 139 |

**Cash (Resource Type)**

| CashAccountID | AccountType | Location |
|---|---|---|
| Ca123501 | Checking | 1st Local Bank |

**CashReceipt (Economic Increment) Event**

| CashReceiptID | Date | DollarAmount | CashAccountID[FK] | ExtAgentID[FK] | CashierID[FK] | |
|---|---|---|---|---|---|---|
| RA14 | 5/1/2009 | $450,000 | Ca123501 | V41 | E111 | |
| RA15 | 5/1/2010 | $500,000 | Ca123501 | I234 | E111 | |
| RA16 | 5/1/2010 | $500,000 | Ca123501 | I235 | E111 | *(Continued)* |

# INFORMATION NEEDS AND MEASURES IN THE FINANCING PROCESS

The most common information customers for the financing business process include top management, investors, creditors, accountants, and auditors. We next analyze each of the entities and relationships in the financing process pattern to provide some ideas about the queries that may be needed to satisfy information needs in the financing cycle. The queries presented are not a comprehensive set of queries (there are simply too many potential queries to list them all); however, the set provided should guide you in creating similar types of queries. To describe queries needed in the financing cycle we use the database tables shown in Exhibits 13–5, 13–9, and 13–10.

**EXHIBIT 13–11** (Concluded)

**DebtFinancingAgreement (Mutual Commitment) Event**

| LoanID | LoanDate | MaturityDate | InterestRate | Amount | CashReqIDFK | CreditorIDFK | OfficerIDFK |
|--------|----------|--------------|--------------|--------|-------------|--------------|-------------|
| L1 | 5/1/2009 | 4/30/2029 | 10% | $450,000 | 3 | V41 | E64 |

**Investor/Creditor (External Agent)**

| Investor/CreditorID | Name | Address | Telephone | Performance Rating |
|---------------------|------|---------|-----------|--------------------|
| V41 | First Chance Bank | 43221 Financial Institute Way | 555-5576 | Excellent |
| I234 | CREF | 1 Retirement Dr. | 555-9988 | Excellent |
| I235 | Schwarb | 852 Mutual Manor Ct. | 555-7312 | Excellent |

**FinancingClerk (Internal Agent)**

| FinancingClerkID | Name | Fidelity Bond Rating |
|------------------|------|----------------------|
| E36 | Diane Bowersox | AA |

Note: Stockflow2 is implemented with CashAccountID posted into CashDisbursement table. Participation7 is implemented with FinancingClerkID posted into CashDisbursement table. Participation8 is implemented with PayeeID posted into CashDisbursement table.

## Resource Queries in the Financing Process

Cash is the resource that most commonly exists in the financing process. Cash is usually tracked by the accounts in which the cash is stored. Cash queries are described in Chapters 8 through 12 so we do not repeat those details here.

## Event Queries in the Financing Process

Users may need information regarding events. The most common events in the financing process are cash requisitions, debt and equity financing agreements, cash receipts, dividend declarations, and cash disbursements. For each of these types of events, users may need any of the following:

- Detailed information about each event instance.
- Detailed information about each event instance that meets specified criteria.
- Summarized information for all instances of an event type for a specified time period.
- Summarized information for only those instances of an event type for a specified time period that meet specified criteria.

Chosen from many other possibilities, the following queries based on the tables in this chapter can satisfy information needs regarding events in the financing process:

- *What dollar amount was requested on cash requisition 3?* Using the CashRequisition table, enter criterion =3 in the cash requisition ID field; display the dollar amount requested field.
- *Which loans bear interest rates > 9%, and what are the dollar amounts of those loans?* Using the DebtFinancingAgreement table, enter criterion >.09 in the interest rate field; display the loan ID and amount fields.

- *How many shares of common stock have been issued as of 5/31/2010?* Using the EquityFinancingAgreement table, enter criteria <=5/31/2010 in the issue date field and =common in the type field; apply the SUM aggregation operator to the #shares field.
- *How many cash receipts occurred in May 2010?* Using the CashReceipt table, enter criteria BETWEEN 5/1/2010 and 5/31/2010 in the date field; apply COUNT aggregation function to the cash receipt ID field.

## Agent Queries in the Financing Process

The agents commonly involved in financing processes are the financial officers who authorize the financing transactions, the investors and creditors from whom financing is acquired, and the cashiers or other clerks who process the cash receipts and cash disbursements. Queries may be needed to obtain any of the following:

- Detailed status information at one or more points in time for each financial officer, investor, creditor, cashier, or clerk.
- Detailed status information at one or more points in time for each financial officer, investor, creditor, cashier, or clerk who meets specified criteria.
- Summarized status information at one or more points in time for all financial officers, investors, creditors, cashiers, or clerks.
- Summarized status information at one or more points in time for all financial officers, investors, creditors, cashiers, or clerks who meet specified criteria.

Some example queries based on the tables in this chapter are as follows:

- *What are the names and addresses of the investors who have been rated as excellent?* Using the Investor/Creditor table, enter criterion =Excellent in the performance rating field; display the name and address fields.
- *Which financial officer has the highest limit for which to authorize debt?* Using the FinancialOfficer table, apply the MAX aggregation function to the authorized debt limit field; display the officer ID field.

### Relationship Queries

Combining information from various resource, event, and agent tables in accordance with the relationships in which they participate can provide much richer data than single table queries. We next discuss queries based on the various relationships in the financing process.

## Duality and Fulfillment Relationship Queries in the Financing Process

The duality relationship set in the financing process connects cash receipts (financing acquisitions) to cash disbursements (financing payments), as it represents exchanges of cash for cash. Because the financing cash receipts may result from either debt or equity financing, the direct duality relationship between cash receipts and cash disbursements is often somewhat ambiguous. Other than identifying what cash disbursements applied to a cash receipt, and vice versa, there is not much information content to be gained from examining the duality relationship in the financing process. Instead it is typically more informative to examine the fulfillment relationships between the financing agreement and the cash receipts and between the financing agreement and the cash disbursements.

In the financing process, each financing agreement (both equity and debt) is associated with at least one cash receipt and at least one cash disbursement. Debt obligations are cash receipts that relate to debt financing agreements. Cash disbursements related to debt financing agreements indicate repayments of debts. Comparisons of the debt obligations to repayments of those debts reveal loans or notes payable balances.

Fulfillment relationship queries in the financing process in general include:

- Identification of unfilled commitment events (e.g., financing agreements for which cash has not yet been received and/or for which cash disbursements have not been made in full).

- Identification of filled commitment events (e.g., financing agreements for which cash was received and cash was repaid according to payment terms).

Based on the tables in this chapter, questions such as the following could be answered via fulfillment relationship queries in the financing process:

- *What is the outstanding principal balance of debt financing agreement L1 as of May 1, 2010?* **Query 1:** The outstanding principal balance for a loan is increased by cash receipt amounts that represent the principal acquired. To find the principal amounts acquired through May 1, 2010, join the CashReceipt and FulfillmentCashReceiptDebtFinancing tables; enter criteria =L1 in the financing agreement ID field and <=5/1/2010 in the cash receipt date field; apply the SUM aggregation operator to the cash receipt dollar amount field. **Query 2:** The outstanding principal balance for a loan is decreased by cash disbursement amounts that represent repayments of principal. To find the principal repayment amounts that occurred through May 1, 2010, join the FulfillmentCashDisbDebtFinancing table to the CashDisbursement table; enter criteria =L1 in the loan ID field and <=5/1/2010 in the cash disbursement voucher date field; apply the SUM aggregation operator to the PrincipalPaid field. **Query 3:** Subtract the sum calculated in query 2 from the sum calculated in query 1.

- *Have any cash receipts occurred that were not related to financing agreements?* Join CashReceipts table to FulfillmentCashReceiptFinancing table with an outer join keeping all cash receipts; include cash receipt ID from CashReceipt table and financing agreement ID from FulfillmentCashReceiptFinancing table; set criteria to IS NULL in the financing agreement ID field.

## Stockflow Relationship Queries in the Financing Process

Stockflow relationships in the financing process represent the connections between cash and the economic events that increase and decrease cash. Some common stockflow information needs in the financing process (among other possibilities) are:

- Which cash account was decreased by a cash disbursement?
- What is the total dollar amount of cash disbursements made from a specified cash account during a time period?
- Which cash account was increased by a cash receipt?
- What is the total dollar amount of cash receipts for a specified cash account during a time period?

Because these types of stockflow queries have been illustrated in Chapters 8 through 11, we do not repeat these details here.

## Reservation Queries in the Financing Process

The **reservation relationship** that is typically materialized in the financing process represents the associations between financing agreements and the cash the agreements commit to acquire and repay. Therefore reservation relationships in the financing process are commonly used in queries to satisfy information needs as to the eventual effect of financing agreements on cash. Some common information needs (among many others) in the financing cycle are

- What dollar amount is a financing agreement committing to acquire for a specific cash account?
- From which cash accounts will any dividend declarations that occurred during a specific time period be paid?
- What is the dollar value of cash reserved by a dividend declaration?
- On what dates is a financing agreement committing to acquire cash?

Based on the tables in this chapter, questions such as the following could be answered via reservation relationship queries in the financing cycle:

- *What dollar amount is financing agreement E1 committing to acquire for cash account Ca123501?* Use the ReservationFinanceAgreementCashAcct table; enter criterion =E1 in the finance agreement ID field and =Ca123501 in the cash account ID field; display the amount reserved field.
- *What is the total dollar amount reserved for cash account Ca123501 by financing agreements during the month of May 2010?* **Query 1:** To determine the dollar amount reserved for cash account Ca123501 by equity financing agreements during May 2010, join the ReservationFinanceAgreementCashAcct table to the EquityFinancingAgreement table; enter criterion =Ca123501 in the cash account ID field and BETWEEN 5/1/2010 and 5/31/2010 in the issue date field; apply the SUM aggregation operator to the amount reserved field. **Query 2:** To determine the dollar amount reserved for cash account Ca123501 by debt financing agreements during May 2010, join the ReservationFinanceAgreementCashAcct table to the DebtFinancingAgreement table; enter criterion =Ca123501 in the cash account ID field and BETWEEN 5/1/2010 and 5/31/2010 in the loan date field; apply the SUM aggregation operator to the amount reserved field. **Query 3:** Add the sum from query 1 to the sum from query 2 to get the total reserved amount for cash account Ca123501 during May 2010

## Participation Queries in the Financing Process

Participation relationships in the financing cycle typically represent the associations between cash requisitions, debt financing agreements, equity financing agreements, cash receipts, dividend declarations, and cash disbursements and the employees who authorize those events (typically financial officers), the employees who accomplish those events (typically cashiers), and the investors and creditors with whom cash is exchanged. Therefore participation relationships are commonly used in queries to satisfy information needs as to the identification of employees, investors, or creditors who participated in financing events or as to the financing events in which specific employees, investors, or creditors participated. Some common financing cycle information needs are

- Which financial officer authorized a cash requisition?
- How many debt financing agreements has a financial officer approved?

- What is the total dollar amount of cash disbursements paid to a specific creditor?
- How many shares of common stock has a specific investor purchased?
- Which cashier processed a specific cash receipt?

Based on the tables in this chapter, questions such as the following could be answered via participation relationship financing cycle queries:

- *What is the name of the financial officer who authorized cash requisition 3?* Join the CashRequisition table to the FinancialOfficer table; enter criterion =3 in the cash requisition ID field and display the officer name field.
- *How many debt financing agreements has Donald James approved?* Join the DebtFinancingAgreement table to the FinancialOfficer table; enter criterion =Donald James in the officer name; apply the COUNT aggregation operator to the LoanID field.
- *What is the name of the cashier who processed cash receipt RA15?* Join the CashReceipt table to the Cashier table; enter criterion =RA15 in the cash receipt ID field; display the cashier name field.
- *What are the name and address of the investor(s) to which the most shares of common stock have been issued?* **Query 1:** To sum the number of shares issued to each investor, use the EquityFinancingAgreement table; apply the GROUP BY aggregation operator to the investor ID field; apply the SUM aggregation operator to the #shares field. **Query 2:** To identify the names and addresses of the investors to which the most shares have been issued, Join the result of Query 1 to the Investor/Creditor table; apply the MAX aggregation operator to the sum of #shares field; display the investor name and investor address fields.

## CONCLUDING COMMENTS

This chapter presented an overview of the activities in the finance process and discussed the extended REA pattern as it is applied to this process. Information needs associated with the finance business process were also described in this chapter, although those identified are not a comprehensive list. An enterprise with an enterprise system based on the REA pattern is able to satisfy most (if not all) of the information needs by constructing queries based on its database tables.

## Key Terms and Concepts

Cash disbursement event, *414*
Cash flow budget, *413*
Cash receipt event, *419*
Cash requisition event, *413*
Cashier, *420*
Commitment event, *411*
Creditor, *410*
Debt financing, *410*
Dividend declaration commitment event, *418*

Dividends, *415*
Duality relationship, *420*
Economic decrement event, *420*
Economic increment event, *419*
Electronic funds transfer, *420*
Equity financing, *410*
Financial officer, *413*

Fulfillment relationship, *420*
Investor, *410*
Participation relationship, *420*
Reservation relationship, *426*
Shares of stock, *410*
Stock issuance commitment event, *414*
Stockflow relationship, *420*

# Review Questions

LO1   R1.   What is the primary objective of the financing business process?

LO2   R2.   How is the financing process related to the conversion process, the sales/collection process, the acquisition/payment process, and the payroll process?

LO1   R3.   What is the difference between a bond certificate and a stock certificate?

LO1   R4.   Which documents are typically used to represent a debt financing agreement event?

LO2   R5.   Identify the resources, internal agents, and external agents associated with each of the following events in the finance process:

   a.   Cash requisition (instigation) event
   b.   Loan (mutual commitment) event
   c.   Stock issuance (commitment to increment) event
   d.   Dividend declaration (commitment to decrement) event
   e.   Cash receipt (economic increment) event
   f.   Cash disbursement (economic decrement) event

# Multiple Choice Questions

LO1   MC1.   Which document typically represents the same phenomena as the cash receipt (economic increment) event?

   A.   Disbursement voucher
   B.   Deposit slip
   C.   Stock certificate
   D.   Promissory note

LO2   MC2.   The financing process represents the point of contact between the enterprise and which set of external business partners?

   A.   Investors and creditors
   B.   Suppliers
   C.   Customers
   D.   Employees

LO2   MC3.   The resource made available by the finance process to the payroll process in a typical enterprise value chain is

   A.   Finished goods inventory
   B.   Machinery and equipment
   C.   Labor
   D.   Cash

LO2   MC4.   Which of the following entities are usually paired in a stockflow relationship in the finance process?

   A.   Cash receipt and employee
   B.   Cash and debt financing agreement
   C.   Cash and cash receipt
   D.   Stock issuance and cash receipt

LO2   MC5.  Which of the following events reflects the commitment of the enterprise to receive and to repay cash provided by a creditor?
   A.  Debt financing agreement
   B.  Dividend declaration
   C.  Cash requisition
   D.  Cash disbursement

## Discussion Questions

LO4   D1.  Describe at least two financing process information needs for each of the following:
   a.  Management
   b.  Finance and accounting
   c.  Investors and creditors

LO5   D2.  What entities and/or relationships most likely need to be included in a query to calculate the loan payable balance for each creditor? (Assume the balance is not stored as a volatile derivable attribute in the creditor table.)

LO4, LO5   D3.  When determining how much cash to keep on hand, what are some of the factors financial officers need to consider, and how can the database tables based on the REA business process level model help them determine a cash budget?

## Answers to Multiple Choice Questions

MC1. B; MC2. A; MC3. D; MC4. C; MC5. A.

# Chapter **Fourteen**

# Enterprise System Risks and Controls

## LEARNING OBJECTIVES

A consideration of utmost importance for enterprise system designers, managers, and auditors is the consideration of risk and control. The objective of this chapter is to introduce some types of risk that occur in enterprises and discuss how these risks may be lessened by controls designed into enterprise information systems. This chapter uses the REA pattern as a framework for identifying types of risks and controls to mitigate those risks. After studying this chapter you should be able to:

1. Describe the relationship between enterprise risks, opportunities, and controls
2. Explain the levels at which enterprise risks occur
3. Use the REA pattern to identify sources of enterprise risk
4. Identify specific controls to prevent, detect, and recover from enterprise risks

## THE RELATIONSHIPS BETWEEN RISKS, OPPORTUNITIES, AND CONTROLS

### Risks

A **risk** is any **exposure** to the chance of injury or loss. Every enterprise faces a multitude of risks. When a risk materializes it threatens some aspect of the entities' operations and more serious risks threaten the ongoing existence of the entity. Every day the news is filled with risks that have developed into major losses, scandals, or total collapses of enterprises. **Threat** is another word some people use to describe these situations because they represent a possible or probable loss to the entity. The following are just a few risks or threats that have plagued many companies:

- Bad decisions by management to discontinue popular product lines.
- Faulty product design that causes costly recalls.
- Fabrication of product quality tests to enhance the value of the company's stock.
- Invasion of a company's network by hackers through the Internet.
- Recognition of revenues a company has not actually earned.

- Overstatement of inventory or operating assets on a company's balance sheet.
- Understatement or misclassification of debt on a company's balance sheet.

Every time one of these risks materializes, critics ask, "Why?" They criticize management for lack of due care. They criticize the auditors for not detecting the problem. They question how such a thing could happen within the enterprise and not be noticed by other people. Risks need to be identified and controlled, but they must be balanced with opportunities, objectives, and the cost of controls. Enterprises must balance operational efficiency with operational effectiveness. Enterprise information systems may sometimes facilitate efficient and effective controls.

## Opportunities and Objectives

Why do individuals and enterprises take risks? Why expose themselves to threats of loss? **Opportunity** and risk go hand in hand. You can't have an opportunity without some risk and with every risk there is some potential opportunity. Typically greater opportunities are accompanied by higher risks, and vice versa. For example, investments in stock are generally riskier than investments in government bonds; those stock investments also provide the potential for greater returns than do the bonds. Individual and enterprise objectives determine the extent to which risks are sought or avoided. Conservative objectives that easily can be achieved require less risk. More aggressive objectives create greater risk as more difficult and complex activities are pursued to achieve them. As an example, say, you have $10,000 available to invest and you do not need this money back until after you retire 40 years from now. If over the course of those 40 years your goal is to simply double your money for a total of $20,000, there is no need to invest in risky investments, as investments that are considered risk-free are likely to double your money in 40 years. If your objectives are more aggressive, such as increasing your $10,000 by 500 percent, then you need to consider more risky investments that have a higher potential return. With every opportunity there is some element of risk. We seek to manage these risks by a system of controls.

## Controls

With every opportunity there is some element of risk. To mitigate the risk of loss while gaining the advantages afforded by risky activity, most enterprises implement a system of **internal controls.** Such controls are activities performed to minimize or eliminate risks. For example, a control to mitigate the risk of stock market investments is to maintain a diversified portfolio rather than holding only one company's stock. Similarly, an enterprise that sells goods on credit rather than requiring immediate cash payment for sales creates an opportunity for additional sales, but also incurs a risk of bad debts. An internal control that may be adopted to mitigate this risk is to check customers' credit ratings before approving sales to the customers.

Internal controls within enterprise systems are increasingly important in today's economy. Because of recent scandals, Congress passed the Sarbanes-Oxley Act requiring that when publicly traded companies issue their annual financial reports, they also must issue reports on their internal control systems. The internal control reports must state management's responsibility for establishing and maintaining adequate internal controls for financial reporting and the reports must include assessments of the effectiveness of the internal controls and the financial reporting procedures. Sarbanes-Oxley further requires auditors

**EXHIBIT 14–1**
**Materiality**
**of Risk**

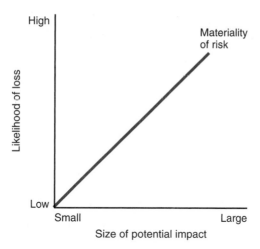

to attest to and report on the assessments made by management in the internal control reports. The AICPA's **Statement of Auditing Standards No. 94** largely established current standards for internal controls.[1] Two important documents in the development of current enterprise risk management and control philosophies were issued by the **Committee of Sponsoring Organizations of the Treadway Commission (COSO).**[2] These documents stress the importance of examining controls at many levels of detail.

Two major concerns regarding controls are the time they consume and the cost. Often multiple controls could each mitigate a particular risk; sometimes the controls differ in cost and effectiveness. So many potential risks exist that it may seem overwhelming to try to control all of them. It may also be cost prohibitive to control every potential risk. Only significant risks for which controls are cost effective should be controlled. The significance of a risk is determined by its impact on the enterprise, and the likelihood of it occurring. *Exposure* is a word some people use to describe the potential impact on the entity, that is, uncontrolled risk. Some people also use the term *risk* in a more narrow sense to describe the probability of a loss occurring. Risks that prevent an enterprise from achieving its objectives are very costly and may have a catastrophic impact on the ongoing viability of the entity. **Materiality of risk,** illustrated in Exhibit 14–1, is a function of:

1. The size of the potential loss and its impact on achieving the enterprise's objectives.
2. The likelihood of the loss.

As either the likelihood or size of the loss increases, the materiality of the risk also increases. With higher materiality comes a greater need to manage risk. In many situations these evaluations can be measured only in rough, order-of-magnitude amounts.

---

[1]Auditing Standards Board, American Institute of Certified Public Accountants, Statement of Auditing Standards No. 94, *The Effect of Information Technology on the Auditor's Consideration of Internal Control in a Financial Statement Audit* (New York: AICPA, 2001).

[2]Internal Control–Integrated Framework (New York: Committee of Sponsoring Organizations of the Treadway Commission, 1992); Enterprise Risk Management Framework (New York: Committee of Sponsoring Organizations of the Treadway Commission, 2004).

Management may choose to ignore risks that have a low impact and a low likelihood of occurrence unless the controls are costless. Controlling all risks to the point of eliminating all potential losses is quite unrealistic and unnecessary. In fact, a commitment to zero risk could render an enterprise totally ineffective because many controls add inconvenience to business processes. Enterprises typically concentrate their control design efforts on risks that have a high impact and a high likelihood of occurrence. Many enterprises choose to purchase insurance to mitigate risks that have a high impact and a low likelihood of occurrence. For risks that have a low impact and a high likelihood of occurrence, management designs controls only if the cumulative costs of the controls are less than the cumulative probable losses based on the risk. The key is identifying and controlling risks in a manner such that the *benefits* of controlling the risks exceed the *costs* of the controls, while balancing enterprise efficiency and effectiveness.

# COMPONENTS OF INTERNAL CONTROL SYSTEMS

The COSO internal control integrated framework discusses five interrelated components of internal control systems: the **control environment, risk assessment, control activities, information and communications,** and **monitoring.** Each of these components is discussed in the following sections.

## Control Environment

*Control environment* sets the tone of the enterprise, which influences the control consciousness of its people. Some people refer to the control environment as the tone at the top. This foundation provides discipline and structure upon which all other components of internal control are built. The control environment includes the following areas:

Integrity and ethical behavior.

Commitment to competence.

Board of directors and audit committee participation.

Management philosophy and operating style.

Organization structure.

Assignment of authority and responsibility.

Human resource policies and practices.

The attitudes and actions of top management largely determine the climate of an enterprise. Consider the environment of one enterprise with top management that has very high standards of moral and ethical conduct, that is committed to hiring competent people and properly training them for their work, that develops an organizational structure where the work of one person is checked by the work of another person, and that is conservative in management style and financial reporting. Contrast this with the climate of a second enterprise in which top management constantly tries to take unfair advantage of their employees, in which people are poorly trained, in which employees' work is poorly defined, and in which management constantly tries to overstate their achievements and minimize their problems. Since the attitudes and actions of lower-level employees typically mirror the attitudes and actions they see in top management, we would expect to find a strong control environment in the first enterprise but a rather weak control environment in the second enterprise.

## Risk Assessment

*Risk assessment* is an element of an internal control system that involves the identification and analysis of relevant risks associated with the enterprise achieving its objectives. Risk assessment forms the basis for determining what risks need to be controlled and the controls required to manage them.

Risk assessment should include consideration of previous company losses and the reasons for those losses, consideration of similar companies' losses and reasons for those losses, and communication with employees about where errors and irregularities are most likely to occur. Historical analysis of past errors and irregularities identifies potential future losses and provides information by which both the probability and the magnitude of the loss may be estimated. Much also can be learned by analyzing other companies' mistakes by examining information available directly from the company or through published literature. Most employees are honest and want to do a good job. They know where errors and irregularities have occurred and have not been reported, and they know where irregularities could occur and not be detected easily. Effective communication with employees may reveal critical information needed for risk assessment.

## Control Activities

*Control activities* are policies and procedures enterprises use to ensure necessary actions are taken to minimize risks associated with achieving enterprise objectives. Controls have different objectives and may be applied at various organizational and functional levels.

Control activities may be classified by function, whether they are used to prevent, detect, or recover from errors or irregularities. The purpose of each control is evident by its name.

- **Preventive controls** focus on preventing errors or irregularities.
- **Detective controls** focus on identifying that errors or irregularities have occurred.
- **Corrective controls** focus on recovering from, repairing the damage from, or minimizing the cost of errors or irregularities.

An **error** is an unintended mistake on the part of an employee while an **irregularity** is an intentional effort to do something that is undesirable to the enterprise. Often much of our attention is focused on irregularities; however, more money is lost as a result of errors than as a result of irregularities.

It is better to prevent an error or irregularity rather than detect it and then have to incur the cost of recovering from the consequences. Because preventive controls are not always possible or cost effective, companies must have a means for determining if the prevention has been effective; therefore detective and corrective controls also are needed. As an example, a control to *prevent* theft of cash by a salesclerk is to have a second clerk assist with each cash sale. This preventive control could fail if the two employees *collude* with each other (i.e., act together to conspire in a **fraud**). Another preventive control that lessens the possibility of **collusion** is to eliminate the use of cash entirely by requiring all payments to be made with a credit card or through an electronic fund transfer. The latter preventive control may not be cost effective. The costs include the transaction costs associated with using credit cards and electronic funds transfers (sellers who accept credit cards pay fees to the credit card companies) and the opportunity costs associated with lost revenues from customers who do not want to pay with credit cards or electronic fund transfers. If the enterprise weighs these costs against the benefit of preventing employee theft, the enterprise may conclude it is an undesirable control. Therefore the enterprise may implement one or more detective and corrective controls to back up the preventive control and ensure its effectiveness. For example, as the sales clerks scan items sold, the cash register prices them automatically. The rule that requires a comparison of the cash in the cash drawer with total sales accumulated by the cash register during an employee's shift is an example of a *detective* control. If the cash in the cash drawer does not equal total sales, we know the employee either pocketed some of the money or made an error in giving change to a customer. An example of a *corrective* control is a policy of deducting the amount of a cash shortage from the employee's pay.

## Information and Communication

The *information system* consists of the methods and records used to record, maintain, and report the events of an entity, as well as to maintain accountability for the related assets, liabilities, and equity. The quality of the system-generated information affects management's ability to make appropriate decisions in managing and controlling the entity's activities and to prepare reliable financial reports.

The information system should do each of the following to provide accurate and complete information in the accounting system and correctly report the results of operations:

1. Identify and record all business events on a timely basis.
2. Describe each event in sufficient detail.
3. Measure the proper monetary value of each event.
4. Determine the time period in which events occurred.
5. Present properly the events and related disclosures in the financial statements.

The *communication* aspect of this component deals with providing an understanding of individual roles and responsibilities pertaining to internal controls. People should understand how their activities relate to the work of others and how exceptions should be reported to higher levels of management. Open channels for communication help ensure that exceptions are reported and acted upon. Communication also includes the policy manuals, accounting manuals, and financial reporting manuals.

## Monitoring

*Monitoring* is the process of assessing the quality of internal control performance over time. This is extremely important as most enterprises are constantly changing their operations to meet new demands in the marketplace and capitalize on new opportunities. Monitoring involves assessing the design and operation of controls on a timely basis and taking corrective actions as needed. This process is accomplished by ongoing monitoring activities by management as they question reports that differ significantly from their knowledge of operations. Internal auditors or system evaluators also accomplish it through periodic evaluations to review internal controls, evaluate their effectiveness, report their results, and provide recommendations for improvement. Information from external entities is also valuable in monitoring internal controls. Complaints by customers or suppliers about billings or payments, reviews by various governmental agencies, and reports by external auditors all provide information on the adequacy of internal controls and how to improve them.

**Performance reviews** are any reviews of an enterprise's performance that provide a means for monitoring. Some of the more common reviews compare actual data to budgeted or prior period data, operating data to financial data, and data within and across various units, subdivisions, or functional areas of the enterprise. An example of a performance review is a comparison of actual production costs of the current period to last period's production costs to identify any significant deviation. Any cost category that deviates significantly from last year should be investigated so the cause may be identified. Another example is a comparison of the dollar value for sales within each region of an enterprise to the quantity of inventory shipped to each region to determine whether the ratio of sales to quantity shipped is similar for each region. If a region's ratio is lower than others, the cause should be investigated—it could be due to theft, damaged inventory, or some other explanation.

The COSO report recommends that evaluation of internal control systems focus first on risk identification, next on identification of mitigating controls, and finally on tests to determine whether the controls are operating effectively. The increased monitoring and attestation regarding internal control systems recommended by COSO and demanded by the Sarbanes-Oxley Act is facilitated by business process and information system designers similarly focusing on risk identification, development of cost-beneficial mitigating controls that can be designed into the business process and/or into the supporting information systems, and then implementation of those controls.

# RISK IDENTIFICATION

Enterprise risks occur at several levels: economy, industry, enterprise, business process, and information process. Table 14–1 illustrates these levels and lists some types of risk at each level. Keep in mind that the risks identified in Table 14–1 are not a comprehensive list. In fact, a comprehensive list is impossible because the environment, technology, and people are constantly changing and new risks continually arise. Also please realize that the categorization of risks is not an exact science. Overlaps sometimes make it difficult to distinguish an economy risk from an industry risk, or an industry risk from an enterprise risk. The most important objective is for you to recognize the risks as potential threats of loss, whether they are economy, industry, enterprise, business process, or information process risks. You must apply critical thinking for risk identification; however, this framework provides guidance for your thinking.

## Economy and Industry Risks

Enterprises do not operate in a vacuum; they operate in an industry that is part of a local economy and also part of the overall global economy. Failure to consider local and global economy risks and industry risks and to adequately address those risks may prove disastrous for enterprises. **Economy risks** include those resulting from war, epidemics, financial market changes, terrorist attacks, and natural disasters such as floods, hurricanes, and

**TABLE 14–1**
**Risk Identification Levels**

| | |
|---|---|
| **Economy risks** | Risks associated with factors that affect the entire economy |
| | Global economic downturns |
| | Wars |
| | Epidemics |
| | Terrorist attacks |
| | Environmental disasters (floods, hurricanes) |
| **Industry risks** | Risks associated with factors that affect the enterprise's industry |
| | Industrywide cost increases |
| | Industrywide decrease in demand for products |
| | Economy risk especially bad for a specific industry |
| | Unexpected competition from another industry |
| **Enterprise risks** | External factors |
| | Increased competition from other enterprises |
| | Reduction of perceived brand quality and/or firm reputation |
| | Crises involving business partners (value system relationships) |
| | Catastrophe that causes an interruption of operations |
| | Merger or acquisition involving another enterprise |
| | Internal factors |
| | Lack of ethics |
| | Low employee morale |
| | Employee incompetence |
| **Business process risks** | Risks associated with actual business process objects |
| | Resources (Rs) |
| | Events (Es) |
| | Agents (As) |
| | Resource-Event relationships |
| | Event-Event relationships |
| | Event-Agent relationships |
| | Resource-Agent relationships |
| **Information process risks** | Risks associated with |
| | Recording information about Rs, Es, and As |
| | Maintaining information about Rs, Es, and As |
| | Reporting information about Rs, Es, and As |

drought. Many of these factors can lead to global economic downturns. Sometimes economy risks particularly devastate selected industries and thereby become **industry risks.** For example, the terrorist attacks of September 11, 2001, contributed to a global economic downturn, but were especially damaging to certain industries such as travel and tourism. Another type of industry risk is widespread cost increases that particularly affect a specific industry. For example, if the cost of raw materials used intensively in an industry increases significantly, the entire industry is negatively affected. Several years ago when the cost of computer memory chips increased rapidly, the entire computer industry suffered decreased product demand because of the higher prices. As the memory chip costs decreased again, product demand resumed. Decreased product demand is an industry risk that is sometimes independent of price increases. Such decreases may result from simple trend shifts (e.g., the waning demand for Beanie Babies) or from the development of superior replacement products developed in another industry (e.g., invention of the telephone replaced much of the demand for telegraph and personal messenger services).

## Enterprise Risks

**Enterprise risks** reflect potential threats of loss to the enterprise as a result of internal and external factors that result from the actions or circumstances of the enterprise itself or of one of its external business partners. Internal risk factors include such threats as low employee morale, lack of ethics in the enterprise, and employee incompetence. These internal risk factors are largely determined by management's philosophy and operating style; therefore interviews with management may identify the extent to which these risk factors represent a concern. If management's philosophy and operating style encourage a high-risk environment, greater risk also exists at the business process and information process levels. Questions that may help to identify a high-risk environment include:

- Is the enterprise committed to hiring competent people who possess the knowledge and skills needed to perform their assigned jobs?
- Does management have a conservative or reasonable approach in accepting business risks and in reporting the financial results of operations?
- If there is a board of directors, are there outside representatives on the board?
- If the entity undergoes an annual audit of their financial statements, does it have an audit committee to oversee the audit?
- Does the company have a well-defined organizational structure with appropriate division of duties and responsibilities and identified reporting relationships so that important activities are planned, executed, controlled, and monitored on a timely basis?
- Do employees understand the company's policies and practices, what they are individually responsible for, and to whom they report?
- Has management developed a culture that emphasizes integrity and ethical behavior?
- Does the enterprise have a whistleblower policy that encourages employees to inform management or the board of directors of fraudulent activities observed in the firm's operations?

Enterprises that can answer these questions in the affirmative likely have favorable control environments. Enterprises that have not taken these and similar steps to encourage integrity and competence face a high degree of internal enterprise risk.

Enterprise risk also results from external factors such as increased competition from other enterprises within the industry, loss of perceived brand quality or firm reputation, catastrophes that cause **business interruptions,** crises involving one or more of the enterprise's external business partners, and risks resulting from mergers or acquisitions. Increased competition may lower the enterprise's market share. Events that cause a perceived loss of brand quality or firm reputation may result in long-term negative consequences for the enterprise (e.g., if quality control fails to prevent a defective batch of products from being sold and the market generalizes the problem to all of the firms' products). All enterprises face some risk of business interruption due to catastrophes such as fire, flood, tornado, power outages, or technology failures. All enterprises also face risks that one or more of its external business partners may experience a business interruption catastrophe that will in turn cause a threat to the enterprise. For example, a warehouse fire that destroys a key supplier's entire inventory and interrupts the supplier's business for several months may cause the enterprise to be unable to fulfill customer orders until an alternative source is found. Another external enterprise risk enterprises sometimes face is involvement in a business combination such as a merger or acquisition. While a voluntary business combination may appear to be an attractive option during negotiations, sometimes plans fail to consider all circumstances and unexpected negative consequences result. The risk of such a consequence is an enterprise risk.

## Business Process Risks

Because the REA pattern represents the reality of an enterprise's business processes, it provides a useful framework to help system designers, managers, and auditors identify **business process risks.** In this section we provide some examples of risks specific to resources, events, agents, and various relationships in the REA pattern for business processes. The examples in this section do not provide a comprehensive list of business process risks; indeed a comprehensive list cannot exist because as controls for known risks are developed, additional means for misappropriating enterprise assets and misstating results of operations for enterprises also are being created that existing controls may not sufficiently mitigate. Thus, although the REA pattern provides a useful framework, we discourage students from adopting a checklist mentality when considering risks and controls.

Business process risks are defined for this textbook as risks associated with actual business process objects, including resources, events, agents, and relationships among resources, events, and agents. Some of the resources most commonly found in enterprises are inventory, supplies, operating assets, and cash. Risks associated with resources include threats associated with theft or loss, obsolescence, waste, and intentional or unintentional damage. Events are classified as instigation, mutual commitment, and economic events. Risks associated with each of these types of events include failure to execute an event that should be executed, execution of an event that should not be executed, or executing an event too soon or too late.

Most risks do not involve resources or events in isolation, but rather involve some combination of resources, events, and/or agents. Relationships that associate resources and events are classified as proposition, reservation, and stockflow relationships. Risks associated with resource-event relationships include execution of an event involving an incorrect resource, an incorrect quantity of a resource, or an incorrect cost or price for a resource. The resource-resource relationship typically defined in the REA enterprise ontology is the linkage relationship between raw material inventory type and finished good inventory type, which represents a bill of materials. Risks associated with resource-resource relationships include an incorrectly specified correspondence of one resource to another resource. An example is a bill of materials for a finished good inventory type that specifies an incorrect raw material or an incorrect quantity of a raw material. Event-event relationships in the REA enterprise ontology include duality, fulfillment, and reversal relationships. The primary risk associated with event-event relationships is incorrect sequencing of corresponding events. For example, if business process policy requires all sales to be accompanied by cash receipts (down payments) equal to at least 50 percent of the selling prices, a risk is that a sale will be accepted without receiving the required cash receipts. Similarly, a risk exists that a cash disbursement may be made without confirmation that goods were actually received for which the cash is disbursed.

Event-agent relationships in the REA enterprise ontology represent participation relationships linking internal and external agents to events. Risks include execution of events involving unauthorized external agents (e.g., sales made to nonexistent customers) or unauthorized internal agents (e.g., cash disbursements made by inventory clerks). Resource-agent relationships reflect custody arrangements such as internal agents being responsible for physical custody of a resource type; risks include unauthorized agents having custody of resources. Examination of single relationships is useful for risk identification; however, full risk analysis also requires simultaneous examination of multiple relationships. For example, queries may be formulated to evaluate whether linked purchase orders, purchases, and cash disbursements are all related to the same vendor. If not, there may be a data entry error or an irregularity that warrants investigation.

## Information Process Risks

**Information process risks** are associated with recording, maintaining, and reporting information about resources, events, agents, and relationships among them. On the surface, these risks may seem very similar to business process risks. The difference is that business process risks have to do with the actual execution of the events and the actual physical resources and agents. Information processing risks have to do with the information that gets recorded, maintained, and reported about those objects. For example, if a sale is made to a nonexistent customer, it is a business process error. If a sale is actually made to an approved customer, but a data entry error is made so that the sale appears to be made to a nonexistent customer, it is an information processing error. Information process risks include recording, maintaining, or reporting information that is incomplete, inaccurate, or invalid. Incomplete information reflects failure to record, maintain, or report information about resources, events, agents, or relationships. Inaccurate information reflects the recording, maintaining, and reporting of data that are incorrect as to the reality they represent. Invalid information reflects the recording, maintaining, and reporting of information about nonexistent resources, events, agents, or relationships. All of these types of information processing risks need to be controlled.

## Controls for Economy and Industry Risks

You may be wondering what an enterprise could possibly do to shield itself from economy and industry risks. These risks can be very difficult, if not impossible, to control. One control that is likely to be cost effective is the gathering and monitoring of enough information to be able to predict trends and product replacements. Enterprises that focus inwardly and tend to ignore the environment in which they operate are likely to be caught unaware by economy and industry risks. Enterprises that focus outwardly and pay attention to industry and economy trends and market demands are likely to be prepared for most shifts in prices and quantities at the economy and industry levels.

## Controls for Enterprise Risks

Like economy and industry risks, external enterprise risks often are difficult to predict and identify and therefore are difficult to control. Constant analysis and awareness of the external environment may help enterprises anticipate and prepare for increased competition.

Strong commitment to quality and extra quality control procedures may help to prevent loss of perceived brand quality or firm reputation; effective responsiveness to the market in case of a quality problem may help to correct any loss of perceived brand quality or firm reputation (possibly at the expense of a short-term financial loss). For example, it may cost a manufacturer a significant dollar amount to recall a production run of a defective product and replace the products at no cost to the customers; however, the cost of not recalling and replacing the products would likely result in a much more costly loss of perceived brand quality and firm reputation. Enterprises may purchase insurance to mitigate some external risks such as business interruptions. They also may create **contingency plans** for transferring operations to a **backup** location during business interruptions. Interruptions of external business partners are more difficult to insure. A supplier whose warehouse burned down may have insurance to replace lost inventory, but usually insurance does not compensate the enterprise that lost money because the inventory was not available when it needed to be issued to the production floor. To help mitigate such risks, enterprises should consider identifying multiple sources for each type of raw material or merchandise inventory they use in their conversion and revenue processes.

Many of the controls for enterprise risks form management's philosophy and operating style. Next we discuss some high-level policies that contribute to a well-controlled enterprise.

### *Human Resource Policies and Practices*

Human capital often is considered to be the most important resource of many enterprises. However, employees who are mismatched with their job responsibilities or who are not managed properly may become more of a liability than a resource. *Human resource policies and practices* relate to hiring, orienting, training, evaluating, counseling, promoting, compensating, and terminating employees.

Sound personnel practices are essential in controlling both operating activities and information processes. This is becoming increasingly important as enterprises empower employees in an attempt to streamline operations and cut costs. The quality of an enterprise's employees directly influences the quality of the goods and services provided to the customers. Generally speaking, competent, trustworthy employees are more likely to help the enterprise create value. Controls that help ensure success in hiring and retaining quality employees include completion of background checks, full explanation of enterprise policies and procedures, clear definition of promotion and personal growth opportunities as well as termination policies, and clear definition of work schedules. Many enterprises have suffered significant losses at the hands of individuals who had histories of incompetence, fraud, or other dishonest acts. Simple background checks could have prevented these losses. The other controls mentioned are summarized in a phrase: effective communication with employees. Employees must understand what is expected of them and they must be equipped with the training and tools they need to meet those expectations. They also need to be very aware of the consequences of not meeting expectations.

## Controls for Business Process Risks

### *Resource Risks and Controls*

Some of the resources most commonly found in enterprises are inventory, supplies, operating assets, and cash. Risks associated with resources include threats associated with theft or loss, obsolescence, waste, and either intentional or unintentional damage.

Most gas stations now allow customers to pay for gas at the pump. These pay-at-the-pump stations automatically bill the customer's credit card and eliminate the need for customers to pay a cashier. All the data about the gasoline sale event (e.g., customer's credit card information, type of gas, quantity, pump location, and station location) are recorded as the customer is pumping gas. Benefits include decreased time customers spend at the station, decreased number of employees needed to run the station, decreased data entry errors, and virtual elimination of nonpaying customers.

*Separation of Duties.*    An important control principle for all types of resources is **separation (or segregation) of duties,** which structures employees' job functions so the work of one employee checks the work of another employee. Effective separation of duties prohibits one employee from performing two or more of the following functions: authorization of transactions involving assets, custody of assets, record keeping, and reconciliation. Separating those functions reduces the opportunity for one employee to steal enterprise assets and to conceal the theft in the normal course of work. Of course, collusion (two or more employees in different positions working together to perpetrate fraud) is still a risk even with separation of duties.

*Resource Theft and Loss: Cash.*    Theft of resources is a rampant problem for many enterprises, costing billions of dollars worldwide every year. Because cash is the most liquid of all resources and is universally desirable, it is particularly susceptible to theft; therefore, enterprises need strict controls over those who have access to cash. Cash is most often stolen by employees, but potentially could be stolen by customers. Restriction of access to cash is the most common preventive control to mitigate loss due to theft. Obviously currency should be kept locked in a container to which only authorized employees have access. In the sales/collection process most enterprises keep cash in cash registers that may be opened only under certain circumstances. Control over the enterprise checkbook is especially important in the acquisition/payment, payroll, and financing processes, as access to the checkbook provides access to the cash in the checking account. Enterprises bond employees who handle cash as a form of insurance. If an employee with an adequate rating from the bonding (insurance) company is proven to have stolen cash from the enterprise, the bonding company recompenses the enterprise. **Bonding** is considered a corrective control. Just as the purchase of automobile insurance does not prevent a driver from being involved in a car accident, bonding does not prevent a seemingly trustworthy employee from stealing cash from the company. Drivers buy automobile insurance so that if an accident occurs, they may be recompensed for the loss incurred. Similarly the purpose for bonding employees is that if a theft occurs, the enterprise may be recompensed for the loss incurred.

Enterprises may take advantage of electronic funds transfers for cash transactions as a means of reducing theft. In electronic funds transfers-in, customers send cash receipts directly to the bank; the bank deposits the cash directly into the enterprise's cash account. In electronic funds transfers-out, the enterprise authorizes the bank to directly transfer funds from the enterprise cash account to a designated vendor. Such transfers also ensure accuracy of record keeping because usually the transaction data are made available to be automatically input into the enterprise information system.

# Case in Point

The bookkeeper for White Electric Company had sole responsibility for the company's checkbook and accounting records. Because of lax controls throughout the company, she felt justified in stealing cash from the company. Her method was quite simple and is illustrated with the following example. She received a vendor invoice for $10,000. She wrote check 5421 for the actual invoice amount of $10,000. However, in the check register she recorded check 5421 as $15,000. She then wrote check 5422 to herself for $5,000 but recorded it in the register as Void. Because she herself performed the monthly bank reconciliation, no one realized what she was doing. Because inventory controls were also lax, apparently no one questioned why the recorded inventory costs were overstated. After guilt feelings overwhelmed her, the bookkeeper hired an attorney and confessed her crime to her employer. She had stolen approximately $150,000 and was sentenced to time in prison. Notice that the risk of her stealing from the company could have been prevented by adequate separation of duties, and could have been detected by requiring that an alternative employee or manager perform the monthly bank reconciliation (because either person would have noticed the mismatched check amounts on the bank statement as compared to the check register). Most current automated enterprise information systems also provide protection against this particular fraud scheme because each check stub and entry into the check register is automatically generated to match the actual dollar amount of the check.

Source: *Red Flags: What Every Manager Should Know about Internal Fraud,* video, Association of Certified Fraud Examiners, 1991.

**Lapping** is a method of stealing cash that enterprises need to control. To accomplish lapping an employee steals cash from a customer payment and delays posting a payment to the customer's account. The employee uses funds from a subsequent customer payment to post to the first customer's account. This process continues with the employee continually stealing from subsequent customer payments to post as prior customer payments. Employees who engage in lapping often attempt to conceal the fraud by writing off as uncollectible customer accounts that have actually been paid. Eventually, lapping becomes so difficult to hide that the perpetrator leaves the company or the lapping is detected.

One of the most important detective controls with respect to cash is the monthly reconciliation of bank statements. Bank statement reconciliation compares details of the inflows and outflows depicted on the bank statement with the details of the inflows and outflows for the same account as recorded in the enterprise information system. Discrepancies in the bank statement versus the records in the enterprise system may reveal fraudulent cash-related activities as well as bank or enterprise errors. An employee with no other cash responsibilities should perform the monthly reconciliation.

Periodic counts of actual cash and reconciliation to account balances in the information system records (similar to bank statement reconciliation) help to detect theft or loss due to errors in petty and on hand cash accounts such as those stored in cash registers.

***Resource Theft and Loss: Inventory, Supplies, and Operating Assets.*** Restriction of access to noncash resources is the most common preventive control to reduce theft of those resources. In enterprises for which inventory, supplies, and operating assets are delivered to the enterprise via common carriers or suppliers, the receiving dock should be secured

Fast-food restaurant managers typically count each cash register drawer's contents before and after each cashier's shift. They compare the difference in cash to the sales rung up on the cash register to see if the amounts agree or if the cashier ended up with an overage (too much) or a shortage (too little) of cash in the drawer. Overages indicate errors by the cashier that cost the customers; shortages result either from theft or from errors by the cashier. Tracking discrepancies over time for each cashier reveals whether a cashier needs additional training or whether the enterprise should conduct additional surveillance to uncover theft by the cashier.

and the goods immediately transferred from the receiving dock to a locked storeroom or warehouse to which only authorized employees are allowed access. Then the goods may be transferred to less secure environments as needed. In enterprises for which merchandise is sold via shipments (e.g., mail order catalog companies or Internet stores), inventory is typically kept locked in the storeroom or warehouse with access limited to authorized employees. In other enterprises customers need to be able to physically examine inventory, so the inventory must be transferred to a less secure sales floor. For high value items, often access is still limited. For example, in retail stores high-priced items small enough to be easily stolen are typically kept in locked display cases and can be examined by customers only under the direct supervision of a sales representative. When supplies and operating assets are made available to the business processes in which they are to be used up, their access should still be restricted when practical. For example, employee offices containing furniture, computer equipment, and other operating assets should be locked when not in use. Buildings in which offices are located should be locked during nonworking hours. Precautions such as tagging each operating asset with a permanent ID tag help to deter theft and to facilitate periodic counts of operating assets and reconciliation of the counts with the recorded assets on hand. As with cash, all enterprise resources should periodically be counted and the balances compared to the recorded balances in the enterprise information system. Discrepancies should be brought to management's attention.

Supplies are the resources employees are most likely to steal from enterprises. Most supplies are small, relatively inexpensive, and easily mixed in with employees' personal supplies. Many employees don't consider personal use of enterprise supplies as theft; and some firms may view personal use of supplies by employees as acceptable. Enterprises that want to monitor supply use typically keep supplies locked in a cabinet, closet, or room that can be opened only under the watchful eye of an employee assigned custody of those assets. The enterprise may require documentation of what supplies were removed and by whom to help detect excessive or unnecessary use of supplies. Such procedures have become more important in recent years, as employees have developed personal needs for more expensive supplies such as printer toner and computer storage media.

A primarily detective control that also may serve as a preventive measure to reduce resource theft is the use of surveillance equipment such as security cameras to identify theft or damage as they occur or afterwards, and to identify those responsible for theft or damage. Frequently surveillance equipment is used in the less secure environments such as the sales floor and employee offices, but also may be used in the more secure storerooms and warehouses.

# Case **in Point**

Cook & Campbell, a construction firm for residential homes, was surprised to find they had one more vacant lot on their financial records than they actually owned at the end of their first year of operations. Upon closer examination they found they had constructed a home on one of the vacant lots and sold it without recording the sale of the lot on the financial records. The lot had actually been sold with the home, but the value of the lot was not included as they priced the home and it was not shown as part of cost of goods sold on the income statement. The anticipated $15,000 profit on the speculative home actually turned into a $20,000 loss as they corrected their mistake.

Tracking the chain of custody of resources is a preventive and detective control for loss. Several technologies exist to assist with tracking the chain of custody of inventory. One is the application of barcodes to inventory and/or inventory containers and the subsequent scanning of the barcode labels as the inventory and/or inventory containers move throughout the enterprise's acquisition and sales processes. An example of using barcodes to track the location and chain of custody of assets with which you may be familiar is that offered by enterprises such as Federal Express and UPS. When you ship a package with one of these enterprises, a barcode is applied to the package. At each location, and when custody of the package changes hands, the barcode is scanned to update the database with the current status of the package in the chain of custody. To enhance customer service, these companies provide customers with tracking numbers that correspond to the barcodes applied to their packages. Customers may enter the tracking numbers on the company websites or via telephone to determine the location and status of the packages.

Radio frequency identification tags (also called smart labels) are another technology available to track the chain of custody of resources. These tags communicate electronically with a reader via radio waves, thus eliminating the need to scan the tags with barcode readers. The readers are connected to a networked information system. Items or containers of items are automatically tracked as they move from location to location. Some envision these tags playing a role in future grocery shopping by allowing shoppers to simply access their shopping carts with their debit or credit cards; put desired items into bags in their carts; and then leave the store with the merchandise. The readers would transmit details to the networked information system and the customer's debit or credit card vendor would be billed for the transaction total.

***Resource Obsolescence and Waste.*** The risk of obsolescence is the likelihood of a resource becoming outdated or superseded by new products. This risk is particularly great for inventory but also is a concern for some operating assets and supplies. Some resources are more susceptible to decreased value due to obsolescence than are other resources. To control the risk of obsolescence, enterprises need to avoid purchasing or producing more inventories, supplies, and operating assets than they expect to sell or use up in a reasonable timeframe. An integrated enterprise system can help to mitigate the risk of obsolescence by shortening the entire cycle from estimating demand for a product to acquiring the raw materials, manufacturing the product, selling the product, and collecting the cash.

Security control equipment is being used in retail stores at cash registers to prevent fraud and promote efficiency. Cash registers and video cameras are connected to, and controlled by, a computer. The computer maintains a record of each transaction and the amount of time the clerk takes to execute it. All clerk activities are videotaped. The computer provides summary statistics at the end of each shift with unusual transactions highlighted based on type or amount of time to execute. Security personnel review the videotape of selected transactions to determine if fraud was present or if a clerk needs additional training.

***Resource Damage: Inventory and Supplies.*** Another risk associated with resources is the risk of damage while in storage or while in transit. Damage could result from various causes, including a lack of climate control, inadequate packaging, careless handling, haphazard placement of inventory on storage shelves, and so on. Well-communicated inventory storage and handling procedures and employee training of those procedures are one form of preventive control for such damage. Insurance is a corrective control; it will not necessarily prevent the damage from occurring, but the firm will be compensated for the loss.

## Event and Relationship Risks and Controls

Business and information process risks associated with events and the relationships in which they participate generally include

- Failure to execute an event that should be executed.
- Failure to record an event that was executed.
- Execution of an event that should not be executed.
- Recording of an event that was not executed.
- Execution of an event at an incorrect time or location, or involving the incorrect resources and/or agents.
- Incorrect recording of event details (such as time, location, affected resources, and agents involved).

We next examine specific risks that fit into these general categories for each type of event in various business and information processes.

### *Instigation Event Risks and Controls*

Some risks reduce the likelihood of the enterprise fulfilling its strategic and operational objectives with respect to its instigation events. Some examples of risk associated with marketing efforts and customer inquiry instigation events include:

- Failure to make potential customers aware of product features that would entice them to buy the product.
- Mistakes made in the advertising or promotions regarding the products or services available for sale.

- A sales call presentation to a customer including products the customer has no reason to be interested in, or for which they have previously declared no interest.
- Inability of a customer making an inquiry to find the information needed about desired products or services.
- Inability to track which customer orders result from each separate marketing effort (tracking is desired to learn which marketing efforts to continue, which to discontinue, and which to further develop.)
- Salespeople spending too much time with nontarget customers; that is, people who never buy anything or who don't buy enough to justify the time commitment of marketing personnel.
- Salespeople spending time doing unproductive things that do not influence potential customers.

Some examples of risk associated with purchase requisition instigation events include:

- Failure to identify needs for resources in a timely manner.
- Requisitioning resources that are not actually needed by the enterprise.
- Requisitioning of resources that do not have the features actually needed by the enterprise.
- Inability to locate a reliable source from which to obtain needed items.
- Failure to approve a requisition for items for which need was appropriately identified.
- Department supervisors may requisition items for which they do not have available funding in their budgets.

This list is only a beginning; many risks exist that may inhibit an enterprise from achieving its strategic and operational objectives for instigation events. The list of possible controls to mitigate risks associated with instigation events is even longer; thus we do not attempt to provide an exhaustive list. However, one major control is an effective enterprise information system. The more complete the design of the enterprisewide database, the more information-related risks are mitigated. For example, if the database is designed in conformance with the REA pattern (and if data are entered correctly and completely) the enterprise can track which instigation events lead to customer orders. Sales and marketing personnel should be able to run queries to effectively identify desirable customers and to help schedule their activities to minimize wasted time. The information system also can accurately report salespeople's activities. Merely recording and reporting the activities performed and the amount of time spent on each activity encourages effective use of time. Similarly, if production schedule data from the conversion cycle are integrated with the acquisition cycle, need for the raw materials involved in upcoming production runs can be communicated automatically. Such an information system also can integrate information linking departmental budgets to requisitions to determine whether funding is available or whether a proposed purchase will cause budget overruns.

### Mutual Commitment Event Risks and Controls

Risks associated with mutual commitment events include:

- Failure to accept an order that both the enterprise and the potential customer would have been willing and able to fulfill.

- Acceptance of an order from an undesirable or unauthorized customer (e.g., a bad credit risk, thus increasing bad debt losses).
- Acceptance of an order for a product or service that is not currently sold by the company and can't be made available.
- Acceptance of an order by an unauthorized internal agent.
- Commitment to provide products or services with an unrealistic delivery date.
- Commitment to provide products or services at an unprofitable price.
- Failure to place a purchase order for items the enterprise needs and can pay for, and which a reliable vendor could fill.
- Placement of a purchase order from an undesirable or unauthorized vendor.
- Placement of a purchase order for items the company no longer needs, or for too many items as compared to the quantity needed by the enterprise.
- Placement of a purchase order by an unauthorized employee.
- A purchasing agent placing an order for a dollar amount that is higher than the authorized limit.
- Failure to provide adequate lead time to vendors when placing orders, leading to impossible situations or leading to exorbitant shipping and handling costs.
- Failure to obtain the lowest possible cost for the highest possible quality items.

Some of these risks can be controlled declaratively within an integrated enterprise information system. For example, the interface can be programmed to prevent placement of a purchase order with an unauthorized vendor, and to prevent acceptance of a sale order from a customer who is not in the system as an approved customer. The interface also can be programmed to allow only items on the approved list of goods and services to be purchased or sold, to allow them to be purchased and sold only by selected internal agents (identified by **passwords** and access codes), to automatically insert the quoted costs and selling prices from the master cost sheet and price list (and possibly to allow adjustments within a specified range), and to automatically calculate line item extensions and total order amounts. Such automation not only improves the efficiency of the business processes but also improves the control over business and information process risks.

### *Economic Decrement Event Risks and Controls*

Because economic decrement events involve an outflow of economic resources such as inventory, this event is particularly susceptible to risks associated with theft of those resources (see *Resource Risks and Controls* earlier in this chapter). Risks associated with sales, shipments, or service engagements in the sales/collection process include:

- Failure to ship goods in response to a sale order commitment.
- Shipment of goods that were not ordered by a customer.
- Shipment of goods by an unauthorized internal agent.
- Shipment of goods to the wrong customer or to an unauthorized location.
- Shipping the wrong product or the incorrect amount of product.
- Shipping poorly packaged products.
- Selecting a poor carrier or route.
- Losing sales due to untimely shipments.

# Case in Point

Marty's Distributing Company is a distributor of alcoholic beverages and soft drinks. Under the precomputerized system, a delivery clerk took a load of beer to a retail outlet and manually prepared a sales slip. There was no independent check on the accuracy of the amount of beer recorded, the extension of quantity multiplied by price, or the summation of the total charge. At the time the computer was installed, the old system and the new system were operated in parallel for two months to verify the accuracy of the new system. During this time many errors were identified, and further investigation revealed the delivery clerk made all the errors in manually preparing the sales tickets. The savings the computer system generated by catching and preventing these errors more than paid for the computer system in less than one year.

An effective integrated enterprise information system can help control several of these risks. The system itself can verify who ships products and to whom they are shipped. Passwords can prevent an unauthorized internal agent from gaining access to the system to ship products. Computer generated address labels can prevent shipping products to the wrong customers and product bar codes can help prevent shipping the wrong products.

Risks associated with cash disbursements include:

- Failure to pay for goods that were received, or making late payments, thus earning a bad credit rating.
- Recording a cash disbursement that in fact did not occur.
- Making duplicate cash disbursements for the same purchase.
- Recording incorrect details about cash disbursements.
- Failure to take advantage of early payment discounts.

**Independent checks on performance** are crucial to mitigate risks in the cash disbursement event activities. Employees other than those who make the cash disbursements can do these independent checks, or the checks may be done by the enterprise system interface. For example, one employee may write checks based on the supporting documentation, and another employee may verify the accuracy of the checks and the entries to record them. Alternatively as the underlying acquisitions are made, the system may generate and record the checks and an employee may verify their accuracy and sign them.

## Economic Increment Event Risks and Controls

Because economic increment events involve resource inflows, these events are particularly susceptible to risks associated with theft (see *Resource Risks and Controls* earlier in this chapter). Risks associated with cash receipts include:

- Failure to receive cash as a result of a sale, or failure to record cash that was received.
- Recording a cash receipt that in fact did not occur.
- Accepting duplicate cash receipts for the same sale.
- Recording incorrect details about cash receipts
- Failure to deposit cash into the bank in a timely manner, or depositing cash into the wrong cash account.

When cash is received in the mail, two employees should open the mail together. One employee should take the money and prepare the deposit and the other person should send a receipt to the customer and record the receipt in the company's information system. The system should compare the deposit total with the total of the receipts to verify their equality. A control to reduce the risk of data entry errors is the use of computer-readable remittance advices. If a customer pays the exact amount of an invoice and returns the remittance advice with the payment, the computer can read the information on the remittance advice and know the amount of the payment and the customer information needed to correctly process the payment.

Risks associated with acquisitions of inventory, supplies, and operating assets include:

- Failure to receive goods in response to a purchase order commitment.
- Receipt of goods that the enterprise did not order.
- Receipt of the wrong goods or an incorrect quantity of goods.
- Damaging goods during unpacking on the receiving dock.
- Failure to receive goods in a timely manner.
- Failure to record acquisitions quickly enough to take advantage of early payment discounts.

Access restriction controls for resource-related theft risks described in this chapter should be enforced for acquisition events. An effective integrated enterprise information system can help control several of the other risks identified. The system can be used during the acquisition event to verify that the goods received were ordered. In an automated integrated enterprise system, acquisitions are recorded in a timely manner (as the goods are received) so that early payment discounts may be taken. The system also may be queried on a regular basis to follow up with vendors regarding unfilled purchase orders (i.e., orders for which goods have not yet been received).

### Economic Decrement Reversal Risks and Controls

Economic decrement reversal events in the sales/collection process should be subject to close scrutiny because they are the alternative to the expected economic increment event and because they involve custody of inventory. Sales returns are sometimes used as a means to cover up theft of cash (for example, without proper controls, a clerk may steal a customer payment for an invoice and then process a sales return for the invoice amount). Other risks associated with sales returns include:

- Failure to accept a sale return for which a customer has a legitimate reason.
- Acceptance of returned goods that originally were not sold by the enterprise.
- Approval of a sale return by an unauthorized employee.
- Recording a sale return that in fact did not occur.

These risks may be controlled with the aid of an integrated enterprise information system. No person without a proper password or access code should be able to authorize a sale return event. Access restriction controls and chain of custody tracking should be enforced for the receipt of the returned merchandise into the warehouse.

### Economic Increment Reversal Risks and Controls

Similarly, economic increment reversal events in the acquisition/payment process are the alternative to the expected economic decrement event and they involve custody of inventory.

Purchase returns are sometimes used as a means to cover up theft of inventory, supplies, or operating assets (for example, without proper controls, a clerk may steal goods and then process a fictitious purchase return for the purchase amount). Other risks associated with purchase returns may include:

- Failure to return goods that did not satisfy the enterprise's needs.
- Return of goods that the enterprise in fact does need.
- Approval of a purchase return by an unauthorized employee.
- Recording a purchase return that did not occur.

These risks may be controlled with the aid of an integrated enterprise information system. No person without a proper password or access code should be able to authorize a purchase return event. Restriction of access controls should be employed in the activities of packaging and shipping the goods back to the appropriate vendor. The integrated enterprise information system may be used to verify who ships goods and to whom they are shipped to help resolve any dispute with a vendor as to whether goods were actually returned. Passwords can prevent unauthorized employees from gaining access to the system to ship products. Computer generated address labels can prevent shipping products to the wrong vendors and product bar codes can help prevent returns of the wrong products.

## Controls for Information Process Risks

Many of the controls for business process risks involved information system controls that overlap with controls for information process risks. Indeed, it is often difficult to distinguish between controls over actual business process objects and the recording, maintenance, and reporting of information about those objects. This section focuses on information processing risks and controls that are reasonably separable from the business process objects themselves.

Although all information processing errors and irregularities are undesirable, those that occur during the recording and maintenance processes are particularly harmful. Why? The adage, "Garbage in, garbage out!" If inaccurate, invalid, or incomplete data are either recorded or maintained, the result is erroneous reporting. Because important decisions regarding the enterprise's strategy and direction are based on reports produced by the system, the errors may prove disastrous.

### System Resource Risks and Controls

In the business process risk section we discussed the need to restrict access to enterprise resources. The enterprise information system is one of the resources to which access should be restricted. Because system resources are used primarily to record, maintain, and report information about business processes, we classify system resource risks and controls into the information process risks and controls category. Critical system hardware such as file servers should be locked in restricted areas; however, other components of networked information systems usually need to be accessible to authorized users to complete business and information processes. Unauthorized access to systems represents a tremendous risk to enterprises, so prevention of unauthorized system access is important. Controlling access is critical when systems have online, real-time transaction processing capabilities. Any computer that is connected to the Internet is vulnerable to attempted

# Case **in Point**

break-ins by unauthorized users sometimes referred to as hackers. Hackers may seek personal gain from intruding into an enterprise's information system, or they may seek only to cause destruction to the enterprise such as has been accomplished by denial of service attacks in recent years. In a denial of service attack, an intruder typically logs into the system and launches an application that inundates the server with logins that overload its resources to serve legitimate users' needs. The most likely way to ensure the secrecy of data stored on a computer is to keep the computer as a standalone (i.e., never connect it to the Internet) and keep that computer locked in a secure place. Most enterprises can't operate effectively in standalone environments; therefore logical access controls for each layer are needed.

**Logical access controls** restrict unauthorized access to the programs and data in systems. Networked information systems have several layers of potential access points, each of which must be secured. Besides controlling access to the enterprise's application software packages, it is also necessary to control access to the underlying database, and to the overall network operating system. If adequate controls are not built into the system at each layer, unauthorized users may gain access to the application software through a back door in the network operating system or in the underlying database. System access controls involve the use of passwords and an **access control matrix.**

A *password* is a unique identifier that only the user should know and is required to enter whenever logging onto the system. Passwords are a weak form of protection. Unless passwords are formally assigned, routinely changed, and protected from use by other people, they quickly get into the wrong hands and provide unauthorized access to the system.

An *access control matrix* identifies the functions each user is allowed to perform and what data and programs the user can access after gaining access to the system. For example, a limited number of individuals are allowed access to payroll data. Some users are allowed to only read data, while other users are given the right to read and update the data. Access controls require users to authenticate themselves (i.e., give evidence that they are who they say they are) by providing something they know, something they possess, or

453

Active-badge technology automatically authenticates users who come within a designated range of the receivers. The badges worn by the users transmit weak radio signals to the receivers, so no physical contact between the badges and the receivers is necessary.

In the past, biometrics authentication was based on comparisons of fingerprints, palm prints, retina eye patterns, signatures, or voices. More recently, a system that recognizes keyboard-typing patterns has been developed. Another technology can reportedly read infrared facial patterns using only a simple video camera for image capture.

Source: R. Kay, "Distributed and Secure," *Byte,* June 1994, p. 165.

something they physically are. Access controls that represent things users know are passwords and **personal identification numbers (PINs).** Access controls that represent things users possess include identification **smart cards or tokens** (see nearby cases in point). Some **biometric access controls** require physical characteristics as input including **voice recognition technologies,** fingerprint identification, retinal scanners, and **digital signature recognition** technology.

Enterprises also can use *terminal identification codes* to prevent access by unauthorized terminals over communication lines. A host computer can require a terminal to electronically transmit its identification code that proves it is an authorized terminal and defines (and limits) the type of transactions the terminal user can perform. The host computer compares the identification code it receives from the terminal with a list of approved terminal identification codes to verify that it is an approved terminal.

**Encryption** is used to protect highly sensitive and confidential data. Encryption is a process of encoding data entered into the system, storing or transmitting the data in coded form, and then decoding the data upon their use or arrival at their destination. This prevents unauthorized access to the data while they are stored or as they are transmitted. Unauthorized users can easily intercept information broadcast over networks by applications that do not use encryption.

*Protecting Against System Failure.* Until we have a fail-safe technology, we must guard against possible failures in the computer hardware and its power source, as well as protect system hardware from the environment. Such failures can result in the interruption of business operations and the loss of data. As a preventive measure, enterprises should properly maintain computer equipment and facilities, and operate equipment in an appropriate physical environment *(environmental controls).* For larger systems, specially prepared rooms are sometimes necessary to house computer equipment. Some enterprises have *backup system components* (e.g., extra disk storage devices, extra printers, and extra communication channels) so that if a component fails, processing can quickly be transferred to another component without interrupting the flow of processing for an extended period of time.

Not only can computer components fail, but the power source for the components also can fail or provide an irregular power supply. The loss of power shuts down the entire operation and any data in temporary storage are lost. Protection from the loss of power usually is provided through the use of special battery units called *uninterruptable power sup-*

# Case in Point

*plies (UPS).* These devices provide battery support and sound an alarm when power is interrupted. This allows needed time to stop computer processes and back up data and instructions (programs). An irregular power supply can damage or destroy the computer hardware. Sudden and dramatic increases in power are called *power surges* or *spikes.* Protecting against surges or spikes involves the use of a *surge protector* or *line conditioning.* Conditioning power lines is sometimes provided by utility companies, but can also be provided by a simple and relatively low cost device called a surge protector.

*Virus protection (anti-virus) software* and *firewalls* are also important tools for protecting system resources. Viruses are malicious software programs that attach themselves to other applications without the user's knowledge. Worms are more invasive, self-replicating types of viruses. When an infected file is executed, the attached virus or worm program is also executed and may cause damage such as deleting files, destroying a hard disk drive, or even crashing an entire system. Enterprises lose millions of dollars each year because of viruses and worms. Virus protection software is designed to search for and destroy known virus programming code. Firewalls are combinations of hardware and software that are used to shield a computer network from unauthorized users or from file transfers of unauthorized types. Firewalls typically provide a higher level of protection than do anti-virus software programs; however, they are not foolproof. Firewalls should be used in conjunction with anti-virus software because firewalls may allow viruses through when attached to files of legitimate types. Keep in mind that virus code writers are always a step ahead of anti-virus code writers; therefore, firewalls and virus protection software provide only limited defenses. Many enterprises with firewalls and virus protection software become victims of new viruses and worms.

## Software Processing Controls

Software processing controls check the accuracy, completeness, and authorization of information to be recorded, maintained, and reported. Two broad categories of software processing controls are **general controls** and **application controls.**

### General Controls

General controls include all controls over data center operations, access security, systems software acquisition and maintenance, and application system development and maintenance. A

# Case in Point

high-level executive who reports to the president of the enterprise (e.g., a chief information officer or CIO) should administer the information system functions of an enterprise. An IS steering committee, composed of several other key officers of the enterprise, should work with the CIO to develop a plan that identifies the strategic use of information technology within the enterprise and prioritizes the development of individual components.

The CIO is responsible for all aspects of the information system functions of the enterprise. This individual makes sure that there is adequate separation of duties and responsibilities and adequate access security, and that the operations of the data center are properly controlled as we have discussed earlier. The other general controls of acquisition, development, and maintenance of both systems and application software are discussed in the next sections.

***Development and Maintenance of Systems and Application Software.*** Systems software consists of the computer programs that make the computer hardware run. They include the operating system, networking and communication software, and various utilities programs to back up and maintain files. *Application software* consists of the programs that process the business events of the enterprise such as the acquisition of goods and services and the production of finished products. Because of the high cost to develop custom software, there is a growing trend to purchase both systems and application software and to modify them as necessary to meet the needs of the enterprise. Care must be taken in specifying the requirements of the software, analyzing available software to see which package best meets the requirements, modifying the software as necessary, and testing individual applications and the entire system to make sure it processes the data accurately.

User departments are generally responsible for developing the list of software requirements. People from the user departments, the systems analysts, and the programmers work together to identify potential software packages in the market and compare their features with those desired by the enterprise. When modifications are required, the systems analysts design the changes and the computer programmers write the code to make the changes. *Test data* are generally used to verify that the programs and the entire system work correctly. Test data are a set of business events to test every logic path within the programs. The correct results from running the test data are developed independently from the system being tested and are compared with the results obtained when processed by the new system. If the new system correctly processes the test data we assume it has been modified correctly. The data control group is responsible for reviewing the testing and the test results, and verifying that they are adequate and that the systems are ready for use.

# Case in Point

This same process must be followed every time a modification is required in a program. The request comes from the user department. Systems analysts design the change, programmers write the code, test data verify that the program functions properly, and the data control group verifies the program is ready for use. Once the modification is complete, it is turned over to the operating people and controlled by the systems librarian. Controls over developing and maintaining a system are very important. The way a system is developed is as important as how it is operated in preventing errors and irregularities.

Financial losses because of software defects are an international problem. As institutions become dependent on electronic funds transfers, the software itself becomes more complex. Individual programmers have taken advantage of this complexity by concealing code in programs that transfer minute amounts from individual transactions to their own accounts. What's the true magnitude of the financial shrinkage due to faulty software? No one knows.

## Application Controls

Application controls apply to the processing of individual applications. These controls ensure that transactions are valid, properly authorized, and completely and accurately processed. Our discussion of application controls is divided into data input controls, processing controls, and file controls.

### Data Input Controls

Some of the most important controls are those dealing with the accuracy and completeness of data that are entered into the computer. Accuracy of input data is checked by event processing rules, data entry verification, and several edit checks.

*Event processing rules* should be built into the system to verify that prescribed business rules are followed when executing an event. Some examples of potential business rules include:

A customer may exist in our database before participating in a related sale event, but it is not permissible to record a sale event without identifying the related customer. That is:

Relationship: Participation

Connected Entities: (0, ) Customer

(1, ) Sale

Products can be shipped (sale event) only after a valid customer order has been taken (sale order event).

457

Sometimes a software defect is intentional. For example, a Manhattan software contractor was fined $25,000 for putting a bug in the software of a law firm. According to the judgment, the contractor put a statement in the program to make it abort when the system reached case number 56789. He planned for the system to fail so the law firm would retain him to fix it for a hefty fee. The law nabbed him. But another consultant earned $7,000 to repair the software.

Source: R. Riehle, "Killer Software: Program Errors Can Kill People, Both Figuratively and Literally, Making Structured Software Engineering Essential," *HP Professional*, February 1994, p. 54.

That is:

> Relationship: Fulfillment
> Connected Entities: (1, ) Sale
> (0, ) Sale Order

Each customer order can have one or more types of inventory associated with it; each inventory type can be involved in many customer orders; and information about inventory types may be entered into the system before any orders are taken.

That is:

> Relationship: Reservation
> Connected Entities: (1,N) Sale Order
> (0,N) Inventory Type

As discussed in Chapter 6, these business rules can be designed into the relational database tables. Event processing rules and other programmed business logic can help enterprises *detect* errors or irregularities, and can sometimes help *prevent* errors. To illustrate detection, consider a mail order company that does not normally have prepaid sales and very rarely incurs cash sales. Because the company gets cash receipts from nonsale sources (such as bank loans), the information system must allow cash receipts to be entered without having previously processed a corresponding sale. A risk exists that a cash receipt that in fact resulted from a sale was not matched to any corresponding sale in the system. A query may be developed to detect whether there are unmatched cash receipts in the system. An investigation could reveal the sale was not recorded in the system (the enterprise's error). Alternatively a query could identify "overmatched" cash receipts in the system—those for which the cash receipt amount exceeded the related sale amounts; such a query could reveal a customer paid for the same sale twice (the customer's error).

Event processing rules also can help *prevent* errors or fraud, if the data input functions are embedded in the business process procedures. In such environments, the rules governing the event and the data describing it can be executed and recorded in real time. The system can note activities that represent exceptions to prescribed rules and send exception messages to a responsible person for review. Based on the authorized person's response, the system can allow or prevent execution of the activity. For example, is a shipment normally necessary to record an order? No, an order event should precede the shipping event.

Is an order necessary to execute a shipment? For many enterprises the answer is yes! The authorization for a shipment is the existence of a valid order. Without a valid order, the shipping event should not be executed. An IT application could deny the execution and recording of a shipment that is not supported by a valid order. When shipping personnel can generate shipping labels only through the system, the likelihood of shipping merchandise without an order is reduced significantly. Notice that if an enterprise does not embed the data entry function into the business process procedures, but instead inputs data after the events have occurred, the system's ability to prevent errors and irregularities is substantially reduced. It can only *detect* rather than *prevent*.

***Data Entry Verification.***   As event data are entered into systems they must be checked to verify the accuracy of the record being updated and the accuracy of the data themselves. Two controls often applied in this area are **closed loop verification** and key verification.

*Closed-loop verification* helps the user verify that the correct record is being processed and updated. It does this by using one input data item to locate the record to be updated and displaying other data about the record so the data entry person can verify the correctness of the record. For example, if a sales order clerk enters a customer number for a customer buying merchandise on account, the computer uses the number to locate the customer record, then display additional customer data (such as name and address) on the computer screen. This way the user can verify that the correct customer record is being updated.

**Key verification (rekeying)** keys input data twice. The first data entry clerk enters the data and a second entry clerk reenters the same data. The computer compares the data entered on the second keying operation with the original data and highlights any differences. The second entry clerk verifies and corrects any differences.

**Edit checks** are incorporated into computer instructions to verify and validate the completeness, reasonableness, and/or accuracy of data. Edit checks can help reduce both operating risk and information processing risk. Their use is not limited to one type of risk or circumstance. Edit checks may be applied to individual fields or to records or batches of records. Several edit checks can be used to check the accuracy, reasonableness, and completeness of individual data input fields. The following overview describes some of the edit check logic used in information systems.

> *Check digit.* A formula can be applied to an account number, part number, or similar standard number to calculate a **check digit.** The **check digit** is appended to and maintained as part of the number (usually as the last digit). For example, suppose we want a five-digit account number (including the check digit) and the first four digits of the account number (based on style, division, color, and product type) are 1534. A check digit formula is used to add the fifth digit. There are several check digit formulas, and one rather simple, but less than adequate, formula adds the account number digits and extracts the second digit of the sum. The resulting account number using this formula is 15343 (the 3 is the second digit of $1 + 5 + 3 + 4 = 13$).

> *Completeness check.* A **completeness check** verifies that all critical field data are entered. It checks for missing data or blanks.

> *Default value.* **Default values** set the field contents to a prespecified (default) value. In some cases the default values may be overridden, while in other cases they may not.

*Field or mode check.* A **field or mode check** verifies that the entered data type is the appropriate mode for a field. For example, if a field is declared as a text or an alphanumeric field, the data input should be alphanumeric (letters and numbers). Other field modes include numeric, date, logical, counters, memo, and embedded objects (such as video, audio, or graphics).

*Range (limit) check.* A **range check** compares entered data to a predetermined acceptable upper and/or lower limit. Data are not accepted without special authorization if the data fall outside the specified limits.

*Validity/set check.* A **validity check** compares entered data against prespecified data stored within the computer to determine its validity. For example, to determine the validity of a user identification number, the computer would compare the entered primary key of the user to a stored list of valid user numbers.

***Sample Record Edit Checks.*** The next level of edit checks examines an entire record, generally a record in the file being updated by business event data. Some of the more common record edit checks are

*Master reference check.* A **master reference check** verifies that an event/transaction record has a corresponding master record to be updated. An error occurs when there is no corresponding master record for the transaction record. For example, there is an error if you input a sale for a customer not currently included in your customer data files.

*Reasonableness check.* A **reasonableness check** verifies whether the amount of an event/transaction record appears reasonable when compared to other elements associated with each item being processed. For example, if an employee is coded as a clerk, it is probably unreasonable that her pay per week is $5,000. Note that a reasonableness check is not the same as a limit check. It might be reasonable for the president to have a weekly check of $5,000. The reasonableness of the pay is based on the relationship between position (clerk versus president) and the amount of the pay, not a fixed dollar amount.

*Referential integrity.* **Referential integrity** is a safeguard to ensure that every posted foreign key attribute relates to a primary key attribute. For example, suppose you have two tables: a Salesperson table and a Sales event table. Since the two tables have a relationship (a salesperson participates in each sale), you must include the primary key attribute of the Salesperson table (e.g., salesperson number) in the Sales event table; salesperson number is a foreign key attribute in the Sales event table. You want to invoke referential integrity to ensure a link between the two tables. Referential integrity prevents writing a sale in the Sales event table without a valid salesperson number from the Salesperson table. It also prevents deleting a salesperson from the Salesperson table as long as the salesperson has sales in the Sales event table.

*Valid sign check.* The **valid sign check** highlights illogical balances in a master file record. For example, a negative balance for the quantity on hand for a particular item in inventory is a likely error.

***Sample Batch Edit Checks.***   The next level of edit checks is for an entire batch of events or transactions. Sometimes business events can be grouped into batches for a period of time, such as one day, and processed together. Controls are needed to make sure none of the events are lost, no unauthorized events are added, and all events are in the proper sequence and correctly processed.

*Sequence check.* A **sequence check** verifies that the records in a batch are sorted in the proper sequence. For sequential processing, which is frequently used with batch processing, the transaction records must be sorted in the same order as the master file's primary key. A sequence check also can highlight missing batch items, such as a missing check.

*Transaction type check.* A transaction type check verifies that all transactions included within the batch are of the same category or type. For example, we would not want the addition of a new customer to be confused with the addition of a new employee.

*Batch control totals.* When transactions are processed in batches, each batch should be dated and assigned a unique batch number. **Batch control totals** are used to verify that all transactions within a batch are present and have been processed. They verify that no transactions were added or deleted during processing. There are several types of batch control totals. Let's use a record that includes a customer number field and an invoice amount field to illustrate three types of batch control totals: hash, financial/numeric, and record count control totals.

*Hash control total.* A hash control total is the sum of an attribute that normally would not be summed because its sum has no real meaning. For example, the sum of the customer number field of all the records in a batch is a meaningless number for purposes other than as a batch control total. But, if it is calculated when the batch is first assembled, the computer can recalculate it after the records have been entered for processing. If the computer-generated sum is the same as the original amount, we have some assurance that all records were accurately processed. If they are not the same, one or more transactions may have been either added or deleted from the batch.

*Financial/numeric control total.* A financial control total is the sum of a financial field, such as the invoice amount, of all records in a batch. Usually, this is a meaningful numeric or financial field. For example, the total of the invoice amounts is meaningful because it represents the increase in accounts receivable and it is useful to evaluate the effectiveness of those taking orders for the day.

*Record count control total.* A record count control total is a total of the number of records in a batch. So if a batch contains 46 records, the record count is 46.

All the batch control totals can be used to verify batch input, processing, and output. For example, suppose a clerk enters 46 customer invoices totaling $14,678.93 in charge sales into a computer file. Also assume that the sum of the customer account numbers on the invoices is 738476846. Once these records are entered into a batch transaction file, the file should include 46 records (the *record count*), the customer number field should total 738476846 (a *hash total*), and the sum of the invoice amount field should total $14,678.93 (a *financial total*). When the records are processed to update the customer receivable master file, the update run should show that 46 records were affected, and the accounts receivable total should increase by $14,678.93.

Batch control totals may be generated by one computerized process compared with another computerized process that uses the same batch as input; in those cases, a hash total is as easy as a record count or financial/numeric control total. Often, however, the initial

**EXHIBIT 14–2** **Batching and Reconciliation Process**

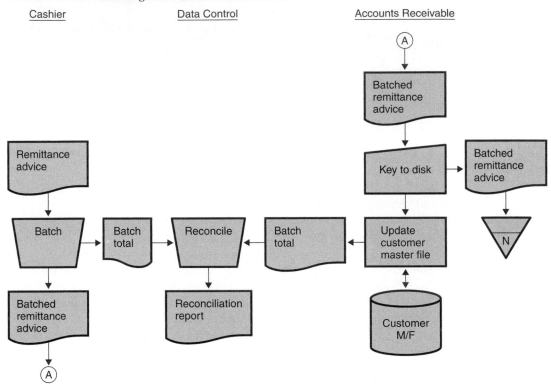

batch control total is generated manually with a ten-key adding machine as the batch is created. The batch control total (usually a financial total, but sometimes a record count) is written on the batch header along with the batch number and date. Once a manual batch control total is computed and the batch is entered into a computerized process, the computer process should generate a control total of the same type (financial, numeric, record count, or hash) and the manual total should be compared to the computerized total. If they match, the enterprise has a reasonable confidence that all items in that batch were in fact processed in the computer system processes. Exhibit 14–2 illustrates an example batching and reconciliation process.

Notice that batch totals do not identify errors in individual records. Batch totals only highlight errors in the group as a whole. Batch totals do not ensure that individual records are correctly updated. For example, if the total of an accounts receivable subsidiary ledger equals the total in a general ledger accounts receivable control account, this does not signify that the postings to the individual customer accounts are correct. It only indicates that the same total amount was posted; some individual items could have been posted to the wrong customer's account!

### *Processing Controls*
Information processing controls are designed to verify that event, resource, agent, and location information are recorded and maintained accurately, completely, and in a timely

manner. They also help ensure the information on reports is complete, properly summarized, and reported to the appropriate people.

*Process controls* verify that the input data are properly recorded in the database and any balances maintained within the system are properly updated. Many of the program development and maintenance controls, data input controls, and edit check controls identified earlier also are used as process controls. The following examples illustrate the application of test data, closed-loop verification, and edit checks to verify process accuracy.

Test data that verify computer programs are functioning properly are an important element in verifying the accuracy of information processing. Once a program is correctly written and tested it is very reliable in performing the same operations again and again.

Closed-loop verification is used when the input data are being processed in an online, real-time mode. For example, closed-loop verification can make sure the customer account being updated is accurate. Because of the mode of processing, this serves as an input and a process control.

Edit checks on the record and batch levels also are used as process controls. For example, a reasonableness check when used in a sequential batch process is a process control. As a transaction is being processed, the computer can compare one element of input with the master record to see if it appears reasonable. If it does not, an error is recorded on the error log. An example of this is a sales order process. Selling 10 computers to a customer with an occupation listed as housewife would not seem reasonable and the transaction would be printed on an error report. If, however, the sales clerk was entering the transaction by an online, real-time process and the sales clerk attempted to execute such a transaction, the computer could perform the reasonableness check as the data are entered and highlight the unreasonableness. In this case it is an input control.

As you can see, many online, real-time controls become process controls when the mode of processing is shifted to batch processing. This explains why real-time processing helps enterprises prevent errors more easily than enterprises that perform batch processing after a transaction has already occurred. With batch processing, error detection is more common than error prevention.

One of the benefits of an architecture based on the REA pattern is the simplicity of data storage and processing. Most event data are stored in a raw, unprocessed form. Processing consists of recording the individual characteristics and attributes about each business event. Most classifications, summarizations, and balances are developed as part of the reporting process. This is much more streamlined and less complex than a traditional processing environment where you have to control not only the input but also a complex posting process to perform classifications, summarizations, and balance calculations. Processing in a REA-based architecture is very simple; it is a direct recording of the event attributes. This allows for straightforward controls. The key to control is making sure the event record is being recorded in the correct file in a timely, complete, and accurate manner. Then we accurately report these data per the request parameters of the information customer.

### *File Controls*

Devices or techniques are available to verify that the correct file is being updated and to prevent inadvertent destruction or inappropriate use of files. Some of these controls include the following:

*External file labels* (as simple as stick-on labels) identify a storage medium's contents. They also help prevent someone from inadvertently writing over the contents of the disk or tape.

*Internal file labels* record the name of a file, the date it was created, and other identifying data on the file medium to be read and verified by the computer. Internal labels include *header labels* and *trailer labels*. Header labels are a file description recorded at the beginning of a file. Trailer labels mark the end of a file and contain control or summary data about the contents of the file.

*Lockout procedures* are used by database management systems to prevent two applications or users from updating the same record or data item at the same time.

**EXHIBIT 14–3**
**Batch**
**Processing**

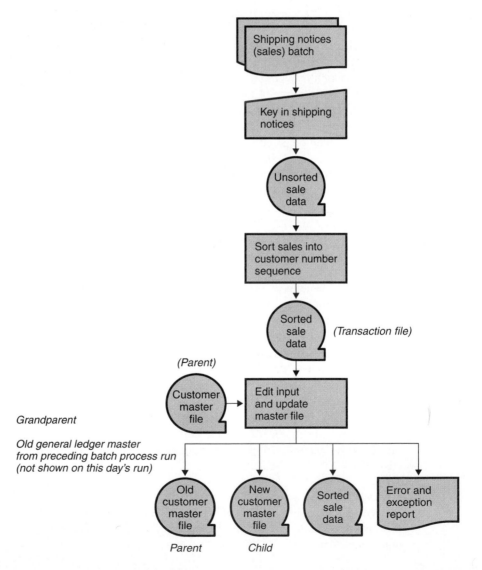

The **read-only file designation** is used to mark data available for reading only. The data cannot be altered by instructions from users, nor can new data be stored on the device.

*File protection rings* allow data to be written on a magnetic tape. When the ring is removed, the data on the tape are protected from being accidentally overwritten.

***Data Loss and File Reconstruction Capability.***   Regardless of the controls created to secure the computer and prevent problems, files are occasionally lost and programs are occasionally destroyed. Therefore, it is necessary to maintain *backup or duplicate copies of current data files, programs, and documentation.* At least one set of backup copies of all these items should be stored at a location that is physically removed from the computer facilities. Enterprises should develop a policy concerning how long to retain backup copies. The length of time depends on the managerial and regulatory requirements of the enterprise. The purpose of backup copies is to allow an enterprise to reconstruct its data should a disaster strike and cause a loss or corruption of data. The basic task is to retain copies of reference (resource, agent, and location) data and event data for use in reconstructing any lost data.

*File reconstruction* involves reprocessing the event or business activity data against the master resource, agent, or location reference data. Enterprises typically update data in either a batch mode or a real-time mode.

**EXHIBIT 14–4**
**Batch
Process File
Reconstruction**

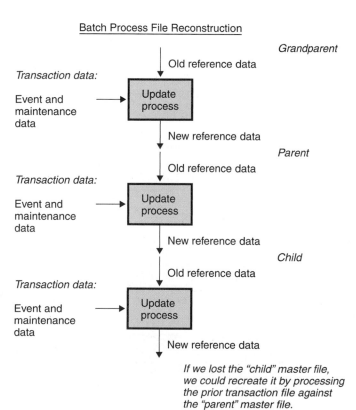

Batch Process File Reconstruction

***Batch Process File Reconstruction.*** Batch processing collects a group of event and maintenance data for a period of time (such as a day) before the master reference files are updated. Processing updates the current version of the master reference file to create a new master reference file as illustrated in Exhibit 14–3. When the next batch of event and maintenance data for, say, the next day are ready to be processed, the new master reference data of the prior run become the current master reference data for the new run. The backup and file reconstruction procedure generally used with batch processing is known as the **grandparent-parent-child approach.** At least three generations of both event/maintenance data and master reference data are maintained (see Exhibit 14–4). If the current version (the child copy) of the master reference file is destroyed or lost, the enterprise can reconstruct it by rerunning the appropriate event/maintenance data against the prior copy of the reference data (the parent copy). If a problem occurs during that reconstruction run, the backup data may be used to reconstruct the parent file. The parent is used then to reconstruct the child and processing continues normally. Batch processing often uses checkpoint controls for applications that take an extended amount of time to process. Some batch processing runs take as long as six to eight hours and if a problem occurs during processing you don't want to have to start again at the beginning.

*Checkpoints* consist of data and program snapshots periodically taken during batch processing. If a hardware failure occurs during a long processing run, the system can resume processing at the last checkpoint, rather than at the beginning of the run.

***Real-Time Process File Reconstruction.*** Real-time processing updates master reference data with new event and maintenance data as the new data are captured as illustrated in Exhibit 14–5. As the event or maintenance data are processed to update the master reference

**EXHIBIT 14–5**
**Real-Time File Processing**

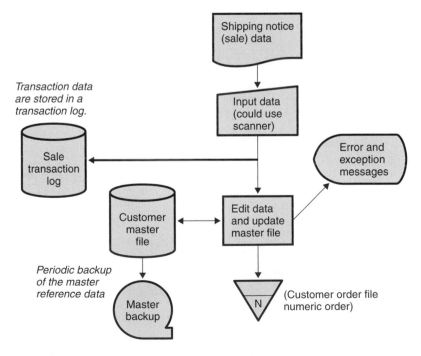

# Case in Point

One day a state's welfare payment system suddenly showed a $15 million shortage. An investigation showed the $15 million left the fund by a direct wire transfer to a Swiss bank account. It was withdrawn from the Swiss bank on the day of the deposit and the account was immediately closed. Further investigation showed the cause of the direct wire transfer was a small section of code (written in machine language) in the welfare payment program that checked to see if today's processing date was the same as a specified date. If they were the same, the $15 million was transferred. The person who had written the program had ceased working for the state agency about a year before the fund transfer, and was believed to be living in Switzerland. This type of fraud was not possible before welfare payments were processed by computer and before the existence of direct wire transfers of funds.

**EXHIBIT 14-6**
**Real-Time Master File Reconstruction**

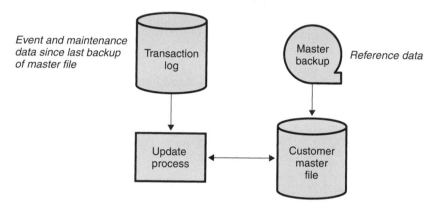

*Event and maintenance data since last backup of master file*

Transaction log

Master backup    *Reference data*

Update process ←→ Customer master file

*The master file backup becomes the master file and it is updated for transactions since the backup occurred.*

data, they also are recorded in a separate *transaction log*. This log is a critical part of the reconstruction process.

File reconstruction procedures must be developed for real-time processing. The transaction log and a periodic copy of the master reference file are the keys to file reconstruction. Periodically the master reference file is duplicated on a backup medium such as disk or magnetic tape. Copies of all event and maintenance data are stored on a *transaction log* as they are entered into the system. At least three generations of both the event/maintenance data and the master reference data are maintained as with batch processing. If the master reference file is lost or destroyed, the first generation backup copy is updated for the activity on the transaction log since the copy of the master reference file was made (see Exhibit 14–6). Once the master reference file is updated, processing continues normally. The three generations allow for additional errors in reconstructing the file. If the first generation is destroyed in reconstructing the file, the second-generation master reference file is used to reconstruct the first generation master reference file. The backup copies of both the master reference file and the transaction log should be stored at a remote site.

The information system captures, processes, and reports information to people throughout the enterprise. The information system and internal controls must be constantly evaluated and updated. As an enterprise changes and as information technology changes, so do the enterprise risks. New technology sometimes brings new risks that people don't even consider as demonstrated by the aforementioned state welfare system.

## CONCLUDING COMMENTS

This chapter introduced the importance of understanding enterprise risks and provided some examples of available controls to reduce enterprise risks. Some of the control examples cited are useful for preventing errors and irregularities, while others are helpful in detecting and correcting errors and irregularities. Just as change has become a constant feature of enterprises and information technology, the need for creativity and innovation in identifying risks and in developing control procedures to reduce risks is becoming consistent across enterprises. The tools provided in this chapter are only a beginning; as new risks arise, new controls also must be developed. The key is to adequately assess risks, determine which of the risks need to be controlled, and design cost-effective controls to mitigate those risks. When measuring the cost of controls, any decreases in operational efficiency and effectiveness must be considered.

## Key Terms and Concepts

Access control matrix, *453*
Application controls, *455*
Backup, *442*
Batch control total, *461*
Biometric access controls, *454*
Bonding, *443*
Business interruption, *439*
Business process risks, *440*
Check digit, *459*
Closed loop verification, *459*
Collusion, *435*
Committee of Sponsoring Organizations of the Treadway Commission (COSO), *433*
Completeness check, *459*
Contingency plan, *442*
Control activities, *434*
Control environment, *434*
Corrective controls, *435*

Default value, *459*
Detective controls, *435*
Digital signature recognition, *454*
Economy risks, *437*
Edit checks, *459*
Encryption, *454*
Enterprise risks, *439*
Error, *435*
Exposure, *431*
Field or mode check, *460*
Fraud, *435*
General controls, *455*
Grandparent-parent-child approach, *466*
Independent checks on performance, *450*
Industry risks, *438*
Information and communications, *434*
Information process risks, *441*

Internal controls, *432*
Irregularity, *435*
Key verification (rekeying), *459*
Lapping, *444*
Logical access controls, *453*
Master reference check, *460*
Materiality of risk, *433*
Monitoring, *434*
Opportunity, *432*
Passwords, *449*
Performance reviews, *437*
Personal identification numbers (PINs), *454*
Preventive controls, *435*
Range check, *460*
Read-only file designation, *465*
Reasonableness check, *460*

Referential integrity, *460*

Risk, *431*

Risk assessment, *434*

Separation (or segregation) of duties, *443*

Sequence check, *461*

Smart cards or tokens, *454*

Statement of Auditing Standards No. 94, *433*

Threat, *431*

Valid sign check, *460*

Validity check, *460*

Voice recognition technologies, *454*

## Review Questions

LO1   R1.   What is a system of internal controls?

LO1   R2.   Distinguish between risk, exposure, and threat.

LO1   R3.   Describe the relationship between risk, opportunity, and objectives.

LO1   R4.   How do you determine the materiality of risk?

LO1   R5.   Should enterprises attempt to control all risks? Explain.

LO4   R6.   Describe separation of duties and responsibilities.

LO1   R7.   Who is ultimately responsible for internal controls within an enterprise?

LO4   R8.   List and describe the five interrelated components of an internal control system.

LO4   R9.   Which type of control is needed more in today's risk environment: prevention, detection, or correction? Explain.

LO1   R10.   If enterprises change from a manual information system to a computerized information system, do their internal control objectives change? Explain.

LO1   R11.   Is it better to build controls into an information system or add them to the system after it is built? Why?

LO3   R12.   What risks do enterprises face with respect to resources?

LO3   R13.   What risks do enterprises face with respect to agents?

LO3   R14.   What risks do enterprises face with respect to events?

LO3   R15.   What is the difference between business process risks and information process risks?

LO4   R16.   What are three means by which system users can prove their identity to the system? Which of these means is least vulnerable to falsification?

LO4   R17.   Explain the purpose of encryption techniques.

LO4   R18.   Describe an application you have used that incorporated some form of closed-loop verification.

LO4   R19.   How do check digits help ensure that field contents are valid?

LO4   R20.   Give an example of a completeness check.

## Multiple Choice Questions

LO2   MC1.   Which of the following guidelines helps in distinguishing industry level risks from economy level risks?

    A.   An industry risk primarily affects the industry in which the enterprise operates, whereas an economy risk affects all industries within the enterprise's local or global economy.

    B.   An industry risk affects all industries within the enterprise's local or global economy, whereas an economy risk is a result of the enterprise not taking advantage of production economies of scale.

C. An industry risk is associated with a specific business object such as a resource-event relationship, whereas an economy risk affects all industries within the enterprise's local or global economy.

D. An industry risk primarily affects the industry in which the enterprise operates, whereas an economy risk is a result of the enterprise not taking advantage of production economies of scale.

LO2    MC2. Which of the following should be classified as an enterprise-level, external risk factor?

A. A global war.

B. Global warming.

C. Employee incompetence.

D. Increased competition from another enterprise.

LO2    MC3. The sudden bankruptcy of an enterprise's largest customer is an example of:

A. An economy level risk.

B. An industry level risk.

C. An enterprise level risk.

D. An information process level risk.

LO1, LO2   MC4. Why is it important for management's philosophy and operating style to encourage a low-risk environment?

A. If management's philosophy and operating style encourage a low-risk environment, lower risk also exists at the economy level.

B. If management's philosophy and operating style encourage a low-risk environment, lower risk also exists at the business process and information process levels.

C. Actually, management's philosophy and operating style should encourage a high-risk environment because that will result in lower risk at the business process and information process levels.

D. If management's philosophy and operating style encourage a low-risk environment then the enterprise will have an ill-defined organizational structure with inadequate division of duties.

LO4    MC5. Virus protection software

A. Provides a higher level of protection than does a firewall.

B. Is executed when an attached virus or worm program is executed and typically causes damage such as deleting files, destroying a hard disk drive, or even crashing an entire system.

C. Is a combination of hardware and software used to shield a computer network from unauthorized users or from file transfers of unauthorized types.

D. Is designed to search for and destroy known virus programming code.

## Discussion Questions

LO1    D1. Why is it important to consider both the costs and benefits of internal controls?

LO1    D2. Is risk 100 percent controllable? Explain your response.

LO4    D3. On January 1, CBU installed a new computer system for tracking and calculating inventory costs. On December 31, at closing, CBU's system reported inventory at $4.5 million for financial statement purposes. At midnight, the auditors performed a physical inventory count and found the inventory total to be $3.5 million. To correct the discrepancy, CBU's accounting staff processed an adjusting entry to reduce inventory by $1.0 million. The next day, two accountants were discussing the events of the previous night. Accountant A was proud of the audit and said it illustrated a benefit of having a good system of internal control. CBU had followed good internal control procedures by having a regular physical inventory count to safeguard a valuable enterprise resource. Accountant A was relieved that the problem was resolved: the financial numbers were corrected before they were reported. In short, he felt successful and thought CBU should feel fortunate to have his accounting staff as control advisors. Accountant B felt differently. She was concerned about the bad decisions that were made throughout the year based on the incorrect inventory numbers. She felt that she and the other accountants should have helped develop more timely and effective system controls. With which accountant's philosophy do you agree? How can you explain the diverse opinions? What policies or procedures, if any, should CBU develop to avoid such problems in the future?

LO1　D4. Some people believe that information technology has made enterprise internal control systems more difficult to design and use. Others believe that information technology has made it easier to control enterprise risks. Which do you believe is true, and why?

LO3, LO4　D5. For each of the following examples of minimum cardinalities (the maximum cardinalities are omitted; you are supposed to consider only the minimum cardinalities) explain the business rule associated with the cardinalities and list the risk of not following each rule.

　a. Sale (1, –) and (0, –) inventory.
　b. Sale (1, –) and (0, –) cash receipt.
　c. Receipt of inventory (1, –) and (0, –) inventory order.
　d. Salesperson (0, –) and (1, –) customer.
　e. Customer (0, –) and (1, –) sale.
　f. Purchase (1, –) and (0, –) vendor.
　g. Shipment (1, –) and (0, –) customer order.

Do these cardinalities suggest a certain sequence of procedural rules for doing business? Explain. What controls should the enterprise consider implementing to control any risk?

# Applied Learning

LO3, LO4　A1. A customer calls a mail order catalog to order merchandise. The order clerk takes the customer's name, mailing address, credit card number, and the merchandise numbers, sizes, colors, and quantities. After hanging up, the order clerk verifies the merchandise numbers given by the client are valid (that the company does indeed sell an item with that number) and checks with the shipping department on availability of the merchandise item.

## Required
　a. What business process and information process risks exist in this scenario?
　b. What controls may be implemented to mitigate the risks identified in part (a)?

LO3, LO4   A2.   ABC recently decided to analyze its expenditures. During the analysis, ABC discovered that all orders for repair services always go to a company owned by the vice president's sister. The repair company has a reputation for high prices and poor service. During the analysis, ABC also discovered that many of its purchases for supplies were delivered to the vice president's home address.

### Required

a. What business process and information process risks exist in this scenario?

b. What controls may be implemented to mitigate the risks identified in part (a)?

LO3, LO4   A3.   A truck driver for a food distributor loads his truck early in the morning according to the invoice purchase orders. He is responsible for picking up COD delivery payments and, on his return trip, for picking up the inventory from major distributors. Currently the POs are handwritten by the floor manager the day before the delivery.

### Required

a. What business process and information process risks exist in this scenario?

b. What controls may be implemented to mitigate the risks identified in part (a)?

LO3, LO4   A4.   Bob owns a small recreational trailer business in a suburban community located close to the mountains. The community is relatively small but growing rapidly. Bob's business is growing, not because of his effective sales style and personality, but because of the growth of the community. Currently, Bob's competition has been nearly nonexistent, but as the area grows he expects to encounter increasing competition. Bob sells mostly trailers for vacationing and camping. When customers arrive on Bob's lot, they are greeted by a salesperson. Depending on the customer's preference, the salesperson either takes the customer on a tour or the customer may roam the lot freely, inspecting trailers at leisure. Because recreational trailers are fairly large-ticket items, customers often leave the lot without making a purchase, only to return another day to purchase a trailer. When the customer decides to make a purchase, the salesperson initiates a series of procedures to properly document the order and sale transaction. First, the salesperson determines the model of the selected trailer and offers the customer a list of options that correspond to the particular model. The customer may (1) purchase a trailer off the lot with no added features, (2) purchase a trailer off the lot with additional features, or (3) special order a trailer that is not currently on the lot. In most cases, customers do not pay cash for their trailers. If, however, the customer pays cash, a simple sales contract is prepared and the customer drives off with the trailer. The majority of the customers use an installment method of purchase. Before an installment purchase is authorized, the customer's credit must be verified to determine creditworthiness. With an installment purchase, an installment agreement is prepared in addition to the sales contract. Bob has arranged financing through a local bank for all installment sales. When an installment sale is made, the bank sends Bob a lump-sum payment equal to the price of the trailer. Instead of making payment to Bob, customers pay the bank plus interest. In either case, Bob receives a lump-sum payment for each trailer sold, whether that lump sum comes from the customer or from the bank. Once the credit is approved, the customer can take delivery of the trailer. This involves a delivery person who checks the trailer before delivering it to the customer. The customer picks up the trailer or has it delivered by Bob.

**Required**

What are Bob's Trailer Sales' instigation, mutual commitment, economic decrement, and economic increment events, and what risks are associated with those events? What are Bob's Trailer Sales' resources, and what risks are associated with those resources? Who are the agents for Bob's Trailer Sales and what risks are associated with those agents? What controls could be implemented to address all of these risks?

LO1, LO4    A5.    A computer operator at the local data processing center decides to visit work on a Monday evening. She has a key to the outside door, and since there is no key required for the computer room, she simply walks into the computer room. The operator is one of the nation's most notorious computer programmer/hackers; she has been convicted five times for manipulating various firms' data files. After opening the documentation bookcase in the corner of the computer room, she finds the procedural documentation, the systems documentation, user manuals, application documentation, and operator manuals. She examines the documentation to understand the payroll program and to find the location of the payroll files. She accesses the information systems library, which is available to all computer operators at all times, accesses the payroll program, reprograms it, and runs a payroll job that creates one electronic funds transfer (to a new account opened by the operator under an assumed name). On Tuesday, the operator transfers the funds to a Swiss bank account and does not show up for work.

**Required**

Prepare a summary that details any internal controls violated in this situation.

LO4    A6.    Review the user documentation for the DBMS you are using for class projects. Prepare a report that documents how the following controls are implemented in the DBMS. You may want to include screen shots where applicable (Alt-PrtSc copies the screen to the Windows clipboard; you may then open a word processor and hit Edit-Paste to insert the screen shot). Note that you may find more than one use of each control. You need turn in documentation of only one use for each type of control.

     a. System access
     b. Completeness check
     c. Default value
     d. Embedding business event rules
     e. Field check
     f. Range or limit check
     g. Validity check
     h. Referential integrity
     i. Valid sign check
     j. Closed-loop verification

# Answers to Multiple Choice Questions

MC1. A; MC2. D; MC3. C; MC4. B; MC5. D.

# Chapter **Fifteen**

# ERP Systems and E-Commerce: Intra- and Inter-Enterprise Modeling

### LEARNING OBJECTIVES

One objective of this chapter is to compare the REA enterprise ontology with current developments in enterprise resource planning (ERP) systems and electronic commerce (e-commerce) in the context of the types of integration introduced in Chapter 1. The prospects for progress in using the REA enterprise ontology as a foundation for intra-enterprise systems (similar to ERP systems) and for inter-enterprise systems needed for seamless e-commerce are discussed. After studying this chapter, you should be able to

1. Compare the goals of current ERP systems with those of the REA enterprise ontology
2. Describe the needs for intra-enterprise and inter-enterprise system integration
3. Identify information integration tools commonly used in practice (e.g., electronic data interchange, extensible markup language, enterprise application integration software, and electronic business extensible markup language) for intra-enterprise and inter-enterprise information systems
4. Discuss strengths and weaknesses of integration tools commonly used in practice for meeting intra-enterprise and inter-enterprise information integration needs
5. Discuss strengths and weaknesses of the REA enterprise ontology as a foundation for meeting intra-enterprise and inter-enterprise information integration needs

# INTRA-ENTERPRISE SYSTEMS: ERP AND THE REA ENTERPRISE ONTOLOGY

**Enterprise resource planning (ERP) systems** are groups of software applications integrated to form enterprisewide information systems. At the time of this writing the major ERP software vendors are Peoplesoft, Oracle Applications, and SAP. ERP systems have their strongest roots in materials resource planning (MRP) system software; however, they also encompass general ledger software, human resource planning software, and other types of software previously considered separate systems. ERP systems originally focused on **back-office applications** such as accounting and human resources. *Back-office* is a term often used in business to describe activities or systems that are seen and used only by people within enterprises; external partners such as vendors and customers usually do not see back-office activities. The systems and activities external partners normally see are referred to as **front-office systems** and activities. For example, activities and systems used in the sales showroom are front-office dealings because customers see and interact with them. Many **bolt-on applications** (software programs that can be added to existing ERP software applications) have been created to allow ERP systems to incorporate front-office applications such as supply chain optimization, customer relationship management, and sales force automation. Non-ERP vendors developed most of these bolt-on applications; however, in some cases the ERP vendors acquired the companies that developed the applications to more fully integrate the products' functionality into their own software. For example, J. D. Edwards (now merged with Peoplesoft) acquired Numetrix in 1999 and YOUcentric in 2001 to add advanced planning system capability and customer relationship management functionality to its software.[1]

The REA enterprise ontology discussed throughout this textbook has been proposed as a theoretical foundation for ERP systems. Therefore it is important to consider the similarities and differences between them. Although preliminary research has compared the core REA model to one specific ERP software package and provided some validation of REA as a theoretical foundation for studying ERP software, the objective in this chapter is not to compare REA to any specific software package.[2] Rather, the objective is to provide a high-level overview of similarities and differences between ERP systems and REA systems. To provide such a high-level overview the goals of each are examined along with the methods by which the goals are achieved.

## Goals and Methods of ERP Software and the REA Enterprise Ontology

Three features may be used to compare some of the goals of ERP software-based systems and REA-based systems: a **database orientation,** a **semantic orientation,** and a **structuring orientation.**[3] We discuss each of these in turn.

[1] J. S. David, W. E. McCarthy, and B. E. Sommer, "Agility: The Key to Survival of the Fittest in the Software Market," *Communications of the ACM* 46, no. 5 (May 2003), pp. 65–69.

[2] D. E. O'Leary, "On the Relationship Between REAL and SAP" (paper presented to the American Accounting Association Annual Meeting, San Diego, CA, 1999).

[3] C. L. Dunn, and W. E. McCarthy, "REA Accounting Systems: Intellectual Heritage and Prospects for Progress," *Journal of Information Systems* 11, no. 1 (1997), pp. 31–51.

### Database Orientation

One goal of both ERP software-based systems and REA-based systems is the achievement of integrated enterprisewide storage, maintenance, and reporting of data needed for decision making. This goal may be referred to as a database orientation; it requires that the following three conditions be met:

- Data must be stored at their most primitive levels, at least for a defined time period.
- Data must be stored only once, and in a way that all authorized decision makers can access the data.
- Data must be stored to allow retrieval in various formats as needed for different purposes.

The most primitive level for data is the level at which the data cannot be further decomposed. For example, total sales for the day is not **primitive level data** because it may be further decomposed into finer levels of detail such as the dollar amounts applicable to each of sales 42 through 89. Similarly the total dollar amounts of each of sales 42 through 89 may be further decomposed into the quantities sold and the dollar unit selling prices for each good or service on each of the sales.

The three database orientation conditions ensure data are stored at the finest level of detail for which decisions may need to be made, so that data may be retrieved and aggregated as needed to make those decisions. The conditions also attempt to eliminate uncontrolled redundancy in the data. Nonintegrated systems (often called legacy or traditional systems) typically record duplicate data about the same object many times (once for each functional area that needs access to the data); thus the data are stored multiple times. For example, in many legacy systems the marketing department records information about customers that have been identified as potential buyers. Once a customer order is received, the sales order entry function (which in a legacy system environment is not usually linked with marketing) records information about the customer from whom the order was received. The sales order entry function may request information about the customer from the credit management function; credit management will retrieve whatever information is in the customer master file and if inadequate information is available to establish a credit rating, credit management may in turn seek and enter additional data from outside sources. Those data are stored and maintained by credit management and are made available to the order entry function only upon request. The sales order entry function typically passes along information about customers to the shipping function and to the customer service function; in those areas the information is entered into their customer master files (either via rekeying or by electronic transmittal). The result is customer data stored in several different customer master files by several different functional areas, which is a maintenance nightmare. Many customers have been frustrated by the fact that when they call their sellers to change their addresses, some mailings from the sellers reflect the changed addresses but other mailings continue to be sent to the old addresses. Such frustration occurs because the customers' calls trigger changes in only one application (that of whichever functional area the customers called) whereas the customers' address is stored in several applications.

In fully implemented ERP software systems and REA systems, data items are stored only once and may be accessed from any authorized functional area in various formats, thus meeting the three database orientation conditions. The extent to which these three database orientation conditions are achieved using ERP software varies for different enterprises depending on whether they use single source ERP software packages, whether they implement best-of-breed ERP solutions, whether they install bolt-on applications in addition to their ERP software, and whether they implement the ERP software enterprise-wide or only in some parts of the enterprises. A single-source ERP solution implemented for an entire enterprise typically maintains a single database and meets the three conditions for the database orientation. The implementation of selected modules of an ERP software package or the installation of a best-of-breed ERP system is less likely to completely satisfy the database orientation. Such an implementation is more likely to store the same data in multiple places because different modules have to overlap to some extent. Bridges similar to the Lego/K'nex connectors described in Chapter 1 may be built to minimize data redundancy and to facilitate data synchronization. However, the retrieval of data from the different modules in combination may be difficult or even impossible. View **integration** for views created with different building blocks may not be seamless.

### *Semantic Orientation*

A second goal of REA-based systems is a semantic orientation. This goal requires objects in the system's conceptual model to correspond as closely as possible to objects in the underlying reality. At first glance both ERP-based systems and REA-based systems share the semantic orientation goal. Horror stories abound of ERP software implementations for which the business processes did not match the software.[4] In fact, ERP system implementations are often regarded as business process reengineering efforts because the business process tasks must be changed to match those supported by the software. Therein lies a subtle difference between REA-based systems and ERP software-based systems. Whereas ERP software requires the business to be changed to match the software, REA tailors the system to match the business's reality. This difference may be necessary so that ERP software can be commercially viable. To date, REA-based systems have been built as proprietary applications as part of custom consulting engagements.[5]

A semantic orientation also precludes the use of artificial constructs such as debits, credits, and accounts as base objects in the enterprise system. Chapters 8 through 13 demonstrated the derivation of many accounting numbers using queries, with no debits, credits, or accounts in the REA-based system. Most ERP software preserves the use of debits, credits, and accounts to satisfy accounting information needs rather than generating the accounting numbers from the underlying economic events and relationships. One probable reason for the preservation of accounting artifacts as base objects in ERP software is market demand; another related reason is lack of education about how to generate accounting numbers procedurally on demand rather than storing them in accounts. Some vendors offer an optional virtual general ledger that is generated on demand, but the market largely rejects that approach and opts for the vendors' hardwired general ledgers that are permanently stored and updated. Whether the market prefers the hardwired general

[4]T. H. Davenport, *Mission Critical: Realizing the Promise of Enterprise Systems* (Boston: Harvard Business School Press, 2000).

[5]J. O. Cherrington, W. E. McCarthy, D. P. Andros, R. Roth, and E. L. Denna, "Event-Driven Business Solutions: Implementation Experiences and Issues. In J. I. DeGross, R. P. Bostrom, and D. Robey, (eds.) *Proceedings of the Fourteenth International Conference on Information Systems,* December 5–8, 1993, Association for Computing Machinery, Orlando, Florida.

ledger approach for efficiency reasons, because of lack of education, because of simple resistance to change, or some other reason is a question for future research. We know only that REA and ERP systems differ to some extent in their semantic orientations.

### Structuring Orientation

A structuring orientation demands the use of a pattern as a foundation for the enterprise system. A pattern-based system design is important to facilitate automated reasoning by intelligent software interfaces to the enterprise system. Academic research is ongoing to develop software applications that can reason with the objects in the REA pattern to aid in decision making. Pattern-based system design is also important to facilitate integration of systems between enterprises. If two enterprises merge their business operations and both used the same pattern-based approach to designing their systems, their systems will be much easier to combine than if they each followed a task-based or haphazard approach. REA-based systems obviously incorporate the REA pattern discussed throughout this textbook. ERP software-based systems do not seem to be intentionally built using any particular pattern; instead they are built to support best practices at the task level. That is, it appears that ERP developers identify the tasks performed by the enterprises that are believed to be most efficient or effective in an industry and build software supporting those tasks. Different versions of the software are created for different industries because the best practices for one industry are not always the best practices for another industry. This reveals a significant difference in the structuring orientations of ERP-based systems and REA-based systems, as most tasks are not used as base objects in REA-based systems.

## Intra-Enterprise Integration

ERP systems themselves are an attempt to integrate applications and data within enterprises, that is, **intra-enterprise integration.** In theory, an ERP system is a single software program that serves the information needs of all users throughout an enterprise. Installed correctly, ERP systems can have a tremendous payback.[6] The five major reasons companies implement ERP are to integrate financial information, to integrate customer order information, to standardize and speed up manufacturing processes, to reduce inventory, and to standardize HR (human resources) information.[7]

In practice many enterprises that have implemented ERP systems have not realized complete system integration. One reason is that many companies have implemented best-of-breed enterprise systems or have implemented only ERP software for part of their enterprises. Best-of-breed enterprise system implementations install different ERP software applications that best meet the needs of different areas of the enterprise. For example, an enterprise may determine that Peoplesoft best meets its human resource information needs, and that Oracle Applications is best suited for its financial information needs, while SAP is ideal for tracking information in its manufacturing processes. Another enterprise may determine that its main integration needs are for financial reporting purposes and therefore decide only to implement the financial module of an ERP software package.

---

[6]C. Koch, "The ABCs of ERP," Enterprise Resource Planning Research Center—CIO, 2002, www.cio.com/research/erp/edit/erpbasics.html.
[7]Ibid.

# Case in Point

In late 1999/early 2000, CMGI had 21 subsidiaries for which financial information needed to be integrated. CIO Jo Hoppe described the monthly process of closing the books based on spreadsheets e-mailed or faxed from the subsidiaries as a horrendous task. Centralized systems became a new priority and CMGI embarked on an ERP system implementation for financial and HR information. CMGI's system integration was greatly improved by the ERP implementation and a new corporate portal that served as a single place to go for information.

Source: E. Prewitt, "Yes, We Had no Integration." *CIO Magazine,* June 15, 2002, www.cio.com.

Within enterprises that have best of breed, partial ERP implementations, or any other nonintegrated information systems, two common integration solutions often are employed. One is the in-house creation of integration programs tailored to the parts of the separate systems that need to be connected. Another is the adoption of packaged **enterprise application integration (EAI) software.** Consider the Lego/K'nex example from Chapter 1. The in-house creation of integration programs is similar to the example of developing a building block with a Lego connector on one end and a K'nex connector on the other end and using it to connect the disparate systems. The use of EAI software is more similar to designing a building block with a Lego (or K'nex) connector on one end and a generic connector on the other end. A typical EAI solution builds bridges from existing applications to a generic central hub that integrates the pieces.

The level of integration used for intra-enterprise systems depends on the goal of the system integration. If the goal is consolidation of information for corporate reporting purposes, integration may be achieved at a high level by creating some sort of shell reporting model and requiring each system to report its results in compliance with that shell. Once each piece is submitted in the shell format, the pieces may be easily combined. Such integration is not as complex as the EAI hub solutions.

ERP systems were originally developed with an intra-enterprise focus. According to David, McCarthy, and Sommer, early ERP systems were inwardly organized.[8] The overall objective was to make information more available and more consistent within enterprises for internal decision-making purposes. Similarly, in its earliest phases REA was inwardly focused. The pattern discovered and applied to each transaction cycle was examined from only one enterprise's perspective. In recent years, the trend for ERP systems and for REA research has shifted to an outwardly organized, supply-chain perspective.[9] The increasing growth of **electronic commerce (e-commerce)** and the increasing benefits of supply chain management have been catalysts for the changing nature of enterprise systems. We next explore the advancements in REA related to e-commerce and inter-enterprise system design.

[8]David, McCarthy, and Sommer, "Agility," pp. 65–69.
[9]Ibid.

# Case **in Point**

## ELECTRONIC COMMERCE SOLUTIONS AND INTER-ENTERPRISE SYSTEM DESIGN

E-commerce is increasingly important in today's global networked economy. E-commerce occurs in various forms; the two most general forms are B2B (business-to-business) and B2C (business-to-consumer). Most people envision B2C transactions when they think about e-commerce; however, most e-commerce activity is actually B2B. If you have ever purchased an item via the Internet using a credit card, then you have engaged in B2C e-commerce (as the consumer). Consideration of ERP systems and REA patterns for a B2C environment isn't significantly different from consideration of ERP systems and REA patterns for a catalog mail order or telephone order environment. In those scenarios a customer inquires about goods or services (or is informed through a marketing event), the customer places an order for goods or services to be delivered, the enterprise delivers the goods or services to the customer, and the customer renders payment to the enterprise for the goods or services. The simple change in communication technology by which the order is placed and/or by which the payment is rendered doesn't change the nature of the business process or the structure of the system needed to capture relevant information.

In B2C commerce the primary differences enabled by electronic technology are the breaking down of time, place, and form barriers. The time barrier is broken in that no longer is consumer access to certain business information restricted to business hours; information may be posted to websites and made accessible 24 hours per day, 7 days per week, 52 weeks per year. The place barrier is broken in that consumers do not need to physically transport themselves to business locations to engage in transactions with the businesses. They can shop from the comfort of their easy chairs with a few clicks of a mouse, and they can obtain product information and products from suppliers around the world from whom they may not have been able to obtain information before the advent of B2C e-commerce. B2C e-commerce also breaks the form barrier in that businesses no longer need to be a particular form or size to attract and satisfy customers. A small enterprise that can't afford a fancy physical storefront may be able to attract customers with a well-designed web-based storefront. Consumers typically do not have automated information systems that need to be

# Case in Point

seamlessly integrated with the businesses' information systems. Thus e-commerce technology advances create little apparent need to change the focus of enterprise systems from an intra-enterprise view to an inter-enterprise view.

In the B2B arena a shift has occurred that requires an inter-enterprise view of enterprise systems. This shift is away from a traditional linear supply chain/value system to the current value webs in which enterprises need information not just about their most direct external partners but also about indirect partners. For example, enterprises today increasingly need information about product demand by their customers' customers. It is difficult to say whether this shift occurred because of advances in technology or whether the increasing information needs driving enterprises toward e-commerce necessitated the technological developments.

Some researchers and practitioners say what we know today as e-commerce began over a century ago with the inventions of the telegraph and the telephone. Indeed a telecommunications infrastructure is necessary to support e-commerce. Other more recent foundations for e-commerce are **electronic data interchange (EDI)** and the Internet. EDI began in the 1960s but wasn't widely used until the 1980s. EDI involves the exchange of data between enterprises in a prescribed electronic format, usually through a VAN (value added network). The VAN connections between enterprises and the software used to accomplish EDI were proprietary and expensive. Enterprises that recognized the need for better and faster information to manage their supply chains justified the expense. Such enterprises realized how much money they had tied up in inventory sitting idle in warehouses and targeted inventory management costs for reduction. Inventory management practices at that time focused on anticipating demand for products and having products available when needed to meet that demand. Enterprises believed that reducing the time it took for upstream supply chain partners (i.e., their suppliers) to process their purchase orders would allow the enterprises to stock lower inventory levels and to better predict downturns in customer demand, thus reducing inventory obsolescence while still meeting customer demand. Large enterprises did benefit from more efficient and effective supply chain management enabled by EDI. In fact, some large enterprises required their suppliers to become EDI-capable if they wanted to remain approved vendors. Some smaller suppliers were unable to afford the investment in the proprietary hardware and software necessary for EDI so they either dissolved their businesses or shifted their business strategies to target different customers.

Many enterprises today still use EDI; however, many efforts in the past two decades have focused on developing standards to make EDI more consistent across industries. In the early years of EDI different industries had different standards, so it was extremely difficult for enterprises whose supply chains crossed industries to use EDI. A decade later the small suppliers that were forced out of business because of EDI would have an easier time engaging in B2B e-commerce with their customers. The Internet eliminated the need for proprietary hardware connections to accomplish EDI, significantly reducing the cost of EDI. Proprietary software was still required to partner with some companies; however, efforts such as Open-EDI attempted to eliminate the need for proprietary bilateral EDI arrangements by creating standards available to all enterprises involved in business transactions.

Cost reduction and process efficiency efforts continue to focus on supply chain issues today, and attempts are still being made to develop standards for inter-enterprise exchange of business transaction data. Customer relationship management bolt-on ERP software applications provide interfaces to allow automated interactions with customers to better satisfy customer information needs. Supplier relationship management bolt-on ERP software applications similarly provide suppliers with self-service capabilities via the purchaser's Internet website. Advanced planning systems and logistics applications are other examples of bolt-on ERP software applications that attempt to make enterprise systems more outwardly focused.[10] Supply chain management for some enterprises has transformed to the extent that a new term has emerged to describe their efforts: collaborative planning, forecasting, and replenishment (CPFR). CPFR is a business technique whereby trading partners agree upon a joint plan and sales forecast; they monitor the extent to which the plan and forecast are met, replenishing inventory as needed, and they recognize and respond to any exceptions.[11]

# INTER-ENTERPRISE SYSTEMS: E-COMMERCE AND THE REA ENTERPRISE ONTOLOGY

The REA enterprise ontology as introduced in this textbook is primarily inwardly focused. How might it be adjusted to shift its focus outward? As described in the previous section, e-commerce requires connections between enterprise systems of upstream and downstream supply chain partners. To achieve CPFR, these connections must be as seamless as possible. Creation of these connections is somewhat similar to view integration. In the view integration chapter, we discussed only intra-enterprise connections. These connections between transaction cycles typically occurred via the resource flows of the value chain. For **inter-enterprise integration,** then, it seems logical that connections between enterprises would occur via the resource exchanges in the value system level model. Let's consider the possibility of connecting two enterprise systems at the value system level.

[10]David, McCarthy, and Sommer, "Agility," pp. 65–69.

[11]J. C. Andraski and J. Haedicke, "CPFR: Time for the Breakthrough?" *Supply Chain Management Review* 7, no. 3 (May/June 2003), pp. 55–60.

Recall the Lego/K'nex toy trains example in Chapter 1. To be able to seamlessly connect two enterprise systems at the value system level would require both systems to be created from the same building blocks. Theoretically REA constructs serve as a great set of building blocks. However, in the short term it is unlikely that either or both enterprises will tear apart their systems and start building from scratch.

Instead Bill McCarthy, the founder of REA, is making efforts to envelope REA constructs in the information exchange standards that will comprise the bridges between enterprise systems. He has served as an influential member of the UN/CEFACT ebXML group whose working documents confirm its adoption of REA constructs as foundational elements of the standards it has created. UN/CEFACT is the United Nations Centre for Trade Facilitation and Electronic Business, established in 1996. Its mission is to contribute to the growth of global commerce by improving the ability of enterprises to effectively exchange products and services. **ebXML** (Electronic Business using eXtensible Markup Language) is one initiative of UN/CEFACT, begun in September 1999 in conjunction with the Organization for the Advancement of Structured Information Standards (OASIS). This nonprofit global consortium focuses on electronic business standards.

EbXML is a set of specifications that provides a standard method by which enterprises may communicate data in common terms. It is similar to EDI but attempts to specify constructs at a higher semantic level. Whereas EDI defines an exact specification for each document used in business exchanges between the linked partners, ebXML expects many variations of each document and focuses on the events underlying the documents. ebXML is a tagging system similar in syntax to HTML (hypertext markup language) and **XML,** languages that are used to create websites. **XBRL** (extensible business reporting language) is also a tagging system tailored to financial statement line items. These tagging systems wrap each data field in a container that identifies what is inside the wrapper; so even if the data fields (building blocks) are different, the containers in which they are enclosed fit together. The attempt to base the EbXML containers on REA constructs is a great step toward encouraging enterprises to use those constructs as foundational building blocks in the long term.

Consider some of the difficulties of inter-enterprise view integration to support CPFR. The process of entity and attribute conflict resolution discussed in Chapter 10 is complicated by the fact that entities labeled as sales/collection cycle phenomena by one enterprise are labeled as acquisition/payment phenomena by the other enterprise. When Enterprise Q sells merchandise inventory to Enterprise R in exchange for cash, Enterprise Q records a sale and a cash receipt. Enterprise R records a purchase and a cash disbursement. To merge these two views, therefore, is a nontrivial exercise. Once merged, the integrated view would include two events, a transfer of goods and a transfer of cash. Each event would need to be related to both Enterprise Q and Enterprise R, with an indication of which enterprise gave up goods to get cash and which one gave up cash to get goods. This merging at first glance may appear relatively simple; indeed the problems are more political than technical. For example, where would the data reside, who would enter the data, who would own the data, and who would maintain the data? The complexities multiply once Enterprises S, T, U, and V are added to the supply web. This textbook does not attempt to solve the problems associated with inter-enterprise view integration. Research on REA as an ontology to support collaborative planning, forecasting, and replenishment is ongoing, and as the research progresses, future editions of this textbook will incorporate the results of that research.

# Key Terms and Concepts

Back-office applications, *476*
Bolt-on applications, *476*
Database orientation, *476*
ebXML, *484*
Electronic commerce (e-commerce), *480*
Electronic data interchange (EDI), *482*

Enterprise application integration (EAI) software, *480*
Enterprise resource planning (ERP) systems, *476*
Front-office systems, *476*
Integration, *478*
Inter-enterprise integration, *483*

Intra-enterprise integration, *479*
Primitive level data, *477*
Semantic orientation, *476*
Structuring orientation, *476*
XBRL, *484*
XML, *484*

# Review Questions

LO1 **R1.** Explain the three conditions that must be met to satisfy a database orientation.

LO3 **R2.** Bolt-on applications and best-of-breed software are both concepts associated with ERP software. What is the difference between these concepts?

LO2 **R3.** What is the difference between intra-enterprise integration and inter-enterprise integration?

LO1 **R4.** What does it mean to have data stored at their most primitive level?

LO2 **R5.** What is the difference between back-office and front-office activities?

LO3 **R6.** To what extent is B2C e-commerce different from B2C commerce?

LO3 **R7.** How has B2B commerce changed with advances in electronic technology?

LO3, LO4 **R8.** Which technology makes information exchange between a small supplier and a large customer more feasible: electronic data interchange or the Internet?

# Multiple Choice Questions

LO2 **MC1.** Which of the following is an example of a back-office activity?
A. An in-store sale of merchandise.
B. Ordering of merchandise from a vendor.
C. Processing of a sale order for a mail-order catalog sales company.
D. Rental of an office building from a landlord.

LO1 **MC2.** Which of the following is a characteristic of a semantic orientation of a system?
A. Data must be stored at their most primitive levels, at least for a defined time period.
B. Data must be stored only once, and so that all authorized decision makers can access the data.
C. A pattern based system design is evident.
D. Objects in the system's conceptual model correspond as closely as possible to objects in the underlying reality.

LO3, LO4 **MC3.** Which of the following technologies provides the strongest level of inter-enterprise integration?
A. Electronic data interchange.
B. ebXML.
C. XBRL.
D. ERP (with no bolt-on applications).

LO4    MC4.  An enterprise has determined that a best-of-breed ERP implementation makes the most sense. What options should the enterprise consider for intra-enterprise integration?

    A. None; the system will automatically be integrated throughout the enterprise because data will be seamlessly transferred among the ERP components.

    B. The enterprise should consider having its IT department design some programs to transfer data between the different ERP components; otherwise it may have to manually rekey data from one package to another.

    C. The enterprise should consider purchasing an enterprise application integration software package that is designed to work with the ERP components.

    D. Both B and C are options the enterprise should consider.

LO3    MC5.  Which of the following statements is FALSE?

    A. The types of events and information needs regarding those events in B2C commerce are similar whether the commerce takes place in an electronic commerce or physical commerce setting.

    B. Electronic B2C commerce breaks down the time, place, and form barriers typically found in a physical commerce setting.

    C. Compared to e-commerce via the Internet, EDI (electronic data interchange) is an inexpensive means for transacting business for small suppliers with large customers.

    D. E-commerce technology advances create little apparent need to change the focus of enterprise systems for B2C from an intra-enterprise view to an inter-enterprise view.

## Discussion Questions

LO1    D1.  How do the semantic orientations of ERP systems and the REA enterprise ontology differ?

LO1    D2.  Do you agree or disagree with the claim that debits, credits, and general ledger accounts are artifacts? Explain why you agree or disagree.

LO5    D3.  Do you believe the REA enterprise ontology provides a valid theoretical foundation for ERP software? Explain why or why not.

LO1, LO5    D4.  Can you think of an alternative pattern to use as a structuring orientation for enterprise systems? Describe the components of your pattern and specify any rules you can identify for the behavior of those components.

LO4    D5.  Explain whether and why you agree or disagree with the following statement: "Now that we have XBRL, real-time financial database reporting (i.e., the reporting of corporate financial results by allowing access to selected views of enterprise data warehouses) can become a reality."

## Applied Learning

LO4    A1.  Choose one of the following types of systems: CRM (customer relationship management), SCE (supply chain execution), ASP (application service provider), SRM (supplier relationship management), VMI (vendor managed inventory), or EAI (enterprise application integration). Conduct library and/or Internet research to find articles describing your chosen type of system. Write an essay describing how that system facilitates inter-enterprise integration. Give an assessment of what level of integration is provided (use the Lego-K'nex analogy if possible).

LO4    A2.    Wal-Mart and Dell Computers are both enterprises that have been lauded for their supply chain management practices. Conduct library and/or Internet research to find articles describing Wal-Mart and Dell. Describe the level of inter-enterprise integration they have achieved, and identify the enterprises with which they have integrated.

## Answers to Multiple Choice Questions

MC1. C, MC2. D, MC3. B, MC4. D, MC5. C.

# Glossary of Terms and Concepts

## A

**Access control matrix**   identifies the functions each user is allowed to perform and what data and programs the user can access once he or she gains access to the system

**Acquisition/payment process**   transaction cycle in which cash or some other form of compensation is disbursed in exchange for goods and services; encompasses all activities associated with the purchase of and payment for those goods and services; also called the "procure-to-pay" mega-process or the expenditures cycle

**Ad hoc querying**   direct retrieval of information by end users from a database whereby the retrieval was not planned (i.e., no preformulated queries or interfaces were developed in anticipation of needing the information)

**Agent**   an individual, department, division, or organization that participates in the control and/or execution of one or more events

**Aggregation function**   a mathematical operation used in querying to summarize information within a single column; also called a vertical calculation

**Application control**   a feature created in a software program to help ensure transactions are valid, properly authorized, and completely and accurately processed

**Areas of responsibility**   departments, sections within a department, or individual employees within a department; used in system flowcharting to clearly identify changes in accountability for a document as the document moves through the system

**Artificial construct**   a thing that is artificially created or developed as opposed to something naturally occurring; also called an artifact

**Attribute**   a characteristic possessed by an entity or a relationship

**Attribute conflict**   differences in the list of characteristics identified as important for describing the same entity or relationship in various view models; resolve in view integration by including a set union of the attributes for the entity or relationship in the integrated view

## B

**Back-office applications**   activities or systems that are only seen and used by people within enterprises; external partners, such as vendors and customers, do not usually see back-office activities or systems

**Backup**   a duplicate copy of a current data file

**Balanced DFD**   data flow diagrams at different levels of detail (e.g., context level and level zero) that are consistent in showing system inputs and outflows

**Base object**   a foundational building block of an enterprise information system; because they are foundational, removal of base objects causes serious problems and requires rebuilding of the system

**Batch control total**   an internal control used to verify that all transactions within a batch were processed correctly

**Bill of lading**   a document that indicates transfer of custody of goods from the enterprise to a common carrier; includes details about how many boxes made up the shipment and the dimensions and/or weight of those boxes

**Bill of materials**   a document that identifies the types and quantities of raw materials needed to create a finished good item

**Biometric access control**   use of biological features such as fingerprints, palm prints, retina eye patterns, signatures, or voices to authenticate users and determine whether to allow them to access a resource

**Bolt-on application**   software programs that can be added to existing ERP software applications

**Bonding**   the process of purchasing insurance on the employees who handle cash for an enterprise; the insurer performs background checks on the employees, determines the likelihood the employees will steal from the enterprise, and agrees to compensate the enterprise in the case of employee theft; primarily a corrective control

**Budget** a plan for future inflows and/or outflows of resources

**Business-entrepreneur script** the stereotypical sequence of enterprise events that says (from the enterprise's point of view) the enterprise gets some money, engages in value-added exchanges, pays back the money, and lives off the profit

**Business interruption** a temporary halt in normal operations due to an incident, such as a threat or catastrophe

**Business process** a term widely used in business to indicate anything from a single activity, such as printing a report, to a set of activities, such as an entire transaction cycle; in this text, business process is used as a synonym of transaction cycle

**Business process level REA model** a representation of an enterprise's resources, events, agents, and appropriate relationships between them within one or more transaction cycles; this conceptual representation is typically used to design the logical enterprise database design

**Business process risks** possibilities of loss and activities intended to mitigate such loss associated with actual business process objects, including resources, events, agents, and relationships among resources, events, and agents

# C

**Cardinality pattern** the complete specification of minimum and maximum cardinalities of the entities that participate in a relationship

**Cash disbursement/cash disbursement economic event** an event that has the effect of decreasing cash; also called a payment

**Cash flow budget** a plan that delineates expected future cash inflows and outflows

**Cash receipt/cash receipt event** an event that has the effect of increasing cash

**Cash requisition event** the identification of need for cash

**Cash resource** usually a list of cash accounts (whether in banks or in petty or on-hand accounts) owned by an enterprise; in essence, a resource type

**Cashier** a person who handles cash transactions on behalf of an enterprise

**Check** a document used to authorize the transfer of cash from one person or enterprise to another

**Check digit** a number that is appended to and maintained as a part of an account number, part number, or other identifier as determined by a predefined formula

**Claim** a timing difference between an economic increment event and the related economic decrement event; receivables and payables are examples of claims

**Closed loop verification** an internal control that helps the user verify the correct record is being processed and updated by displaying details of the record the user should recognize as belonging to the record; e.g., display of a customer's name upon the user entering the customer number

**Collusion** two or more employees acting together to perpetrate a fraud

**Column** the data values of an attribute (field) for various records (rows) in a database table

**Combined entity key posting** a logical level implementation compromise whereby a single foreign key is placed into a table to represent two or more different relationships

**Committee of Sponsoring Organizations of the Treasury Commission (COSO)** a committee of the Treadway Commission that issues reports with guidance/requirements as to components of internal control systems and methods of evaluating internal controls

**Commitment event** an event whereby an enterprise becomes obligated to engage in a future economic event

**Comparison operator** in querying, operators used to compare a variable to a value; common comparison operators are *less than, equal to, greater than, not equal to, greater than or equal to,* and *less than or equal to*

**Completeness check** an edit check internal control that verifies that all critical field data are entered; only verifies that some value has been entered for each field; does not verify accuracy

**Composite attribute** a characteristic that is a combination of other characteristics

**Concatenated primary key** a unique and universal identifier for an entity or relationship that is made up of multiple attributes

**Conceptual database model** a representation that depicts the important objects and relationships between the objects that must be captured in a database; is independent of any hardware, software, or even any type of software

**Conceptual level modeling compromise** the use of less than ideal representation in a conceptual model because of an inability (e.g., inadequate measurement technique) or lack of need to completely and accurately represent an object

**Conceptually congruent events** two or more events that are inseparable, that always occur simultaneously

**Consume stockflow** a relationship between a resource and an economic decrement event whereby the resource is partially used up by the decrement but still exists when the decrement is complete

**Context** the circumstances or setting in which an event occurs; determines which script is invoked in attempting to understand and make predictions about the event

**Context diagram** the highest level data flow diagram; represents a single system and provides the scope of the represented system

**Contingency plan** an approach to be followed in case of a future business interruption or other emergency

**Contract** an agreement that commits two or more enterprises to engage in one or more future exchanges of resources

**Control activity** one of COSO's five interrelated components of an internal control system; a policy or procedure used to ensure necessary actions are taken to minimize risks associated with achieving enterprise objectives; may be preventive, detective, or corrective in nature

**Control environment** one of COSO's five interrelated components of an internal control system; "the tone at the top"; the foundation that provides discipline and structure upon which all other components of internal control are built

**Conversion process** transaction cycle in which materials, labor, machinery, and other resources are transformed into finished goods or services; also called the manufacturing cycle

**Copy of entity** a duplicate representation of an entity placed in a separate position on a conceptual model; must be marked as a copy and have no attributes assigned to it to avoid the creation of duplicate database tables

**Corrective control** a control activity that focuses on recovering from, repairing the damage from, or minimizing the cost of errors or irregularities

**Credit memorandum or credit memo** an internal document used to communicate to the accounting department that a journal entry needs to be made with a credit to the customer's account receivable; a copy may

be given to the customer to confirm the account balance was decreased

**Creditor** an external agent (business partner) from whom the enterprise borrows cash and to whom the enterprise repays cash

**Customer** an external agent (business partner) to whom an enterprise sells its goods and services

**Customer order** information in the customer's own format regarding what goods and services the customer is committing to purchase from an enterprise

**Customer statement** a document that summarizes the economic transactions for a customer and reflects the customer's account balance status

# D

**Data flow diagram** a graphical representation whose primary purpose is to illustrate the logical flow of data in a system

**Data flow diagram symbols** the notations used in a graphical representation whose primary purpose is to illustrate the logical flow of data in a system; four types of symbols are used: squares for data sources and destinations, circles for processes, arrows for data, and parallel lines for data storage

**Data manipulation language** the specification of operations to be performed on one or more data fields to obtain additional information; may create aggregations, horizontal calculations, subset selections, and so forth

**Data type (field property)** (in Microsoft Access) specification as to what kind of data values may be entered into a database table's column

**Data value** the actual entry in a cell of a database table

**Database orientation** a goal for integrated enterprise-wide data storage that requires data to (a) be stored at their most primitive levels, at least for a defined time period; (b) be stored only once, and such that all authorized decision-makers can access the data; and (c) be stored so as to allow retrieval in various formats as needed for different purposes

**Database window** (in Microsoft Access) a screen that depicts the components of the selected database (e.g., tables, queries, forms)

**Datasheet view** (in Microsoft Access) a mode that presents a relational table or a query result in row/column format

**Date constraint** a restriction placed on a date field in a query to limit the query results to include only records for which the date values meet the restriction

**Debit memorandum**   an internal document used to communicate the need for a journal entry to debit (decrease) the enterprise's accounts payable balance for a supplier to whom goods were returned

**Debt financing**   a mechanism for acquiring cash whereby the enterprise borrows cash from one or more external business partners for a specified period of time and with the agreement that the enterprise will pay a specified interest rate as well as repay the principal balance

**Decision/management events**   activities in which managers, employees, and external users make decisions about planning, controlling, and evaluating business processes

**Decomposition**   division of processes on a data flow diagram and into more detailed subprocesses

**Default value**   a software option that sets a data field's contents to a prespecified (default) value; in some cases the default values may be overridden, while in other cases they may not

**Deposit slip**   a document used to summarize the cash receipts that are added to an enterprise's bank account at a specified point in time

**Derivable attribute**   a characteristic of an entity or a relationship that can be calculated based on the values of other stored characteristics

**Design view** (in Microsoft Access)   for relational tables, a mode that displays details about the fields of a table and allows the user to specify various design parameters such as which field(s) comprise the primary key, whether a field is set to required data entry, and the data type for a field; for queries, a mode that depicts the logic of a query in QBE format

**Detective control**   a control activity that focuses on identifying that errors or irregularities have occurred

**Digital signature recognition**   a technology that compares a user's signature to a stored digital representation of the user's signature to authenticate the identification of the user

**Direct deposit**   a cash disbursement (economic decrement event) made to an employee via electronic funds transfer from the enterprise's bank account to the employee's bank account

**Disbursement voucher**   an internal document that authorizes the transfer of cash from an enterprise to an external business partner

**Dividend**   a portion of enterprise earnings that is paid to shareholders

**Dividend declaration commitment event**   a commitment to a future economic decrement event in the equity financing cycle; a legal obligation of the enterprise—once a dividend is declared the enterprise is required by law to actually pay the dividend

**Document/procedure flowchart**   a graphical representation that depicts the movement of and processing procedures for documents through a system

**Duality relationship**   the causal link between a give (economic decrement) event and a take (economic increment) event

**Dynaset** (in Microsoft Access)   a query's result; looks and behaves like a table but is not actually stored as a table; it is generated as a view each time the query is run

# E

**ebXML**   Electronic Business using eXtensible Markup Language; a set of specifications that provides a standard method by which enterprises may communicate data in common terms

**Economic decrement event**   an activity that decreases one or more resources

**Economic decrement reversal event**   an activity that undoes a previous event that had decreased a resource; therefore, the reversal event increases the resource

**Economic event**   an activity that either increases or decreases one or more resources

**Economic increment event**   an activity that increases one or more resources

**Economic increment reversal event**   an activity that undoes a previous event that had increased a resource; therefore, the reversal event decreases the resource

**Economy risks**   threats of loss associated with factors that affect the entire economy, and control activities that mitigate such threats

**Edit check**   a control incorporated into computer program instructions to verify and validate the completeness, reasonableness, and/or accuracy of data

**Electronic commerce (e-commerce)**   use of electronic technology to facilitate or accomplish business exchanges

**Electronic data interchange (EDI)**   the exchange of transaction-level data between enterprises in a prescribed electronic format, usually through a proprietary value-added network

**Electronic funds transfer**   a form of payment that reduces human involvement with cash by having customers electronically transfer funds from their personal bank accounts directly to the company's bank account

**Employee** an external business partner with whom the enterprise exchanges cash for labor; also serves as an internal agent acting on the enterprise's behalf

**Employee knowledge and skills** resources an enterprise is obtaining together with employee labor, but which the enterprise usually is unable to "own"

**Encryption** a process of encoding data entered into a system, storing or transmitting the data in coded form, and then decoding the data upon their use or arrival at their destination to prevent unauthorized access to the data while they are stored or as they are transmitted

**Enforce referential integrity** (in Microsoft Access) a choice selected in the relationship layout to determine whether the referential integrity principle will be enforced in a relationship between two tables as the user enters data into the database

**Enterprise** an organization established to achieve a particular undertaking involving industrious, systematic activity; may be profit driven or charitably motivated

**Enterprise application integration (EAI) software** a software solution that builds bridges from existing applications to a generic central hub that integrates the pieces

**Enterprise resource planning (ERP) system** a group of software applications integrated to form an enterprise-wide information system solution

**Enterprise risks and controls** threats of loss to the enterprise as a result of internal and external factors that result from the actions or circumstances of the enterprise itself or of one of its external business partners, and control activities to mitigate such threats

**Entity** an object that has either a physical or conceptual existence

**Entity conflict** discrepancies in the labeling of entity sets in different views; may result from synonyms (same entity set given two different labels) or homonyms (different entity sets given the same label)

**Entity integrity** a principle in the relational database model that requires the primary key of each tuple (row) to contain a non-null value; guarantees the uniqueness of entity instances and enables proper referencing of primary key values by foreign key values

**Equi-join** a join that combines the tables together based on a common attribute, keeping only those rows for which the data values of the common attribute match exactly; also called an inner join; accomplishes a set intersection of the tables

**Equipment** a resource that gets partially consumed in machine operations in the conversion process

**Equity financing** a mechanism for acquiring cash whereby the enterprise issues shares of stock in exchange for cash

**Error** an unintended mistake on the part of an employee or external business partner

**Event** an activity within an enterprise that needs to be planned, controlled, executed, and evaluated

**Event activity roll-up** the aggregation of a group of event records into a single summary entry; an implementation compromise made at the physical level after transaction data are entered into the database once the historical detail is no longer needed

**Exchange** a trade or swap of resources between two parties

**Exposure** the potential impact of a threat of loss on an enterprise, i.e., uncontrolled risk

**Expression Builder** (in Microsoft Access) an application within Microsoft Access that assists the user in creating horizontal calculations within queries

**Extended business process level REA model** the business process level of the REA enterprise ontology that includes commitment events, instigation events, and appropriate relationships in which those types of events participate

**Extension** the rows in a relational database table; they represent the specific instances that are members of the entity or relationship set

**External agent** a person or organization with which an enterprise trades resources; also called external business partner

**External business partner** a person or organization with which an enterprise trades resources; also called external agent

# F

**Fact** the pairing of a candidate key data value with another attribute data value; facts are found in a table's extension (rows)

**Field** a column in a relational database table

**Field or mode check** an instruction in a computer program that verifies the entered data type is the appropriate mode (e.g., text, numeric, date) for the field into which the data are entered

**Field property** (in Microsoft Access) defines the type of data that are allowed to be entered into a column of a database table

**Financial officer** internal agent who authorizes events in the financing process

**Financing process** transaction cycle in which cash is exchanged for cash at a later point in time; may include debt and/or equity financing

**Finished goods** the resource(s) produced in a production run event in the conversion process; the type of inventory into which raw materials, labor, and equipment are transformed

**Firm infrastructure** support value activities in Porter's generic value chain; activities that support the entire value chain (e.g., general management, planning, finance, accounting, legal, government affairs, quality management)

**Flow line** a symbol on a flowchart used to indicate the movement of a document, a physical object, or data to the next point in a system

**Flowcharting conventions** guidelines to be followed in preparing a system flowchart

**Flowcharting symbols** specific notations used to communicate constructs on a system flowchart; numerous symbols are used to represent different constructs

**Foreign key** an attribute from one relational database table that is added as a column in another relational database table to establish a link between the two tables

**Fraud** an intentional effort to cause harm to an enterprise; an irregularity

**Front-office systems** systems and activities that are typically visible to external partners such as customers and vendors

**Fulfillment relationship** associations between instigation and commitment events whereby the commitment events fulfill the instigation events, and associations between commitment events and economic events whereby the economic events fulfill the commitment events

# G

**General controls** all controls over data center operations, access security, systems software acquisition and maintenance, and application system development and maintenance

**Generalization** a relationship between a supertype and its subtype entities; often called an "is-a" relationship

**Grandparent-parent-child approach** a backup and file reconstruction procedure generally used with batch processing that maintains at least three generations of both event/maintenance data and master reference data; if the current version (the "child" copy) of the master reference file is destroyed or lost, the enterprise can reconstruct it by rerunning the appropriate event/maintenance data against the prior copy of the reference data (the "parent" copy); if a problem occurs during that reconstruction run, the backup data "grandparent" copy may be used to reconstruct the parent file; the parent is then used to reconstruct the child, and processing continues normally

**Group by** a querying function used to create subgroups to which aggregations may be applied; a means for creating subtotals

# H

**Homonym** a word used to designate multiple different things

**Horizontal calculation** a row computation in a query that combines data from two or more separate columns of one or more tables

**Horizontal subset of a table** a part of a table that includes only some of the table's rows, but includes all the columns

**Human resource management** support value activities in Porter's generic value chain; activities involved in recruiting, hiring, training, developing, and compensating all types of personnel

**Human resources process** transaction cycle in which cash is exchanged with employees for labor; also called the payroll cycle

# I

**Implementation compromise** deviation from the identified ideal information system design due to practical considerations, insufficient measurement techniques, and other constraints

**Imprest cash account** a checking account that normally maintains a zero balance and is often used for payroll; enterprise transfers total payroll amount from a regular checking account to an imprest account; individual paychecks are drawn on the imprest account; a positive balance indicates employees haven't cashed paychecks; a negative balance indicates a mistake likely occurred; either situation warrants investigation

**Inbound logistics** primary value activities in Porter's generic value chain; activities associated with receiving, storing, and disseminating inputs to the products or services

**Independent checks on performance**   verification of accuracy of an employee's performance by a different employee (or by an automated procedure)

**Industry risks**   threats of loss associated with factors that affect an enterprise's industry, and control activities that mitigate such threats

**Inflow**   the flowing in (receipt) of a resource to an enterprise

**Information and communication**   one of COSO's five interrelated components of an internal control system; prescribes features of the information system to ensure information quality and also prescribes open channels of communication to ensure employees understand what is expected of them in achieving internal control objectives

**Information need**   a situation for which data are required, e.g., as input to a decision

**Information process event**   a workflow activity that records, maintains, or reports information about one or more operating events

**Information process risks**   Risks associated with recording, maintaining, and reporting information about resources, events, and agents and controls to mitigate those risks

**Information retrieval**   repossession or capture of data that were previously entered into a database or other data storage structure

**Information system**   the network of all communication channels used within an organization, including all paths by which enterprise employees and business partners impart, process, and receive information (e.g., conversations, documents, calculations, fax transmittals, computer technology)

**Inner join**   a join that combines the tables together based on a common attribute, keeping only those rows for which the data values of the common attribute match exactly; also called an equi-join; accomplishes a set intersection of the tables

**Instigation event**   an activity in which need for a resource is identified; typically the event that starts a transaction cycle

**Integration**   the combination of parts into a whole

**Intension**   the columns in a relational database table; they represent the attributes of the entity or relationship set; also called the schema of the table

**Inter-enterprise integration**   the connection of separate systems across two or more enterprises

**Internal agent**   an individual, department, or division within an enterprise that participates in the control and/or execution of one or more events

**Internal business process**   a series of activities that achieve a business objective within an enterprise; a transaction cycle within an enterprise

**Internal control**   an activity performed to minimize or eliminate risk

**Intra-enterprise integration**   the connection of separate systems within an enterprise

**Inventory**   a resource; goods purchased or manufactured by an enterprise and offered for sale to customers

**Inventory type**   a resource type; a category of goods purchased or manufactured by an enterprise and offered for sale to customers

**Investor**   an external agent with whom the enterprise exchanges partial ownership of the enterprise for cash

**Irregularity**   an intentional effort to cause harm to an enterprise; a fraud

# J

**Job time ticket**   a document that indicates starting and stopping times and descriptions for labor operations performed on a specific date by a specific employee; the document's number often serves as an identifier for the labor operation event; also called a time track document

**Join**   to combine separate but related tables by linking them on their common attributes; one of the three primary relational algebra operators discussed in this book

**Join properties window** (in Microsoft Access)   a screen that appears when a user double-clicks on a join line to reveal whether the join is an inner join, a left join, or a right join; a user can change the join type in this window

# K

**Key verification (rekeying)**   the keying of input data twice, with the computer comparing the two entries and highlighting any discrepancies for correction

# L

**Labor acquisition event**   an economic increment event in which employee labor is purchased; each instance covers some time period; often represented by a timecard document

**Labor operation**   an economic decrement event that uses up the employee labor resource

**Labor type resource**   a resource-type entity set that represents a list of the kinds of labor activities that can be performed in labor operations

**Lapping**   a method of stealing cash whereby an employee steals cash from a customer payment, delays posting a payment to the customer's account, and then uses funds from a subsequent customer payment to post to the first customer's account; the process continues with the employee continually stealing from subsequent customer payments to post as prior customer payments

**Left join**   a combination of tables based on a common attribute that includes unmatched records from the first table in the join and does not include unmatched records from the second table in the join; a partial outer join

**Level zero DFD**   a high-level (just under context level) representation that depicts only the very high-level processes within an information system

**Linkage relationship**   an association between two resources to represent the fact that one of the resources is composed of the other; in the conversion cycle this provides a means for identifying the materials a finished good is composed of and the types of labor that are needed to produce a finished good

**Load (high and low)**   the percentage of data values for an attribute that are non-null; if most cells in a column have actual values, the load is high; if most cells in a column have null values, the load is low

**Logical access control**   restricting unauthorized access to the programs and data in systems

**Logical level implementation compromise**   an implementation compromise made when converting a conceptual model into database objects

**Logical model**   in database design, a model into which the conceptual model is converted once the type of database software to be used has been chosen (e.g., relational or object-oriented); hardware independent and somewhat software independent (if relational is chosen as the database type, then any relational software may be chosen but object-oriented software may not)

**Logical operator**   Boolean search terms used in queries to define which records are included in the query result (examples include AND, OR, and NOT)

# M

**Machine operation**   an economic decrement event that partially consumes a machine in the conversion cycle

**Margin**   the difference between value and cost in Porter's generic value chain model

**Marketing and sales**   primary value activities in Porter's generic value chain; activities associated with providing a means by which customers can buy products or services and the means for inducing them to buy

**Marketing event**   an activity such as a sales call, advertising campaign, or promotion intended to inform customers about products and/or services and persuade them to trigger the sales/collection process; an internally instigated instigation event

**Master reference check**   verifies that an event/transaction record has a corresponding master record to be updated

**Materiality of risk**   a function of the size of the potential loss, its impact on achieving the enterprise's objectives, and the likelihood of the loss

**Materialization of task as entity**   a conceptual model level implementation compromise in which an activity that could be reengineered is established as an entity (base object)

**Mathematical operation**   a calculation that manipulates data values

**Maximum participation cardinality**   represents the maximum number of times each instance of an entity set may participate in a relationship; legal values are one and $N$ (many)

**Minimum participation cardinality**   represents the minimum number of times each instance of an entity set must participate in a relationship; legal values are zero (optional participation) and one (mandatory participation)

**Model**   a representation intended to serve as a plan or blueprint for something to be created; an object that represents in detail another (usually larger and more complex) object; used in systems design to help control complexity

**Monitoring**   one of COSO's five interrelated components of an internal control system; the process of assessing the quality of internal control performance over time and taking corrective actions as needed

**Move ticket**   a document typically used in the conversion cycle to indicate the actual use of raw materials (i.e., the materials issuance event)

**Mutual commitment event**   an event that obligates an enterprise to participate in at least two future economic events, one that increments a resource and another that decrements a resource

# N

**Name conflict**   a form of entity conflict in which two different entities are assigned the same name or a single entity is assigned two different names

**Noncash related economic event**   an activity in which a resource other than cash is increased or decreased

**Null to zero (Nz) function** (in Microsoft Access)   a Microsoft Access procedure used in querying that treats null values as if they are zeros

**Null value**   a blank cell in a database table; a cell into which no data has been entered

# O

**Object**   a thing that has a physical or conceptual existence

**One-fact, one-place rule**   a principle in database design that prohibits a pairing of a candidate key value with another attribute value from appearing multiple places in a database table and also prohibits multiple pairings of candidate key values with other attribute values in the same place; helps to ensure well-behaved relational tables

**Open purchase order file**   a repository that contains information about purchase order events that have not yet been fulfilled by purchase events; a collection of unfilled purchase orders

**Open purchase requisition**   a purchase requisition that has not yet been fulfilled by a purchase order

**Open sales invoice file**   a repository that contains information about sales events that do not yet have related cash receipts

**Open sales order file**   a repository that contains information about sale order events that have not yet been fulfilled by sale events; a collection of unfilled sale orders

**Operating event**   an activity performed within a business process to achieve enterprise objectives that does more than just communicate information (e.g., economic events, commitment events, and some instigation events)

**Operations**   primary value activities in Porter's generic value chain; activities associated with transforming inputs into final products or services

**Operations list**   a document that identifies the labor types needed to create a finished good; captures the same information as the linkage relationship between labor types and finished goods

**Opportunity**   a potential for reward

**Outbound logistics**   primary value activities in Porter's generic value chain; activities associated with collecting, storing, and physically distributing products or services

**Outer join**   a combination of tables based on a common attribute that includes unmatched records from both sides; accomplishes a set union of the tables

**Outflow**   the flowing out (disbursement or distribution) of a resource from an enterprise

# P

**Packing slip**   a document that identifies the goods that have been shipped to a customer

**Parameter query** (in Microsoft Access)   a query in which variables are used in lieu of data values as part of the query's selection criteria; allows the user to specify the data value to be used each time the query is run, thereby allowing reuse of the same query many times for different decisions

**Participation cardinalities**   represents business rules for how many times an instance of an entity set is allowed to participate in a relationship

**Participation relationship**   an association between an event and an internal or external agent

**Password**   a unique identifier that only an authorized user of a system or application should know and that the user is required to enter each time he or she logs onto the system; a weak form of protection; a logical access control

**Pattern**   a template or configuration from existing scenarios that can be used to make sense of other scenarios

**Paycheck**   a document representing a cash disbursement (economic decrement event) to an employee

**Payroll clerk**   an internal agent responsible for accomplishing the cash disbursement event in the payroll transaction cycle

**Performance review**   a review of some element of an enterprise's performance that provides a means for monitoring (e.g., comparison of actual data to budgeted or prior period data; comparison of operating data to financial data; and comparison of data within and across various units, subdivisions, or functional areas of the enterprise)

**Personal identification number (PIN)**   a numeric identifier used as a logical access control to authenticate a user; similar to a password

**Physical database model**    a working database system that is dependent on the hardware, software, and type of software chosen during the design stages

**Physical level compromise**    an implementation compromise made when entering the logical database objects into a database software package to create the working database

**Picking slip**    a document that identifies the goods that have been taken out of the warehouse and made available to be shipped

**Posted key**    an attribute of a database table that is added to another database table to create a link between the tables

**Preventive control**    a control activity that focuses on preventing errors or irregularities either from occurring or from being entered into the enterprise information system

**Primary key attribute**    a characteristic that uniquely and universally identifies each instance in an entity or relationship set

**Primary value activities**    the events that create customer value and provide organization distinctiveness in the marketplace; events viewed as the critical activities in running a business

**Primitive DFD**    the lowest level (most detailed) representation of a system process; cannot be further decomposed

**Primitive level data**    data that cannot be decomposed into any component parts

**Procurement**    a support value activity in Porter's generic value chain; the function of purchasing inputs to a firm's value chain

**Production employee**    an internal agent involved in labor operations and production runs in the conversion process; a worker who participates in the manufacture of finished goods

**Production order document**    a document that captures information about a production order event

**Production order event**    an event that represents the enterprise's commitment to engage in a future economic increment event (a production run) that will increase the finished goods resource

**Production run**    an economic increment event that increases the quantity of a finished goods resource

**Production supervisor**    an internal agent who authorizes events in the conversion cycle

**Project**    a relational algebra operator (pronounced pro-JECT' rather than PRO'-ject) that specifies a vertical subset to be included in the query result

**Proposition relationship**    an association between an instigation event and a resource or resource type; often specifies quantity and proposed cost or selling price for the item(s) identified as needed

**Purchase**    an economic increment event in which services or the title to goods transfers from a supplier to the enterprise; also called an acquisition

**Purchase order**    a mutual commitment event in which a supplier agrees to transfer title of goods to the enterprise at an agreed upon future time and price and the enterprise agrees to pay for those goods; a document reflecting the terms of the mutual commitment event

**Purchase requisition**    an instigation event in which the need for goods or services is identified; an internal document that communicates this need to the enterprise purchasing function

**Purchase return**    an economic increment reversal event in which the title to goods previously transferred from a supplier to the enterprise is transferred back to the supplier

# Q

**Query**    a request for information submitted to a database engine

**Query by example (QBE)**    a type of query interface intended to be more "point and click" in nature than is SQL; in this interface the user creates a visual example of what tables and fields should be included in a query result and specifies any calculations to be included

**Query grid** (in Microsoft Access)    the lower half of the QBE view into which fields are dragged and in which aggregations or horizontal calculations may be created to establish the desired logic for a query

**Query window** (in Microsoft Access)    the screen in which queries are created; user may toggle back and forth between QBE design, SQL design, and Datasheet (result) views within the query window

# R

**Range check**    an instruction in a computer program that compares entered data to a predetermined acceptable upper and/or lower limit and rejects data that fall outside the specified limits unless special authorization is obtained

**Raw material**    an input resource in the conversion process that is completely used up in the transformation to finished goods

**Raw material issuance**   an economic decrement event involving the using up of raw materials in the production process; the raw materials are usually transformed into finished goods and lose their own identity and nature in the process

**Raw materials requisition**   a commitment event whereby the inventory clerk or warehouse supervisor commits to the production supervisor to transfer materials from the materials warehouse to the production floor; assumes the raw materials are available within the enterprise and reserves them for use

**REA core pattern**   the original version of the REA model at the business process level; includes resources, economic events and agents, duality relationships, stockflow relationships, and control (participation) relationships

**REA ontology**   a domain ontology founded by Bill McCarthy at Michigan State University that attempts to define constructs that are common to all enterprises and demonstrate how those constructs may be represented in an integrated enterprise information system. The REA ontology is made up of four layers: the value system, value chain, business process, and task levels.

**Read-only file designation**   a property used to mark data as available for reading only; the data cannot be altered by instructions from users, nor can new data be stored on the device

**Reality**   that which exists objectively and in fact

**Reasonableness check**   an instruction in a computer program to verify whether the amount of an event/transaction record appears reasonable when compared to other elements associated with each item being processed

**Receiving report**   a document that lists the items and the quantities and condition of each item received in an acquisition event; the receiving report identifier is often used as the identifier for the acquisition event

**Reciprocal relationship**   a relationship between a commitment to an economic increment and a commitment to an economic decrement; the commitment level equivalent of the duality relationship; in the conversion cycle, represents a schedule of what is to be produced and what will need to be used and consumed in the production process

**Record**   a row in a relational database table

**Redundancy**   in database design, duplicate storage of the same information

**Reengineering**   the redesign of business processes or systems to achieve a dramatic improvement in enterprise performance

**Referential integrity**   a principle in relational databases that requires a value for a foreign key attribute to either be null (blank) or match exactly a data value in the table in which the attribute is a primary key

**Relational algebra**   the original data manipulation (querying) language that was constructed based on set theory and predicate logic as part of the relational database model; primary operators include Select, Project, and Join; however, other operators are also part of the relational algebra

**Relational database**   a collection of tables that meet the criteria of the relational model

**Relational model**   a logical level database design model developed by E. F. Codd based on set theory and predicate logic; primary constructs are relations (tables) that represent entities and relationships between entities

**Relational table**   a relation; a two-dimensional storage structure (i.e., a storage structure with rows and columns) that represents either an entity or a relationship between entities and that adheres to relational principles such as entity integrity, referential integrity, and the one-fact, one-place rule

**Relationship**   an association between two or more entity sets

**Relationship conflict**   a discrepancy in the assignment of participation cardinalities or in the label used to name the same relationship in different view models

**Relationship layout** (in Microsoft Access)   a window in which relationships between tables are visually depicted

**Remittance advice**   a document (usually the portion of a customer invoice or statement that says "return this stub with payment") that advises the enterprise the customer is remitting payment; often used as the identifier for a cash receipt event

**Rental**   an economic decrement event that does not involve the transfer of title of goods, but instead involves a transfer of the right to use goods for an agreed upon length of time; begins when the right to temporary possession of the goods transfers from the lessor to the lessee and ends when possession of the goods transfers back from the lessee to the lessor

**Repeating group**   multiple facts stored in one place; the same value of a key attribute field associated with multiple values of another attribute

**Representation**   a surrogate for something; a symbol that closely resembles the actual construct; the closer the resemblance to the real object, the better the representation

**Request to return goods** notification to a supplier of the enterprise's dissatisfaction with goods that seeks permission to return those goods in lieu of making payment (or in exchange for a refund)

**Required data entry (field property)** (in Microsoft Access) a choice specified in table design view; a user will not be allowed to enter a record into the table without including a value for any field(s) for which this property is set to "yes"; a user may leave any field except the primary key field(s) blank for which this property is not set to "yes" (Microsoft Access automatically enforces entity integrity so there is no need to set the required data entry field property to "yes" for primary key fields)

**Reservation relationship** an association between a mutual commitment event and a resource or resource type; often specifies quantity and budgeted cost or selling price for the item(s) involved in the agreement

**Resource** a thing of economic value (with or without physical substance) that is provided or consumed by an enterprise's activities and operations

**Resource flow** the increase or decrease of a resource as the result of an event

**Resource inflow** the increase of a resource as the result of an event

**Resource outflow** the decrease of a resource as the result of an event

**Reversal relationship** an association between an economic reversal event and a resource or resource type; often specifies the quantity and cost or selling price information for the item(s) involved in the event

**Right join** a combination of tables based on a common attribute that includes unmatched records from the second table in the join and does not include unmatched records from the first table in the join; a partial outer join

**Risk** an exposure to the chance of injury or loss

**Risk assessment** one of COSO's five interrelated components of an internal control system; the identification and analysis of relevant risks associated with the enterprise achieving its objectives; forms the basis for determining what risks need to be controlled and the controls required to manage them

**Row** the data attribute values that apply to a single instance of an entity or relationship set as represented in a relational database table

# S

**Sales call** An internally initiated instigation event; typically involves a sales representative calling on a customer, either via telephone or in person, to describe the features of one or more products or services

**Sales invoice** a document used to communicate to a customer the fact that the enterprise has fulfilled a commitment to transfer title of goods to the customer; sometimes also serves as a request or reminder for the customer to fulfill its commitment and remit payment to the enterprise

**Sales order** a mutual commitment event in which the enterprise agrees to transfer title of goods to a customer at an agreed upon future time and price and the customer agrees to pay for those goods; a document reflecting the terms of the mutual commitment event

**Sales return** an economic decrement reversal event in which the title to goods previously transferred to a customer transfers back to the enterprise

**Sales/collection process** transaction cycle in which goods or services are exchanged to customers or clients for cash or some other form of compensation

**Schedule** a mutual commitment event in the human resource business process wherein the employee agrees to provide labor as specified in the schedule and the enterprise commits to pay the employee the contracted wage rate for the labor provided

**Schema** the column headings, or intension, of a relational database table

**Script pattern** a sequence of events that typically occur in combination with each other

**Select** a relational algebra operator that specifies a horizontal subset to be included in the query result

**Select-From-Where** the format of SQL queries; the Select clause specifies a vertical subset to be included in the query result; the From clause specifies which table(s) are to be queried and any subgrouping to be done; the Where clause specifies a horizontal subset to be included in the query result and, if multiple tables are included, helps to define the join

**Semantic orientation** a goal of REA-based systems that requires objects in the system's conceptual model to correspond as closely as possible to objects in the underlying reality

**Separation (or segregation) of duties** the structuring of employees' job functions such that one employee is prohibited from performing two or more of the following functions: authorization of transactions involving assets, custody of assets, record keeping, and reconciliation; reduces the opportunity for one employee to steal enterprise assets and to conceal the theft in the normal course of his or her work

**Sequence check**   a control used to verify the records in a batch are sorted in the proper sequence and/or to highlight missing batch items

**Service**   primary value activities in Porter's generic value chain; activities associated with providing service to enhance or maintain the value of the products or services

**Service engagement**   an economic decrement event in which the enterprise transfers services to a customer

**Service type**   a kind of service an enterprise has the ability to provide to customers; a resource type

**Shares of stock**   units that represent the holder's right to share in various ownership interests of an enterprise

**Show Table window** (in Microsoft Access)   a screen from which the user may choose which table(s) to include in the relationship layout or in a query

**Simple attribute**   a characteristic of an entity or relationship that cannot be further decomposed into component characteristics

**Smart card or token**   a logical access control that authenticates a user through a hardware device combined with a log-in password process; the smart card generates a random code that changes at predetermined intervals and must be matched against the host system; the user must also enter a password to gain access to the system

**SQL view** (in Microsoft Access)   a mode for viewing the underlying SQL statement for a query; even if a query was created in QBE mode, Microsoft Access generates a corresponding SQL statement that the user may view to evaluate the query's logic

**Statement on Auditing Standards No. 94**   an auditing statement that largely established current standards for internal control

**Static derivable attribute**   a derivable attribute for which the derived value will not change if additional transaction data are entered into the database

**Stock issuance commitment event**   an equity financing agreement that commits an investor to provide a determinable cash dollar amount (stock proceeds) on a specified date

**Stockflow relationship**   an association between an economic event and a resource or an association between an economic reversal event and a resource; often specifies quantity and actual cost or selling price for the item(s) involved in the event

**Stovepipes**   functional areas structured such that the only pathways for communication are at the top (i.e., between the managers of each area); also called functional silos

**Strategy**   an enterprise's planned course of action for achieving an objective

**Structured Query Language (SQL)**   a query language developed to enable the performance of multiple operations in a single query and to use a standard format for every query statement (Select-From-Where) to simplify the task of query development

**Structuring orientation**   a goal of REA-based systems that demands the use of a pattern as a foundation for the enterprise system to facilitate automated reasoning by intelligent software interfaces to the enterprise system

**Sum**   the mathematical total of a column of numerical data values

**Supplier**   a person or organization from which an enterprise purchases goods or services

**Supply chain**   the entire network of enterprises (e.g., retailers, wholesalers, transportation firms) involved in providing a particular product or service to an end customer

**Support value activities**   in Porter's generic value chain, activities that facilitate accomplishing the primary value activities

**Symbol**   something that stands for or represents something else

**Synonym**   a word that has the same meaning as one or more other words

**Syntax**   the formatting rules of a query language (and also other types of languages)

**System flowchart**   a graphical representation of the inputs, processes, and outputs of an enterprise information system; includes details about the physical as well as the logical aspects of the system components

# T

**Task level REA model**   a task is a workflow step or activity that may be changed or eliminated without fundamentally changing the nature of the enterprise and therefore should not serve as a foundational element in an enterprise information system; task level models in the REA ontology are graphical representations of workflow processes for which there is no identified pattern

**Technology development**   support value activities in Porter's generic value chain; the know-how, procedures, or technology embedded in processes that are intended to improve the product, service, and/or process

**Threat**   a situation or event that causes possible or probable loss to a person or enterprise

**Timecard**   the primary document prepared by the enterprise in conjunction with the economic increment event; may be completed on a daily, weekly, or other basis; is typically completed by employees and approved by supervisors; lists the times employees started working (punched in) and stopped working (punched out) for each day in the covered time period

**Token**   an individual object; token-level representation uses a separate token for each individual instance in the piece of reality that is being modeled

**Training**   the provision of education to employees to further develop their skills and/or knowledge

**Transfer duality relationship**   an association between economic increment and decrement events in which the resource(s) decremented are traded for the incremented resource(s)

**Transformation duality relationship**   an association between economic increment and decrement events whereby the resource(s) decremented are changed into the incremented resource(s), i.e., the incremented resource(s) are created from the decremented resource(s)

**Tuple**   a row in a relational database table

**Type**   a category into which individual objects may be classified; type level representation uses one type to represent as many individual instances as fit the category

**Typification**   a relationship between an entity and an entity type; allows for storage of characteristics of entity categories

# U

**Use stockflow relationship**   a relationship between a resource and an economic decrement event whereby the resource is completely subsumed by the decrement (i.e., the resource is completely used up)

# V

**Valid sign check**   an internal control used to assess whether a field's sign (positive or negative) makes sense; used to highlight illogical values, particularly balances in master file records

**Validity check**   an internal control in which a comparison is made between entered data and prespecified stored data to determine whether the entered data are valid

**Value chain**   the interconnection of business processes via resources that flow between them, with value being added to the resources as they flow from one process to the next

**Value chain level REA model**   a representation that depicts the interconnected business processes for an enterprise, the resource flows between the processes, and the duality relationships within each process

**Value system**   an enterprise placed into the context of its various external business partners such as suppliers, customers, creditors/investors, and employees

**Value system level REA model**   a representation that depicts the resource exchanges in which an enterprise engages with external business partners

**Vendor invoice**   a document sent by a supplier to the enterprise to communicate the fact that the supplier has fulfilled its commitment to transfer title of goods to the enterprise; sometimes also serves as a request or reminder for the enterprise to fulfill its commitment and remit payment

**Vertical calculation**   a computation that is a summarization of data values within a single column; also called an aggregation function

**Vertical subset of a table**   a part of a table that includes only some of the table's columns (but includes all the rows)

**View integration**   the process of combining separate conceptual models into one comprehensive model

**View modeling**   the creation of conceptual models to represent separate parts (usually transaction cycles) of an enterprise

**Virtual close**   the ability to produce financial statements without actually closing the books; often touted as a benefit of ERP system software

**Voice recognition technology**   used for internal control, creates a digital representation of a person's voice and stores it in a database; to access a resource the person speaks into a device; the spoken voiceprint is compared to the stored voiceprint and the person is denied access if the voiceprints do not match

**Volatile derivable attribute**   a derivable attribute for which the derived value will change if additional transaction data are entered into the database

# W

**Withholdings**   employee pay amounts retained by the employer to remit to governmental or other agencies on behalf of the employee (e.g., social security, income tax, health insurance premiums)

**Workflow**   detailed procedural steps and activities used to accomplish events and business processes in enterprises

# X

**XBRL**   Extensible Business Reporting Language; a tagging language used to identify data values of business reporting line items such as financial statement elements

**XML**   Extensible Markup Language; a tagging language used in the creation of websites

# Index

**A**

Abstraction relationships, 55
Access, 137–149
Access controls
    and acquisition events, 451
    biometric, 454
    logical, 453–454
    matrix, 453–455
Accounting, 33
Accounts; *See* Cash accounts; Checking
    accounts
Accounts payable; *See also*
    Acquisition/payment process
    cash disbursement (*see* Cash
        disbursements)
    defined, 289
    electronic data interchange, 481–484
    electronic funds transfer (*see* Electronic
        funds transfer (EFT))
    individual supplier balances, 301–303
    total dollar amount query, 288–293
Accounts receivable; *See also* Sales/
    collection process
    in applied learning, 118–119
    balance data, 103
    null values, 235–237
    queries, 231–237
    and sales/collection, 231–237
Ackoff, Russell L., 11–17
Acquisition event set, 46
Acquisition/payment process
    activities, 260
    applied learning, 117–120, 157–159,
        307–309
    cash disbursement, 273–275, 289 (*see
        also* Cash disbursements)
    concepts and terms, 305
    control activities, 443–444, 446, 451
    and conversion process, 346
    database design, 263
    decrement events, 273–275
    defined, 43
    duality relationships, 269, 288–293, 303
    e-commerce, 481–484
    EDI, 481–484
    entity relationship diagrams, 263, 314
    and financing process, 43, 410
    flowchart, 70
    fulfillment relationships, 295–297, 298
    and human resource process, 43,
        386, 387
    increment events, 269–272

Acquisition/payment process—*Cont.*
    information needs, 279–280 (*see also*
        Queries, acquisition/payment)
    and labor costs, 355
    main concerns, 273
    modeling example, 63–81
    objectives, 260–261
    overview, 260–262
    purchases, 269–272
        returns, 270, 275–278 (*see also*
        Purchase returns)
    in REA model, 25, 28–29, 262, 304
    reengineered workflow, 92–93, 274
    reimbursement, 95–96, 102
    reservation relationships, 299
    revenue/acquisition integration,
        325–327
    review and discussion, 305–307
    risks, 449–450, 451
    stockflow relationships, 269, 294–295
    three-way match control, 7
    time factors, 269
    in value chain model, 46, 304
    in value system model, 304
Acquisitions
    defined, 269
    recording, 269
Active badges, 454
Ad hoc querying, 161–162
    in QBE, 174–189
Advertising
    risks, 447
    in value system, 40, 41
Agents; *See also* External agents;
    Internal agents; Participation
    relationships
    in acquisition/payment events,
        262–263, 287–288
        queries about, 299–300
    attributes, 67
    in business process modeling, 64, 69–70,
        72–74
    cardinality, 69–70
    and commitment events, 82
    and decrement events, 212
    definition, 24
    implementation compromise, 321
    in instigation events, 203–204
    and production runs, 349
    in REA model, 24, 29–30
    relationships between, 84–85,
        365–366
    and resources, 84–85

Aggregation functions
    AVG, 173, 400
    COUNT, 400
    MAX, 173
    in QBE, 184–187
    in SQL, 173–174
    SUM, 324, 425
Allowances, 217–219, 275–278
American Institute of Certified Public
    Accountants (AICPA), 433
AND
    in QBE, 180
    in SQL, 172
Andraski, J. C., 483n
Andros, D. P., 478n
Annotation, in flowcharts, 100, 101
Application controls, 457–468
    data input, 457–462
    file controls, 463–468
    processing controls, 462–463
Application software
    data entry controls, 457–462
    definition, 456–457
    development, 456
    file controls, 463–468
    maintenance, 456–457
    processing controls, 462–463
Approvals, in flowcharts, 102
Archive files, 103
Areas of responsibility, 101, 102; *See also*
    Responsibility
Arrows, in flowcharts, 101
Artificial constructs, 9, 478
Artificial intelligence, 386
Assets, 443; *See also* Fixed assets; Operating
    assets
Assignment relationships, 365–366
Association relationships, 365–366
Assumptions
    information needs, 11–14
    interdepartmental communication,
        14–16
    for inventory costs, 334, 336–337
    MIS user role, 16–17
Asterisk, 225
Attributes
    of acquisition/payment events, 264–275,
        308–309
    of agents, 67
    assignment of, 64–67, 74–77
    in business process model, 53
    candidate keys, 124
    of cash, 65–66

Attributes—*Cont.*
  cash accounts, 389, 413
  cash disbursements, 274–275, 324,
    395–397, 420
  cash receipts, 217, 324
  cash requisitions, 413
  composite, 54
  conflicts, 313
  of conversion events, 347–356,
    382–383
  of debt financing agreements, 414
  definition, 122
  derivable, 54, 321–324
    volatile, 54, 389, 478
  descriptor, 76
  of duality relationships, 66–67, 288–289
  of economic events, 66–67
  of entities, 65
  of equity financing, 415
  of events, 66–67
  foreign key, 123
  for human resources, 407
  of instigation events, 204, 264
  of labor requisitions, 390
  of labor schedule, 392
  labor type/finished goods, 369
  for machine operations, 359
  of mutual commitment events,
    206, 266
  non-key, 76
  notation, 56, 64–65
  primary key, 53–54, 76, 123
    concatenated, 54, 56
  of production order events, 359–361
  for purchase returns, 275
  of raw material requisition, 363
  for raw materials/finished goods, 367–368
  in relational databases, 122–123
  of relationships, 65, 135–137, 231
  of resource acquisition, 269
  of resources, 65–66
  of sales calls, 204, 228–229
  sales/collection examples, 157–158,
    308–309
  of sales returns, 218
  simple, 54
Audit committees, 434
Auditors, 432–433
Authorization
  and control environment, 434, 443
  for purchases, 449
  queries about, 376–377, 424, 427
  for raw material issuance, 353
  risks, 441, 449
  for sales returns, 218
Automobiles, 37
Average unit cost, 294–295, 334–335
Averages
  in QBE, 184–186
  in SQL, 173

AVG
  in QBE, 184–186
  in SQL, 173

**B**

Back-office applications, 476
Background checks, 442
Backup files, 103, 465, 467
Backup locations, 442
Backup systems, 454
Backus-Naur form (BNF), 56
Badges, 454
Balance forward, 217
Balanced DFDs, 111
Balances; *See also* Cash balance
  cash receipts and deposit, 451
  data storage, 103
  of financing agreements, 425
  high value assets, 445
    case, 446
  of individual suppliers, 301–303
  outstanding principal, 425
  risk/cost of controls, 434
Bank statements, 444; *See also* Financial
    statements
Barcodes, 446
Base objects, 8, 9, 91
  tasks as, 30
Batch control totals, 461–462
Batch edit checks, 460–462
Batch processing
  controls, 460–462
  data reconstruction, 465–466
  description, 105, 346–347
  flowchart, 462
  quantity needed, 369–370
  queries, 373–374, 374–375
Batini, C., 56n, 312n
BETWEEN, 172
Bill of lading, 211, 275
Bill of materials, 367–368, 377, 440
Biometric access controls, 454
Boards of directors, 434, 439
Bolt-on applications, 476, 478, 483
Bond certificates, 414–415
Bonding, 55, 215, 443
Boolean operators, 172, 180
Bostrom, R. P., 478n
Brand, 439, 442
Bridges, 478, 480, 484
Broken lines, 101
B2B commerce, 482–483
B2C transactions, 481–482
Budgets
  and financing process, 413
  and human resources, 390, 399
  and requisition events, 448
Building
  acquisition/payment queries, 279–285

Business-entrepreneur script, 25
Business events; *See also* Commitment
    events; Economic decrement events;
    Economic events; Economic
    increment events; Exchange events;
    Instigation events
  control of, 436
  core, 28–30, 59–64
  decision management, 86
  defined, 24
  information events, 85–86
  operating events, 85, 86
  risks, 440, 447
  software processing, 457–459
  support activities, 38–39
Business interruption, 439–440
Business level REA model, 25
Business process modeling
  applied learning, 34, 88–89, 256–258,
    307–309
  attribute assignment, 65–67, 74–77
  cardinality assignment, 67–70, 78–81
  constructs, 52–55
  core pattern, 59–63
  extensions, 82–86
  focus, 25
  key concepts, 86
  notation, 55–59
  purpose, 92
  review and discussion, 87–88
  steps, 63–70
    RSWS example, 70–81
  *versus* task level, 91–94
  validation, 70
Business process reengineering
  acquisition/payment, 92–94, 274
  applied learning, 11
  discussion, 33
  and ERP, 478
  and information process events,
    85–86
  *versus* paving cowpaths, 6–8
  and task level model, 91–92
Business process risks, 440–441, 442–452
  in applied learning, 471–472
Business processes
  acquisition/payment process (*see*
    Acquisition/payment process)
  analysis (*see* REA (Resources-Events-
    Agents) ontology)
  and business solutions
  cash in, 65–66, 79
  and commitment events, 82
  conversion process (*see* Conversion
    process)
  decisions (*see* Decision process)
  defined, 24, 42
  example enterprise, 25–30
  extended enterprise process
  financing (*see* Financing process)

Business processes—*Cont.*
    human resources (*see* Human resource
      process)
    integrated, 324–333
    internal, 38
    internal resource transformations, 44 (*see*
      *also* Production runs)
    linking (*see* Linkage relationships)
    organizational structure, 434, 439, 443
    in REA model, 25
    reengineering (*see* Business process
      reengineering)
    relationships between (*see* Relationships)
    review, 32–34
    risks, 432–433, 440–441
      controls, 442–452
    RSWS example, 70–80
    sales/collection (*see* Sales/collection
      process)
    strategic analysis, 27–30, 36
    terms and concepts, 32
    value chain analysis, 24–25, 27–30,
      35–39, 42–47
Business rules, 142, 457–459

**C**

Calculations
    of accounts payable total, 288–293
    accounts receivable, 232
    average employee wage, 400
    averages, 173, 184–186
    cash balances, 224–225, 324
    of cash disbursements, 400
    with dates/time, 177, 372
    in flowcharts, 98
    of labor, 386
    of manufacturing costs, 347, 372
    margin, 36
    with null values, 235–237
    past due invoices, 177
    payroll, 401
    in QBE, 177, 184–187, 324, 330 (fig.)
    of quantity on hand, 224, 328–333
    quantity sold, 187
    sales call duration, 229
    in SQL, 172–174
    of supplier balances, 301–303
    vertical, 173, 175
    weighted average unit cost of inventory,
      294–295, 334–335
Candidate keys, 124
Capital appreciation, 414
Capital tools, 118
Cardinalities
    and application controls, 458
    assignment of, 67–70, 78–81
    and business rules, 142
    and duality relationships, 70, 79
    and foreign keys, 127, 132, 142

Cardinalities—*Cont.*
    maximum and minimum, 54, 158–159
      (*see also* Maximum participation
      cardinalities; Minimum participation
      cardinalities)
    notation, 54, 57–58
    participation, 54–55, 67–70, 78–81
    patterns, 125–135
    and risk (exercise), 471
    for stockflow, 67–69, 78–81
Casanave, C., 8n
Cascade updates (MS Access), 145–146
Cash
    attributes, 65–66
    in business process model, 65–66, 79
    disbursements, 79 (*see also* Cash
      disbursements)
    for dividend declarations, 416
    employee handling, 215–217
    from external sources (*see* Financing
      process)
    in human resource process, 389, 398–399,
      401, 403 (*see also* Cash
      disbursements)
    payment management, 215–217
    in REA model, 28–29
    as resource, 40, 71–72, 413
    theft prevention, 435–436, 443–444
    tracking, 399
    unapplied, 217
    in value chain model, 42–47
    in value system model, 40–42
Cash accounts
    attributes, 389, 413
    check digit, 459
    control activities, 443–444
    and debt financing, 414
    in ERP *versus* REA model, 478
    and financing process, 413
      queries, 425, 426
    and human resources, 389, 399, 401
Cash balance
    calculation of, 224–225, 324
    for enterprise, 325–327
    queries, 389
    update triggers, 283
Cash disbursements
    in acquisition/payment process, 70–72,
      273–275, 289
    attributes, 274–275, 324, 395–397, 420
    in business process model, 29
    calculation of, 400
    and cash, 79, 324
    controls, 73, 441, 450
    data storage, 103
    database compromises, 319, 321
    and debt financing, 414
    in financing process, 45–46, 420–422,
      424–425, 426–427
    in human resource process, 395–397

Cash disbursements—*Cont.*
    queries, 400, 401, 403
    relational tables, 324, 420–422
    risks, 441, 450
    and suppliers, 80
    time factor, 273–274
    and total cash balance, 224–225
    in value chain model, 45–46
Cash flow, 409, 415
Cash flow budget, 413
Cash receipts
    in applied learning, 88–89
    attributes, 217, 324
    and cash balance calculation, 324
    controls, 451, 458
    and date, 324
    in financing process, 419–420
      queries, 423, 424–425, 426–427
    as increment events, 213–217
    by mail, 451
    null values, 235–237
    relational tables, 217, 324, 421
    risks, 440–441, 450–451, 458
    and total cash balance, 224–225
Cash refunds, 217–219, 275
Cash requisitions, 413
    queries, 423, 426–427
Cash resource, 71–72, 413
Cashiers
    controls, 445
      case, 447
    in fast food restaurants, 445
    in financing process, 419–420
    fraud by, 444
    queries, 424, 426–427
Catastrophes, 440
Categories, mapping to, 21
Ceri, S., 56n, 312n
Change management, 9
Charitable donations, 41
Check digit, 459
Check register, 444
Checking accounts, 443–444
Checkpoints, 466
Checks; *See also* Edit checks
    master reference, 460
    payment type, 273, 444
      in applied learning, 119–120,
      157–159
      in flowcharts, 97, 102
    on performance, 450
Chen, P. P., 56n
Chen notation, 56, 57, 59 (table)
Cherrington, J. O., 478n
Chief information officer (CIO), 455–456
Claims, 62
Closed loop verification, 459, 463
Codd, E. F., 122, 163
Collaborative planning, forecasting, and
    replenishment (CPFR), 483, 484

Collections; *See* Sales/collection process

Collusion, 435, 443

Columns, 122–123
calculations within, 173

Combined entity key postings, 321

Commitment events; *See also* Mutual
commitment events
in conversion process, 349, 359–361,
361–365
human resource process, 392–393
and instigation events, 242
queries, 375
as REA extension, 82
relationship between, 366
and resources, 82, 244–247
stock issuance, 414
time factors, 375

Committee of Sponsoring Organizations of the
Treadway Commission (COSO),
433–437

Communication
and controls, 436
instant messaging, 456
interdepartmental, 14–16
of irregularities, 435
links, in flowcharts, 101
of personnel policies, 442
of roles and responsibilities, 436
telecommunications, 482

Communications networks, 101

Comparison operators, 172

Comparisons, 437

Competence, 434, 439

Competition
and risk, 435, 439, 441
and value, 36–37, 39

Completeness edit checks, 459

Composite attributes, 54

Compromises; *See* Implementation
compromises

Computer viruses, 455

Computers, 445, 449, 453–455; *See also*
Application controls; Software;
Terminals

Concatenated primary key, 54, 56, 125

Conceptual data model; *See also* REA
(Resources-Events-Agents) ontology
applied learning, 157, 340–343
compromises, 318–320
and logical model, 122–137
applied learning, 157–159

Conceptually congruent events, 319–320

Condensation, 12–13

Connected entities, 56

Connectors, 100

Constantine, L., 106

Construction company, 446

Consume stockflow, 359

Context, 23–24

Context diagrams, 110

Contingency plans, 442

Continuous processes, 347

Contracts, 82; *See also* Mutual commitment
events

Control activities; *See also* Controls
in acquisition/payment, 443–444,
446, 451
assets, 443
cases, 443, 445
for cash accounts, 443–444
for cash disbursements, 73, 450
comparisons, 437
decrement events, 450
reversal, 451
financing process, 443
increment events, 451
reversal, 451–452
for information systems, 452–455
for instigation events, 448
prioritization, 437
sales/collection, 437, 443, 444, 460
and shipping, 444–445, 449–450
types, 435–437

Control environment
description, 434–435
information systems, 448–449, 454
software, 455–468

Controls; *See also* Internal controls
applied learning, 471–473
for business process risks, 442–452
on cash account data, 459
on data input, 457–462, 463
for economy risks, 441
for enterprise risks, 441–442
gas station example, 443
for industry risks, 441
and REA model, 463
review, 469–471
and risk impact, 433–434
for software, 457–468
application controls, 457–468
general controls, 457–459
terms and concepts, 468–469
against theft, 442–447, 451
time factors, 433, 436
types, 435–437 (*see also* Corrective
controls; Detective controls;
Preventive controls)

Conversion process; *See also* Queries,
conversion process
applied learning, 380–383
batch size, 369–370
batch *versus* continuous, 346–347
and commitment events, 82, 349, 361–365
control activities, 442, 446
cost calculation, 347, 372
cost of operations, 349
decrement events, 348–349
labor operations, 353–358
machine operations, 358–359
raw material issuance, 351–353
defective product runs, 442

Conversion process—*Cont.*
definitions, 43, 345
duality relationships, 348–349, 353,
373–374
and employees, 350–351, 373
entity-relationship diagram, 348
and human resource process, 387
increment events, 347, 348–351
industry risks, 438–439
internal resource transformations, 44
(*see also* Production runs)
monitoring, 437
objective, 45
and other processes, 346
in REA model, 25, 346
review, 378–380
schedule, 82
standards, 367, 369
terms and concepts, 378
in value chain model, 46, 201 (fig.),
346–349
in value system model, 346–349

Cookie example, 347–378

Copies
of entities, 318
in flowcharts, 97–98

Core business events, 28–30, 59–64

Core pattern
description, 59–63
examples, 60–63
extensions to, 82–86

Corrective controls, 435–436, 443, 447

COSO (Committee of Sponsoring
Organizations of the Treadway
Commission), 433–437

Cost of goods sold (COGS), 336–337

Cost of operations, 347, 349, 372

Cost(s)
of controls, 433–434, 434–435, 468
of conversion process, 347,
349, 355
of goods sold, 337 (fig.)
and industry risk, 438–439
of inventory, 334, 336–337
overstated, 444
weighted average unit, 294–295,
336–337
of labor, 202, 355
of manufacturing, 347, 372
monitoring, 437
old, 336
in purchasing, 449
shipping and handling, 449
of software development, 456
and supply chain, 483
and value, 36
weighted average unit, 294–295,
334–335

Cott Co., 481

COUNT, 400

Cowpaths, paving, 6–8

Credit cards
  as control, 435–436, 443
  payments with, 213–214, 273
Credit memorandum, 219
Creditors
  queries, 424, 426–427
  in REA model, 24, 39
  in value chain level, 39
  in value system level, 41–42, 410
Credits
  alternative approach, 8
  in ERP *versus* REA models, 478
Crow's Foot notation, 58, 59 (table)
Custodial functions, 419, 443, 445
Custody, chain of, 446
Custody relationships, 365, 441
Customer inquiries, 448
Customer orders
  application controls, 458
  as commitment events, 206–207
  risks, 448–449
Customer purchase order, 206
Customer statements, 214, 217, 451
Customers
  bad credit risks, 449
  in business process model, 52
  and controls, 437
  data redundancy, 477
  database identifiers, 123–124
  differing requirements, 210
  in e-commerce, 481–482
  feedback from, 39
  nonexistent, 441
  nontarget, 448
  and payments, 217
  in REA model, 24
  repeat business, 80
  and sales call table, 204–205
  and salesperson, 84–85
  theft by, 443
  and value, 36–37
  in value chain analysis, 39
  in value system model, 42

**D**

Data; *See also* Attributes; Fields; Files
  access controls, 449, 453–454
  completeness, 459
  for conversion process, 349, 353
  in data flow diagrams, 106–107
  default values, 459
  detail level, 477
  encryption of, 454
  in flowcharts, 97–98, 99–100, 101
  incomplete, 103
  *versus* information, 14
  information process events, 85–86
  loss of, 465–468
  from multiple business processes, 324–338
  numeric, 459–460, 461, 478

Data—*Cont.*
  primitive level, 477
  for production runs, 349
  redundancy, 4, 477 (*see also* Redundancy)
  reference information, 98
  for sales orders, 206
  sources and sinks, 106–107
  storage, 98, 102–105, 467, 477–478
  tagging, 484
  from tasks, 91
  for testing, 456, 463
  timeliness, 105, 459
  verification of, 457–462
Data entry
  controls, 457–462, 463
  errors, 441, 452
  in MS Access, 148–149
  rekeying, 459, 481
  required, 142–143
  and risks, 441
  for sales orders, 205–206
  typing patterns, 454
  verification types, 457–462
Data flow diagrams
  applied learning, 117–120
  balanced, 111
  constraints, 107–110
  context diagrams, 110
  *versus* flowcharts, 102, 112–115
  levels, 110–112
  logical and physical, 106
  payroll example, 112–115
  review, 116
  rules, 107–109
  sales/collection example, 110–111
  symbols, 106–107
  terms and concepts, 115
Data manipulation language, 169
Data modeling, conceptual, 122, 135–137,
      318–320
Data processing; *See also* Information systems
  batch processing (*see* Batch processing)
  input controls, 457–462, 463
  on-line, 105
  real time, 105, 463, 466–468
  report-time, 105
Data types
  dates, 460
  listing, 460
  in MS Access, 140–141, 177
  numeric, 459–460, 461, 478
  verification of, 460
Data values
  calculations, 172–174 (*see also* Derivable
      attributes)
  in column, 123
  for dates, 172, 177
  load, 125
  ranges, 190, 460
  sorting on, 173–174
  textual, 141

Database design; *See also* Implementation
      compromises; Relational databases;
      Relational tables
  and application controls, 457–462
  applied learning, 153–159, 340–343
  attribute types, 52–55 (*see also* Derivable
      attributes)
  cardinalities, 54–55, 67–70, 78–81
  conceptual model, 122, 135–137,
      318–320 (*see also* REA (Resources-
      Events-Agents) ontology)
  data values, 123
  default values, 459
  detail level, 73
  duality relationsips, 133
  entities (*see* Entities)
  entity integrity, 123–124
  foreign keys, 123, 125–126 (*see also*
      Foreign keys)
  implementation compromises,
      318–323
  and information retrieval, 162–163
  logical model, 122–137
  model types, 122
  in MS Access, 137–149
  null values, 123–124, 125–126, 132,
      320–321
  physical model, 122, 137–149
  primary keys, 53–54, 76, 123
      concatenated, 54, 56, 125
  redundancy, 124–127, 132
  referential integrity, 123 (*see also*
      Referential integrity)
  storage structure, 54, 61–62, 321–323
  and tasks, 91
  view integration, 312–318
  view modeling, 311–312
Database orientation, 477–478
Database window (MS Access), 140, 143
Datasheet views, 179
  in MS Access, 148–149
Date/time field, 372
Dates
  and accounts payable total dollar
      amount, 290
  acquisition, of fixed assets, 285
  calculations with, 177, 372
  and cash balance calculation, 324
  and cash receipts, 324
  as data type, 460
  data values, 172, 177
  for delivery, 449
  and individual supplier balance, 303
  in inventory dollar cost, 335
  and MS Access, 372
  and production runs, 349
  ranges, 190
  testing, 235
Davenport, T. H., 478n
David, J. S., 346n, 467n, 480, 483n
Debit memos, 275

Debits, 8, 478
Debt financing
　and cash disbursements, 414
　cash receipt event, 419
　definition, 410
　as mutual commitment event, 414–415
　queries, 423, 424, 425, 426–427
　and risk, 432
Decision/management events, 86
Decision points, 100
Decision process
　and ERP, 479, 480
　and information, 13–14, 171–172, 452
　and REA model, 27–30, 36, 480
　risks, 431
Decision support systems, 386; *See also*
　　Enterprise resource planning (ERP)
　　systems
Decomposition DFDs, 110
Decrement events; *See* Economic decrement
　　events
Decrement reversal events, 217–219
Default values, 459
Deferred revenue, 232
DeGross, J. I., 478n
Delivery dates, 449
Dell Co., 482
Demand, 446
DeMarco, T., 106n
Denna, E. L., 478n
Deposit slips, 215–217, 419–420
Derivable attributes, 54, 321–323
　cash balances as, 324, 389
　volatile, 54, 389, 478
Descriptor attributes, 76
Design; *See* Database design
Design view, in MS Access, 140, 177
Detail(s)
　incorrect recording, 447
　level of, 73, 400, 477
　types, 21n
Detective controls, 435–436, 444, 446–447
　in software applications, 458–459
DFD; *See* Data flow diagrams
Diagrams; *See* Data flow diagrams;
　　Flowcharts; REA (Resources-Events-
　　Agents) ontology; Value chain model;
　　Value system model
Digital signatures, 454
Direct access data storage, 104–105
Direct deposit, 395
Directors, 434, 439
Disbursement vouchers, 273
Disk storage
　in flowcharts, 98
　and processing method, 105
　types, 104–105
Dividend declarations
　as commitment event, 415–418
　queries, 423, 426–427
Dividend payments, 414

Documentation; *See also* Data flow diagrams;
　　Flowcharts; Paper documents
　of cash receipt event, 419–420
　of cash requisitions, 413
　for computer backup, 465, 467
　and control, 432, 436
　for disbursement vouchers, 273
　of errors, 435
　of event details, 447
　file labels, 464
　of labor acquisitions, 394
　of labor need, 390
　of labor schedule, 392
　of personnel policies, 442
　receiving reports, 218–219, 269, 273
　of roles and responsibilities, 436
　of supply removal, 445
　of tasks, 30, 91–92
Documents
　copies of, 97
　in flowcharts, 94, 97–98, 101–102
　organization of, 98
　paper, 97–98, 103
Dollar cost value, 334–335
Domain ontology, 23–24
Donations, 41
Dotted lines, 100
Duality relationships
　in acquisition/payment, 70, 269,
　　288–293, 303
　attributes, 66–67, 288–289
　cardinality, 70, 79, 349
　in conversion process, 348–349, 353,
　　373–374
　customer/supplier, 210
　and database design, 133
　decrement events, 212
　definition, 43
　and exchange events, 63–64, 66
　in financing process, 420, 424–425
　and fulfillment relationships, 241–242, 295
　in human resource process, 400–401
　increment with decrement events, 269,
　　288–289
　in labor acquisition, 394
　labor cost/payroll, 202
　purchase/cash disbursement, 319
　purpose, 348
　queries about, 231–237
　risks, 440–441
　in sales/collection process, 231–237,
　　253, 289
　in value chain model, 45
Dunn, C. L., 9n, 476n
Dynasets, 179

**E**

ebXML, 484
Economic decrement events
　in acquisition/payment process, 273–275

Economic decrement events—*Cont.*
　and agents, 212
　in conversion process, 348–349
　　labor operations, 353–358
　　machine operations, 358–359
　　raw material issuance, 351–353
　in financing process, 420–422
　in human resource process, 387, 395–397
　and increment events, 269, 289, 349
　merchandise transfers, 208–209
　and mutual commitment events, 206
　reversal, 217–219, 275, 451
　risks and controls, 449–450
　in sales/collection process, 207–213,
　　237–241, 253
Economic events; *See also* Exchange events
　for acquisition/payment process, 70
　attributes, 66–67
　business model example, 62–64
　cardinality, 67–68, 79
　and commitment events, 242
　noncash-related, 82
　relationship between, 62
　and resources (*see* Stockflow)
　risks, 440
Economic increment events
　and acquisition/payment process, 269–272
　　reversal, 275–278
　in conversion process, 347, 348–351
　and decrement events, 270, 289, 348–349
　in financing process, 419–420
　in human resource process, 393–395
　and mutual commitment events, 267
　reversal, 200, 219, 275–278, 451–452
　risks and controls, 450–451
　in sales/collection process, 213–217, 253
　and stockflow queries, 237–241
Economy risks, 437–438, 441
EDI; *See* Electronic data interchange (EDI)
Edit checks, 459–462, 463
EFT; *See* Electronic funds transfer (EFT)
Electronic commerce (e-commerce),
　　481–484
Electronic data interchange (EDI), 481–484
Electronic funds transfer (EFT)
　as control activity, 435–436, 443
　in financing process, 420
　in human resource process, 395
　in increment event, 217
　risks, 457, 467
Employees; *See also* Human resource
　　process; Labor
　average wage, 400
　bonding, 55, 215–216, 443
　cash handling by, 73, 215–217, 273
　compensation, 442
　competence, 434, 439
　computer access, 452–455
　in conversion process, 350–351, 373
　evaluation, 366, 442
　expense reimbursement, 95–96, 102

Employees—*Cont.*
  health insurance, 42
  hiring, 442
  integrity and ethics, 434, 439
  knowledge and skills, 386, 389
  positions, 73
  promotion policies, 442
  queries about, 400
  in REA model, 24
  reporting relationships, 439
  as resources, 389
  roles and responsibilities, 436
  segregation of duties, 439, 443, 444
  supervisor relationship, 365–366
  terminating, 442
  theft by, 442–447
  training, 442
  in value chain, 39
  in value system, 26–27, 41
Encryption, 454
Energy, 40, 454–455
  utilities, 40
Enforce referential integrity (MS Access),
    146–147
Enterprise; *See also* Business processes; REA
    (Resources-Events-Agents) ontology
  defined, 1
  functional areas, 5–6
  organizational structure, 434, 439, 443
Enterprise application integration (EAI)
    software, 480
  applied learning, 486–487
Enterprise resource planning (ERP) systems;
    *See also* Integrated enterprise
    information systems
  applied learning, 486–487
  best-of-breed approach, 479–480
  bolt-on applications, 476, 478, 483
  bridges, 478, 480
  corporate reporting, 480
  customization, 9
  degrees of integration, 2–5
  and e-commerce, 481–484
  and general ledger, 478–479
  and industries, 479
  and inter-enterprise applications, 481–484
  objectives, 479
  and obsolescence risk, 446
  partial implementations, 478, 479–480
  people issues, 9
  and REA ontology, 8–9, 475
      database orientation, 477–478
      semantic orientation, 478–479
      structuring orientation, 479
  and reengineering, 478
  review, 485–486
  task *versus* pattern approach, 479
  terms and concepts, 485
Enterprise risks, 439–440, 441–442
Entities
  attributes of, 65

Entities—*Cont.*
  cardinalities, 54–55, 57–58, 67–68
  conflicting, 312–313
  connected, 56
  copies of, 318
  defined, 52
  detail level, 73
  in ERP *versus* REA models,
      478, 479
  hierarchies, 55
  labor type resource as, 389, 395
  materialization of tasks, 318–320
  mutually exclusive, 321
  name conflicts, 312–313
  nonmeasurable, 318
  notation, 56
  and sales instigation events, 203–205
  status data, 103
  subtypes and supertypes, 55
  task materialization, 318–320
  typification, 55, 73
  view integration, 312–318
Entity activity roll-ups, 323
Entity integrity, 123–124
Entity relationship modeling
  for acquisition/payment, 263
  applied learning, 380–383, 406–407
  for conversion process, 348, 380–383
  description, 52–59
  financing process, 412
  human resources, 388
  *versus* relationship layout, 146–147
  for sales/collection, 203
  and view integration, 312–318
Entity sets, 52
  members of, 52–53
Entrepreneurial scripts, 44; *See also* Scripts
Equi-joins, 165–168
Equipment
  acquisition/payment queries, 284
  control activities, 445
  and conversion process, 349, 359
  tracking, 349, 359
  in value system level model, 40
Equity financing
  attributes, 415
  commitment events, 414–418
  definition, 410
  increment events, 419–420
  queries, 423–424, 425, 426–427
  and risk, 432
ERP; *See* Enterprise resource planning (ERP)
    systems
Errors
  in batch processing, 462
  data entry, 441, 452
  detecting and preventing, 435
  exception reporting, 458–459
  logs of, 463
  past, and risk, 435
Ethics, 434, 439

Event categories, 39
Event-driven systems, 8, 105
Event processing rules, 457–459
Event triggers; *See also* Instigation events
    production orders, 366
  for updates, 224, 284, 413
Events; *See also* Business events
  attributes of, 66–67
  in REA ontology, 24
  selection of, 252–253
  simultaneously-occurring, 319–320
  and tasks, 91
Exception reporting, 458–459
Exchange events; *See also* Economic events
  in acquisition/payment process, 70
  attributes, 66–67
  barter, 40–41
  in REA model, 63–64
  timing, 62
  in value chain, 45
Executable files, 103
Executive information systems (EIS), 480
Expenditures cycle; *See* Acquisition/Payment
    process
Expense reimbursements, flowchart example,
    95–96, 102
Exposure, 431, 433; *See also* Risks
Expression Builder (MS Access), 187
Extended business process model, 82–86
Extensible business reporting language
    (XBRL), 484
Extensible marking language (ebXML), 484
Extension, 122–123
External agents
  and acquisition/payment, 269–270, 287
      queries, 299–300
  attribute assignment, 67
  in business process modeling, 64,
      72–74
  and cardinality, 69–70, 80
  and commitment events, 82
  and controls, 437
  in financing process, 413
      queries, 424
  in human resources, 386, 390, 394–395
      queries, 400
  and internal agents, 365–366
  risks, 441
  in sales/collection, 212, 213–214, 217,
      218
      queries, 230, 246
External business partners, 37–38,
    40–41, 439
External file labels, 464

**F**

Facial patterns, 454
Fast food restaurants, 61, 445
Feedback, 39, 459, 463
Field checks, 460

Fields; *See also* Data types; Data values
  properties (MS Access), 140–142, 177
  in relational databases, 122
  required, 142–143
  tagging systems, 484
File controls, 463–468
File protection rings, 465
File servers, 452
Files
  archives, 103, 323
  computerized, 98, 463–468
  controls, 463–468
  executable, 103
  in flowcharts, 98
  headers and trailers, 464
  history, 103, 323
  labels, 464
  lockout procedures, 464
  and media type, 104
  off-line, 98
  open invoice, 232
  open purchase order, 295–296
  open sales order, 243
  read-only, 465
  reconstruction, 465–466
  storage and access, 477–478
  types, 98, 103
  virus-infected, 455
Filtration, 12
Financial/numeric control totals, 461
Financial officers, 413, 414
  queries, 424, 426–427
Financial reports, 436, 439
Financial risks, 449–452
Financial statements, 436, 444, 484
Financing agreements, 414–419
  queries, 423, 425, 426–427
Financing process
  and acquisition/payment process, 43, 410
  and cash accounts, 413
    queries, 425, 426
  cash disbursement queries, 424–425,
    426–427
  commitment events, 412, 414–419
  control activities, 436, 443
  decrement events, 420–422
  duality relationships, 420, 424–425
  entity-relationship diagram, 412
  in entrepreneurial script, 44–45
  increment events, 419–420
  information retrieval (*see* Queries,
    financing process)
  instigation events, 412, 413–414
  and labor, 387
  objective, 410–411
  and other processes, 410 (fig.)
  in REA model, 25, 411–422
  relationship types, 420
  review, 428–429
  risk management, 443
  terms and concepts, 427

Financing process—*Cont.*
  in value chain model, 410
  in value system, 410
Finished goods
  conversion process, 345
  in custody relationship, 365
  detail level, 371
  as increment event, 349
  and labor types, 317, 367, 369
  and raw materials, 317, 366, 367
  and risk, 440
  in value chain, 346
Firewalls, 455
Firm infrastructure, 39
First-in-first-out (FIFO), 334
Fixed assets
  in flowcharts, 100
  queries, 285
  tracking, 349, 359, 371
Flow charts
  off-line processing, 99
Flow lines, 100–101, 107
Flowcharts; *See also* Data flow diagrams
  annotations, 100, 101
  applied learning, 117–120
  approvals in, 102
  areas of responsibility, 101, 102
  arrows, 101
  automation, 99
  basic concepts, 94
  batch processing, 462
  calculations in, 98
  communication networks, 101
  connectors, 100
  conventions, 101–102
  copies, of documents, 97–98
  creation of, 94
  *versus* data flow diagrams, 102,
    112–115
  data storage types, 98, 102–105
  decision points, 100
  discussion, 115–116
  expense reimbursement, 96
  extended REA pattern, 83, 84–85
  flow lines, 100–101, 107
  limitations, 102
  manual operations, 99
  operating asset acquisition, 264
  purpose, 94
  register tapes, 98
  review, 115–116
  symbols, 94–101
For-profit organizations, 36
Ford Motor Co., 7–8, 274
Foreign keys; *See also* Referential
    integrity
  and business rules, 142
  and cardinality, 132, 142
  example, 123
  and load, 125–126
4 Levels, 24–25

Fraud
  collusion, 435
  electronic fund transfer, 467
  examples, 444, 467
  lapping, 444
  whistleblowers, 439
Front-office systems, 476
Fulfillment relationships
  acquisition/payment, 266n, 269, 295–297
  application controls, 457–458
  in conversion process, 363, 375
  and decrement events, 212
  in financing, 412n, 415n, 419n, 420, 425
  in human resources, 391n, 394, 394n
    queries, 402
  queries, 241–243, 248–250, 295–297, 375
  risks, 440–441
  in sales/collection, 212, 241–243,
    248–250
  services, 241–243
Functional areas
  and risk management, 439, 443, 444
  and stovepipes, 5–6
Functional silos; *See* Stovepipes
Furniture
  acquisition/payment queries, 279–284
  control activities, 445

**G**

Gane, C., 106
Gas station examples, 319–320, 443
Gaudin, S., 456
Geerts, G. L., 8, 20, 24, 43, 60, 82, 84
General controls, 455–457
General ledgers, 478–479
Generalization, 55
George, J., 107–109, 108, 110*n*
Goodwill, 41
Government services, 40
Grandparent-parent-child approach, 466, 467
Grocery shopping, 446
GROUP BY
  in QBE, 185–186, 333
  in SQL, 173–174

**H**

Hackers, 452–453
Haedicke, J., 483n
Hammer, M., 6–7, 11
Hardware controls, 445, 454–455
Hash control totals, 461
HDC notation, 58, 59 (table)
Header record, 464
Health insurance, 42
Hierarchies, 55
Hildebrand, C., 482
Hiring practices, 442
History files, 103, 323
Hoffer, J., 107–109, 108, 110n

Hollowell, G., 8n
Homonyms, 313
Horizontal calculations, 175
Horizontal subsets, 163
    examples, 164–165
Human capital, 389, 442
Human resource process
    and acquisition/payment, 43, 386, 387
    agents, 386, 390
    applied learning, 406–407
    average employee wage, 400
    and cash, 389, 398–399, 401, 403
    commitment events, 392–393
    control activities, 73, 442, 443, 450
    and control environment, 434
    and conversion process, 346
    decrement events, 395–397
    duality relationships, 400–401
    entity-relationship diagram, 388
    increment events, 393–395
    information needs (*see* Queries, human
        resources)
    instigation events, 389–392
    labor schedules, 389, 390, 392–393
    objective, 387
    and other processes, 387, 397
    payroll cycle, 385, 389, 393–397 (*see also*
        Payroll process)
        extended REA model, 388
    personnel, 385, 389–395, 442
        queries, 401–404
    REA model, 25, 387–397
    review, 404–406
    software, 4, 304, 479
    terms and concepts, 404
    time factors, 394
    training, 9, 442, 447
    in value chain, 39, 386–387
    in value system, 386

I

IBM, 4
Identification tags, 446
Identification technology, 454
Identifiers, 56, 123–124; *See also* Primary
    keys
Identity loss, 457
Implementation compromises
    applied learning, 340–343
    concepts and terms, 338–339
    conceptual level, 318–320
    logical level, 320–321
    physical level, 321–323
    review, 339–340
Imprest cash accounts, 389, 399
    queries, 401–402
Inbound logistics, 39
Increment events; *See* Economic increment
    events
Independent checks, 450

Industries
    and ERP software, 479
    risks, 438–439, 441
Inflow, 39–43
Information; *See also* Data
    accuracy, 441, 452
    and controls, 436–437
    at corporate level, 480
    for customer inquiry, 448
    *versus* data, 14
    and decision process, 13–14
    erroneous assumptions, 11–17
    flow of, 61–62, 100
Information and communications (as control),
    436
Information customers
    acquisition/payment process, 279
        (*see also* Queries, acquisition/
        payment)
    assumptions about, 11–17
    conversion process (*see* Queries,
        conversion process)
    financing process (*see* Queries, financing)
    human resources (*see* Queries, human
        resources)
    sales/collection process (*see* Queries,
        sales/collection)
Information event risks, 441, 452–455
Information events, 85–86
Information needs, 11–14, 312
Information overload, 12–13
Information process events, 85–86
    *versus* operating events, 86
Information process risks, 441, 452–455
    in applied learning, 472–473
Information retrieval; *See also* Queries; Query
    By Example (QBE); Structured
    Query Language (SQL)
    accuracy, 174–175, 191, 235
    applied learning, 196–198
    approaches, 161–162
    calculations, 172–174
    efficiency, 323
    horizontal subsets (SELECT), 164–165
    incorrect result, 174–175
    multiple business processes, 324–338
    from multiple tables (JOIN), 165–169
    from relational databases, 162–163
    review, 192–195
    sorting, 173–174
    terms and concepts, 191–192
    vertical subsets (PROJECT), 164
    and views, 312
Information systems; *See also* Enterprise
        resource planning (ERP) systems
    and bank statements, 444
    base objects, 8, 9
    *versus* computer technology, 1–2
    as control, 13–14, 436, 448–449
    controls on, 452–455, 457–463
    data files (*see* Files)

Information systems—*Cont.*
    defined, 1, 436
    degrees of integration, 2–5
    event-*versus* view-driven, 8
    executive (EIS), 480
    integrated (*see* Integrated enterprise
        information systems)
    main functions, 12–13
    management (MIS), 11–17
    risks, 431, 467
    separation of duties, 444
    stovepipes, 5–6
    threats, 431
Infrastructure, 39
Inner joins, 165–168
    in QBE, 182–183
Input devices, 97
Input documents, 97–98
Input-output symbols, 94–99
Input-process-output, 95–99
Instance, 52–53
Instant messaging, 456
Instigation events
    in acquisition/payment, 262–265
        queries, 295–297, 298
    and commitment events, 206, 242
    control activities, 447–448
    in financing, 412, 413–414
    in human resources, 389–392
    in REA ontology, 82–85, 388
    and resources, 244, 298
    risks, 440, 447–448
    in sales/collection, 202–206
Insurance
    health, for employees, 42
    and risk management, 434, 442, 447
    in value system, 40
Integrated enterprise information systems
    applied learning, 11–17
    best of breed approach, 479–480
    bolt-on applications, 476, 478, 483
    bridges, 478, 480
    as control, 447–452
    controls on, 452–455
    database orientation, 477–478
    defined, 1–2
    and e-commerce, 481–484
    erroneous assumptions, 11–17
    partial implementations, 478, 479–480
    review, 10–11
    terms and concepts, 10
Integration
    defined, 2
    degrees of, 2–5
    inter-enterprise, 482–484
    intra-enterprise, 479–480
    of revenue/acquisition cycles, 325
        in applied learning, 357–358
Integrity, 434, 439
Intension, 122
Inter-enterprise integration, 482–484

Internal agents; *See also* Employees
  in acquisition/payment, 269, 287
  attribute assignment, 67
  cardinality, 69–70, 79–80
  and commitment events, 82
  in conversion process, 350–352,
    363, 365
    queries, 373, 376–377
  and economic events, 64, 214
  and external agents, 365
  in financing, 413, 419–420
    queries, 424
  in human resources, 386, 390, 394–395
    queries, 400, 403
  identification of, 72–74
  queries about, 229–230, 246
  relationship between, 365
  risks and controls, 441, 449
  in sales/collection, 203, 206, 212
    queries, 229–230, 246
Internal business process, 38; *See also*
    Business processes
Internal controls
  components, 434–437
  documentation, 432, 436
  exercises, 471, 473
  responsibility for, 432
  three-way match, 7
Internal file labels, 464
Internal resource transformations, 44; *See*
    *also* Production runs; Transformation
    duality relationships
Internet, 452–453, 456
Intra-enterprise integration, 479–480
Inventory; *See also* Stockflow relationships
  in acquisition/payment process, 270–271,
    279–283
  in business process model, 66, 72
  control activities, 437, 442–447, 451–452
  and conversion process, 349–350
  cost of, 336–337
    average unit cost, 294–295, 334–335
  damage, 447
  and decrement events, 212
  dollar cost value, 334–335
  integrated supply chain, 482–484
  and minimum cardinality, 78
  obsolescence, 446
  quantity on hand, 224, 284, 324–333
  relational tables, 271
  risks, 439–440, 442–447
  and sales/collection, 221–228, 237–241,
    244–247
  and sales returns, 217–218
  of service providers, 202
  total cost, 336–337
  tracking, 371
  in value system model, 40
  warehouse management, 481
  weighted average unit cost, 294–295,
    334–335

Inventory type
  in acquisition/payment process, 270
  attribute conflict in, 313
  and decrement events, 212–213
  as entity, 66
  quantity on hand, 224, 284, 324–333
  queries, 238–241, 244, 294, 298, 299
  as resource, 40
  and sales call table, 204–205
  weighted average unit cost, 294–295,
    334–335
Investors
  queries, 424, 426–427
  in REA model, 24
  in value chain level, 39
  in value system level, 41–42, 410
Invoices
  *versus* balance forward, 217
  as decrement events, 211
  in flowcharts, 97–98
  open, 231
  past due calculation, 177
  and payments, 217
  remittance advice, 214
  from vendors, 269, 273
Irregularities, 435, 436, 437
IS NULL, 172


**J**

J. D. Edwards, 4, 304
JD Edwards One World, 304
Job time tickets, 355
JOIN
  examples, 165–169
  in QBE, 181
  in SQL, 171–172
Join properties window, 183
Joins
  in cost of inventory, 337
  in quantity on hand query,
    324–333


**K**

Kay, R., 454
Key verification, 459
Keyboard typing patterns, 454
Knowledge bases, 386, 389
Koch, C., 479nn


**L**

Labels, 446, 464
Labor
  calculations, 386
  in conversion process, 349
  costs of, 202
  definition, 386
  requests for, 389
  tracking, 371, 386–387, 399

Labor—*Cont.*
  in value chain model, 46, 346,
    386–387
  in value system model, 40, 386
Labor acquisitions, 393–395
  queries, 399–400, 401–404
Labor operations, 349, 353–358, 366
  queries, 371–372, 373–374
Labor requisitions, 389–392
  queries, 399–400, 403
Labor schedule, 389, 390, 392–393
  queries, 399–400, 402–404
  relational tables, 393
Labor type
  in applied learning, 406–407
  attributes, 355, 356
  and finished goods, 367, 377
  *versus* labor operation, 353–356
  quantity needed, 369
  queries, 398–399, 401–403
  as resource, 389, 395
Land, 285
Lapping, 444
Last-in-first-out (LIFO), 334
Lead time, 449
Left joins, 168–169
  in QBE, 183
  in SQL, 171
Legacy systems, 477
Legislation, 432–433
Legos/K'nex example, 3–5
Level-zero DFDs, 110
Levinson, M., 481
Light, L., 453
Linkage relationships, 361,
    367–371
  queries, 377–378
Load, 125, 132–133, 320
Lockbox method, 217
Lockout procedures, 465
Logical access controls, 453–454
Logical level compromises, 320–321
Logical models, 122–137
Logical operators, 172
Logistics, 39; *See also* Supply chain


**M**

Machine operations
  costs of, 349
  as decrement event, 361
  flowchart symbols, 99
  queries, 371–372, 373–374
  and reciprocal relationships, 366
  relational tables, 360–361
  in script example, 46
Machinery
  acquisition/payment queries, 285
  in conversion process, 349
  tracking, 371
Magnetic tapes, 98, 104, 105

Maintenance, of software, 456–457
Management information systems (MIS), 11–17
Management philosophy, 434, 439
Managers
  communication needs, 14–16
  and control environment, 434, 436
  information needs, 11–14
  and MIS, 16–17
Manual operations, 99
Manuals, 436
Manufacturing; *See* Conversion process; Queries, conversion process
Many-to-many relationships, 127–128, 135–137
Margin, 36, 38–39
Marketing; *See also* Sales/collection process
  control activities, 448
  events, 202
  risks, 447–448
  as value activity, 39
Master files
  description, 103
  reconstruction, 465–468
  storage media, 104–105
Master reference checks, 460
Material, 46
Material requisitions, 361–365
Materiality of risk, 433–434
Materialization of tasks, 318–320
Mathematical operations, 172–174; *See also* Calculations; Numeric data
MAX, 173
Maximum participation cardinalities, 54–55, 57–58, 132; *See also* Cardinalities
McCarthy, W. E., 8, 9n, 19n, 20, 24, 25, 43, 59–60, 62, 84, 312n, 476nn, 478n, 480, 483n, 484
McKay, D., 455
Measurement
  and database design, 318–319
  of department performance, 14–15
  of employee knowledge/skill, 386
  for labor, 355, 390
  of labor type, 403
Merchandise; *See also* Finished goods
  in flowcharts, 100
  high-value, 445
  transfer of, 208–209
Mergers and acquisitions, 439–440, 479
Microsoft Access, 137–149; *See also* Query By Example (QBE)
  cascade updates, 145–146
  database window, 140, 143
  datasheet view, 148–149
  date/time fields, 372
  design view, 140, 177
  *versus* entity-relationship diagram, 146–147
  expression builder, 187
  field properties, 140–142, 177
  information retrieval (*see* Query By Example (QBE))

Microsoft Access—*Cont.*
  inventory queries, 226
  null values, 235–237, 293
  outer joins, 304
  parameter queries, 188–189, 190, 233
  physical database model, 137–149
  referential integrity, 145–147
  relationships, 144, 148
  required data entry, 142–143
  Show Table window, 178–179, 187
  SQL query in, 187–189
  SQL view, 175
  terms and concepts, 150, 192
  wizards, 138
Miller, J., 8n
MIN, 173
Minimum participation cardinalities; *See also* Cardinalities
  assignment of, 67–70, 78–81
  description, 54–55
  and foreign key posting, 132
  heuristic exception, 78
  notation, 57–58
MIS; *See* Management information systems
Mission, 36
Mode checks, 460
Model car analogy, 20
Models; *See also* Business process modeling; REA (Resources-Events-Agents) ontology
  applied learning, 33–34
  conceptual data, 122, 135–137, 318–320
  purpose, 19–20
  review, 32–33
  task level, 91–94
  terms and concepts, 32
  value chain, 42–47 (*see also* Value chain model)
  value system, 40–42 (*see also* Value system model)
Monitoring, 436–437, 441
Move tickets, 353
Mutual commitment events; *See also* Commitment events
  for acquisition/business, 265–268
  in queries, 295–297, 299
  definition, 82
  in financing process, 412, 414–419
  homonyms, 313
  and instigation events, 206
  and labor schedule, 392–393
  queries, 402
  risks, 440, 448–449
  sales/collection, 206–207
  shipping, 206, 266

**N**

Name conflicts, 312–313
Navathe, S. B., 56n, 312n

Networks
  communications, 101
  value-added (VAN), 482
Nike Co., 482
Noncash related economic events, 82
Normalization, 122–137
NOT, 172
Not-for-profit organizations, 36
Notation
  of attributes, 56, 64–65
  cardinalities, 54, 57–58
  conceptual data model, 55–59
  Crow's Foot, 58, 59 (table)
  data flow diagrams, 106–107
  flowcharts, 94–101
  for relationships, 56
Null to zero (Nz) function, 235–237, 333
Null values; *See also* Required data entry
  compromises, 320–321
  in foreign keys, 123
  and information retrieval, 168–169
  and joins, 168
  and load, 125–126, 132
  in MS Access, 235–237, 293
  as primary key, 123–124
  in SQL, 172
Numeric data, 459–460, 461, 478

**O**

Object patterns, 22–23
Objectives, 432, 437
Objects; *See also* Base objects
  categories of, 20
  in flowcharts, 100
Obsolescence, 446
Off-line data storage, 98
Off-line processing, 99
O'Leary, D. E., 9, 476n
On-line manual input device, 97
On-line processing
  description, 105
  *versus* real-time, 105
  symbol for, 99
One-fact, one-place rule, 124
Ontology, 8; *See also* REA (Resources-Events-Agents) ontology
Open-EDI, 483
Open invoices, 231–232
Open purchase order files, 295–296
Open purchase requisitions, 295
Open sales invoice file, 231–232
Open sales order file, 243
Operating assets
  in acquisition/payment, 264, 270, 285
  risk management, 444–446, 451
Operating events, 85
  *versus* information process events, 86
Operating style, 434, 439
Operation Research, 14n

Operations, 39
Operations list, 367, 377
Opportunity, 432
  loss of, 436
Optical character readers, 99
OR
  in QBE, 180
  in SQL, 172
Oracle, 4, 304, 479
Order to cash mega-process; *See*
    Sales/collection process
Organizational structure, 434, 439, 443
Orientation, 442
Outbound logistics, 39
Outer joins, 168–169
  and MS Access, 304
  in SQL, 171
Outflow, 39–43
Outsourcing, 37n
Overhead, 72

**P**

Packing slips, 210, 275
Paper documents, 97–98, 103
Parameter queries, 188–189, 190
  and accounts receivable, 233
Participation cardinalities
  assignment, 67–70, 78–81
  description, 54–55
  and foreign keys, 132
  heuristic exception, 78
  notation, 57–58
Participation relationships, 269
  acquisition/payment process, 263n, 266n,
      269, 272n, 278n, 299–300
  application controls, 457
  and association relationships, 366
  attributes, 246
  conversion process, 348, 350–351, 353,
      356, 359
    queries, 376–377
  financing process, 415n, 419n, 420, 421n
    queries, 426–427
  human resource process, 391n,
      394–395, 394n
  queries about, 246–248, 299–300
  risks, 441
  in sales/collection process, 212, 246
Passwords, 449, 453
Patel, D., 8n, 24n
Patterns; *See also* Value chain model; Value
    system model
  background, 59–60
  cardinalities, 125–135
  core, 59–63 (*see also* Core pattern)
  and ERP software, 479
  object versus script, 22–24
  at task level, 91
  in typing, 454
  uses of, 21–24

Paving cowpaths, 6–8
Paychecks, 389
Payments
  with checks, 97, 102, 273, 444
  with credit cards, 273
  as increment event, 213–217
Payroll clerks, 400
Payroll cycle, 385, 389, 393–397
  extended REA model, 388
Payroll process
  in applied learning, 406–407
  calculation, 401
  cash accounts, 389
  flow chart *versus* DFD, 112–115
  and labor costs, 202
  *versus* payroll cycle, 385
  in value chain model, 46
PeopleSoft, 4, 304, 479
Performance
  independent checks on, 450
  measures, and communication, 14–16
  reviews, 437
  of suppliers, 287
Personal identification numbers (PINs), 454,
    460
Personnel, 385, 389–395
  queries, 401–404
Physical database models, 122
  Microsoft Access implementation,
      137–149
Physical level compromises, 321–323
Physical workflow, 61–62
Picking slip, 210
Planning, 367; *See also* Enterprise resource
    planning (ERP) systems
Porter, Michael, 36, 38–39
Posted keys, 134, 146, 175
Power, electrical, 40, 50, 454–455
Preferred stock, 415
Prepaid expenses, 289
Preventive controls
  access restriction, 443, 444–445
  definition, 435
  ERP as, 446
  in software applications, 458–459
Prewitt, E., 480
Price lists, 98, 103
Pricing, 449
Primary key attribute, 53–54, 76
Primary keys
  and acquisition events, 269
  and attribute conflict, 313
  concatenated, 54, 56, 125
  as foreign keys, 123
  notation, 56
  null values, 123–124
  telephone numbers, 123–124
Primary value activities, 38–39
Primitive DFDs, 110
Primitive level data, 477
Privacy issues, 53–54

Process controls, 462–463
Process symbols, 99
Procure-to-pay process; *See*
    Acquisition/Payment process
Procurement, 39
Product numbers, 459
Product replacements, 441
Product risk, 431
Production employees, 350–351
Production order documents, 359–361, 367
Production order events, 366
  queries, 371–372, 375–376
  relational tables, 360–362, 366
Production runs
  in batch *versus* continuous
      processes, 347
  commitment to, 359–361
  as increment event, 349–351
  queries, 371–372, 375
  relational tables, 349–351
Production supervisors
  participation relationships, 350–351,
      353, 356, 360
  queries, 376–377
  responsibility relationships,
      365–366
PROJECT, 163
  example, 164
  in QBE, 177–179
Promissory notes, 414–415
Property, 40
Proposition relationships, 244, 440
  acquisition/payment process, 298
  attributes, 244
Purchase orders
  in applied learning, 119–120
  as commitment event, 265–268
  control activities, 441
  and disbursement vouchers, 273
  forms, 206
  queries, 286–287, 441
  risks, 449
  in sales/collection process, 206
  time factor, 266n
Purchase requisitions, 266n
  control activities, 448
  as instigation event, 262–264
  queries, 298
  relational tables, 266
  risks, 448
  unfilled, 295
Purchase returns
  as increment reversal event,
      275–278
  queries, 299, 300, 303
  and requisitions, 270
  risks and controls, 451–452
Purchase(s)
  and cash disbursements, 319
  goals, 260–261
  relational tables, 272

Purchasing; *See also* Acquisition/Payment
  process
  and cash disbursements, 319
  interdepartmental communication, 14–15
  REA model, 29

**Q**

Quality, 431, 439, 442
Quantities; *See* Cardinalities
Quantity on hand, 224, 284, 328–333
QBE; *See* Query By Example
Queries; *See also* Query By Example (QBE);
    Structured Query Language (SQL)
  approaches to, 161–162
  existing, 178–179
  from multiple business processes,
      324–338
    cash balance, 324
    cost of inventory, 333–338
    inventory quantity on hand,
        324–333
  null value compromise, 320–321
  result, 179
  reusability, 189–190, 191, 389
  saving, 179, 187
  testing, 235
Queries, acquisition/payment
  agent queries, 287–288
  duality relationship, 288–293
  event queries, 285–287
  fulfillment, 295–297
  individual supplier balances,
      300–303
  participation, 299–300
  proposition, 298
  relationship queries, 288–304
  reservation, 299
  resource queries, 279–285
  stockflow, 293–295
  unfulfilled purchase orders, 451
Queries, conversion process
  agents, 373
  duality relationship queries, 373–374
  events, 371–373
  finished goods/labor type, 377–378
  fulfillment relationships, 375–376
  participation relationships, 376–377
  raw materials/finished goods, 377–378
  reservation relationships, 376
  resources, 371
  stockflow relationship, 374–375
Queries, financing process
  agent queries, 424
  duality relationships, 424–425
  event queries, 423–424
  fulfillment relationships, 425
  participation relationships, 426–427
  reservation relationships, 426
  resource queries, 423
  stockflow relationships, 425

Queries, human resources
  agent queries, 400
  duality relationships, 400–401
  events, 399–400
  fulfillment queries, 402
  participation queries, 403–404
  reservation queries, 402–403
  resource queries, 398–399
  stockflow queries, 401–402
Queries, sales/collection
  accounts receivable, 231–237
  agents, 229–230
  cash receipts/sales amounts, 458
  duality relationships, 231–237
  events, 228–229
  fulfillment, 241–243, 248–250
  multiple relationships, 246–250
  participation, 246
  proposition, 244
  reservation, 244–246
  resource, 221–228
  stockflow, 237–241
Query By Example (QBE), 174–190
  accuracy, 174–175, 191
  aggregation functions, 184–187
  applied learning, 196–197
  calculations, 177, 184–187,
      324, 330 (fig.)
  cost of goods sold, 337 (fig.)
  displaying result, 179
  existing queries, 177
  field properties, 177
  fixed asset query, 285
  inner join, 182–184
  inventory queries, 226, 228, 334–338
  JOIN, 181
  AND and OR operators, 180
  PROJECT, 177–179
  purchase order date and amount, 288
  quantity on hand, 331–332 (fig.)
  query grid, 175, 179
  query window, 178–179
  relationship layout, 175–178
  review, 192–195
  saving queries, 179
  SELECT, 179–181
  sorting, 184–186
  SQL view, 175, 187
  supplier performance rating, 288
  terms and concepts, 191
  window size, 179
Query grid, 175, 179
Query window, 178–179
Quotes, from vendors, 320

**R**

Radio frequency identification tags, 446
Ranges
  data verification, 460
  of dates, 190

Raw materials
  control activities, 442, 448
  custody relationship, 365
  as decrement event, 349, 351–353
  and finished goods, 366, 367, 377
  issuance of, 352, 353
    queries, 371–372, 373, 374
  level of detail, 371
  requisitions for, 361–365, 366
    queries, 371–372
  risks, 440, 442, 451
  supply chain integration, 482–484
REA (Resources-Events-Agents) ontology;
    *See also* Business process modeling;
    Value chain model; Value system
    model
  and accounting, 33
  applied learning, 11, 88–89, 256–258,
      307–309, 380–383, 406–407
  business process level, 478
  and controls, 463
  core pattern, 59–63 (*see also* Core
    pattern)
  and data processing, 463
  description, 8
  detail levels, 24–25
  and ERP, 8–9, 475, 478–479
  example, 25–30 (*see also* Robert Scott
    Woodwind Shop)
  extension, 82–86
  and inter-enterprise applications,
      483–484
  purpose, 29, 92
  review, 10–11, 87–88
  and strategic analysis, 27–30, 36
  terms and concepts, 10, 86
Read-only files, 465
Real-time processing, 105, 463, 466–468
Reality, 19–21
Reality-to-category mapping, 21
Reasonableness checks, 460, 463
Receipt, of goods, 269–272
Receiving reports, 218–219, 269, 273
Reciprocal relationships, 366, 412n
Recognition technology, 454
Reconciliations
  of bank statements, 444
  and flow charts, 98
  and risk management, 443, 444
Record count control totals, 461
Recording events, 85, 443, 446–448;
    *See also* Data entry
Records (in relational databases), 122–123
Redundancy
  and consistency, 4
  data rekeying, 459, 481
  and database design, 124–127, 132
  in ERP and REA, 477
  and information overload, 12
Reengineering; *See* Business process
    reengineering

Reference files, 98, 103
Referential integrity
  and combined entity key postings, 321
  defined, 123
  in event processing rules, 457–459
  in MS Access, 146–147
Refunds, 217–219
Register tapes, 98
Relational databases; *See also* Database
      design; Relational tables; View
      integration
  applied learning, 153–159
  cascade updates, 145–146
  information retrieval, 161–169 (*see also*
      Queries; Query By Example (QBE);
      Structured Query Language (SQL))
  logical models, 122–137
  records, 122–123
  relational algebra, 162, 163–169
  review, 151–153
  software for, 121–122, 137–149, 169–174
  terms and concepts, 150
Relational model, 122, 163
Relational tables
  for cash accounts, 413
  and cash balance calculation, 324
  for cash disbursements, 324, 420–422
  for cash receipts, 217, 324, 421
  for cash requisitions, 413–414
  for financing agreements, 418
  horizontal subsets, 163–165
  for integrated revenue and acquisition,
      325–327
  for inventory acquisition events, 271
  labor operations, 356
  for labor requisition, 390–392
  for labor schedule events, 393
  for machine operation, 359–360
  for production order event, 359–362, 366
  for production run, 349–351
  for purchase requisition, 266
  for purchase returns, 275–278
  raw material issuance, 353
  for raw material requisition, 363
  reciprocal relationships, 366
  for resource queries, 371
  for sales calls, 204–206
  for sales events, 215–216
  for sales orders, 208
  for sales returns, 219
  vertical subsets, 163, 164
Relationship layout
  in MS Access, 144–147
  in QBE, 175
Relationship sets, 52–53
Relationships; *See also* Duality relationships;
      Fulfillment relationships; Linkage
      relationships; Participation
      relationships; Referential integrity;
      Reservation relationships
  abstraction, 55

Relationships—*Cont.*
  agent/agent, 84
  agent types/agent type, 365–366
  for agents, 69–70, 84–85
  assignment, 365
  association (responsibility), 365–366
  attributes, 135–137
  cardinality, 54–55, 57–58, 67–68,
      78–81
  cash disbursement/payroll cycle, 397
  cash receipts/sales, 458
  commitment events/resource, 244–247
  conflicts, 312, 313
  custodial, 365, 441
  customer/sales rep, 84–85
  defined, 52–53
  between economic events, 62, 70,
      212, 269
  for economic events, 68–70
  between exchange events, 63–64
  extra, 304
  for finished goods, 366, 367, 440
  hierarchical, 55
  and information retrieval, 165–169
  instigation/commitment events, 242
  for instigation events, 204, 244
  inter-enterprise, 484
  for labor, 367, 390–392, 394
  many-to-many, 127–128, 135–137
  in MS Access, 144–148
  mutually exclusive, 321
  notation, 56
  payments/invoices, 217
  position/pay, 460
  for purchases, 268, 275–278, 303–304
  raw materials/finished goods, 366, 440
  reciprocal, 366, 412n
  for resources, 68–69, 84–85, 244
  sales/collection, 84–85, 231, 244–250 (*see
      also* Queries, sales/collection)
  of sales events, 204, 206, 219, 460
  supervisor/employee, 365–366
Remittance advices, 214, 451
  lack of, 217
Rental acquisition, 269–272
Rental agencies, 201 (fig.)
Rental agreements, 265–268
Rentals, 206–207, 209–210, 269
Repeat business, 80
Repeating groups, 124–125
Report-time processing, 105
Reporting, 85–86, 480
Reporting structure, 439
Reports; *See also* Documentation; Queries;
      Receiving reports
  of acquired items, 218–219, 269, 273
  as control activities, 436
  and control environment, 434
  corporate level, 480
  financial, 436, 439
  in flowcharts, 97–98

Reports—*Cont.*
  manufacturing (*see* Queries, conversion
      process)
  sales by inventory type, 238–241
  sales returns, 218–219
  stockflow, 218–219
Representation
  abstraction levels, 20–21
  applied learning, 33–34
  and attribute notation, 65
  flowchart symbols, 94–101
  review, 32–33
  terms and concepts, 32
  uses, 19–20
Reputation, 41, 439, 442
Requests to return goods, 275
Required data entry, 142–143
Requirements analysis, 456
Requisitions
  for cash, 413
      queries, 423, 426–427
  for labor, 389–392, 399–400, 403
  open, 295
  for purchase, 262–264, 266n
  for raw materials, 361–365
  time factors, 266n
Reservation relationships
  in acquisition/payment, 299
  attributes, 244
  and conversion process, 361, 365, 376
  in financing process, 426
  in human resources, 402–403
  risks, 440
  in sales/collection, 244–247, 248–250
Resources; *See also* Labor type; Raw
      materials; Stockflow; Stockflow
      relationships
  acquisition/payment, 269, 270
      queries, 279–285, 294–295, 298, 299
  and agents, 84–85
  attributes of, 65–66, 269
  in business process modeling, 64
  and cardinality, 67–69
  cash as, 40, 71–72, 413
  and commitment events, 82, 244–247
  control activities, 442–447
  and conversion process, 349–350, 352
      queries, 371, 374
  damage, 447
  data requirements, 353
  and decrement events, 212
  in financing process, 413, 423
  flow of, 40, 45, 63–64, 71–72
  and (not)for-profits, 36
  in human resources, 389, 395
      queries, 398–399
  immeasurable, 318
  individual items *versus* type, 350
  and instigation events, 244
  internal transformations, 44 (*see also*
      Production runs)

Resources—*Cont.*
machines as, 358–359
obsolescence, 446
for operating assets, 270
for planning, 367
in REA ontology, 24–25, 27–29
relational tables, 371
risks, 440–447, 448, 450–451
selection of, 252–253
types of, 40, 442
in value chain model, 304
resources
in value system, 40–42
Resources-Events-Agents (REA); *See* REA
(Resources-Events-Agents) ontology
Responsibility
areas of, in flowcharts, 101, 102
and control environment, 432, 434,
436, 439
in financing process, 412n
for information system security, 455–456
for internal controls, 432–433
of production supervisor, 350–351
relationships, 365–366
Responsibility relationships, 365–366
Restaurants, 60–61, 445
Returns
of purchases, 270, 272n, 275–278 (*see
also* Purchase returns)
of sales, 212, 217–219, 451
Revenue
deferred, 232
integrated, with acquisition, 325–327
Revenue process, 346
Revenue transaction cycle; *see*
Sales/collection process
Reversal relationships
in acquisition/payment, 270, 272n,
275–278
decrement, 217–219, 275
increment, 219, 275–278
risks, 440–441
in sales/collection, 212
Riehle, R., 457, 458
Right joins, 168
in QBE, 183
in SQL, 171
Risks
applied learning, 471–473
assessment of, 435, 468
in cash disbursements, 441, 450
for cash receipts, 440–441, 450–451, 458
and debt financing, 432
in decrement events, 449
reversal, 451
in decrement reversal events, 451
definition, 431
and duality relationships, 440–441
enterprise, 439–440, 441–442
increment events, 450–451
increment reversal events, 451–452

Risks—*Cont.*
information-related, 431, 441,
452–455, 467
instigation events, 447–448
management of, 432–433 (*see also*
Controls)
materiality of, 433–434
mutual commitment events, 448–449
and objectives, 432, 437
*versus* opportunity, 432
in product, 431
in purchasing, 7–8
review, 469–471
in sales/collection, 431, 439, 440, 444,
448–449
and shipping, 447, 450
in software, 457
system resources, 452–455
terms and concepts, 468–469
time factors, 440–441, 446, 447, 449, 450
types, 431–432, 437–442
Robert Scott Woodwind Shop (RSWS)
business process model, 70–81
core pattern, 62–63
example REA model, 25–30
value chain model, 43–47
value system model, 37–38, 40–41
Robey, D., 478n
Rockwell, S. R., 312n
Roll-ups, 323
Roth, R., 478n
Rows, 122–123
RSWS; *See* Robert Scott Woodwind Shop

**S**

Sales allowances, 217–219
Sales calls
attributes, 204, 228–229
duration, 229
as instigation events, 202–204
queries about, 228–229
relational tables for, 204–206
risks, 448
Sales/collection process
and accounting, 219, 231–237
applied learning, 88–89, 117–118,
153–157, 256–258
congruent event example, 319–320
control activities, 437, 441, 443,
444, 460
and conversion process, 346
data flow diagrams, 110–112
database design, 203
decrement events, 207–213, 253
reversal, 217–219, 451
decrement reversal events, 217–219, 451
defined, 43
duality relationships, 231–237, 253, 288
e-commerce, 481–484
entity-relationship diagrams, 203, 314

Sales/collection process—*Cont.*
fulfillment relationships, 241–243,
248–250
increment events, 213–217, 253
and industry risk, 439
information retrieval (*see* Queries,
sales/collection)
instigation events, 82, 202–206
inter-enterprise, 484
model sequence, 252–253
mutual commitment events, 206–207
and other business processes, 200–202
participation relationships, 246
proposition relationships, 244
REA model, 25, 202–219
reservation relationships, 244–247,
248–250
returns, 217–219, 451
revenue/acquisition integration, 325–327
review, 254–255
risks, 431, 439, 440, 444, 448–449
stockflow relationships, 237–243,
246–248
terms and concepts, 253–254
in value chain, 46–47, 200–202, 253
in value system model, 252–253
Sales events
application controls, 457, 458
attributes, 65
cardinality, 68
in e-commerce, 481–482
relational tables, 215–216
Sales invoices, 211; *See also* Invoices
Sales orders
attributes, 206
*versus* customer orders, 206
data entry, 205–206, 460, 463
queries about, 241–243, 244–250
relational tables, 208
Sales representatives
risks, 448
and sales call table, 204–205
Sales returns, 217–219, 451
Sales total
as derivable attribute, 54
in QBE, 186–187
in SQL, 173–174
Salesperson/customer relationship, 84–85
SAP, 4, 304, 479
and REA model, 9
Sarbanes-Oxley Act, 432–433
Sarson, T., 106
Scenes, 44–45
Schank, Roger, 19n, 60
Schedules; *See also* Labor schedule
and commitment events, 82, 366
communication of, 442
and control activities, 448
queries, 372, 399–400
Schema, 122
Script patterns, 23–24

Scripts
applied learning, 88–89
of financing process, 44–45
restaurant examples, 60–61
review, 33
and value chain, 25
writing, 44
Security cameras, 446–447
Segregation of duties, 439, 443, 444; *See also*
Independent checks
SELECT, 163
and aggregation functions, 173
example, 164–165
in QBE, 179–181
in SQL, 170
SELECT-FROM-WHERE, 169–170
Semantic orientation, 478–479
Separation of duties, 439, 443, 444
Sequence, 91–92
Sequence checks, 461
Service agreements, 206–207, 265–268
Service engagements, 241–243
Service providers
decrement events, 209
labor costs, 202
in value chain, 201 (fig.)
Service types, 212–213
Services
acquisition of, 269–272
allowances, 275–278
as value activity, 39
in value system, 40
Shares of stock, 410, 415
queries, 427
Shipping
application controls, 457, 458–459
and barcodes, 446
case, 450
control activities, 450, 452
costs, 449
damage during, 447
decrement events, 210–211
delivery dates, 449
and increment events, 270
as labor cost, 202
and mutual commitment events, 206, 266
and purchase returns, 275
risk management, 444–445, 449–450
risks, 449, 450
and sales returns, 218
Show Table window (MS Access), 178–179, 187
Simple attribute, 54
Simultaneous events, 319–320
Skills, of employees, 386, 389
Smart cards, 454, 455; *See also* Tokens
Smart labels, 446
Social security numbers, 53–54
Software; *See also* Application software;
Enterprise resource planning (ERP)
systems
anti-virus, 455

Software—*Cont.*
death by, 457
development costs, 456
enterprise application integration
(EAI), 480
for flowcharts, 94
general controls, 455–457
intentional defect, 458
maintenance, 456–457
for relational databases, 121–122,
137–149, 169–174
system *versus* application, 455–456
Sommer, B. E., 476n, 480, 483n
Sorting
in QBE, 184–186
in quantity on hand query, 333
in SQL, 173–174
Specific invoice, 217
SQL; *See* Structured Query Language
Standards
for auditing, 433
for conversion process, 367, 369
for EDI, 483, 484
Statement of Auditing Standards No.
94, 433
Static derivable attributes, 54, 321–323
Stockflow, 43
Stockflow relationships
acquisition/payment process, 269,
294–296
attributes, 238
cardinality, 67–68, 78–81
in conversion process, 374–375
equipment and machinery, 359
in financing process, 420, 423n
queries, 425
in human resources, 394, 401–402
in REA model, 64
risks, 440
in sales/collection, 212–213, 217–219,
237–243, 246–248
Stocks; *See also* Equity financing
issuance of, 414
preferred, 415
proceeds, 414
repurchases, 414
shares of, 410, 415, 427
Stovepipes
applied learning, 11
description, 5–6
discussion, 11
review, 10
Strategic analysis, 27–30, 36; *See also*
Decision process
Strategy, 36
Structured Query Language (SQL)
applied learning, 196–198
asterisk (*), 225
average, 173
calculations, 172–174
comparison operators, 172

Structured Query Language—*Cont.*
fixed asset query, 285
inventory queries, 225–228
in MS Access, 175, 187–189
PROJECT example, 170
purchase order query, 286–287
in QBE, 175, 187
review, 192–195
SELECT examples, 170, 226,
229–230
with PROJECT, 170
sorting, 173–174
supplier performance query, 287
syntax, 169–174, 191, 225
terms and concepts, 191
totaling sales, 173–174
tutorials, 191
Structuring orientation, 479
Subscenes, 44–45
Subtypes, 21n, 55
SUM, 173, 324, 425
Sunbeam Co., 481
Supertypes, 21n, 55
Supervisory relationships, 365–366
Suppliers
authorization, 449
average delivery time, 177
balance calculation, 301–303
and cash disbursement, 80
control activities, 441
and controls, 437
defined, 39, 42
in example model, 72, 80
integration with, 482–484
and mutual commitment events, 265
performance query, 287
queries, 299
quotes from, 320
risk management, 442, 449
in value chain, 29, 39
in value system, 24, 37–38,
40–41, 42
Supplies
acquisition/payment queries,
279–283
control activities, 444–445, 447, 451
custody of, 445
damage, 447
in flowcharts, 100
obsolescence, 446
risks, 451
Supply chain
applied learning, 486–487
defined, 24
inter-enterprise management,
482–483
and value system, 24, 37–38
Support value activities, 38–39
Surveillance equipment, 446–447
Suspense files, 103
Sutherland, J., 8n, 24n

Symbols
data flow diagrams, 105–106
for flowcharts, 94–101
relationship symbol, 45
uses, 19–20
Synonyms, 313
Syntax, 169
for parameter queries, 190
System flowcharts, 94–102; *See also*
Flowcharts
System requirements, 456
System software, 456
Systems
physical attributes, 112–115
risks and controls, 452–455
view-*versus* event-driven, 8

**T**

Tables; *See also* Relational tables
logical model, 122–135
in MS Access implementation, 141–148
subsets, 163–169
Tagging systems, 484
Tapes
in flowcharts, 98
as media type, 104, 105
Task level
applied learning, 117–119
*versus* business process modeling,
91–94
discussion, 116–117
and ERP software, 479
purpose, 91
in REA model, 25, 30
review, 115–116
system flowcharting, 94–102
Tasks
and database design, 30
defined, 25, 91
and events, 91
materialization, 318–320
unmeasurable, 91
Tax tables, 98, 103
Taxes, 41
Technology development, 39
Telecommunications, 482
Telephone numbers, 123–124
Templin, N., 37
Terminal identification codes, 454
Terminals
as input, 97, 98
as output (display), 99
Test data, 456, 463
Tests, 431; *See also* Quality
Theft
case, 444
of cash, 435–436, 443–444
controls, 442–447, 451
by customers, 443
by employees, 442–447

Threats, 431–432; *See also* Risks
Three-way match, 7
Time factors
acquisition recording, 269
cash disbursements, 273–274
and commitment events, 265, 296, 375
and controls, 433, 436
and core pattern, 62
credit card payments, 273
of data entry, 459
and data updates, 105
delivery dates, 449
and e-commerce, 481
file reconstruction, 465–466
and human resource process, 394
and increment events, 269
lead time, 449
and mutual commitment events,
265, 296
and obsolescence, 446
requisition and purchase order, 266n
risks, 440–441, 446, 447, 449, 450
sequence, 91–92
simultaneous events, 319–320
Time tracking, 355
Timecards, 394
Tokens, 20–21, 454, 455
Totals; *See also* Balances; SUM
in QBE, 186–187
record count, 461
in SQL, 173–174
Tracking numbers, 446
Trailer records, 464
Train analogy, 3–4
Training, 9, 442, 447
Transaction cycle; *See* Business processes
Transaction files, 103
Transaction logs, 467
Transaction type checks, 461
Transfer duality relationships, 349
Transformation duality relationships, 349
Treadway Commission (COSO), 433–437
Trends, 441
Tuples, 122–123
Types, 20–21
Typification, 55, 73

**U**

Unapplied cash, 217
United Nations, 484
Updates
cascade (MS Access), 145–146
closed loop verification, 459
lockout procedures, 464
to master file, 104–105
in MS Access, 145–146
in nonintegrated systems, 477–478
triggered, 224, 284, 413
Use stockflow relationship, 350–351
Utilities, 40

**V**

Valacich, J., 107–109, 110n
Valid sign check, 460
Validity checks, 460
Value
automobile example, 37
and (not)for-profits, 36
in script, 25
in value chain model, 45
Value activities, 38–39, 44; *See also*
Conversion process
Value added networks (VAN), 482
Value chain, 37–39
Value chain model
and acquisition/payment, 46, 304
applied learning, 50, 381–383
cash disbursements in, 45–46
and conversion process, 46, 201 (fig.),
346–349
financing process, 410
focus, 24
and human resources, 39, 386–387
and margin, 36
precursor, 62
review and discussion, 48–49
RSWS example, 27–30, 71 (fig.)
sales/collection, 46–47, 200–202, 253
script, 25
steps, 42–47
terms and concepts, 48
and value system level, 24, 40 (fig.), 44
Value system, 35–37
Value system model
and acquisition/payment, 304
applied learning, 33, 50
and conversion process, 346–349
financing process, 410
focus, 24
government services in, 40
human resource process, 386
objects, 25
review, 32–33, 48–49
RSWS example, 26–27, 71 (fig.)
and sales/collection, 252–253
steps, 40–42
terms and concepts, 48
and value chain level, 24, 40 (fig.), 44
Variance analysis, 367
Vendor invoices, 269, 273; *See also* Invoices
Vendors; *See* Suppliers
Vertical calculations, 173, 175
Vertical subsets, 163, 164
View-driven systems, 8
View integration
applied learning, 340–343
inter-enterprise, 484
in partial ERP implementations, 478
review and discussion, 339–340
steps, 312–318, 338
terms and concepts, 338–339

View modeling, 311–312
Virtual close, 323
Viruses, 455
Voice recognition, 454
Volatile derivable attributes, 54, 389, 478

**W**

Warehouses
    control activities, 446
    and ERP system, 481

Water, 40
Weighted average unit cost, 294–295,
    334–335
Wheatley, Malcolm, 9
Whistleblower policy, 439
WIP Job (Work in process), 46
Withholdings, 395
    queries, 401
Work in process (WIP Job), 46
Workflow, 61–62, 91–92, 92–94

**X**

XBRL, 52, 484
XML, 52, 484

**Y**

Yourdon, E., 106